# Contemporary Authors

## Autobiography Series

ISSN 0748-0636

# *Contemporary Authors*

## Autobiography Series

**Adele Sarkissian**

Editor

*volume* **5**

GALE RESEARCH COMPANY • BOOK TOWER • DETROIT, MICHIGAN 48226

Copyright © 1987 by Gale Research Company

Library of Congress Catalog Card Number 84-647879
ISBN 0-8103-4504-8
ISSN-0748-0636

# Contents

# Preface

Each volume in the *Contemporary Authors Autobiography Series (CAAS)* presents an original collection of autobiographical essays written especially for the series by noted writers. *CAAS* has grown out of the aggregate of the Gale Research Company's long-standing interest in author biography, bibliography, and criticism, as well as its successful publications in those areas, like the *Dictionary of Literary Biography, Contemporary Literary Criticism, Something about the Author, Author Biographies Master Index,* and particularly the bio-bibliographical series *Contemporary Authors (CA),* to which this *Autobiography Series* is a companion.

As a result of their ongoing communication with authors in compiling *CA* and other books, Gale editors recognized that these wordsmiths frequently had "more to say"—willingly, even eagerly—than the format of existing Gale publications could accommodate. Personal comments from authors in the "Sidelights" section of *CA* entries, for example, often indicated the intriguing tip of an iceberg. Inviting authors to write about themselves at essay-length was the almost-inexorable next step. Added to that was the fact that the collected autobiographies of current writers were virtually nonexistent. Like metal to magnet, Gale customarily responds to an information gap—and met this one with *CAAS.*

## Purpose

This series is designed to be a congenial meeting place for writers and readers—a place where writers can present themselves, on their own terms, to their audience; and a place where general readers, students of contemporary literature, teachers and librarians, even aspiring writers can become better acquainted with familiar authors and make the first acquaintance of others. Here is an opportunity for writers who may never write a full-length autobiography (and some shudder at the thought) to let their readers know how they see themselves and their work, what carefully laid plans or turns of luck brought them to this time and place, what objects of their passion and pity arouse them enough to tell us. Even for those authors who have already published full-length autobiographies there is the opportunity in *CAAS* to bring their readers "up to date" or perhaps to take a different approach in the essay format. At the very least, these essays can help quench a reader's inevitable curiosity about the people who speak to their imagination and seem themselves to inhabit a plane somewhere between reality and fiction. But the essays in this series have a further potential: singly, they can illuminate the reader's understanding of a writer's work; collectively, they are lessons in the creative process and in the discovery of its roots.

*CAAS* makes no attempt to give an observer's-eye view of authors and their works. That outlook is already well represented in biographies, reviews, and critiques published in a wide variety of sources, including *Contemporary Authors, Contemporary Literary Criticism,* and the *Dictionary of Literary Biography.* Instead, *CAAS* complements that perspective and presents what no other source does: the view of contemporary writers that is reflected in their own mirrors, shaped by their own choice of materials and their own manner of storytelling.

*CAAS* is still in its youth, but its major accomplishments may already be projected. The series fills a significant information gap—in itself a sufficient test of a worthy reference work. And thanks to the exceptional talents of its contributors, each volume in this series is a unique anthology of some of the best and most varied contemporary writing.

## Scope

Like its parent series, *Contemporary Authors,* the *CA Autobiography Series* aims to be broad-based. It sets out to meet the needs and interests of the full spectrum of readers by providing in each volume twenty to thirty essays by writers in all genres whose work is being read today. We deem it a minor publishing event that more than twenty busy authors are able to interrupt their existing writing, teaching, speaking, traveling, and other schedules to converge on a given deadline for any one volume. So it is not always possible that all genres can be equally and uniformly represented from volume to volume. Of the twenty writers in Volume 5, about half are novelists and half are poets. Like most categories, these oversimplify. Only a few writers specialize in a single area. The range of writings by authors in this volume also includes books of nonfiction as well as work for movies, television, radio, newspapers, and journals.

## Format

Authors who contribute to *CAAS* are invited to write a "mini-autobiography" of approximately 10,000 words. In order to give the writer's imagination free rein, we suggest no guidelines or pattern for the essay. The only injunction is that each writer tell his or her own story in the manner and to the extent that each finds most natural and appropriate. In addition, writers are asked to supply a selection of personal photographs, showing themselves at various ages, as well as important people and special moments in their lives. Barring unfortunate circumstances like the loss or destruction of early photographs, our contributors have responded graciously and generously, sharing with us some of their most treasured mementoes, as this volume readily attests. This special wedding of text and photographs makes *CAAS* the kind of reference book that even browsers will find seductive.

A bibliography appears at the end of each essay, listing the author's book-length works in chronological order of publication. If more than one book has been published in a given year, the titles are listed in alphabetic order. Each entry in the bibliography includes the publication information for the book's first printing in the United States and Great Britain. Generally, the bibliography does not include later reprintings, new editions, or foreign translations. Also omitted from this bibliography are articles, reviews, and other contributions to magazines and journals. The bibliographies in this volume were compiled by members of the *CAAS* editorial staff from their research and the lists of writings provided by many of the authors. Each of the bibliographies has been submitted to the author for review. When the list of primary works is extensive, the author may prefer to present a "Selected Bibliography." Readers may consult the author's entry in *CA* for a more complete list of writings in these cases.

Each volume of *CAAS* includes a cumulative index that cites all the essayists in the series as well as the subjects presented in the essays: personal names, titles of works, geographical names, schools of writings, etc. The index format is designed to make these cumulating references as helpful and easy to use as possible. For every reference that appears *in more than one essay,* the name of the essayist is given before the volume and page number(s). For example, W.H. Auden is mentioned by several essayists in the series. The index format allows the user to identify the essay writers by name:

Auden, W.H.
Abse **1**:24, 31
Belitt **4**:60, 65
Bourjaily **1**:68
Bowles **1**:86
Grumbach **2**:208

Howes **3**:143
Jennings **5**:104, 110
Jones **5**:118-19, 120, 121, 123
Kizer **5**:146
Settle **1**:311

For references that appear *in only one essay,* the volume and page number(s) are given but the name of the essayist is omitted. For example:

*CAAS* is something more than the sum of its individual essays. At many points the essays touch common ground, and from these intersections emerge new mosaics of information and impressions. *CAAS* therefore becomes an expanding chronicle of the last half-century—an already useful research tool that can only increase in usefulness as the series grows. And the index here, for all its pedestrian appearance, is an increasingly important guide to the interconnections of this chronicle.

## Looking Ahead

All of the writers in this volume begin with a common goal—telling the tale of their lives. Yet each of these essays has a special character and point of view that set it apart from its companions. Perhaps a small sampler of anecdotes from the essays ahead can hint at the unique flavor of these life stories.

**Elizabeth Jennings,** describing how she came to know and love London: "I had some very exciting meetings with great and eccentric writers. The most memorable was tea with T. S. Eliot in the tiny room at Faber's which they called 'Uncle Tom's Cabin.' I was so awed that I cannot remember if I drank the tea or ate the biscuits which were brought in for both of us. Eliot did indeed seem 'an aged eagle' because he was very tall and had a slight stoop."

**Mervyn Jones,** recalling a visit with Sigmund Freud: "I was already keen on history, and I showed genuine interest in Freud's collection of antiquities, all displayed in glass cases in what practically amounted to a small private museum. Suddenly, Freud started giving me pieces from the collection—one, then another, and eventually four.... He desisted only when my father pointed out that we might have trouble with the British customs.... Freud then went on to tell me, with great seriousness, that archaeology would be an excellent career for a young man with my interests. (I was only thirteen, but he didn't condescend to children.)"

**Andrew Sinclair,** recounting some of the risks of filmmaking: "On one catastrophic occasion, I found myself in Athens with the two weightiest actors of them all, Orson Welles and Oliver Reed. I was trying to shoot a modern Faustian legend. The English stock market crashed, the producer ran away, and I was left with two megaliths who took my credit card out of my pocket, sat me between them in the best restaurant in town, consumed every dish in the place and twenty-two bottles of wine during the next fourteen hours, while they were discussing who would murder me first."

**Robin Skelton,** on his friend Geoffrey Keynes: "Staying with Geoffrey [at his home in Hampstead] was itself an education. The house was filled with paintings and fine prints, and crammed with books from all centuries.... I was introduced to the wonders of William Blake and Samuel Palmer, and Geoffrey took me to first nights in London, especially to the ballet.... I met fascinating people, including Siegfried Sassoon, who slaughtered me at croquet, and who scared me silly in London by dashing across streets in full traffic as if he were still leading a charge in the trenches."

**Colin Wilson,** on his early problem of earning a living: "I tried working in the office of a wine company, then in the office of a spare-parts garage; but it was so obvious that I detested the drudgery that both sacked me within weeks.... I decided to try to save rent by buying a tent and sleeping outdoors. The first night, I erected the tent on a golf course in north London, but it was too obviously conspicuous. Then a friend suggested the obvious solution: a waterproof sleeping bag. It was, in fact, a kind of rubber envelope that went over the ordinary sleeping bag. When it rained, I could pull a kind of hood up over my head, and sleep warm and dry."

These brief examples can only suggest what lies ahead in this volume. The essays will speak differently to different readers; but they are certain to speak best, and most eloquently, for themselves.

### Acknowledgments

A special word of thanks to all the writers whose essays appear in this volume. They have given as generously of their enthusiasm and good humor as of their talent. We are indebted.

# Authors Forthcoming in *CAAS*

**Mulk Raj Anand** (novelist, short story writer, nonfiction writer, and critic)—As an eminent guide to the culture and life of India, Anand has increased the world's understanding of the great Asian subcontinent through such powerful books as *Untouchable* and *Confession of a Lover.*

**Dee Brown** (historian and novelist)—Popularly and critically acclaimed for *Bury My Heart at Wounded Knee,* Brown writes primarily about the historical exploitation of the American West—of the Indians, of the land, and of the natural resources.

**Philip Jose Farmer** (science fiction novelist and short story writer)—A three-time winner of the Hugo award, Farmer introduced innovative themes and techniques to the sci-fi genre in works like his "Riverworld" and "World of Tiers" series.

**Leslie Fiedler** (critic, novelist, poet, and editor)—Fiedler is one of today's most distinguished, and often controversial, literary critics. His well-known writings include *Love and Death in the American Novel* and *The Last Jew in America.*

**Nikki Giovanni** (poet and essayist)—In verse collections like *My House* and the recent *Those Who Ride the Night Winds,* Giovanni creates poetry that mirrors her life-long concern for the rights and dignity of black people.

**Nat Hentoff** (novelist, critic, journalist, and editor) —The wondrous music of jazz and a passion for civil rights have been consistently present in such Hentoff books as *The First Freedom* and *Jazz Is.* Novels like *The Day They Came to Arrest the Book* have exposed many readers to the continuing struggle for social justice.

**Jessica Mitford** (essayist, journalist)—Her *American Way of Death* and *Kind and Unusual Punishment* are muckraking masterpieces. Equally renowned for her autobiographies, Mitford is a writer of good humor, profoundly concerned with civil liberties.

**M.L. Rosenthal** (poet, critic, and editor)—Already an established critic, Rosenthal published his first book of poetry at age forty-seven. He has written several verse collections, in which he creates a unique mix of his public and personal concerns in an urban landscape.

**Karl Shapiro** (poet, critic, editor, and playwright)—Shapiro broke from his early award-winning work in his watershed verse collection, *The Bourgeois Poet,* and in controversial criticism, such as his *In Defense of Ignorance.*

# Contemporary Authors
## Autobiography Series

# Jonathan Baumbach

*1933-*

## THE STORY SO FAR

I am born. I was born on July 5, 1933, in Brooklyn, the first son, the only son for twelve and a half years, of Harold and Ida Baumbach. My mother taught grade school, fifth grade as I remember—never to advance, never to graduate—while my father stayed home and painted pictures. Although my father was in the house, was home and not home, a succession of maids and mother's helpers looked after me until I was old enough to go to school. We moved about like sagebrush, changed location with upsetting regularity, moving, it seemed, almost every year, until 1940 when my parents bought a free-standing brick house in an area of Brooklyn called Boro Park. The grade school I attended, P.S. 208, was in East Flatbush—it was a public school with an experimental program for bright children—and I travelled alone by bus to school from the age of seven on. The trip took thirty minutes, sometimes longer. I got on the bus at Forty-eighth Street and Eighteenth Avenue and got off at East Forty-eighth Street and Avenue D three miles away. When I missed the bus, or the bus was late, my father drove me to school. I was a lonely, self-reliant, independent (no doubt, frightened) child with a rich fantasy life.

I can surmise certain things about the experience of these early years—memory of feelings is closed off—from the surviving evidence. After first grade, in which I was an exemplary student (my true nature in disguise), I became a disciplinary problem, my behavior worsening (old report cards stand as evidence) with each succeeding year. According to my reports, I lacked appropriate restraint, talked out—joked, I believe—without raising my hand and receiving sanction to speak. I "lacked respect for the rights of others," which may have been another way of saying the same thing. I was a hardened case at P.S. 208, incompletely school-broken. Still, no matter how disrespectful or depraved my behavior, I was not the worst in class. The first worst, the negative star, was a boy named Robert Schlitt, who, as I remember, retained the distinction unwaveringly (perhaps I eclipsed him once or twice) from first grade to eighth. I was the class clown, willing to do anything, to sacrifice reputation and respect, for a laugh. I was, what was later to be known as, a wiseass. My teachers, if the surviving report cards are an indication, never cracked a smile.

Says evidence, I clamored for attention at school,

*Young Jonathan Baumbach on the shoulders of his grandfather, Isaac Zackheim, about 1935*

not getting enough of what I felt myself to want at home. The pattern is classic: I was a shy, lonely child with a hunger for celebrity. A spotlight was required to validate my presence.

It was also important to me to be accepted by my classmates, to be considered "a regular guy" particularly so because I felt myself (and still do) irregular—an outsider—which may be an aspect of my identification with my father's role as artist. It has stayed with me, this feeling. Even among friends, even among other writers, I still feel myself an outsider. (Is it that I am not quite at home, even now, in my own house, in the various metaphorical houses I inhabit?) I played every sport, distinguished myself in some, failed to fulfill promise in others, was a relentless, self-defeating competitor.

At school when we were asked from time to time what our fathers did—they almost never asked about

*Jonathan with father, Harold, and mother, Ida, 1936*

almost can't do without, have been a major influence on me as a writer. They occupy me, the good and bad alike, like secret dreams.

I was an only child for almost twelve and a half years, for as long as it takes (longer probably) to feel like an only child. I was at summer camp when I learned to my shock during my parents' visit that my mother was pregnant. My brother Jim was born November 10, 1945. It was a belated loss of space for me, the first and not the last. My second brother, Dan, was born November 12, 1948. I looked after Jim when he was small, more like a parent (my mother was teaching, my father painting) than a brother. I gave Danny less attention, couldn't be responsible indefinitely for the vagaries of my parents' behavior. My brothers, as it turned out, were the first of three sets of children I've had direct responsibility for. I feel, looking back, that I've been some kind of father almost all of my life.

Having gone to a grade school that none of my street friends attended, I decided to go to a local high school, a place called New Utrecht, which was almost as far from where I lived (in another direction) as P.S. 208. New Utrecht was a major adjustment for me. P.S. 208 was an eighth-grade school—one of the rare ones in Brooklyn—so I entered high school in first term,

our mothers—I used to make things up to seem more like the others, embarrassed to say that my father occupied himself painting pictures. Making art was not, I thought, an acceptable thing for a father to do. Fathers, as everyone knew, were in business, or lawyers, or doctors, or accountants, or schoolteachers, or firemen, or dentists. So, when put on the spot, I had to invent things for my father to do so he would not seem different from other fathers, so his son would not seem different from other sons.

I read as a child beyond the call of requirement, mostly novels, reading everything I could find in the library of whatever author attracted me at the moment. This was before television, or before television was in general currency. I remember seeing television for the first time in 1944 at a war plant called Air King where my father worked as a draftsman during the war. (My father is a draftsman, I could say in class without feeling I had given some terrible family secret away.) If I read a lot, I also spent a significant part of my life going to movies, went to a double feature at least once a week, usually to my local theater, which was the Culver on McDonald Avenue, went ritually Saturday afternoons with a friend or friends, sometimes alone. No matter whom you had come to the theater with, once the movie started you were alone with it in the dark. Movies, which I love to this day, which I

*Jon, age three*

while my neighborhood friends were still in junior high. I entered high school knowing no one in my class. I was small at fourteen, had not grown in three years, had metamorphosed from one of the taller kids in school to one of the shortest. If I thought myself an outsider at 208, I must have felt beyond the pale at New Utrecht, which is an overpopulated city high school with students of greatly varying abilities. Perhaps a third of those attending New Utrecht were there because the law required it.

So I am fourteen, undersized, shy, in a situation wholly unlike the one I had known for eight years. And I have no friends at my new school. There is no one there I knew before arriving. I am at a new school with no one I know.

This is what I remember of that time. In the lunchroom, which is virtually unsupervised, this my first full day, someone steals my lunch bag when I go on the cafeteria line to get a container of milk. Steal is perhaps not the right word. It is more game than theft, my lunch passed back and forth, kept away from me for as long as I pursued it. I knew what to do. I took on the smallest of my tormentors, fought fiercely with contrived abandon, fought him until outsiders separated us. I relied on the fight being stopped before matters went too far, though my manner suggested I would fight to the death. I was viewed as out of control by my tormentors—a reputation I cultivated—which meant it was inadvisable to mess with me.

The lunchroom at New Utrecht was at best unpleasant, at worst a source of dread. Was it possible—I hardly remember now—that boys and girls were separated? It must have been so. That's why there were so many fights and so much noise. Sexual energy was displaced into bravado and small violence. Condoms (I was innocent as to their real use at the time) were blown up like balloons and batted about from table to table. It was because the girls were not there, were on the other side of the check-out counters, their shadowy presence a taunt to our awareness of ourselves, an unseen provocation. I've heard people from small towns talk about their high-school days as being among the happiest of their lives. I mostly hated high school. A public New York City high school in the late forties and early fifties was a horror show. When I did my time in the army (1956-1958), it recalled my high-school days to me with a terrifying déjà vu. One bureaucratic oppression is very much like another.

And maybe high school wasn't really as bad as I felt it to be that first difficult year. It's possible that much of my unhappiness had to do with lowered self-esteem, with loss of attention at home, with conventional teenage malaise. Although the academic work in high school was undemanding except in petty ways, I didn't distinguish myself particularly (not in the first two years), achieved a kind of invisibility which may have been my real goal. To seem smart was to attract the wrong kind of attention at a school like New Utrecht. To be thought of as a "brain" was to be viewed as a freak, was to set oneself up for disparagement. Mediocrity was an acceptable disguise. After a while ambition got the best of me.

Most of my neighborhood friends arrived in high school during my second term, but they had skipped a year in the special classes of junior high and so started a term ahead of me. I did better in my second year and better still in my third. My two best subjects—that is, the two subjects I scored highest on—were math and English. Where could such a combination lead me?

This is what I remember of high school, this most: longing after girls in various classes and being too shy, too fearful of rejection, to ask them for dates. My romantic life at fourteen was centered in fantasy. I rehearsed private scenarios in my mind. Some girl I fantasized myself in love with would be attacked by a thug (his intention never fully clear to me) and I would come by in the nick of time and save her, putting the villain away (as in Hollywood films) with one perfectly thrown punch. My reward would be a kiss—my aspirations as metaphorical as the adult behavior I had observed in movies of the forties. I would receive her gratitude, which is to say her notice (she would see I was worthy of her) and, so it followed in the fantasy, her undying love. Women fell in love with men who rescued them, I somehow thought, men who saved them from terrible unnameable fates, a feeling I've not to this day fully outgrown. (I've been saving or trying to save women ever since with predictably disastrous results.) Heroes, said the code I studied, and only heroes, were worthy of a good and beautiful woman's love. My romantic life would have been a lot less troublesome over the years had this absurd notion not been so deeply ingrained in me. I was a movie hero passing invisibly among the mistreated women of the world, awaiting appropriate occasion.

I put this down as it comes to me, as memory evolves. I am fifteen now, have grown three inches in the past year. My face is breaking out, I am razor thin, and wear my hair, says evidence of photos, in what was called a pompadour. Such is the message of evidence. Memory says otherwise and clearly is to be discounted.

This too. I remember the following with particular clarity. I was a member of the service squad at New Utrecht—it sounds surrealistic in the retelling—and was assigned to guard one of the entrances to the building. My responsibility was not to let anyone in without an appropriate pass. I took my command seriously,

*Baumbach at seventeen*

turned away anyone who didn't have official entry. One day some tough kid warned me that if I didn't let him in, his friends would get me on the way home from school. I didn't doubt him, but I still wouldn't let him by. It was my job, wasn't it? not to. For a while I was careful to go back and forth from school among a group of friends, was wary of walking the two blocks to the bus stop alone. After a few weeks, I forgot about the ostensible danger. Travelling in a group—I was always more or less a loner—was not my style. When I least expected it, my way was barred by two boys, the one who had tried to get in, and a considerably larger companion. "Why didn't you let my friend in the school?" the bigger one says. Something like that. I don't remember how I explained myself except to say that I was under orders not to let anyone in. Some friends of mine came along and I escaped (escaped what?) with the warning to let them in, either or both, the next time they appeared. There was no next time. I requested a change of assignment and someone else, someone perhaps more permissive, took my place at the door.

I wrote for the school newspaper during my second year, did feature articles and later, a weekly column, a mix of verbal play and ironic observation. They were perhaps embryonic versions of what I would do later on. I thought of myself as a writer, as someone who was destined to become a writer, and what I wrote, I imagined, was in the service of a long-term commitment. That may have been an illusion, but it was an illusion that sustained me.

Though in many ways a ragtag place, New Utrecht had a distinguished English department, which was fortuitous for me. The teacher I learned the most from was Arnold Horowitz, whom I had for fifth-term Honors English. Mr. Horowitz, who had been a working journalist, was less academic and more sophisticated than anyone I had studied with before. He gave me my first and only 100 in English, which was a combination, I suspect, of encouragement and irony. He knew that grades were beside the point so gave me the grade I wanted to believe I deserved, took me at my most grandiose valuation of myself.

I didn't date much in high school, went to dances with friends, tried to pick up girls with little or no success. Often shyness manifested itself in bravura. I would perform, do comic routines, as much for my friends as the girls I was trying to impress. I drew blank stares from my audience as if I were talking a foreign language only superficially like their own. Being thought a fool inspired me to greater foolishness. Looking back on it, I can see that the showing off was more a way of keeping distance than making contact. I was still a virgin at seventeen.

Women, fair to say, were a mystery to me. Ours was a male-oriented household. When my brother Dan was born, we outnumbered the women in my family by four to one. Also my father was the dominant figure in our family, his career as a painter of orchestrated concern to us all. As wives of artists at that time tended to do, my mother lived vicariously through my father's career. She held us together, though over the years she became increasingly self-effacing. Mostly, the girls in my classes seemed like creatures from another planet to me. I was fascinated and mystified by them, made sense of them through fantasy. I went on occasional dates while in high school, mostly double dates, some blind, though I have only dim, generalized recollections of the experiences. My friends and I bragged about fantasized (and real) successes with girls, monitored each other's experience as a form of vicarious education.

I had particular difficulty asking a girl for a date over the phone, was painfully vulnerable to rejection. I used to make my calls from my father's studio, the one place in the house where I could have complete privacy. I remember pacing around the large room to work up my courage, rehearsing my approach. I wouldn't allow myself to leave the studio until I had completed the call I had set out to make. The preliminaries were often easier than anticipated, the chat about school and parents and homework and movies. It was the asking for the date that was hard, the risking of rejection. And when the girl said, as she sometimes did, that she was busy, I could never be sure whether she was telling the truth or putting me off. I tended to accept all refusals as rejections, almost never called a girl again who had been unavailable the first time. I suspect I tended to ask for dates in a way that was so willfully noncommittal that I invited misunderstanding, seemed to be asking for nothing at all.

Solving the mystery of the other sex may have occupied me as much or more than my course work, which made only marginal demands. One obsesses most about one's failures. The word "failure" suggests that victory and defeat were at issue, which was often the case. The game was called "making out." Boys wooed and pursued, and girls led us on and held us off, and sometimes surrendered. Where it was a badge of success for a boy to sleep around, it was an indication of bad character for a girl to be promiscuous. This was the fifties. I didn't know at the time, a reluctant participant in the game of making out, how little of what went on had to do with real sexual feelings.

Sex was a contest for us, a test of strategies. You either won (got laid) or lost (got turned down) or reached some plausible compromise (petting or oral sex), which temporarily satisfied both sides. For the sake of form, I carried condoms in my wallet, some packages more worn with disuse than others, awaiting elusive opportunity. My secret aims were essentially romantic. I wanted to be loved and admired. Sex, which seemed to require artful deceptions, was a secondary aspiration. I was seventeen, sixteen or seventeen, entering my final year at high school.

I spent the summer I turned seventeen as a waiter at a place called Camp Tohone. It was 1950. The Korean War was raging. One had to sign a loyalty oath in high school—a recent law emerging from the anticommunist panic—in order to graduate. For a variety of mostly nonpolitical reasons, I refused to sign. Two other boys went along with me. I suspect that it was my idea, that I was the leader behind this quixotic protest. I was opposed to the war but that was only part of my reason for refusing the essentially pointless and vulgar gesture of signing. It seemed to me an act of patriotism—of heroism—not to sign. If I were really disloyal, went my argument, I would sign in order to disguise my disloyalty.

We were invited separately to a meeting with the assistant principal and reasoned with, cajoled, and finally threatened. A letter was sent home to our parents to be signed and returned. We were warned that we would never be able to attend college, that our lives would be ruined. It sounds horrendous as I report it now, but the pressure brought to bear on us to sign this unconstitutional document, this document wholly out of keeping with the spirit of American democracy, was very much an aspect of the times. It would please me to report that I held out against this bureaucratic harassment, but ultimately I gave in. I knew I would capitulate after the others had signed—my imaginary heroism only went so far—though I held out for another week. Giving in made me feel worse about myself than if I had not made the stand at all. I had learned the necessity for compromise, and the self-contempt such compromise engendered in one who aspired to be perfect.

I graduated sixth in my class at New Utrecht and ended up going to Brooklyn College despite scholarships to two Ivy League colleges. Reasons: I had inherited my father's reverse snobbery and thought Brooklyn College a more appropriate place for me. Also, my parents were broke at the time and could offer me virtually no money toward college. Also, Brooklyn College, which was completely free to New York City residents, had a reputation in the fifties for being one of the best undergraduate schools in the country. Whatever my reasons, I regret the missed opportunity of going to an out-of-town college. I was born in Brooklyn, had lived most of my life in Brooklyn (there was a year and a half in Manhattan when I was small), and here I was at seventeen and a half going to college in Brooklyn. I had been to New England during summers as a child and upstate New York almost to the Canadian border, but I had not been further west than Pennsylvania or further south than Maryland. I was an urban provincial.

The summer after high school (I had completed one term of college), I worked for a month selling Good Humor ice cream on one of those tricycles, then hitched around the country with a friend, going wherever rides would take us. It was an attempt to experience something of the country outside of Brooklyn and Manhattan. As it turned out, our travels were limited to the northeast, to territory we both had explored to some extent before. I don't remember many of the details of the trip beyond the fact that we had some adventures with girls, and that I was more innocent than I wanted to be when I returned after Labor Day to my parents' home in Brooklyn.

I turned eighteen that summer and had to take an army physical, a preliminary one, in order to be rated for the draft. I was 1-A. The Korean War hung over us, controlled our lives. To assure completion of college, I signed up for Air Force ROTC, a new program at Brooklyn, with the idea of becoming a pilot. After only one term of playing soldier on campus, I relinquished my career as pilot. I saw no reason for military training on a liberal arts college campus, and I didn't want to be complicit in the militarization of civilian life. The Korean War had been used as an excuse for the violation of civil liberties on a number of fronts at home. I would take my chances on the draft. I saw myself as the loyal opposition in a bad time—McCarthy had just begun his tacky reign of terror—a civil libertarian, a spiritual anarchist. I took a romantic view of my invisible private role.

I was a romantic at nineteen, a moral sentimentalist in the guise of a street-wise, street-tough kid. I tried on identities like new secondhand clothes. My idea of myself: the mysterious stranger. I was the one beautiful women, unknown to themselves, were waiting to meet. Apart from my secret identity, I read three books a week, went to the movies as if it were a form of worship, played basketball and tennis, wrote plays and poems. I became interested in acting, did theater reviews for the college newspaper, auditioned for college plays, appeared in *Winterset* and *The Long Voyage Home* and *The School for Scandal*. I liked acting, but I was probably too self-conscious to be really good at it. Acting was an extension of my fantasy life, a trying-on of new selves.

I began to write plays, thought myself a playwright for a while. I divided my time among a variety of seemingly incompatible interests. I wanted to write plays, I wanted to write novels, I wanted to act, I wanted to be a tennis player, I wanted to make movies. I did most things as if there were records to be broken, some unsung heroism to be achieved.

Social life at school was more involving than the actual courses I took. I hung out among friends in the college cafeteria, debating real and imagined literary issues. I was nineteen. To support myself, I worked fifteen hours a week in the college bookstore, I posed for my father's painting classes. So I spent most of my day at the college working, attending classes, rehearsing plays, arguing with friends, and stayed away from home for as long as I could invent reasons to stay away. My brothers were seven and four, and though I loved them, I needed to be free of the responsibility of raising them. I needed my own life.

After resisting the obvious pressures (and perhaps yielding to them after the fact), I began to go out with the daughter of friends of my parents, a girl I had known all my life. Her father was one of my father's two closest friends. They lived in Boro Park less than a block away from us. We got together after a summer as counselors in the same camp, a summer in which we avoided getting together. We had been friends, something like siblings (friends and strangers) and it took a

while for the terms of things to change. As I see it now, aside from short-lived summer romances, S was my first girlfriend, the first girl I went out with for an extended period of time. There seemed a rightness about our getting together. That is, our relationship had the appropriateness of cliché. That we would get together despite our parents' pressure in that direction gave it a romantic aura in reverse—the romance of anti-romance. It was like getting to the obvious by contriving to avoid it. Anyway, that was the narrative of my fantasy.

S was a musician, played the guitar and sang, gave recitals, took pleasure in being the center of attention. I remember carrying her guitar case for her and resenting my role. I remember being obsessed with her, thinking myself in love, but at the same time not liking her very much. Her narcissism, I suspect, warred with mine. It disturbed her that I was not musical, couldn't carry a tune, couldn't identify the Beethoven symphonies she liked to hum to me on the subway as a test. If we were fated to get together, we were not fated to go on together for very long. We dated for little more than a year (perhaps a year and a half), though it seems longer than that in emotional time. She ultimately went off with a friend of mine, a guy I had introduced her to. I didn't regret losing her, not so much that (our relationship was a succession of crises that staled after a point), as I regretted that she preferred someone else. It was loss that I mourned, but not her loss in particular. Once S was lost to me irrevocably, it was a relief to be free of the obligation of pursuing her. As I look back on it, I can see that I've had a predilection for narcissistic women. S was only the first.

In my junior year, I wrote a one-act play that was produced at the college. I directed the play and ended up taking over the lead role when the original actor left to take a part in something else. It may have been that I was too demanding as a director and drove him off. The play, as I remember it—no copies of it survive, was a kind of Restoration comedy in contemporary setting, a succession of one-liners that aspired to wit.

The mostly favorable reception of the play confirmed me in the view that I was a playwright. I wrote poems and stories as an undergraduate, but my real bent, as I saw it, was the writing of plays.

I am trying to remember what it was like to be twenty, have only the vaguest sense of what or who I was. (I was a small pond in a big fish.) At about the time my play was being done, I became friends with a girl named Naomi, whom I would marry the following year. She was an English major who wrote fiction, dark and very pretty, someone I had known casually for a while. We spent a lot of time together, not going to classes, sitting on the grass in some not quite private corner of the campus. After a while, we went to her place in the afternoons. Her parents didn't get home as a rule until after six. It was after we started going together that I learned that she had a longtime steady boyfriend, a childhood sweetheart. (Or did I know that all along? Was that part of the attraction?) We saw each other only during the week—the weekends reserved for the real boyfriend. (I was the illicit lover.) In the beginning, the other boyfriend didn't matter to me, or at least I kept it (him) from mattering. I was the preferred one, she said. Occasionally, when the real boyfriend was away, or doing something else, I would go out with Naomi on a weekend night. Finally, I pressed her to make a decision between us. She promised to break off with the real boyfriend, though when they were together she was unable to tell him. So we went on for a while in this heightened state, seeing each other surreptitiously as if we were Romeo and Juliet. I mention this at length because the illicit has been a factor—a powerful factor—in many of my relationships with women. I liked being the secret lover. (The fantasy pattern is classic: I was again and again winning my mother away from my father.)

After Naomi broke up with the real boyfriend, whom she depended on in various ways (was dependent on), I had no choice but to take his place. I had won, but I felt vulnerable to the inevitable successor to my former role. I felt like one of Shakespeare's usurper kings; I had initiated the pattern that would be my own undoing. Apart from metaphor, I worried, had cause to (Naomi still kept his picture in her wallet), that the displaced boyfriend was now the secret lover. In the heat of so much neurotic fever, it was inevitable that we decided to get married. I was twenty; she was nineteen.

We were in love—I think that's true—but I suspect the real reason we got married was to move out of our parents' houses. We were both looking for an occasion to get out. And then there was another element, a further irony. After we had decided to get married, Naomi got pregnant. Although our positions tended to change from discussion to discussion, mostly I wanted to have the child and Naomi didn't. Shortly after our marriage—a month or so after—Naomi had an illegal abortion. It was done in a doctor's office (after hours), and without an anesthetic. I held her hand through it—that is, she held mine, squeezing my hand when the pain became unbearable. It was a nightmare and remains vivid to me even now.

Our marriage never recovered from the trauma of the abortion. My first day in graduate school at Columbia University, I came home to find a good-bye note from Naomi. She had gone home to her parents, couldn't handle it, whatever it was. This was the second time she had left me, the second and final time. The game of marriage was over. I tried in perfunctory ways to reestablish contact, called her every few days without making connection. For a while, Naomi wouldn't even come to the phone to talk, her parents protecting her from herself, insisting that she didn't want to speak to me. (First love: second loss.) I refused to call it quits, stayed on in our grim basement apartment, listening for footsteps. The marriage was annulled after about two months of separation. At twenty-one, I was a formerly married man, whose marriage (given the logic of annulment) officially never existed.

After the break-up of my first marriage, I threw myself into the writing of a three-act play. I carried my notebook with me everywhere, wrote on the subway, wrote in restaurants, wrote in classes. I avoided pain, or tried to, by keeping busy. I gave up my basement apartment in Brooklyn and took a furnished room near Columbia, moved through a succession of furnished rooms. I liked being at Columbia and I liked being on my own. I remember thinking, while grieving over the loss of Naomi, that this was the best year of my life.

I entered the MFA Program in Theater Arts at Columbia in January 1955. That summer I took a job writing the daily newspaper at Grossinger's Country Club. I had had part-time jobs throughout the year and had essentially supported myself since I was eighteen. The Grossinger's job was in continuation of that necessity, though substantially different from the kind of jobs I had taken during the school year. In conjunction with a colleague, I wrote a mimeographed newspaper called the *Daily Tattler,* whose purpose was to publish the names of guests (and celebrity visitors) in a flattering context. I used to interview guests at meals—generally at lunch—getting their names and professions. The guests were mostly single women, mostly women in their thirties, looking to meet men. The interviewing was the aspect of the job I liked least. I was shy at intruding on strangers while they were eating. Once, a woman put the key to her room in my hand when we shook hands. It was flattering, but I was too high-minded (too scared perhaps) to accept her implicit offer. After getting out the daily newspaper, I was on my own time. I played tennis (once with Jackie Robinson, who was a guest during All-Star break), and swam in the Grossinger's pool, had free run of the facilities of the resort. During cocktail hour, I mingled with guests. That too was an aspect of my job. I was part of the social apparatus of the hotel. While the job was a pleasure—a dream job really—it bothered me that I was a kind of gigolo.

One day I passed an attractive woman, clearly more sophisticated than the usual run of guests, sitting on a bench, waiting for someone, looking mildly forlorn. Always available to women in distress (women mistreated by other men), I introduced myself, sat down and talked to her. Perhaps she smiled at me first. She was not a guest, not a paying guest as it turned out, was waiting to see the guy I worked for. I entertained her in his absence. She was just out of college, worked as an editor of children's books for Harper and Row, seemed knowledgeable and smart about matters that interested me. I gave her a copy of my play to read, left her on her bench, less forlorn than before though still waiting.

She returned my play to me that evening and I asked her if she liked it. She studied the question before answering, said, "I like you." The dialogue is extremely clear in memory, left an inescapable impression. She left after a few days and I took her number. It was an eventful summer in my life—the summer of '55, the summer I turned twenty-two. I played a set of tennis with the great baseball player Jackie Robinson, and I met a woman I would eventually marry.

The play I wrote at Columbia for my thesis, *The One-Eyed Man Is King,* was produced at the Theater East the following spring by Orion Productions. I understudied the lead and planned to go on one night myself, though when the time came I decided against it. On occasion the director threw me out of rehearsals, became upset with my interference. The actors changed lines; I wanted the play read exactly as written. The play on stage often seemed very different from the one I thought I had written. I rued the lack of control I had over my own work. The play in performance seemed to me a collaboration that to some extent excluded me. Although I was grateful to have my first play performed, it was in many ways a disillusioning experience. I had difficulty then, as always, making appropriate compromises.

Shortly after the play completed its limited run (March through June, I think), I was drafted into the army, let myself be drafted rather than go on for a Ph.D. If you managed to stay in school until you were twenty-six, the army no longer wanted you. I chose the army over a Ph.D. assuming that it would be a richer experience for a writer, accepting the philistine belief that physical experience is somehow more real than the intellectual life.

The authoritarianism and incompetence of the army, the combination of the two, surprised me. This was 1956. It was between Korea and Vietnam, between our two major follies. The training was slack. It was not the ordeal that made the army difficult to take, but the stupidity and boredom. The stupidity and

meanness—the gratuitous harassment—were the worst aspects of the training. What the training achieved—I wonder in retrospect at the consciousness behind it—was a kind of demoralization that prepared one for dying. One longed for something to do that was challenging, that made one feel useful or even used.

I spent ten days of idle processing at Fort Dix, then was sent to Fort Knox, Kentucky, an armor fort, for Infantry Basic Training. A run-down World War II barracks was rehabilitated—the locks taken off the doors—for our arrival. Our cadre of NCOs had never conducted Basic Training before, and had little gift for teaching army skills. We were not prepared to fight in a war after our training; at best, we had been sufficiently dehumanized to be willing to put our lives on the line without complaint. If other soldiers at other forts received the kind of training I received, one can understand the debacles of Korea and Vietnam. My advanced training was at Fort Huachuca, Arizona, an army electronics proving ground that had almost no functioning electronic equipment at hand. My battalion was commanded by a major who had been removed in Korea for unnecessarily exposing his troops to fire.

In the last week of Basic Training, I married Elinor Berkman in a small—very small—ceremony in Louisville, Kentucky. Ellie gave up her job as a chil-

*With son David*

dren's book editor at Random House (she had gone there from Harper's) to join me at Fort Huachuca. Our first child, David, was born on the fort in 1957. After living several months in a chicken coop shack about ten army-town miles from the fort, we rented the cowboy house on a ranch in Elgin, Arizona, an idyllic spot—the setting for a movie (filmed when we were there) called *3:10 to Yuma*. On weekends, on three-day passes, we went to Mexico, to Nogales, which was sixty miles away, and watched bullfights. I wrote a scenario for a short film on bullfighting, though maneuvers interceded and I never got a chance to film it.

While in the army, I finished a second play, wrote two short stories, and two film reviews for the magazine *Film Culture*. I was discharged in April 1958, three months early, in order to return to school. With a wife and child to support, I needed to find some way of earning a living. I entered the Ph.D. program at Stanford University, which I had visited during a period of leave from the army. After the army, Stanford seemed like paradise, and I completed the degree, while teaching one or two courses a quarter, in three years. If I hadn't gone into the army, if the army hadn't sent me to Arizona to become, of all things, a pole lineman, it is unlikely that I would ever have found my way to Stanford. Though I wanted to write, I had spent five years away from writing, had postponed my career circumstantially.

My recollections offer a roseate view of my time at Stanford, which I immediately distrust. It seemed wonderful—liberating—in contrast to the relative oppressiveness of the army. I did a dissertation on the contemporary American novel under Wallace Stegner, a subject that might not have seemed respectable at most other universities. In preparation, I read almost every novel with claim to importance in the past twenty years. It was, though I didn't know that then, a kind of apprenticeship for me as a fiction writer, a way of coming to terms with my immediate literary past. My thesis was called "The Theme of Guilt and Redemption in the Post—Second World War Novel" and included chapters on Robert Penn Warren, Saul Bellow, Bernard Malamud, William Styron, J. D. Salinger, Flannery O'Connor, Ralph Ellison, and Wright Morris—an attempt at giving a critical overview of the American novel between 1945 and 1960 by concentrating on eight exemplary works. An expanded version of my thesis was published as *The Landscape of Nightmare* by New York University Press in 1965. I am one of the rare and lucky people who enjoyed writing his Ph.D. dissertation. It is a personal reading—a writer's reading—of eight writers who mattered to me a great deal at the time.

I neglect to mention my private life at Stanford. I'll get to that later, or not at all. I made a number of friends who have remained friends. My daughter, Nina, was born at a hospital in Redwood City, California, on July 12, 1961—a month before we were to leave for Columbus, Ohio. The best of the teaching offers I had was at Ohio State University, and I started there—leaving Stanford with some reluctance—in the fall of 1961. Although I enjoyed my time at Stanford, I was desperate to start writing again. I had managed two stories while doing graduate work. I was ready to start a novel.

For a city of its size—over five hundred thousand—Columbus, Ohio, is a cultural backwater, offers its residents relatively few distractions. Consequently, it's a good place to write. I spent my first year at Columbus writing a novel, wrote in my office every free moment I could get. What I remember most about the experience was the exhilaration of completing the novel. As soon as I sent the book off to an agent, freed of its burden, I began another novel. An editor at Random House liked the book, but wanted to publish my second novel first (I had about a hundred and fifty pages). My second novel was *A Man to Conjure With* and was published by Random House in 1965, a few

*Daughter, Nina*

*With son Noah, 1969*

months after NYU Press had brought out *The Landscape of Nightmare: Studies in the Contemporary American Novel.* My first novel, the one that attracted the attention of Random House in the first place, was by agreement never published.

Though stylistically my own, *A Man to Conjure With* showed the influence of the books I had been reading. It was relatively conventional in form, was distinguished perhaps by its dream passages. It got mostly favorable reviews, was published in England and Italy. It got a wonderful advance comment from Bernard Malamud, which appeared on the cover of the English edition. I haven't looked at the novel in a long time, have moved so far away from it (a departure certain admirers of that book never forgave me for) that I can barely remember having written it. When I finished it, while I was writing it, I sensed that it was a considerable advance over anything I had done before.

When *A Man to Conjure With* came out I was living in New York City and teaching at NYU (uptown campus). Let's move back a few years, return to Columbus, Ohio. It is 1963, the year of John Kennedy's assassination. Ellie and I have become increasingly estranged. I

have become involved with a graduate student at Ohio State, a married woman (a married child-woman), who is assisting me in a graduate course in modern drama I am teaching. She reminds me in certain ways of my first wife, a compelling attraction. We split up when I leave Ohio State to take a teaching job at NYU, and I assume I won't see Georgia again. While I have gone East, she has gone West—to a new branch of the University of California at La Jolla to complete her Ph.D. Several of the English Department faculty have gone to La Jolla to start the school's humanities program. We say good-bye. It is 1964. I return to New York City after having been away since 1956. The distance between us makes serious our separation—we are three thousand miles apart.

Still, we keep in touch, write to each other every day, the distance between us seeming to intensify our connection rather than dissolve it. Words have always had enormous power in my life. Language codified our romance. Love was never so real until it was spelled out on the page.

*The Landscape of Nightmare* and *A Man to Conjure With* both came out in 1965—the book of criticism in the spring, the novel in the fall. It was not the celebratory time it might have been. As my career as writer moved forward, my life seemed to be moving in reverse. I missed Georgia. My marriage to Ellie was in increasing disarray. The problem was that I couldn't bear the idea of leaving my children, of no longer living in the same house with them. Yet I couldn't go on living the way I was. I had been postponing the inevitable next step, hoping my life would resolve itself.

In 1966, when I took a teaching job at Brooklyn College, I separated from Ellie and moved into a one-room apartment in Brooklyn Heights. Georgia was in New York, had also taken a teaching job at Brooklyn College. Eventually, I found a larger place in the Heights I could afford (alimony and child support took more than half my take-home pay), a four-room floor-through on State Street in in an early nineteenth-century frame house. After a while, Georgia gave up her apartment in Greenwich Village and moved in with me. With some sense of risk, Georgia and I were married in June 1968. We had at that time the same therapist, a man named Clifford Deutscher. I don't think we would have ever gotten together without him. We had gone through a great deal—I omit the difficulties, the innumerable break-ups along the way—to get to where we were. We had earned the right to be together, I thought.

What remained difficult, what never got easier and never had ease, were the weekly Saturday visits with my children. A visiting father, I discovered, is less a parent than a part-time entertainer, a song-and-dance man with a stale routine. I did my best and failed at the job, took Nina and David to museums and baseball games and movies and out to dinner and in to dinner, and all of us remained discontent. If they were difficult during these visits, as they often were, carrying as they did the burden of their mother's resentment toward me, I was reluctant to discipline them. I did not want to lose their favor—I wanted (how could I not?) to be liked by my estranged children. The implications of the divorce (joint custody which was not then an alternative would have made considerable difference in our lives) were traumatic for the children and painful to me. It seemed a cruel arrangement, made worse by my guilt and Ellie's bitterness. I felt for the longest time that I had lost my children. Only recently—they are both in their twenties now—have I become close to them again.

Time begins to move at a quicker pace. In 1968, I published my second novel, *What Comes Next,* with Harper and Row—the novel coming out (edited by David Siegal) a few months after my marriage. *What Comes Next,* which is in part a response to the Vietnam War, is a novel about public and private violence and is my darkest, most pitiless book—the manifest demon of my psychotherapy. It got a long appreciative review in the *New York Times Book Review,* though had a small sale. It is the first of my novels to be directly influenced

by films, and it was taken on option by the director Ulu Grosbard with the provision that I write the screenplay. I had mixed feelings about doing the screenplay because it meant postponing work on the new novel I had started. As a writer, I was no longer interested in *What Comes Next,* had already solved the problem of the material, had discovered the novel's form. Still, Ulu's was not an offer I could pass up. To work on a movie was something I had wanted to do for a long time.

As with most movie projects, the film of *What Comes Next* never got made. I wrote two extended treatments, virtual screenplays, which Ulu showed around, but the people who had the money didn't see it as a sufficiently commercial project. I have the sense that the writing of the screenplay, the thinking of action in terms of image, had some influence on the novel I would write next. That was the most positive aspect of what turned out to be a frustrating experience.

I remember that I was writing a piece on the New York Knicks for *Esquire* at the time, relating the obsession of being a fan with the obsession of being a writer. Georgia seemed to have an endless pregnancy, carried beyond term, and labor had to be induced. I was in the delivery room, a vicarious participant, when my son Noah was born on September 3, 1969. I was enormously pleased to have another child, and Noah in particular. It was an elation comparable to what I felt

*Baumbach (left) with son Noah, and Robert Towers with daughter Sara,*
*Oxford, England, 1973*

when I completed my first novel. This time, I was ready to be a father. If you do something over and over again, you generally get better at it.

Also, I had broken through as a writer, had written a book that was a notable advance over anything I had done before. It was called "Dreambook" initially and it was composed of forty (thirty-three in the final version) cinematic dreams. The novel was held together by recurring configurations—the same things happening again and again to the central character in different metaphoric disguise. I was greatly pleased with the book—it realized its intention, it was the book I wanted to write, it was mine—and so I was dismayed at the difficulty it had in finding a publisher. No one seemed to know what to make of it. My agent, Candida Donadio, sent it around for over two years (I kept making lapidary changes) and it garnered something like thirty-four rejections. It may have circulated three years or even four. The title changed. It became "Jack in the Box," then "Reruns." New editors looked at it; old editors looked at it again. "Reruns" remained an orphan.

The myth was and remains (against persuasive evidence to the contrary) that all good novels eventually find a publisher. Why was I having so much difficulty with *Reruns?* Was it the nature of the book? It seemed to me extremely accessible, entertaining even. I had been giving readings from it for over a year to enthusiastic response. On five occasions, young editors wanted to publish the book only to be overruled from on top. Publishing houses were becoming more cautious perhaps, wanted fiction that was recognizably commercial. I was advised to be patient. The problem was I couldn't get into another book, was stuck, while *Reruns* was homeless.

The story of how the Fiction Collective got started has been told so many times, it has ceased to be interesting or even true. I discovered that my problem with *Reruns* was not unique, that a number of other writers whose work I admired, had had similar experiences. After close to a year of discussions, we decided to form a publishing cooperative for serious fiction. To publish the kind of fiction—risky, imaginative, original—that most commercial houses seemed not to want to chance. *Reruns* came out with the Fiction Collective in October 1974, three years after its completion.

I served with Peter Spielberg as co-director of the Fiction Collective for its early years, despite myself became a self-taught publisher. Overseeing each of the steps of *Reruns'* production was almost as exhilarating in its own way as being in the delivery room at Noah's birth. I had become part of the process of making a book, a process which had always seemed somewhat magical to me. *What Comes Next* was out of print a year

*"On my fortieth birthday." Introducing Noah to the British Museum, London, 1973*

or so after publication, despite its favorable reviews. Twelve years after its first printing, *Reruns* is still in print, still in certain bookstores, is taught occasionally in university courses, is available to be read. It has sold more than twice the combined sales of my first two novels. A further irony: publishers who rejected it in the first place have referred to it as a classic while rejecting more recent work for not being in the same "classic mode" as a book that had been turned down thirty-four times.

The year before *Reruns* came out, I had published a story in *Partisan Review* called "Drool," about a baby who stands on his father's lap and tells him a story. Listening to Noah who was learning to speak, I became fascinated by the cunning language of children, which is rich with metaphor. I did a sequel to "Drool" called "Babble: The Baby's Second Story," which was published in *Esquire.* It was after I had written the third story, "Pagina Man," that I had decided to make a novel—something like a novel—out of the Baby stories. Often snatches of Noah's private conversation set off the idea for the next segment of the Baby's adventures. I was writing a novel, I realized, about a child's imagination and the discovery (the invention) of language. *Babble,* as it was finally called, is a small book about almost everything. Although a few commercial publishers were interested in *Babble*—three of the sections had appeared in *Esquire*—I elected to do the book with the Fiction Collective. *Babble* was published to notably little attention, to what seemed like absolute silence, in 1976. It was the first book of mine not to be reviewed in the *New York Times Book Review.* I was told by one of the editors that it had been sent out for review, but what had come in had been "too stupid to print." I was too polite to say that that had never been a detriment to publication in the *Book Review* before. Nor did I ask why they had sent it to someone who was not adequate to the book. The fact is, that once the Fiction Collective had stopped being news, its books began to get ignored by the media. That the Collective had almost no advertising budget began to take its toll.

My son Nicholas—called Nico—was born on March 10, 1975, almost eighteen years after my first son, David. At this writing, I have four children between the ages of eleven and twenty-nine. When they all get together, which is reasonably often, I permit myself the pleasurable illusion of being a kind of patriarch. It is like having still another career.

The career that supported me was teaching. It made possible my writing the kind of books that were important to me regardless of commercial implications. In 1973, the year the Fiction Collective was conceived, Mark Strand and I created a graduate program in Creative Writing at Brooklyn College, which I've co-directed with Mark Strand and later with John Ashbery. I take pleasure in the teaching, feel that it complements my career as a writer rather than undermines it. I've tended to write in the mornings—usually from eight to twelve—and do my teaching and reading of student work (and reading for the Fiction Collective) in the afternoons and evenings. My schedule used to be fairly rigid. As I've gotten older, I've allowed myself more time off from work. Obsessions, like all addictions, die hard. There was a period of over two years where I didn't miss a morning of writing, which is to say a morning communing with my typewriter. On Christmases, I tended to work two hours instead of

*Son Nico*

*Nico and Noah in Maussanne, France, 1979*

four, a gesture in deference to tradition. Wherever I've lived, I've tended to have studies away from the main action of the household. Like my father when I was a child, I was home and not home. I must have been a difficult person to have around.

In 1974, I began to do a regular film piece for the *Partisan Review*. I had done my share of reviewing over the years, both of books and films, but this was the first reviewing on a regular basis I had done. I preferred (and prefer) reviewing films to books and particularly liked the idea of discussing movies in an intellectual journal. In 1976, I believe, I was elected to the National Society of Film Critics. In 1982 and 1983, I served as its chairman. So I was doing three things (pursuing three careers) that gave me great pleasure— writing fiction, teaching fiction-writing, and writing about films.

We are moving inexorably toward the present, which recedes even as I approach it. I received a Guggenheim Fellowship in 1979 and I spent with my family most of the year in the south of France, Noah and Nico attending school in the country town of Maussanne. In the same year (it seems as if there are certain key years in my life), I had two books published—the novel *Chez Charlotte and Emily* and a book of stories called *The Return of Service*. If *Reruns* can be seen as my breakthrough novel, *Chez Charlotte and Emily* might be

seen as the fulfillment of that line of pursuit. It is a novel about imagined experience—the imagining of experience—and the relationship between the teller and the tale. I've only seen one or two discussions of it in print that even come close to reading the book I think I've written. Even sympathetic pieces seemed to miss the point, which was disheartening.

The novel and the book of stories confirmed my position among the writers of "experimental fiction," the putative oddballs and cranks, who refuse to give the tired but deserving reader what he presumes he wants. My identification with the Fiction Collective and with nonrealistic fiction seemed to estrange me even further from the publishing establishment. I was behaving, in a wholly different context and time, like the kid who refused to sign the loyalty oath (a law long since revoked) in high school. I didn't know what was good for me then and I still didn't, and I still don't.

In my Guggenheim year in the south of France— it seems like only last year—I wrote a novel about an estranged son visiting his father in London. The novel has three separate but related narratives that play off one another—the son's story, the father's story, and the screenplay the father is writing. It is a somewhat less adventurous book than *Chez Charlotte and Emily*, but it is not a signing of the loyalty oath either. *My Father More or Less* was published by the Fiction Collective in 1982.

*Chatting with Robert Coover in his garden in Deal, England, 1978*

*Three charter members of the Fiction Collective: Russell Banks, Clarence Major, and Jonathan Baumbach*

Recently, I've worked more and more in short forms. Having come to the short story after the novel, I have a special affection for that form, a form I arrived at late and with insufficient respect. What I like about the short story is that it is closer to the poem and what I've been about all along—this a new discovery for me—is the making of novels with the language and texture of poems. A second collection of my stories—I think of the book as all of a piece—came out in May 1987. The title story is *The Life and Times of Major Fiction*.

I continue to do the same things as if my life had the pattern of an obsessive fiction with a repetitive motif. The point is to keep it fresh for as long as I can. The particulars of my life have changed in the past year and a half. Georgia and I, after about eighteen years together, have separated. We have agreed on joint custody and I live with Noah and Nico half of every week, which is almost sufficient, which is an acceptable compromise. I put in as much energy and take as much pride in being a father as being a writer. For a while, single parenting kept me from writing as much as I had in the past, but for the last six months I've worked well. I've just completed a new novel, and am writing between novels, this compacted autobiography, the work in hand. My best work lies ahead of me, I feel. And with that awareness, the sense that there are surprising things inside of me I've yet to discover, I continue to do what it seems I've always done. I continue

to imagine language on a blank page.

---

## BIBLIOGRAPHY

### Fiction:

*A Man to Conjure With.* New York: Random House, 1965; London: Gollancz, 1966.

*What Comes Next.* New York: Harper, 1968.

*Reruns.* New York: Fiction Collective, 1974.

*Babble.* New York: Fiction Collective, 1976.

*Chez Charlotte and Emily.* Madison, Wis.: Fiction Collective, 1979.

*The Return of Service* (short stories). Urbana and London: University of Illinois Press, 1979.

*My Father More or Less.* New York: Fiction Collective, 1982.

*The Life and Times of Major Fiction.* New York: Fiction Collective, 1987.

### Nonfiction:

*The Landscape of Nightmare: Studies in the Contemporary American Novel.* New York: New York University Press, 1965; London: P. Owen, 1966.

### Plays:

*The One-Eyed Man Is King,* first produced at The Theater East, New York City, 1956.

### Editor of:

*Moderns and Contemporaries: Nine Masters of the Short Story,* with

Arthur Edelstein. New York: Random House, 1968; second edition published as *Moderns and Contemporaries: Twelve Masters of the Short Story.* New York: Random House, 1977.

*Writers as Teachers/Teachers as Writers.* New York: Holt, 1970.

*Statements: New Fiction from the Fiction Collective.* New York: Braziller, 1975.

*Statements Two: New Fiction,* with Peter Spielberg. New York: Fiction Collective, 1977.

# Wayne C. Booth

*1921-*

## THREE UNFINISHED PROJECTS

*Wayne Booth*

I've always liked that account by Mark Twain of the turning point of his life. When he was twelve and a half his father died—but that wasn't the turning point. The major event was, he claimed, his deliberately contracting the measles, to get rid of his fear of contracting the measles. He almost died, and his mother, to keep him out of further mischief, apprenticed him to a printer—and that of course led inevitably to his becoming a great comic writer.

Our lives are full of such turning points, real enough even if material for comedy. And when we finally are tempted by autobiography, we fish about among them to find the most reasonable explanation of how on earth—and that's where we seem always to have been—we ever got *here*. I have a friend who claims that nobody ever writes an autobiography until he or she (usually it's a he) knows where *here* is. If you know where you are at last, you know who you are, he says, and you can conduct a reasonable search for the turns in the path you've followed. But if you are more like me, not entirely sure yet where you are or who you want to be when you grow up, you will either write several autobiographies or none.

I've tried several, and I now offer samples from three of them.

## I

### *The Resistance to Yielding*

The turning point of my life was my father's death, when I was six. I discovered that this was so when I found myself writing an autobiography, to be called either "Yieldings" or "Unselvings," about six months after my eighteen-year-old son, Richard, was killed by a car, on the open road, by a "nurse" (so we were told) who stopped and identified herself to police but who never so much as dropped us a note to express her regret. After months of the inevitable shock, grief, anger, and guilt, and after several imaginary heart attacks—hoping that I too might die though flatly rejecting suicide—I suddenly felt strangely liberated, more fully freed from anxiety than I could ever remember: the world was new again. I had survived the worst, and I sat me down, in our bleak little apartment in Putney (London), and turned out maybe three hundred pages (don't ask me to count them now: I've not even looked at them for sixteen years) explaining that the goal of life was to get to feel the way I then felt.

As I remember it—no, I will *not* go now and check; where *are* those pages, anyway?—I portrayed a mature, nay wise, forty-eight-year-old man whose deep experience of love and grief had freed him to *yield*—to yield to further and fuller love of his family; to yield to his teaching and writing in ways less anxious than in the past; and finally to yield even to God's cruel ways. I felt that I had at last earned the right to "stand up in meeting and bear my testimony of thanksgiving" for the gift of life—including the life of that wonderful son, and even his unthinkable snuffing out.

As I saw it—as I can *almost* see it now—yielding, difficult and loaded with suppressions as it was for me, was a lot easier than it was for someone like my wife who had not had practice at it. I had been given a head start, at the age of six, with the shock, grief, guilt—perhaps even anger?—in response to my father's

death:

*September 28, 1986:*
It was not long after my sixth birthday when my father, after one year in his new job teaching "Agronomy," took to his bed with Addison's disease and died, after two weeks that I only dimly remember as horrible. My mother, a devout Mormon, had always believed that if she prayed with "a sincere heart and contrite spirit" her prayers would be answered. She prayed with all her heart that he would live, prayed many times with me and no doubt many times in private, and he died. I had of course prayed too, as coached by Mama, and I doubt very much that I was coached to conclude, "Not my will but Thine, Oh Lord."

My mother managed to yield, in a way: that is, she soon coped. Left with two children, no money, and a scarred faith, she began, only five months after "Daddie's" death, to teach elementary school.[1] But she told me years later that "for a long time I couldn't really pray." I can remember many a night when I could hear her sobbing in her bedroom. I had thus lost not just my father but the cheerful, confident, secure mother she had been. Until my son was killed, I often dreamed, in strict obedience to Freud, that I had killed "a man" and buried him in our back garden. The police were about to figure it out and dig up the body, and I would be . . .

Then, less than a year after my father's death, Mother's mother—my next favorite person—was killed with a clumsy appendectomy. We moved to join my bereft grandfather's family—and the little boy who had been the center of the world found himself in a family of seven, disciplined at table and in my chores by a grieving, dour grandfather, welcomed at home after school by a resentful, slovenly "hired girl." I often wept myself to sleep, crying, "I want my Daddie," and I often dreamed, just as I later dreamed about

---

[1] She soon became principal, began earning college credits, became first a teacher-trainer, then after taking her M.A., the head "Counselor for Women" at Brigham Young University. Have you ever thought of what it would mean to accumulate three years of college credit, while working full-time and managing a family without a mate? My heart goes out to those single parents who are attempting similar feats today, often, I'm afraid, without the communal and family support that Mother had.

my son, that the lost one was not dead after all. Bliss! And then to wake to the "farm forever fled from the childless land."

That sort of experience gives good training in what to expect from life: unhappy surprises. If you've found your loving and doting father and mother suddenly replaced by an unyielding and anxious grandfather and an overworked and indeed seemingly absconded mother, you will never again assume that things are going to go your way, or that you are in charge, or that your relation to whatever is in charge can be solved with simple cheerfulness and goodwill.

So: I had expected, in the depths of my unconscious, the unthinkable. What I had not expected—what seems strange even now, is that within a few months of Richard's death I would come to feel a positive exhilaration in laying out my reasons for accepting it and embracing the world in which the unthinkable is normal. What did I then claim to have yielded to, other than the "other" to Whom I felt glad to relinquish my self?

To yield, in my definition at the time, meant to give up one's "self," to engage totally with something other than self which then, by virtue of the yielding, yielded back a new and larger self. The business of life, I had come to feel, was to transcend the limits of one's accidental individuality, with its destructive infusions of self, self, self; the task was to engage so totally with the not-self as to erase all boundaries.

As isolated individuals we do not usually choose our "turning points": the moment when our parents met, the moment when we were conceived, the circumstances of our birth and setting forth, our schools and friends, the childhood diseases that did or did not maim us, the illnesses that did or did not kill off our parents. More fundamentally, we did not choose, could not in our wildest ambitions even dream of imagining what it might mean to choose the essential natural conditions that create life itself: the Way Things Work. We find ourselves—as I only later learned that Heidegger puts it—"thrown" into an existence beyond our control. Pray as we will, the conditions of our "thrownness" persist.

The one central choice of life for everyone, then, is whether to "accept the toss": whether to yield to the Great Unyielder and try to move *with* Him/Her, or to try to go it alone, pretending to an absurdly impossible, in-dividual autonomy. As G. K. Chesterton says somewhere,[2] the most important thing to know about

---

[2] I've really tried to find it, but the precise quotation eludes me.

any person is how that question will be addressed and answered.

My joy, writing in grief at age forty-eight, a joy that I can now only fitfully recapture, came largely from the discovery, as I looked back over my five decades, that I had in fact yielded, and could happily continue to yield, to various representations of the "Other." I was of course aware that in some theologies the "Other" has no representatives: "He" is totally *other*. But that was not my theology: the God that I had rediscovered and fitfully yielded to in 1952-53 (see Autobiography II below) was to be best known precisely *in* representatives, and in yielding to those representatives one yielded to Him/Her. Who or what were they?

### *Family*

(Now surely is the moment to get out that typescript after all and find whether I was at all successful in beating down that Old Nick, Ego. Yes, here it is, at the bottom of the stack of diaries. And here is a section boasting about how I have yielded myself one hundred percent to my family—and *here* is the necessary ironic discounting, labelled "For ego section: family????" Can you trust me to quote honestly from the embarrassing stuff in these autobiographies, and in the journals they in turn quote from—just as I wrote it, without the cleanings-up that the old ego would like to impose? I'll indicate all elisions, but I'll not provide a "sic" for *every* error or egregiously misguided moment. Do trust me.)

*October 30, 1969 (*aetat *forty-eight):*
All right, then: we're trying here for a way of injecting a little reality into all this abstraction. And if we're to do that without undue distortion, we have to work a bit at being honest. This section was planned, in a moment of madness, as one more step in my unselving: how I have mastered, or—let us not be too obviously arrogant—nearly mastered, the destructive drags and pushes of the unschooled ego. I *was* an egotistical bastard; now I have put away childish things.

Well, we shall see. Try out the following, as the portrait of the purged ego, 1969.

*Scene: The meanly furnished living room of our Putney flat. We (Phyllis, his* [sic] *wife; daughters Katherine [21] and Alison [15] and myself) have just returned from dinner . . . Katherine and Phyllis want to crochet & knit, if I will read to them. I agree to read, either* Dubliners *or my journal from thirty years ago, whichever they prefer. Hint, hint. They agree to listen to the journal.*

*Wayne:* Well, I'll read you some stuff I haven't re-read since I wrote it, written in '44 after my return to Provo from my mission—stuff about meeting Phyllis that I just re-read today. OK?

*Silent, knitting assent.*

*Wayne:* "Feb. 4, 1944. In the two weeks since my return [from my two years as a missionary, years in which I had abided more or less strictly by the Church's rules against being alone with a woman], I've had good visits with [I list four former teachers] . . .; dates with N_____ M_____ and L_____ Q_____, the former dull, the latter rather interesting; but neither had anything to encourage further investigation. N_____ is much the more intelligent and better educated, but withal she is pedestrian: I could never think of things to say to her once we were married. She has the right opinions, she knows music well, but that must be only a starting position for enjoyable association; she makes it all seem so final. Besides (and I suspect much more important than anything else, she simply does not attract me physically; nor does L_____."

You understand, I'm just selecting here, stuff about girls. There's a lot of *good* stuff here about the war, about literature and the imagination, about my own fears about lacking creativity. But I'll skip onward:

"Feb. 19, 1944: Life in Provo in Feb. 1944 is pleasant for a young man. There are hundreds of attractive girls and practically no fellows. The quest for a mate is delightful if perplexing—and one can retreat into selfish personal pleasure and forget the war for hours at a time. . . ."

"Feb. 23, 1944: Extra! I have found two—not one but two—girls who genuinely understand and appreciate music. One of them was here last night listening to Haydn's D Major and Beeth's [sic] C♯ Minor quartets. No, I am not indulging . . . in wishful courting. She really knew what was going on. . . ."

I'll skip some stuff here . . . about my unfulfilled plan to write, on my birthday, a "long critique of myself"; ah, here's the embarrassing bit [I was looking for]:

"March 18, 1944: Critical thinking doesn't go well with finding a mate. Emotionally I am set for marriage; rationally I cannot (a) justify marriage for me at the present time [dangling before the draft] or (b) find a girl to suit. Phyllis Barnes may remove both difficulties simply by destroying my critical faculties. I rather hope she does.

"Girls are like institutions: they are necessary to carry on the business of the race, but no one representative of them will bear intent investigation.

"Experimental data: Phyllis received a subscription [from me] to the *New Republic* on her eighteenth birthday. If I marry her [which I did, two years later], now a seemingly strong possibility, the experiment may be pronounced a success. Further data: she listens without complaint to my records—last night two hours of them—and makes an attempt to respond to my conversation. All fine, but—maybe I expect too much from an eighteen year old."

*The hero looks up from his reading to discover that he has not amused his hearers. Two of the women are glaring at him.*

*Katherine:* Dad, that's terrible!

*Wayne:* Well, yes, I know. But of course he is making fun of himself.

*Phyllis:* He isn't either. He's simply arrogant. Conducting an examination. That's what happened to my appreciation of music—I've always been having to prove that I was doing it your way.

*Wayne (already hurt):* Oh, no, no. You've got it all wrong. The young man is teasing. Look at that phrase:
"Experimental data." He wasn't writing that seriously. He was making fun of himself. He really was.

*Phyllis:* No, he wasn't, not really.

*Wayne (trying to affect a bantering tone):* You're not *really* angry about that, are you? I thought it would *amuse* you. Here, here's a better one (*a bit frantic now*). Listen to this:
"April 13: Phyll and I had a fine easter picnic, and we were together all day Sunday: Bach's Passion, Mendelssohn's violin concerto, and stuff." Well, that wasn't the one [I was looking for]. Oh, here it is:
"June 18, 1944, Camp Roberts, Calif.: At the very great risk of making a fool of myself, I'm going to give briefly the details of my love. I thought I was in love with Phyllis

long before last week-end. I didn't say much about it here, because the entries prompted by my seeming love for Aileen [a few years before] seem so absurd now. After last week-end, tho, the need or desire for concealment completely disappeared. I am completely and irrecoverably in love. In the time honored manner of poets, my mind is filled constantly with thoughts of her and with plans for us . . ."

[And on he goes, for a full paragraph about the love, with lots of words like conjugal, aesthetics, ethics, religion, religious rites, spiritual contracts, humor, passionate spiritual communion—but as she points out when they discuss it calmly next day, not a word about *her*.]

*The hero looks up, embarrassed at the tone, but sure that he will have satisfied all critics with his irony. He has not. Phyllis still looks angry, though she doesn't say much. The hero is completely discombobulated, because though he doesn't know very much, one thing he does know is that when Phyllis thinks he is at fault the chances are 99 to one that he is at fault.*

So I've given you mainly evidence of how little success I had in yielding up the egocentrism to love and to family, as if you needed more evidence than the fact that I am writing here, in 1986, about *me*. We'd get only slightly less discouraging results if we went on through the draft of "Yieldings," to find what I said about
—*Work:* the effort to record something of those rare wonderful days when you look up from the page, in the late afternoon, and realize that you have managed to forget your *self* for six hours straight—but how do you *record* that? I made a stab at it, but you don't want to read that now.
—*Music:* the inescapably purple passages about how it feels to become totally absorbed in playing chamber music, when the group goes well together: the total yielding to your always clumsy but still excited sense not of what *you* want but of what *Beethoven* wants. Somewhere in my files there is a half-article "On Learning Thumb Position on the Cello at the age of 50"—a bit lighter attempt at what I treated quite solemnly in '69.
—*Teaching:* the inherently implausible accounts, convincing only to me, of the rapturous hours when a class takes over—when we all together seem to have forgotten that we are all separate. Oh, yes, I'm doing a book on that subject—another book that may never get finished.

And finally:
—*Supreme Power and Act,* the great *I Am,* to Whom I sometimes, in meditation, yield up my self: If the other accounts of yielding are embarrassing and inherently paradoxical—"I will as a self now show you a self getting rid of itself"—"effing" about the ineffable is even more unpersuasive. "Yieldings" quotes me as a young missionary, just after I had read William Ernest Hocking's *Meanings of Death and Life,* following a period of rising skepticism about religion, fed doubts by people like Bertrand Russell and Sinclair Lewis:

A totally new hope and happiness has come—not unallayed by further questions, but nevertheless happy and hopeful. Hocking gives the first really intelligent discussion I have read on immortality from the positive side [this from a young man who had "read" most of the dialogues of Plato during the previous three years!]. His arguments were especially convincing because I have had some of the mystical experiences he uses to prove his points.

The autobiographer of 1969 had a momentary hope that he had found evidence of unselving in that young missionary, but he read on: "I have long been troubled by the feeling that I *am* more than I seem, that there is something about *my* self-consciousness beyond the idea anybody could ever get from my explanation of it." The aspiring missionary's italics give him away. What he has managed, in his meditations, is not an unselving at all but a self-aggrandizement. His ego—he now wants to believe that he believes—will endure forever, and it's a better one, he thinks Hocking has taught him, than anybody he knows has cottoned onto yet. Except perhaps his mother.

I'm afraid that the middle-aged grieving father did not do much better. The *feeling* of yielding, of having won through at last, was genuine enough, but the language seemed too often to suggest an absurd self-advertising, worse than Mailer's and lacking the saving grace of Mailer's open egotism and metaphorical flamboyance. Though there were many moments of sheer ecstatic embrace of the Giver of all Gifts, as I wrote in freedom on that tiny table in that drab flat, the first autobiography could not really get itself written because the project it tried to report on was and is incomplete.

## II

### *A Modernist Repents*

The second autobiography, begun some years after the other one failed to get completed, might better be called *Grappling* than *Yielding*. It was to be called "A Modernist Repents," and it was to show the three-stage saga of a representative twentieth-century figure who moves from secure traditional beliefs first to an exhilarated and threatening modernism, and then on to a deconversion *from* modernist dogmas and *to* . . .—well, of course, to the new synthesis that was just about to emerge from my new electric typewriter. But that one also remains unfinished, I think because I could never decide which of my present original and profound post-modernist opinions could bear the weight of having to replace the profound appeals of my modernist mentors. But I have no doubt that it would make a whale of an autobiography, if only I could get the third act into shape.

## Act I: The Truth.

In 1921, the boy is born into the heart of the nineteenth-century. He comes into consciousness surrounded by loving people who teach him that the Bible is literally the word of God, that Joseph Smith has restored the one True Church after two millenia of apostasy; that since he is male and of the lineage of Ephraim he will—provided he minds his p's and q's—someday become a God of his own world and people it with his very own offspring (no doubt propagating polygamously), just as Jehovah did when he peopled his very own world, this one. At the age of twelve, when he became a Deacon in the Aaronic Priesthood, he believed, or would have said that he believed, not only all this, but everything else that he was told about the history and principles of the Church of Jesus Christ of Latter-day Saints. On the surface this meant mainly that he could stand up in Testimony Meeting and "bear his testimony to the truthfulness of the Gospel, and to Joseph Smith as a true prophet and to the Book of Mormon as the word of God." He did that, many times though in shifting forms, from the age of ten or twelve until he went into the army at twenty-three. But beneath those surface beliefs that at one time seemed all important, there were deeper teachings not quite so easily classified as peculiar to Mormons:

(1) "Mankind," with the help of female "helpmeets," is eternally progressing. Progress is the fundamental principle of the universe. "As man is, God once was; as God is, man may become." Until his college years, the young man never heard anyone suggest that the world is not getting better all the time; he lived hopefully, in a world exactly like that of William Ellery Channing a hundred years earlier:

. . . the happiest feature of our age . . . is the progress of the mass of the people in intelligence, self-respect, and all the comforts of life. What a contrast does the present form with past times. . . . [T]his revolution is due in a great degree to religion, which, in the hands of the crafty and aspiring, had bowed the multitude to the dust, but which, in the fulness of time, began to fulfil its mission of freedom. . . . It was religion which armed the martyr and patriot in England against arbitrary power, which braced the spirits of our fathers against the perils of the ocean and wilderness [my mentors would have added "and of crossing the plains"], and sent them to found here the freest and most equal state on earth (*Self-Culture*, 1838).

Since his life was filled, as he came to consciousness, with vivid accounts of World War I (the photographic images made vivid in a stereopticon), and since he came into adolescence with the Depression in full flower and soon faced the horrors of Fascism (only much later the horrors—and attractions—of Stalinism), he must have known more cognitive dissonance than the record shows, as he clung to that idea of progress. But I can now remember no hint from anyone, until late in my college years a professor suggested that I read Bury's *Idea of Progress* (1932), that everything was not on the whole getting better and better.

(2) Most obviously, the idea of progress applies to oneself. The purpose of life is to improve oneself, both by doing good works and by learning how God's world works. "The Glory of God is Intelligence." "Mankind cannot be saved in ignorance." Already at my birth, I was taught, I had been far up and away on an eternally inclined plane with no beginning and no ending; I had earned the right to birth by opposing Satan in the war in Heaven, and my job in life was to keep on climbing that inclined plane so that after death I could go on climbing it even unto the condition of Godhood, which would itself be exercised by continuing upward on that inclined plane. Thus though I never read a novel by Horatio Alger, let alone the sermons of Channing, and though I always thought of such beliefs as peculiarly Mormon, I in fact imbibed the most characteristically American of all theologies: through hard work, application of shrewd calculation, and sheer natural endowments (including the great fortune of being one of God's blest from the beginning of time), one can prove that nothing is impossible with the Lord. Faith the size of a mustard seed can move mountains. And one gets better at the moving all the while.

(3) Of course all of this means that pessimism, or

anything remotely resembling a "negative attitude," is wicked. Basically, everything is all right. Things are working out. In the long run nothing is amiss. *The Power of Positive Thinking* was read by everyone in my family, along with *How to Win Friends and Influence People* and a host of little books filled with homilies like this:

> Two artists entered a beautiful park on the morning of July 5th. The park was "messed up" with paper napkins, candy boxes, banana peelings, cigar stumps—the litter of National Patriotism.
>
> Each artist painted a picture. One didn't see the candy boxes, the banana peelings, the tips of cigars. He saw beauty in nature—the landscape, the trees and sky mirrored in the glassy lake. His was a magnificent picture! The other saw the paper napkins, and banana peelings. He lacked the genius to look around them, and so they got into his picture. It was spotted with cigar boxes and refuse of this sort and that. He saw the rubbish.[3]

The boy memorized stories about how if you look at them right, weeds are simply wild flowers. In the "Two-and-a-half Minute Talks" that he gave in Sunday School, he imitated his elders in telling how the pessimist sees a glass of milk and says "it's half empty," while the optimist sees the same glass and says "it's half full."

When the Depression wiped out in a bank closure the tiny insurance payment my mother had received on my father's death, she was crushed—but she had no permissible language to express being crushed. She could hardly even talk of a Depression. We all were taught that "no good Mormon has ever gone on relief." "If you really want a job, you can find one." "It's only those who don't keep their lives in order (and especially those who do not pay their ten percent tithing) who get hit hard by the Depression." We sang:

> Put your shoulder to the wheel, push along;
> Do your duty with a heart full of song.
> We all have work.
> Let no one shirk!
> Putcher shoul-der to the whee-el.

Once his voice had changed, the boy sang the bass line for that hymn hundreds of times, loud enough so that everyone could tell what a good part-singer he was.

---

[3] Leo J. Muir, *The Upward Reach.* Los Angeles, 1930, p. 45. I later encountered Muir himself as the president of my mission—a generous-spirited, wildly undisciplined intellectual who was very good at calling rubbish rubbish.

And he believed, devoutly, what the song and others like it said: hard work became a kind of religion in itself. I still am tempted to think that no matter how bad a piece of writing is, it will somehow be redeemed if I've sweat blood over it.

(4) The wheel you put your shoulder to is not just yours: salvation lies within the community, through following communal paths. You do not find your salvation by soaring off into the wild blue yonder on your own, intending "to forge in the smithy of your soul the uncreated conscience of your race." Instead, you steadily circle back toward the center of your group—your family, your congregation (the "ward" and "stake,"), your Church, and just possibly your country (he never knew anyone who even thought of fleeing to the Left Bank; "back east to the University of Chicago" was about the most daring trip imaginable, except to go as a missionary wherever sent). You find in your group the corrections for any idiosyncracies or selfish errors you may pick up along your path. It is true, of course, that God gave us our earthly bodies so that, through exercising free choice, we could learn how to be strong autonomous creatures, capable of governing worlds of our own. Free agency is our most precious gift—it was precisely on the question of whether to give it to us that Satan rebelled and was expelled from the heavenly hosts. But free agency is properly exercised only when it yields the right results: conformity to the group's norms. A later parodist was to satirize one president of Brigham Young University by having him say, "I want every faculty member to exercise his free agency, and I'm going to see to it that you do." The boy was taught that he should feel blessed, protected, even in a sense insured against disaster, by the steady surround of community: a blessed community, chosen by God to carry the chalice of truth into the Millennium. And he should be willing to practice *obedience* to the leaders of that community.

(5) What all of this amounts to is that you are subject to a central divine command: you have an immense, daily, hourly burden of responsibility to make of yourself what you can. Your soul *counts* as one of the eternally important units. Your *history* counts; you should keep a record of every day (at fourteen he started keeping that journal you've already heard from). What is more, you have a duty to probe the world to discover what is good in it for you. Your group does not yet have all that you need—not only does God progress, which means that the Church depends on "continuous revelation," but YOU *must* progress, and one way you do that is by getting an education. Education will yield the good things of God's plan, and those include—in some versions at least—the world's art and music and literature. You should of

course not go too far: you should spend more time reading the three basic scriptures than you spend on secular literature. Still, secular literature contains a lot that will be valuable to you. You should remember the "Thirteenth Article of Faith," given to Joseph Smith by the Lord—especially the last sentence:

> We believe in being honest, true, chaste, be-nevolent, virtuous, and in doing good to all men; indeed, we may say that we follow the admonition of Paul—We believe all things, we hope all things, we have endured many things, and hope to be able to endure all things. If there is anything virtuous, lovely, or of good report or praiseworthy, we seek after these things.

In short, in the twenties and thirties of this much-cursed century, that boy was given not only a place in the world but a place in the cosmos. Whatever anxi-eties he felt ("Mother, am I conceited?" "Why am I not popular?" "Why do I have those guilty dreams?") were his own fault. When he felt depressed, as he often did through adolescence, he knew who was to blame.

## Act II: The Religion of Modernism.

How could a lad fed such wholesome cheerful be-liefs find himself, by his mid-twenties, fallen into high modernism? How could he become, in only about ten years (from fourteen to twenty-four), an "atheist" and "socialist," reveling in the works of Shaw, Kafka, Wells, Voltaire, Samuel Butler; a cultural relativist who thought that sociologists and anthropologists could explain every one of his values and who would argue, at least on Mondays, Wednesdays, and Fridays, that "it's all just the way we were brought up"; a wor-shipper of art as the last, indeed, the only firm value; a pessimist, more likely to quote Gide or Kierkegaard on the human prospect than Hocking on immortality? How did he learn to see his salvation pretty much as a scrabbling for a highly individualized, indeed atomized "culture" that the Mormons had somehow denied him even as they pretended to honor it?

The change was so enormous that I can only de-scribe it as a conversion. It is important to remember, though, that I am moving now through only one of three—and possibly more—autobiographies, the "in-tellectual" one about professed beliefs. What was actu-ally going on beneath the surface formulations, I no doubt do not fully understand even now: that con-verted "atheist" went on teaching adult Sunday School classes until the age of forty-two; that skeptic about all values became an absolutely devoted family man, a totally committed monogamist; that cultural relativist

became a committed anti-Nazi, anti-anti-Semite, anti-racist, and passionate devotee of the value of inquiring into "truth" through teaching and scholarship.

What modernist beliefs had he substituted for those I described in Act I? For each of them I could claim to find a "turning point." But neither of my ma-jor conversions occurred in quite so schematic a way. Act II—the embrace of modernism—included hun-dreds of moments of reversion to the beliefs and prac-tices of Act I. Most of the "turning points" that follow carry with them ambiguities: echoes of Act I, foresha-dowings of Act III. But there is one that in its clarity of focus cuts most sharply:

"The turning point of my life" came when I was stationed in Givet, France, in November of 1944, awaiting assignment to a combat unit. I had been clas-sified and trained as a "clerk-typist" but I was to be used as an infantryman. The Repl-Depot sergeant had said so as soon as we arrived at Givet: "All right you guys. Get it out of your fucking heads you're going to be clerks. You're going in as fucking riflemen, see?" We could hear the bombardments in the distance; we be-lieved him. But then they lined us up to get into the trucks moving us to the front, and they called off the names—Adamson, Anderson, Baker, Banderzinsky. Here, here, here, here.

"Booth!"

"Here!"

"You're not going. You're going back to Paris as a fucking typist."[4]

Somebody had seen on my record that I could type 80 words a minute. I was taken over to headquar-ters, I was given—oh bliss—a bunkbed in place of my straw tick on the ground, and after lying around for a few days, guiltily missing my former buddies, I was trucked back to Paris.

On that cold, rough trip I thought hard, and re-corded the "thinking" like this:

> *November 22, 1944:*
> It appears that Bob [a buddy with two chil-dren] and Dean will probably go into combat as riflemen. I was taken out of the Co. at the last possible moment. I always had a super-stitious faith that "something would happen" to keep me from combat—that "my abilities would be recognized." Now that m. a. have b. r. (I will be doing straight typing, requir-

---

[4] Actually the diaries reveal that this memory coalesces the events of several weeks. The announcement of the return to Paris came long after the announcement that I was to be "saved" as a clerk-typist of some kind. But for our purposes here the remembered version is more important: we are dealing in three mythic structures for a life that is steadily recreating itself.

ing absolutely no ability) I have lost the faith: it was practically chance all the way, and adverse fortune could throw me into combat tomorrow. . . . Mack Cunningham [a high school friend] would say, "There is some power overseeing your destiny, or this would not have happened." Poppycock! I'll admit that I had one brief moment—may I never cease to be ashamed—of thinking, "This is what I deserve. T. Y. and I & Max & Howard are not being killed. J____, a less responsible, less spiritual person, *was* killed. Perhaps ____" But immediately I recovered myself and felt ashamed for allowing my ego to play such tricks on my sense. The thousands of men—better men than I—who have died in this war should be given a special assignment to haunt me for eternity. And may . . . [my buddies] never hear of my arrogance. . . . It is arrogance of the most unforgiveable sort to think God would preserve me, without wife & children, without a nature that suffers greatly under inconvenience, and allow to be killed men with families, men who *do* suffer (for example, R____). No, it was the working of chance . . .; I feel guilty about it, undeserving, disappointed about not being able to observe myself in danger—and exuberantly happy at being out of the worst part of the mess.

No doubt this "turning point" was abetted by the first one, the death of my father. How could I have ever believed, living with that disillusioned mother, that an interventionist God is in His Heaven and all is right with the world? Was I, then, simply going through the motions, from age six to age fourteen (when the first overt questioning began), whenever I "bore my testimony"? Was I simply pretending, showing off, hypocritically conforming? I can remember asking Professor A. C. Lambert at Brigham Young, when I was nineteen, what I could do about "not having a burning testimony"? He hedged: "There are different kinds of testimony. Some people are just not the kind that get a 'burning.'" So by then I was deeply troubled—long before I agreed to serve my two years as a missionary, long before my experience in Givet.

But surely *the* turning point of my life toward skepticism occurred long before, when I chose the Booths as one of two families to be born into. My father, son of a contented and not very successful farmer who was son of a reluctant and incompetent farmer (actually "doctor" for a hundred-square-mile area, though with no formal training), himself wanted to be a farmer—a scientific one. He and his family all had

intellectual aspirations—even a strong critical bent. My Grandfather and Grandmother Booth, who inevitably became very important to me after my father's death, were "readers," from families that valued reading and indeed all kinds of learning. My Great-Grandfather Booth, the "doctor"/farmer, was reputed to have brought the first chess set into Utah—a set that I still own. I have early memories of my gruff, sardonic Grandfather—no chess player, he—mocking teachers of our town for failing to think for themselves. He loved to catch out the high-school teachers of history or mathematics in some fact or process that they should have known: a date from the Civil War, a method of calculating fractions in your head. My Grandmother Booth had her own critical bent. As a passionate Republican surrounded by Democrats, a great reader and quoter of anti-Roosevelt lore, she was scornful of most people in American Fork for their failure to read and think. While my Mother's family, the Claysons, would never criticize anybody or anything, the Booths would even sometimes criticize some of the Church's general authorities; Grandfather's sister had married one of them, and the whole family knew just how human those pious Authorities could be. Story-telling time in that family was a joy—when Grandfather and his brothers and sister—the one who lived in Salt Lake with her "Apostle"-husband—would regale us with astonishing stories of old heresies and misdeeds. Were not the seeds of my later embrace of modernist heresies planted there?

The Claysons were much more given to conforming, but they gave me a mother and later a sister (Lucille Booth Bushnell) whose example of an unlimitedly yielding love for others offered me the best single antidote there is for the ravages of abstract thinking and the religion of culture. In a sense Mother had lost her faith (though she never gave up her strict observance of surface codes, or her verbal agreement that Mormonism is "the only true church"). But she went on living her deepest faith to the hilt—something like "love is all we have but it's enough." Living that faith, even when she seemed to me to have absconded, she convinced me that I would be loved no matter how far I pushed the critical spirit of the Booth side. But that is to get ahead of my story—she laid the ground for Act III, not Act II. The point here is that once the Great Authority had let us both down, and once I was old enough to start thinking about that let-down rather than simply weeping about it, I simply began to ask questions "like a Booth," to her great distress. "Wayne C., you have such a good head—if you only wouldn't *criticize!*"

But surely the real turning point toward Act II, building on the groundwork of those Booth-family anecdotes, came when I had Luther Giddings as my chemistry teacher in high school. A non-Mormon, a man with a genuinely critical mind, a man who set aside time for himself each week to read whatever books were being talked about in the national press, he not only inspired me to become a scientist, a "chemical engineer," but led me to read Aldous Huxley, Sinclair Lewis's *Arrowsmith*—whatever was on the scene. I can't remember that he led me to read anything written before about 1900, except Mark Twain; it was all "liberal," all "critical." I would leave those sessions in his office, the hour or two of talk after all the other students had left, resolving that "some day I'm going to be able to think as well as he can":

*November 3, 1937:*

> Talked to Mr. Giddings about religion, Mormon's beliefs, meat eating, & the word of wisdom etc. He thinks that beyond any possibility of a doubt there is a god, but that he [does the pronoun refer to the God that exists or to the one that Giddings himself would like to be? The diarist's lower case is I think significant] would not require so much attention as most people seem to think but would merely expect people to live good lives. Choir practice, after play practice. Home and to bed, 8:59.

No, on further thought I'd say that the turning point toward Act II was my encounter with M. Wilford Poulson, professor of psychology at BYU. Poulson had been born and raised near my home town, as a devout Mormon. He had gone "back east" to take an M.A. in psychology at the University of Chicago, and then he came back to Utah carrying—nay, proudly flaunting—"the scientific method" and "the higher criticism," a critical apparatus that increasingly led to difficulties at a place like Brigham Young University.

Poulson had early begun to collect materials important to Church history. Much of it seemed in those days to be dynamite against the Church; it threw so many doubts on the official Church account of our origins. These days the Church seems to have discovered that no historical account is really terribly dangerous. Most devout believers, it turns out, will simply obey when told how to accommodate or reject any new historical find. Why had that not been true for me? For me, the slightest flaw in the official story was devastating. Poulson would take me into his basement and show me books that Joseph Smith could have read and that sounded suspiciously like sources for the Book of Mormon; speculative studies by Harvard professors about Joseph Smith's disturbed psyche; evidences that the Doctrine and Covenants (Joseph Smith's revela-

tions directly from God) existed in many editions, some of them quite incompatible with others.

By 1941, when people began to talk about my serving as a missionary, I had concluded that the origins of the Church were murky indeed, where they were not flatly different from what the Church claimed. Certainly Joseph Smith had no gold plates when he "translated" the Book of Mormon: a decision that felt like the most important I had ever made. Indeed, under the gentle probing of Poulson, Karl Young, P. A. Christensen, and A. C. Lambert, all of them active in the Church, I had abandoned one "essential" point after another, including any notion that Joseph Smith was to be fully trusted in what he said about *anything*. Was he therefore a fraud, or only self-deceived? Poulson would not say, but I can say that the largest share of my intellectual energy for something like two decades went into trying to decide just how much of what I had been taught in Act I had to be scuttled. When I added all those doubts, which might be called abstract, to my objections to the Church's official downgrading of all "Negroes" (they had been "neutrals" in the War in Heaven, had then been cursed as descendents of Cain, and therefore did not *yet* deserve to hold the priesthood),[5] I had every reason to refuse to "go on a mission" to help convert people to the Church. (It is significant to me now, and a bit embarrassing, that the Church's denial of equal status to women seems never to have figured in my objections until quite recently!)

Under any other kind of mentor, at any other university, I would perhaps have made a clean, sharp break. Under Poulson I learned complexities and ambiguities. I learned (though years later I had to learn it again) that Churches are not to be judged strictly by a literal reading of their historical origins. Unlike most of my friends who in their youth bought modernism as they scrapped traditional religion, I found myself in a prolonged battle within myself that still in effect goes on; though I am currently resisting attendance in four different denominations—the Mormons, the Catholics (that one is easier under the present Pope than it was a few years ago), the Quakers, and the Jews—it is mainly the Mormon appeal that comes to me at church time on Sunday morning (now in fact the time when my wife and I play chamber music with friends). But to talk of returning to *any* church is already to spill over into Act III.

A daily battle over a mythic past as idiosyncratic and complex and recent as Mormon history does not exactly place a man in the center of world thought.

---

[5] I meet members now who deny that the Church ever taught such stuff. What memory-chutes we all employ!

There were advantages, of course: for example, I had the excitement of facing up to Darwinism with as much shock and challenge as I would have felt if I'd been Darwin's contemporary, and I read Ernest Renan with the same thrill that he produced in his Victorian readers. Every intellectual challenge that the great world had faced since about 1820 was new to me; ancient controversies that would have bored many of my more sophisticated contemporaries were to me novel and exciting.

But the advantages could not entirely compensate for the lonely anguish of the battle as it went on, especially after I was in the "mission field," nor the ways in which it slowed down (or permanently prevented) intellectual growth and training that I now long for: I know, for example, little history (other than Mormon history), and have trouble distinguishing one Greek myth from another. For these and other holes in my learning it's slim compensation to have a pretty good grasp of what happened, say, when Joseph Smith claimed in later years to have found some further plates, this time *brass* ones, and "translated them" as ancient scriptures (the Kinderhook plates).

It is in fact a peculiar, ambiguous fate to spend weeks, months, years, trying to settle questions that most thinkers have never even heard of. Who cares—not even most Mormons now care—about whether Brigham Young actually authorized the Mountain Meadow massacre or the scapegoating of Lee? Who cares whether he deliberately betrayed Orderville, that wonderful little village of Mormon communists who believed that they were practising the absolute laws of God's "united order"? Who cares whether the Temple ceremonies for the dead have been changed beyond recognition, or whether, even in their changed form, they are moral or immoral? By the 1980s, there are far more scholars, Mormon and non-Mormon, who care about such questions than did then; there is now an international community of historians of Mormonism that simply did not exist when I was fighting my personal battles. But in my time, it was a lonely business—or rather, a *secret* business practiced by only a coterie of those who could be trusted.

*Scene: Summer, 1941, the northwest corner of the BYU farmland, where the head sluicegates of the irrigation system lie. I have been manipulating those sluicegates for three summers, irrigating the farm and surreptitiously reading my pocket Plato, waiting at the end of the furrows for the water to arrive. This evening, "old" Poulson [probably then ten years younger than I am now] has stopped his car, seeing me pulling at a headgate. I go to his car, stand with one rubber hipboot on his fender, and we talk, talk*

*through the beautiful sunset, on into the twilight, slapping mosquitoes, talking, talking about the Church.*

*Poulson:* "Don't throw out the baby with the bath water. You keep leaping ahead into areas you know nothing about. The fact that some Church leaders are hypocritical and that the policy on race is benighted doesn't mean the Church is valueless. Every institution has limitations. Surely you're not going to say that because the Church claims to be divinely led, and its leaders are clearly not divine, it must be worthless judged in human terms.

*Wayne:* No, but I don't see any reason to . . .

*Poulson:* You shouldn't be looking for reasons *to* do a rebellion. You should be looking only for reasons *not to.* [And with one stroke he plants the seeds of one main branch of my *Modern Dogma and the Rhetoric of Assent*]. Here you are, raised in a marvelously vital tradition, surrounded by an astonishing number of good, intelligent, energetic people who have found a way to organize their lives effectively. Believe me, that is something rare in the world. And you come along and ask them for reasons *to* join them in what they are doing!

*Wayne:* But I just can't bear even to sit in meetings without speaking up when somebody talks vicious nonsense. Last Sunday they were talking about personal devils, and some of them seemed really to believe that stuff.

*Poulson:* Well, what I said when they called me on the carpet in Salt Lake about that one is, "Of course I believe in personal devils. *All my devils are personal!*" Don't you see how unimportant it is whether you call it the devil or some other word for the source of our viciousness?

*The "old" man, lonely, hated by many students for his nagging rigors in the classroom, mistrusted by the Church and University authorities, owner of "the best collection of books on Mormon history," talks on into the dark, perhaps feeling blessed to have a student who likes to discuss as much as he does; the twenty-year-old boy, chilling in his wet socks inside the leaky boots, worn out after twenty hours on the job, changing from one foot to the other, exhilarated beyond description: this is what life can be, this is one of the great times—I'll talk forever if he'll only go on.*

*Wayne:* But don't we have a right to hope for an institution that is at least honest with itself? I just wish I had a cause that I could give myself to as fully as the full believers— my father and mother, my grandparents— have given to the church.

*Poulson:* Well, you may find it, if you try hard enough. All you would have to do is just put your mind to rest and let your emotions take over. *This* one could itself easily become that for you, if you wanted it to badly enough. The Church has plenty of members just like that: all causes do. What they lack is devoted men who still can think. And this Church has a lot of those, too. And what it needs is a corps of missionaries who know a lot about what's wrong with the Church—and who don't care, because they know that it can be an instrument for good in their hands. Just keep saying to yourself, "Show me a *better* church."

*In the dark now, a moon not quite ready to rise, the stars bright as they never are bright today, the old man's gray hair faintly visible inside the car, the deep slow voice pours out into the night. The dirty fingernails, which in spite of the boy's own increasing and deliberate slovenliness often distract him in the daytime, are invisible now: there is nothing but the prophetic voice and the silver glow.*

*Wayne:* Are you suggesting that I should go on a mission?

*Poulson:* Why not? If you could work not to dunk people under the water in the greatest possible numbers but to take them where you find them and to help them grow—why not? Can you think of a better way to spend two years than setting out to help other people, with no concern for your own welfare? That's what the missionary system is, at its best— though of course it seldom works at its best. But you might, if you worked hard, and if you thought hard, and if you could keep from worrying too much about your own reputation—you just might make a real difference for a lot of people.

Teachers like Poulson kept me at the double task of deconversion and reconversion: freeing myself from the dogmas and then freeing myself from the anti-dogmas that can bind with equal harm. It was not much

later, already on my mission, that I quoted George Eliot in my journal:

> When I was at Geneva, I had not yet lost the attitude of antagonism which belongs to the renunciation of *any* belief—also, I was very unhappy, and in a state of discord and rebellion towards my own lot. Ten years of experience have wrought great changes in that inward self: I have no longer any antagonism towards any faith in which human sorrow and human longing for purity have expressed themselves; on the contrary, I have a sympathy with it that predominates over all argumentative tendencies. (Gordon Haight's biography, *George Eliot,* p. 331).

Still, nothing that those wonderfully complex teachers at "the 'Y' " could do could save me from that simple moment in Givet, when I decided that God was not, and that religion had nothing for me. I think now that the moment of total doubt was inevitable: one has only to look at how few intellectuals of my time escaped it to see that it was simply in the works. All Poulson and the others could do was to postpone the hour, by persuading me to accept the call to go on a mission, hoping to "liberalize the Church from within." Though I had plenty of trouble with doubts during my two years as a missionary in the Midwest, the daily effort to make that mission *count* for something like Poulson's idea slowed me down considerably in my steady drive to become a total modern. In fact I went on struggling between belief and doubt well into my twenties, my deconversion sluggish indeed compared with that of most modern intellectuals who have cast off a religious upbringing.[6]

Nevertheless, the deconversion occurred, as it has occurred for tens of thousands of other bright young men and women who would have claimed, like me, that they were "thinking their own thoughts, in critical independence." By the time I returned to the University of Chicago in 1946—I had taken a few courses there while doing the mission, perhaps a unique privilege in mission history—I had replaced the five beliefs of Act I with another set entirely. In retrospect what I believed then seems a a jumble of incompetencies and incomprehensions, though at the time we all talked of ourselves as just about the first really enlightened gen-

---

[6] Most of them report their discovery of atheism with a sentence or at most a paragraph. Bertrand Russell, whose diary, written at sixteen, is far more sophisticated than mine at twenty-five, gives many pages to his wrestling with the angels, but he often reported on it later as if it were the simplest thing in the world to see that God could not possibly exist. See the indexes to the three volumes of his *Autobiography.*

eration in history. What I did not believe could of course be more easily summarized than what I believed: I had, or so I thought, rejected everything in the belief-package of Act I except for the importance of family and art and a kind of last-ditch hope of extending justice in the world.

—In place of a belief in eternal progress underwritten by God, I saw us rapidly regressing, quite probably doomed to destroy ourselves in some further war; and there was no God to care about our doom. (A "professed atheist," I was rather careful about where I did the professing: certainly not in the adult Sunday School classes that I went on teaching.)

—In place of the belief that my individual soul was eternally important, progressing toward Godhood, I saw myself as fighting alone (well, almost alone: there were a few others in the saving remnant, my wife, for example), on behalf of values that Bertrand Russell and a host of others had taught me were entirely man-made. I can remember precisely the day on which I faced the appalling realization that "it does not matter what I do, as long as I feel all right about it" (the specific issue was sex, but of course I generalized it to all behavior). Indeed, I felt that just about all true thinkers would agree with me—those modern thinkers I had read earlier, defenders of religion like Jung, Bergson, Rudolf Otto, and Rufus Jones simply hadn't caught on yet.

I can remember how shocked I was when it turned out that some people at Chicago held to standards after all. A colleague got one of his first-year students pregnant. Her parents complained, and to my great surprise *the University kicked him out.* And a couple of people I talked with about it even said that they agreed with the administration: Assistant Professor Z——— had done something wrong, genuinely wrong. I really had come to believe—so loose was all the talk in those days—that since values were only subjective, how we behaved was simply our personal preference—so long as we didn't (as the current joke went) do it in the street and frighten the horses. (I should add that through all this, as throughout my married life, I had no affairs with other women. Am I the last "intellectual" alive who has practiced a wholehearted monogamy? And are you suspicious about any autobiography—or any three autobiographies—in which sex figures so distantly?) The point is that I had decided that all values were invented, not grounded.

—In place of an abhorrence of pessimism, I had entered a world that mocked optimism, and indeed most of the virtues, like cheerfulness, public service, open altruism, that tend to accompany optimism. Of course all of us young "liberals" had our own little code of behavior: you ought to join the Co-op; you ought to

support the new FM station; you ought to mock your professors' follies and praise their virtues as little as possible; you ought to support advanced scientific research like Kinsey's (my wife and I dutifully reported for interviews for the first Kinsey report); you ought to oppose bigotry; you ought to support socialism. But above all, thou shalt not praise the Universe or any of its works. It—the great non-ground and non-center—is running down and will ultimately be an indiscriminate mess of just plain *entropy.*

—In place of salvation-within-a-community, salvation achieved by making oneself as much *like* other "good" people as possible, I had now embraced a notion of individual fulfillment: "salvation" by seeking my own true differences and cultivating originality and creativity. I have recently treated at some length the modern invention of the isolated self (Chapter Eight of *The Company We Keep,* forthcoming), and so won't go into it here.

My changed notion of my "self" provided perhaps the biggest single distinction between Act I and Act II: what was once *essentially joined* was now *essentially disconnected.* Whatever alliances I might make, like my wonderfully fortunate marriage to the Phyllis Barnes who beautifully shattered all of the arrogant young man's abstract categories, were against the grain of things: we are all alone, trying, for the most part ineffectually, to make contact. In Act I, we all had been *in essence* together, separated only by accidents that might be overcome. A corollary of my loss of belief in that communion was of course a total repudiation of any notion of obedience to authority or respect for institutional traditions.

—In place of my constructing a history of a self with a fate that counts in the great scheme of things, a self that tried to "get ahead" with a comforting sense that it is God's will that one should do so, I now had left only the dangerously self-destructive dregs of that ambition: I still must get ahead, because that is what *I* must do: to get ahead is what one does in this world. Get ahead of the others, or they will get a head of yours—your scalp. Though in practice I continued to have many moments of glorious engagement with learning for its own sake, in theory I was going into graduate work for my own advancement—what else was there to do anything for?

## Act III: A Modernist Repents.

Like BYU from 1938 to 1941, or my mission from 1942 to 1944, the University of Chicago from 1946 to 1950 could be placed into either Act II or Act III, depending on which professors and fellow students I chose to emphasize. It was a stirring place to be, then as now; it was flooded with returning GIs who were eager to get an education. And it had representatives on campus of every conceivable intellectual and political position, including not only a smattering of Stalinists and (as I learned later) a couple of crypto-Nazis, but also an influential group of powerful critics and philosophers so thoroughly steeped in pre-modern thought as to make you wonder, sometimes, if they knew what century it was. In short, the University was very Modern and very anti-Modern, subjecting me to conflicting influences that I cannot even now clearly distinguish.

The followers of the avant-garde—I choose my phrase carefully—were perhaps most prominent. In some discussions it was almost more than one's life was worth to reveal ignorance of Whatever-Seemed-Most-Advanced. Just about everybody I met was an "atheist," most were "socialists," some were Communists, all were passionate about modern art and literature—indeed about every "modern" manifestation. I discovered Eliot and Pound—and for a young man who had carried Virginia Woolf's *The Years* and Anaïs Nin's *Under a Glass Bell* in his duffle bag two years before, that was a very late discovery. I had already discovered Joyce back in 1943, reading *Ulysses* on my own (the best way to begin with it: no skeleton keys, no mythological parallels), in the Mission office, because a professor had mentioned it. But most of my excited reading in the Army had been in the Army's cheap editions of classics—*Tom Jones, Tristram Shandy, Bleak House.* The army did not, as I remember it, distribute Ezra Pound or Djuna Barnes!

In a contrast that I did not see clearly at the time, I also met at the University a group of teachers who had a deep philosophical and classical training and whose joy in life was found in undermining modernist clichés. Steeped in Aristotle, Plato, Aquinas, Spinoza, Kant, and Dewey (they knew them all by heart, or so it seemed to me), they soon revealed to me just how shallow my reasoning had been, both in my periodic defenses of religion and in my "decision" that it was not for me. I can remember Elder Olson saying one day, in a brief discussion after class, that "anybody who has really thought about it knows that the God whose existence is proved by the philosophers really exists, though that's not the same God you were brought up on. In fact, you'll discover—once you think about it—that you believe in His existence, too." Shock. Humiliation. "But I don't have time, now," I would say to myself, "working for my Ph.D. with a dissertation on *Tristram Shandy,* to think this through. Here I am, teaching an adult Sunday School class for the Mormons, thinking of myself as a grand subversive, and yet

all the time maybe I'm not—maybe—" and the whole thing got more or less postponed while I worked for a year or so on "The Self-Conscious Narrator in Comic Fiction before 1760," completed in 1950.

The turning point of my life occurred in 1952 when I received a Ford Faculty Fellowship to allow me to "read the major philosophers on 'value theory,' " *on my own.* Few grants in American foundation history can have been weirder: the Fordies worked up this program to help ease the job shortage during the Korean War (can that be true?), and I applied for a year of free reading time—and got it! I began with the pre-Socratics, moved through Plato and Aristotle and some Augustine and Anselm, on through a good swatch of Aquinas, all of Spinoza, lots of Leibniz, Hume, and Locke; not much Berkeley (though enough, as one might say), and on to Kant, then, skipping almost all other continentals, to Whitehead, Dewey, and Santayana. What a year. I wasn't very far along in it before I knew that my vocabulary for inquiry about "deep questions" had indeed been pitifully inadequate, and I came out of the year skeptical of most of what I had embraced as a modernist; if I was not exactly what most people would think of as a "believer," I was even further from what most people would think of under terms like "atheist" or even "agnostic." Ever since 1953, when I returned from that Ford year not to Haverford College but to Earlham College (a wonderfully "Quaker" institution that figures largely in the longer version of "Yielding"), whenever I've found myself arguing with atheists (like my good friend LL), I've wanted to say, with great condescension, "Go read those *big* guys steadily for a year, and then we can talk."

Many of the somewhat-smaller defenders of religion who had earlier helped to postpone Act II now naturally came back into their own: ranging, you might say, from Harry Emerson Fosdick as the most vulnerable, through G. K. Chesterton as the cleverest, on to Rufus Jones and William Ernest Hocking and Albert Schweitzer and Mahatma Gandhi, on "up" to Rudolf Otto—and then on to a host of theologians I had never even heard of until Act III was well under way: Charles Hartshorne, Bernard Lonergan, Richard Niebuhr[7] and many another.

Actually, the turning point of my life was going to Earlham College in 1953, just after all that philosophical reading, and living for nine years in something like a religious community: nine wonderful years among

---

[7] In Act II his brother, Reinhold, had of course figured. Because of his political stance you could attend to him, in Act II, simply by wiping out the religious edges. Richard was never mentioned by anyone in my hearing until about 1975.

the Friends—people who, while professing a baffling variety of Christian orthodoxies and heresies, along with Theosophy, Buddhism, Judaism, and—slightly later—Transcendental Meditation, really worked at the job of building a loving community. I attended the Meetings for Worship, both the official College Sunday Meeting, a curious blend of two radically contrasting branches of Quakerism, and the Clear Creek Meeting, a full-fledged "silent" meeting where no one spoke until moved to by whatever spirit seemed worthy of obedience. I spoke "from the silence" several times over the years, deeply moved each time. But I am sure that I was rebuked at least once, with great obliquity, when Allen Hole, one of the "weightier" of the traditional Friends, rose to express his worry that we were becoming a bit un-Quakerly, in fact in danger of becoming indistinguishable from "Deists."

Whether the beliefs of Act III are "deist" or "theist," they are certainly not very clear and not the sort of thing to be properly summarized in a brief account. Do I believe in God? Yes and no. Do I believe in immortality? Yes and no. Do I believe in Christianity? Yes and no. How about Judaism? Yes and no. Do I believe in conformity to communal and traditional norms, and in obedience to authorities? Yes and no. (I learned a lot about the use and abuse of authority in my five years as dean of *the* College. But those years deserve a fuller account than I gave in *Modern Dogma and the Rhetoric of Assent* or can give here.) Which form of which denomination comes closest to . . .? To which I have to give the unsatisfactory reply, "Though there are no doubt many false and destructive religions, there are also many true and constructive ones, many revelations of God's truth. If you will allow me to define 'true' and 'constructive,' I will even argue that one can measure the truth by its power to construct lives. And if you think that that sounds like crude utilitarianism, you haven't understood a word of what I've said."

The trouble is, though, that Act III doesn't come out with clear, unequivocal beliefs of the kind I held—sometimes—in Acts I and II. No doubt that is why I've not been able to finish this second autobiography either. Just as I didn't really arrive at a point where I could convincingly yield to—what?—so I have not arrived, at sixty-five, at a coherent set of beliefs to supplant the modernism that died a fairly rapid death in 1952-53. Still, when I run over those original beliefs of Act I, my present views are closer to them than to their opposites in Act II. I'll say a bit more about that at the end of the third autobiography.

### III

*The Making of a Rhetorician*

The first two autobiographies exist, more or less: piles of manuscript of books that will never be printed. The third is brand new, coming into being here before our eyes. It is even more abstract than the second: an account of my life as a producer of books and articles. It is in its abstraction a bit like the autobiography Einstein wrote for the Library of Living Philosophers, which turned out to be almost entirely an impersonal, scientific account of the discovery and meaning of his theories of relativity.

> "Is this supposed to be an obituary?" the astonished reader will likely ask. I would like to reply: essentially yes. For the essential in the being of a man of my type lies precisely in *what* he thinks and *how* he thinks, not in what he does or suffers. Consequently, the obituary can limit itself in the main to the communicating of thoughts which have played a considerable role in my endeavors.
> ("Autobiographical Notes," in *Albert Einstein: Philosopher-Scientist*, Evanston, Ill., 1949, p. 33.)

From this perspective, my first two autobiographies consist almost entirely of the kind of thing Einstein chose to leave out. Coming to the third, I discover a "self" a bit like his in kind—that is, the man dissolves into that part of his work that a public has responded to. As Einstein abstracted "the physicist," I abstract "the rhetorician," or perhaps what should be called "the rhetorologist": a creature who seems to have existed only in the library or seated at a typewriter; a post-modern inquirer almost all of whose writing was done well into Act III—that is, after the deconversion from modernism; an increasingly "public" figure who found himself succumbing, sometimes, to ambition, to a sense of competition with critics he had formerly not respected or not even heard of; in short a "figure" some of whose lineaments would not only have surprised but offended the man he was before starting on *The Rhetoric of Fiction* at the age of thirty-five, and some of whose failures shame me now.

What turned me from the single-minded *teacher* I had elected to be in rejecting the academic big-time and going to Earlham College in 1953, toward the aggressively hard-working teacher/*scholar* that I am now? At Earlham I was totally free from pressures to write or publish. I had elected to immerse myself wholeheartedly in a *teaching* college in a Quaker setting where learning how to "yield" was a central concern. I then elected, following some wonderfully liberating years, to try to write the kind of books that ultimately led to an appearance in a volume like this. That election cost a great deal to my family, to those (imagined) freshman students who never even met me because I had to some degree absconded, [8] and at least for a time to my lifetime project of combatting a rapacious ego. Nobody would have invited me to this occasion for my glorious but partial success in "yielding" to the Great I Am; nobody would have invited me as "representative figure in converting to and then deconverting from high modernism." What was the turning point toward the belated "vocation" that leads us to this moment?[9]

First I should note the vocations, the "callings," that I had resisted earlier. Surely in one or another of these I would have succeeded quite wonderfully, though I doubt that I would ever have succeeded as the "doctor" or "dentist" that my mother sometimes talked about.

As an adolescent and young man, I had made firm decisions, one after the other, to become:

—A salesman, perhaps even a supervisor of salesmen. An uncle from booming LA told me, in about 1932, that that was where the action was. (I wonder what his expression for that would have been.)

—A journalist. At fifteen I became the stringer, in American Fork, Utah, for the *Salt Lake Tribune*, and I kept at it for at least six months. I can't remember much about the articles I wrote, though I do remember that those anonymous and brutal editors in Salt Lake accepted a few features. The editor kept me miserable, though, with rejections, and even more with what seemed like furious, contemptuous corrections fired back at me: "Don't say 'He died of heart failure.' *Everybody* dies of heart failure." "Godammit, go look up 'implied' and 'inferred.'" "There's no such word as 'irregardless.'" "The word is 'proved,' not 'proven'!"

—A chemical engineer. If Luther Giddings was a chemist, I wanted to be a chemist—but one who made more money and did more research than any high-school teacher could.

—A radio announcer. By the age of fifteen, I prided myself on my deep bass voice, and after getting a couple of compliments about the way I read the service over the sacramental bread and water, I decided that nothing could be so glorious as captivating unseen audiences in the way that favorite CBS announcers man-

aged to do. I even got a job as an apprentice announcer at KOVO, Provo, in 1940 or 41, and I really had a ball, or so I thought—until, for reasons I never figured out, I was fired, just dropped without a word. Was it because I never allowed any platter just to play by itself but always took some time introducing it with a clever original joke or pun or hilarious comment on the orchestra—a premature d.j.?

—A musician. I had found that I could pick up instruments and learn to play them quickly, fast and loud. I sang bass in a lot of quartets and choirs. I played clarinet in a lot of bands and orchestras. I even taught beginners, one rather miserable summer, how to play the saxophone—without really knowing how to play it myself. I spent a lot of time throughout adolescence sitting at the piano and teaching myself how to play Bach and Beethoven and Chopin, very badly. I made up lots of songs. I had even learned something of how to *yield* to a classical symphony or string quartet, after some years of hypocritical half-listening to the Sunday afternoon broadcasts of the New York Philharmonic and chamber groups that visited the BYU campus. So why not become a musician?

—A novelist. This one came quite late, really only toward the end of graduate work in 1948 or 49. Working on *Tristram Shandy* it occurred to me—twenty years ahead of my time—that what the world needed was a fine piece of metafiction like Sterne's (the term did not exist yet, but never mind). So after I got my first job, at Haverford College, I spent what spare time I had writing a novel about a man writing a novel to be submitted "in partial fulfillment of the requirements for the Ph.D." in the Writing School at the University of Iowa. *Farrago* had a lot going for it, including some juicy stuff about polygamy in Utah ("my" imaginary grandparents, like Tristram's imaginary parents, naturally suffered lots of sexual contretemps). It was never finished, after early chapters failed to win a prize in the *Furioso* fiction contest in about 1952 or 53.

I've tried others over the years—am in fact still thinking about getting around to trying to revise a current one, *Cass Andor; or, Pessimism* (get it?). But there's something wrong with my ego (that has been clear to you for some time, I assume): whenever I encounter some setback, like a rejection slip, I put the stuff away instead of digging in. Unlike William Golding (say), who went on revising *Lord of the Flies* again and again until a publisher would finally accept it, I nurse my wounds and turn back to writing what everyone seems eager to publish: my criticism. (But again I'm ahead of my story).

—A General Authority in the Mormon Church, one of "the Twelve." In spite of one obvious obstacle—my family was not in any of the genealogical lines that

---

[8] I did go on teaching freshmen almost every year—but the total number has been much fewer than if I had resisted the life of a publishing scholar.

[9] Perhaps the point should be underlined like this: Almost nobody these days publishes a first scholarly book as late as the age of forty. Everyone is forced to do it earlier or be fired (if employed at a place that aspires to have "publishers" on the roster) or do it not at all (if at a place that stresses teaching and allows no time for writing). My kind of "postponed" scholarly career was unusual at the time and is even rarer today.

figured in most choices made in Salt Lake City—I was clearly just the sort they needed: a fluent not to say garrulous talker; a serious student of the scriptures; a deeply and visibly spiritual young man who could (if the truth were known) do a lot better job of overwhelming congregations with religious emotion than most of the "Brethren" who visited us from headquarters. At fourteen, I had felt some annoyance in realizing that Joseph Smith had *already* at my age preempted the prophetic slot; there was not much I could hope for in that line, now that the gospel was fully restored. But to become one of the Twelve Apostles, or perhaps even Prophet, Seer, and Revelator—it's surely not unthinkable. So why not become—well, at least a Church Leader?

The answer was clearly that college teachers, and especially English teachers, led more interesting lives, the most interesting of all. It was not that my hours with English teachers had been more interesting than my hours with Giddings, in high school, or with Poulson, after psychology class. I simply discovered what Giddings and Poulson had been really teaching: obviously it was "English" without their quite knowing it: how to read and talk about important books and ideas. Giddings had not been *paid* to do what my marvelous Freshman English teacher, Karl Young, was paid to do: follow ideas wherever they wanted to go. To be paid, even paid badly, for doing what P. A. Christensen did in his Milton and Chaucer and Advanced Composition courses—that would be to do a kind of end run around the stultifying forces I had been recently reading about and learning to call "bourgeois." I could be paid simply for being an intellectual.

The notion of writing academic books of any kind, let alone books of rhetorical criticism, was nowhere in sight. I had never read one: why should I think of writing one? The only writing I ever imagined myself doing, through the college years, was novels, poems, short stories, perhaps the *New Yorker* kind of humor—certainly never anything like works of rhetorical criticism.

What was it that turned me, then, to puzzling about rhetoric—not just the rhetorical side of narrative but the seemingly more ordinary but equally complex rhetoric that we talk and write to each other and that we "composition" teachers claim to teach?[10] Well, of course you can find zigs and zags very early. Even if

you discount the origins of my great-grandparents' conversion to Mormonism in heated hermeneutical discussion of the scriptures, my setting was always in the midst of argument:

> *1933-41,* aetat *twelve to twenty: Mother:* Wayne C., you know I think you have a good mind, but why do you have to prove it to me every day, three times a day. If only you wouldn't *argue!*

> *1937: Grandmother Booth:* Well, *I* think you should be a lawyer. You *argue* like a lawyer. Your father, you know, when he was in the army, took on the defense of a buddy against a court-martial charge, and he won the case, just by studying the army's lawbooks in advance on his own. He would have made a fine lawyer, and you'd make an even better one.

But really the turning point of my scholarly life, the point when I discovered who I really was to *be,* occurred in Miss Gene Clark's English class, in my junior year in high school. We had read somebody's essay on scientific method and objectivity, and golden-haired, lush-bosomed, twenty-three-year-old Gene Clark said to the class—I now wonder what could have been her pretext—something like this:

> And in my view there is one student in this class who *sometimes* actually exhibits *something* like the spirit of objectivity we're talking about. And that's Wayne C. He is really trying to figure out how things work, he really listens to opinions he doesn't like . . ."

and on for a few more minutes in similar vein. Absolute bliss. Ecstasy.[11] Determination to *earn* that praise. Determination to believe *nothing* until I had proof. Determination to show the world just how objective I could be. Determination to "read all the great books," "learn Latin and Greek and the other main languages. I'm going to find all the truth that it's possible to find."

I didn't have the words "scholar" or "critic" or "rhetorician" for what I had in mind, and I can remember puzzling about how I could become like Miss Clark while becoming a chemist like Mr. Giddings.

---

[10] "Rhetoric" is a weasel-term, with literally thousands of definitions. For here I shall mean by "rhetorical studies" any inquiry that concentrates on how people get together through symbol systems, or why they so often fail to. The rhetorician studies people communicating and inquiring *together,* subordinating when necessary scientific, philosophical, poetic, and historical interests.

[11] Only much later did I realize what that kind of comment must have done to my chances for the much coveted "prize" of being "representative boy" at the end of the senior year. How I longed to be voted "representative," while pursuing critical, even sarcastic ways that made it impossible. Here again we find the stories overlapping: in a culture that advertises "representative boy" as the supreme prize, much more highly coveted than "valedictorian," how is a man to learn anything about "yielding" his ego to *any* other?

Was she teaching English or science?[12] But there was no doubt in my mind, as I pumped my bicycle home that noon, chanting "I've won her, I've won her," that I had become somebody, in somebody's eyes, and I would become somebody, in the eyes of the world, and I would do it by hard thinking.

The desire to think hard about what other people said and wrote was of course underlined by the switch to "English" in college. My chemistry teachers in college did not seem at all like Luther Giddings: my English teachers did seem like him and like Miss Clark, so after two years of pretending to put chemistry first, I switched to "English"—without the slightest idea of what the choice entailed. My vocation, my calling—and I think that those terms are not too strong for it—was simply to become a "teacher of young college students." It was only much later that I saw that what I wanted to teach them could be best summarized with the word "rhetoric."

But the major turning point in my life as a rhetorician came with my two years as a missionary. If you become a missionary for the Mormon Church and you have a "testimony" only to the social value of the Church, not to its unique divinity, you give yourself a daily rhetorical problem. It would be a relatively simple problem if your only point was to conceal your true opinions; then "rhetoric" in the popular sense of verbal trickery would perhaps serve your needs. But if you want to be a genuine *missionary,* with a deep conviction of your role as radically different from that of your fellow missionaries, you must learn a different rhetoric: the art of mediating between your own views and the world, the art of discovering in your circumstances what the possibilities for transformation are—including the possibilities for your own increased understanding. Some would still call that a hypocritical art, since it often entails withholding some of what you believe. But though you may be forced occasionally to practice a deplorable and cowardly hypocrisy, much of the time you will find yourself doing—rhetoric.[13]

A Mormon missionary usually must deliver some kind of public speech several times each week. He will present his version of "the principles of the gospel" in a variety of contexts thousands of times during his two years: to auditors ranging from university groups through businessmen's service clubs and their ladies' auxiliaries (they *were* divided by sex in those days) to high-school assemblies, Future Farmers of America conventions, and even some meetings of puzzled and semi-literate adherents to this or that new fringe cult.[14] And he will live and converse and pray with hundreds of fellow missionaries, some of them strict-interpretationists ("God dictated every word of all three of our 'Standard Scriptures,' "), some of them total unbelievers and backsliders, sent on missions to reform them, and some of them really quite supple and subtle hermeneutical artists, though none of them will have heard the words "hermeneutics" or "the higher criticism."

In short, by throwing who I was in 1942 into a maelstrom of "alterity," I found myself having to "translate," hour by hour, what I *wanted to say* into *what I presumed could be heard.* Since my professed purpose was "to liberalize the system from within," I had given myself some high rhetorical tasks.

I was reading at a furious pace, everything I could get my hands on—reading hurriedly and ineptly, of course, as I only later realized after meeting those disciplined minds at Chicago, but reading freely and with passion; I felt that I "had a lot to say" and I knew that I had a lot more to puzzle over. I read not just newly discovered religious writers—Chesterton, Newman, Harry Emerson Fosdick, Ernest Jones, William Ernest Hocking, Jung—but a wide range of skeptics and iconoclasts and political radicals who prepared me, unawares, for Act II (above): Bertrand Russell, Marx, Freud, Anna Louise Strong, *Partisan Review, Politics,* Shaw, Wells. Much of my energy went into keeping a voluminous—and of course somewhat pontifical—journal that tried to join these disparate voices, and into little abortive essays about this or that theological, ecclesiastical, or political problem. (There are some comments on literature, music, and the paintings I discovered at the Art Institute in Chicago, but nothing along those lines nearly as serious as my efforts to grapple with religious, ethical and *rhetorical* questions). I poured the stuff out night after night, unable to talk plainly about my half-baked ideas with anyone, yet often reporting on the problems raised when, in the daylight hours, I sought alternative languages that might reconcile superficially opposing views.

---

[12] I don't believe I had the word "philosophy" in my vocabulary until I read Will Durant's *Story of Philosophy* some years later. At BYU in those days, there were no philosophy courses and no department of philosophy. Durant was first published in 1926, when I was five. But he came my way very late.

[13] I have written a bit about the productively hypocritical side of rhetoric in my forthcoming book, *The Company We Keep*).

[14] In one month, in the summer of 1942, the Mormon Male Quartet, with me as bass and (usually) as chattering MC, sang an average of three engagements a day, including the convention of the Society for the Preservation and Encouragement of Barber Shop Quartet Singing of America. We wowed the SPEBSQSA, or so the *Daily News* reported, in July or August—the truth is that I can't find that headline about our "taking over" the convention. There's rhetoric for you.

*January 29, 1942* [*one month "in"*]: Last night we . . . showed our film [about "the Gospel"], and we had a very pleasant evening talking to four people who came. Several interesting points about my reaction:

1. I warmed up—too much—to *my* religion as I told more and more about it.

2. I tended to tell them "*we* believe" certain things that I don't believe at all; I would catch myself often being untrue to myself.

3. What was worse, I even seemed to like some of the things I said which I did not believe.

All this is against my purpose here. I did keep [it] in mind quite well: when the man and woman of the house started arguing about the honesty of ministers, I was able to stop the argument. I emphasized as much as I could the place of the teachings of Jesus in the doctrine of our Church.

*February 18, 1942:* My senior companion and supervising elder [both of them about my age, but longer in the mission field] do not hesitate to lie about their ideas in conversation with non-members. They put up a rather liberal front, in fact, so far as they are able. . . . Consequently I am able to say much in our gos[pel] cons[versations] that I could not say elsewhere: they [my companions] usually think I am merely "appeasing." Thus I can say [to outsiders], "Of course, we are agreed that by far the most important thing about any religion is its effect on the lives of the members. The stimulation it gives to better and happier lives is so much more important than the form of the ordinances that they really don't matter." The boys think I am only soft-soaping when I am really giving my ideas.

But they are not always satisfied. Monday night in talking to Presbyterians we found that they have a second baptism when the person feels "saved"; the first baptism is mostly a time of pledging on the parents part. Well, I thought this very reasonable and fine, and also thought it similar to our system of christening (or "blessing") and [then holding our] "second" baptism at 8 yrs. of age. I said so. When we got home they both reprimanded me for being too "anxious to make people think we are not different." After a short period of rebuttals, somewhat hypocritically softened, I bit my lip (figura-

tively) and went to sleep.

This figurative lip biting is becoming a daily practice for me, but it does not get easier with repetition.

Incidentally, [Elder M——— thinks it] "blashphemous" [sic] for me to think the God of the Old Testament cruel and less loving than Jesus, because "Jesus *is* the Jehovah of the O.T."

*March 1, 1942:* (While I write, my companion, Carpenter, is talking in my left ear about how President Woodruff received a direct revelation to start the sugar industry in Utah.) Incidentally, I have so far kept myself from discrediting myself with rashness—have managed to keep dishonest, in other words—in this [new] district. My opinions still have weight, as a consequence. Do the ends justify the means in this case, granted I get the desired ends? I wonder.

Into his already troubled mind there burst—a novel, Sinclair Lewis's *Elmer Gantry*, with its portrait of Frank Shallard, the hypocrite.

*March 10, 1942:* In Frank Shallard, Lewis incorporated much of me and my problems. Born in a religious family of strict constructionists, he entered a ministerial school and, through his refusal to overlook Biblical inconsistencies, met an agnostic professor who showed him more and more inconsistencies. He became tormented with doubts about staying within the church, but rationalized himself into taking his degree "in order to liberalize the church from within." (This cut was so accurately aimed at me that I was caught off guard: I had been feeling so proud of my similarities to Shallard (since obviously Lewis felt sympathetic toward him) [original punctuation]. He became a Reverend, but was always giving emasculated speeches and prayers, always rationalizing, always yearning for honesty. Finally he is kicked out of his church position, and joins some social workers—but finds they are as hypocritical and grasping as his former "religious" associates. . . .

He read the same books I have read—Renan's *Jesus*, White's *History of The Warfare of Science & Theology*, etc.—and his troubles with foolish bigots were very similar with mine. He was more courageous than I, and a better scholar, but his problems were much the same.

As I read the journal now, that forlorn struggler seems even more deeply troubled than he quite realizes. He goes on for two more pages and then, three days later, confesses to a long list of troubles raised by that book (could I bear to re-read it now?), including doubts about God's existence but concluding with a promise to be "more apprehensive of dishonest concessions where unnecessary" and more careful to "keep myself honest at least to myself." Yet soon (March 25) he sounds thoroughly confused:

Have I lost all spirit? At home I would have stood up to him [a missionary spouting bigotry] . . . Here I sit making affirmative noises. I rationalize to myself and say, "I now know that nothing is to be gained by arguing with fools: I am merely being wise." But I know that it is really the desire for peace, cowardly peace.

By God, I refuse to remain all my life in compromising silence. . . . The men of history I admire are those who have stood by their convictions at all costs. Galileo capitulated, earning contempt. I daily capitulate, earning daily self-contempt.

Even in my letters I am spineless: to religious correspondents I make myself out as a God-fearing, though slightly liberal, missionary, happy in my work. To my agnostic correspondents I bend a little backwards the other way.

My real attitude changes frequently, which shows my wishy-washiness. Any old idea, well decked out, will attract me, for at least a day or so.

The Q. for the Historical Jesus [Schweitzer] is really a fine book—and gives me plenty of chance to observe my vacilation [sic] in action. I just haven't the originality to form an opinion of my own. . . .

All is not black: I've made some lightheaded converts to the Soviets. I brought Strong's *The Soviets Expected It* home [here], and two of the boys have been raving about Russia since. But they'll change to anti-Russian the first contact they have with an anti-Russian book.

And on he went, confused, guilt-ridden, quixotic—but unwittingly practicing at the most basic level the art of rhetoric. Within a few months his journal entries exhibit less despair, a bit more confidence, and bit more mastery of the problems.

*July 19, 1942:* Tonight we sang for a small congregation, Church of Christ, and the Minister, a young student, had us to his apartment after. An intelligent conversation ensued, and with what I thought were very cleverly balanced statements I kept the other missionaries from making fools of themselves.

Example:

Maughan said, "We believe that we [the Mormons] have all religious truth."

I, hurriedly: "That is, *available* truth and truth understandable by us in our present state of development."

Maughan satisfied, student satisfied, incident closed.

By mid-August he sounds like this:

I'm conducting a missionary class for five days. Nine of us are studying "Prophecies of the Old Testament in the Light of Present Developments" at the request, and *under* the outline of, President Muir. I'm afraid that it's a little out of my line, to put it mildly [actually it was out of the Church's main line, too, being based on Egyptian numerology].

But much to my pride, I have swallowed it and undertaken to make worthwhile [sic] out of the silly material. . . . This involves a great deal of juggling and thus careful preparation. . . . The elders resent any obvious departure from the outline and especially if they detect any departure from "church" position.

I gave a preliminary lecture yesterday morning on the "occasional" fallibility of scriptural interpretations . . . . Immediately they were on me. "I'm sure," said Grant, "that the church authorities would not use a scriptural interpretation if it were not strictly correct and true."

There was a time when I would have stuck by my critical guns—but not now. In the best "liberalizing from within" style, I backed down and went on with the rest of the lesson.

I can't even say, as Kant did: "I believe many things that I dare not say, but I have never said things without believing them."

Everytime I am dishonest with my true opinions in that way I have a very difficult time of it talking myself into believing it necessary.

But of course he went on talking to himself, and to the others, talking, talking, talking, writing, writing,

writing, for the full two years. Can anyone wonder that such a young man would discover, in his middle years, that he had been "doing rhetoric all the time, without knowing it"? By the time I encountered the rhetorical pluralism of Richard McKeon (what he called philosophical semantics), a systematic effort to intertranslate philosophies rather than asking them to cancel each other out, I was ripe for the harvest.

The rest of this third autobiography is pretty much in the public record, except insofar as it is not yet finished. Each book has been the best summary I could provide for what I—the scholar, leaving "I" the person more or less to one side—believed or cared about at that time. Though they reveal changes from the first book (1961) to the present one (1987? 1988?), they have all been about how we manage to get together, sometimes, in our efforts to reach a human truth, and why we so often fail to. Underlying it all has been that worrisome rhetorician's credo: "Though the quest for 'Truth' is important, it is less important than the quest for 'Understanding.' It is better for two people to understand each other, even in joint error, than for one of them to hold the truth unwilling or unable to share it with the other." Even *The Company We Keep: Ethical Criticism and the Ethics of Reading,* which is in part a search for some truth about the ethical effects of narrative, has become in effect a *rhetoric* of ethical questions about our narrative encounters.

## IV

My three autobiographies cannot be drawn together into an integrated picture of a single authentic self, one that after long effort I could claim as the core of all this diverse experience. I believe that I have a *soul* or a *character,* not a self, and that soul, that "social psyche," is inherently a kind of society, a "field" in which the many other souls I have encountered exist in animated (that is, en-souled) conversation. In "Yieldings" I inevitably failed to yield completely, because as a tiny fragment of All That Is, I was and am inherently pledged to keep up *my* end of the conversation: the only way to yield completely would be to die—and even after death each of us lives on in ways far too complex ever to be traced. Yet in my better moments I know that I have indeed yielded, not only to "the others" who, because I have taken them in, are indistinguishable from me, but to the "Other" Which/Who carries on the supreme Conversation with us moment by moment. At the Center of things, as through every point of the circumference, acts the Principle: "There is nothing that exists by itself except One Thing Who/Which is not in any intelligible sense a *thing* at all; whatever tries to exist by itself is doomed.

What Is, is Relation (at *least* Trinity, but why not, as William James and the Mormons have suggested, more?): Relation and His/Her/Their offspring, other relations." "I" thus yield to the Relation Who made and makes "me," and I try to serve Him/Her/Them by understanding as many relations as I can, including the many within "me."

That makes an inherently unresolved resolution to each of the three autobiographies: in Act III I have discovered the quite unmodern (traditional? post-modern?) social soul and I yield to a Soul that asks me to continue my vocation as student of rhetoric. I receive no promises from Them of any more precise or positive outcome down the line. But it is clear that most of what I now believe could be more easily translated, by some supreme rhetorician, into the five beliefs of my early youth than into the still common commonplaces of high Modernism or most versions of postmodernism.

---

## BIBLIOGRAPHY

**Nonfiction:**

*The Rhetoric of Fiction.* Chicago: University of Chicago Press, 1961. Second Edition. Chicago: University of Chicago Press, 1983.

*Now Don't Try to Reason with Me: Essays and Ironies for a Credulous Age.* Chicago: University of Chicago Press, 1970.

*Modern Dogma and the Rhetoric of Assent.* Chicago: University of Chicago Press, 1974; Notre Dame, Ind.: University of Notre Dame Press, 1974.

*A Rhetoric of Irony.* Chicago: University of Chicago Press, 1974.

*Critical Understanding: The Powers and Limits of Pluralism.* Chicago: University of Chicago Press, 1979.

*The Harper and Row Rhetoric,* with Marshall Gregory. New York: Harper, 1986.

*The Company We Keep: Ethical Criticism and the Ethics of Reading.* Berkeley, Calif.: University of California Press, 1987.

*Occasions for Rhetoric: The Vocation of an English Teacher* (essays and speeches). Forthcoming.

**Fiction:**

"Selections from Susan Dunham's *Cass Andor, or Nihilismism: The Last Anti-Novel.* Ed. W. Clayson Booth." *Chicago Review* 32, no. 1 (Summer 1980): 49-88.

**Editor of:**

*The Knowledge Most Worth Having.* Chicago: University of Chicago, 1967.

*The Harper and Row Reader: Liberal Education through Reading and Writing,* edited with Marshall Gregory. New York: Harper, 1984.

# Daniel Fuchs

*1909-*

## THE TENDER COMEDY OF TIME

In the late summer of 1945, soon after V-J Day, without the knowledge of anyone, I was on the island of Santa Maria in the Azores, on my way home from Germany and France and the war. I had managed to wangle a passage by luck, through a military clerical bungle which I took hold of and turned to my advantage. My travel orders and flight priority-number were irregular but good enough to get me home if no one examined them closely. This was the first leg of the flight over the ocean. There was a bluish haze, a smoke, hanging in the sky against the thickly overgrown mountain. The sunlight here was intense. The mountain rose up steeply before us. It seemed to take up the whole island; when we came in for the landing, we had been handed inflatable jackets so that we'd be kept afloat if the plane overshot the tiny airstrip and spilled us into the sea.

We stood in strung-out clusters outside the plane on the airfield, waiting on the pleasure of the flight personnel. They were civilians under contract to the Army Transport Service; they kept to themselves and had nothing to do with the military people they were flying. There were three generals among us, the only passengers to have seats, three great upholstered chairs lashed in a row to the metal eye-sockets imbedded in the deck of the plane. The generals didn't know one another. They didn't speak. They were, all three, extremely handsome, tall, big-boned, and well-built. There was a sallow, bearded individual, a secret agent perhaps, a government expert; he wore a sort of linen duster over his clothes, kept both hands jammed in the pockets of this garment, and looked like the photo of Marcel Proust on his deathbed. There was a slender GI in green fatigues, with a blood-stained bandage around his head. He had been in a traffic accident on the drive out to Orly Airport; the jeep he had been driven in had backed into the high tailboard of a French truck. The rest of us were unmemorable, soldiers and sailors mixed in with junior officers of both services.

There was no estimated time of departure, no preliminary signal given, no count-off or warning. When the civilian pilots came sauntering out of wherever they had gone to retire to, they simply got on board without a backward glance and the plane took off. That was why we were all strung out in the

*Fuchs, at right, with shipmates at Fort Barrancas, Pensacola, Florida, about 1945*

open on the airfield in the heat, ready to file in and not be stranded. I stood hidden in the largest of the groups. My idea was to lose myself in the background and do everything I could to avoid notice and detection. The island of Santa Maria, on that particular day, with its unwavering, incredible sunlight, was the most beautiful place I had ever been to.

At the Goose Gander Air Base in Newfoundland, the second stop and with one last leg to go, while we loitered outside the plane, again waiting on the pilots, it suddenly became apparent that the injured GI was no longer with us. He had wandered away. I, who might just as well have done nothing, went looking for him—out of superstition, to appease whoever there is to be appeased. The GI had gone to the PX on the base. The PX was in a barn of a building a good distance off the tarmac and away from the plane, and when I was inside the barn there was more time used up while I searched and tried to find him. He was standing at the magazine rack, reading, in his green fatigues, with his bloody head. He looked startled and confused when I grabbed him, and clearly had no idea what I was doing with him. I pulled him away from the magazine stand, led him out of the building, and then hustled him over the field and to the plane as fast as I could make him go. In a matter of minutes the flight crew came by.

We flew on, now in darkness. The tall, silent generals were back in place, sitting Indian file in their row of chairs. Gear and cargo were heaped together in the middle of the plane, the mass held fast by a system of steel-tipped poles locked in the eye-sockets of the floor planks. We lay sprawled on the deck against the cargo, found blankets, and kept warm. The injured GI loomed before me. "You want my comic book?" he asked me, offering me the gaudy colored packet he had bought. I said no, thanked him, and he walked away, unruffled and erect. There was the smell of fire in the plane, of wood smoke. The flight engineer came out of the cockpit and started looking around and checking, but it developed the fire was down below us, a smouldering forest fire in the desolation there, and not in our plane.

I lay back on the deck. Everyone around me was dozing or asleep but I was wide awake. I waited in the quiet for the flight to end, safe, lulled by the power of the plane and its throbbing rhythm.

My wife and I stood in the lobby not far from the opened door of the theatre office, talking to the theatre manager, or the theatre employee on duty, who had come out to meet us. It was the dead hour of the weekday matinee, a hot New York City summer day, the picture playing behind the shuttered lobby doors, nobody entering the lobby, no ticket-buyers at the window of the box-office booth outside on the baked-out, littered sidewalk pavement. My wife wore a pale blue piqué maternity dress, a natural straw hat with a small brim. We were going to the hospital to reserve a room and make arrangements for the baby that was coming, and, on our way to the hospital that day, we stopped at the theatre, the Rialto Theatre on Broadway, to see if we could catch the coming attraction of the picture that was due the following week. The picture was based on a *Collier's* magazine story by me. It was the first thing of mine to be filmed, the first connection I had with Hollywood and the motion picture studios, and even though the picture wasn't playing and wasn't due for another week, since we were in the area anyway, we came by to look at the posters in the glass-enclosed cases and take in the picture's trailer.

The theatre manager—he was wearing a summer shirt with half sleeves—told us the feature inside had another hour to run before the coming attractions came on. He was unnerved by my wife's fine materni-ty dress, by the straw hat. He didn't know what to

make of the two of us, what we were doing there in his movie-house, why we had this interest in coming attractions, and I could see he didn't know whether to believe us when I said that we'd be back.

We went down to the hospital. It was the small, Catholic-run French Hospital, about two dozen blocks south of the Rialto Theatre, so it was possible for us to make the reservation, sign the papers, and return in time for the trailer we wanted to see. "This is the room I would choose for myself if I were having a baby," the young nun, who was taking us around, said when she showed us a large corner room with windows on three sides, but we settled on a more modest, less expensive accommodation.

The general story idea was mine and I recog-nized bits of dialogue, but it was all surprisingly strange and unfamiliar to me, as though we were looking at the trailer of somebody else's picture and not one in which I had had some part. It was an RKO picture with small stars in it, but I was more im-pressed with it than I expected to be or wanted to be, secretly disturbed because I sensed that the things they were doing in the picture were the real goods, homely, homemade, authentic, and out of my sphere.

"Being a sucker for a long shot, nothing delights

*Susan Fuchs*

us more than seeing Germany and Russia shaking hands, Poland besting the theoretically irresistible Nazi war machine, a Joe Penner comedy being rated in these columns as one of the funniest comedies of the season," the *New York Times* critic, Frank Nugent that year, wrote in his review. This was when the Hitler-Stalin pact had been signed just weeks earlier; Nugent's review appeared on September 13, 1939. Poland was still fighting at that time, still standing off the *Wehrmacht,* but the resistance collapsed soon after, fourteen days later, and the country was partitioned.

These movie-makers were naturals. Their inventions and jokes, their ways of coming at the material, were strictly their own. For example, the picture, which was called *The Day the Bookies Wept,* had to do with some taxi drivers who pool their money and buy a racehorse which they turn over to one of their number, Joe Penner, to train, putting their trust in him because he is marvellously adept with the pigeons he has raised all his life and loves; and to demonstrate his unusual gift, an animation sequence was inserted—a flock of paper-cutout pigeons flying in V-formations at Penner's command, wheeling to the left, swooping to the right, doing barrel-rolls, Immelmanns, loop-the-loops. The animation was combined with live action, and I wondered how they had hit on such a concept and knew it would be funny. I could see them chortling among themselves as they worked up the notion and tried it out, and of course the reason I was bothered and had secret misgivings was that what these people did seemingly so effortlessly and well was unknown territory to me. The female lead in the picture playing opposite Penner was Betty Grable, then at the start of her career, fresh and buxom.

The theatre manager watched us as we turned to leave. He had been with us through the trailer, the three of us standing at the rear of the theatre, looking at the screen. He was still at a loss. He wanted to give us back our money—we had paid admission to get in. The next day the afternoon paper, the *New York Sun,* printed a brief item in one of its movie columns about us, saying a couple had walked into the Rialto Theatre, paid full admission, watched the coming attractions, and then walked out.

The house, a mansion with its numerous cool, quiet, beautiful rooms, lay in the tree-darkened section above Sunset Boulevard in Beverly Hills, in the flat just where the sharp rise of the hills begins. I was taken through the house on occasion and as we passed along, I would steal glances at the silent, imposing furnishings, everything polished and in place; I saw the shining, spic-and-span backstairs

serving pantries, the interesting, odd-shaped other utility rooms which, with their household paraphernalia, were also tucked away in the back of the house. What struck me was the thought that this extensive establishment, with its grounds and gardens, was all at the pleasure of a single person living there alone, a bachelor, without family. It seemed strangely excessive and caught my imagination. As if to put the spaciousness to use and not let it be wasted, or to atone and make amends, there was a standing arrangement for guests to come drifting by at will over each weekend. People came and left during the course of the day, a steady flow, some staying on, new arrivals turning up to enliven the proceedings. A houseman or the Mexican maids brought out trays of lemonade, and it was a more or less continuous entertainment going on from the end of work at the studios on Saturday afternoons until Monday, when the work started all over again.

The host, the production head at one of the studios, had a casual way with his guests, whom he didn't greet or interfere with. He went threading past them, always on the move, busy with some plan or errand on his mind, a group of three or four friends of his invariably following and keeping up with him to abet him in whatever he was up to. He was more a ringleader with his retinue than a host, and left his guests to make themselves at home and enjoy themselves on their own. Among the people following him on these marches was the brother of his former wife, an intimate after the divorce and sorrows; on one weekend when I was there, the host's former mother-in-law was present, a still youthful-looking, attractive woman, a member of the party just like anyone else. She wore a tan gabardine suit with a tight skirt that showed off her legs. Myself, I stood on the fringes of the assemblage and looked on at the guests, some of them celebrities recognizable to me on sight, for example, the tennis champion Bill Tilden. He was then past his prime but still enormous at the net—he was a towering, remarkably rangy man, with broad shoulders and a great armspread that made him impassable at the net, certainly in the competition he met on the tennis court at this home. After the games, he would play bridge, and won.

Here and there among the company were individuals who had taken great pains with their appearance. They were all dressed up, even in the heat of the day, and held themselves with a stiff, self-conscious dignity, on display, obviously expecting to be seen. For some reason these people were usually found in couples, standing together, husbands and wives. There were certain guests, performers whom I had never seen and so didn't know by sight and who were remote to me until I found out what their names were—somebody nearby, looking at them, and, like me, wondering, would inquire in a whisper, "Who is that?" and I would overhear the answers—and then the names would come to me with a start, names I had seen on billboards in New York, on elevated train stations while I waited for the train, the leads in the Schwab and Mandel Broadway musical comedies, in Shubert operettas. I used to watch a middle-aged gentleman, one of the regulars there—he would drop out, miss a week or two, reappear and be seen again. He was portly, careworn and gloomy, of medium height, wearing European shoes with raised heels, and to my astonishment I discovered, after I had been watching him for some time, that he was a famous professional ballroom dancer, half of an internationally known team.

The last novel I had written before we came out to Hollywood was a book called *Low Company*. This was the same title of an English book, an autobiography, written by a man who had robbed banks and been in prison. The duplication made for some confusion. (My book was called *Neptune Beach* in the English edition; the Englishman's became *Angels in Undress* in this country.) And just as the word had gone out identifying the Schwab and Mandel musical-comedy performers, say, or the ballroom dancer, so the word got around about me, erroneously, that I had been a bank robber, had been in jail, and so on. My wife, who often went with me to the gatherings at the Beverly Hills house, one Sunday happened to pass a group standing on the open terrace which overlooked the tennis court. I was playing in a doubles game down there. "He doesn't look like an ex-convict, does he?" an MGM producer said to the others with him, and my wife realized they were talking about me.

"That's why they favor us," she said, when she told me about the incident. "And because we're young, younger than they are."

When my mother was dying and I went back east to see her, as I sat by her bed and we were together, talking and falling silent, at one point she said, "Has Susie changed?", meaning how did my wife look.

I said no, that I was fond of her and to me she looked the same. ("Oh, you're the man that loves his wife," a New York reporter, interviewing me, once said to me, in wonder.)

Sometimes, alone, I hear my mother's voice calling me: Daniel.

The story departments covered books, English and American, wrote up synopses, distributed the

*Susan Fuchs and sons at Corral Beach near Los Angeles, "as it used to look." Tom (center) is now a television writer and head of Fuchs Productions in Hollywood. Jake is Professor of English at CSU, Hayward.*

mimeographed lists of summaries to the different producers on the lot, and, with the katzenjammer consistency that followed me and my false criminal reputation, I was assigned, when I went to work at the studio, to write on gangster pictures. What probably entered into it was that my studio was Warner Brothers, which specialized in these movies (Edward G. Robinson, Cagney, Raft), and I was eagerly asked for by many of the producers, although when I started to talk to them, in story conferences, about the gangsters I had witnessed on the streets and around the tenements in the Williamsburg, Brooklyn, district where I grew up, and outlined what I proposed to do, they stared in disbelief and lost heart—they asked me what kind of gangsters was I talking about, who were these people? In any case, the first picture on which I had my name as a screenwriter was a gangster picture, *The Big Shot*, with Humphrey Bogart, produced by a fastidious but thoroughly courteous and kindly man (his name was Lord!). It's been a lasting curiosity to me that I have absolutely no recollection of the content of this picture on which I had labored, not an isolated scene, a frame. A good thirty years later, on a Sunday afternoon, I met Lauren Bacall at the beach house of a friend, who led me over to her on the sand, introduced me to her, and said I had a story which he thought it would amuse her to hear. "I suppose you want to tell me about Bogey," she said, when my friend left us. But it wasn't about Bogart. It was about her and me, about another Warner Brothers picture, *Storm Warning,* and it was plain to see she had no recollection of the incident and of me.

This other Warner Brothers picture was about to start, the sets built and standing on the stages, the cast assembled, all in readiness, except for Bacall who balked flatly. She wouldn't do the part. The producer, Jerry Wald, busy with ten or twelve other projects as well as the final pre-production details on this picture, with more pressing down on him than one man could bear, asked me to take over and reason with her—to discuss the script, spend the time, promise changes, appeal and win her over. But when I sat down with her in Wald's office that day and faced her, I said if she didn't like the script and honestly felt the part was not good for her and would do her harm, then she was right to refuse the assignment and I told her, "Don't do it." She straightened up in the chair, got her things together, rose, and walked out of the room, without changing her expression or responding. I had worked with Wald on an earlier picture, *The*

*Hard Way;* it had been a happy time—everybody liked the picture, it had had a nice success—and Wald and I had developed a warm relationship, but when he saw what I did, with all his other troubles distracting him, he blew up and told me it was the last time he would let me talk to a star.

It was a serious predicament the studio was in, with people on salary and the costs rising. Steve Trilling, Jack Warner's executive officer—he was a rather undersized man, with a rosy, clean complexion and an ever-cheerful manner—came hurrying over, now in a state of some alarm, but Wald swiftly reassured him. Wald tapped the side of his temple with his finger—he had not been caught off-guard, he said. He said he knew Bacall was out, that she wouldn't budge and it was useless to count on her, and that he had been working secretly in the background with another star in reserve—he had had dinner last night with Ginger Rogers at Romanoff's and had sold her on the picture; he had told her the whole script as they dined, had gone over her key scenes with her, she had loved them, and they had her. She was—as it happened, as Trilling knew—between pictures, available immediately, so there

*A break during the filming of* Storm Warning. *From left: Jerry Wald, Ronald Reagan, Ginger Rogers, and Stuart Heisler. (Copyright © 1951 Warner Brothers Pictures, Inc. All rights reserved.)*

would be no loss of time or delay. Trilling took a few moments to absorb the news and was smiling and calm again, halfway out the door to go back and tell Warner all was in order, when he suddenly stopped, the gladness gone. "Jerry," he said, "Jerry, you were with me last night. You had dinner with me at Romanoff's."

Wald worked in a tumult of activity. That was his way. He had pictures shooting three and four at a time, more in different stages of preparation, sat with writers all day long, made mistakes, mixed illusion with fact, and went boiling on. Norman Krasna, his onetime partner, said he was like a dentist who had a mania to fill every cavity in America. (I was in the room one day when he was on the phone selling an actress he wanted for one of his pictures, not mine, pounding hard, telling her in confidence that she had the leading part even though Crawford was supposed to be the star, that Crawford had no inkling of what was going on and that she would steal the picture away from her—all the while unaware that he was speaking to Crawford at the other end of the line and not the actress he believed he was conning.) He was overweight, a fast eater, a fast talker, always trotted, never walked, had a wild streak of imagination, and a young man's headlong, rousing ardor that marked what he did, and enchanted.

The strange thing was that Rogers wound up in the picture. The picture went into production without delay and was released on schedule, *Storm Warning*, with Ginger Rogers, Doris Day, Ronald Reagan, and Steve Cochran.

*Fuchs, photographed by director Robert Parrish (seen in mirror)*

Robert Parrish

T‌he jumble, the comic turnabout and surprise, the levity—a magazine editor I knew said this strain of comedy in my stories was Middle-European in character, typically Viennese, and that I got it by inheritance, since my father, coming from Vienna, was Viennese. Howard Moss, in an essay on my three Brooklyn novels, wrote, instead, that my comedy was my way of dealing with the humiliation that infested the lives of the poor people I wrote about; that I neither romanticized them nor inflicted them with the additional insult of my pity. Mr. Moss was exceedingly complimentary and God knows he admired my twist of humor and approved, but in his very examination (whose clarity and pace I would not dare to praise) were the reasons why in time this humor of mine began to irk me. The brave jollity—it increasingly seemed to me—was an evasion; it dodged and skidded around the truth and would not meet it fairly; it was the device by which a writer, working at tangents and using satire, did not say straight-out what there was to say, and avoided responsibility. The

mirth, this "combination of the real with the absurd" (Mr. Moss's phrase), this thing I did so well and so constantly—it would slip in on me unbidden, when I thought I was writing an altogether different kind of story—became a fixation and weighed on me. I was tired of making fun of the people in my stories, hitting them off, as I did, easily and without conscience. I was, in the end, in the peculiar position of a writer whose forte was a quality he secretly disliked and wanted to lean on less and less and not at all, and who, on the other hand, had no other special talent or great idea to offer in its place.

My father—what else?—didn't come from Vienna and wasn't Viennese. He was born in Russia. He was brought over by his father when he was eighteen; and even though he arrived in this country at an early age, and spent time in the Midwest, in St. Paul, and wasn't Viennese, his manner retained an old-world, courtly flavor. When he had a whiskey, there was a glass of seltzer water on the side for a chaser, a crust of bread to go with it. "And you are his inspiration when he composes his stories?" he asked my wife, showing her the deference that, according to his thought, was due a young woman. He was always at a remove, keeping his distance, keeping to himself, not wanting attention paid to him. He smoked with the contentment of the solitary smoker observing the passing scene; his left eye was heavily lidded, half-closed, because he held his cigarette in the left corner of his mouth, and smoked often. He had a curving, old-fashioned mustache, which he tended, in his style. He washed his hair every morning, using a bar of the yellow Octagon kitchen soap.

He had the news- and candystand concession in the Whitehall Building at 17 Battery Place, at the tip of Manhattan—it was one of those booths you see as you enter the lobbies of the tall New York City office buildings. My father's building, considered a sky-scraper at the time, faced the open New York Upper Bay (and the Aquarium before it). Steamship lines had their offices there and in the nearby area, and some of the less prominent companies—the Consu-lich Line, White Star—employed him to fit out a ship's library with periodicals. We went together in the late Saturday afternoons, after he locked up his small place of business, I to help and accompany on those out-of-the-way Brooklyn and New Jersey piers. I followed along as he trudged with the bundles of magazines; we walked into the ships over the crew's bridge on the dock, past the hard metal bulkheads, the storerooms in the interior, the waxy sides of beef hanging in a row from the overhead hooks. At Christmas time, executives in the building or their secretaries came down to the lobby and gave my father holiday gift-orders to be filled—five pound boxes of chocolates, Page and Shaw, Park and Til-ford. My father handled the deliveries himself, which was the way he did it or had to do it, and I went with him on those exhausting expeditions, late at night, long after work, dropping off the parcels one by one at their different destinations. We found ourselves on strange, outlying El stations, waiting in the winter cold, the only people on the platforms, for trains which so late at night, it seemed to us, might never come. The Upper Manhattan residential sections, where many orders took us, were totally unknown to us and proved a maze—we had never been in such surroundings before. We wandered crosstown on foot in the icy dark, retracing our steps, blundering, checking the directions on the slip of paper, while the wind racketted down the dead, empty streets and smashed against the multistoried apartment build-ings.

"You will send up to the Club" [the Whitehall Club in the building], my father said to me, and listed

the publications on order—*Spur, Country Gentleman, Yachting,* the *Tatler.* During the High Holy Days, on Yom Kippur, my father would open the newsstand for me and then hurry back to spend the day in prayer at his synagogue. He was telling me the things I had to attend to the next morning when I would be taking his place. "A man will come down from Booth and Flynn [a construction company in the building] and you will give him what he wants—he will tell you. At nine o'clock the German consul comes to work in his office. He likes to pick up the morning papers himself, so you should have them ready when he comes, also the *Journal of Commerce,* the *Wall Street Journal,* and the two German papers." He named them and then held up. He read my mind, sensed the resistance in me, how the German names of the foreign-language papers grated on me. This was now in the middle thirties, the wretchedness fast taking form. My father hovered, hidden in the haze of his cigarette smoke, reflecting, remote. "If when he comes and you see him, if you can't stand the sight of him, spit in his eye," he said.

The consul appeared the next morning, as my father said he would. I had the papers ready for him on the counter. He picked them up and was almost past me, when he looked up and stopped. "Where is the old gentleman?" he said.

I said my father was at temple.

"Oh, yes, I see. Would you wish him a happy New Year for me?" he said, and moved on. He had been civil, a preoccupied, slender man, nothing out of the ordinary, blond, not yet middle-aged, in a fresh grey business suit.

There was a worn groove on the cabinet door below the newspaper counter. The groove was a foot wide, smooth and polished, the bare wood showing, and it interested me the other times I noticed it when I spelled my father, because I couldn't imagine how the hollow had come about, what had caused it—the door opened clear and there was nothing it could possibly come in contact with. But as I sat in the booth that morning, facing the daylong wait ahead of me, chagrined with myself on account of the consul (saying temple to the man and not synagogue), I saw the answer.

The booth was a cubicle, a closet, cluttered on all sides by the cabinets where my father kept the stock— the chewing gum and candy boxes brought in from the jobbers. There were tied-up bundles of maga-zines underfoot. There was just enough room to turn around in, and no more. I was wedged in a corner, sitting on a high stool, on top of a pile of newspaper returns, aching to get myself through the day, when I noticed that my leg, crossed at the knee, was bobbing up and down, ceaselessly, the toe of my shoe fitting exactly in the niche where my father, imprisoned over the years, had ground out the smooth, well-worn groove.

My father had been a furrier. He developed the furrier's lung disease, became incapacitated, no longer had a trade, and was destitute, all this while still a young man, not long before I was born. My uncle Hymie, who ran four open streetcorner newsstands in Harlem, came down one day with the news of a new building under construction, almost completed, a skyscraper, that he said might be a solution and my father's salvation. Hymie wanted my father to sell newspapers at the construction site, to station himself at the wooden temporary shacks where the architects worked, where the engineers, the building managers, the real-estate agents came and went—there would be enough to guarantee a flow of customers. My uncle, a lusty bruiser of a man, a doer, said he'd break my father in, fix him up with the newspaper delivery men, and, best of all, he said, when the building was finished, there would be booths in the lobby, one of them a place for a newsstand, and with luck, if the building people liked him, my father could get the concession. My mother told us later, when we were grown, how the three of them, young people, sat in the dark, in the stealth, putting their heads together, turning the idea over, hoping and plotting. The first night, when my father came home after the day's trial, he spread the money he had taken in on the table and, with the shades pulled down, my mother pressing close at his side, they counted the pennies and nickels to see how much it came to and if they would be able to make a living for themselves and their children.

The elementary school I went to in Williamsburg, P.S. 19, had two units—the old building and the new one. After the first two grades, the pupils were moved up and went on to the New Building. The Old Building—one of the earliest, the nineteenth built in Brooklyn—was a small, red-brick structure, with almost no playground space. I was waiting outside the small building for the gates to open and the classes to begin, so I was six or seven at the time. I was standing on the sidewalk across the street from the school. A street peddler with a horse and wagon carrying a load of country apples was getting ready for the day's work. He had one of those great brown paper bags which he had marked up for a sign: 7 lbs—25 cents, in big numbers, and I was watching him fix the sign over a stick nailed to the sideboard of the wagon. There was a sudden, monstrous thud, a rush of air knocking me forward on my feet. The street peddler turned

around to see what it was. *"Veiber, gevalt!"* he cried, with all his heart, in horror and fright.

A housewife, cleaning her windows on the fifth floor of her tenement building, sitting on the windowsill, had lost her balance and fallen to the pavement just beside us.

When I was born, while my mother was still busy with me in the flat—where she had had me just four days earlier—my brother George, at the age of five, was pushed off the roof and killed.

I don't know what effect the two tragedies had on me. It may be that I have a deep-seated fear of heights without knowing it, that I picked the Navy to go into during the war because I feel safer and at home on the water (although, as it happened, as might be expected, I never went to sea on a naval vessel and a portion of my military service, such as it was, was spent on planes). The fact is I am clinically unable to sit through those scenes where actors are on high, narrow building ledges ready to jump or taking chances on high towers or clinging to the perpendicular sides of mountains; I go through physical contortions, my legs shiver and freeze, and I

*Jacob and Sara Fuchs, at the grave of their young son George*

*The "four youngest Fuchs," about 1914: the twins, Helen (holding doll) and Eli, in the chair, Henry on the left, and Daniel on the right*

turn away from the picture in the movie house or on television and won't look at it even though I know, as I do, that these thrilling moments are made with process screens and when the window ledges are just a few feet off the floor of the studio sound stages.

We moved. The house—where I was born, where George was killed, on Rivington Street in the Lower East Side of Manhattan—became fearsome and hateful. It was a superstition on the East Side for people to abandon the premises they were living in when misfortune struck, but I think my mother left out of misery, because she was unable to undo what had happened and had to do something. We went to New Lots, far out in Brooklyn. The New Lots section was largely undeveloped and unpopulated. There were ditches and pits. They filled with water when it rained and were a constant danger and dread—children could fall into the pools and drown, as in some cases that were widely talked about they did. And so we moved now to Williamsburg, to a five-story tenement on South Second Street, on the first floor in the front.

The tenement with its many families, six on each floor, was an undiscovered country. On the fourth floor, an enormous fat woman, Mrs. Likker, lived with her grown sons, also in the front, three stories above us. She had a malady that accounted for her bulk and, with her asthma, made it impossible for her to lie

down or sleep in a bed. She sat all day in a chair in the front room looking out at the street and seeing what was going on; I used to imagine her at night, sitting in the blackness above us, sleeping or awake, waiting for the morning and the new day to start. I once caught sight of Mr. Borden in the hall, walking down the steps with a plain, small wooden box, a coffin, in his arms; one of his children, an infant, had died and he was taking it out in the afternoon for burial. Mrs. Leparbler held court. She was an attractive woman, but ailed and seemed unable ever to get well, an invalid. She persevered. Neighbors came in to sit at her bedside. They made tea for themselves and she entertained. "Alexander," she would say to her husband—he was a postal clerk, "if you would be so good, if you are not too tired, would you go into the kitchen and empty out the pan under the ice-box"; if it was neglected, the pan overflowed and the tenants below complained. "Marianna, sing 'Eli-Eli' for the company," Mrs. Leparbler would say to her eight-year-old daughter, home from school, and position the child near her at the head of the bed. Mrs. Steinberg lived on the first floor, at the other end of the landing from us. She had diabetes. She was always carefully dressed, never in a house dress. Her home was spotless. Her rooms were in the back, getting the sun, and the floors and furniture shone with light.

I went on walks by myself, to Broadway under the El (the Brooklyn Broadway), drawn to the shop windows there—the ties, the haberdashery. There was a pool parlor on Grand Street Extension, a broad, cobblestone thoroughfare running at a slant from the Williamsburg Bridge Plaza; almost every night a group of young men would be practising complicated tap-dance steps on the sidewalk outside the pool parlor, and I was often there, looking on as they put in the effort, matching the combinations with one another and improving them. I had a route. I took in the street sights at night, the Mary Sugar Bums at the garbage cans with their bags of belongings, the men fornicating with women pushed up against the wall in the dark doorways of vacant stores. I would linger at the open doors of bakeries at night, watching the bakers with their hairy, whitened arms kneading the dough, punching the clumps into rolls, sliding the raw dough into the ovens on the flat wooden paddles.

When I was eleven or so, I was playing ball with some friends in the street outside my house. The ball got away and sailed into the sidewalk, hitting a man who had been loitering with two or three others at the entrance to the building. The man grabbed the ball and started to throw it over the roof. I jumped up in front of him to stop him, missed, and was astounded to find him coming down at me. I ducked and danced as he went after me. Mrs. Klingsberg, at her window on the first floor, went into a paroxysm of rage, screaming at him to leave me alone and raising such a din that he and the men with him were swiftly cowed. They gathered themselves together and quietly walked away.

They were pimps, strong-arm men, keeping the ground clear for the brothel that was operating upstairs in the tenement.

I was on Rodney Street on the way to South Third, dawdling along on one of my aimless walks, after school, when I came upon a killing, a gangster murder. It was daytime, a warm day, people on the street sitting on folding chairs and on the stoops. The first sign I had of impending danger was the glimpse I caught of Blackie, the cop on the beat. He was hated, a heavyset, low-slung, swarthy man, a sneak who always had to be watched when he appeared on the scene—his specialty was to rush in on the sidewalk crap games, send the crapshooters flying, and scoop up the coins and bills on the pavement for himself. There was a candy store on the corner of South Third; it was one of those places that had an open counter facing the street, where people bought carbonated drinks and malteds. Blackie was moving forward when suddenly he stopped dead short and wouldn't go further. I looked up to the corner. There was a car in the middle of the street, someone still at the wheel, two men emerging with pistols in their hands. The people on the sidewalk parted. The man at the candy-store counter cringed and did not attempt to escape. I looked back at Blackie. He bolted, running hard with his chest close to the ground, frantic to get out of sight. He reached the corner at Grand Street Extension and was gone.

The violent incidents of one kind or another—the many street accidents and the clamor and turbulence that arose around them, the vicious fist fights that erupted almost periodically, the husbands and wives settling their differences in public, brawling in the street—were part of the commotion that provided a daily spectacle and was the reason, I suppose, for the walks I took. The crowded streets had an excitement for me, satisfying an instinct I wasn't even aware of at the time. My interest, I felt, was authentic, strong and sound, and to be trusted; I felt, when I undertook to make my way as a writer, that if a subject genuinely interested me, there was a chance it would interest others, that there was nothing else to go on. I freely used the sights and happenings, which had absorbed me, in the three novels I wrote in my twenties, but the books, when they came out, were a

disappointment. They failed, had no sales, attracted few reviews. Some years afterward, I was with a friend, talking about the old days in Williamsburg, and I told him about the killing I saw on South Third Street. My friend said what a good story it was, why didn't I write it? Of course I had.

The actuality wasn't enough. I had to find a way of compelling the reader, of drawing him in and holding him fast. I faced the exasperating, elusive problem of form. In the movie business, the stress was on continuity. We made step-sheets and outlines. We wanted the actuality, the news, material that was intrinsically interesting, but we knew it was the plot-line that inveigled the people in the movie-house, that caught them off guard and surprised, that tumbled them around and kept them captive until the finish. The problem, the process, has apparently become much harder, more exasperating and demanding than ever. A director in a trade-paper statement cautions that the onlooker now will "out-think you, will outguess you all the time," and had better not be underestimated. The audience nowadays is savvy, wants the story told in quick flashes, in quick cuts, dispensing with dissolves: a character is seen walking to his car and—a jump cut, no transition—is driving away. "Let people reach for it. Let them add it up," the director advises new moviemakers.

"The author tells about sideshow people, fortune-tellers and the like," a reviewer wrote of one of the novels. "As soon as he finds out why he wants to write about people of that sort, he may write a good novel." I knew why I wanted to write about them—people were a wonder and a fascination. Or maybe he meant that my people—"people of that sort"—were unsuitable and not to be written about. What made it more difficult to understand what he meant and wanted was that I hadn't written about sideshow people at all—I think he got the fortune-telling idea from a blowsy corsetiere in my novel and that he mixed up the setting of the novel—a seaside Brooklyn residential neighborhood—with Coney Island. But the reviewer was inconsequential and a pain. It remained for the author to arrange or discover the necessary pattern, to implant the ideas and motifs organically, so that they could develop naturally and carry the reader or viewer along irresistibly, including even the fellow who glanced through my novel, and others of his sort.

We spent the days with no certain direction in mind, following a routine that seemed to have sprung up and taken shape by itself. There were those vacant, sunny afternoons when I came home from school, dry-lipped, wearing my shirt and tie, another day gone; there was the strange stillness and feeling of solitude in the rooms of our flat when, as it sometimes happened, nobody was home and I was alone there for a spell. At the end of June, when school was over for the summer vacation, we went to the country, to board on a farm in the Catskills. My mother took the four youngest of us with her—the twins, Eli and Helen, my older brother Henry, and myself; the two oldest boys, Rupert and Julie, were left behind to shift for themselves with my father. Coming home from one summer in the country, as we trooped down the street—the bedding, the trunk, the pots and pans to arrive later on by Adams Express—my mother saw Julie and Rupert waiting for us at the tenement building, and, with a sudden lift at the heart, going up quickly, she flung her arms around Rupert, throwing herself against him and holding him, while all the time Julie hung back, motionless and sick, and looked on. Some many years later, I recalled the incident to Rupert, but he didn't remember any part of it and didn't want to believe that Julie had been hurt by it, that he had been the cause of Julie's hurt. My mother, when we were growing up, was slim, standing straight and unafraid, with a good, full bust that had nourished each of us. She had a European woman's style and flair and grasp of the realities; she had a sense of drama. She was bold, impulsive, warm, and independent. I myself was somewhere, in the order of the family, between the twins and George. My mother had no time for me. She was forever busy, taken up with the house, fussing with the twins, and she went by me, until in the spring one year I fell seriously ill. I had double pneumonia and pleurisy. My mother cleared out the front-room parlor, removing all the furniture and putting in a bed. The door was kept closed, only my mother going in and out. The room was just for me over the number of days that I lay there, surviving the pneumonia and pleurisy and then resting and getting well again, while my mother tended me. I was content. Everyone was away at work or at school. I listened to the street noises, the wagons going by with their load of fruit or potatoes or flowers, the peddlers calling out. I had my mother all to myself, so I knew, when we came home from the country that day, what Julie missed and Rupert had.

She had a special tenderness for him. He was her first born and in danger. He sat at the piano, our Fischer upright, and played the songs that were popular at the time. He played by ear. He had the natural gaiety that came from strength and being loved. He went with girls. He had gone to Commercial High School, later called Alexander Hamilton—

(Julie had gone to Boys, a Latin and mathematics school)—and had won an essay contest in his senior year but had been disqualified, the English teacher claiming the essay had to have been plagiarized. He sat Rupert down in an empty classroom, gave him a theme and an hour to write it up in, and locked the door. Rupert came out with the finished new essay, won the prize again, was complimented by the principal, and then turned around and slugged the English teacher. He was expelled and never graduated. He was good with cars, then fairly new in Williamsburg and something of an excitement—he owned a Hupmobile which he had patched up and put together, and once drove around in a four-door Marmon touring car. He serviced the big Mack Bulldog trucks for a heavy-industry company, worked for trucking firms on the docks at Wallabout Market in Brooklyn and on the New Jersey docks, carried identification papers on him, was mixed up with gangsters and was employed by them. He had a battery and ignition shop on Bedford Avenue for many years, and soon after he went into this business for himself, he was sought out by the bootleggers who ran their boats out of Sheepshead Bay, not very far from the shop in Brooklyn. The boats slipped out at night on regular runs to ships anchored in the Atlantic, loaded up in the dark, and brought the liquor back to shore. Rupert never went out on the boats. He made his repairs on the engines and magnetos while the boats were tied up at their moorings, and stayed out of trouble; when Prohibition was ended, he worked, again on a legitimate basis, for Vannie Higgins, a man who controlled much of the laundry business in Brooklyn and had a fleet of delivery trucks that needed to be cared for. I used to meet some of the hard characters that hung around my brother's shop for one reason or another and were friends of his. I had become a schoolteacher, and on Saturdays or after classes during the week, I liked to walk over to Pratt Library, which was part of the Institute there and open to the general public. This took me across Bedford Avenue and I would stop in at the shop on my way. The men knew I was a schoolteacher, Rupert probably told them I was a writer, too, and they would never have anything to say and were intimidated by me. One day when I came by, there was a lull. The shop was deserted. I went looking for my brother in the garage the building owners maintained behind the row of shops and stores that lined the street. He was there by himself in the big empty place, in his woolen watch cap and heavy, grimy work clothes, riding around on a bicycle that he had found somewhere.

I had the License No. 1, which meant I could teach in the city's elementary schools (although there were no appointments; I taught as a substitute, a permanent-substitute). Henry, my older brother, couldn't get past the examination for the High School English license; all he had was the substitute license which allowed him to fill in sporadically if an English teacher somewhere was absent and the principal wanted to call him. Henry had had Pott's disease, tuberculosis of the spine. His spine had stopped growing with the disease, so that he was stunted in height, not more than five feet four. He had disproportionately long, powerful arms, a powerful chest, and extremely broad shoulders. He was a stalwart, easily the leader among us when we were boys on the block. He stood up to cops; when we made our fires on a winter night, scarring the street pavement, and the cops sneaked up, cracking our ears with their gloves, we all ran but Henry held his ground, taking them on, arguing and taunting. If I was in a fight and he came by, he would brush me aside and finish the scrap in minutes. He could not pass the High School English Test and it perplexed him as much as it made it impossible for him to teach what he loved and make his living. He could not understand why he failed, and stubbornly returned each year to try again.

The exam was drawn out over a period of days and weeks—written tests in teaching methods and in the subject, oral tests, interviews. He had no trouble with the written sections—he was magna cum laude, Phi Beta Kappa, New York City College—and passed, without exception, in the top three in each of the years. It was the oral or the interview that trapped him. After the fourth or fifth attempt—I tried not to think of the examinations and never knew the exact number—he decided to appeal to the State Board of Education people in Albany. I dragged along on the trip because he should at least have someone with him. He stood up before the state officials and made his speech, saying how qualified he was, how much English and American literature meant to him, how often he had passed the written with the highest marks, but he soon lost his place, was floundering miserably, didn't know what he was saying, rambled desperately, and kept pushing on—they were not listening to him, one of them sprawled out on the chair, drinking milk from a carton through a straw. On the railroad station, as we waited for the train, it finally came out of me—I explained it was his appearance, that he was deformed. He stared at me, shattered, unbelieving and bewildered.

"Why did you tell him?" my mother said to me, in tears, when we got home.

I taught at P.S. 225, lying between Brighton Beach and Manhattan Beach in Brooklyn and serving the children of both those lively communities. It was a blessed school, the teachers and the children. The principal was Sol Branower, a brilliant man who properly had no business being an elementary principal and should have been moved up long ago; he had been blocked by Board of Education politics at one time and was now held down by the Depression, which limited advancement and promotions in the city educational system. Out of boredom, he would suddenly start the bells clanging through the building and pull a fire drill, filling the streets all around with masses of children; or he would find a pretext and call a quick, unscheduled assembly to brighten up the day. I ran the school newspaper for him, the *Brighton Beacon,* and taught the fourth grade. The young men and women at 225, my colleagues—the ones with permanent tenure and the permanent-substitutes on day-to-day substitute pay—were similarly affected by the Depression, locked in grade-school classes or forced to take substitute work since nothing better was available, so they were a highly unusual bunch. It is an unexaggerated fact that they were select, overqualified, a prize collection of teachers. They came to work each morning shining with health and vivacity, and the school throbbed. My books, as they came out, each sold a total of two hundred copies. The members of the faculty, the principal, the two assistant principals, and Miss Merican, the clerk in the office, bought sixty of them, which I duly autographed.

Late at night, near midnight, the phone rang and the voice at the other end, in a whispery, carefully modulated tone, said he was Jed Harris and was I the author of *Homage to Blenholt,* a novel he much admired. If the name of Bergotte made the Narrator in Proust jump like the sound of a revolver shot fired at him point-blank, then the name of Jed Harris—coming to me in the apartment my wife and I were living in in Brooklyn—had an equivalent and even wilder effect. I had seen the name on the shingle hanging at the entrance of the ornate, flowery Empire Theatre on Broadway—A JED HARRIS PRODUCTION—at a time when the name was a distant entity, when it didn't enter my head that I would ever have a personal connection with him and get to know him. Just a few years earlier, I had been in the balcony of the Cort Theatre, watching in wonder *The Green Bay Tree,* a distinguished hit which he had produced and directed, with a performer who moved throughout the play with the sustained delicacy and precision of a life-sized puppet. I had seen many Jed Harris productions. His celebrity and doings were things I read about in the theatrical columns of the daily newspapers. He represented an exciting uptown-Manhattan world that I longed to be a part of but had always felt was out of my reach and not meant for me.

After school the next day, I made the long subway trip from Brighton Beach to the Empire Theatre. I found my way through the labyrinthine passages within that ancient, fabled structure and reached a row of bare, murky rooms, on an upper floor above the backstage dressing rooms, which were Jed Harris's offices. He was then casting the Philip Barry play *Spring Dance,* and the anteroom was crowded with a number of young actresses in riding costume. An assistant, his stage manager, when I told him my name, knew who I was, said I was expected, and led me to the producer's private office at the end of the row.

He was unshaven. He had hooded, sleepy eyes; a contemptuous mouth; an emphatic, bony, greenish jaw. He wore a turtleneck pullover under his jacket, dispensing with the need of a shirt and tie. He lay back in his swivel chair with both feet up on the desk and I saw he had holes in his shoes. He said he had enjoyed my novel—it was all about his uncles, he said—and that it might be worth my while to dramatize it under his supervision. He talked at length about the content of the book, reviewing certain incidents with full understanding and appreciation, other incidents in original ways I had not thought of. He said I had written the novel around the wrong character, that the dramatization should center on Munves, a secondary figure in my story, and not on Max Balkan, my main character. He did not explain why he objected to Balkan. "You're sitting there, disturbed," he said, "because it weighs on your mind that there are people outside waiting to see me and you're here taking up the time and keeping them from me." That was true. "You're a person of talent, something none of the individuals in the anteroom happen to be or know anything about, and you shouldn't distress yourself on principle. Your sympathy is wasted and doesn't benefit the other party in the least and your work will suffer."

The Empire Theatre was on Fortieth Street, on the edge of the garment district, and he later took me to a long, narrow, rectangular restaurant, squeezed in between two manufacturing buildings—a restaurant the garment workers went to—where he continued to divert and instruct me. He told me not to put my forearms on the table. He warned me against the tops of tables in restaurants; he said they were dirty and if you rested your arms on them, your sleeves picked up stains. He instructed the waiter, too. There was a

small altercation. The waiter wanted Harris to pay the check at the cashier's stand near the door, according to the custom at this place. Harris firmly insisted on having the waiter carry the check and the money down to the cashier, said he didn't care what their practice was or how they did it here, and prevailed. The bill was for eighty-five cents for each of us—the waiter brought back three dollars and change out of the five-dollar bill Harris had placed on the saucer. Harris had dismissed the actresses at his office some time before we left for the restaurant; when the stage manager, who had had the job of dismissing them, fumbled for an excuse and said he didn't know how to put it to them after they had been waiting all afternoon, Harris had said, with the same cool insistence and disdain, "Tell them I'm not in the mood."

He next took me to a quietly imposing, red-brick townhouse off Fifth Avenue, a short distance above the Arch in Washington Square. The living quarters, which extended the length of the first floor of the house, glowed with light and color. The impression was that of a stage set designed by Dreyfus or Mielziner except that the furnishings here were real and solid—the sofas, the dark gleaming tables, the drapes, the glossy wood floors and the rich carpets lying on them. A housekeeper in service uniform, who had let us in, stood by. Two beautiful, black, standard-sized poodles were released from somewhere in the back and came jumping forward eagerly to greet Harris. His whole face broke out with pleasure as he fondled them. He spoke with a new effusiveness. He told me how much dogs meant to him, that the big, standard-sized poodle was the most intelligent of the breeds; he said it was well-known that dogs took on their characteristics by association, depending on the person who spent time with them, and that the dogs he owned were always bright and accomplished just from being with him. But it was clear that the two frolicking with him now weren't his and that this wasn't his home. The dogs, the fine modern townhouse belonged to somebody else, and Harris was obviously a guest or visitor.

The considerable fortune he had once had was gone, lost in the stock-market crash, with the Depression. The run of hits, which hadn't failed him in the past, sputtered and seemed to have come to a stop. His downfall was part of the current notoriety around him, frequently mentioned, but in my eyes it did not lessen his achievement nor did the attraction he had for me diminish. It was absorbing to be on the scene and see him now in disgrace. On one of my after-school trips to the theatre, I walked into the middle of a brutish exchange going on in his office. The young stage manager there was confronting Harris, giving him back-talk—apparently he had been asked to do some task not to his liking and had refused. "I don't have to do that kind of work on the salary you're paying me which is zip," I heard him saying. He turned his back on Harris, quit on the spot, didn't stop to pick up a book or a personal possession, and walked out. The amazing thing was that Harris appeared to be completely untouched by the incident, above it and uninterested.

In meeting him, I was particularly curious about certain plays of his which had long intrigued me. They were productions marked by a highly stylized refinement of taste and feeling, rigidly controlled, of a distinction all his own—they were his productions of *Uncle Vanya, Our Town, The Green Bay Tree, Serena Blandish*—and I wondered if, in being with him, I might be able to find some clue or secret of personality that accounts for such outstanding creative work and makes it possible. But the mean selfishness, the lack of balance, the plain boorishness that I saw in him jarred with the quality of those plays and left me confused. I did not see how the two, the man and his work, came together.

Harris, asserting himself constantly, did all the talking. He didn't listen or hear anything you said; if you asked a direct question, he might wander off and not reply. And as he indulged himself and went on talking, as I took it all in in this strange one-sided relationship I had with him, the realization came to me that he saw himself in a certain light, that this idea he had of himself drew him out of himself and was apart from him. It was not the ordinary egotism and arrogance that people accused him of and had against him. He believed unshakeably in the instinct of his genius, a belief instilled in him by the smash hits of his young manhood, one after the other—*Broadway, Coquette, The Royal Family, The Front Page*—all by the time he was twenty-eight, and to him the fantasy he lived in was real.

He phoned, always late at night, to summon me to the office. I lost Saturdays. He kept me up late and it meant nothing to him that I had to make the morning line-up in the schoolyard the next day or, for that matter, that I needed time to do the dramatization. We didn't talk about the dramatization. (I remember one last reference by him and that one quickly passed over and forgotten.) He had no special regard for me. He wanted me around with him in those days because he didn't like to eat alone, because I was unimportant and of no account and he could be off his guard with me, and felt safe.

He was shrewd enough to know that he was acting badly, and he would make the attempt at times—with the people preparing the new Barry play, with others—to restrain himself and conform, but the hate in him broke loose, he couldn't help himself, and he would come out with the jibes, doubling and redoubling his excesses. "The most loathsome man I'd ever met," a noted actor, a half century later, said of him. ("My revenge on Jed Harris was complete.") He used people shamefully, but they were using him, too, he once pointed out to me in an angry burst, getting the good of his brains and strength; he said they wouldn't be there if not for what they got out of him, that none of them were saints.

"What am I doing?" He was being jocular now, arch, mimicking me. He was letting me down—I had finally finished the dramatization and had turned it in, and he was now mocking my aspiration, my disappointment to come. "Why do I go schleppin after it? What have I got to do with it? O, a movie sale! O, Delancey Street [the birthplace of the young ambitious sons of immigrant Jews]. O, Hart Schaffner and Marx, the Champs-Élysées, and a fine Dusenberg motor car. Sweetie, this thing is no good." He was holding my typed-up dramatization in his hand. "I don't have to read it. I can tell just from holding it. The experienced playreader always can tell what's coming just from the weight and feel of the manuscript." He smiled, joking, not joking, baleful. He was standing before me. He had lost interest in the project long ago. He waited a moment, to see how I was taking it, the eyes in his head two living creatures perched there. "Now you'll go around like everybody else and say what a terrible man I am."

I said no, I wouldn't. In the case of Proust's Narrator, who had been aroused by the name of the famous author Bergotte, the pistol-shot excitement collapsed with their meeting—the great man in person proved to be a squat, commonplace figure and all illusion was dispelled. But Harris had not failed me. He had put on a continuous show. It had been a revelation, all new to me—the recklessness, his commitment to his star, the fierce expenditure of energy and the turbulence he created around him. I was stirred by the example of the rage in him, by his compulsion to destroy himself, and I felt I had no claim on him or right to complain. He owed me nothing. I was indebted to him and had no bitterness.

I had finished the dramatization during the Easter vacation. Toward the end of the summer of that year, with the approach of the new fall school term, when my wife and I were living in the country, I received a communication, in a plain brown envelope, from the Board of Education officially informing me that I was at last granted an appointment as a regular teacher. I was told that since I had taught for seven years as a permanent-substitute, my probationary period was considered completed and I would start with permanent tenure from the outset. I was further informed that my wages were to be calculated on the basis of the accrued seven-years annual increases and I would therefore start on eighth year teacher's pay. I decided not to accept the appointment.

I was tied down to a publisher's contract which I had signed when I was twenty-three years old and couldn't get out of. (The Author's Guild had made a study of these contracts, had listed thirty-two different abuses, and said my contract was the only one they had ever seen with all thirty-two of them.) I suddenly found I wanted no more to do with the publisher or with the novel I had been working on that summer.

I put all that behind me—the teaching, the novels, the disappointments. I struck out on my own and was successful from the beginning. I wrote story after story. I broke up my unfinished novel into stories. The letter from the Board of Education and the appointment had inflamed me. There was an exhilaration in me, something of the joke that flickered in Jed Harris, on which he subsisted, and which perhaps had carried over to me. The money that came in delighted me; it was a preoccupation and pursuit as enjoyable as any other.

The stories I wrote for *The New Yorker* put me in a company I admired with all my heart and brought me esteem. The ones I did for the large-circulation national magazines were even more rewarding. I went afield. I was able to write about heroic characters, people who manipulated their destinies and who lived and battled on a scale of grand values.

I wrote about wrestlers, prizefighters, theatrical people, trapeze artists, and many horse-racing stories, four of them a year. One day I read of a trainer who as a boy had been a pigeon-fancier. I got the notion of a group of cab drivers who band together, buy a racehorse, and turn it over to train to one of their number who has tended pigeons all his life. The magazine *Collier's* called the story "Crazy Over Pigeons." My original title was "The Day the Bookies Wept," and this was the title RKO used on the movie, with Joe Penner and Betty Grable, the coming attraction of which my wife and I saw that summer afternoon, standing at the rear of the theatre, with the house manager beside us.

Say three times, say three times . . . . I go to the synagogue once a year, on the anniversary of my father's death, to recite the memorial prayer, the *Yahrzeit.* I sit there during the long, drawn-out morn-

*Grandchildren, from left: Anya, David, and Sarah*

ing service, unable to read the Hebrew text but following it in the English translation that runs alongside it in the prayer book. The reader stands before us at the Ark and doles out the story of Abraham and Isaac. " 'I see the wood, the stones, the sacrificial bed, but I don't see the sacrifice,' Isaac said to Abraham and Abraham suffered. The Angel from the Lord appeared before Abraham and said he has shown he loves the Lord, he has shown he fears the Lord, and is released from his vow. The lamb came out of the thicket." As the reader reaches the reprieve and Isaac is saved, we all speak out in unison, saying it three times, as required, "The Lord is good. The Lord is one. The Lord is merciful." The reader takes it up again, now on the making of perfume. " . . . . . And add one maneh of myrrh, Rabbi Nathan says, then add three manehs of frankincense. If there is no frankincense, let him use cloves. If he overdoes the cloves, reprimand him, punish him. If he uses honey, remove him . . . ." He drones on, we join in at the appropriate junctures, until he comes to the summation of this section, and now we call out the last line, the fervent plea with which the prayer ends: "O, make me pleasant to the Lord!"

To be pleasant to the Lord, to praise Him and win His favors, to be strong and happy. I watch the old men I am with—there are a dozen of them—as they rumble on and parley with the Lord, still hungry for life, hanging on, and I suddenly realize, not entirely with amusement, that I think of them as old codgers, of another generation, when in fact none of

*Charlotte Granet*

*Daniel Fuchs*

them are much older than I am and some not even as old. I let them rumble on. I don't follow the text. I think of the time when it was all spread out for us, when the days seemed limitless and we spent them without reckoning, when we took the bad with the good because we were always certain better was ahead and that our fortunes would change. I think of the deceitful nature of time, that there is no way we can go back and start all over again from the beginning, that there is no use pining, and I turn my mind to other things—to the lawns and gardens and flowers we have here, to the sight of the sky as the sun comes up in the east, to the faces of my grandchildren, to the drives I like to take on the desert, on Interstate 5. I imagine for the moment that I am on the desert again, on another one of my excursions, and I find myself smiling. A surge of good cheer rises within me. I feel that all that I have and remember is alive and will last forever and I tell myself that I will outrace time and will go on as if also forever, with no end to life in view, just as the road that I am travelling on in my revery stretches out before me to a far distant horizon and beyond.

*BIBLIOGRAPHY*

**Fiction:**

*Summer in Williamsburg.* New York: Vanguard Press, 1934; London: Constable, 1935.

*Homage to Blenholt.* New York: Vanguard Press, 1936; London: Constable, 1936.

*Low Company.* New York: Vanguard Press, 1937; also published as *Neptune Beach.* London: Constable, 1937; also published as *Förlåt Oss Våra Synder.* Stockholm: P.A. Norstedt & Soners, 1938; also published as *Spelunka.* Warsaw: Państwowy Instytut Wydawniczy, 1968.

*Stories,* with Jean Stafford, John Cheever, and William Maxwell. New York: Farrar, Straus, 1956; also published as *A Book of Stories.* London: Gollancz, 1957.

*Three Novels* (includes *Summer in Williamsburg, Homage to Blenholt,* and *Low Company*). New York: Basic Books, 1961; also published as *The Williamsburg Trilogy.* New York: Avon, 1972.

*West of the Rockies.* New York: Knopf, 1971; London: Secker & Warburg, 1971; also published as *Na Zachód Od Gór Skalistych.* Warsaw: Państwowy Instytut Wydawniczy, 1977.

*The Apathetic Bookie Joint* (short stories). New York: Methuen, 1979; London: Secker & Warburg, 1980.

**Screenplays:**

*The Big Shot,* with Bertram Millhauser and Abem Finkel. Produced by Walter MacEwen, Warner Brothers, 1942.

*The Hard Way,* with Peter Viertel. Produced by Jerry Wald, Warner Brothers, 1943.

*Between Two Worlds,* based on the play *Outward Bound* by Sutton Vane. Produced by Mark Hellinger, Warner Brothers, 1944.

*The Gangster,* based on the author's novel *Low Company.* Produced by Maurice King and Frank King, Allied Artists, 1947.

*Hollow Triumph,* based on the novel by Murray Forbes. Produced by Bryan Foy, Eagle Lion, 1948.

*Criss Cross,* based on the novel by Don Tracy. Produced by Michael Kraike, Universal Pictures, 1949.

*Panic in the Streets,* based on the story by Edward and Edna Anhalt; screenplay by Richard Murphy; adaptation by Daniel Fuchs. Produced by Sol C. Siegel, Twentieth Century-Fox, 1950.

*Storm Warning,* with Richard Brooks. Produced by Jerry Wald, Warner Brothers, 1951.

*Taxi,* with D.M. Marshall, Jr.; based on the French motion picture *Sans Laisser d'Adresse* written by Alex Joffe and Jean-Paul Le Chanoi. Produced by Samuel G. Engel, Twentieth Century-Fox, 1953.

*The Human Jungle,* with William Sackheim. Produced by Hayes Goetz, Allied Artists, 1954.

*Love Me or Leave Me,* with Isobel Lennart. Produced by Joe Pasternak, Metro-Goldwyn-Mayer, 1955.

*Interlude,* with Franklin Coen; based on the story by James Cain and Dwight Taylor. Produced by Ross Hunter, Universal, 1957.

*Jeanne Eagels,* with Sonya Levien and John Fante. Produced by George Sidney, Columbia, 1957.

# George Palmer Garrett, Jr.

*1929-*

*At Camp Chaffee, Arkansas, early 1950s: Sgt. George Garrett kneeling, far right*

Two men dressing. They are wearing GI undershorts and shiny dog tags like necklaces. They are freshly shaved and showered. Their hair is cut short on top and sidewalled. They are flat-stomached and hard-muscled. Two American soldiers in a large high-ceilinged room located in the heart of an old *Luftwaffe* barracks a little to the south of the city of Linz. It's a fine, stone, permanent barracks, the best these two American soldiers have lived or will live in. Waxed and shiny hardwood floors; high clear windows overlooking a grassy parade ground. There are maybe half-a-dozen cots, neat and tight, perfectly made up, shiny green footlockers with names and serial numbers painted on the lids of each. There are large, ample, wooden wall-lockers which the Krauts left behind, left open now with GI uniforms, khaki at this season, the olive drabs recently packed away, hanging perfectly in strict prescribed rows.

The two soldiers are carefully and awkwardly dressing, their twin cigarettes casting veils of pale smoke from a butt can. Awkwardly because they do not wish to sit on and muss up their beds while dressing. If they sit, to lace up boots for example, they will use a footlocker for a chair. Their khakis are tailored snug and crisp from starched ironing, creases as straight and keen as a razor's edge. Their brass—collar brass and belt buckles—glitters. (They put their buckles on backwards to save them from scratches; for they will be wearing pistol belts, too.) Their cordovan-dyed jump boots are spit-shined and glossy. They have put in white laces and will be wearing white gloves, too, and a white chin strap on their simonized helmet liners. Red artillery scarves instead of neckties. The blue-and-white TRUST patches, worn on the left shoulder and proudly set off with a flashy white cross-stitching, to show that they come from the old 351st Regimental Combat Team in Trieste, have now been removed and replaced by some bland patch or other. (Whose shape and color and meaning I have long since forgotten.) Indicating that they are serving in Austria. But anyone with a trained eye and any interest would know right away that they come from somewhere else. Most likely TRUST, but maybe from the Sixth Infantry in Berlin which affects some of the same singular style: dyed black web equipment, pistol belts in this case with each and every one of their brass eyelets buffed to remove the paint and grit to the metal and give it a high, bright shine, confirmed with clear nail polish; first-aid pouches hung on the left hip, and an ammo pouch, holding two full clips of .45-caliber cartridges, worn up front just to the right—two eyelets over I seem to recall—of the belt buckle. On the right hip they hang a gleaming dark leather holster holding the .45 pistols which they have been issued for today. Last of all, each puts on a brass whistle on a chain, attached to left shirt-pocket button, and an arm-band—MP for Military Police.

There is no MP unit up here near Linz. Which, except for the Four Power City of Vienna, deep in the Russian Zone, is as far forward as Americans are. Just across the river, the dirty old Danube, from the Ruskies. There are said to be some forty thousand of them over there. Over here we have a Reconnaissance Battalion, an old outfit which has been here a good while, an Infantry Battalion and ourselves, the Twelfth Field Artillery Battery (separate). In theory we have come here in response to the fact that they have suddenly, and for no discernible reason, moved those forty thousand combat troops into positions on the other side of the river. Should they decide to come across, to attack, that is, it is our function in this advanced post to try to delay them for a period of between fifteen minutes and half an hour. That will give the main body of American forces in Salzburg, and farther west in Germany, time enough to take their defensive positions.

These two men have drawn MP duty on a quiet Saturday in springtime. Fully dressed and ready, they will be briskly inspected by somebody or other, the Officer of the Day most likely, or maybe the Sergeant of the Guard; then they will pick up a jeep at the Motor Pool and drive into the city.

It is a clear, bright day. And now these two, coming outside from the barracks, are jointly astonished to see a ring of distant snowcapped mountains all around. It has been so gray and close, wet and foggy, since they got here, that they never knew there were any mountains within sight until this minute. They don't say anything. What is there to say? They

are old-timers, short timers in the Army now. It is not that they are not surprised. It is that they are continually astonished by everything. They don't speak, but they stop in mid-stride. They stand there and just look around. The young Corporal allows himself to whistle softly between his teeth.

"Let's go," the Sergeant says then. "We're fixing to be late."

They move off side by side, in step.

I cannot remember the Corporal's name for the life of me.

The Sergeant, of course, is myself.

*

All things considered, this autobiographical piece is one of the most difficult things I have ever tried to write. Why is that? I can think of a couple of reasons, which could probably go along with a whole cloud of vague and less-realized ones.

For the first reason, I have to tell you a story. Years and years ago, in 1962 I think, but it could have been 1963, right after the publication of the second volume of his masterpiece, *The Civil War: A Narrative*, Shelby Foote came to the University of Virginia for a week-long residency. One day he visited my creative writing class. He talked awhile, then fielded questions. Aware that he had known William Faulkner well, and as a friend, one of the students asked him what William Faulkner was really like.

"Have you read the books?" Foote asked back. "Yes, sir."

Well, then, Foote went on to answer, that was it. That is all there is. William Faulkner had finally become what he had always wanted to be—his work. Nothing more and nothing less. He offered up his life, gave it all, and by the end of it there was nothing (nobody) left living outside separate and distinct from the books.

And there it was, a precise and articulate formulation of exactly what I, myself, hoped for, vaguely dreamed of, without—until then—knowing the example for it. Ever since then the shape of that idea, the perfection and the purity of it, has haunted me. If only, somehow, I would be able, would be *permitted* to write works into which "the real me" (whatever that might be) could vanish forever, wholly transformed, leaving only ghost and flesh, finally mere shadows, behind. As a former competitive runner, I knew by heart and honored the runner's ideal of spending all of one's energy so perfectly and adroitly as to be able to cross the finish line exactly one step this side of unconsciousness. Let my whole life be only in my work and everywhere equally, whether in a long knotty novel or in the four verse-lines of a brisk

*George and Susan Garrett on their wedding day,
June 14, 1952*

epigram.

It was never, never once for a minute, my ambition *to be a writer.* Rather to be, for some supremely transcendent moments, anyway, the work itself. Measured against that ideal, my "real" life, even at its finest moments, seemed shabby, inconsequential, irrelevant. And even now, in middle age, I have not entirely discarded that judgment, though it is modified and moderated. For one thing, I live, I discover, in a very different world than William Faulkner's, one where his example, taken literally, makes less sense. For another, I cannot deny that my real life includes others, is inextricably involved in and with the lives of others who are in no way inconsequential. A wife of thirty-five years at this writing; three grown children; a mother of eighty-seven; sisters and cousins and all kinds of kinfolk. Many of whom I love more than my life or my work, either. And who, because they happen to be who they are, have never once required of me that I should make any such choice. Then, too, I have lived a good long time since that day in class and have lived and learned and (yes) changed a little. For instance, one of the things I have learned is that, almost in spite of myself, but always whether I wanted it so or not, the

plain facts of my life, the *facts* and not merely the ghostly shadows of it, have slipped quietly into the heart of all my work. It may be (I certainly hope so) that I, alone, could ever recognize them in their motley disguises; but they are there, nevertheless. No denying that. In other words, in this late middle age I never really imagined arriving at, it has at last come home to me that there is no known way that I can ever disappear, truly and completely into my work. By the same token, in truth I move along as naked as the fairy-tale emperor in his new clothes in everything I have ever written. And that is the measure of the truth of what I write. My pride and joy being that nothing I have ever written, be it ever so humble and slight, lighthearted and frivolous, graceful or inept, contains more or less of the truth of myself than any other piece of my work. To that extent, then, I guess I have succeeded. If only by turning Shelby Foote's proposition inside out.

Now then.

As if in contradiction to all of the above, there is the unpleasant fact that, at some time following my

*George and Susan Garrett in Vienna, Austria, 1954*

*The Garrett children: William, Alice, and George, 1983*

fiftieth birthday, I began to allow myself to feel hurt that somehow or other I had never quite managed to receive really serious recognition for my work. A most curious mid-life crisis! Ironic, too, for it had never seriously troubled me before then, and I couldn't understand those writers I knew of (many) who cared about such things. For thirty years, longer, I had kept on working and thinking that, one way or another, things like that would just take care of themselves. Knowing that it was mostly out of my

hands, anyway. Knowing that I had far too much work I wanted to do in a lifetime to waste any time and energy worrying about such things. And, besides, I had told myself when the subject had, in spite of all good intentions, slithered into my consciousness, I was not at all sure what recognition really means or what I might mean by it. I believed that I did not mean prizes, awards, honorary degrees, and the other conventional honors. Not fame and/or notoriety. As a competitive athlete in several sports (not very good, just pretty fair at best), I had learned and knew well the enormous differences and discrepancies between popular reputation and reality. Between truth and symbolism, facts and official images. One of the athletes' worst insults, usually proffered with a condescending concern was: "That poor bastard believes his press clippings." I am not at all sure what I meant by recognition. I was, of course, too intensely aware of all the signs, even the least and most subtle hints of some kind of credible and acceptable recognition, acceptance by the powers that be. That knowledge was, for a time, a source of pain and could have led straight to downtown Paranoia, if permitted to. I was looking (I told myself) for something I already knew exists in the worlds of athletes, musicians, performers of all kinds, even doctors and lawyers and Indian chiefs—an honorable and enduring respect for honorable work, regardless of its fortunes (either good or bad fortune) in the marketplace. Regardless of its fate (good or bad) at the hands of critics and reviewers. In one sense this was a ridiculous notion; for I also knew

*Garrett in his office at the University of Virginia, 1965*

*From left, poet Henry Taylor, novelist Jesse Hill Ford, and George Garrett at the celebrated Hollins Conference, 1970*

that many of my favorite poets were practically unknown, unknown especially among the favored few in the Literary Establishment. Most of my favorite novelists were unknown. Likewise the playwright whose work I admired most. That is, I had plenty of evidence if any were needed, that, in the literary world at least, justice is as rare as any unicorn. Because I had long been and remained a teacher, I kept up, as best I could, with the work of others, my contemporaries. And I made an effort to keep an open mind and an open spirit about all of it, especially when I was faced with work built upon the foundation of very different assumptions and prejudices from my own. This seemed the very least that that rare and lucky being, a free artist in a free country, could try to do. Moreover, it seemed to me, no artist can even begin to make anything worth having without having learned the tested and active virtues which arise from an open mind, an open heart, an open spirit . . . .

How could I possibly learn anything of value from the simple confirmation of my own acquired assumptions and hidden, sometimes secret prejudices?

At some point, then, following my fiftieth birthday, I began to realize that I had not earned and now probably would never earn that special kind of recognition which I had foolishly imagined came not like some prize or medal or winning lottery ticket, but instead was simply bestowed on every surviving and working professional writer as it was in every other field of endeavor I knew anything about. I was coming close to the age when all of the males on my father's side of the family had died. (On my mother's side the men lived long.) Too many things began to seem valedictory.

I have many good friends and true, a good many of whom are writers whose love and trust and respect mean much to me. But for a time the indifference of many others, and (yes) the hostility of a few, wounded me. It was my own fault. I let it happen. In boxing it is a foul to hit a fighter when breaking from a clinch. But the ancient rule, always repeated by referees, is—"Protect yourself on the break." If you don't and you let yourself get tagged and hurt, there's nobody but yourself to blame. For a while, then, in my early fifties, I perceived that my whole professional life and career had been a boring waste of time and surely an unfit subject for any piece like this. I fretted and let myself get furious at being ignored, raged at real and imaginary slights. Indulged in self-pity. Which experience and education and the only worldly code (not to mention my religion) I knew and lived by named an utterly contemptible emotion. Adding guilt to the shame of it. My Christian faith, challenged strongly by the world, the flesh, and the devil, made this form of despair less sinful than ridiculous. A hard truth. For I think we fear the ridiculous more than many other real dangers.

In the rollicking, riotous 1960s I had already found myself in other kinds of troubles. Developed,

*Garrett and poet Brendan Galvin*

and finally overcame, a genuine addiction to amphetamines. Smoked far too much, two or three packs a day. And then there was booze which has been a family problem. I drank a lot. And then, after fifty, sometimes, in the late, last, darkest, drunkest hours, I came closest to (close enough to taste the bitter breath of it) despair. Sometimes—yet not even with the very slight honor of doing so seriously—I tickled myself with childish ideas of suicide. All a brutal and grotesque absurdity. I know it now and, indeed, knew it then. And I was learning lessons, too. For instance, I discovered that, occasionally during bad times, I was, for the first time in my life, consumed by envy. Before that the cliché, "consumed," had been nothing more than that. Now it was a living metaphor. I could feel it happening. And for the first time I began to understand and to pity all the truly envious people I had known. What had been faintly ridiculous became no less foolish, but nonetheless sorrowful. The old Church Fathers had been right about that, too, as ever and always. Envy is truly a deadly sin. Sometimes at night when I woke and couldn't sleep, I put myself back to sleep not by counting sheep but by summoning up the innumerable rejections, slights, insults, put-downs, bad reviews, and bad times I had endured. After all, everything I had ever written had been rejected at least once or twice, usually more than that and hardly ever with any civility or politeness. (Nevertheless, as I did not choose to remind myself then, everything had also been, sooner or later, published.) The trouble with this gesture of self-inflicted ridicule was that I began too late in life. There were too many bad things (and bad people) to remember. I had forgotten half of them and was already into the habit of forgetting. It had always been my comfortable good intention to forgive and forget. But now I was forgetting before I had a chance to forgive. Acts of forgiveness, like acts of love or courage, have a right time and place. Or they do not take place. So be it. Self-pity turned into laughter in the dark. If I couldn't remember the thousand-and-one injuries I wished to redress, how could I possibly expect anybody else to? All of my wounds seemed to have come from pratfalls.

At best my head was cloudy and confused. Why bother to pick up a pen, to slip a piece of paper into my typewriter if, no matter what I might write (good or bad), the results and rewards would be the same? A fighter going into a fixed fight does not worry too much about the tightness of his shoe laces or how well his hands are wrapped.

Nevertheless I kept working, sometimes in slow motion and with limbs of lead, but always working. I had finally finished *Death of the Fox,* then went on working on other things while a dozen or so major publishers rejected the novel outright and *not* very politely. It took a good while to find Sam Vaughan, then at Doubleday, who was interested enough to publish it. I'll always be grateful to him for that.

This gloomy depression (more inward than outward; for I continued to smile and to do my teaching jobs and to pay my bills) continued until . . . . Yet even in the worst of it I managed to accomplish some work with some regularity—fiction, criticism, one thing and another. Poetry suffered most. Poems came to me fewer and further apart. But there were still a few, enough to keep hope alive. And I was, ironically perhaps, teaching some of my finest students. Some of whom have now become fine writers. Teaching them everything that I could except this one terrible truth I believed I had learned. Until . . . and here is no great flash of insight. No sudden and shining moment of revelation. It was simply a slow-dawning awareness that, even as I worried over it, I have passed by the point where any of it can matter much. Of course, I can still be injured by being, for example, rejected or, from my point of view, unfairly or inaccurately criticized, ignored, and left out. Only the last cold, the real *rigor mortis,* the final dark and final silence, can cure the last shreds of those minor and prideful pains. But no matter. What has eased and lightened my burden (in this purely secular problem) is the understanding that no amount of generous recognition, the kindness of perfect strangers, coming now can ever make up for or take away the injuries already done to myself by myself and by others. Right or wrong (and I know now, too, that it is not for me to judge), all but a few—and how I shall always cherish these precious few!—have paid no attention to my life's work for the nearly forty years since I began to publish it. But every other artist, even the most celebrated, has to admit to the same thing. All numbers, all but the precious few, are false. There are only the precious few. And they are an everlasting blessing, not earned, but freely given. The living ones all know who they are. I shall not embarrass them by claiming their names. Among the dead, who are now safely beyond all praise or blame, I am grateful beyond all measure and telling to a host of kinfolk, to teachers and coaches and trainers. Even to certain superior and commanding officers. And there are writers I owe much to. I am especially grateful for the good interest, for the loving kindness, for encouragement and companionship to the following late friends: Marianne Moore and Babette Deutsch, John Ciardi and John Hall Wheelock, R. P. Blackmur and Rolfe Humphries, William Goyen and Roger Rath.

*Norman Mailer and George Garrett, University of Michigan, 1984. Critic John Aldridge is in the left background.*

Do you see how it is? My loneliest bad times were deeply self-deceptive. We are never nearly as alone as we think we are. As we sometimes wish to be.

I am fifty-seven at the moment of this writing. All of the males on my father's side, for at least two or three generations back, were dead before they reached this age. Perhaps my being here means I have inherited my maternal genes and will live long enough to grow up if not to grow wise. Anyway, I am now again, I hope and pray, freed from the debilitating and familiar fever and chills of self-induced self-pity. Almost beyond arousal from the outside. No one—not publishers, not critics, not even peers—has that kind of power over me now. Power, true power, power with any force and meaning, derives from the twin capacities to punish and to reward, to deliver pain and pleasure. Either alone is false and empty, not power at all. The notion that I have now somehow passed beyond the power of any kind or form of reward to please or to soothe me is profoundly liberating. Like the ladies in Boston who do not shop for them because they *have* their hats, I already have my good friends and true, those whom I admire without reservations, those whose admiration means everything to me. I have my good friends and I know who most of my enemies are. I am able to do my work and I have plenty of work to do.

And now I feel, at last, that I can also write down a little bit about my own life and times without shame or apology.

A word more and I am done with this part of my confession. Why? Why wash dirty clothes in public? Why tell secrets with signal flags for all to read? In part for the catharsis of it, sure. But also, believe it or not (and I do not care a damn if you believe it or not),

because I feel that I am here, briefly, representative of all the wonderful writers, living and dead, I know of (and there are many, *many*) who did not get a fair shake or a fair hearing. Here, for some reason, I am invited to tell my story, to make my case. Very well, then. I owe them all, honestly and in honor, some part of this piece dedicated to the proposition that the roof and foundation of not only art, but civilization itself would collapse and fall to ruin without the unceasing and enormous effort of a multitude of good workers who are unknown, and probably always will be. I spent too long as a common soldier not to know the truth of that. Here, then, I am their representative, and they are my large and honorable constituency.

Shall we continue?

\*

In a strictly literary sense the completion and publication of the novel *Poison Pen* is the outward and visible sign of that inward and spiritual liberation. I had been writing bits and pieces of it for more than twenty years. More for my own fun and games than anything else. But now it seemed possible, manageable as a piece of work, in and of itself. And there was an excellent small publisher, Stuart Wright, a friend, who was adventurous enough (and interested enough in me) to publish it, quietly and elegantly. It is a hard-knuckled, hard-nosed book in many ways; but it is also, I can justly claim, a funny book and a little testament to my own latest, Houdini-like escape from the world, the flesh, the Devil, and myself. What kind of a book is it? Well, if you will get hold of a copy and open it up to page 162 you will find *The Oxford Classical Dictionary* definition of *Satire* (*Satura*) as something which

> may be broadly defined as a piece of verse or prose, or prose mingled with verse, intended to improve society by mocking its anomalies, and marked by spontaneity, topicality, ironic wit, indecent humor, colloquial language, frequent use of dialogue, constant intrusions of the author's personality, and incessant variety of tone and style.

That about covers it from the point of view of the author's intentions. For the reactions of others, I am willing to accept the very first one to appear in the *Kirkus Reviews:* "A brilliant, merciless, shapeless, many-layered, some-splendored kazoo concerto."

Go see for yourself.

\*

They pass by the gate guards and turn left on the highway heading for Linz. You can be sure that without a word, a glance or a nudge, they are both smiling for at least a moment. They sit in the front seats of the jeep, the Corporal driving, very straight, feeling almost fragile as they seek to keep every crease and part of their uniforms crisply unwrinkled. They want to be sharp-looking downtown. They like to show the local girls, whores and shackjobs, and hamburger bandits, that Americans in uniform can look every bit as sharp as (everybody says) the Krauts did. Going out of the gate and turning left and north, they both smile into the breeze.

They are thinking about the moment they first arrived at that gate maybe a month or so ago. How they left Trieste secretly by night. Went first to a staging area in the pine woods near Pisa. The rumor was they were going to Greece, somewhere like that. Who knew? Anyway, they painted over all the unit numbers on all the vehicles. Got rid of patches and anything identifying them as coming from Trieste. They were loaded on trucks with all the canvas laced tight and sent off in small convoys, a few at a time, up north through the Brenner Pass and into Austria. Nobody, except ranking officers, knew where they were headed until they actually got there. Except, of course (as ever and always) somebody goofed. Somebody forgot or never knew that the vehicles of the Austrian command, alone of all commands in the U.S. Army, did not use the large white star, on each side and on top of the hood, as an identifying marker. For all our care and secrecy we were known at once as convoys coming from elsewhere by our gleaming white stars. Every spy between Pisa and Linz would have noted our coming and going. So that when we arrived at the old *Luftwaffe* camp and some guy in the outfit turned on his battery-powered portable radio, we picked up, from the Russian side, in good English, "Greetings to the men of the Twelfth Field Artillery on their safe arrival at Linz."

But that is not worth the smile they are smiling. What has them grinning is the subject of women.

When we pulled out of Trieste suddenly, the group had to say good-bye to their girlfriends and semi-permanent shackjobs. Some of these couples had been together for years. Some of them had children, illegitimate, of course, because it was an extremely difficult and complex process for a GI to marry a Triestine woman. It was not encouraged. Nevertheless it was a wrench for all of them. A time of tears and gloom. Promises to write. Promises to meet again, somehow, some day. The gloom lasted for a few days over in the tent camp near Pisa, until it began to dawn on all the guys that wherever they

went next—to Greece or North Africa or the freaking South Pole—they would be starting over. A new deal. All new girls. So by the time we were loaded, that's all the guys (especially the bona fide lover boys) could think and talk about—the new and improved stuff, strange nookie! they were going to be enjoying very soon. Try to imagine their crestfallen surprise, surprise for all of us, when we pulled up at the main gate of the new camp and found a whole big bunch of women from Trieste just standing there, waving their handkerchiefs (Yoo-hoo!). Somehow, and easily enough, they had found out our Top Secret destination and, overcoming all obstacles and boundaries, beaten us there. I'm telling you, there were long faces and faint smiles in the trucks.

*

This essay is not turning out to be either exactly a straightforward or a chronological retailing of my life and times (such as they both may be). That kind of version can only be found in my own official *curriculum vitae*, the basic academic resumé that I use all the time. (When you are a serious candidate for the Tomb of the Unknown American Writer, you almost always have to furnish folk with a resumé.) The plain facts are there. Some of them. With, of course, a strongly academic emphasis.

Missing are things like the dozen or so mostly unskilled manual-labor jobs (though they would have to include some high points, calling for some skill, like bartending and truck driving) I have made a sort of a living from and will again, too, if I have to.

Missing is the clarinet I played and practiced on for years and years, from early childhood until early manhood. A fine B-flat instrument made of Madagas-

*Classical guitarist Susan Garrett rehearsing for a concert at the University of South Carolina, 1972*

*Larry D. Petersime*

car ebony and brightly equipped with German silver keys. Finally, sometime in high school, I abandoned it, saying to myself that of course I would come back to playing it someday. And of course did not, have not; though I still today own the same instrument and have carried it with me with each and every move from one place to the next. I can barely make a clear and decent sound on it nowadays, but I believe it taught me much. And not least among things learned is a profound respect and admiration for musicians as well as a love of music. Good music of all kinds well performed. Also my wife is, among other things, a first-rate musician.

Missing from my resumé are all the sports, the athletics which occupied, at times, almost all my time and energy and desire. Beginning first with swimming—I learned to swim before I was two years old. And ending with college football where by the end of it I was as wrapped in tape as any mummy from injuries of every kind. A David playing without benefit of miracles on a field full of Goliaths, I ruined both knees, broke both feet, and covered my body with cloudy bruises. I recollect long afternoon-hours spent in the steam and stink of the training room, then hobbling back to the dormitory, fresh tape binding me here and there, reeking from the scents of a medley of salves and liniments, groaning (quietly, quietly, a smile fixed on my face lest anyone should suspect my pain) as I passed by the tennis courts where there were crowds of young white men all in white and all of them trim and handsome and graceful, not Goliaths, not a one, but everyone of them a Scott Fitzgerald (this was, after all, Princeton). They flaunted what I had to admit was style. I can still hear, by an exercise of grim willpower, the crisp, tingy sounds of tennis balls and rackets meeting each other in autumnal air. Can still summon up the slow-fading of late-afternoon light, the scent of woodsmoke from somewhere not far; likewise the odor of leafsmoke—for they still burned their leaf piles in those days. And in the midst of all this a boy-man mummy who would cheerfully have leapt into a burning leaf pile if he could have vanished into the thick, pale gray smoke of it.

Even in football, though, overmatched or not, there were moments. Moments of joy on practice and playing field . . . .

Many other things are missing on my resumé also. For instance the two wonderful years (1960–62) when I worked with the Alley Theater in Houston and their excellent group of actors and their superb director, Nina Vance. Not a day during that time that I didn't spend some time at the theater, before or after work and in the evenings, watching rehearsals

*A scene from the play "Garden Spot, U.S.A." by George Garrett, produced at the Alley Theatre, Houston, Texas, 1962*

and productions, talking with and listening to the actors. I wrote two plays, one (*Sir Slob and the Princess*) for children and their children's theater, and one for grown-ups called *Garden Spot, U.S.A.* which ran its full month in the theater's season and did all right. It was written for and around that particular company and that particular stage—a theater in the round created in an abandoned fan factory. To have a play produced and directed by Nina Vance was its own reward.

Under what I call the "Miscellaneous" heading of my resumé I mention working for a time as a screenwriter for Samuel Goldwyn, Jr. I do not mention the several stages of several Goldwyn films I worked on. Only one of these, *The Young Lovers,* was actually produced and released. All in all it wasn't half bad, and it was Peter Fonda's first starring role. The best actor in the movie was the wonderfully gifted and funny late Nick Adams. He was so good that I rewrote his part completely after we were already shooting to take advantage of some of the things—impersonations of old movie stars, for instance—he could do so well in real life. He was the best thing about the picture. It's still shown on television and in the 16mm circuit once in a while. I gather they have cut Nick Adams's footage back as far as they can, to

*Poster for the Stonecoast Writers' Conference, 1982*

make Fonda look better.

I do not mention in my resumé a couple of free-lance films I worked on which were produced and released. One, cowritten with a couple of my students, R.H.W. Dillard and John Rodenbeck, was *Frankenstein Meets the Space Monster*. It has been honored with a Golden Turkey Award as one of the one hundred worst films of all times. It turns out to be a special favorite of editor and scholar Michael Weldon. Who says with enthusiasm in his book, *The Psychotronic Encyclopedia of Film:* "You really owe it to yourself to watch this—it's *the worst.*" If you ever do watch it, try to see it on TV. It's one of the very few films I know of which is greatly improved by regular commercial interruptions.

I don't mention, either, *The Playground* (Jerand Films, 1965) which picked up some nice notices here and there, including a rave from *Cue* magazine and a nice review from Bosley Crowther of the *Times.* For awhile, maybe ten years, it was something of a modest cult film at colleges. It was a strange film, an absurd comedy about American attitudes towards death and dying; but it was elegantly photographed and edited, by Richard Hilliard, and not bad at all.

My resumé gives lists of names and places, but there are always lives behind all those things. There are colleagues and neighbors, friends and enemies, good times and bad. There are places of great weight and importance in this lifetime. Rome, for example,

where we lived for a year and a half, thinking always that we would return soon. Now, almost thirty years later, still hoping that time will come again. Out of that time have come many poems and stories and even *The Holiday Guide to Rome.* Which I did anonymously for a few hundred dollars (badly needed) in 1959 and which, though mildly updated, has been in print, errors and all, ever since. There are houses: The house my father built in the Depression in Orlando, Florida; the 1780 house in York Harbor, Maine, which my wife inherited, making our children the fifth generation of the same family to live in that house; the wonderful old country house near Roanoke with its spectacular view of the Blue Ridge Mountains and its high sleeping porches which seemed like tree houses; the four houses in Charlottesville, Virginia, and the bad times and good times there.

Enough . . . !

My resumé offers all sorts of facts, though only some of the facts, and is as accurate as memory and goodwill can make it. With all of its absences and ellipses, its strict limitations, it may at least serve as a guide to help make some sense out of this brief and fragmentary autobiographical essay.

\*

One thing about the selected bibliography at the end of this essay. Its literary facts. It lists the books in order of publication, but, of course, can tell nothing of their composition, transformation, publication, reception, etc. Well, then. Briefly. Some came easily and quickly. *Which Ones Are the Enemy?* took three full weeks to write; *Death of the Fox* and *Poison Pen* were twenty-year projects. Many things on the list started out to be something quite different from what they became. For example, the novel *Do, Lord, Remember Me* was, in its finished version, twice as long as it now is. I still think of it as, truly, half of a book. All books on the list were rejected by more than one publisher. As to reception by the establishment critics and reviewers, what is there to say? Whimsically different. Some were prominently noticed and some were not. *Death of the Fox,* for example, was never reviewed in the daily *New York Times* and was reviewed in the *Times Book Review* many months after publication. Still, *Publishers Weekly* said, simply enough, "One of the finest novels we have ever read." Can't do much better than that. On the other hand, a few years later, *Publishers Weekly* did not even choose to review *An Evening Performance* which offered my new and selected short stories from thirty years. A glance at the reception of these works would conclude it has been hit or miss, depending on many variable things. As for myself, though I am always grateful for any favorable notices, I cannot say that any notice, positive or negative, has in any way helped me as a writer. I know the flaws and weaknesses of my work better than anybody. I have chosen to live with them.

\*

Barring some major crime involving American GI's, and even in that case they will work mainly as liaison with and for the local Austrian police, the actual duties of these two soldiers are more in the line of Courtesy Patrol than anything else. They will patrol the town, check various well-known bars and public places, looking for GI's who are drunk or disorderly. Most of these, if any and if possible, they will not arrest, but simply carry back to the barracks. They will correct uniform violations. They may spot check for ID cards, passes, and papers. Mostly they will be a visible and symbolic presence of the American intention to maintain some kind of order. Mostly, except for the boredom, it is good, clean duty and not a bad way to pass the time.

Once in town, they check in on the basic radio network, linking themselves, more or less and depending on the equipment, to the camp, to the local Austrian police, and to other patrols. They stop briefly at the station of the local police. Who are friendly enough and who are not, at this time, holding any GI's under arrest for anything. These would have to be taken back to the camp and the Stockade there.

The Corporal wonders if the cops are planning a "floor show" tonight. Sometimes on a Saturday night the Austrian cops will round up all the whores they can find and try to discourage them from practicing their profession in Linz. They do this by taking them into a large empty room about the size of a basketball court and stripping them bareass and beating them black and blue with rubber truncheons. It is quite a sight, something to behold. It doesn't seem to have much effect, though. A few days later the same whores are back on the streets. Tonight there will be no "floor show."

Now they take a turn or two slowly driving up and down some of the main streets; then they go down to the bridge across the Danube and the checkpoint on our side. There are two conventional checkpoints, one on each side, American and Russian. The Twelfth Field has drawn the duty, for this month, of manning the American checkpoint; so our pair on patrol stop by to say hello to some guys from the outfit. Theoretically there is, by treaty, free access for troops both ways. We can go across the Russian Zone into the Four Power City of Vienna on the train,

the Mozart Express, with American flags painted on the cars and with soldiers armed with grease guns guarding each car. And with a proper pass, American soldiers can cross the bridge and pass through the Russian checkpoint and vice versa. Every day or so this right is tested. A vehicle of some kind will be sent across to the other side. After passing the checkpoint the vehicle, having scored its legal point, will turn around and come back. The two soldiers in the jeep might be asked to do this by the Lieutenant on duty. But they are not; a truck went over and back this morning. They are relieved. It can be a . . . touchy situation. The Russians are, to us, very strange sometimes. Once, for whatever reason, they suddenly closed the checkpoint and barred an American military truck at gunpoint. Because the bridge is narrow the driver had to back his way to our side again. Our lieutenant called in, according to his strict instructions, to his commanding officer. And the news went all the way up the mysterious chain of command. After a while a Russian jeep came roaring up to their checkpoint: driver, Russian officer, two enlisted men in back. Out jumped the officer who conferred briefly with the other Russian officer on duty there. Then they drew their pistols and shot the two soldiers who were guarding the checkpoint. At which point the two enlisted men jumped out of the jeep, removed the weapons and equipment from the dead guards and— one, two, three, heave-ho!—threw their bodies off the bridge and into the Danube. Whereupon the new guards took up positions at the barrier.

The funny part (can you believe there is a funny part) is this. When the young and green American Lieutenant saw what happened, he drew his pistol, shouted at his own men to follow him, and raced across the bridge to . . . to do *what*? He had just witnessed a crime, no question. But, pistol or no pistol, outrage or not, it was a double murder outside of his jurisdiction. The Russian officers were sympathetic to his feelings, but nonetheless amused. In halting English they tried to explain that somebody had to be punished for the mistake of closing the checkpoint to our right of access. They pointed out that the two soldiers, whose bodies had long since vanished in the flow of the river, were only Mongols (as were the two new replacements) and wouldn't be missed by anyone. Anyway, there were millions more where they came from . . . .

My own firsthand experience came from having to instruct my unit in the Russian use of land mines and booby traps. It was supposed to be an area of my expertise. I knew a little, mostly self-taught, but not much. But nothing had prepared me for the chaotic and totally irrational ways and means of the Russian

Army with land mines. Every other army in the world (for many good reasons) makes and uses mines for a specific purpose. For example, an anti-tank mine won't go off when a man walks over one. Maybe they have changed now, and I hope so, but in those days a cat, probably a mouse, could set off any Russian land mine. That's kind of crazy. Then there is the matter of the big bang. Every other army in the world uses mines which contain enough explosive, and no more, to do the job they are intended for. The Ruskies had mines that, stepped on by one man, or one mouse, would blow up a football field. To what purpose? Terror, I reckon. Except a combat soldier with any experience at all is not going to be terrified by a bigger bang. It's the death he fears, not the noise of it. Another example: In every other army in the world only fairly high-ranking officers, usually of field grade, can authorize laying down a mine field. It must be mapped and is usually clearly marked. The danger of it to one's own troops outweighs any value of secrecy. In the Russian army, in those days at least, a squad leader, a corporal, or a sergeant, could lay mines without telling anyone and without mapping or marking them. Very often they had to leave them

right where they were, unseen and unknown, when they advanced or fell back. This didn't slow up the Germans much, but nobody will even venture a guess as to how many Russians were blown up in World War II by their own mines. Huge numbers. No matter. Plenty more where they came from.

Today the experts wonder why the Russians have built missiles with huge, "dirty" warheads, many megatons beyond any remotely conceivable destructive value. Counterproductive in the sense that they will create enormous dangers for their own people in the fallout. It makes no sense, but it is the same philosophy they had with land mines and Mongols.

We shoot the breeze with the guys at the checkpoint for a few minutes. Then we head back into Linz.

"Hey, let's get something to eat," the Corporal says.

"Suits me."

\*

What can I appropriately say about my own family? First, that on both sides they came here early. First of all to Maine and South Carolina. Well before the Revolution. All of them except (ironically) a pair of brothers named Garrett who came from Devon late, a couple of decades before the Civil War. (My wife's family came even earlier, descended directly from the line of the Mayflower's carpenter—John Howland.) Our names were (among others) Hunt and Holmes and Palmer on one side; Vanderhorst, Legare, Manigault, Morrison, and Toomer on the other. There were English, Dutch, French, Welsh, Scotch, and Irish bloodlines. Mine was and is a large family and mostly they have lived long lives. Except for those who were killed young in the wars. We have fought in all the wars, from the French and Indian Wars through Vietnam. Still most survived those wars and lived long lives. So that as a child I sat on laps and listened to the stories of kinfolk who were Confederate veterans. There were plenty on both sides of that war, but I never met any of the Yankee veterans.

And there were both slaveholders and abolitionists. Just so, also, as a child I heard the stories of more than one Black woman who had been born into and lived in the times of slavery. Even now all of American history seems close in time and a matter of flesh and blood concern. I own a rusty Civil War dress sword, worn by one ancestor, a Yankee naval officer. I have a fine, twisted toasting fork given as a personal present from George Washington to another ancestor. There is a good gold watch dating from the middle of the nineteenth century and a set of aviator's wings from

*General O.H. Palmer, Garrett's great-grandfather*

World War I. Some very old bits and pieces of furniture. For example, a tiny and intact footwarmer, holes in the top and a little drawer to hold the hot coals, which one ancestor in Maine took to church on cold Sundays. Some cups and silverware, some brass buttons and pieces of jewelry, patches of cloth and old toys. That kind of thing. Not preserved, only accidentally kept. And not much really. It has never been the practice of our family, on either side, to look back much. Life is for now and the future. There is some pride in the past, to be sure and, I like to think, some immediate, honest, no-nonsense understanding of it. But if they had been creatures content with the past, they would never have come over the dangerous ocean to the dangerous wilderness in the first place.

Much closer in time, of course, and still present in a few old photographs, there were the large family groups on both sides. Many uncles and aunts and, therefore, a multitude of cousins. My own immediate family consisted of two sisters. And an older brother, who died at birth, but who has been, always and perhaps strangely, a haunting presence in my life. Our house and our lives were never empty or isolated from the constant presence of kinfolk. And we always

*Some of the Garrett family, mid-1930s: from left, Francene, George (the author's father), Suzanne, Evelyn, Alice (grandmother), Oliver, and Helen*

travelled a lot—with all the difficulties and adventures of making trips in those days when most Americans were not nearly as freely mobile as they are now. We didn't so much visit as go and stay a good while with one another. And they with us. One or two regular journeys I remember well. To visit Grandmother Garrett in Sandwich on Cape Cod: by train from Orlando to Jacksonville; then by ship, the old Clyde Mallory Line, two days to New York; transfer to an overnight boat on the Fall River Line. Change in Fall River to the train again and go to Buzzards Bay. Where we would be met. Picture it. All of us, together with some friends and cousins and, likewise, the Black maid, Hattie, and some of her family. Or perhaps to Papa's, my grandfather, Colonel William Morrison Toomer, and his place in the mountains of North Carolina. By train and several changes and finally up into the mountains with two locomotives, one pushing and one pulling. Stopping, a flag stop, at the Post Office at Naples, North Carolina, to disembark in dusty confusion amid piles of luggage and to the considerable amusement of local loafers and children who were startled when the train stopped there.

There were some interesting uncles: a cavalry officer who became one of America's first military pilots; a tap and ballroom dancer, who danced in several Broadway shows and on the great ocean liners while those bright floating palaces still crossed the Atlantic; a first-rate professional golfer; a very good musician or two. There was even a professional guide

*Grandfather, Legh Garrett, U.S. Navy, 1877*

and mountain climber who disappeared forever into a sudden blizzard long before I was born. There were even some writers on both sides of the family. My aunt Helen Garrett wrote some marvelous children's books and won awards for them. My uncle Oliver, a much-decorated survivor of infantry combat in World War I, became a first-rate newspaperman with the old New York *Sun* and then a screenwriter in the early days of talking pictures. He kept on, wrote dozens of movies, some of them very good indeed, helped to found and was president of the Screenwriters Guild. He was *somebody.* And he was my godfather. Owned fast bright cars and was (to my young eyes) always in the company of fast, bright, beautiful women. Knew Fitzgerald a little, Faulkner and Hemingway pretty well. And wrote several of the best short stories I've ever read about World War I. Also a couple or three Broadway plays. On the other side was my grandfather's cousin, Harry Stillwell Edwards, of Macon, Georgia, whose brief novel of Reconstruction, *Anaeus Africanus,* has, over the years, quietly sold a couple of million copies and whose other work, mostly in the final decades of the nineteenth century, won him some recognition. I never met or saw him, but I heard all kinds of family stories about him. One that stuck like a stickabur, and one I liked a lot, was how Edwards, who was then postmaster of Macon, won a $10,000 *Chicago Tribune* prize for his novel *Sons and Fathers.* Now that was plenty of money, still, when I first learned about it. But in the last years of the nineteenth century it was a huge sum, really, an enormous sum to fall into the hands of a southerner of most modest means. One who, by the way, my grandfather always claimed owed him a modest sum

*Colonel William Morrison Toomer, maternal grandfather, 1950*

of money. Edwards evidently didn't choose to repay it. Instead, as family story had it, chose to rent a Pullman car, fill it with family and friends, and then take them all to New York City. Where, together, they managed to spend it all in a fortnight. Then back to Macon and life at the PO.

Well, then, no lack of what we now call "role models" for me in those days.

But above all, the two most powerful influences and examples, somewhat contradictory, were my grandfather Toomer and my father. Both lawyers and very good ones—my father probably a great lawyer. It was accurately reported that in his lifetime Grandfather made two fortunes and spent three. In his halcyon days he had a ninety-foot steam yacht, the *Cosette,* a lean and very fast yacht, a stable of racing and trotting horses (which he sometimes drove) and some very fine automobiles. A brief story about cars will have to do for Papa. How he had five sons and they would "borrow" the cars for the day while he was eating breakfast. So he would buy another car. Finally had six, so that one would always be left over. Driving himself to work one day, crossing the high

*The Toomer family, Jacksonville, Florida, about 1925*

bridge over the St. John's from Ortega to Jacksonville, he stalled. Couldn't get the car started. Tried and tried while horns blew and traffic piled up. Finally, in a brief fury, he removed the keys, dropped them over the side of the bridge into the river and walked to work. Point of the story, though, is that nobody knows what became of the car itself. He never mentioned it again.

Here a few words, all too few, about my father. For a beginning we had his library—an overflowing library of thousands of books. Books of all kinds in bookcases and piled on tables everywhere in the house. Everybody, all of us, read and read. I remember reading Kipling and Stevenson and Dickens and Scott sooner than I was really able to. And I could earn a quarter for reading any number of hard books my father believed everybody ought to read.

There were many things, more than the love of reading and writing and the gift of the ways and means to enjoy both, which he taught me by example. Athletic teaching was the one thing that he could not do for me. He had been an athlete and, I am told, a very good one, playing ice hockey and rowing in school and college. And he had led, for a time, a rugged physical life, dropping out of MIT to work in Utah as a copper miner. He wanted to be a mining

*George Garrett at age seven with mother, Rosalie, and baby sister, Alice, 1936*

engineer someday, but midway his money ran out; so he went to work in the mines out west; and he hoped to save enough money to go back to school. He had a slightly mangled left hand, missing two full fingers, and bulked, powerful shoulder muscles and a sinewy eighteen-inch collar size to show for his hard years as a miner. He had his charter membership in the United Mine Workers framed and on the wall; and in the attic there was a dusty old metal suitcase full of one kind and another of ore samples he had dug out himself. But he was crippled; for he had a bad left leg and a limp left arm. Neither of which greatly impeded his apparent vigor and energy and, indeed, were scarcely noticeable unless he tried to hurry, to run, or to leap up out of a chair. His lameness came in part from an injury and in part from a severe case of polio which had almost killed him. Now he could still swim—an awkward, but powerful sidestroke; and he learned to play a pretty good game of tennis, hobbling it is true, but overpowering many good players with a hard backhand and a truly devastating and deadly forehand. He also had a quality possessed by one of his tennis heroes, Bitsy Grant. Somehow or other, in spite of all awkwardness and all disability, he would manage to return almost anything hit at him. He was hard to ace and you couldn't often get by him. When I was a boy, he was a ranked player, fairly high on the ladder of the local tennis club. Once or twice, over those years, he and a partner were number one, tops in doubles. None of which meant anything to me at the time. I was still young enough to be horribly ashamed of all that clumsy, awkward hobbling about. Young? I *still* wince with embarrassment to recall it; though now I have to believe that my youthful shame could never have equaled the embarrassment of his often younger and always more graceful opponents.

By the time I was born, he was a prominent, controversial, daring and, in fact, feared lawyer, fearless himself. Together with his partner he ran the Ku Klux Klan, then a real political power, completely out of Kissimmee, Florida. And lived to enjoy the victory. Took on the big railroads—the Atlantic Coast Line, the Florida East Coast, the Seaboard, and the Southern—and beat them again and again. Tried not one, but any number of cases before the U.S. Supreme Court. Yet, at the same time and always, gave hours and hours of time, without stint, to those who were once called downtrodden. Especially to Blacks, who were more downtrodden than most anyone else. When Black people came to see him at home, they came in by the front door and sat in the living room like anybody else. And nobody said a word about that or any of his other social eccentricities. Because most of them, white and Black, respect-

*The Garretts in Orlando, Florida, 1943: George, Sr.
and Rozanne at rear; Alice and George, Jr.
(with "Winston") in front.*

ed him and depended on him. Those who did not
respect him were afraid of him. With good reason.
Once in my presence (for, by his practice, all the
family was included in anything that happened at our
house) a deputation of lawyers from the various
railroads offered him a retainer, much more money
than he earned, in effect *not* to try any more cases
against them. He didn't wait or consider his reply,
though he surprised all of us by being polite. He
thanked them for their flattering interest. He allowed
as how it was a generous and tempting proposition.

"I would be almost a rich man," he said. "But
what would I do for *fun?*"

And, laughing, he more shooed them than
showed them out the door.

One of the many things I hope I learned from
him is the courage of generosity. He was a proud
man, a tough and unsentimental man; but, true to the
code of his family and ours, he believed that our first
and primary duty in whatever vocation we found
ourselves was always service. The opposite of service
was not self-serving (much too mild a word), but pure
*selfishness.* I have too often forgotten his good example, but it is always there to be remembered. And I
am grateful for that inestimable gift.

\*

Everywhere the Twelfth Field went we had our
special hideouts. In Trieste we had a hole in the
wall called the Poker Bar. Here we had found and laid
claim to the *Gasthaus* of the little farm village of
Leonding, a few miles outside of Linz and close by
the rifle range, an old one going back to the bright
and colorful Austro-Hungarian Empire days. Which
is how we found it in the first place, marching out
there to fire qualification on our M-1's and carbines.
A big sprawling place (large for such a small village);
quiet, dark, low ceilings; a kind of cave with a long
wooden bar and with huge, round waxed oak tables.
Here we held our Battery party a couple of weeks
ago—plenty of booze, a show all the way from
Germany with a stripper, a couple of acrobats, a
magician, and a trained-dog act. And here, out of the
brightness of the spring afternoon we stand at the bar
eating *Holstein Schnitzels,* the ones with a couple of
fried eggs on top and drinking frosty steins of dark
beer. The *Schnitzels* are fine here and so is the venison
they serve with a wine sauce. We are standing, still
trying to preserve our khakis from wrinkles. There
are a few old guys playing cards at one table, nothing
more going on.

We bullshit with the owner who is not much
older than we are, though he looks a generation
older. He speaks good English. He fought the Russians in the East and then was a prisoner in Siberia for
a few years. We swap Army stories. Our guys have
mixed feelings about the Krauts, but everybody
respects them as soldiers. He is telling us about how
his father, who is still alive, and how even some of
these old cardplayers remember Hitler who lived
here in Leonding as a child. Hitler's father was a
customs officer who had owned a farm and lost it and
moved into the village when Hitler was six years old.
The boy would come to the *Gasthaus* in the evening
and get a bucket of draft beer for his father's supper.
They can remember that. They remember, too, how
he used to whistle, coming and going. He could
whistle tunes very well, they say . . . .

He would come into this same room and stand
right here where we are standing waiting to get his
bucket of beer. A funny feeling for us now.

We like this *Gasthaus* because they treat the guys
from the Twelfth Field well here. Even our very few
Black soldiers in the newly integrated American army.
Other places, especially in the city, are not so friendly
to the Black soldiers. Once they go to a place it gets a
name, and none of the locals will go there. And they
shun the prostitutes who go with Black soldiers. We
don't care one way or the other what they do. Except
where it concerns our own outfit. There is no color
line in the Twelfth Field.

While we stand there eating, stuffing our faces
with good food, he tells us how (he believes) he

survived in the labor camp in Siberia by counting calories and judging and doling out energy. Most of the time they lived on soup. The whole trick was to try to gain energy from the soup, not to spend more getting it than a serving of soup contained. It was always a matter of energy, not hunger. People who didn't know any better ran and jostled and wrestled each other for extra helpings when there were any, using up far more energy in the process than they would gain. They filled their bellies and they died sooner than the rest.

We nod with straight-faced understanding as we wolf the veal and eggs and swallow the rich, sweet, delicious local beer.

It is not that we are utterly insensitive. But we are young and strong and (as yet) undefeated. We cannot seriously imagine surrendering to anybody.

*

My resumé indicates the schools and colleges I attended. But, like most resumés, begins late, with high school. Before that there was kindergarten at the Cathedral School of our Episcopal cathedral—St. Luke's. The only memory I have of that school is of the rhythm band—drums, triangles, tambourines, etc. Ourselves in white with white hats and blue capes. Making a joyful noise. Then two years in a tiny private school, without a name, I think, but called "Miss Call's," for its founder and chief teacher who taught us all together, first grade on up through eighth or ninth, in one large room of an old house facing on a lake. I think it must have been Lake Ivanhoe, the edge of Orlando in those days and still pure enough to drink, spring-fed and unpolluted. Those years, only a couple before something happened and she had to close the school and I moved over to the public schools, must have been the most important, educationally, of my life. Because, you see, we were all doing our different lessons and assignments in the same room. And I picked up a lot, so much, in new interests and knowledge of new subjects, just from being around the older children. I was never, really, a good student then or later. But I was never afraid of learning or embarrassed about it, either.

My clearest memory of Miss Call's is how on one day we were all herded outside to stand by the curb on the sidewalk to watch as the President, FDR of course, rode slowly past us in an open car like one of my grandfather's. We waved at him. He waved back.

When I think of the President, I think also of my father who was a dedicated Democrat (as I am, in spite of all their foolishness) and, like so many, a great admirer of FDR. The reason I think of them together, though, has nothing to do with ideology or politics. My father gave about half of his working time to *pro bono* work for the poor. And he would take and win cases when nobody else would—even, or perhaps especially, militant organizations which professed to represent one group or another. He was, then, a man who did many good works, generously, without expecting or taking any credit for it. He made up for it, anyway, by charging his rich clients the largest fees you can possibly imagine. "They feel better," he used to say about the rich, "when they have to pay a lot for something. It matters to them." Anyway, when he died in 1947, I, as the male heir, was called on by a delegation from the Black community. They brought flowers and presents. "We feel just the same as we did when our President died," they told me.

After Miss Call's I went to the public schools in Orlando. To Delaney Street Grammer School (also attended, a little earlier, by Mary Lee Settle), which was two long blocks from home. Then, later, Cherokee Junior High School, about twice that distance. Both were close enough to come home for lunch if I felt like it or forgot my lunch money. Both were close enough to run home to safety if I had to. Oh, plenty of playground fighting (for survival) at both schools. But mainly my time was spent in the rough and tumble of Delaney Park, half a block from the place where I lived, a large green grass, cleared field (with a huge hole in the ground where a municipal swimming pool had once been planned and promised). Where a loose-knit gang of us played the sport of the season every afternoon and all weekend (except for church). Which was mostly a continual game of tackle football, played without any equipment except for odd bits and pieces. Softball took over for a while in the summer. There were a couple of concrete courts, but tennis never really caught on except for girls. All shapes and ages and sizes we played football. Once, more by accident than anything else, we scrimmaged against the Cherokee varsity football team which was getting ready for its big rivalry, the game against Memorial from across town. They had full equipment and a full team. There were, that day, only nine of us; so we had to borrow two of them. They had playbooks and real plays. We made ours up in the huddle, drawing diagrams in the dirt. And we beat the pants off of them. Then they borrowed our best players (alas not I) and put them on the starting lineup against Memorial. And won the game, too.

In high school, at Sewanee Military Academy and then at Hill School, sports were more organized. And I played as many sports as much as I could: football, boxing, swimming, and track. I was never especially good at any of these. Swimming was easiest for me; boxing was my best sport. But there were odd

*Garrett, Sewanee Military Academy, 1944*

payoffs, anyway. To this day, I am convinced that the only reason I was admitted to Princeton was that I was a member of the Hill football team which soundly beat the Princeton freshman team. At Princeton I played regular and then lightweight football until I was too banged up to play anymore. Then I returned to the pleasures of books, to reading and writing.

Just before graduation—finally! after some interruptions—from Princeton in 1952, I married Susan Parrish Jackson of Philadelphia in Philadelphia. The minister who married us had once won a gold medal in the low hurdles at the Olympics. So much for athletics, the passion of my youth.

Actually, truth is I learned more lessons from athletics, especially the contact sports, than anywhere else. School of hard knocks taught me most. Learned more about myself and the hard, deep lessons of survival. I think I was prepared for most of the pains and disappointments life showers over us (one and all) like confetti in a crazy parade. Except for the fact that most of the literary people I have met, except for that precious few, my friends, lack the character, courage, courtesy, and decency of the average jocks I have known. But, I suppose, nothing could prepare someone for the small-minded, mean-spirited, malice-ridden, rodent-like nastiness of the *literati*.

Similarly I was educated and prepared for everything but happiness. Did I mention my marriage? I did that. But I did not go on to say that we have lived

happily ever after. And we have done just that. Which is no small thing, and a very great blessing, in these bitter seasons of a cruel and brutally dangerous century, "this all-hating world," if I may borrow some words from Richard II.

\*

Now then, full of good food and beer and full of goodwill towards humankind, one and all, our two soldiers have driven into town, parked their jeep in a reserved space and are taking a stroll around the *Bahnhoff*. They will check the papers of a few GI's who are arriving or departing. They will caution a soldier or two to button up a shirt pocket or tighten up a necktie. And they will watch the trains come and go. The weather is really fine and dandy, couldn't be better. Nice and warm and getting warmer with the afternoon. The air is scented with springtime. Or is it the little bouquets of flowers so many people seem to be carrying? The girls are in their light dresses already. Splendid, if a little pale from winter. Sap stirs in the limbs of the Sergeant and Corporal.

Unusually crowded today. They are separated by the crowds. No matter. They will meet up sooner or later on one of the platforms or back at the jeep.

Alone, I stroll, not strut, out of the great barn of a building (most GI's call it the *Barnhoff*) into the sunlight on a platform. People, crowds of them, smiling and jabbering, waiting for a train. Even if my German was good enough to understand more than a

*Sgt. 1st class George Garrett in the 12th Field Artillery barracks, Free Territory of Trieste, 1953*

few rudimentary phrases, I could not hear what they are saying. Somewhere nearby, though I can't yet see it, a brass band is playing cheerful *oompah* music. Deafening and delightful.

Must be a local holiday of some kind. Now I am closer to the band. I see the middle-aged musicians, their cheeks chipmunking as they play. I am standing close by the huge bass drum. Which keeps a steady rhythm. Heart of an agitated giant.

This band is of an age which would allow them to have played all through the War. I wonder if they did that.

Now, even as I hear the shrill scream of the whistle, I see all the faces in the crowd turn towards the track where a train is coming, slowly, with sighs of steam, easing into the station. To my amazement I see their faces, all of them, change entirely in a wink of time. A moment ago they were animated, smiling. Now each mask of flesh is anxious and searching. And, as if at an order, they all begin to cry. I have never been among a huge crowd of weeping people before. Sobs and tears all around me. Stunned and lost, I feel, out of empathy (and perhaps out of a military reflex), tears well up in my own eyes. I am one of them, I am one with them, though I do not know why.

Now many in the crowd are holding up enlarged photographs, placards with names printed large on them. Like some kind of grotesque parody of a political rally.

The doors open and out of the train, helped by porters, here come, one after another, many of them with crude canes and crutches, a raggedy company of dazed, shabby, skinny, scarecrows. They are weeping also, some of them. Others study the crowd, searching for familiar faces with hard looks and dry eyes. The band is deafening. Next to me the bass drum pounds and pounds.

In time, very soon, in fact, I will learn that they are the latest contingent of Austrian veterans from the Eastern Front, returning home from Siberia. The Russians are moving slowly, in their own inexorable, patient, glacial fashion, towards a treaty here in Austria (as I will learn much later), if not a war first. Part of that movement is to let some of the scarecrows, who have somehow managed to survive until now, come home.

But here and now I know nothing of that and care less. I see a homecoming of the defeated and the wounded. Some greeted with great joy, with flowers and embracing. Some, as always, alone now even at home—though I see schoolchildren have been assigned the duty of making sure that everyone gets a greeting and some flowers.

*George Garrett, Jr., 1984*

I stand there knowing one thing for certain—that I am seeing our century, our times, close and truly. Here it is and, even among strangers, I am among them, sharing the moment of truth whether I want to or not.

An American Sergeant stands in the swirling crowd with tears rolling down his cheeks. He will be gone from here soon, first miles, then years and years away. But he will not, because he cannot, forget this moment or himself in it, his share of this world's woe and joy, the lament and celebration of all living things.

---

## *SELECTED BIBLIOGRAPHY*

### Fiction:

*King of the Mountain* (short stories). New York: Scribner, 1958; London: Eyre & Spottiswoode, 1959.

*The Finished Man.* New York: Scribner, 1959; London: Eyre & Spottiswoode, 1960.

*In the Briar Patch* (short stories). Austin: University of Texas Press, 1961.

*Which Ones Are the Enemy?* Boston: Little, Brown, 1961;

London: W.H. Allen, 1962.

*Cold Ground Was My Bed Last Night* (short stories). Columbia: University of Missouri Press, 1964.

*Do, Lord, Remember Me.* Garden City, N.Y.: Doubleday, 1965; London: Chapman & Hall, 1965.

*A Wreath for Garibaldi and Other Stories.* London: Hart-Davis, 1969.

*Death of the Fox.* Garden City, N.Y.: Doubleday, 1971; London: Barrie & Jenkins, 1972.

*The Magic Striptease* (short stories). Garden City, N.Y.: Doubleday, 1973.

*The Succession: A Novel of Elizabeth and James.* Garden City, N.Y.: Doubleday, 1983.

*An Evening Performance* (short stories). Garden City, N.Y.: Doubleday, 1985.

*Poison Pen.* Winston-Salem, N.C.: Wright, 1986.

**Nonfiction:**

*James Jones* (biography). San Diego: Harcourt, 1984.

**Poetry:**

*The Reverend Ghost* (in *Poets of Today IV* ), with Theodore Holmes and Robert Wallace, edited by John Hall Wheelock. New York: Scribner, 1957; London: Scribner, 1958.

*The Sleeping Gypsy and Other Poems.* Austin: University of Texas Press, 1959.

*Abraham's Knife and Other Poems.* Chapel Hill: University of North Carolina Press, 1961; London: Oxford University Press, 1961.

*For a Bitter Season: New and Selected Poems.* Columbia: University of Missouri Press, 1967.

*Welcome to the Medicine Show: Postcards, Flashcards, Snapshots.* Winston-Salem, N.C.: Palaemon Press, 1978.

*Luck's Shining Child: A Miscellany of Poems and Verses.* Winston-Salem, N.C.: Palaemon Press, 1981.

*The Collected Poems of George Garrett.* Fayetteville: University of Arkansas Press, 1984.

**Plays:**

*Sir Slob and the Princess: A Play for Children.* New York: French, 1962.

*Enchanted Ground.* York, Me.: Old Gaol Museum, 1982.

**Editor of:**

*New Writing from Virginia.* Charlottesville, Va.: New Writing Associates, 1963.

*The Girl in the Black Raincoat: Variations on a Theme.* New York: Duell, Sloan & Pierce, 1966.

*Man and the Movies,* with W.R. Robinson. Baton Rouge: Louisiana State University Press, 1967.

*Film Scripts One* (includes *Henry V, The Big Sleep,* and *A Streetcar Named Desire*), with Jane R. Gelfman, and O.B. Hardison, Jr. New York: Appleton-Century-Crofts, 1971.

*Film Scripts Two* (includes *High Noon, Twelve Angry Men,* and *The Defiant Ones*), with J.R. Gelfman, and O.B. Hardison, Jr. New York: Appleton-Century-Crofts, 1971.

*New Writing in South Carolina,* with William Peden. Columbia: University of South Carolina Press, 1971.

*The Sounder Few: Selected Essays from "The Hollins Critic,"* with R.H.W. Dillard and John Rees Moore. Athens: University of Georgia Press, 1971.

*Craft So Hard to Learn: Conversations with Poets and Novelists about the Teaching of Writing,* with John Graham. New York: Morrow, 1972.

*Film Scripts Three* (includes *The Apartment, The Misfits,* and *Charade*), with J.R. Gelfman, and O.B. Hardison, Jr. New York: Appleton-Century-Crofts, 1972.

*Film Scripts Four* (includes *A Hard Day's Night, The Best Man,* and *Darling*), with J.R. Gelfman and O.B. Hardison, Jr. New York: Appleton-Century-Crofts, 1972.

*The Writer's Voice: Conversations with Contemporary. Writers.* New York: Morrow 1973.

*The Botteghe Oscure Reader,* with Katherine Garrison Biddle. Middletown, Conn.: Wesleyan University Press, 1974.

*Intro 5,* with Walton Beacham. Charlottesville: University Press of Virginia, 1974.

*Intro 6: Life as We Know It.* Garden City, N.Y.: Doubleday, 1974.

*Intro 7: All of Us and None of You,* with James Whitehead and Miller Williams. Garden City, N.Y.: Doubleday, 1975.

*Intro 8: The Liar's Craft,* with Stephen Kendrick. Garden City, N.Y.: Doubleday, 1977.

*Intro 9: Close to Home,* with Michael Mewshaw. Austin, Tex.: Hendel & Reinke, 1978.

A fairly complete checklist of published writings by George Garrett—"George Garrett: A Bibliographical Chronicle, 1947-1980," by Stuart Wright—is available in *Bulletin of Bibliography* 38, no. 1 (January-March, 1981), 6-19, 25.

# George V. Higgins

*1939–*

*George V. Higgins, 1986*

I suppose there must be as many ways of looking at fiction as there have been people who have looked at it. Some of the results are cockeyed, of course, tortured prose that torments the prose supposedly under inspection (that is why the proper reaction to interpretation that seems nonsensical to the reader is to discard it promptly—one's instincts in that respect are generally correct), seeking to impose a semidoctrinal approach that vitiates the good writers's entire purpose, and the good reader's, too. The first obligation of the writer is to entertain, to tell a story. There is no standard measure of goodness, of course, which rather complicates the matter, but that circumstance is also liberating. It frees

readers to determine entirely subjectively what they want to read, writers to follow as blindly as they choose whatever muse may call.

Writers need data. The surest way to win a reader is to divulge new information on a point of interest. It doesn't matter whether the writing is fiction: All writing is gossip; all readers fishwives. Bombarded as we now are with all sorts of information, we crave most the writing that makes sense of it, even if the sense is wrong. The function of contemporary fiction is to impose coherence upon events that seem—and are—frighteningly random, so that as we digest each new dispatch from John Updike about the most recent vicissitudes in Rabbit Angstrom's life, we come away with an improved awareness of what's happened in our own.

The writers I most admire are those who have taken the trouble to inquire how the world works. Charles Dickens knew London—Parliament, the Old Bailey, and its other institutions—because he had studied the City himself. John O'Hara knew New York high life, and Pennsylvania small towns, because he had seen them up close. William Faulkner's scrutiny was microscopically encompassing, if that is not an oxymoron; his vision really only comprehended the declining Mississippi society that he studied all his life, but it identified each detail with a clarity that made his stories of its members universally illuminating. F. Scott Fitzgerald, I think, was ill served by his early recognition as chronicler of the Jazz Age; famous and rich while he was still quite young, he was able to languish among the smart set on the Riviera, acquiring no fresh resources of experience except those essentially narcissistic sensations he and his wife, Zelda (Sayre), suffered as results of their hedonistic life. For Gerald and Sara Murphy, luxuriating in the fortunes rolling in from his family's Mark Cross luggage stores, it was a beautiful life. But for Fitzgerald, it was a disaster. He didn't learn anything. The man could write like an angel, and once—*The Great Gatsby*—he did just that. But once, as that great hack Jacqueline Susann declared, is not enough, not enough for a career.

When I was in college I fell under the spell of mythic and psychological theses of literary interpretation. I read much more Freud and Jung than was probably good for me, and after the Jung immersion surfaced into the writings of Sir James George Frazer (*The Golden Bough*), Jessie Weston (*From Ritual to Romance*), and Robert Graves (*The White Goddess*). I suppose it was all T. S. Eliot's fault, cribbing the Fisher King as he did, pied-pipering whole generations of literati down the winding lanes of his own obsessions, but it was fascinating to me at the time and probably greatly amused my indulgent professors when I applied all my newfound arcana to such as Geoffrey Chaucer.

At least I hope it did: Literature in each of its occupational disguises—reading, teaching, writing —seldom pays enough to warrant doing it for money. If we're not going to have any fun at it, we should find something else to do. The first time I saw what might be disparaged as a "lit-crit" review of one of my books, I was first amazed and then delighted: The critic had determined that Mob contract-killer Jackie Cogan was a Christ-figure who moved through death to redemption—other people's deaths, to be sure, but still death to redemption. I began to be grateful that Chaucer never read my papers about his *Canterbury Tales*. He would've been convulsed.

After that experience—thirteen years out of college—I became somewhat more respectful of the biographical approach to literature—"What porridge had John Keats?"—that I'd formerly disdained. Not convinced that it contained the talisman for understanding of what every writer does; there is no talisman, I think—it was more a matter of becoming willing to grant that there may be something to it after all. You will search in vain for evidence that I've ever been a contract killer, or even a volunteer, but it's definitely relevant to a fair reading of *Cogan's Trade* to know that I prosecuted hired guns—among other miscreants—for seven years, and got to know those folks. It's not necessary to know that, I hope—the notion that the reader must research the writer in order to appreciate the writing is to me repugnant. If, in order to read Shakespeare, I must first read Holinshed; then after reading Holinshed I must read and study all his times; and then of course learn context of all those historians; by the time I reach *Macbeth*, my vision will be gone. I think—or hope—that the intelligent reader can enjoy my work without knowing a damned thing about me, or where I got the idea for it, and at the same time I think it likely, but not certain, that the reader who happens to have some such notion may find some additional illumination of a given episode. Not that that illumination will by any means neces-

sarily be the one I had in mind when the characters took off and I started writing; only that the reader's enjoyment may be heightened. Keep in mind when reading anything with my byline on it that you are the second reader; if I had not enjoyed writing it, or wanted to know how it came out, I would have stopped writing it, and thrown it away, and you never would have seen it.

In the spring of 1962, Irving Howe conducted a seminar for Stanford University graduate students bent upon intensive study of the works of Nathaniel Hawthorne and Herman Melville. The syllabus was daunting, requiring of the prudent seminarinarian not careful study of the masterful performances (Hawthorne's fictional biography of the unfortunate Hester Prynne; Melville's fishing story), but Hawthorne's *Blithedale Romance* and Melville's *Pierre*. The professor was daunting, too; Mr. Howe, at least in those days, was a prepossessing man, capable of rudeness and protective of his eminence, not noticeably inclined toward gracious waiver of the privileges his rank conferred when he smelled impudence from mere novices. We sat there under his hegemony, frantically conjuring up "insights" from bad books which provoked few, ever conscious that our projected applications for financial aid and coveted assistantships might very well be shrivelled by a mean comment from him. We were not happy scholars.

I was not, at least. That seminar stood out in a thoroughly disagreeable year as an especially anomalous and pointless exercise. Mr. Howe, later the 1976 recipient of the National Book Award for his *World of Our Fathers*, was simultaneously intensely Jewish and insistently socialist, inclined to dogmatize. His politics accounted for his selections of the two utopian, visionary, tractarian, dull novels written by Hawthorne and Melville in the throes of similar political ideologies and enthusiasms. I guess they did, at least—I can't imagine any other motive to explain those assignments.

His ethnic sensitivity I presume now to have been the wellspring of his evident disdain for a Boston College graduate whose round face and surname lent credence to suspicions he was Irish Catholic. Keep in mind that this was less than a decade after the Red-baiting era that crested in the middle fifties, symbolized by such great Americans as Senators Pat McCarran of Nevada and Joe McCarthy of Wisconsin, turbulent secular priests pronouncing career-ending anathemas upon people who shared at least some of Mr. Howe's views. I was young then, far from home for the first time, innocent of the fact that by being Irish Catholic I was guilty by big-oted association with those crusaders. I didn't know about the anti-Catholicism then, if not now, fashion-able as the intelligentsia's version of anti-Semitism. Slouching sullen in my chair, hearing the birds in the palms outside herald in song an unearned spring's arrival to a land that knew not winter, I lis-tened without recourse or right of reply (then, not now) to a prejudiced ideologue from New York pon-tificate in Palo Alto about the mind, the morals, the ethics, and the character of New England, the place where I grew up.

That unsettling experience, one of many fur-nished without let or hindrance to me by that uni-versity and state (do you know what they do out there? They list "lobster" on menus when crayfish is what they've got), in that dispiriting year, carried with it, I suppose, the merit of abrading the surface of the certitudes I had harbored until then, about what I am and where I come from. It also served, with the rest of Stanford's many courtesies, to make a quietus of my initial plans to live my life as a West Coast academic. For this English major, at least, the best poetry of June of 1962 was that proclaimed by the public address system at San Francisco Interna-tional Airport, announcing the departure of Ameri-can Airlines' direct flight to Boston.

Since then a kindlier fate and somewhat better judgment than combined to cause me to choose Mr. Howe's seminar have on a good many occasions brought me back to Logan Airport in East Boston to depart New England, but always temporarily. I visit other places; this is where I live. The minds and the characters, the morals and the ethics, that one finds in New England have their faults and defects, but we are orderly when right and ashamed when we are wrong. We have a sense of decency. To a degree at least, we seem to have a better sense of who we are and what we ought to be than I have seen else-wheres in their inhabitants. We know what evil is.

By one tradition, of course, evil is reputed to exist solely in the eye of the beholder. So I suppose I had better pause here and go back to the begin-ning, to the sources of my eyes.

The end of World War II released gasoline and tires to civilians like my father, and eliminated at the same time what I suspect had been the expla-nation he and my mother had until then made to my maternal grandmother, Evelyn Montgomery, for failing to pay visits in the summer to her home in Hinesburg, Vermont. For the millions who have never heard of it, and with excellent reason, the center of Hinesburg in the late forties consisted of a

creamery, Lantman's IGA general store, a Mobil gasoline station, the Congregational church, and the public school. Thirty miles or so south of Burling-ton, it was more or less a part of Richmond, a wider spot in the road to the north.

In the summer the Green Mountains collected heat and stored it in the valleys of Hinesburg, where it lay undisturbed by anything more than the occa-sional, vagrant hot breeze. The Jerseys in the pas-tures were lethargic, even for cows, and the maple leaves seldom stirred. I suppose I was six, maybe seven, when my father and mother loaded me and the baggage into the blue-and-white 1941 DeSoto and headed north from Rockland, Massachusetts, with a grim resignation perceptible even by a child. We arrived in early evenings, on those visits that be-came detestably annual and remained so until I reached puberty (although that milestone was not the reason that they stopped—I don't know what that reason was, but I was grateful for it), and after Coca-Cola from juice glasses on the screened porch behind the grapevines guarding against intrusion by any fugitive breeze, the youngest of the three trail-hardened pilgrims was taken up the brown-painted staircase—the railing was made of one-inch steel pipe—to his lumpy bed in the room at the north-west corner of the house, under the red tin roof which had conserved the heat all day especially for him. The single window to the north was open on the wan pretense that there might be a cooling breeze, and it served admirably the convenience of abundant pollen from the surrounding fields. Much later, when I first read about the owls bearing away the farm from "Fern Hill," I knew two new things instantly: Dylan Thomas was a wonderful, lyrical poet, and; he did not have allergies.

Fairly early the next morning for a normally late-riser, my father, in his annual up-tempo imita-tion of Pontius Pilate washing hands of us, would back the DeSoto down the steeply inclined gravel tracks of the driveway, cramping the front wheels to the limit in order to avoid hanging up the undercar-riage on the steeper incline upward to the roadway at the foot. If my eyes by then had not been swollen shut by allergic reaction, I would cry as I stood on the lawn and watched him desert my mother and me for a full two weeks of something approaching penal incarceration in Boredom Penitentiary. My mother was more restrained and did not show her dismay, but if either of us could have gone back home with him, abandoning the other hostage, either would have done so at once. I will accord to the late Evelyn Montgomery the *carte blanche* extended to all dece-dents not known to have been convicted of major felonies, and content myself with the observation that she was an unhappy woman, and therefore a difficult one. It was not her fault, either, that her old car didn't work, and there was really no place to go in it anyway. But those circumstances all had much to do with the fact that her company and isolated village attracted few outsiders who had any other choice.

Evelyn had come from Ireland as a girl, whether alone or accompanied I do not know, bringing with her one trunk she still had when I met her. She was of Protestant stock. With childish heedlessness I rejected her importunate offers to provide me with an oral inventory of the contents of that trunk and the history of her life, begun across the sea before Bismarck invaded France in 1870, perhaps one of many slights by me and others accounting in part for her disposition. She met her husband, Roy, in time to give birth to my mother, her first child, in 1909. There is some doubt whether Roy's ancestry was Scottish or Irish, but none on the point that he was a Roman Catholic until she insisted that he renounce popery when he married her.

Not withstanding that religious ductility, he seems not to have proven an especially felicitous marital catch. He was an unregenerate financial opportunist, capitalizing (but not very successfully) on what he learned circulating through the state as a dairy inspector by purchasing *seriatim* one broken-down operation after another, moving his family in, spending a few years working them and himself to their nubs in order to fix up the places, then selling off the now-spruce home and barns to acquire another wreck. I remember Evelyn saying that "Roy always made money on his deals, but . . . ," and letting her voice trail off. I can finish the sentence now for her, with some confidence: ". . . treated his family like a bunch of intrastate Joads who never did settle down."

While that was going on in Vermont, south of Boston what seems strikingly like a mirror image of it was in progress. My paternal grandfather was born in North Abington, one of five brothers and one sister, in 1876. His father, Arthur, was an Orange Protestant, probably from Londonderry, converted to Green Catholicism by his wife, Mary. Charles J. Higgins was the sunniest, hardest-working, most generous and compassionate human being that anyone who met him will admit to having seen. He married Annie, who gave him no competition whatsoever in quest of such respect, and they had one child, my father, in 1906.

Therefore, when my mother, raised as a Protestant, married my father, raised as a Catholic and a fiercely believing one, she converted back to the faith her father had renounced to marry her mother, leaving the final family score of defectors at Romans 2 (Arthur and Doris), Protestants 1.

For several strong reasons valid in their times, my father and his father, and their various pastors at Holy Family Church were inclined to take grim satisfaction from that sort of tally. While my grandfather commenced his adult life in the second phase of Irish assimilation into American economic life with fewer and smaller handicaps than his father had confronted, a more genteel but flourishing nativist prejudice still influenced his whole life. He progressed against it nicely, from hardware store clerk to hardware store owner, to tax collector, to town treasurer, to treasurer of the Rockland Cooperative Bank—only by much hard work done in furtherance of indissoluble alliances with other ambitious young men of Irish Catholic heritage.

A prime principle of their league was not to forget their own, not only their own families, but also their fellow Micks not gifted with their luck or wit. His priests believed, his friends believed, and he believed as well, that mutual aid and loyalty were the only hope that any of them had.

Charlie Higgins kept that creed for more than eighty years, some of them the decade after the Crash of '29. That was what accounted for the stream of mourners who tramped through his wake at his house (no funeral home wakes for real Irish, no matter how much grief; my father said he'd haunt me if I did that to him, and by God I didn't do it—I have got some sense). Most of them were people of modest circumstances in 1955, men and women in their sixties, their eyes filled with tears, grasping my fifteen-year-old hand in both of theirs, often embracing my nonplussed father, telling him who understood and me, who then did not: "During the Depression, Charlie Higgins saved my house. I couldn't pay the mortgage and my taxes, see, and I went up to see him, and I told Charlie all my troubles, and he said: 'Jim, don't worry, we won't take your house. We know you'll pay up when you can. Go home and don't worry.' " And when better times arrived, that is what they did. Of course if Charlie were around today, overlooking delinquent property taxes due the town, carrying delinquent mortgages at the bank, he would be indicted in short order and remanded to custody.

But then again, of course as well, if Charlie were around today, he might not dare to do it. There are many more laws now than there were then, a bewildering array of exquisitely technical statutes enacted to meet needs perceived during the gradual and continuing erosion of *ad hoc*, unwritten sanctions against wickedness. The strong secular creed of solidarity enforced in Charlie's day by churchmen and parishioners alike imposed upon the recipients of compassion obligations fully as solemn as it did upon grantors. My grandfather's standing in the community rested upon his decency to the temporarily needy family. That family's standing rested no less upon its justification of his trust when better times came back. As he and his fellow members of the upstart Mick bank board would not have dared to ape the callousness of the Protestant bankers they had challenged with their venture, so the Rockland Co-op's borrowers would not have dared to dishonor or abuse their trust. Ostracisim yawed for offenders in either camp. There was less need for statutes to punish banking wickedness, because their was less likelihood that irregular banking practices would result in losses to the bank.

The material rewards of the settled lifetime Charlie spent with his family in shoetown Rockland, while not great by worldly standards, were markedly better than the ones that Roy spent gypsying from farm to Vermont farm with his. Charlie's family had been able to help him through two years of business school, my namesake granduncle through medical school, my father's namesake uncle through enough college to teach school, and my other granduncles as well into steady trades. Charlie's relative prosperity secured not only a full A.B. for my father at Boston College, but also an M.A.

Those generational improvements in educational credentials, though, did not bring with them automatic access to better opportunities. Resourcefulness was still required. In the forties and fifties my father encountered in his professional career in public education, evidence sufficient to persuade him his religion barred him from the executive positions he coveted. He overcame that bigotry with a modified version of the strategy my grandfather and his friends had employed to start the bank, channeling the energy of his resentment into electioneering among the increasing numbers of Irish Catholic teachers joining what is now the Massachusetts Teachers Association, becoming its treasurer. He went back to Rockland to secure his principalship from a five-member school board including three Micks, succeeding another Irish Catholic who had died in office (thus swapping, not so incidentally, the English teacher's position that was his joy and passionate metier for the greater status he perceived in a grueling, tedious, administrative post).

Until her marriage my mother had been a teacher, too, which is something akin to saying that Elizabeth I was of royal lineage before she became Queen. What she temporarily gave up when I arrived (she returned to teaching as soon as I started school myself, serving as a "substitute"—meaning that she usually taught all five days each week, but each day in a different grade) was the occupation, not the vocation. While neither she nor my father had planned to replicate his parents' decision to stop with one child, that was how matters turned out. The consequence was that I started school well before I started school at four-and-a-half (not an unusual thing today, in this era of Montessori, but a rare and definite advantage then). Since my father had been luckily too young to be eligible for death in World War I, and was luckily too old (and far too fat) for martyrdom in World War II, I spent virtually all of my childhood waking hours being taught. I was not aware of this at the time (though I rather surmise that they were), so that made the learning not only palatable, but even interesting.

Today I am hard-pressed to say whether the inaccessibility of Dr. Vladimir Zworykin's 1923 invention (the iconoscope, precursor of the eye of today's TV camera) to the common man detracted from or improved that early education. My children have grown up with television as a given, but they also read as voraciously as I did, and at each stage of their lives have been far more sophisticated than I was at the same age. My guess is that my parents would have seized upon the gadget sooner than they did—it was around 1950 when we got our first one; I was about eleven—if it had been affordably available, and that they would have allowed me to consume it on much the same terms that they allowed me to share their reading, and their arguments (I am using *arguments* here in the Socratic sense: staking out a position and defending it, not so much to gain a position of moral or intellectual superiority as to determine whether one has the facts straight and has interpreted them correctly). They treated me as an adult when I was a little kid. If they read it, and I wanted to read it, I could go ahead and read it. Since they read not just for learning, but for pleasure, that is what I did—the *Atlantic Monthly* tonight, low-rent detective novel tomorrow, the *Saturday Evening Post* when it arrived, Arthur Conan Doyle day after, John P. Marquand's newest next week, John O'Hara's after that. Catholic they were in outlook, and catholic in practice, too.

I suppose that eclecticism is the etiological explanation for my belief that the subjective approach to literature—writing it or reading it—is the only reliable guide (even though it's so maddeningly permissive). Much of the stuff that I thought I had read almost certainly went over my head—and probably a good thing, too, considering that much of it was junk. I profligately disbursed my allowance on pulp magazines—*Saga, Argosy, True*—and until mean reporters determined that Bridey Murphy was a hoax, actually believed that reincarnation had been proven. But because I also had access to supplementary funds for the purchase of books and magazines, I could also buy *Field and Stream*, and there, utterly by chance, encounter a reprint of a story called "Big Two-Hearted River," by a writer named Ernest Hemingway whom I had somehow missed. Which sent me to the library, at the age of about twelve, to see if he had written any other stuff, as indeed he had, and I was mesmerized for weeks (and as I still am). The librarian did not wholly approve of such fare for children—she was one of those dried-up old bats who let no one in the stacks; we called her "The Lone Ranger"—but she was also one of those people who disapproved of the fact that I called my mother "Doris" and my father "John"—a practice they deemed sensible enough, inasmuch as those were their names—and her veto was soon overridden. Their view was that if I thought I was old enough to read it, I was old enough to read it.

Soon enough, probably too soon, I decided (though distracted by the Vargas girls in *Esquire* and Marilyn Monroe starkers in the early *Playboy*) that if it was this much fun to read, it must be ecstasy to write. Somewhere or other I had acquired the information that magazine editors did not read handwritten submissions. This meant I had to learn to type. Rockland High School (this was before my father became principal, in my sophomore year) offered no typing course to what were then known as "college students" (meaning that was what we were preparing to be) until junior year. But my father, working at home as treasurer of the teachers' association, had never learned how to type either, and he typed all the time. Since he didn't know how to type, he demolished typewriters regularly, and the association replaced them as he required. My father's typewriter, by remarkable coincidence, was pronounced unfit for further duty within days of my first assaults upon it, and was promptly replaced. Magically the deceased machine was returned to life at his expense, and then at great cost to my mother's rest, the wee small hours of the morning in our house were made hideous by the sounds of my struggles with the Smith Corona manual portable. I sent out my first story when I was fourteen.

It came back. It came back a lot of times. So did my first novel, which I wrote when I was fifteen. I began to believe that I had inadvertently gone into the boomerang business. But I also believed that I was having more fun making boomerangs, if that's what I was doing, than I'd ever had doing anything else, and therefore I did persist.

It is a confession, not a boast, when I say that I continued to persist for the next seventeen years in willful typewriter abuse. At least as much as any other writer, I am an egotist if not a solipsist. The whole premise of the trade is the scribbler's obsessive conviction that what he or she has to report from the backyards of personal consciousness is *important*. The writer believes that the world will be a better place after its residents have read what he or she is writing. No one disbelieving that could ever write a thing. That is what justifies keeping one's mother awake down the hall until three in the morning (John was a deep sleeper, and could have gotten his rest in the Blitz): What I am doing is important work. It has to be done, and it has to be done *right now*, and it doesn't matter how selfish you or anyone else choose to think I am, because I am going to do it. Right now.

It helps, if the one obsessed also aspires to some semblance of a normal life, to have a metabolism that operates smoothly at the tach redline. I inherited my mother's, which refuses to idle. In high school I was able to perform creditably in the not-too-demanding courses, earn varsity letters in sports (e.g., baseball) that real athletes (football players, basketball players, sprinters *et al*) disdained, and edit the school paper and yearbook, while writing all the time, because I didn't need much sleep. That is not a boast, either, because I had nothing to do with it. Rockland was still rural enough, forty years ago, to offer space ample for small-game hunting and freshwater fishing. Reed's Pond's a dry hole now, and the pickerel are gone, and thus so also are the opportunities to act out (inadequately) Hemingway's travelogues. A friend of mine lived in a white house that had a big maple tree in the yard. His father installed a chain hoist on a thick limb, and we all got grease-covered overhauling Ford flathead engines from the junkers our friends drove. My father had been indoctrinated by his father in the sacred mysteries of the Boston Red Sox, and (perhaps the only mean thing he ever did to me) inculcated the same devotion in me. We played touch-football in the street in the fall, engaged in dangerous BB-gun war games (nobody lost an eye, but it wasn't our fault; those Red Ryder carbines had no range), and when the hormones kicked in, chased the girls with excitement (many were caught, and had to get married, but none, I admit, by me).

And then, in September of '57, I went to Boston College, and the whole world was new. It caught me by surprise. I had always known I would go there—my father told me so, and I did what he said. I applied a year before high-school graduation, was accepted, and that was the end of that. In the spring of '57 a Harvard recruiter, nervous about the dearth of small-town high-school applicants, visited Rockland High School and told John I should go to Harvard. My father said he couldn't afford it—which was true—and the recruiter offered a scholarship equal to the difference in tuitions. John and Doris and I discussed the matter at dinner. The discussion was short. We turned it down flat. We were right.

Boston College in the late fifties—and today; I keep in touch—was a most remarkably exciting place. Because my father assured me I could do anything I wanted (I like to think he was right, but he probably was wrong), and because he wanted me to be a doctor, I enrolled in pre-med. It was agony. Useful agony, perhaps, given my adult trade—grudgingly I learned a lot of science, and nothing a writer learns is wasted—but agony nonetheless. I wasn't any good at it. Hotshot graduates of small high schools are at seventeen accustomed to being the best in their classes; it wounds their feelings to strive, to seek, to know, and then to yield. It wounded mine, at least. It was not until the middle of my junior year that I conjured up the courage to defy my father and shift over to English, where I'd wanted to be all along. There was precedent for a pre-med editor of the *Stylus* literary magazine at BC, but it was not one I cared to underscore. I wanted to spend all my time reading real stuff: Chaucer under Ed Hirsch, Graham Greene for Dick Malany, Andrew Marvell for Dick Hughes, Shakespeare for Al Duhamel, boring them senseless with 100-page term papers, and driving Leonard Casper nuts with my long short-stories.

They treated me and my classmates as equals. Francis Sweeney, S.J., was faculty moderator of the *Stylus*, in charge of assuring that none of the obscenity and scatology we designed to print got published. We went up the front and down the back, hollering and yelling, and he treated us as intellectual equals. Not in knowledge, no, or power, but in intellect. Just as my parents, now that I think of it, had always treated me. When I won the *Atlantic's* college contest in fiction in 1960, those teachers seemed more

pleased than I was, and that redoubled my pleasure. They thought writing was important. They agreed with me.

And then I went to Stanford, to meet the likes of Howe. Nothing had prepared me for that. My middle-class upbringing, only briefly interrupted by those dreaded Vermont trips and the "vacations" we took when my father attended NEA conventions in such places as St. Louis and Miami Beach, and four years at BC had by June of '61 implanted in my marrow some trace element which to this day affects every judgment that I make. In September of '61, regrettably for me, I was not aware that this had happened, but by the following December, after a mere three months at Stanford, among California heathen, I knew it all too well. I came home for Christmas like a prisoner on work-release, and when it came time for me to return to California after the holidays, I went with deep pain in my heart. Also in my belly, as it turned out—when I made my escape from that wretched place in June of '62, I had copies of hospital records to enlighten doctors at home, should my bleeding ulcer recur. There is this to be said for bleeding ulcers, though: If you time them right, they can keep you out of combat in Vietnam, and that is what mine did.

I'd spent my college summers driving a truck for Coca-Cola, in Brockton, Massachusetts. I liked the job and it paid well (for those days—$149 a week). John was not delighted when I returned to it. He negotiated a waiver that would allow me to teach English to Avon (Mass.) high-school students despite my lack of course credits in educational methodology (I could pick those up at Bridgewater State College at night). I concluded from my lukewarm receptions at the U.S. Information Agency, the CIA, and the J. Walter Thompson advertising agency that mongrel English majors were not a hot commodity, except in teaching, which I didn't want to do. I took the road most travelled by such misfits, and went into the newspaper business. From October 1962 through May 1963, I quarreled with several superiors at the *Providence* (R.I.) *Journal*, bucketing around in a grey secondhand 1959 Triumph TR-3 (which taught me the meaning of patience when it balked at starting in cold weather) and then in a black, new, TR-4 (which taught me the meaning of penury).

Then came that spring morning when my mail at the Warwick office of the *Journal* consisted of two letters; a phone call came in while I read them. The first of the letters was from the man who supervised the suburban bureaus; he took me to task for an error that I had not made, saying something along these lines: "You're trying to run before you can walk. You're not Scotty Reston yet." The second was from the publisher of the *Journal*, complimenting me on an editorial page piece; he said it was "as good as anything James Reston's ever done." The phone call was from Ed Tunstall, deputy New England bureau chief for the Associated Press in Boston. He inquired whether I would like to become the AP's first correspondent in Springfield, Massachusetts. I accepted. I wrote a letter of resignation from the *Journal*'s staff. I went across the street to the photocopying machine in the City Hall. I copied the publisher's letter and the supervising editor's letter, twice each. I copied my resignation twice. I put a copy of the editor's letter and a copy of the resignation in an envelope and mailed it to the publisher. I put a copy of the publisher's letter and the original of my resignation in an envelope addressed to the supervising editor. I gave the copy of the resignation to the *Journal* bureau chief. He said I was making a big mistake. (I'd been making $69 a week, base pay, working for the *Journal*, and taking nothing but grief—which, to be sure, I was returning with interest. The AP was offering $89 a week, no grief, my own show, and the chance to show what I had. You can see what I mean about writers being solipsists; every writer is an only child, even those that aren't. Nothing but a bunch of show-offs, smoked Virginia hams.) I laughed at him. He's a nice man. He laughed back. We still correspond.

I learned a lot in Springfield. I could have learned the most permanently valuable part of it in almost any city in the world, if I could've gotten a job. The best creative writing school in the whole world is the Associated Press, where you'd better not make it up. AP teaches: facts and speed. It leaches the self-indulgence out of your prose. It doesn't matter if you write the most eloquent report of a plane crash that history has ever recorded, not if your story clears the wire five minutes after the OSN (opposition). By the time your aureate prose hits the member papers' City Desks, the OSN's will be set in type, and running page one, above the fold. AP enforced the KISS rule: "Keep It Simple, Stupid." When young writers ask me today how they should proceed, I tell them: If you possibly can, get a job with the Associated Press. And also today, when reviewers are cruel, I know very well that I'm a crackerjack rewrite man, and if all else fails I can always go back to the Associated Press. And *that* is bragging.

Another thing I learned in Springfield was insistence on discretion. It has been the hallmark of the New England communities where I have spent

enough time to gain a sense of place. Now, I am not here suggesting that a young newspaperman in his novitiate at the *Providence Journal* embarks upon eight months' residence in Rhode Island with powers of observation superior to those of an examiner from the Federal Deposit Insurance Corporation assigned out of Washington for the same period to the same place. Or that a year in Springfield, covering western Massachusetts, qualifies anyone as an expert on the manners and mores of people west of Worcester. What I am suggesting is that the reporter has to concentrate as best he can those powers of observation which he happens to possess, and to develop as rapidly as possible a working understanding of what goes on in a new place, and what people there think of it—unless he really likes being reamed out by the copy desk when he gets something wrong. And, further, that the dependence of his continued employment upon his ability to make good use of his occupational right to interrogate total strangers from all walks of life implies a further incentive to glean as much as he can from what they say of what they think. He enters his new town surrounded at his new post by garrulous gents and ladies (whom he deems elderly at fifty-one or so) adjured by the generous traditions of the trade to conduct—free, gratis, and for nothing—crash courses in the local history. If he is shrewd, he listens, and if he isn't shrewd he listens anyway, because reporters tell good stories and they're fun to collect, like old coins.

If you listen to those stories, and remember them as well, you will not only have good times on slow nights, but at greater leisure perceive what looks a lot like a common thread. That *leitmotif* is that no matter what the stated offense that brought somebody down, the secular punishment that followed was either for flouting the consensus, or rank hypocrisy. Nothing I heard and saw later, prosecuting and defending here, changed my view on that. I think you can get away with quite a lot in New England, as a good many of us do, if you are discreet enough to do it privately and never boast that you are doing it and getting away with it, or claim that you aren't doing it. The Reverend Mr. Dimmesdale knew that; his whole life in Hawthorne's *Scarlet Letter* was destroyed anew each time he saw Hester with her A, because he in his position was impliedly announcing he himself was pure of lust. Since the community never caught on, he quite properly finished himself off. Good story, that—pure New England, too.

The Mafia trials that I watched as Springfield AP correspondent, that summer of '63, had great effects upon me. The immediate effect—since the AP office was in City Hall, much closer to the Hampden Superior Courthouse than the UPI (OSN) office north on Main Street—was that they enabled me to provide superior coverage to AP members. That attracted more AP members, which meant that the bureau was no longer a loss-leader—it was making money. The intermediate effect was that glimmerings of reality appeared before my eyes (and the ultimate effect was that I decided to go to law school).

I hated law school. It was boring. I had to study a lot of stuff that didn't interest me at all. What I needed was the rules of evidence and the rules of criminal procedure, and the diploma that would enable me to take the bar exam. But to get the diploma, I had to pass Trusts and Estates, and Commercial Law, and Civil Procedure, and Labor Law, and a whole bunch of other courses that intrigued me about as much as a three-year seminar in square dancing. So I did it, griping all the way, and I learned a lot.

I emerged from law school, still equipped with John's and Charlie's experience, into a cold February afternoon of 1967, with snow blowing down the canyon of Boston's Milk Street, with: a 1961 A.B. from Boston College; a 1965 M.A. from Stanford University; a law degree expected in June of 1967 from the Boston College Law School; a wife who wanted to have children soon; the sickening residue of a bad interview with a worse lawyer who had offered me sixty-five dollars a week to do scut work for him; no other job prospects or promising leads; and all my prejudices intact. I encountered Walter Jay Skinner (now a Boston federal judge), whom I had come to know in 1963 when he as an Assistant Attorney General prosecuted the Hancock Raceway cases in the Hampden Superior Court in Springfield. When he committed the blunder of asking me how things were going, I told him. Those trials had done much to inflame my judgment that my destiny in life was to try cases. Now here I was, almost ready to do that, and I couldn't get a job.

"Elliot Richardson's hiring staff," Jay said, of the new Attorney General. "Why not apply to him?" And all of my gloomy bitterness at nearly everything in the world came out in one sour response along approximately these lines: "Oh, sure," I said. "Yankee Republican. I bet he's really beating the bushes for Irish Catholic Democrats without political connections. Can't find enough of them."

Jay Skinner's a nice man, nice enough to be harsh when the situation dictates. "Why don't you grow up?" he said. "That stuff's all gone by. Elliot doesn't care."

He didn't, either. And when he was succeeded by Robert H. Quinn, Democratic Speaker of the Massachusetts House of Representatives, chosen by that body to complete Richardson's term in 1969, I discovered to my further gratification that the highly political Mr. Quinn did not expect the resignations of Mr. Richardson's appointees, or any reduction of their prosecutorial zeal, but rather wished that they remain in place for as long as they wanted, party renegades or no.

Such signal but far from singular demonstrations of decency from unexpected quarters over the years demolished many of the self-defensive certitudes that I inherited from forebears. Their credence of those certitudes in their own times was surely justified, but sometime before I reached the point in my life where my efforts to make my way called for their application, those certitudes became obsolete. Without for a moment meaning to imply that ethnic, religious, and racial prejudices are things of the past in New England, I have to posit the fact that I have either not suffered their application, or else have been too dense to see what was done to me. I prefer the former hypothesis. In the occasional contemplative moment, I have wondered whether there might perhaps be other areas in which my own empirical data indicate that some ideas I always trusted have also become obsolete. I have decided that there are.

Those coastal differences in decadent behavior that bothered me at Stanford I think attributable to the disparity between the two regions in likelihood of community disapproval for shameful acts, and the consequent ability of the actors to commit them without shame. Sin has always been pleasant, and therefore most of us have sinned. But in New England there was then and remains today a strong if reduced community consensus that when the self gets out of control, it had better be discreet. It is perfectly all right to remark that consensus as a lingering remainder of bluenose Puritanism, in my case and many others intensifed by an Irish Catholic upbringing of that Jansenist subspecies. It is permissible as well to sneer at all its public manifestations, whether egregious (Boston Mayor Raymond Flynn's leadership of censors enraged by local production of *Sister Mary Ignatius Explains It All for You*) or moderate (protests by Irish Americans convinced that *Globe* cartoonist Paul Szep, portraying a leprechaun as a rat in an anti-IRA panel, would not have taken similar liberties depicting a Jewish villain of whom he disapproved), and it is indisputable as well that an element of hypocrisy is often involved in the enforcement of a public morality. But as Harvard's James Q. Wilson has so often pointed out, the enforcement of personal codes of morality and ethics, whatever their defects, first by the family and then by the community, is the engine which drives the machinery of social order. When those codes, however repressive, begin to break down, as they did about twenty years ago, the burdens of law enforcement increase geometrically.

It is in the nature of humankind, I think— *vulneratis in naturalibus, spoiliatus in supernaturalibus* —to seek limits on behavior. When there are no visible limits, when the keenest eye cannot discern a probably informal punishment for previously merely shameful behavior, the more timid among us will behave shamefully, while the boldest will be piqued by the temptation to investigate whether there exist formal punishments for criminal acts. During the second of my three years as an Assistant U.S. Attorney in Boston, the presentencing reports prepared by the probation office on convicted defendants so regularly recorded ineffectual or utterly absent paternal influence of the subjects in their formative years that then-U.S. Attorney (now U.S. District Judge) Joseph L. Tauro and I began to keep an informal log of such entries; after six months or so, when the 93 percent incidence of such findings had been steady for a while, we stopped, and declared our suspicions confirmed. If, as my children have occasionally alleged, I am rather more vigilant of their comings-in and their goings-out than is strictly necessary, that is a part of the reason.

I am not sure I could marshal social reinforcements somewhere else to make such vigilance effective. The New England code of acceptable behavior, though marked by repeated infractions, remains in my estimation relatively sturdy, and however censorious and frequently irritating, accounts in considerable part for the fact that life here is more orderly than I have found it elsewhere. We have retained a sense of decency, still powerful enough to prompt even those flouting it, and getting caught, to feel a sense of guilt.

Writers need context. If the context permeates the writing, then the writer can dismount confidently from the high horse of judgment, allow the characters to tell the story, and leave it to the readers to make the moral judgments. What I try to do, when I write stories, is stay the hell out of them, avoid making judgments, and leave the reader to decide whether the characters have behaved well or badly. I think that's the way it should be. Reading's a participatory sport, just like jury duty. The person

*Martyn J Adelman*

*Higgins, a 1986 portrait*

doing it should call the close ones, and the ones that aren't so close, as well.

Molière equated writing with prostitution: first you do it for love, then for a few friends, and finally for money. Molière left something out: You have to be very lucky to make money doing something that you love.

## BIBLIOGRAPHY

**Fiction:**

*The Friends of Eddie Coyle.* New York: Knopf, 1972; London: Secker & Warburg, 1972.

*The Digger's Game.* New York: Knopf, 1973; London: Secker & Warburg, 1973.

*Cogan's Trade.* New York: Knopf, 1974; London: Secker & Warburg, 1974.

*A City on a Hill.* New York: Knopf, 1975; London: Secker & Warburg, 1975.

*The Judgment of Deke Hunter.* Boston and Toronto: Atlantic-Little, Brown, 1976; London: Secker & Warburg, 1976.

*Dreamland.* Boston: Little, Brown, 1977; London: Secker & Warburg, 1977.

*A Year or So with Edgar.* New York: Harper, 1979; London: Secker & Warburg, 1979.

*Kennedy for the Defense.* New York: Knopf, 1980; London: Secker & Warburg, 1980.

*The Rat on Fire.* New York: Knopf, 1981; London: Secker & Warburg, 1981.

*The Patriot Game.* New York: Knopf, 1982; London: Secker & Warburg, 1982.

*A Choice of Enemies.* New York: Knopf, 1984; London: Secker & Warburg, 1984.

*Penance for Jerry Kennedy.* New York: Knopf, 1985; London: Deutsch, 1985.

*Imposters.* New York: Holt, 1986; London: Deutsch, 1986.

*Outlaws.* New York: Holt, 1987; London: Deutsch, 1987.

**Nonfiction:**

*The Friends of Richard Nixon.* Boston and Toronto: Atlantic-Little, Brown, 1975.

*Style versus Substance: Boston, Kevin White, and the Politics of Illusion.* New York: Macmillan, 1984.

---

Portions of this essay appeared in the *New England Journal of Public Policy* (Summer/Fall 1985) and are used here with permission.

# Elizabeth Jennings

*1926-*

I was a clumsy child, always falling down stairs, rushing into furniture, running when it would have been more sensible to walk, a constant worry to my parents. Yet, somehow, I generally fell lightly. My first fall happened when I was a baby, working my way along a passage on my pot; there was a nursery gate but some careless person had left it open. So, typically, down I tumbled. I can remember very clearly being picked up off the stone floor of the pantry and having butter rubbed into my napper. I was quite unhurt.

I have had five head injuries in my life but only two in the home where I was born in Boston, Lincolnshire. It was and is a very flat county, where sugar beet is an important crop. Also Boston is close to Spalding, where rows and rows of shining, upright red, yellow, and white tulips are grown. All this part of Lincolnshire was called Holland and it is no wonder that I became extremely muddled about the real Holland, the country of the Dutch people which lay across the North Sea. It too was flat and it also grew magnificent tulips.

My father was a doctor. He had done all his medical studies at St. Thomas's Hospital in London which is situated opposite the Houses of Parliament. His father was the chief pharmacist at the same hospital but I never met him; he died in his early fifties when I was only two years old. My mother, not given to sentimentality though an extremely gentle, easily hurt woman, has often told me that he was a joy to have in the house. His wife was a very different kind of person.

I am glad I spent my first six years in Boston because this gives me a deadline for my memories. People sometimes say to me, "You don't remember that. Somebody told you." They are wrong because I can recall with great keenness the smell of honeysuckle, the first flower that I remember. It is, in a way, for me what the little madeleine cake was to Proust; it is the starting point for a great cluster of memories, things seen, touched, tasted, and heard.

My sister is two years older than I am and, talking to her recently, I noticed that she has very different detailed memories from mine. A poet's childhood is usually a great storehouse of exciting events, passions, throngs of touchings and handlings. Wordsworth, of course, is probably the greatest English poet who

would share this view adamantly.

The second time I bumped my head (and cut it) was when I was four and, as usual, as a result of rushing into a room and hitting a low chair. I remember having the cut stitched up; it was quite painless. My last childhood head injury really was unpleasant and painful. I cycled into a tree—head down as usual—when I was nine and the next thing I remember was being carried into the house. I realize now that my father was observing me after this episode to see if I had concussion. I was put to bed and my mother was reading to me from *The Blue Fairy Book* when I started vomiting. This was a clear indication that I was concussed. The following day a consultant visited me and said I must sleep with my head sloping and stay in a dark room for three weeks.

The day I was visited by the parish priest really alarmed me and, when my sister, quite correctly, said, "You'll die after this," I let out a very loud yell!

*Elizabeth, three-and-a-half years old*

I am enlarging on these illnesses (there were plenty of others) because I feel fairly convinced that a lot of poets are physically clumsy. Auden was a perfect example of this; every room he lived in was soon a chaos of books, papers, records, and even cats. Yet he wrote with extraordinary dexterity, elegance, and metrical and verbal skill. It does seem then, that perhaps clumsiness—I was called in my family "A member of the Awkward Squad"—makes potential poets particularly eager to achieve order in their work, to shape a world where there is civilisation, purpose, and reason.

Of course one can think of poets who were very skilful at manual labour or even at painting. Blake and David Jones spring to mind. Keats, as a doctor, could not possibly have been clumsy, nor, in a different way, was Chaucer since he worked in a high position in the fourteenth-century customs and tax office. And, of course, Shakespeare—who breaks all known rules—must have been expert at many activities from shooting and acting, to selecting from Holinshed or Plutarch, or some other source, the precise material he needed for, say *Julius Caesar* or *Henry V.* I am not saying that clumsiness or any other affliction makes a poet but I do think (again with Auden) that the deeps of a poet's imaginative sources are sometimes plumbed because he is not simply compensating for his physical disadvantages—Byron's club foot, Pope's small stature, Eliot's early shyness with women—but rather that most human gifts have their acute disadvantages and it seems quite possible that some even minor physical defects may actually strengthen a poet's mind and its expression. If one believes in the Fall of Man which, as a Roman Catholic I do, then this makes very good sense. To put it in simpler terms, you have to pay for your gifts.

I was a very late developer; I did not read at an early age but, as far back as I can remember, I created cities or even worlds in which I lived a rich imaginative life. I created a secret brother whose name was Jack Baycock. I had no brother and longed for one but I think that the creation of Jack went deeper than that. He was the signpost to the life of my imagination; he pointed the way to worlds which had almost no boundary.

I must have been at most four years old when I created or found Jack. In Boston he inhabited the greenhouse. I used to talk about him to my sister and parents and nanny and they did not tease me about him, which says a lot for their good sense and understanding.

I enjoyed nursery rhymes but not more than prose stories which were read to me. But I was fascinated by stories about families such as *Little Women, Little Men, What Katy Did,* and later the E. Nesbit novels. Yet my

*At age four*

most clearly remembered images of those years leading to my fifth birthday are highly visual—bright green asparagus beds, yellow and red roses, pink hollyhocks, the grey stones of rockeries, our nursery with its white walls and furniture. Even today, I sometimes wish that I were a painter because painting and drawing, whether abstract or representational, give one so much more freedom. And yet it was, on the other hand, the discipline of form, metre, and rhythm which gripped me when I first began to hear poetry as poetry, not just a pattern of words and sounds.

When we left Lincolnshire my sister and I were driven to Bristol to stay with my mother's parents while she and my father went to Oxford to look for a house. Much later I learned that he had taken a drop in salary because he wanted to give us both a good education. There can surely be few debts more gratefully owed to a parent than the gift of a splendid education.

In the car on the way to Bristol I was crying quietly in the backseat. When this became evident my parents began to inquire tenderly what was the matter. The tears then fell in floods and I managed to sob, "I miss Ethel." Ethel was our nursery governess and I certainly cannot remember feeling any great devotion to her while she was with us. I soon recovered from this rather unusual form of homesickness and I remember the thrill of eating lunch in an hotel. What the first course was I cannot remember but the second (dessert) was cherry pie.

Oddly I have no recollection of any scenes of tears or anguish when my parents left us with our grandparents. They lived in a large, tall house near the Bristol downs; its largeness was not a childhood fantasy, for my mother was one of nine children, all but one younger than herself, and five of them were still living at home. My grandmother was a beautiful woman: childbearing had done no harm to her for there had always been plenty of servants. My grandfather was the Bank Manager of the Bristol main Midland Bank. He was a very tall, slender man who painted in his spare time and also collected pewter. He was a fine freshwater and seawater fisherman. He never lost his temper and I recall vividly his teaching my sister and myself to play darts.

I have heard it said that painting changes to poetry in two generations; it is probably just an old saying but my great-grandfather had been more than a competent painter in oils, so maybe there is a fragment of truth in that saying. In Bristol my sister and I shared a room with my youngest aunt, Ruth. She seemed extremely old to me but she cannot have been much older than twelve or thirteen. Her life was consumed by a passion for horseriding and, I thought even then, that her features were beginning to take on an equine look! I remember that one night she told us of a terrible riding accident that her teacher had endured. I said, "She must have suffered as much as Jesus." My aunt was horrified by this statement and told me I should not say anything so blasphemous. This was a ridiculous reaction because I was telling the worst sort of suffering that a child could think of.

Christmas came soon and with it my father and mother who told us they had found a fairly large, newly built house in Oxford. Immediately after Christmas we were driven to Oxford. My mother showed us what would be both our day nursery and night nursery. She opened the doors of a white cupboard and showed us all our toys beautifully arranged in it. However, all I said was, "Where is my blue car catalogue?" My poor mother said, "Oh, how dreadful, I threw it away. I didn't know you cared for it so much, darling." I did not repine for long.

The first time we went into Oxford with its great streets of colleges and shops, my mother unwisely jumped off a bus at the traffic lights and there my sister and I were, standing scared stiff like a pair of waifs on the steps of the bus. However, my mother ran after us and rescued us and then took us into Woolworth's. In the early thirties, everything still cost only threepence or sixpence in our old currency. There was a magical toy department with china and celluloid dolls of every size and shape, boxes of magnificent doll's furniture, clockwork cars and locomotives, and dozens of other

desirable playthings. Later I was to buy a violin, strings and bow and all, for the then princely sum of one sixpence.

But we were soon to discover an even more dazzlingly magical toy shop called *De la Mare's*. There you could purchase beautiful tiny things for dolls and dolls' houses—"silver" tea sets, tiny cakes, boxes of three tablets of scented soap, miniature telephones, bookcases with books in them, radios, chairs, tables, baths, wash basins, and uncountable other fascinating delights. To this day I am an ardent collector of small things.

But Oxford was by no means to prove totally joyful. In mid-January we were sent to a Catholic private school. The only school I had been to in Boston was a nursery school run by a charming, patient, and always happy Miss Pilcher. All I had done there was to crayon pictures, play the triangle in a little band (I always yearned for a drum!), and collect frogs and lizards. This new school was to prove to be the first "prison-house," as Wordsworth called such places. It was run by two Catholic ladies who were pioneers in that they were not nuns. On the face of it this does sound reassuring, since nuns are (or were) notorious for being strict, didactic, and zealously religious. However, one of the teachers employed by these two ladies was more imbued with false piety than any reactionary nun.

Almost from the first week I felt ill at ease at this school. I cannot remember exactly when I learnt to read but I was certainly a late starter. In every lesson I felt out of my depth, as if I were struggling hopelessly

*Elizabeth, while a student at a Catholic private school, about 1935*

against a fierce tide of well-intentioned but highly misguided teaching. For example, one of the two headmistresses had constructed a system for learning grammar which was supposed to simplify it. For me it proved complex to the point of almost total incomprehension. This lesson was not made easier by the fact that pupils of all ages from six to seventeen attended this lesson, which was given in a general sense of awed hush.

But much worse than the lessons were the educational and moral notions of a younger teacher. One day, I miraculously got all my arithmetic sums correct. This mistress proved highly sceptical about this and asked me if my sister had helped me; I lied, out of fear, and said "No," whereupon the teacher in question learnt the truth from my sister. What followed was to prove my first unhappiness about my "Cradle Catholic" religion. I was taken into a small room and kissed (out of forgiveness); I recoiled and to this day cannot endure the smell of powder on another's face. I was still only six years old so could not go to confession. However, my sister and I were taken along a distance of about half-a-mile to the nearest Catholic church "to tell God we were sorry." Why my sister was forced to go to confession I shall never know. I knelt before the tabernacle and made an Act of Contrition. I did not feel angry with God, only a deep sense of muddled fear.

My sister flourished at this school and was highly successful at work and games. Gradually I began to accept the fact that I was an idiot, a moron, one incapable of learning anything. Soon I started to steal small objects I did not even cherish or want—a card from a teacher's English lesson, small useless pieces of someone else's toy train set. In short, I was on the way to becoming a classic case of juvenile delinquency. My father must have felt sure that there was more in me than appeared evident, for he decided to change our school.

In those days Catholic children were forced to go to a Catholic school if one was available. My father showed great moral courage when he went to one parish priest and said, "I am going to send the children to the Oxford High School." The priest, somewhat flustered, replied, "I shall have to get the Archbishop's permission." "Whether you get it or not," replied my father boldly, "I shall move them to the High School." That act of bravery of his was certainly the turning point in my life. If he had not made it, I might not be writing this brief autobiography of a poet at this moment.

The new school, the Oxford High School, was a wonderful place. I was put in a class with many girls a little younger than me because that spring I had had concussion while riding a child's bicycle, and my parents were afraid that I might easily get bad headaches if I were put into a higher form. From the moment I stepped into that classroom I felt a vast awakening; a true liberation was upon me.

We were taught English language and literature, history, geography, and French by a slim, lively teacher called Miss Wilson. She was a great teacher, drew me out, opened up my imagination, and taught me the wonder of knowledge. I think I was probably her favourite but none of the other girls took this out of me (there were no boys at this school then). I loved *Julius Caesar* but I did not really like poetry much then; I did not think of Shakespeare as a poet! Everything came easily to me and I experienced the happy truth that I was really quite an intelligent child of ten. However, I was soon having accidents and illnesses. One day, when we were playing a somewhat violent game called Wild Horses, I emerged from the bottom of a heap of children with an almost broken right arm. This was called a green-stick fracture because a child's bones have not yet become hardened even at the age of ten.

The only way I could be made to stay still was to be kept in bed with a big sling on my arm. I had a long table beside my bed covered with model cars, farm animals, a doll's house, and almost every small toy I possessed. Typically kindly, Miss Wilson wrote me letters and sent me easy lessons to do. After three weeks I was back at school but only to succumb to what was then called congestion of the lungs.

But apart from illnesses this was a happy time for me. I began to win prizes for the year's work. I did not become adolescent until I was fifteen but I began to love poetry when I was thirteen. One day in an English literature class we read G.K. Chesterton's great battle poem "Lepanto"; I was gathered up and carried away. I felt a strange new excitement and I went home and wrote a very enthusiastic essay. In my Term Report our wonderful English teacher wrote, "Latterly she has developed a taste for poetry."

I had developed more than a taste; I was experiencing a new passion. We soon went on to study Wordsworth, Coleridge, Keats, and Shelley. When I read Keats's "Ode on a Grecian Urn,"

Thou still unravished bride of quietness,

or Coleridge's *Ancient Mariner,*

And ice, mast-high, came floating by,
As green as emerald.

or Wordsworth's sonnet written on Westminster Bridge,

Earth has not anything to show more fair

my spirit and senses were quickened. I had entered into my own kingdom.

It was at this time that I began to write verse itself, and very bad it was! But at least I was trying to use strict forms such as sonnets, ballads, and odes. At this time too, when I was so receptive to every kind of sensuous and intellectual stimulus, I had my first "crush," as it was sometimes called, on a girl older than myself; I suppose she was only seventeen but of course in childhood a year is a whole epoch.

Nancy Waters (that was her name) was tall, had straight, thick black hair, and a beautiful complexion. I was in the incubating period of love but this was love most certainly. Nancy had taught me the Girl Guide Law but it was not until one of the girls in my form told me that she liked me that I realized how very much I admired and was awed by her. She once sent me a message in Morse on April 1st and I had to ask a friend to decode it; it said, "April Fool!" There is a natural and unique purity in love like this. I did not want to talk to Nancy, let alone touch her; I was only grateful if I could watch her and worship her from far off.

Before I became adolescent I began to have religious doubts and difficulties. The first of these came upon me quite suddenly when I was lying on my bed one hot summer afternoon. For no reason that I can remember I suddenly thought, "What really is the Holy Ghost?" I thought at once of a huge bird (I had not at that age, of course, read Gerard Manley Hopkins's great poem "The Windhover," in which an analogy is drawn between a bird and the Holy Ghost). A child is always literal-minded, and of course I at once thought, "The Holy Ghost can't be a bird." After that doubt or difficulty dozens of others besieged me and I was helpless before the attacks. The parish priest, a convert who had been to a great English public school, Winchester, and to Oxford University, tried to deal with each doubt as it came along. I continued to practice my religion but I think that only the reading and writing of poetry and my hero-worshipping lightened these years before I entered adolescence some months after my fifteenth birthday.

From that time I began to find that mathematics was very difficult. Like many children I had a capacious and totally reliable memory. As long as I could learn up a book full of geometrical theorems, I could reproduce any of them in an examination the following day. But when it came to applied mathematics or algebra, I was totally lost. I continued to love and to be good at English literature and history and, though no linguist, I could learn French, Latin, and Greek very swiftly. By the time I was fifteen I was studying biology and dissecting rabbits and dogfish. The stench of these

and the formaldehyde they were pickled in nauseated me and I could not eat meat or fish for several months. I was squeamish always, quite unlike my sister who loved all science and would have made a very good doctor had not marriage claimed her.

At this time I had begun to send out my verses in long brown envelopes. Back they came relentlessly through the letterbox. They deserved to be rejected but I was greatly warmed one day when a rejection slip from the *New English Weekly* (long since dead) contained the hand-written words, "These poems show talent."

Most of my teenage years were spent during the Second World War. Oxford was "a safe area" and so my mother not only had to have evacuees for a time from a London school but also one of her sisters and her husband who was then working at the Ministry of Information in London. She was dreadfully overworked and had little help with maids or charwomen and by this time also had my father's mother (the subject of one of my later published poems) who was a difficult old lady. From the age of thirteen to eighteen I became quite impervious to tears because my grandmother would nag us at mealtimes and my father would chide her. She would then burst into tears.

It is shameful that because Oxford was in a "safe area" my worst recollection of the war was hunger. There were very few sweets, and sugar, butter, and almost everything else were severely rationed. However, apart from this my life went on much as usual. I was often in trouble at school but for very minor offences. For example, I was once sent out of the room for whistling in a drawing lesson, where (such was my bad luck) I was found by the headmistress who would give me the extra punishment of staying in for "break," as recreation in the playground was called, the following day. I always used to wonder what happened if you stole or swore or committed some really serious crime! One day I had a real physical fight in the playground with a girl who led a gang of young Marxists. I knew they were atheists. I was skinny but the girl I fought was wiry and she held my wrist and was about to twist it when, mercifully, the bell rang.

Soon I was in the Lower Sixth Form and working for my entrance examination to St. Anne's College in Oxford. I decided to study English but I needed extra coaching in that as well as in Latin. I had a childish conviction that at Oxford I could acquire all knowledge. I took the word "university" quite literally. I passed my entrance exam in the February before I went up to St. Anne's in October.

This is the time to say something of my rapidly developing passion for the theatre. As a small child I had owned two theatres, and when I was a very young fifteen a friend of mine and I wrote alternate scenes of a play called *The Spell of the Desert*. Of course we wrote ourselves long "star" parts, which was probably the reason why our other friends were not too eager to play the "bit" parts.

Two years before my entrance into St. Anne's I had been taken in a school party to see John Gielgud in *Macbeth*. He became my actor hero from that day to this. It seems an odd, horrific play in which to discover an actor whose work I would love for the rest of my life. (I now from time to time enjoy a delightful correspondence with Sir John. He writes most vivid and witty letters.) But of course Gielgud's Macbeth was no ranting, bloodthirsty, ambitious, ruthless power-seeker. He was a sensitive, highly imaginative power-seeker led on by his ambitious wife. I heard the famous Gielgud voice with its infinitely variable tones, its subtly altered tempos, its pure magnetism.

Just before my first term at Oxford began, I saw John Gielgud again, this time in Congreve's *Love for Love* and then in what turned out to be his last *Hamlet*. His company came for two weeks to the vast theatre in Oxford and played to packed houses every night. My father took my sister and myself and we sat in excellent seats in the dress circle. I can only say that for weeks after seeing Gielgud's *Hamlet* I was utterly obsessed by the play and his interpretation of it. I say with absolute honesty that this *Hamlet* was not only the greatest theatrical experience of my life but also the greatest aesthetic one. To this day I remember the utterly compassionate way in which Gielgud said, "Alas poor Yorick" and "There's a special providence in the fall of a sparrow."

I nearly went down (as leaving the university is called in Oxford) on my first day when I was told I must translate a piece of Anglo-Saxon verse in *one* week. Anglo-Saxon is virtually a foreign language. Somehow I managed to overcome this seemingly insuperable task. Oxford at once was a place of excitement for me. Although I soon abandoned my hope of acquiring all knowledge, I did join a number of societies—religious, philosophical, and literary. I also acted in a one-act play of Noel Coward's, *Hands across the Sea,* for the Experimental Theatre Club. I attended the high-powered philosophical society called the *Socratic Club* every Monday evening, though I was much too over-awed ever to open my mouth. C.S. Lewis never failed to attend this society and sat quietly in a corner until almost the end of the meeting. He would then, in one or two simple sentences, gently and courteously dispose of some particularly fatuous piece of pseudo-thinking.

C.S. Lewis also gave lectures every Saturday morning to a packed Magdalen College Hall. He would give learned but lucid *Prolegomenon* to Medieval

or Renaissance literature. Countless people who were not even studying English literature attended these masterpieces of the art of lecturing undergraduates. C.S. Lewis helped to open their minds, forget their prejudices, and allow them to feel the kind of awe they had mostly lost in their early childhoods.

No lectures were obligatory but I never missed any of C.S. Lewis's. Lord David Cecil was also a popular lecturer and a natural English eccentric. He would enter a lecture hall with hair and papers flying in all directions. He too made compulsive listening; he loved his subjects so much whether they were the English Romantic poets or Jane Austen. Stories about him and his family became legends. One likely one was that when a tradesman's boy delivering groceries came to the backdoor, Lord David Cecil answered the bell. The boy said, "May I see your mistress?" whereupon the wildly attired aristocrat replied in his characteristic high-pitched voice, "I live with my wife." Another story went about which declared that, when one of Lord David's young sons was asked what he wanted to be when he grew up, he said, "I want to be a neurotic like Daddy!"

These are jokes. There was plenty of very enjoyable seriousness at Oxford. I was up at the university at a very lucky time. The famous Jesuit Father Martin D'Arcy was the Master of Campion Hall then. I remember being sent to him with religious doubts and difficulties. He evidently spotted at once that I was genuinely troubled, because he took all my queries about Aquinas and Berkeley and so on with perfect gravity and answered them all in a beautifully simple way.

I met my first boyfriend during this first term. His name was Francis, and we met at a tea party given for new undergraduates at the University Catholic Chaplaincy. Francis invited me to lunch at the restaurant of the Oxford Union, the University Debating Society.

Because of the war I had never been to a London theatre or to any of its art galleries. Fortunately for me I became friends with another student of my year; her name was Justine O'Sullivan. She lived in London and I spent much of the vacations of my first year in London. I saw John Gielgud's *Hamlet* again, this time in London's most beautiful theatre, the Haymarket, which is all blue and gold inside. London was a revelation for me. As a child I had always felt that it was a great centre where all the artists, actors, and great men and women of my country lived. So it appeared to me.

Justine's mother somehow got us tickets in the back stalls for one of the great postwar theatrical occasions at the New Theatre (now called the Albany); it was Shakespeare's *Henry IV, Part One* with Ralph Richardson as Falstaff and Laurence Olivier as Hotspur. The auditorium was as star-packed as the stage, and I went round getting autographs (in my tiny university diary) of John Gielgud, Malcolm Sargent the conductor, Noel Coward, and James Agate, a very noted theatre critic. They were all charming to me. I must have looked very young and callow.

I fell in love for the first time during the winter vacation of my third year at Oxford. It was at a party and it was also love at first sight, at least on my part. I am a romantic and always have been. During the course of this party there was an indoor team-game, and Stuart (the man in question) picked me first for his side to my huge gratification. He was seven years older than me and had been a prisoner of war in Japan during the Second World War. He was slim then and had dark brown eyes and slightly wavy dark brown hair. Far from being disillusioned by imprisonment, he discovered a deep interest in Buddhism.

Falling in love for the first time has a unique magic. It pervades your whole being, it makes you feel almost levitated, and you feel warmly and delightfully well disposed towards the whole world. I did not see Stuart again until he invited me to tea with him at Keble College. At that time he was writing rather good poems, but these never came to anything. This was in the spring term of my last year and now, of course, love took over from work. When spring really began we spent a lot of time punting on the river. Stuart's home was in Oxford so I saw a great deal of him during the six-week vacation before the summer term.

A few days before my nine papers in the Honours School of English Language and Literature, I opened my *Anglo-Saxon Reader* and had a very unpleasant shock. It seemed once more like a foreign language to me. However, my memory was still very good and I "mugged up," as we say, on all my subjects and learnt quotations from every period of English literature, which I hoped to fit into some of the countless questions awaiting me.

Every morning of the examinations Stuart brought me a different-coloured carnation and every evening at 5:30 P.M. when I came out of the day's second paper, he gave me one glass of Pimm's Number One, a long, gin-based drink. Then he sent me home. During these five days my father gave me a sleeping pill each night. I do not know what it was called, but it had no after-effects and I used to wake up mightily refreshed at about 7:30 every morning and learn quotations by heart.

I had so looked forward with every hope to the end of Finals—balls, parties, every kind of celebration—but I had not reckoned on the vast exhaustion,

nervous and physical, which I felt after the papers were over. But youth is resilient and I soon recovered. All through the following summer months (when I celebrated my twenty-first birthday) I saw Stuart every day. We punted, canoed, swam in the Thames and Cherwell, and he also took me up to London for exciting days.

It was he who introduced me to Chinese food, and with him I saw *Oklahoma!* at the Drury Lane theatre. My Finals' result came out that July. I was very lucky indeed to get a Second Class. Although Stuart was so much older than me, he still had another year at Oxford; there were special courses for ex-servicemen. I naturally wanted to be up too. I decided to do a further degree, a B.Litt., as it was called, on *Matthew Arnold as a Romantic and Classical Poet*. I had not, however, reckoned on the very difficult preliminary exam.

It was during the seminar in which we were taught Court Hand-Writing that I met Kingsley Amis. He introduced me to jazz and we spent hours in record shops, and also went to the cinema sometimes. Kingsley was writing a lot of poems then. He was a humorous and enchanting companion and had decided views on everything to do with literature. He detested the theatre and Milton and most classical music but he never teased me, at least never unkindly, about my more conventional tastes. Neither of us knew that he was married and I engaged at this time! But our friendship never turned into any kind of love affair.

Kingsley began to read and admire my poems and he and another young man, now long forgotten, put five of my early ones in the annual *Oxford Poetry* published by the world-famous bookseller Blackwell's. I failed my B.Litt. exam and decided to get a job in London. During this year at Oxford I had become very interested in other young men (as I've already said, I was a late developer). Stuart was my first love but now others were claiming my attention. One in particular, called Peter Chettle, a law student at University College, and also another ex-serviceman attracted me very much and this seemed to be mutual.

Although my engagement was rapidly becoming fraught, I still wanted to be in London while Stuart was there. He had now finished his Oxford Finals in English Language and Literature and had enrolled at the London Institute of Oriental and African Studies. The world of the East was his real passion.

I worked with an advertising agency as a copywriter. I obtained the job through meeting someone in the firm. I would write headlines and copy for Richard Shops and Simpson's Sportswear. I found that this activity made my style extremely relaxed and slick, because I was by now having poems published here and there in London magazines such as the *Spectator* and the *Poetry Review*. There was not really sufficient work for me in the agency. I sat in a tiny room with a very temperamental lady much older than myself. I was not allowed to speak to her while she banged out her copy on a very noisy typewriter. She also used me as an errand-boy (or girl!) and got me to take her clothes to the dry cleaners and to deliver sandwiches to her while she sat under a hair-dryer.

That July was one of the unhappiest in my early life, because I was not only virtually fired from the agency but my engagement broke up. Although I was no longer in love with Stuart I still missed him and, because I was publicly engaged and wearing a zircon-and-diamond engagement ring, I found it very painful being asked frequently when I was back in Oxford and living at home, "When are you going to be married?"

A pleasant young man reading history took me out a great deal very soon, and we would go for long walks and look at old churches, but I was not in love with him. That Christmas he sent me Walter de la Mare's anthology entitled *Love* and within it placed a Pre-Raphaelite reproduction on a postcard called *Love Locked Out!* I was, after a few sad months without work, now working in the Oxford City Library in a physically demanding job for a very small salary.

This turned out to be ideal in many ways; undergraduates who were interested in my poetry and who also usually wrote poems themselves would come in and invite me out for my brief tea-time or for dinner and a play or film. It was at this library that I began to meet young men who have become famous since— Geoffrey Hill, Adrian Mitchell, the American poets Donald Hall and Adrienne Rich, and other English poets such as Anthony Thwaite, Alan Brownjohn, and others. So this was a hectic time. I wrote my own poems, as I still usually do, late at night.

Gradually I was assembling enough poems to make a full-length book, but I had not as yet found a publisher. Thanks to Michael Hamburger, the poet and translator who mentioned me to her, Janet Adam Smith, the literary editor of the *New Statesman,* had accepted some of my poems. It has always been necessary in England to have appeared in magazines before a publisher will take on the risk of a whole volume of poems. At this time there was a private printer who lived in a small village called Eynsham outside Oxford. He started printing and publishing a series of small pamphlets which held about eight or nine poems. This was the Fantasy Press Poets series, and my work was in the first pamphlet which cost sixpence in predecimal currency. It is now a very valuable series because it included in its list Philip Larkin, Geoffrey Hill, Adrienne Rich, Donald Hall, Adrian Mitchell, Anthony

Thwaite, Kingsley Amis, and many other writers who are now famous.

Oscar Mellor, the owner of the press, decided to produce a full-length book of my poems—forty in number. I was very excited about this and had the good fortune to receive an Arts Council Prize with it for a First Book of Poems written within a certain period. So began for me what can only be called "the star treatment." Local and London photographers and journalists came to the Oxford City Library to take photographs and to interview me. *Time and Tide* and the *Spectator* wrote to ask me for articles and book reviews.

I was then twenty-seven and as I try to see myself thirty-odd years ago, I find it hard to decide what sort of effect this fame had upon me. It excited me certainly and I was somewhat elated. I don't believe, however, that it changed my attitude toward other people. If I was conceited, this wasn't evident to others. I did, however, begin to feel that I ought to have at least one poem or book review a week in one of the big London journals, including those I have already mentioned as well as the *Times Literary Supplement* and the *Listener*.

Almost at the moment when I won the prize for my *Poems* volume, John Lehmann, who had included a poem of mine in the first recording of his BBC radio literary programme called "New Soundings," was about to publish the first number of the *London Magazine*. He included three of my poems in the first issue along with some of Thom Gunn's early poems. T.S. Eliot wrote a special introduction. Stephen Spender was also about to start *Encounter* and he too wrote to ask me for poems.

The poems I was writing at this time still showed some influence of Auden and Robert Graves but there was a clarity, a kind of lyrical innocence which I still find valid today. I never caught Auden's own voice, luckily, but I learnt from him something that has proved invaluable to me ever since, even when I have not been able by any means always to follow his example; it is to try to find the precise but unexpected adjective. This habit is everywhere apparent in Auden's work but I will cite only one example which appears in his celebrated poem "Lullaby" that begins, "Lay your sleeping head, my love." What I am speaking of resides in "thoughtful children." A lesser poet might well have written "thought*less* children."

Although I was having much success with my work at this period—the early 1950s—I was always worrying whether I could keep up the standards which I felt were demanded of me. A second book of verse is always a hazard. Critics are waiting to pounce and declare, "It doesn't live up to the promise shown in her first book." If you have enlarged your scope in the matter of theme and form you are unlikely to win even then, for journalists will say, "She is uneasy with her new subject-matter."

I did have a number of such reviews for my second book, *A Way of Looking,* but it did not matter because something very wonderful happened to it. It won me the Somerset Maugham Award in 1956. This award stipulated that the recipient "spend at least three months abroad in a country of his or her choice studying the manners and customs of a foreign people." This prize was then worth £400 but it was quite enough money in those days for a person to live comfortably (planes and trains included) for longer than three months. In fact I brought £80 home to England! I was given three months—April, May, and June—unpaid leave of absence from the Public Library.

I am quite sure that I owe the happiest and most worthwhile time of my life to this award and I shall always be grateful to Somerset Maugham for his generosity. I had spent four days in Rome once on the way to a holiday in Sorrento and it had given me a tantalising taste of that great city. When my mother saw me off at Heathrow I shed a few tears; after all, going alone abroad for three months is quite an adventure for a young person of only thirty. I had a lot of resilience then and was soon talking to an old lady in black who was going out to Rome for the ordination of her son who was at "the late vocation" seminary called the Beda.

I was travelling very light, just a small suitcase, a small grip, and a typewriter. Everything it was possible to buy in nylon I had purchased. I have always had my baggage opened in Rome when I have carried a typewriter. This time I was furious because a grubby customs officer simply put his rather dirty hands into my suitcase and lifted up and down my lovely, clean new clothes. Of course there was no trouble with guns and drugs then, and Rome's airport was then Ciampino, which was not far from the city. As soon as that unique smell of Italy, composed of dust, flowers, and heat, entered my nostrils I felt transformed. On my first full day in Rome however it rained and I needed my thick coat and warm sweater and, to my indignation, eventually was forced to buy an umbrella.

My pensione was on the penultimate floor of a huge building in Via Venti Settembre. It was called Pensione Wacker. The street was wide and quiet and rather like our Whitehall in London. Mine was called "a garden room" because it was very quiet and I never heard anything except the sound of cars being hosed and the very distant noise of traffic. I was in a wonderfully central position, within walking distance of Santa Maria Maggiore and the Spanish Steps, the Quirinal Palace and the Piazza Venezia. In those early days I

wandered alone round Rome armed with a map, a guidebook, an Italian Phrase Book, and a tiny dictionary. There was one great nuisance—the men who followed me. I could not go anywhere without knowing that a man was about nine yards behind me. I could not sit down in any park or garden for a second without a young man apparently shooting out of the ground, well-dressed and well-barbered. It infuriated me.

I was soon looking for a shop where I could buy soap flakes, and for a laundry. One day I saw an old lady standing in her doorway carefully and rhythmically ironing. "I shall take my shirts and summer frocks to her," I decided. I would not use my introductions for at least a week; it would have seemed a sort of admission of defeat if I had done so. Instead, I began to learn about the churches and ruins of Rome and to begin to chatter in very ungrammatical Italian. The Italians are a wonderfully courteous people; when I managed just a few halting words they would smile and say, "Bravissimo," which, of course, encouraged me to go on. The French are not polite in this way. They correct you the moment you make a mistake.

Even in the rain I discovered the intense beauty of Rome—the Borghese Gardens, the Palatine Hill with its crowd of cypresses, the Piazza Navona with its Bernini Fountain, the foot of the Spanish Steps with its flower-sellers and with John Keats's house which still looks inside exactly as it must have done when he lived there, coughing, longing for Fanny Brawne, but always writing.

I used to eat in trattorias where you always found good pasta and wine and a linen napkin, even in the cheapest. I was sitting in a tiny one when I wrote my first poem in Rome, a small lyric which ended:

> How someone on his elbow turns
> And in the moon's long exile here
> Touches another in the night.

I would have felt slightly guilty, I think, if I had written nothing at all in my first week in Rome.

After about a week I used my first introductory letter. It was to a duke who had written a book in English for my then publisher, André Deutsch. He took me to the Rupe Tarpea Jicky Club, the first nightclub I had ever been to. The Duke was a man of great charm and courtesy. He looked at the scantily clad women on the tiny stage and declared, "I've never seen so many ugly women in my life!" I was enjoying gazing at a handsome young man playing an accordian.

The following day the Duke took me to the Villa Borghese to see the sculpture and then in a carrozza to Trastevere, the oldest part of Rome where there were two famous restaurants where Spaghetti Carbonara was served.

A few days later I wrote to Princess Caetani, a great patron of literature in many languages. She published *Botteghe Oscure* and had put some of my poems in one of its numbers. A day later I was called to the telephone at about nine o'clock in the morning. I said, as is the Italian habit, "Pronto, pronto," and a voice with a slight American accent invited me to luncheon the following day in her palace in the Via Botteghe Oscure.

In one of my best summer dresses (the weather had greatly improved by now) and feeling extremely nervous I walked along to the Piazza Venezia from which the Via Botteghe Oscure led, and was greeted by a butler wearing white gloves. He took me in a lift up to the vast apartment in which the Princess and her ninety-year-old husband lived. I was intensely shy all through the luncheon, but afterwards Princess Caetani talked to me about poetry, Italy, publishing, and so on. She also introduced me to her young American assistant, Eugene Walter, who became a great friend and introduced me to many writers, English and American, most of whom seemed to be writing the script for a new *Ben Hur*.

Ten days after my luncheon with Princess Caetani, I went to confession in Santa Maria Maggiore, one of the four great Basilicas. For many centuries the Dominicans, called Canons Penitentiary, had been hearing confessions in this great church. There were about eight "boxes" and I had found one which gave a name which was indisputably English—Father Tindal-Atkinson. This confession was an unforgettable experience because it brought me spiritual happiness for the first time in my life. I said that perhaps I had drunk a little too much wine and the gentle voice said, "One over the eight or nicely thank you?" I had never had a laugh in the confessional before. But this priest was clearly also a very holy man and I soon got to know him as a friend as well as a confessor. He took me to many parts of Rome and outside Rome which I would never have discovered for myself—the Villa Guilia in the Borghese Gardens which held the great collection of Etruscan art, Anzio, now once more a fishing village (it had been one of the landing-places in the Second World War), and to Ostia Antica.

Rome was becoming a place that I fell in love with. I gabbled Italian and received great courtesy from all Italians. Nobody thought it odd that I was a poet; on the contrary, the simplest people thought it wonderful. I made friends with a little family who kept a trattoria just round the corner from my pensione. Maria, the wife, insisted that she was a "Leopardi" (her maiden name) "non Stefanini." Her husband, Gino, waited at table but also painted.

Easter came late that year and the weather cleared for the blessing "To the City and the World" from the then Pope, Pius XII.

I felt that for the first time in my life I was becoming a whole and happy person and I think I was aware of my good fortune. I wrote a number of poems in Rome which appeared in my third book, *A Sense of the World*. They included *Fountain, St. Paul Outside the Walls* (another of the four Basilicas), and *Letter from Assisi*. I went to Assisi for ten days after Rome and loved the utter peace there; I do not think it is so peaceful now. A fortnight in Florence came next. I had four weeks still left free and of course I went back to Rome for them. I had an unforgettable train journey through Tuscany into Umbria. My last week on Somerset Maugham's magnificently generous award was spent with an English friend in Paris. I was so deeply in love with Rome that I never came to like Paris very much, though I did enjoy Montmartre and the day we went to Chartres. But Paris is really a northern city and Rome a southern one, and I was made for the South.

I returned to my job at the Oxford City Library determined that I would soon leave, though not for some months. My three months in Rome in 1957 had cost only £320 and this included flights and first-class train travel. I spent the remaining £80 on a holiday in Rome in September. That is a beautiful time. The grapes are out and nuts and slices of red melons are sold at almost every street corner. When I returned from this two-week spell of autumn magic, I gave up my job but did not actually leave until the end of February 1958. I then went for thirteen weeks in Rome on my own money, beginning in early April. This, I suppose, was my second honeymoon with and in Rome.

My poetry was changing slowly. It did not cease to be mainly lyrical but my subject matter extended to religious themes. I also experimented with many forms, including the prose poem. But all this was not a deliberate choice on my part; it was an unconscious process. Now and then I have deliberately made experiments with poetic forms and occasionally the result has been successful. I was not a free-lance writer for long after I returned to Oxford from my thirteen weeks in Rome in 1958. That summer I was offered a job as general reader to the very fine and long-established London publisher Chatto and Windus. I did not particularly want the job but I accepted it after thinking the matter over during an August Bank Holiday weekend. On the Tuesday I wrote to the directors and took their offer on the condition that I did not start to work until early October. I had, as I told the directors, promised myself the whole of September in Rome.

At this time Chatto and Windus, which had been

*Elizabeth Jennings, about 1966*

a publisher for over a hundred years, was in its true heyday. Its list was splendid and formidable, for Chatto's then included the Hogarth Press, the publishers started by Virginia and Leonard Woolf. Leonard Woolf came into the office one day a week. One of his authors was Laurie Lee, whose best-seller *Cider with Rosie* was published during my time with Chatto's. Many turgid theses on English literature used to arrive by almost every post. The reason for this was that Chatto's had a splendid list of literary critics including William Empson and F.R. Leavis.

The great joy for me was that Cecil Day Lewis, the poet, came in every other week. He became a wonderfully kind friend, and much later I was to spend two Christmases with his wife, Jill Balcon, and their son and daughter. Daniel Day Lewis is now, at twenty-eight, a famous young actor and film star.

Work was hard because I had to read so many literary theses and borderline novels. However, all the directors and the younger members of the staff were delightful and sympathetic. But as I was writing a book about mysticism and poetry called *Every Changing Shape*

at this time, I slowly became worn out. I went home to Oxford every weekend to get on with my book. I could not work in the evenings in London, mainly because I had been reading and writing reports on books all day long. But also there were so many parties and films, and plays on in London to which I went. I would meet Stephen Spender, C.V. Wedgwood, the historian who became a close friend later, John Lehmann, among many others.

I came to know and love London more than ever before. There was no violence in the late fifties and early sixties and you could wander through Soho at night with complete safety. I had some very exciting meetings with great and eccentric writers. The most memorable was tea with T.S. Eliot in the tiny room at Faber's which they called "Uncle Tom's Cabin." I was so awed that I cannot remember if I drank the tea or ate the biscuits which were brought in for both of us. Eliot did indeed seem "an aged eagle" because he was very tall and had a slight stoop. The other most exciting literary meals were two luncheons with Edith Sitwell at her Sesame Club in Grosvenor Street (near the American Embassy). I had given her a well-deserved good review for a fine two-volume anthology of British poetry which she had selected and edited. I received a glowing letter from the Sitwell villa near Florence in which this remarkable lady said I must lunch with her when she returned to London.

I was extremely nervous before I arrived because I had heard that she did not care for other women poets. I took her a large bunch of flowers and found her not only kind but gentle and, as the Italians would say, *"molto simpatica."* She expressed an interest in an essay about Edwin Muir which I had contributed to the *London Magazine* and promised that she would read his poems carefully. More to the point and wholly enchanting, she invited me for luncheon on the following Friday too. Her Jesuit confessor, Father Philip Caraman, who had received her into the Catholic Church, was present at the first meal.

At Chatto's there was often much to laugh about. The directors knew I worked hard and was one of the first arrivals in the office in the morning, so the long, witty conversations with Geoffrey Barry, the man in charge of publicity, who had an office next to mine, were always tolerated. Sometimes an unwittingly funny novel would arrive and I would send it to him to read. I still remember a long Australian saga called *Bail-Up at Wantabigy* in which a madman took pity on his victim and raped her instead of murdering her! These were the days before violence and permissiveness had even begun.

I stayed for two years at Chatto's. Halfway through my second one I woke up with a pain in my stomach such as I had never felt before. Like so many doctor's children, I did not seek medical advice. In fact I did just about the most stupid thing I could have done, took painkillers which contained aspirin and sucked the strongest mint tablets I could find. But I was also suffering from more than physical illness. I would find myself sitting through a funny film with hot, silent tears pouring down my cheeks. In short, I was cracking up.

As I had more free-lance work to do than I had ever been given before, I decided I must leave. But I left Chatto and Windus with reluctance for I had made many friends there and, indeed, in many other parts of London too.

I was unhappily in love at this time but, looking back now, I realize that a few great friendships were to prove more important in my life than any passion, infatuation, admiration, or mere physical attraction would ever be: such friendships have become the deep, fertile roots of my life ever since.

When I left Chatto's I had five books to write, edit, or translate. They were a new book of poems to be called *Song for a Birth or a Death*, *Let's Have Some Poetry* (a book for children about poetry), *British Poetry 1940-60* to edit, a British Council pamphlet about current poetry, my big book about poetry and mysticism (called *Every Changing Shape*), and Michelangelo's *Sonnets* to translate. I was also reviewing novels for the *Listener*. But soon I was quite seriously ill with gall bladder. The next two decades were dogged by illness and illness is such a boring subject; but I always went on writing and am doing so to this day as I approach, with a certain horror, my sixtieth birthday.

I think my work has changed greatly since my early lyrics. I have used many poetic forms in recent years, from the ballad and sonnet to free verse and, occasionally, the prose poem. I do not travel as much as I used to but seven years ago I spent two wonderful weeks in Tuscany in a remote little town called Bibbiena. It is situated in the most pastoral part of Italy and I went in a sun-drenched May. Arezzo is half a mile away by car and Florence, where I gave a poetry reading, about two hours. I found that my Italian came back rapidly. When you are in love with a city or a country its language becomes part of you. I live in Oxford now and meet many young people who want to be writers. I also go to Stratford-on-Avon a great deal to see Shakespeare and to meet my friends there. I have a deep need to hear Shakespeare. It always restores and revitalizes me. Last year my fourteenth book of poems, *Extending the Territory*, was published; it contains many poems about my childhood because recently my Lincolnshire childhood has become more and more vivid to me. Maybe this is a sign of old age,

*Jennings, about 1976*

but I somehow don't think so.

---

## BIBLIOGRAPHY

**Poetry:**

*Poems*. Oxford, England: Fantasy Press, 1953.

*A Way of Looking*. London: Deutsch, 1955; New York: Rinehart, 1956.

*The Child and the Seashell*. San Francisco: Feathered Serpent Press, 1957.

*A Sense of the World*. London: Deutsch, 1958; New York: Rinehart, 1959.

*Song for a Birth or a Death, and Other Poems*. London: Deutsch, 1961; Philadelphia: Dufour, 1962.

*Penguin Modern Poets I,* with Lawrence Durrell and R. S. Thomas. Harmondsworth, England: Penguin, 1962.

*Recoveries.* London: Deutsch, 1964; Philadelphia: Dufour, 1964.

*The Mind Has Mountains.* London: Macmillan, 1966; New York: St. Martin's 1966.

*The Secret Brother and Other Poems for Children.* London: Macmillan, 1966; New York: St. Martin's, 1966.

*Collected Poems, 1967.* London: Macmillan, 1967; Chester Springs, Pa.: Dufour, 1967.

*The Animals' Arrival.* London: Macmillan, 1969; Chester Springs, Pa.: Dufour, 1969.

*Lucidities.* London: Macmillan, 1970.

*Hurt.* London: Poem-of-the-Month Club, 1970.

*Folio,* with others. Frensham, England: Sceptre Press, 1971.

*Relationships.* London: Macmillan, 1972.

*Growing-Points: New Poems.* Manchester, England: Carcanet New Press, 1975.

*Consequently I Rejoice.* Manchester, England: Carcanet New Press, 1977.

*After the Ark* (for children). Oxford, England and New York: Oxford University Press, 1978.

*Moments of Grace.* Manchester, England: Carcanet New Press, 1979.

*Selected Poems.* Manchester, England: Carcanet New Press, 1979.

*Winter Wind.* Newark, Vt.: Janus Press, 1979; Sidcot, England: Gruffyground Press, 1979.

*A Dream of Spring.* Warwickshire, England: Celandine, 1980.

*Italian Light and Other Poems.* Eastbourne, England: Snake River Press, 1981.

*Celebrations and Elegies.* Manchester, England: Carcanet New Press, 1982.

*Extending the Territory.* Manchester, England: Carcanet New Press, 1985.

*In Shakespeare's Company.* Warwickshire, England: Celandine, 1985.

*Poets in Hand: A Puffin Quintet,* with others. Harmondsworth, England: Penguin, 1985.

*Collected Poems.* Manchester, England: Carcanet New Press, 1986.

**Nonfiction:**

*Let's Have Some Poetry!* London: Museum Press, 1960.

*Every Changing Shape.* London: Deutsch, 1961; Philadelphia: Dufour, 1962.

*Poetry Today, 1957-60.* London and New York: Longmans, Green, 1961.

*Frost.* Edinburgh and London: Oliver & Boyd, 1964; New York: Barnes & Noble, 1966.

*Christianity and Poetry.* London: Burns & Oates, 1965; also published as *Christian Poetry.* New York: Hawthorn, 1965.

*Seven Men of Vision: An Appreciation.* London: Vision Press, 1976; New York: Barnes & Noble, 1976.

**Editor of:**

*New Poems, 1956: A P.E.N. Anthology,* with Dannie Abse and Stephen Spender. London: M. Joseph, 1956.

*The Batsford Book of Children's Verse.* London: Batsford, 1958.

*An Anthology of Modern Verse, 1940-1960.* London: Methuen, 1961.

*A Choice of Christina Rossetti's Verse.* London: Faber, 1970.

*The Batsford Book of Religious Verse.* London: Batsford, 1981.

*In Praise of Our Lady.* London: Batsford, 1982.

**Translator of:**

*The Sonnets of Michelangelo.* London: Folio, 1961; Garden City, N.Y.: Doubleday, 1970.

# Mervyn Jones

*1922-*

*Young Mervyn Jones playing chess with father, Ernest, about 1930*

Never, at any time of my life—in childhood, in my schooldays, or when the crucial decisions of early manhood had to be made—did I consider a future as anything but a writer. I don't remember when I learned to read, but it was certainly well before I started school. I always preferred reading to playing any sort of game. After my mother had tucked me into bed and switched the light off, I waited for her to go downstairs and switched it on again. When this stratagem was detected, I took to reading by a flashlight held beneath a tent of blankets. As I grew older, the habit was encouraged and I was given books for Christmas and birthdays; I don't remember, either, when I first began to take pride in my library. While other boys might take generals, explorers, or pioneer aviators as their heroes, mine were invariably writers.

If asked why I became a writer, I generally answer, "Because I couldn't do anything else." Although I intend this to be received as a joke, or a piece of evasive modesty, it contains a large element of truth. At school, I sat through the science lessons in a state of groping bewilderment. I was hopeless in the art class and never managed to draw a chair so that it looked like a chair. I could respond to music, but never

learned to play an instrument; and I couldn't, by any process of self-delusion, claim to be "musical." I showed little aptitude for abstract thought, especially of a logical or systematic nature. I was, and I still am, defeated by every kind of mechanical device, and I've long ago resigned myself to being among those who ineluctably put on the windshield wiper when it gets dark and the lights when it starts to rain. Since the word processor became fashionable, people who meet me sometimes inquire whether I use one, but nobody who knows my characteristics and capacities would put this question.

Of all the autobiographies I have ever read, the one that evokes the most familiar echoes for me is Sartre's *Les Mots*. It is the story of a boy who was not merely fascinated by words but dependent on words. I too was that boy. Like Sartre, I was small, physically unattractive, graceless, and clumsy. Like him, I was unpopular with others of my age and unskilful in forming relationships. Like him, I suffered from loneliness, but also sought it, following an instinct for solitude. The love of words—the passion for words—was his salvation, as it was mine. Words are the playthings, the pets, and indeed the best friends of such a child.

*Ernest and Katherine Jones*

I have lived, ever since, in a world peopled by words. For the true word-lover, each word has a personality of its own—a quality of insistent power, or modest simplicity, or flamboyant beauty, or exotic strangeness—beyond its literal meaning. All writers have favourite words, which they repeat with compulsive frequency. We even confuse human beings with words, and are attracted to them through their names. I fell in love, briefly, with a girl called Sasha Krinkin. Later, I fell in love with a girl called Kari Polanyi. Eventually, I fell in love with and married Jeanne Hartley-Urquhart. It's possible, of course, that she agreed to marry me because the surname of Jones offered her relief from this sonorous appellation.

I was born and spent my childhood in London and have lived there for most of my life—continuously, now, since 1955. I shouldn't endorse Dr. Johnson's famous dictum, and I can understand the pleasures of a country life, but I am by immutable temperament a big-city man, and I shouldn't be happy to live anywhere but in London, Paris, or New York. My father, Ernest Jones, was one of the pioneering generation of psychoanalysts, and is best remembered today as author of the standard biography of Sigmund Freud. My mother, born Katherine (or Katerina) Jokl, regarded him with humble reverence, but was entitled to pride in her own intellectual attainments; she had taken a Ph.D. in economics, no common achievement for a woman in 1918, and later took a degree in philology—words! Since she was Jewish, I entered the world as a Welshman by patrilineal law and a Jew by matrilineal law. I am grateful to my parents for endowing me with this double identity. It's true that I know only a few words of either the Welsh or the Hebrew language, and I can write only in English; but that has been the medium of many admirable Welsh and Jewish writers.

One of the questions that I've regularly been called upon to answer is: "What was it like being the son of Ernest Jones?" I can honestly say that it was like being the son of anyone else—or rather, of any father whose distinction in his own sphere must have been obvious to a growing child, whether he might have been a lawyer or a historian. Whether because he could see that I had no scientific aptitude, or because he had scruples about instilling beliefs in me by the authority of fatherhood, he never expounded the principles of psychoanalysis unless I asked a direct question. I read some of Freud's books on my own initiative, but that was at a period when I was voraciously and unsystematically reading anybody whom I thought I should know about, from Plato to Shaw. As a parent in the home, Ernest Jones was kindly, necessarily remote because he was always very busy, and distinctly old-fashioned (he was forty-three when I was born, and most of my school-friends had fathers whose attitudes and habits struck one as more contemporary). Although the drawers of his desk, as I discovered when I took a peek, might be crammed with the obscene verses and pornographic sketches produced by patients, sex was a subject avoided in the family circle; I had to learn about it from playground whispers just like any other boy. On rare occasions he told a mildly off-colour joke, recalled from his student days, but in such circumlocutory language that it required decoding. I must have been about ten, I think, when my father, in the course of reading aloud from a translation of Dante's *Inferno*, came to the phrase: "wallowing in excrement." Naturally, I asked, "What's excrement?" Ernest Jones gave an embarrassed cough and replied, "What goes down the lavatory."

His literary tastes were old-fashioned, too; he seldom read novels but preferred those that told a straightforward story, such as works by Trollope. There was one poet whom he read and re-read whenever he had the leisure; this was Browning, whose psychological insight impressed him. "Modern" poetry—that is, the work of poets of the Auden generation,

*On holiday in Wales, with father and sister, Gwenith, about 1925*

*Ernest Jones at the wheel of his Wolseley, 1927*

whom I read with fascination as a boy in the 1930s—was incomprehensible to him. Social life (mainly through his friendship with James Strachey, Lytton's brother) brought him into contact with Virginia Woolf and others of the Bloomsbury circle, but he didn't read their books. He was once asked—so he told me years later—whether psychoanalysis could do anything to help D. H. Lawrence with his problems; his reply was that nothing could be done for a man who had the misfortune to be married to Frieda.

The other question that I've frequently encountered from those who know of my parentage is: "Did you ever meet Freud?" I have, indeed, a clear memory of meeting him, and I am quite sure that it was on Easter Sunday, 1935. My father, never a man to waste time, took the family (my mother, my younger sister and me) to High Mass in the Vienna cathedral in the morning, and we visited Freud in the afternoon, thus encountering the fountainhead of Austrian anti-Semitism and the country's most famous Jew in the same day. I was already keen on history, and I showed genuine interest in Freud's collection of antiquities, all displayed in glass cases in what practically amounted to a small private museum. Suddenly, Freud started giving me pieces from the collection—one, then another, and

eventually four. My impression was that generosity was an uncontrollable passion with him, as avarice or acquisitiveness might be for a different man; he desisted only when my father pointed out that we might have trouble with the British customs. I still have the gifts, of course. One of them is an Etruscan statuette of exquisite beauty and, I've been told, considerable value. Freud then went on to tell me, with great seriousness, that archaeology would be an excellent career for a young man with my interests. (I was only thirteen, but he didn't condescend to children.) I haven't followed his advice, but I've no doubt that it was good advice; thirty years later, I made a friendship with an archaeologist—his speciality was Early Christian Ireland—and spent three happy and absorbing holidays working as a volunteer with the trowel. I've sometimes wondered whether Freud's antiquarian enthusiasm revealed a shade of regret that he hadn't become an archaeologist himself—a recognition, perhaps, that it was something like psychoanalysis, but less difficult and painful. I wish I'd sought my father's reaction to this theory, but I never did.

At roughly this time in my life—to be exact, in September 1934—I was sent to a boarding school in

*Ernest Jones in his later years*

the English Midlands, where I spent five years. I wasn't happy there—no British writer has ever admitted to being happy at school—but I have cause to be grateful to the English teacher, a poet called Wilfred Bosence, who provided me with encouragement and astringent criticism in well-judged proportions. I was writing poetry, palpably derivative of Auden or Spender, but I think I realised by the time I left school that, if I had a future as a writer, it would be in prose. I had come across an anecdote that made me ponder. "It must be terribly difficult to write poetry," a gushing lady said to Paul Eluard. "No, madame," he replied, "it is either easy or impossible."

I sat the exam for a history scholarship to Oxford and was given a place at Queen's College. I didn't really want to go to Oxford; the musty atmosphere of inherited traditions, the rigorous enforcement of absurd rules, and the regrettable paucity of girl students all struck me as severe drawbacks. Adolf Hitler, by launching the Second World War, ensured that I never did go there. My mother had chosen August 1939 for a visit to the United States, and took me with her. The morning of September 3 found us at the New York

World's Fair, about to enter the "World of Tomorrow" pavilion, which was replete with technological marvels promising to bring about a new age of ease and plenty. Someone who had been listening to the radio informed us that Britain and France were at war with Germany. Since there was nothing we could do about it, we went on to see the World of Tomorrow.

Within the next few days, it was decided that, as I wasn't yet of military age, I should stay in the neutral U.S. and enter an American university instead of Oxford. I was too late to get into Columbia, but New York University accepted me. "NYU downtown" was (and still is) a solid building with the aspect of an antiquated textile mill facing Washington Square, which was favoured in those days by courting couples and chess-players rather than by junkies and alcoholics. My spirits rose as soon as I went to register; on a quick count of the visible sample, more than half of the students were girls.

I majored in history, grasping the opportunity to learn something about American history, which was virtually ignored in British schools. Among English people who consider themselves educated, I'm still exceptional in being able to distinguish between Andrew Jackson and Andrew Johnson. However, I took a keener interest in the English courses taught by two remarkable and iconoclastic professors, Edwin Berry Burgum and Margaret Schlauch. It is to Burgum's course on the modern novel (from Balzac to Faulkner, if I remember rightly) that I owe most of my knowledge of the resources and techniques of prose fiction. According to Burgum, the most significant writers of

*Trapped by snow in the Alps, 1934. Jones is on the right, between his father and mother.*

our age were Proust, Mann, and Joyce. I duly read *Du Côté de Chez Swann* and *The Magic Mountain;* I had already read *Ulysses,* although it was banned in Britain, in a copy printed in Paris and smuggled across the Channel, which is still one of the treasures of my library. Schlauch gave a lecture on *Finnegans Wake,* which had just been published, expounding the theme of Anna Livia Plurabelle and the complex meanings of the letters A L P. A student raised his hand and said that, so far as he knew, A L P stood for American Labor Party. Schlauch beamed and replied that he was beginning to grasp how to read Joyce.

Away from college, I went to a seminar on poetry organised by the League of American Writers. The tutor was my idol, W. H. Auden. He worked by giving us exercises; one of them, based on a device used by Dante, was to write an allusive line to identify a character, beginning: "He who . . ." Auden himself wrote of Churchill: "He who wore many hats and in Epping Forest spoke frequently of battleships." (Epping Forest is a woodland on the fringe of London, in the parliamentary district then represented by Churchill.) It's a pity that this wonderfully Audenesque line doesn't take its place in the *Collected Poems.* Once, Auden invited me to tea at his apartment in Brooklyn Heights. I made my way there with feelings oscillating between delight and trepidation, having heard rumours about his indiscriminate sexual appetites. But he behaved with perfect decorum; I now know from the biographies that he had just then fallen in love with Chester Kallman.

I was in New York for two thoroughly enjoyable years, and I've no doubt that the right time to spend

*With cousin Fred Bauer and violinist Mirian Soloviev, Santa Monica Beach, 1941*

*Mervyn and Jeanne Jones on their wedding day, 1948*

two years in New York is between the ages of seventeen and nineteen—at least, for a young person of the male gender. I returned to England to join the Army, submitting perforce to a prolonged postponement of my literary ambitions. In the course of the next few years, I took part in the Normandy invasion; was taken prisoner in Holland and spent the last phase of the European war in an Oflag; and then spent a year in India, observing the expiration of the British Raj. To answer another question: "How did you write your first novel?", I can reply, "By being the only officer in India who didn't sleep in the afternoons." It was a long and overambitious war novel, of the kind that scores of young men were producing in the first year of peace. It was rejected all round and never published, an experience which depressed me at the time but of which I can't complain. More often than the public knows, a writer's "first novel" is actually not the first attempt, but the first to reach a publishable standard.

My first published novel—it appeared in January 1952, a month before my thirtieth birthday—was called *No Time to Be Young.* It was a story of growing up in the thirties. The central character and narrator, a girl called Anne Beckton, was the same age as the author and also had a double identity, but English/French instead of Welsh/Jewish. I decided that this character should be a girl simply in order to dis-

*The author in his thirties*

tance myself from direct autobiography. In subsequent years, however, I've written several novels in which events are seen, and sometimes narrated, from a woman's point of view, and I've been complimented by reviewers and readers—including women—on my ability to get inside a woman's skin. I can't honestly say that I find it very difficult (perhaps it's either easy or impossible). A man, or at least a heterosexual man, is likely to have devoted a good deal of time to observing and studying women, and it follows, if he is a writer, that he knows more about women than about men and is naturally inclined to make use of his knowledge. I noted with interest recently that Bernice Rubens—a writer who is a friend of mine, and who is definitely heterosexual—said in an interview that, when she is impelled to write in the first person, it's always as a man. But another possible explanation is that the creative process brings the feminine side of my nature (and the masculine side of Bernice's nature) to the surface. If so, I'm content with having a double identity in that sense, too.

When it appeared, *No Time to Be Young* received favourable reviews from C. P. Snow, John Betjeman, and V. S. Pritchett, and no young writer could ask for

a better start than that. I went on writing steadily—too fast, I daresay—and by 1955 I had four novels to my credit. My publishers, the house of Jonathan Cape, treated authors in a gentlemanly style. The manuscript was received without comment and printed without alteration, just as a tailor might make a suit if given the material. Editing, in those days, was regarded as a nasty American custom. My fourth novel was rather poorly reviewed; the chairman of Cape, over a lunch a few years later, said, "Yes, as a matter of fact, we never liked that one very much." The hardback edition always made a modest profit, with which the firm was content. There was no talk of subsidiary rights. It didn't occur to me that the gentlemen at Cape ought to sell my books to a paperback publisher, and I don't think they ever tried.

One of the pleasures of being a writer was that I made friendships with other writers. It is traditionally believed that, whereas French writers all know one another and meet constantly in cafés, British writers live in remote cottages and avoid the company of colleagues. In my experience, this picture is much overdrawn. The main difference is that French writers discuss literary and philosophical theories, while my friends in London talk about the problems of survival, and also about who's sleeping with whom and whose marriage is breaking up. (One of my friends is brooding on a scheme to put his finances on an even keel by producing an annual reference book called *Who's With Who*.)

In the year when I was writing *No Time to Be Young*, a young woman arrived in London from Southern Rhodesia, of all places, with an infant son, money for a few weeks' rent and food, and the manuscript of a novel. This novel was soon accepted and was an instant success, as it deserved; one could reasonably maintain that *The Grass Is Singing* is the best first novel ever written (since *Wuthering Heights*, anyway). When I met Doris Lessing, it seemed almost miraculous that this brilliant writer should also be a highly attractive *femme de trente ans*, with eloquent brown eyes and a fetching gamine hair-style. I was dazzled, but I had enough sense to realise that an affair with Doris would be a full-time occupation, and certainly not a leisure amusement for a married man. We became, and have remained, friends.

Naturally, I bought (or occasionally reviewed) all Doris's books on publication, and I have a complete set on my shelves, including *Retreat to Innocence*, a novel which she decided to disown—wrongly, in my opinion—and doesn't list among her published works. In 1983, she turned up at my house with a copy of *The Diary of a Good Neighbour*, by Jane Somers. This was the

*With children in Wales, 1957. From left to right: Jacqueline, Conrad, and Marian*

novel which she wrote and submitted to publishers under a pseudonym, as a sort of acid practical joke. Cape, her British publishers, rejected it; but her American publisher, Bob Gottlieb of Knopf, recognised the style at a glance and called her up to say, "Hey, Doris, who are you kidding?" It seemed to me that the novel was unmistakably Lessingian, but of course I was in on the secret—a secret which I managed to keep, despite my relish for gossip, until Doris chose to blow the story. The copy on my shelves is inscribed: "For Mervyn and Jeanne—Jane Somers (Doris Lessing)—16th July 1983." Doris must have known that she was presenting us with an investment, but I intend to keep the book, along with the Etruscan statuette, the banned *Ulysses,* the first edition of Auden's *Spain,* and other treasures.

I wasn't making a living from my novels, but I was getting by on a combination of journalism, writing radio scripts on history and geography for the Schools Service of the BBC, and various kinds of hackwork. I have never particularly resented the necessity of hackwork; it seems to me that having to turn your hand to jobs that you find tedious is a fair payment for the privilege of an independent life. After my first novel came out, the editor of a women's magazine called me up and asked me to write short stories for her. Admonished by my wife not to be cynical about it, I tried to write as well as though I were working on a novel, but I had to give this up. Whenever a story contained the least vestige of literary merit or plausibility, the editor

infallibly spotted it and struck it out. After a time, she started supplying me with the plots, which she must have dreamed up herself. I preferred to listen to them over the phone rather than to go to her office, for it wasn't easy to keep a straight face. With practice, I was able to write a story in a day, thus earning what was then the equivalent of a bus-driver's wages for a month. The golden rule for a writer is that, since real writing is invariably underpaid, hack writing must be overpaid.

Even with the aid of these devices, however, I still wasn't making an adequate income, and we now had three children. In 1955, I was offered a job on a political weekly, *Tribune,* and accepted it. The opinions that *Tribune* represented were those of the left wing of the Labour Party; the guide and inspiration was Aneurin Bevan, while the editor was Michael Foot. They were both remarkable men, whom one could whole-heartedly admire for the vision and sincerity of their beliefs, but both unfitted by temperament for politics in the baser sense of the word. Bevan never became leader of the party; Michael did ultimately become leader, only to undergo a disastrous defeat at the hands of Margaret Thatcher in the 1983 election. At the time when Bevan was running for the leadership against the right-winger Hugh Gaitskell, I heard through the journalistic grapevine that every single uncommitted Labour member of Parliament had been invited for a meal or drinks at Gaitskell's home. Bevan didn't invite anybody to his

*Aneurin Bevan, Doris Lessing, and Jeanne Jones. Attending a party at the Royal Court Theatre, London, 1959*

home except his chosen friends, a varied and interesting collection who included the painter Graham Sutherland, the playwright Benn Levy and his wife Constance Cummings, and the jazz-band leader Jack Hylton. Obviously, such a man wasn't about to win the required votes.

Bevan had himself edited *Tribune* at an earlier period—during World War II—and he was able to pass on an important piece of advice: Don't make jokes, especially if they involve irony. Bevan's irritation had been aroused by the writings of Lord Vansittart, who ascribed all the misdeeds of the Nazis to the innate wickedness of the German character, as manifested throughout history. Bevan, therefore, filled a page of *Tribune* with an account of the evil record of the Scots, putting in Macbeth, the Massacre of Glencoe, and whatever else he could think of (and with gleeful contributions from his wife, Jennie, who was Scots herself). The mail on Monday morning brought ten letters—nine from Scots cancelling their subscriptions, and one from an Englishman which began: "At last someone has dared to tell the truth."

I stayed at *Tribune* for four years. We had a tiny staff, and I wrote—under my own name or pseudonyms—practically everything: political editorials, reports from the South Wales coalfield or the Glasgow slums, book reviews, theatre criticism, and even reports from our American correspondent (we hadn't got one at the time). The work was exhilarating, but it was demanding. I wrote only one novel during these four years, and saw little prospect of writing another. It's possible to write a good novel in evenings and weekends if the working days are filled by a routine job at a bank or an insurance office, but scarcely if you have a job that makes a continual call on your mental and emotional energies. I found, indeed, that my novel-writing muscles had temporarily atrophied. Even after I left *Tribune*, it was difficult to get back into harness. I wrote two nonfiction books, which could be described as elongated journalism; I took on hackwork; and I produced a novel which Cape judged to be unsuitable for publication. In fact, I didn't get a novel published between 1957 and 1965. I may have benefited from the interval, but it didn't feel like that at the time.

No sooner had I successfully regained my novel-writing rhythm than, in 1966, I was offered another job. (The only jobs I've ever had are those which were offered to me, and I've invariably failed to land those I applied for.) I was making a reasonable income and I had resolved never to let myself be immured in an office again, but this job was on the *New Statesman,* and that was special. It was, for a long and golden period between the 1930s and the 1970s, the weekly that everybody who claimed to be intelligent and alive to events, and to have a liberal or radical outlook, simply had to read. I had been reading it myself since the age of twelve; it had given me my first appearance in print in 1945. I was familiar with the office in Great Turnstile, having often entered it as a free-lance. The clinching factor was that the editor, Paul Johnson, was offering me a viable salary for working three days a week—an arrangement that I couldn't very well reject. In the end, however, I stayed for only two and a quarter years. Regular office work and commuting definitely don't suit me.

I shared a room with Francis Hope, a wonderful companion, who never quite achieved the recognition that his talents merited and who was killed in the crash of the Turkish DC-10 in 1974. (It is strange how often I've met people who lost friends or relatives in that unforgotten disaster.) On a hook behind the door, there was—and had been for as far back as anyone remembered—a shabby old raincoat, reputed to have been left there by H. G. Wells. According to legend, any man who went out wearing it was sure to pick up a woman. Francis and I treasured the legend, but we didn't put it to the test, and we were cautious about repeating it. The dawn of modern feminism was already brightening the horizon. Years later, the building was sold and demolished. To the best of my knowledge, the Wells raincoat vanished in the wreckage.

Although the *New Statesman* wasn't a wealthy paper, it was richer than *Tribune* and could afford to send me abroad. In 1967, Greece fell victim to the dictatorship of the colonels. Greek democrats in exile approached the *New Statesman* and offered to arrange meetings with the underground resistance in Athens. I booked a package holiday, and was instructed to wait in my hotel room until a woman called up. She would say, "This is Alkystis—d'you remember? We met at the beach last year," to which I should reply, "Why, sure—let's get together." The so-called Alkystis was in fact a French girl called Michèle, mistress of a Resistance leader. She was new to underground life, and when I answered the phone she said, "This is Michèle—I mean Alkystis." However, we straightened this out and she picked me up every evening in the hotel bar, which was regularly used by whores. I doubt if this was the wisest arrangement, for Michèle was too attractive to look like an Omonia Square whore, and the real whores could well have been part-time police informers. Still, I don't think I was followed as I accompanied her to interviews in unfashionable apartments with drawn curtains. I spent my days in the museums; few tourists can have studied classical and Byzantine art more assiduously.

Outwardly, Athens looked fairly normal, though less lively than I'd found it on previous visits. When I was leaving, I got into conversation in the airport-departure lounge with an American tourist who said that he saw no signs of the alleged dictatorship. Somewhat irritated, I asked, "What did you expect to see—tanks on the streets?" The man replied, "Why, yes. You see, I come from Detroit."

I was flying to Israel, and staying in Jerusalem. It was only a few months since the Jewish and Arab sectors of the city had been united, thanks to the Israeli victory in the Six-Day War. The space below the walls of the Old City, pleasantly landscaped today, was a vacant and untamed no-man's land, and unlit at night. Malcolm Muggeridge, whom I knew in *New Statesman* circles, was in Jerusalem, making a television film about the life of Jesus, and was staying at the American Colony Hotel. The American Colony is a district in East Jerusalem, originally settled by some sort of born-again American Christians, and the hotel was an Arab establishment. The beds and chairs were extremely uncomfortable, the food was appalling, but the hotel hadn't been in any way modernised and was as pictur-

esque as a Bedouin tent. It had rapidly become a favourite with the Israeli intelligentsia, who declared that if they could get a peace treaty they would give back everything but the American Colony. I wasn't at all surprised to find Malcolm there.

"Come to dinner," he urged. "There'll only be the film crew and Graham—he's in town for some reason." He hung up before I could ask what Graham this was. Soon after I had reached the hotel and sat down in one of the rickety cane chairs, a man clutching a bottle appeared between the bead curtains and announced, "I've brought some whisky, Malcolm." It really was Graham Greene; reality was echoing his novels. If I'd had an instamatic camera, the picture would have been another treasure.

In the course of a recent controversy, Greene had written in a letter to the London *Times* that he would rather live in the Soviet Union than in the United States. I took the opportunity to ask whether he meant it. "God forbid that I'd ever have to live in either," he said, but Malcolm declared that he was dodging the question. A gleam was discernible in his pale blue eyes. "Well," he said, "if I lived in the Soviet Union I'd be able to smuggle my books out, like Solzhenitsyn. That would be worth it, wouldn't it?"

My current novel, at that time, was *John and Mary*. It had only two characters: a young man and a young woman who meet at a party, spend the night together at the man's apartment, and go through the following day making up their minds whether to stay together or not, and in fact getting to know each other. A reviewer commented, "One is almost tempted to think that Mervyn Jones set himself the task of writing a whole novel within the framework of the famous classical unities of the drama." For once, the reviewer was absolutely right. I had approached the book as a technical exercise, or—I might say—a bet with myself.

It was also a topical novel, belonging distinctly to the 1960s. Of course, it wasn't unprecedented in history for a man and a girl to meet and proceed without delay to make love. What marked the book as a sixties novel was the assumption that this was normal behaviour for two people who didn't in other respects regard themselves as unconventional. "Not a moral tale," the *Sunday Telegraph* warned its readers. The *Observer* reflected: "The new freedom brings its own received modes of conduct and assessment." The review in the *Aberdeen Express* read thus:

> John and Mary are strangers. They
> meet at a party, and go to bed together!
> They wake up, STILL strangers!
> But they take the rest of the weekend to

put all that to rights.

They make love again.

That, briefly speaking, is what *John and Mary* is all about.

Yes, sir, it's a lot to achieve all in one weekend. A sign of the times, perhaps?

The novel marked a step forward for me, being the first of my books to be published in the U.S. (The American reviewers weren't so puzzled by it.) Another unprecedented event was that I received an offer from someone who wanted to make a film out of it. When my agent informed me of this, I said, "The man must be crazy." Indeed, one could scarcely imagine a less filmable novel. All the action—if it could be called action—was confined within a small apartment. The content consisted of the speculations and meditations of the two characters, with a small amount of rather laconic dialogue. The sexual activity occurred before the story began and after it ended. The nearest approach to a dramatic moment was when Mary accidentally broke a glass. Who would pay to see a movie of that?

Still, the director who was bent on pursuing this rash project, Anthony Harvey, was said to be very talented, and when I met him he assured me that he wanted to stick closely to the book. He proposed to shoot the film in a real apartment, not in a set (obviously, it would be a low-budget film, appealing to discriminating audiences in a few art houses). He hadn't found an actor for John, but he had invited Glenda Jackson to play Mary and she had agreed. This was great news. I was quite as much in love with Glenda Jackson as I had been with Sasha Krinkin and Kari Polanyi and Doris Lessing. I had seen every play in which she'd appeared since her debut with the Royal Shakespeare Company a few years earlier, and I was a paid-up member of her fan club. She was also a highly intelligent person with a keen and faultless understanding of how a writer's mind works. How did I know this? She lived in the next street to me. Meeting in the corner store, we told each other how much we looked forward to the movie.

I signed the contract and banked the money (not a vast amount of money, but it was going to be an art movie). After that, nothing happened for a year and a half. I heard nothing from Mr. Harvey; Glenda heard nothing from Mr. Harvey. Then an American friend sent me a cutting from a movie trade-journal. A film of *John and Mary* was being made, not by Anthony Harvey—apparently, he had failed to get enough backing and had disposed of the rights—but by Twentieth Century-Fox. The lovers would be Americans and their encounter would be relocated to New York. Mary would be played by Mia Farrow, and John by Dustin

Hoffman. Somebody had written a screenplay.

I thought that I'd like to see the screenplay. My agent explained that I had no right to see it, but he had a friend in the London office of Twentieth Century-Fox who would smuggle out a copy if I kept quiet about it and returned it quickly. I read it with mounting incredulity. Rather than a film set in New York, this was going to be a film about New York. John and Mary, whose occupations had been unspecified in my novel, were provided with suitably modish jobs—he as an interior designer and she as a receptionist at an art gallery. They met at a singles bar, then a fashionable innovation. There was a lengthy scene at a party (to which, in the novel, John was invited but didn't go) complete with psychedelic lights, drug-induced hallucinations, unusual sex experiences shot from odd camera angles, and such "sixties" touches. Considerable attention was given to an earlier girlfriend of John's (briefly mentioned in the novel) and an earlier lover of Mary's (entirely invented). This person, a liberal congressman, was seen vacationing with Mary in Jamaica, getting into difficulties with his wife, and confronting an audience who criticized his stand on the Vietnam war. The climax of the film was a sequence in which John searched for Mary all over New York, providing opportunities for interviews with various typical citizens, caustic remarks by the legendary taxi-driver, and a wide range of uptown and downtown scenery.

News of the project began to get around. If I went into a pub patronised by journalists, I was likely to be asked: "How's your film going?" and I had to explain that I was in no way involved, if only to avoid paying for all the drinks. I genuinely had no idea how the film was going, and was fully prepared to hear that it had been abandoned as a disastrous experiment. Visitors from New York brought rumours, which might or might not be based on fact. It was said that Hoffman and Farrow disliked each other and never exchanged a word off the set. (This, I reckoned when I ultimately saw the film, could well be true.) It was also said that Hoffman, Farrow, and everybody else taking part in the production had been forbidden to read my novel; this was almost certainly true.

Then, one fine day, the film critic of a London newspaper called me and asked what I thought of the film. I replied that I was hoping to see it when it was completed. After an incredulous pause, he said, "But, Mr. Jones, we've all seen it."

I was shortly leaving for India on a trip for the *New Statesman,* so I decided that I must make an effort to see the film ahead of the Bombay critics. After pleas from my agent, I was notified that I could attend a trade showing. Jeanne and I duly went along; we had a vague idea that somebody from Twentieth Century-

Fox might shake hands with us when we gave our names at the door, but nobody did. When it was over, nobody asked for our comments, so we went home. Some days later, a friend, Spiros Mercouri—being Melina's brother, he moved in film circles—told me that the publicity director of Twentieth Century-Fox was desperately trying to get hold of me. I remarked that he could find me in the London telephone book. "Oh," Spiros said, "he wouldn't do a thing like that."

A line that sometimes recurs in my mind is spoken by Gaev in *The Cherry Orchard:* "I am a man of the eighties." Most of us are imbued with the outlook, the tastes, and the habits of a period that we have found especially congenial; and I'm willing to agree that I am a man of the sixties. In the hard, bleak times through which we're now living, that decade is much derided for its excesses and absurdities. Some of us weren't unaware of the absurdities at the time, and yet we felt that it was genuinely a time of liberation. For writers in particular, we were blessed by liberation from a whole network of constraints, taboos, hypocrisies, and enforced evasions. In Britain at least, the sixties began at a precise moment: three o'clock in the afternoon of November 2, 1960. At that moment, in the Central Criminal Court, the Clerk asked the jury, "Do you find that Penguin Books Limited are guilty or not guilty of publishing an obscene article?" The foreman replied, "Not guilty." An outburst of cheering and clapping from the public galleries was quickly suppressed.

Since Victorian times, it had been an offence to publish a book that might "tend to deprave and corrupt persons likely to read it." However, since a revision of the law made in 1959, no offence could be found if the book—depraving and corrupting though it might be—contributed to "science, literature, art or learning, or other objects of general concern." Thus, it was open to the defence to call witnesses (such as writers, literary critics, professors, and even bishops) who would declare that the book in question qualified as a work of literature. Penguin made their new edition of Lawrence's *Lady Chatterley's Lover* a test case, and won.

The upholders of decency weren't beaten, however, and resorted to the strategy of prosecuting books which, they hoped, couldn't possibly be depicted as valid literature. There followed, through the 1960s and into the 1970s, a series of trials in which, to everybody's surprise, the jury always returned a Not Guilty verdict. Credit for this belonged primarily to the lawyer who conducted the defence in most of the cases, John Mortimer. He was himself a writer, and had made enough money from his plays (and, incidentally, from writing the remarkable screenplay of *John and Mary*) to have

retired from legal work, but stuck to it from a genuine love of the law and the courts. A jovial and witty man, John came across to the jury as a reassuring figure, while the prosecuting counsel looked by contrast like a humourless fanatic. John's line, to paraphrase, was: "We're all grown-ups, aren't we? We like a bit of a sexy read, don't we? What's all this fuss about? What harm is it going to do?" Time and again, it worked.

There was at that time a magazine called *Oz* (because it had originated in Oztralia) which incarnated the spirit of the counterculture. The authorities prosecuted one of its more outrageous issues, and I was among the writers requested by John Mortimer to give evidence for the defence. I couldn't honestly say that the stuff was well written, but I reeled off a little spiel about freshness, vitality, and what not. John made his classic winding-up speech, and *Oz* was acquitted.

Another prosecution, a few years later, was of a book called *Inside Linda Lovelace,* which purported to be the autobiography of Linda Lovelace, star of the porno movie *Deep Throat.* The content was a zestful description of her varied and ingenious sexual activities, in which apparently she had engaged with enthusiasm and delight. Linda Lovelace herself wasn't in court, of course (although in effect it was her way of life that was on trial), and anybody who read the book was bound to suspect that it had been ghostwritten by some cynical hack. We did the customary spiel about freshness and vitality, and John Mortimer chalked up another acquittal.

I was due to give evidence on a Wednesday. When I arrived at the court, John told me that the case was running behind the timetable, and asked me to come back on Friday. "What about Thursday?" I inquired. The court would be in recess, John explained, because the judge was due to see his doctor and hear the result of his cancer tests. I appeared, therefore, on the Friday. The prosecuting counsel's strategy was to read out, in a slow and laborious manner, passages from the book with detailed accounts of oral sex, anal sex, multiple sex orgies, and so forth, and ask the witness how he could justify them. During this process, I was aware of the judge gazing abstractedly into empty space. In the light of the verdict that he must have heard from his doctor, it really couldn't matter to him whether a libidinous American girl enjoyed sucking cocks or not. I was glad to step down at the end of this chilling experience. Some months later, I met John Mortimer at a party. "Haven't seen you since the trial," he said. "The judge croaked, you know."

Several years later, again, the former Linda Lovelace—this had never been her real name, obviously—came out with a book called *Ordeal,* in which she described how she had been held prisoner by her evil genius and forced to take part in sex acts which she loathed. According to some commentators, this showed that John Mortimer and the rest of us had all been fooled. Yet, so it seemed to me, *Ordeal* also made an impression of having been ghostwritten, perhaps by another cynical hack, perhaps even by the same one. What the ultimate truth about Linda Lovelace may be, I shouldn't care to say with any certainty. I remain as firmly opposed as ever to all censorship and to the prosecution or banning of any book whatever, regardless of its literary merit or lack thereof. In fact, one of my reasons for taking this attitude is that censorship is a bad alternative to criticism and controversy; one hesitates to attack a book that may be denounced by an intolerant and illiterate authority. Some books that describe themselves as "erotic" fill me with revulsion, based as they are on contempt for and degradation of women, and it's clear to me that the movement called Women Against Pornography is making a very cogent point, now that what used to be a minority culture has become big business. I don't, however, propose to appear in the Central Criminal Court as a witness for the prosecution.

Meanwhile, I was continuing to write novels. After my tenth, I parted company with the house of Cape, with a minimum of acrimony. They felt that I had been given sufficient opportunities to write a book that would be a real commercial success, and if I hadn't done so yet, then I was never likely to. I

*Mervyn Jones, about 1975*

couldn't argue against this proposition, since I'd never imagined that I was that kind of writer. By now (I write in 1986) I've had four publishers, a record that might be compared to four marriages, and might similarly be viewed as rather excessive. The record can be summarised as one separation by mutual consent, one divorce on my initiative, one divorce demanded by the other party, and one autumnal union which, I hope, will endure until my authorial demise.

Ironically, the years that followed my departure from the house of Cape witnessed my rare successes. *Holding On,* the novel for which I'm probably best known among English readers, was published in 1973. It was the story of a stevedore in the London docks from his birth in 1900 to his death in 1970, and of his family, with episodes describing the General Strike, the two World Wars, and various social and political changes. The time, I suppose, was right for this kind of reflective, elegiac chronicle; perhaps readers sensed that there wasn't much more English history to come. Anyhow, the book sold well and was made into a television serial. The script was discussed with me and I was allowed to come to rehearsals, so this was a more pleasing experience than the film of *John and Mary.*

While this was happening, news came that Simon and Schuster wished to publish the book in the U.S. and were offering a large advance—large, I mean, by my modest standards. Fulsome, flattering letters began to arrive from the editor who was in charge of it. Since she is now pursuing a different career, I'll call her Maria, which isn't her name. She did have a number of requests, one of which was to change the title. Her suggestion was *Make Glad the Day.* As I hadn't yet met Maria, I couldn't imagine why she considered this idiotic title to be suitable for a sober, realistic novel about working-class life; eventually, I agreed to *Twilight of the Day.* Her next request was to bowdlerise, or clean up, the text. "My biggest concern," she wrote to Richard Simon, my agent, "is that Mr. Jones's beautiful book get the widest possible readership. And, according to our sales force, this is much more likely to happen if they can say that the book doesn't have any words that a female reader would find objectionable." I read this with bewilderment, since the year was 1974; five years had gone by since *Portnoy's Complaint* was a best-seller, and most American females of my acquaintance were using words that I considered rather crude. Attached to the letter was a three-page list of improvements and substitutions. I accepted most of them, though some were expressions that could never have been uttered in the East End of London.

Soon, Maria wrote to say that she was coming to London and looked forward to having dinner with me, and that she was authorized to offer $50,000 for the rights to my next two books. Richard advised me not to be trapped into such a deal, since the books would undoubtedly have to conform to the taste of the Simon and Schuster sales force. He was right, obviously, but I asked him to be present at the dinner to stiffen my backbone. We gathered at an Italian restaurant in Soho. Alarmingly, it was soon noticeable that Maria had a poor head for Chianti, of which one carafe after another appeared on the table. Richard had sent her the typescript of the novel I had just finished, *Strangers,* and I asked whether it was acceptable as one of the books in the programme. When she said that it wasn't, the discussion was at an end so far as I was concerned; I thought then, and still think, that *Strangers* was a better novel than *Holding On.* But Maria, nudging her chair closer to mine as she progressed from wine to brandy, raised the offer to $60,000. With considerable relief, we guided her out to the street and put her in a taxi for the London Hilton. Then I hailed another taxi to go home; it isn't every day, after all, that one enjoys the luxury of turning down $60,000. I never heard from Maria again. Before the American publication of *Holding On* (or *Twilight of the Day*) she had been fired.

My next novel was *Lord Richard's Passion.* The theme was a man's obsessive, incurable love for a woman whom he is fated never to possess. The title was a mistake—one has no right to expect readers to take a novel called *Lord Richard's Passion* seriously—but, once it had occurred to me, I couldn't resist it. "It is not clear," said a reviewer sternly, "to what extent the author wishes us to accept it as straight-up historical romance and how far it is tongue-in-the-cheek pastiche." I hadn't really intended the book to be either romance or pastiche; I was exploiting the conventions of the Victorian era, especially the well-worn conflict between love and ambition, for an ironic purpose. Readers of *Holding On,* having accepted that I was at home with the dockers of the East End, were surprised to find me writing sympathetically about an aristocrat who enjoyed a cavalry charge in the Second Afghan War and held office under Lord Salisbury. Other readers, who regarded my accurate grasp of contemporary life as my strong suit, wondered why I was reaching into the past. I don't, in point of fact, feel much affection for the Victorian period; as a historian *manqué,* I find the seventeenth century much more interesting. But the story I wanted to tell had to be placed in a time when emotional candour between men and women was impeded by formidable obstacles, and when no one understood the sufferings of a young woman who was terrified of sex. The unexpected outcome was an offer from another major American publisher, this time Knopf. When I went to New York and met the Knopf editor who had picked up my novel, she said, "What

we like about it is that it's so incredibly pre-Freudian." What my father would have said about that, I can imagine only too well.

Neither Simon and Schuster nor Knopf ever published another novel by me. In my experience, American publishers (I've had transient affairs with five of them) are averse to permanent relationships with writers. Still, my earnings from these three books—*John and Mary, Holding On, Lord Richard's Passion*—ensured that, for a halcyon period of about six years, I was making enough money as a novelist and had no need to give my time to journalism or hackwork unless I felt like it.

The trouble with money, from a writer's point of view, is that it comes when it isn't needed and doesn't come when it is needed. If $x$ represents the income required to support a satisfactory standard of living, without extravagances but without anxieties, then the sad truth is that it's possible to make more than $x$, and all too easy to make less than $x$, but impossible to make $x$ itself. When a novel is successful, it may well attract a film option (even if no film eventually results), be chosen by a book club, and be serialized in a magazine in Sweden or Brazil. Indeed, all three of these things can happen simultaneously. But when the book isn't successful, none of them will happen. The successful and the unsuccessful book have demanded the same amount of writing time and sweat—and the former, the writer probably knows, isn't a better book. I once proposed to my publisher that the firm should

*At family celebration of author's sixtieth birthday, 1982*

pay me a modest salary to write a novel a year, and keep any profits that might arise from lucky breaks, such as big paperback sales, TV versions, or films. Of course, he thought I was joking.

To date, I have written—or, to be precise, had published—twenty-two novels, one book of novellas, and six nonfiction books. Reviewers sometimes describe me as an "accomplished craftsman," or in similar phrases, but I don't claim that I know much more about writing novels than I did when I toiled over the first chapter of *No Time to Be Young,* and only recently I spent two months on a false start which had to be abandoned. A novel can't be written by following set rules or precedents; each book, each chapter, and virtually every sentence is a new venture and presents fresh problems. Nor is there any objective criterion of success; if a bridge carries the required load it's a good bridge, but a writer can never be sure of having written a good book, even if the critics say so. For us, it is eternally true that a man's reach must exceed his grasp (one of Ernest Jones's favourite quotations from Browning). Beyond each book, there is always the un-

attainable ideal of the book as it would have been written if the same theme had been taken up by Stendhal or Dostoevsky; and even for them, one can assume, there was the tantalising gleam of a better *Chartreuse de Parme,* a better *Brothers Karamazov.* As you deliver the product to the publisher, you can only say, "This is as good as I, with such talent as I possess, can make it." I've long ago relinquished any dreams of rising to the stature of Stendhal or Dostoevsky—or, for that matter, Doris Lessing—but I still work at the writing as though the quality of my book were of supreme importance to the world. One thing is certain: anyone who is resigned to writing a second-rate book will write a tenth-rate book.

All writers have favourites among their books, which don't often coincide with their successes. A book that I regard with lingering affection is *Two Women and Their Man,* published in 1982. For one thing, I was pleased with the title. The two women were the wife and the mistress of a magnetic but rather stupid man; he imagined that the former knew nothing about his affair with the latter, while in reality they were good

*At the unveiling of plaque commemorating the former home of Mervyn's father, Ernest, the pioneer psychoanalyst, 1985. From left to right (omitting children): daughter Jacqueline, wife Jeanne, brother Lewis, daughter Marian, Mervyn Jones, son Conrad, sister-in-law Julia, nephew Stephen*

*With Jeanne in India, 1985*

friends and regularly met to discuss him. Soon after I'd finished the book, I happened to be in Dublin and was invited to a party where I met the wife and the mistress of a well-known public figure. It was clear that they were good friends. A novelist is gratified when his speculations are confirmed by reality; invention is not, or shouldn't be, our aim.

The setting for *Two Women and Their Man* was a part of rural Wales which I knew slightly, though I had to do some walking there to get my topographical details right. I placed my story in 1939, a time when this was still a self-contained region with unimpaired traditions, religion was a powerful force, and sexual immorality incurred stern disapproval. Events are recalled in turn by the three characters (alternating narration, a device that I had adopted in *John and Mary*, is a handy literary form) who are supposed to be exerting their memories many years later. For reasons of plot, the cottage rented by Estelle (the mistress) had to be at the end of a dead-end road, directly beneath a steep-sided mountain, Arenig Fawr. The cottage really existed, though when I walked up to it I found it empty. I made Estelle's lover remark at the end of the book that nobody ever stayed long in the cottage and it was mostly bought by outsiders. While the book was in the press, we went out to dinner with London friends and

were introduced to a professor (a sinologist, it appeared) and his wife, who started talking about their cottage in Wales. Questions elicited that it was at the end of a dead-end road, beneath Arenig Fawr. I didn't leave the dinner party without an invitation to spend a night in Estelle's cottage. I arrived—like Estelle—on a foggy night when the mountain was invisible, but in the morning the summit stood out against a blue sky—as it had for Estelle. I've had other such curious experiences in the course of my writing life, but this is the most striking among them.

I surprised myself, on the whole, by setting a novel—for the first time, and it was my twentieth novel—in Wales. Despite my natal inheritance as a Welshman and a Jew, the shaping of my life has made me a Londoner, and I've generally found it natural to set my books in London. But some kind of unconscious process, suppressed for many years, must have been demanding a recognition of allegiance. A couple of years later, again without planning it, I was setting another novel in Wales. This time, I chose the part of Wales where my son had gone to live, and where my grandsons are now learning Welsh in the village school. The novel was about the return of a wanderer who has spent a lifetime in the Far East, and I used the working title of *Coming Home*. I intended to give it more thought and change it to something more original; there had been C.P. Snow's novel *Homecomings,* Harold Pinter's play *The Homecoming,* and Doris Lessing's book about Africa, *Going Home.* Yet, in the end, I let the book appear as *Coming Home.* The title said something—to the reader, and to me.

---

## BIBLIOGRAPHY

**Fiction:**

*No Time to Be Young.* London: J. Cape, 1952.

*The Last Barricade.* London: J. Cape, 1953.

*The New Town.* London: J. Cape, 1953.

*Helen Blake.* London: J. Cape, 1955.

*On the Last Day.* London: J. Cape, 1958.

*A Set of Wives.* London: J. Cape, 1965.

*John and Mary.* London: J. Cape, 1966; New York: Atheneum, 1967.

*A Survivor.* London: J. Cape, 1968; New York: Atheneum, 1968.

*Joseph.* London: J. Cape, 1970; New York: Atheneum, 1970.

*Mr. Armitage Isn't Back Yet.* London: J. Cape, 1971.

*Holding On.* London: Quartet, 1973; also published as *Twilight of the Day.* New York: Simon & Schuster, 1974.

*The Revolving Door.* London: Quartet, 1973.

*Lord Richard's Passion.* London: Quartet, 1974; New York: Knopf, 1974.

*Strangers.* London: Quartet, 1974.

*The Pursuit of Happiness.* London: Quartet, 1975; New York: Mason/Charter, 1976.

*Scenes from Bourgeois Life* (novellas). London: Quartet, 1976.

*Nobody's Fault.* London: Quartet, 1977; New York: Mason/Charter, 1977.

*Today the Struggle.* London: Quartet, 1978.

*The Beautiful Words.* London: Deutsch, 1979.

*A Short Time to Live.* London: Deutsch, 1980; New York: St. Martin's, 1980.

*Two Women and Their Man.* London: Deutsch, 1981; New York: St. Martin's, 1981.

*Joanna's Luck.* London: Piatkus, 1984.

*Coming Home.* London: Piatkus, 1986.

**Nonfiction:**

*Guilty Men, 1957: Suez and Cyprus,* with Michael Foot. London: Gollancz, 1957; New York: Rinehart, 1957.

*Potbank.* London: Secker & Warburg, 1961.

*Big Two: Life in America and Russia.* London: J. Cape, 1962; also published as *The Antagonists.* New York: C.N. Potter, 1962.

*Two Ears of Corn: Oxfam in Action.* London: Hodder & Stoughton, 1965; also published as *In Famine's Shadow: A Private War on Hunger.* Boston: Beacon Press, 1967.

*Life on the Dole.* London: Davis-Poynter, 1972.

*The Oil Rush.* London: Quartet, 1976.

**Translator of:**

*The Second Chinese Revolution,* by K.S. Karol. New York: Hill & Wang, 1974; London: J. Cape, 1975.

**Editor of:**

*Kingsley Martin: Portrait and Self-Portrait.* London: Barrie & Jenkins, 1969; New York: Humanities Press, 1969.

*Privacy.* Newton Abbot, England and North Pomfret, Vt.: David & Charles, 1974.

# Carolyn Kizer

*1925-*

*Grandfather Frank Kizer, as Fire Commissioner (third from right in third row), about 1893*

## I

The first Kizer—or Keyser as it was then spelt—to leave the home of his ancestors in Holland was the Reverend Dirck Keyser, son of Gerrits Keyser, a silk merchant in Amsterdam. He came to Germantown, Pennsylvania, as a Dutch Mennonite preacher in 1690, bringing his wife and three children," wrote my father in a memoir which he has left to me. "Dirck Keyser's sons took to farming, down in the Shenandoah Valley in Virginia, west of where the city of Washington was to be built a hundred years later.

"There, succeeding generations changed the Dutch 'Keyser' to 'Kizer,' and dropped names such as Dirck and Gerrits for English Bible names such as John, Simon, and Joseph. There they farmed the land

and raised large families. In 1809, my great-grandfather Joseph Kizer . . . made a horseback journey into western Ohio, and there he selected 160 acres in the deep woods of what was later Champaign County, where his descendents still farm the land." After obtaining a patent signed by President Jefferson, he moved his wife and two little children and their household goods to Ohio, then a journey of six weeks. "There, within a year, their third child, my grandfather Benjamin, was born to them." His son was Frank Kizer, who married Mary Hamilton, Scots daughter of a Springfield physician whose family, like the Kizers, came from Virginia. A year later, in 1878, my father was born.

My grandparents settled on a farm which had been given them by my great-grandfather as a wedding gift. Grandfather had not wanted to be a farmer, but he had only had a year at Oberlin College, and now his father insisted that he settle down. He stood it for four years, and then managed to sell the farm back to his stern, disapproving father, and set up as a small-town merchant. Farm life hadn't agreed with my father either. He was subject to severe hay fever and must have been allergic to practically everything on the farm. And he hated farm food: the enormous platters heaped with meat and potatoes and liberally slathered with gravy to satisfy the farmhand's appetites nauseated him. (At home we rarely had meat, we never had mashed potatoes, and never gravy.)

Father's first memory was of the farm, when he couldn't have been older than three:

> "One day I climbed into the pig pen to see the new litter of baby pigs, and the mother pig bit me," Father said. "So I kicked the pig. Just then my father came around the corner of the barn and saw me. And because I had kicked the pig he gave me a whipping. I felt the terrible injustice of this, and decided to run away from home. I didn't get very far, as my legs were short, and I soon settled down behind a haystack in the near field. Pretty soon my mother came to the back door and began calling to me, 'Ben! Ben! Come to supper now!' I'm sure I had been in that field all of fifteen minutes and I was dying of hunger, but nothing would induce me to speak. 'Ben! Ben!' Mother kept calling, 'Where are you, Ben?' I could bear it no longer. 'I won't anser!' I cried."

Like Father's people, Mother's, both the Ashleys and the Warrens, came from Virginia; but they were of English stock. My grandfather William Washington Ashley was a descendant of the first Earl of Shaftesbury, Anthony Ashley Cooper, and of the elder brother of George Washington. My grandmother Carolyn Warren descended from one Martin Warren, who fought in the Revolution, after which he settled in Missouri, founded the town of Warrensberg, and spent the rest of his life as a blacksmith. (Thanks to Martin Warren, Mother was able to join the Daughters of the American Revolution at the time they barred the great singer Marian Anderson from their hall in Washington, D.C., solely because she was black. Mother joined so that she could raise some serious hell about this outrage, a quite characteristic act compounded of fury and glee.)

Grandfather Ashley was orphaned as an infant, and one of my mother's stories which made a great impression on me was of how her great-aunt Eliza, who was engaged to a Union captain, Richard Merriweather Box, used to drive a buggy through the

*Maternal grandmother, Carolyn Warren Ashley, in Montrose, Colorado, 1888*

Southern and Union lines during the Civil War, with the baby beside her on the seat, to visit her fiancé.

Carolyn Warren, for whom I am named, was a beauty, with black hair, dead white skin, and violet eyes. "She despised her nickname," my mother told me. " 'Care-worn!' she would cry, in her soft Southern accent, 'I'm *not* care-worn!' " (I wonder if my aversion to nicknames stems from hers. I coped with this as a child by simply refusing to answer if addressed by anything other than my full name.) Like my Kizer grandmother, she was a year or two older than Grandfather, and self-conscious about it. She was an ardent Democrat, and he, like most doctors, a staunch Republican. "He called her 'mouse-ears,' " Mother said, "and she called him 'donkey-ears.' " Grandfather graduated in the first class of Belleview, Mother told me, and shortly after he began to practice medicine they moved to the Colorado mountains because both of them had tuberculosis. There my mother and her brothers were born, one right after another. Poor Grandmother! By the time of her early death, right after my youngest uncle was born, she must have been care-worn indeed.

"In St. Paris, from 1881 to 1890, my father spent

the hardest, most toilsome years of his life," my father wrote, "in a desperate attempt to make a go of an enterprise that was doomed from the start." For one thing, he had stocked fine china, which was his special pride, but no one would buy it. "Farms, not china were the hobby of those who had money. Bit by bit, the noose grew tighter. Finally, when my father was thirty-three, he could go on no longer. He was forced to turn everything over to his creditors." His humiliation over this disgrace marked him for the rest of his life. "To him it seemed important that the Kizers, whom he thought of as the oldest and best family in the region, had never had a failure among them. Father had secretly thought himself smarter than the others, sure to carry the credit of the family to greater heights." The only thing to do was to move far, far away. So Grandfather headed west, and stopped at the little town of Spokane, in Eastern Washington.

"Ouray, the little town where we grew up, was high in the Colorado Mountains—12,000 feet," Mother said. (It was more like 7,800, but Mother had a highly developed dramatic sense, and 12 sounded better.) "It never occurred to us that skis were for recreation; we used them to get around on most of the year. And sledding too—although sometimes we sledded for fun. One Sunday when we should have been in church, the five little Ashleys dragged their sled way up the side of the mountain, and we slid all the way into town; the doors of the Episcopal church were wide open, and the service was going on, the choir was singing, as the sled shot down the center aisle and bumped up against the altar!" (I visited that little church last summer; the door faces away from the mountain and it would have been impossible to enter in that fashion.)

Grandfather Kizer's first job in Spokane was as a clerk in a grocery store. But soon he became book-keeper and office manager for a wholesale butter-and-egg distributor. He was an attractive man who made friends easily, in his church and in the Republican party. In less than three years after arriving in Spokane, he became one of three City Commissioners. I have a wonderful photograph of Grandfather as Fire Commissioner, presiding in civilian clothes over his firemen, who look as funny as Keystone cops. Because he was a public official, my grandfather managed to escape the calamitous results of the panic of 1893; but Frank Kizer had dreamed of returning to St. Paris, Ohio, in triumph, a successful man in a frock coat and a silk hat, to obliterate forever the memory of his disgrace. Every effort by every family member was bent towards this goal; the little boys worked at odd jobs; my grandmother, after her normal thirteen-hour day, baked bread at night for the boys to peddle the next day. But only a year after the panic Spokane was in the midst of a wild mining boom. Speculators poured into town; new mining companies were quickly organized, and wiser heads than Grandfather plunged into dubious investments. Finally, Grandfather couldn't resist: he resigned as city commissioner, and bought into a mine called The Lily May. He lost everything, including the top hat and the new frock coat.

"Your grandfather was the doctor for the towns of Montrose and Telluride as well as Ouray," Mother told me. "Those were terrible times. If a miner was injured in an accident, the company just fired him. No workman's compensation or insurance or anything like that. His family was lucky not to starve. And when the miners tried to strike, the company would lock them into boxcars and shunt the train from Ouray to Montrose to Telluride and back again. The women would run down to the tracks and try to throw them food and bottles of water. The men were just packed into those cars like the Jews under Hitler." And when the miners were hurt, my grandfather tried to patch them up, most of the time without being paid anything. All this made a lifelong radical out of Mother.

The second ruin of Grandfather Kizer was, as my father put it, the last blow. "When he was only forty, my father suffered a stroke. Instead of the handsome, affable, magnetic man I had always known, my father was an invalid, bewildered, deeply self-critical, pathetically dependent on the rest of us." (A characteristic of both my grandfathers was that they were rotten businessmen. Whatever they touched turned to dross, the difference being that Grandfather Ashley was a successful doctor and brilliant diagnostician. God knows what my poor grandfather Kizer should have been! At any rate, I inherited their impracticality; the women in my family were the shrewd and provident ones.)

Shortly after that, Grandfather, who was also growing deaf, was walking on the trestle bridge over Hangman's Creek where supposedly he failed to hear the train coming behind him. He was instantly killed. (Of course one wonders about suicide, although it seemed clear that this supposition had not occurred to his son.) My father had to drop out of school to become the sole support of the family, which included a younger brother and sister. In addition to selling newspapers on the streets of Spokane he went to work as a bookkeeper in a hardware store (and when he left, he was succeeded by a lad named Henry J. Kaiser, for whom my father was general counsel when Kaiser was building Grand Coulee Dam—leading, obviously, to endless confusion).

"The next three and a half years were the bitterest of my life," my father wrote. "The one thing I wanted above everything else was an education. I was deeply rebellious, not against my father, but against the fate that had involved me in his second ruin. I could see no escape."

"This is a picture of the most beautiful girl in Ouray," Mother said. "The whole family lived in a two-room house. Her little brother was an idiot who was kept chained to a bedstead in the front room." He babbled and drooled, and had no control over his bodily functions. "She could never bring friends home because of her brother. All the boys were in love with her, but she wouldn't see any of them. As they both grew older, she became more and more desperate, and finally she ran away and went on the streets. There was nothing else for her to do."

In addition to working a seventy-hour week at McGowan Brothers hardware store, my father found additional employment reading aloud to an Episcopal clergyman and to a few elderly lawyers and judges who had fled the South in the days of Reconstruction. They were the town's intellectuals, men of large learning and extensive libraries. "This nourished my love of books," Father said. "No one else had these beautiful volumes, row on row, covered in red leather with the names stamped in gold on their spines! So I determined to become a lawyer, so that I could have such a library for my own."

My mother and her two brothers, Rob and Charles, often spoke of my grandfather Ashley as a stern disciplinarian. One day when Rob and Ray, the two oldest boys, were still very young they met the owner of the livery stable and chorused, "Hello, Sam!" My grandfather happened to overhear them, and instantly dragged the boys off to the woodshed for a severe whipping. "Never again do I want to hear you call a grown man by his first name!" The boys protested that they didn't know that Sam *had* a last name, to no avail. Forty years later, they were still bitter about this. But to the granddaughter who visited him and her uncles in California, Grandfather was soft and indulgent. I still remember from the age of six or so when I had been begging for more candy, Grandfather saying, "Oh, let the baby have what she wants!" and the long long look which my mother and

my uncle Rob exchanged. I can't help but believe that the lifelong insecurities of that handsome and gifted generation grew in part from the harshness and severity of my grandfather's discipline. On the other side, I think that my father's enormous self-confidence developed under the aegis of a gentle father and an adoring mother.

With less than two years of high school and none of college, Father determined to enter the Law School of the University of Michigan, which in those days you could do without having an undergraduate degree. "I camped in the office of the President until he would see me," Father said. "He just laughed at me and turned me down. So I went back every morning at eight o'clock and sat in his office, till finally I wore him out, and he admitted me. 'Now I hope I've seen the last of you,' he said. 'Well, no,' I told him. 'Now I want you to admit my brother Don.' He just threw up his hands, but eventually he let Don in as well."

"When I was seventeen," Mother said, "I was chosen to ride on the float in the annual parade. I already had a white organdy dress for church, but Mother made me the most beautiful sash I had ever seen: turquoise blue silk with a long bow in the back.

*Mother, Mabel Ashley, at seventeen*

When I rode on the float I was so proud! I waved at the crowd standing along the street, and dropped my new embroidered handkerchief. A rough-looking miner picked it up and put it in his pocket." The next day, she went with her father to the mine, where one of the miners had had an accident. At the mine entrance stood the man who had picked up her handkerchief, and fixing her "with a lewd grin," he masturbated into it. "So I went home and took my beautiful blue sash that I loved so much and I opened the door of the stove and pushed it in and burnt it up."

Father had a desperate time at college. Having saved every penny while he was working in Spokane to keep his mother going, he now took on a variety of jobs to support himself, including digging ditches and writing theses for the other, lazier men. I have in my possession his little account book, where a typical entry is, "Collar turned: one penny." I always weep when I read it. He was tall, thin, undernourished, and frail. Inevitably, the life of unceasing labor and study caught up with him. His whole system rebelled: what food he ate he vomited up, and he went blind. A

*Author's mother, age twenty-nine, in 1909*

fellow-student from Spokane, Ed Powell, nursed him and read case notes aloud to him in these, his darkest hours. This forged a friendship that lasted all their long lives as practicing attorneys in Spokane. After a rest of several months that winter, he regained his sight. "And the doctor told me never to take stimulants—coffee, tea—to go easy on meat, which I didn't care for anyway, not to smoke and never to drink. And get plenty of exercise." He took this advice and lived by it for the rest of his life. He walked, hiked, climbed. Well into middle age, he could still walk forty miles. As soon as he returned to Spokane, he began to carry a cane, for pleasure. And I suspect he thought it made him look more mature. He carried it all his life; it was his totem, his hallmark: swinging his cane as he strode along Second Street on his way to the office. If by any chance he mislaid it, strangers would come up to him in the street, saying, "Mr. Kizer, where is your cane?"

When Mother was thirteen her own mother died. This was a wound to my mother that never healed— and which was passed on to me. "When my mother died, I never forgave myself for being impudent and disobedient. If anything should happen to me, I wouldn't want you to have that burden of guilt." The message was, of course, "Be good, or else!" When Rollin, her favorite brother, sustained an injury on the football field, he became paralyzed for life, which was a decade until he was twenty-six. He became the family saint: winsome, spiritual, beautiful. And, like all the Ashleys, he was endowed with—or developed, lying helpless day after tedious day—extraordinary intuitions, perceptions, ESP, call it what you will. "Charles [Mother's youngest brother], almost as soon as he could walk, looked after Rollin: washed him, fed him, turned him over in bed. Later, Charles might be on the dance floor miles away, and he would drop the girl right in the middle of the floor and run out, saying, 'Rollin wants me.' " And Rollin did.

One night, my grandfather, who had gone up the mountain to deliver a baby, didn't return and didn't return, and everyone was worried. " 'It was a breach birth, and twins, and the horse has gone lame. Dad will be home about five in the morning. He's dead tired,' Rollin said." And so it was, Grandfather staggering in, heaving off his muddy coat, and telling them about it, word for word, at five in the morning.

My father graduated from Michigan Law School, Phi Beta Kappa, in 1902, was admitted to the Michigan Bar, and returned to Spokane to practice law for the rest of his life. Meanwhile Mother was going to the University of Colorado, in Boulder, to get her degree in Biology. The last time I looked, she was still on the walls of the Pi Phi House in Boulder, in a group picture, the very model of a glorious Gibson Girl. Then Grandfather, who had remarried and started a second family, moved the whole tribe to California. Mother went on to get her advanced degree in Biology at Stanford, in 1904.

Mother had wonderful stories about teaching kindergarten in San Francisco for Chinese tots, and running a summer camp for impoverished children near Muir woods. My favorite San Francisco story concerns a time when the Powell Street cable snapped, and the cable car slid all the way down the steep hill, to crash into a waiting truck at Union Square. An ancient Chinese inquired of Mother, "Whatsa molla? Stling bloke?" But for the most part, their stories of childhood and growing up had ceased, to be replaced by fragmentary memories called up at odd moments. There was something like a twenty-year hiatus until they met each other, and the family romance began.

Father proposed to Mother on a sofa on the balcony of the famed Davenport Hotel, two weeks after they had met, he then being a widower in his late forties, Mother a spinster in her early forties. This bench was a shrine of my youth, often revisited. Father jokingly suggested to Mr. Davenport that he be permitted to buy the sofa; sometime in the sixties it disappeared.

I came along not too long after their marriage, conceived, I was told, on March 12, at Lake Louise, in Canada. On the night I was born, December 10, my father went for a long walk under the stars while my mother was in labor, and then went home and wrote me a letter, to be delivered on my eighteenth birthday.

> Your mother had just been taken to the delivery room, where she was given over to the care of doctors and nurses among whom she was to endure the travail of your birth, while your father was sent out into the night. . . . There was no moon nor a cloud in the sky, and in that crisp, sparkling air, the stars were at their nearest to earth. Sirius was there, high in the south; Capella was there, low in the northwest, near to her setting; Vega was there, just risen in the northeast; and well up in the east was Arcturus. The four brightest, most beautiful of all our stars, so rarely to be seen together, were shining down upon your birth. . . . It is at just such poignant mo-

*Mabel Ashley at forty-five*

ments as these that the voices of the Universe become articulate to us. It is when our spirits are stabbed broad awake that we can listen, that we can feel the everlasting arms of the God at the heart of all being. Why do I tell you this? You too will suffer pain, emotion too keen for the human breast to bear alone. When it comes, when it seems unbearable, walk out of doors if you can. There will be the wind of the dawn, or the sun of noonday, or the stars of night. There will be the pine trees and the hills, or perhaps the sweet rain. . . .

I believe that that is the closest my father ever came to poetry. He lived so energetically in the world that I am afraid that I came to feel that Mother was in sole charge of the poetic, artistic part of my life—this despite the fact that he read aloud to us every night of our lives when we were at home, beginning when I was five or so. If you should be mad enough to want your child to grow up to be a writer, I can guarantee this method, doubled in my case because Mother read aloud to me too.

Me. I. Who was I? I found a slip of paper in the

book of my early life which my mother so scrupulous-
ly kept. It reads, in part, "Eleanor Ashley Kizer, Isabel
Ashley Kizer, Evelyn Ashley Kizer, Sylvia Ashley
Kizer, Janet Ashley Kizer," and finally, "Carolyn
Ashley Kizer." And by each name are a number of
initials; evidently Mother's friends voted on the
names! I am glad that "Carolyn" won. I am one of
those rare people who has always been fond of her
name. However, it has occurred to me that bits of
Eleanor (queenly, imperious), Isabel (the cold selfish
villainess), Evelyn (wishy-washy old Evelyn), Sylvia
(unpredictable wood-nymph), and Janet (reliable
horse) were digested by my psyche as well. From
childhood through adolescence when I would come
down to breakfast, Mother frequently inquired, in
tones of irony, "And who are we this morning?"

It may be another sign of my shaky sense of
identity that I had not one imaginary playmate but
four: Ling, Ding, Kootoo, and Grease, or Greece.
Ling was the dominant one (and where I got those
Chinese names I have no idea), a boy, as were Ding
and Kootoo (who, it is conceivable, was Japanese);
Greece was a girl who lived in the water tower across
the river that I could see from my bedroom window. I
believe that the boys were in residence. I remember
shouting at our phlegmatic, literal-minded laundress,
Mrs. Anderson, "Get up! Get up! You are sitting on
Ling!" I can still see the look of somewhat bovine
bewilderment on her good face as she rose heavily
and looked behind her at an empty chair.

I have often been asked how I managed not to be
crushed by two strong, articulate, and dominating
parents. Long ago I found a formula for replying to
such queries: "Inside this body of a road-company
Valkyrie is a small, bedraggled brown sparrow." Like
all such formulae, it is a lie with a kernel of truth. One
way of handling my family situation was by parroting
the opinions of my parents. We were an intensely
political family, and as I was one of those repellant
children who was allowed to dine with the grown-ups,
I felt free to express opinions on the news of the day
about which I was only superficially acquainted, no
doubt to the disgust of visitors.

And visitors we had aplenty, many of them
distinguished and internationally famous. During my
childhood, the trip across America was still by train,
and a long trip it was: a night and a day from New
York to Chicago, and then two more days and nights
to Spokane, at which point many people felt the urge
to break the trip. The fame of the Davenport Hotel,
and the spreading fame of Mother's talents as a
conversationalist and cook, as well as Father's wide
acquaintanceship in the world of letters, the law and
state, regional and national planning, brought us a

*Father, Benjamin H. Kizer, at age fifty*

rich social life, in contrast to the bland, complacent,
unintellectual, and almost wholly Republican society
of Spokane.

Why, you may ask—as Mother often did—were
two people of their outstanding talents supposed to
be content to live in relative obscurity in this small
provincial town? Father's stock answer was that most
of the United States had been despoiled by willful and
greedy men—damaged almost beyond repair—and
that the West still had a chance to avoid the mistakes
which had so damaged Europe and the rest of
America. His dedication to city, county, state, and
regional planning stemmed from this passionate
belief. (At one time he had eleven letterheads for
everything from the National Society of Planning
Officials all the way down to the city planning
commission; he headed all of them at one time or
another, having started most of them.) His dream
collapsed with the onset of World War II, when
planning lost all its priorities, and the aftermath,
when books such as Friedrich Hayek's *Road to Serfdom*
equated planning with socialism, which led inevitably
to communism, and the death of civilization as we
know it. Father never gave any indication that he
realized that the West, our pristine West, was going
to end up as squalid as the rest of the country. As he

grew older and older, and seemed destined to live forever, I prayed that his fading sense of reality protected him from the knowledge of the worst excesses of the free-enterprise system as it tore up his beloved West.

But at any rate, his indefatigable letter-writing and his passionate interest in planning and international affairs brought these streams of interesting people to our house in Brown's Addition, where they took a break before entraining for Seattle and the Pacific Coast. I will mention only a few of them, the ones who made a lasting impression on me. My husband, an architect and planner, enjoys telling people that Lewis Mumford taught me about sex. You would think that my mother the biologist might have filled me in, as she had a couple of generations of girls at Mills and San Francisco State, where she headed the departments of Biology, but no. I fear that my dear mother subscribed to the fantasy that ignorance is protection. (Father coped with the whole topic in his inimitable way by pressing on me the *Collected Works* of D. H. Lawrence, which indeed I devoured, and which may have had the somewhat salutary effect of protecting me during World War II from the kinds of boys who said, "I'm shipping out tomorrow, and I may never come back." In retrospect, I wish I had honored the wholesome fears of some of them, but I was too hung up on Lawrence

and what I thought of as the sanctity of sex.)

At any rate, Lewis, who had formed a fast friendship with my father through correspondence, arrived in Spokane when I was ten or so; we went out to our cabin at Hayden Lake, and in the course of taking me for a walk Lewis discovered that I knew absolutely nothing, despite Lady Chatterley (expurgated edition). He proceeded to enlighten me—which was the last information I received until I entered college, and some kind medical students at Harvard put me to bed on their couch and dumped a comprehensive medical text on the coffee table beside me.

We had a number of Chinese visitors in those days during the Japanese invasion of Manchuria and later the Chinese mainland; they were scouring the country's campuses to plead the Chinese cause. I remember the scholar and musicologist T. Z. Koo, a man of great beauty (and I've always been a fool for a pretty face) who wore long gowns of pale blue or grey silk, with white stockings and black cloth shoes. He usually carried a bamboo flute in his hand, and could be persuaded to perform infinitely poignant and melancholy folk airs on it. (He is also the hero of the "Likee fishee?" story which has gone round the world—and indeed his English was without flaw.) But the philosopher Dr. Hu Shih made the deepest impression on me (it's easy to tell, because I can

*"My father, in the Reed College dining room, whence all but he had fled (in the 1960s).
He was a Regent of Reed for over thirty years."*

remember speeches and conversations word for word though memory may fail me about nearly everything else).

One day we drove Dr. Hu down to Washington State College, in Pullman, a couple of hours south of Spokane. I was deeply impressed by his speech to the students and faculty because of the calm, detached tone in which he recounted the horrors of the Japanese invasion—rape, pillage, murder, destruction—and members of his own immediate family had been victims. He spoke of the necessity of stopping the Japanese, and then took a long view of how they should be treated after defeat: with the generosity of honorable men. On the way home, very emotional still, I protested, "Dr. Hu! How could you sound so calm?" "Because, my dear, it was not my own feelings I wished to arouse, but yours." I like to think that this lesson has remained with me all my life, not in my conversation—that would be too much to ask of one who inherited her mother's capacity for indignation—but in my work.

In addition to an assortment of philosophers, architects, and planners, we had a number of interesting English visitors, including Harold Laski, Vera Brittain, and Marjorie Strachey, one of Lytton's sisters. I blush to recall that when Laski inquired about the future of a politician then much in the news, I blurted out that I didn't think he could ever be successful, he was so small and he had a silly mustache, and he wore a hat that didn't fit him. As this was a dead-on description of Laski himself, I certainly didn't get any award for tact. But from what I subsequently learned of Laski, he was without tact himself, and deserved some of his own medicine. After the war, Mother and I visited Miss Brittain and her husband, George Catlin, at their home in Cheyne Walk. As shortages of almost everything were still a feature of English life in 1947, Mother had taken them a rather lavish package of tinned meat, butter, cookies, and other good things. These they refused in no uncertain terms, to my mother's deep humiliation. "As we are part of the Socialist Government which is demanding sacrifices of our people, we cannot accept gifts which would better our own lot." Speaking of tactlessness, I wondered why they hadn't just thanked Mother for her thoughtfulness and then quietly given away the food to the hungry. I think I began to believe that tactlessness was a prominent feature of British Socialism.

I remember Miss Strachey less well, perhaps because we didn't see her again after that initial visit. But I do remember that she subsequently sent me a set of the novels of Thomas Hardy. By a piece of bad luck, I began with *Jude the Obscure,* and like so many

Benjamin H. Kizer

*Vachel Lindsay, Pullman, Washington, 1925*

others before me, when I reached the part about the hangings in the attic, I threw the book across the room. Now if she had sent me the poetry. . . .

But in addition to these visitors—our lifeline to the outside world—we had a guest for whom my father was responsible for a number of years. In the spring of the year after I was born, Vachel Lindsay ran an ad in a literary review inquiring, in Vachel's often inflated and dramatic style, if there was anyone out there who would care to exchange bread for poems. My father at once answered in the affirmative—and I believe his was the only response which Vachel received. Father enclosed a train ticket (coach) from Gulfport, Mississippi, to Spokane, Washington. Vachel packed up his hundreds of books, notebooks, scrapbooks, and manuscripts in Gulfport and in Springfield, Illinois, and shipped them to the Davenport Hotel. Privately, Father had made an arrangement with Louis Davenport, sole owner and proprietor, to house Vachel in a pleasant suite of rooms on the top floor, charging him the nominal sum of thirty-five dollars a month, Father to contribute the rest from his own slender pocketbook, unbeknownst to Vachel.

It is worth a moment's digression to speak of Louis Davenport, an unusual man even if this were all that we knew about him. In the great Spokane fire of 1889, which virtually destroyed the city, young Louis Davenport (I believe that that was not his name then; it was something Armenian) had set up a tent and a flapjack stand on one of the ruined blocks and was doing a thriving business feeding the inhabitants, including miners, lumbermen, their families, prostitutes, and assorted scalawags. Legend has it—Mr. Davenport's legend anyhow—that a gypsy fortune-teller showed up and insisted on reading his palm. "You will be *vairy* rich and successful," she said, rolling her gypsy eyes, "if you build a hotel on this *vairy* spot, so long as your hotel is filled with singing birds, living fish, water fountains, and fresh flowers."

And so it came to pass. The Davenport was an amazing establishment for the small-town America of that day. As I was growing up, it was in its prime: Between the pillars in the lobby were hung cages of beautiful singing canaries; fires burned all day in the massive fireplaces at either end of the lobby; and in the center was a large fountain surrounded by masses of living blooms. (It is significant that the hotel prospered until Mr. Davenport died, the hotel was sold, and a series of subsequent owners eliminated the birds, the fountain, the flowers, the fish in their tanks, and the fires in the fireplaces. And the hotel, growing ever shabbier, has been in trouble ever since.)

When Vachel moved into the Davenport, all coins that passed through the hotel were washed and polished until they gleamed like new. Every incoming guest received flowers and a basket of fruit. Vachel brought with him one of his own large paintings, entitled *The Tree of Laughing Bells*, which Louis Davenport hung in a prominent place on his elegant mezzanine.

Every Sunday morning my father would walk from our house at 202 Coeur d'Alene, right at the end of Second Street, all the way down to the hotel, where he would pick up Vachel. They would walk for hours, along the banks of the Spokane River, or on the Rimrock, overlooking the valley. Vachel, an enthusiast if there ever was one, was at this time infatuated with the architect and medievalist Ralph Adams Cram, and Cram's concept of "the walled town," a utopian city whose ramparts would shut out invaders. Vachel fancied that Spokane, surrounded

by rocks and scrub pine and fields, could be such a town. Vachel had had his dreams of Springfield, his hometown, but they had come to nothing. Now, perhaps, if Spokane could be made to listen to Vachel as he preached his Gospel of Beauty to men's clubs, the Elks, the Chamber of Commerce—whose program directors, always desperate for luncheon speakers, particularly those who charged no fee, were happy to invite Vachel to speak—if Spokane could be made aware of Beauty, then she might approach the ideal of Cram's and Vachel's fantasies.

When I was barely able to toddle I sometimes accompanied the two men. There are snapshots of the three of us in the family album, Carolyn self-consciously holding up one Mary Jane-shod foot. Vachel had told me that I had "Della Robbia toes." I had no idea what kind of toes these were but they sounded special, so special that I thought they might be visible through my shoes. The snapshots help to restore my memories (though I believe that they also suppress the genuine visions in favor of the printed ones). But I truly remember Vachel's great gusts of laughter; it was an extraordinarily loud, braying laugh that must have echoed for miles across the valley—and his nonstop, uninterruptible discourse. What a talker the man was! I have noted with indignation that some accounts refer to Vachel as a drinker. Nothing could be further from the truth. Like Father, he never took a drink in his life. But unlike Ben Kizer, Vachel never outgrew his puritan origins. It's understandable that people might think that he drank, because he became intoxicated by his own language: his voice would rise and rise until he was shouting. I don't remember many of the words, but I will remember the tones until death silences all.

One night Percy Grainger came to the house. He had known my father for some time, Father being chairman of the symphony board and responsible for booking the artists who appeared with it. It was always exciting to have Percy visit. Like Vachel, he was a highly dramatic, even florid, personality, though far more attractive than Vachel, who was, in truth, a plain and gawky man. Vachel believed that these qualities made him resemble his idol, Lincoln, though it is difficult for an objective outsider to see the resemblance. Percy would appear for dinner, dazzling in white tie and tails before his concert, and would insist on clearing off the table between courses. Percy protested his democratic spirit in all things, to the consternation of a succession of German maids who would fall back against the walls when Percy swept into the kitchen with a pile of plates.

On this particular night, Vachel, Percy, and my parents had been to a lecture by a young Englishman who had recently returned from Africa, where he had studied tribal drumming. He came back with them to the house, and I was permitted to come downstairs in my Doctor Dentons because my mother believed that children should be included in Special Occasions, which were more important in forming the infant sensibility than Regular Hours. There was an enormous fire blazing on the hearth, and the young Englishman was sitting crosslegged in front of it with an assortment of drums. I remember his quiet voice as he began softly, tentatively, to drum. Suddenly, Percy sprang to the piano and began to play his "Zanzibar Suite," recently composed. In a moment Vachel leapt up and began his chanting:

> Then I saw the Congo, creeping through the
> black,
> Cutting through the jungle with a golden
> track. . . .

All the lights had been turned out, and Vachel's face blazed in the firelight:

> Mumbo-Jumbo will hoo-doo you,
> Mumbo-Jumbo will hoo-doo you,
> Mumbo-Jumbo . . . will hoo . . . doo . . .
> you.

All my life I have lugged an old blue silk hatbox from one to another of the places I have lived. In it, along with my grandmother's, my mother's, and my own christening gown and other antique treasures, is a tiny Bible. In it, Vachel has inscribed, in his characteristic scrawl, large, round, and black, "To Carolyn, from the man who usually writes on barn doors, but can write on an angel's penny." And somewhere in every house I have owned are some framed drawings, product of Vachel's "word game." This entailed Vachel writing out the signature of the person in question, and then turning that signature into a portrait. My favorite is Elizabeth Barrett Browning, ringlets and all, a dead likeness. Vachel would have loved to have been an artist, and he kept coming back to drawing for all of his fevered life. But his gifts in this genre were limited, and most successful when linked to literature, as with the word games.

I think that people have been inclined to overestimate Vachel's influence on my becoming a poet. I think that from a very early age I sensed Vachel as a man frighteningly flawed, a man stubborn, obsessed, blind to the realities of the crass American towns where he sang his songs and preached his beliefs, whose citizens laughed at him and thought him a buffoon. And who ultimately destroyed him. No, the chief influence came from another direction. Vachel had a sister named Olive Wakefield, a missionary in

China. I remember Vachel reading her letters aloud; I remember Mother saying that Vachel wrote what was, to her, his best poem, "The Chinese Nightingale," on our living-room sofa. I remember Mother reading aloud to me the translations of Arthur Waley. Through Mother, and Vachel, and Mrs. Wakefield, whom I never knew except through the excitement which her letters caused, I acquired my unending devotion to Chinese poetry.

Of course, Vachel was a limited poet, limited in some of the ways in which Sandburg was, and for some of the same reasons: they were both obsessed with the idea of being American, a kind of crippling chauvinism which blinded them to the importance of what was happening in Europe: the French symbolists, Eliot, Pound. But even with his limitations of judgement, and I suppose ultimately, of talent, I often wonder what Vachel's life would have been like if he had been born forty years later. By the time he was grown, the Main Street Babbitry of small-town America would have diminished; poets no better than he would read poetry to jazz in San Francisco clubs to wild acclaim.

Vachel was the precursor of Dylan Thomas, to whom all poets owe everlasting gratitude for making popular our chief source of income: poetry readings. At his best, the companion for children, the child that was and is me, Vachel was a magic man. My own children demanded that I play Burl Ives singing Vachel's poems, over and over until the records were worn out: "The moon's the North Wind's cookie / he bites it day by day . . ." Singing:

> There was a little turtle
> He lived in a box
> He swam in a puddle
> He climbed on the rocks
>
> He snapped at a mosquito
> He snapped at a flea
> He snapped at a minnow
> And he snapped at me.
>
> He caught the mosquito
> He caught the flea
> He caught the minnow
> But he didn't catch me.

I remember Vachel's answer to a reporter who asked him how long he planned to stay at the Davenport. "Till the ants carry me out grain by grain through the keyhole," he said.

And I remember standing by his knee as Vachel almost whispered these words to me:

I heard a cricket's cymbals play,
A scarecrow lightly flapped his rags,
And a pan that hung by his shoulder rang,
Rattled and thumped in a listless way,
And now the wind in the chimney sang . . .

"Life is the west-going dream-storm's breath,
Life is a dream, the sigh of the skies,
The breath of the stars, that nod on their
pillows
With their golden hair mussed over their
eyes."
The locust played on his musical wing,
Sang to his mate of love's delight.
I heard the whippoorwill's soft fret.

I heard a cricket carolling,
I heard a cricket carolling,
I heard a cricket say: "Good-night, good-
night,
Good-night, good-night . . .good-night."

## II

In an early poem of mine called "By The River-side" (the only poem, so far as I know, that takes its epigraph from the cover of the telephone directory: "Do not call from Memory. All numbers have changed"), I speak of the house where I grew up, at 202 Coeur d'Alene. For many years the house had been owned by a Dutch bank, and passed from one bank president to the next, along with a hefty sum for remodelling. So wings were added, rooms closed off (for example, there was a fascinating closet five feet off the floor, about ten feet deep, with a stained glass window at the end; Mother kept rolls of wallpaper and carpeting in it), and windows cut through walls. Mother said that, architecturally, it was a stew. But for a child growing up, it was a dream of a house. Those mysterious corridors, that peculiar back staircase, those deep and multitudinous closets! It was always a stimulus to a burgeoning imagination, and has continued to haunt my dreams.

The Freudian belief that an old house symbolizes Mother seems just right to me (although like many another woman, I check out when it comes to Freud's theories concerning women; however, penis envy to females of my generation meant that if you had one, you too could be a Rhodes Scholar or visit Mt. Athos). Perhaps especially so in my case because my mother was old, old enough to be my grandmother: haunted, mysterious, full of hidden passages and unexpected adventures. Every Hallowe'en, from the age of five or so, I was given a party. The most

*202 Coeur d'Alene, the house in Spokane (which no longer exists) where Kizer grew up*

wonderful feature of this event was Mother, dressed as a gypsy, telling our fortunes, and at some point leading all the little children, blindfolded, up and down and around the house. It was an extraordinary experience, being totally lost and disoriented in one's own home. I've always blessed my luck in growing up there, with her, instead of in a box-shaped tract house or an apartment.

Hallowe'en wasn't the only occasion we celebrated. Virtually every notable day on the calendar (with the exception of Mother's Day, which my mother viewed with contempt, as do I) was commemorated in some fashion, and always by handmaking something: May baskets on May Day, filled with a handful of limp flowers and weeds gathered by my grubby fingers and then hung on the doorknobs of the neighbors. Easter! My first poem written on my own, I believe, without an assist from Mother. It was sent to Bishop Cross, with whom I was in love from the age of seven or so. This early passion had something to do with the way his face reminded me of the high-laced shoes that he and my father wore, and I too at times, for weak ankles. The poem was intended as a strictly personal communication, and I was unspeakably shocked when Bishop Cross read it aloud from the pulpit on Easter Sunday. (The only line in it which had any merit at all compared the Easter lily to the angel who appeared at Christ's grave.) No one, especially the bewildered Bishop, could understand why I wasn't pleased by the publicity.

Perhaps this is the time to say a word about Religion. My father was descended from Quaker stock who became converted to Methodism late in the nineteenth century. I remember when I saw the film of Jessamyn West's *Friendly Persuasion:* there was a scene in the Quaker meetinghouse when the little children, in the dead silence of the service, heard the enthusiastic singing of the Methodists down the road, and leaned wistfully out the window. So that was how it happened! Thanks to his mother's training, my father knew the Bible backwards and forwards, and could quote Scripture verbatim. One of the delights of my childhood was listening to my father's up-to-date version of the plagues of Moses. They were deliciously funny, and I begged for them over and over again, correcting him when he altered or omitted a word until he became heartily sick of them. (Neither of my parents, skilled raconteurs, could understand why I never tired of hearing their stories.) These stories obviously influenced my artistic life: one of my early paintings is of the house where Peter's wife's mother lay sick of a fever. It shows a small contemporary cottage painted blue, with a Ford

flivver parked neatly beside it.

However, by the time I came along, Father had ceased being a Methodist, or anything else, although I believe that he still believed in God, and believed in Jesus as leader, poet, and prophet. The chief remnant of his early training was song. Father had a high, thin, Methodist tenor, and when he was feeling especially pleased with life he would break into a doleful hymn tune. Mother loved to tell how, on their honeymoon, he kept singing, "How tedious and tasteless the hours / Since Jesus no longer I see, / Sweet prospects, sweet birds, and sweet flowers / Have *all* lost their sweetness for me." Mother was a nominal Episcopalian, although from time to time, feeling dissatisfied, she would try something else. I wrote about it not long ago:

> For awhile my mother was a believer in
>   Coué
> so as a child I chanted, "Every day
> in every way, I am getting better and
>   better."
>
> Later in my youth
> Mother moved on to The Church of Truth
> which Mrs. Weinstein led, and at her nod
> we sang, "Be still and know that I am
>   God . . ."

But both parents were deeply devoted to the Right Reverend Edward Makin Cross, Episcopal Bishop of the enormous diocese of central and eastern Washington, Idaho, and Montana, as I recall. He was involved in a consuming life work: to build a Gothic cathedral designed by the architect Harold Whitehouse on a hill in Spokane. Although I had not been attending Sunday School, it was brought to his attention that I was praying a good deal (a habit I have never lost), and that he was prominently featured in those prayers. A letter from him at that time reads in part, "Of course, we have to remember as we pray that God's 'no' is just as much an answer to prayer as is God's 'yes,' so always the central theme of our petitions must be, 'Thy will be done.'"

It was about then that he had a serious talk with my parents, in which he pointed out that not sending me to Sunday School was really depriving me of choice, not giving me the freedom they supposed. I had to know what I was rejecting before I could intelligently reject it. This argument, worthy of a Jesuit, proved compelling, and I was duly baptized, with the Bishop and his wife as my godparents—and I've been an Episcopalian ever since! I have two dear writer friends who go to church along with me: George Garrett and Denise Levertov, whose father was a converted Anglican clergyman. I don't think that the three of us would care to be grilled on just what articles of the Nicene Creed we accept. Let's just say that in a world of increasing chaos and violence—or perhaps one should say, "of chaos and violence that we know about"—the stately order of the service is a solace and comfort. And, like my dear father, I love to sing hymns! But I must say that the new Prayer Book, which has mucked up the lovely old cadences without any substitution of clarity, is an abomination to a faithful lover of language, and its ubiquity has cut down on my church attendance, alas. If only the church had listened to Wystan Hugh Auden!

Speaking of Auden, we had in common the fact that the first book either of us was given was *Come Hither,* edited by Walter de la Mare. My copy was presented on January 3, the day I was named. Perhaps it was in being read to from that winsome book that I learned the name of Thomas Love Peacock. At any rate, I fell in love with that combination of words and sounds, and used to sit on the potty shouting, "Thomas Love Peacock! Thomas Love Peacock!" a production number which I have recorded in a poem called, "What Was in a Name." But more than de la Mare's anthology I loved his "children's poems" (unaccountably omitted from his *Collected Poems),* and I still do:

Ann, Ann!
    Come! quick as you can!
There's a fish that TALKS
    In the frying pan.
Out of the fat
    As clear as glass
He put up his mouth
    And moaned 'Alas!' . . .

\*

Has anybody seen my Mopser?—
A comely dog is he,
With hair the color of Charles the Fifth
And teeth like ships at sea;
His tail it curls straight upwards,
His ears stand two abreast,
And he answers to the simple name of
    Mopser
When civilly addressed.

("The Bandog" by Walter de la Mare. Quoted by permission of the Literary Trustees of Walter de la Mare and the Society of Authors as their representative.)

\*

'Come!' said old Shellover.
'What?' says Creep.

'The horny old Gardener's fast asleep;
The fat cock Thrush
To his nest has gone,
And the dews shine bright
In the rising Moon;
Old Sallie Worm from her hole doth peep;
Come!' said old Shellover.
'Ay!' said Creep.

\*

It's a very odd thing—
As odd as can be—
That whatever Miss T. eats
Turns into Miss T. . . . .

\*

I know a little cupboard
With a teeny tiny key,
And there's a jar of Lollypops
    For me, me, me. . . .

I have a small fat grandmama
With a very slippery knee,
And she's the Keeper of the Cupboard
With the key, key, key. . . .

\*

'Grill me some bones,' said the Cobbler,
    'Some bones, my pretty Sue;
I'm tired of my lonesome with heels and
    soles,
Springsides and uppers too;
A mouse in the wainscot is nibbling;
A wind in the keyhole drones;
And a sheet webbed over my candle, Susie,
    Grill me some bones!'

Irresistible poems! How sad that today's children are deprived of their magic and mysteriousness. Although that most haunting of de la Mare's poems in *Peacock Pie* has come to the attention of one or two younger people. When I read Michael Ryan's poem "Gangster Dreams" not long ago, I said to him, "Aha! You've imitated de la Mare's "Song of the Mad Prince"! and he was a little surprised that someone had spotted his homage to an obscure piece.

Mother kept a record of my reading up until the age of eight, and in addition to some of the usual children's books of that day there are many volumes of poetry and poem anthologies. But the name of Gertrude Stein does not appear there, although a poem of hers was, I believe, the first work which I had by heart—called "Grass":

Be cool inside the mule,
Be cool inside the mule,
Be cool inside, with a monkey tied,
Be cool inside the mule.

As you see, it entailed no great feats of memorization. In the meantime, Father had been reading me Kipling's stories, all of Jane Austen, and a great deal of poetry, especially his favorites, Poe and Keats. Father read aloud in a voice that throbbed with feeling. It made Mother nervous. She would jump up from her sewing at the slightest excuse, and make her escape, while Father remarked, "Mabel! Can't you sit still for a few minutes?" I've referred before to my father as "the last of the red-hot romantics." I suppose his demanding life at the office and at the bar didn't allow much scope for the deeply ardent side of his nature, that ardor which, among other things, made him always a passionately loving husband.

Even very early on I believe I preferred my mother's style. Along with Arthur Waley's translations, she read me a great deal of Robinson Jeffers (whom I think she had known slightly in her California days) and even more Whitman. My mother had the most beautiful voice, creamy, deep, and resonant; she didn't need and didn't attempt histrionics. I didn't much care for Poe, and it wasn't till later that I realized that it was his mechanical rhythms and his Gothic sentimentality that repelled me. (It was clear to me by the time I was in the eighth grade, when the teacher required everyone in the class to memorize a poem. They nearly all chose quatrains: the shortest works they could find. But a classmate, Jack, and I memorized the whole of "The Raven," which we used as an accompaniment to a soft-shoe shuffle.) Keats seemed very beautiful and very alien, and I wished that Father's reading didn't make me as uncomfortable as Mother was. Perhaps I sensed that Keats was a poet I could not emulate. Now the letters would have been a different matter, but I probably wasn't ready for them.

As a child, I suffered from severe allergies: asthma, hay fever, and eczema. Much of the time when Father read aloud, I was flaked out on the living-room sofa, trying to be as passive as possible, and concentrating on breathing. I am sure that part of Mother's and my discomfort was our sense that Father, quite unconsciously, was attempting seduction—verbal seduction to be sure—but even so, damaging I have no doubt. It must have been particularly trying for my mother, who was so extraordinarily intuitive, and a seething mass of insecurities as well. She often referred to the intellectual bond between my father and myself, as if she, poor inferior creature, were shut out. I did my best to disabuse her of this nonsense. For one thing, she was certainly our intellectual equal, surely our imaginative superior, and—far more important—my deepest

bond was always with her.

Around eight I launched into serious reading. (I have a typed list, again, which my mother kept.) Mother loved to tell of finding Shaw's *Mrs. Warren's Profession* under the bathmat in the toilet, where, like many children, I had gone to find much-needed privacy. Of course she realized that I didn't have the faintest idea of the situation on which the plot turned. But at that point I was so infatuated with the way that Shaw's mind worked that I could put up with a good deal of incomprehensibility. Mother's list of my favorite plays, made when I was twelve, includes most of Shaw, seven plays of Barrie, three of Milne, and Pirandello's *The Play's the Thing.* I had been putting on plays for some time, my own, and scenes from works I admired. Mother (of course) saved the program from a production when I was eleven, which consisted of the balcony scene from *Romeo and Juliet,* a "Vaudville" (dancing dolls which I had made out of large tassels), *Portrait of a Gentleman in Slippers* (Milne), and "Walt Disney Cartoon & Poetry Reading (if we have time)."

Mother's comment at the foot of the program: "This was killing!—and extraordinary at the same time. The only audience was Ben and me and the maid whom C. insisted on coming, and rows of dolls and paper dolls. She made all the stage settings. The one for the balcony scene was lovely. Dolls took all the parts and Carolyn recited the lines behind a screen, almost all from memory."

Activities such as these prompted Mother to have a real stage built for me in the basement. She also provided a trunk full of marvelous clothes and props—including a big, blue, ostrich-plume fan which I still have: swathes of velvet and chiffon, bits of fringe, embroidery, and all sorts of exotic headgear from Mother's colorful premarital past. Of course with this kind of encouragement and equipment I was off and running. I pressed the neighborhood children into acting, ready or not, under my imperious direction.

This may be the moment to point out that, in case it has not already been made clear, my peers did not find me adorable, unlike a few adults, particularly my parents and a few selected teachers and tolerant friends of the family. The few friends I had I ruled by tyranny and bribes (Mother's cooking, Mother's parties, Mother's inventive ideas for having fun), by what I felt was the Divine Right of the spoiled only child. My only close friend in early childhood lived across the street; her name was Virginia Marshall, known as Bunny. For a number of years I bullied Bunny to my satisfaction. Her only mild revenge was in possessing a Shirley Temple doll, frills and all, which was said to resemble her, and which my mother thought tacky. (I had ethnic dolls, Indian squaws, and—to her credit—a black baby doll named Rosy Posy which Mother had to special-order from a factory.)

One night we had had an unusual snowfall, along with heavy winds, and when I woke up I found that the wind had blown a great heap of snow up against the garage. I rushed out after breakfast and began to build an igloo. When Bunny came over later in the afternoon, I had a nice passageway carved out which led to an interior space, and I had fixed the outer and inner surfaces with water, which promptly froze. I coaxed the poor child into crawling through the tunnel to the little room, which I had furnished with a toy telephone, a dish or two, and some apples. Soon after she had entered, I sealed off the entrance with more snow and left her there. So that I am not considered a total sadist or potential murderer, it really didn't occur to me that the child would be so paralyzed with fright that she wouldn't simply knock a hole in the wall and crawl out. When I sauntered back an hour or two later, I discovered her still there and let her out, puffy-faced, weeping, and freezing. Bunny never played with me again. I missed her a great deal—rather in the way that whites missed blacks when slavery was abolished—but by her own little Emancipation Proclamation she gained my permanent respect, as walking home from school I would gaze at the hedge enclosing her yard, a hedge as impenetrable as any fortress.

But there was another friend whom I managed to keep until I left Spokane, a local character called Wild Willie Wiley. One day when I was eight, Mother found me missing, and went out on the front porch, where she saw this young person with a white-blond "boyish bob" sitting on the front seat of a rattletrap open car, an Overland, next to a nearly naked man with a long bushy beard, wearing only a singlet of bobcat fur. Many a mother would have freaked out at this spectacle, and indeed Willie spent a lot of his time in jail, having been run in by parents who failed to understand the fascination that this harmless man had for children to whom he was always generous and kind. My mother was made of stronger stuff; and her intuitions told her that I had nothing to fear. Willie had been sickly in his youth, and had taken up semi-nudity as a way of building up his strength. And indeed he was solid as a rock, with a deep, leathery tan the year round. When Willie died in 1956 I am happy to say that my conservative hometown, never too kind to him while he lived, turned out for his funeral: more than three hundred people visited the funeral home, "in business suits and work clothes, in white gloves, pigtails, and bobbysox," according to a local columnist. And there is a memorial stone to Willie in a Spokane cemetery.

It didn't occur to me until just now that Willie and Vachel were soul brothers; with some similarities to my father as well, with his regimen of daily morning exercises, his nearly vegetarian diet, and his emphasis on a healthy body. And I wonder if Willie wasn't responsible in part for my continuing attraction to oddballs, free spirits, and eccentrics. In this respect, too, I was my mother's child; my father didn't really notice whether people were eccentric or not!

## III

Mother managed to sneak me into public school while I was still five, knowing that, with my December birthday, I would be held back a year if she waited until I was six. I attended the Washington School, a gloomy old pile so prisonlike in appearance that it haunted my dreams for years. I remember the sense of relief I felt when I awoke and realized that I was grown up! It was about fifteen long blocks from our house, and like most children I took my lunch. However, my lunches bore little resemblance to those of the other children. Describing them to friends later on, I exaggerated only marginally when I said they could consist of Breast of Chicken under Glass. Take it from me, they were gourmet all the way. Naturally, this set me apart, as did my hand-knits, my old-fashioned hair styles, and my voracious appetite for reading. Nothing could be done about the latter, but occasionally I was able to swap my exquisite and nutritionally balanced lunch for the ambrosial contents of Joey Lindsley's brown bag: a peanut-butter and jelly sandwich on Wonderbread (forbidden to our house; every Sunday we crossed the river to the aromatic bakery of the Seventh Day Adventists, to purchase our homemade bread for the week), cherry jello with bits of canned fruit and tiny marshmallows embedded in it, and a big hunk of Mrs. Lindsley's featherweight chocolate layer cake, whose memory makes me salivate right now.

Because of Mother's dread of tuberculosis, which had caused both of her parents to migrate from the South to Colorado soon after they were wed, and which had run riot through Mother's own generation, I had been scientifically over-vitaminized since birth. Daddy was just past six feet tall, and Mother five eight, very tall for her generation. So the combination of genes and systematic feeding made me always at least a head taller than my peers. I'm not hard to spot in class pictures, with my hair like a blown dandelion, in the back row, overtopping the others.

In those antediluvian days, women teachers in my State—and they were always women—lost their jobs if they married. And we were, of course, deep in the Depression. So for teachers we had a series of "old maids," none of them younger than forty, and a number of them, it was said, over seventy and dying their hair. It is remarkable how many of these women, lonely, tired and overworked—usually with an invalid mother or a feckless sibling or two to support—managed to be habitually kind, interesting, and dedicated. We had one psychopath in seventh grade, Miss Mead, who warped several generations of children before being committed to the madhouse, but the rest were, by and large, angels. Miss Odell, my first-grade teacher, had taught the mothers and grandmothers of many of my classmates, and ended up being adored by five generations.

And Miss Odell, like most of my teachers then and later, loved me back. I was reading fluently when I entered school, and I had been trained to read aloud as well. My classmates divided roughly into thirds: one-third middle-class children like me from Brown's Addition, one third from Fort Wright, the army post, and one third from Peaceful Valley, which was what passed for a slum in Spokane: a poor but pastoral enclave under the hill along the banks of the Spokane River. The army brats did fairly well in school but they took no interest in mental exercise. The poor kids, often hungry and wretchedly clothed, particularly miserable in our bitter winters, frequently had all they could do to concentrate on their lessons. Of course my teachers loved me, and like my parents, spoiled me. As far as I can recollect, I never did homework. I got up my lessons in study period, or faked my way through question periods, while beamed upon and held up as an example. Only Miss Griffith, my sixth-grade teacher, made any attempt to discipline me. I think she felt that somebody better try. And she sharply cross-questioned me at every turn, exposed me when I was bluffing, and constantly challenged me to do better work commensurate with the extraordinary advantages of my upbringing. Single-handedly she could hardly hope to reform me, but it is significant that whenever I returned to Spokane after I left for college I never failed to visit her.

Perhaps my most vivid memory of grade school is of Miss Mead. She was habitually scornful of the poor children from the Valley, although deferential to me and to Joe Lindsley, whose father was a Superior Court Judge, and to the army kids whose fathers were officers. One day she flew totally off the handle and began to berate the Valley children:

"Do you know that you're nothing but trash, the worst of trash?" she hissed, and began flailing at them with her ruler and screaming, "Trash!" over and over again. Joe Lindsley and I rose as one from our seats and told her to stop it. Then we marched into the principal's office, where she soon came panting after us. I no longer remember how the matter was settled although both Joe's and my mother became involved. There was some kind of a truce, and Joe and I were unpunished. She managed to control herself then, but I know that she went on abusing children long after Joe and I had graduated from all our schools. I still see the foam on her lips and the rictus of her terrible smile, and wonder how many lives she damaged.

The summer of 1936 was an important one for me in several ways. We attended a conference of the Institute of Pacific Relations in Yosemite, saw old friends like Dr. Hu Shih, and made new ones, particularly among the other Chinese delegates, the Russians, and the Japanese. The wife of a Chinese delegate, Mrs. Sze, gave me a ring cut from a single piece of Imperial jade which I treasured until it was stolen thirty years later. I have a snapshot of myself dressed by Mrs. Takianagi in her purple kimono. But by all means the most significant encounter was with the family of the Russian journalist Vladimir Romm, the Washington correspondent for *Isvestia.* The Romms had a little son, George, a couple of years younger than I, and the Romms and the Kizers tramped in the Yosemite woods together, fed squirrels, admired giant redwoods, and picnicked from boxes prepared by the staff of the Awahnee Hotel where we were luxuriously housed. My mother noticed and remarked on the deep and passionate bond between the senior Romms; further, she commented on Mrs. Romm's seeming anxiety about her husband. "When he goes away for an hour or two, they embrace as if they would never see each other again," Mother remarked, prophetically. Before the conference was over Romm was suddenly called back to Moscow. There ensued many tears and much frenzied packing, and the Romms departed in haste and obvious perturbation.

The following January we were horrified to learn that Vladimir Romm had been arrested, tried, and convicted in the infamous Moscow conspiracy trials. Romm had "confessed" to having been the contact man between Trotskyite comspirators in Russia and Trotsky himself. The editor of the *San Francisco Chronicle,* who had also been a delegate to the Yosemite conference, said that Mr. Romm had confessed to personal participation "in something which never happened and in which it would have been physically impossible for him to have played the part to which he has 'confessed' " [sic]. We never heard what became of him; presumably he was killed. And I never knew what became of my friend George, though I have asked many people many times over the years.

My family discussed this over and over again. Why had Romm gone back when it was obvious, in retrospect, that he was in deep trouble? Perhaps it was his clear conscience, his misplaced belief that some measure of honor and decency still pervaded the system of which he was a part. And what a price he paid for this naivete. Interestingly enough, Vladimir Romm's naivete served to protect my own, just a few years later, when I attended a college where a number of my teachers were Marxists and a few were communists. And some of my fellow students called themselves communists. At that time in our history you couldn't be an American Communist without sedulously following the twists and turns of Soviet policy. Stalin owned and operated American Communism, whether all members of the Party admitted it to themselves or not.

But, idealist that I was, and having vivid memories of the Depression when I was a child—apples sold on street corners, milk running in the gutters, a procession of the poor begging at our door (the screen door of our kitchen had a mysterious mark on it which we learned indicated that the lady of the house was always good for a free meal; indeed Mother kept a great big stock pot simmering on the back of the stove, to which she added meat and nourishing vegetables to fill up empty stomachs)—it would not have been unusual for me to have been tempted by communism, and its avowed mission to help the wretched of the earth. From this Romm saved me. And "socialist realism" in the arts played a part as well. When schoolmates lent me copies of the *Masses* or the *Daily Worker*, I have to confess that I found the literary and art criticism hilarious; if they were serious I was certainly not. I confess that aesthetics has played as important a part in my politics as in my religion.

Later in 1937 I received letters from China from Mr. Fred Sze and his wife, in belated answer to my own. His of September 28 tells me that Mrs. Sze and the children had left for the country just days before the Japanese attack on Shanghai, "so they have been spared the horror of a devastating war which I have been witnessing daily for the past month and a half. . . ." But the letter of this wealthy, delicate, and sheltered woman, written just before Christmas, tells of a perilous trip of three days and nights, when the Japanese bombed their train; she and the children hid under the walled gate of a city while a bomb was dropped about thirty yards away. "The detonation was truly frightful. Thank God we got thru safely!" My peaceful Spokane had been invaded by the terrors of the big world. I remember walking home from school up Second Street, with its large houses and wide green lawns, the spidery sprinklers turning lazily in the sunlight, hearing the voice of Hitler from the open windows: that harsh, hypnotic, terrifying voice pouring from each radio, so that someone who knew German would not have missed a word. And the even more terrifying, mechanical, ritual response from a hundred thousand throats: *"Sieg Heil! Sieg Heil! Sieg Heil!"*

Recently I wrote a poem in which I mentioned a "recurring nightmare" of that period which went on for some years:

> Jackboots on the stairs, the splintered door
>            just before dawn,
> And the fascists dragging Daddy out of bed,
> Dragging him down the steps by his
>     wonderful hair;
> The screams as his spine cracks when he hits
>     cement.
> Then they make him brush his teeth with his
>     own shit.
> Though I know this is the price of bravery,
> Of believing in justice and never telling lies,
> And of being Benjamin, the best
>     beloved. . . .

I believe that part of this dream (O, be quiet, Freudians!) had to do with my sense that my father, although possessed of great moral courage (among other acts, he had defended Americans of German ancestry who were persecuted during World War I—and remember, the villain of that war was another Kaiser), was not physically courageous—and neither am I. (So the dream would seem to be a rare example of my identification with my father.) I remember my mother's and my silent suffering at the dinner table when Father regaled us with a blow-by-blow account of his latest visit to the dentist. And the slightest scratch or wound let him to carry on as if he'd had an amputation without anaesthetic. This was in contrast to my mother's stoicism in regard to her painful ailments, both real and psychosomatic. She postponed having her gallbladder removed for a couple of years, until I was eight, believing that she might not survive the operation and anxious that I not become an orphan until I was older. She suffered excruciatingly from colitis for the rest of her life, and I don't believe that she ever slept through the night. On the occasions when I arose in the dark hours, I was often aware of her endless, lonely pacing.

Related to the postponement of her visit to the Mayo Clinic was the conflagration in the driveway in our backyard, when my mother burned every scrap of her correspondence, her journals and notebooks as well. Why? Mother had had a "past." Father had been a virgin when he married the first time, at thirty-six, and had had no other loves beside his first wife and my mother. Mother, on the other hand, had many amorous adventures, including the most serious affair of her life, in her forties before she met my father. (She used to warn me about that when I was still a child: "Watch out for your forties! If you fall in love then it can nearly kill you." Of course she was right—but who heeds such warnings? And it nearly killed me.) She was afraid that if she died, Father would go through her papers—and perhaps at a later time I would as well. I don't believe my father, the least jealous of men, would have been upset, and I know I wouldn't have. I have never ceased to regret this erasure of her past, particularly those years of which she never spoke.

When I entered the eighth grade of the Washington School, my teacher was a spiritual and emaciated spinster (though the word is now out of fashion, it was absolutely appropriate then) named Miss Whittaker. Even the crudest children adored her; having survived Miss Mead, we were somewhat stunned by the rule of love. She wore the same dress day after day, month after month, its detachable collar and cuffs always fresh and neatly pressed. One morning she appeared in a new dress: light blue with white dots. And as one we stood up and cheered. I have not forgotten the way she blushed with pain. How terribly poor she must have been, that gallant woman.

I also remember the music period, when we listened to ancient records on a temperamental wind-up Victrola which tended to run down before the end of the record and howl dolefully like a wounded beagle. And we sang as well. Our repertoire consisted, in the main, of Negro Spirituals. Here we were, as far from the Old South as we could get, geographically, singing,

"All the darkies am a weepin' / Massa's in the cole, cole groun'," singing of the days when our black hearts were young and gay as we hoed that corn and cotton, of how we longed to be carried back to Ole Virginny, "where this old darkie's heart am long to go." Dear suffering Jesus! Perhaps if a single black child had attended school with us, these words might have ceased to be abstractions, and Joe and I might have led another rebellion.

Halfway through that year, my parents transferred me to Havermale Junior High School, across the river, chiefly because of the reputation of the principal, a progressive teacher receiving a great deal of attention because he had instituted what he called a "free day": Every Friday we could choose which classroom we wanted to spend time in. It worked remarkably well as I recall, at least so far as I was concerned: Being a longtime victim of "Math anxiety," and having been given the only grade lower than an A in my life in Algebra, I would work out in the mornings with my math teacher, Noble F. Leach. Until he entered my life I had equated the study of Math with a visit to the dentist. After he explained things and straightened me out, I would dash for the Art room and spend the rest of the day happily drawing and painting. My favorite, though, was Arthur Biggs, a distant relative of the late organist, for whom we sang in the chorus and in operettas. I had tiny solo parts, and I like to think that I might have had bigger starring roles had it not been for the presence of a pretty girl named Patrice Munsil who walked off with all the leads.

Most of the children at Havermale were not well-off, and I was deeply embarrassed at being driven to school in our Buick, so I made a deal with Mr. Priebe, our splendid German gardener, to take me to school in his rattletrap Model-A. I don't know that this deceived anybody, but it made me feel better. After Havermale, Patrice and I both transferred to Lewis and Clark High School, back on the right side of the river—the very same school from which my father had had to drop out as a lad. It was a huge establishment whose principal feature was the Thursday morning pep rally at which we sang fight songs and cheered on the football or basketball team, depending on the season. Occasionally these sessions featured Patrice's singing "The Bell Song," from *Lakme*, or other ambitious arias which her ambitious mother had prompted her to learn, as vital to a precocious career which began with lessons in artistic whistling.

But that summer before moving over to high school, Patrice and another, older girl named Josephine Rangan and I responded to a newspaper ad calling for chorus members for the touring San Carlo opera company which was about to perform in Spokane. Soon we were being interviewed by Maestro Colantoni, a minute Italian who seemed to be part genius-entrepreneur, part charlatan, and part the unlucky victim of circumstance. I vividly recall his account of an outdoor performance of *Aida* which perhaps terminated his career in the land of his birth. He made use of animals including elephants, and his description of the great heaps of dung which they produced, followed almost immediately by the corps de ballet, who slipped in shit, fell down, collapsed, and caused the curtain to be rung down apace was a mixture of high comedy and bitter grief. The current enterprise seemed to be put together with adhesive tape, spit, and a prayer.

But it was a glorious opportunity for us! Patrice and Josephine were cast in small roles; I lied about my age (and Patrice must have done so too) and became a member of the chorus. In *Cavalleria* I actually had two lines of my own to sing. But that was of minor importance. The great thing was learning the operas: *Carmen, Cav* and *Pag, Traviata, Trovatore.* Fifty years later I can still sing along with *Cav* and *Pag,* and bits of *Trovatore* stick with me—but glorious *Carmen!* I can sing the whole thing, including the overture! Most of the stars of the company were, to put it bluntly, over the hill, with the possible exception of the tenor, whose handicap was that he was nearly a midget, despite his four-inch built-up heels. The baritone, however, was a figure to whom I attached my nebulous adolescent feelings. My mother found this hilarious, which wounded me deeply, as I had been wounded not long before when she laughed at my vows to remain unmarried forever. Sandro Giglio couldn't have been younger than fifty; later, when I saw French films starring Jean Gabin, I recognised the type. He had the remnants of a fine voice, and he could act. All in all, it was a romantic summer, for which I bless the memory of Maestro Colantoni.

One benefit for me was to be taken into the bosom of Josephine's large Italian family, with whom I spent many happy evenings around the old upright piano, singing operas straight through, every member of her family taking part. I'm afraid I drank some homemade chianti, having helped tread the grapes for it in my bare feet. (I don't remember Mother making any comments about purple ankles. She was good about things like that.) So I had a glimpse of a very different life-style, materially poorer than our own, but full of laughter, joy, and song. Not much later, Josephine went on to the San Francisco Opera, and Patrice, at eighteen, had the spelling of her last name changed, won the Metropolitan auditions and joined the Metropolitan Opera Company.

My immediate future was far less glamorous. I've said, more or less in jest, that all I learned in high school was how to type, and that is virtually true. No science, no math, and no foreign languages. It is not surprising that I applied to Sarah Lawrence College, probably the only institution unconventional enough to accept me. My high-school graduation exercises may have had something to do with this happy outcome: As usual, I had woefully neglected my history homework, and feared that I might flunk

History and fail to graduate. So for ancient Mr. Teakle, my teacher, I stayed up most of one night and wrote a poem about the necessity of American intervention in World War II. (The previous spring I had won a medal from the Veterans of Foreign Wars for an essay on "Permanent Peace for America." Prophetic I was not.) All during my school years I was surrounded by conservative children and teachers. I battled Mr. Teakle and indeed the entire class on everything to do with economics and politics. To calm the waters, our jest was that the only thing we agreed on was that Spokane needed a sewage disposal system. Now the poem, called "Stars through the Perilous Night," impressed Mr. Teakle enough to pass me, and impressed the principal sufficiently that the poem ended up being chanted by my entire graduating class during commencement. And, for an hour, I felt that I was one of them.

Someone sent the poem to the then popular journalist Dorothy Thompson, who ran part of it in her daily column. This attracted the attention of the editors of the *Ladies' Home Journal,* who ran the entire poem in the magazine, along with a picture and a brief biography of me. From this I received more than five hundred letters. (This must have totally overwhelmed my mother's curatorial impulses, for they have all disappeared.) Later, after I had been admitted to college, the poem was set to music and performed on "The Prudential Family Hour," a popular radio program, and sung by a cast of hundreds. I remember very little about this entire experience, except that it frightened me severely, as I knew I wasn't ready for all this attention. I was at least bright enough to know that as far as my writing was concerned, I didn't know what I was doing. And it wasn't for another thirteen years, until I studied with Theodore Roethke, that I found out. My writing teacher at college was Genevive Taggard, who either threw my poems in the wastebasket or suggested that I send them to a magazine. Explaining how to make a good poem out of a bad poem was quite beyond her powers. So for the next few years I had to rely on lucky accidents rather than learned skills.

In my sophomore year, however, I wrote a poem which I thought good enough to submit to the college literary magazine. Miss Liddell, the advisor, an elderly blonde with Shirley Temple ringlets, promptly rejected it. "Send it to the *New Yorker* dear," Genevive said, in her languid way; I did, and they took it. So I felt justified in going back to Miss Liddell and announcing the acceptance. "Well, we have very high standards, dear," she replied. The poem was published, and then reprinted in the overseas edition of the magazine which was sent to the armed services abroad, as we were now at war. And eventually I received another five hundred letters or so, from servicemen. (Many years later, I mentioned to the poet Ruthven Todd that I had had a poem in the *New Yorker* at age seventeen. "It wasn't very good," I said, hoping he wouldn't look it up. But he did, and announced, "You were right. It wasn't very good." So perhaps Miss Liddell was vindicated.)

I think the importance of all this was that I began, very tentatively and shyly, to think of myself as someone who might become a poet. The materials were all in place: my family, my imagination, my reading. Now all I needed was to learn how to do it. But something else of importance occurred to me when I was eighteen. It seems to confirm Erik Erikson's theory about a pivotal experience or decision which alters the course of a life. I have no idea what event or series of events, internal or external, brought this on. I only know that at this point I decided that I didn't like myself very much: I was narcissistic, selfish, and self-absorbed. Other people, their pains, delights, and problems impinged on my consciousness only peripherally. "Well, you're just going to start behaving like a nice, decent, generous human being, and if you keep it up long enough and hard enough, it will become internalized, and you will really be that person without play-acting or hypocrisy."

The interesting part about this decision was that I fully believed that major artists were, by and large, not very nice people, and that if I continued as I was, my chances of becoming a real poet were probably much better than if I embarked on this conscious campaign of self-improvement. Nevertheless, I stuck to it. Of course psychologists will say that I had deep inner doubts of my own talent; feminists will say that this was a way of avoiding competition in the ruthless world of men. My own tentative psychological interpretation is that, once again, I chose sides and once again I chose Mother rather than Father.

At my rate, riddled with self-doubt as I was, utterly bewildered about my identity (so much so that I used to joke that I was afraid to look in the mirror for fear that nobody would look back), ignorant of life and unskilled in my craft, still I was ready to fare forth. Product of my parents, and what they had told

me of their parents and their beginnings, influenced by their stories, beguiled by their voices, taking my place at the end of their family myths, I was the child of their childhood as well as my own.

Everything that was to come—war, love, marriage, separation, loneliness, children, the death of those I loved—was simply going to be added on to the person I was already. Oh, eventually I would figure myself out, more or less. And in about twenty-five years I would be able to say with Chaucer's Criseyde, "I am my owne woman, wel at ese." But by then, at eighteen, the material from which I would make my poems was in my head and in my hands. The rest is encounters, episodes, and events. They can wait. . . .

---

*BIBLIOGRAPHY*

**Poetry:**

*Poems.* Portland, Ore.: Portland Art Museum, 1959.

*The Ungrateful Garden.* Bloomington, Ind.: Indiana University Press, 1961.

*Five Poets of the Pacific Northwest: Kenneth O. Hanson, Richard Hugo, Carolyn Kizer, William Stafford, and David Wagoner.* Seattle: University of Washington Press, 1964.

*Knock upon Silence.* Garden City, N.Y.: Doubleday, 1965.

*Midnight Was My Cry: New and Selected Poems.* Garden City, N.Y.: Doubleday, 1971.

*Yin: New Poems.* Brockport, N.Y.: Boa Editions, 1984.

*Mermaids in the Basement: Poems for Women.* Port Townsend, Wash.: Copper Canyon Press, 1984.

*The Nearness of You.* Port Townsend, Wash.: Copper Canyon Press, 1986.

*Carrying Over* (translations). Port Townsend, Wash.: Copper Canyon Press, 1987.

**Editor of:**

*Woman Poet—The West* (poetry editor). Reno, Nev.: Women-in-Literature, 1980.

*Leaving Taos,* by Robertson Peterson. New York: Harper, 1981.

*Primitive Places,* by Muriel Weston. Beattle, Wash.: Owl Creek Press, 1987.

(Continue on next page.)

*Kizer, as bride in 1948*

*With fellow writer David Wagoner, 1959*

*Editing* Poetry Northwest, *1965*

*Children, from left: Ashley, Jill, and Scott, 1954*

*Publicity photograph of author for Poetry
International 70, held at Queen Elizabeth Hall*

*With friend and poet Naomi Lazard and noted Urdu
poet Faiz Ahmad Faiz, in Hawaii, 1980*

*Maureen Hurley*

*Kizer ("and the world's longest forefinger") in
conversation with Galway Kinnell, 1982*

*At her marriage to John Marshall Woodbridge, 1975*

*Daughter Ashley*

Mary Randlett

*Daughter Jill, at seventeen*

Burda, San Jose Mercury News

*Carolyn Kizer, "the day I won the Pulitzer, 1985."*

# James Koller

*1936-*

## FIFTY YEARS

*James Koller, 1980*

Leslie Burhoe

I t is said today that we invent ourselves. We pick from all that is offered those things that make up what we come to think of as ourselves. Some believe that it makes sense to afford one's self as many possibilities as one can—see as much, know as much. Others see life as a very simple thing, where what really matters is shown to nearly all. The way it seems to work is that you learn the simple things after you've tried everything else.

My children will read this. Maybe more than once. Some of them read the poems even now. Because I am their father. Because maybe in all this writing there is something that will make for a continuity. At least they will know that I too was young once, and like me they will grow older, and know that it is hard to see things as uncomplicated as one once did.

Writing this is like pulling off the road to check the map. This is where I am. I came this way—it might have been easier to go another way, but there were things I had to see—and this seems to be where I'm going next. (Things aren't always as they seem.)

Others have been here before. I hear their voices—it is good to listen, to know what makes things as they are, then to do what *you* do. "Just do what you think right. You can do anything you want to do, if you're willing to pay the consequence."

Judge me by what I believe, how well I have done what I set out to do. Judge me by my own standards—to judge one by another's standards is only to establish what differences exist.

Each time and place offers a road of its own. My cousins lived on a farm. Their bedrooms contained their beds, little more. There were no rugs, no storm windows, snow came in around the rags stuffed in the broken panes. The house was heated by wood or corncobs. Water was hand-pumped from a cistern. Everybody worked everyday—fieldwork, chores, housework. Work was what life was about; it was meaningful because it was necessary—what you worked at turned directly into those things you ate, wore, your heat. Anything you were able to sell went to buy those things you didn't raise or make that you had to have to keep it going. In the city, in the towns that were becoming suburbs, most worked at jobs that took them away each day. They were jobs that didn't make sense—it was hard to see how they were necessary. All you could get out of it was money. The best you could hope for was that you were doing something you liked doing. I grew up with more than I needed. I knew it. I admired those who had less—the less the better—because everything they had was necessary. Everything was needed. It all made sense when you worked for what you needed.

Those who people one's life contribute their input into that life—they too have a heavy hand in inventing you, as they imagine you, and as you play off that image. As you change, or think you want to change, you find yourself meeting new people, making new friends, who will reenforce those changes, allow you to see yourself as you want to be seen. You retain those friends who see you as you want to be.

When one remembers, the sensations, feelings, thoughts, pass again, a *remembered now,* that one carries into all nows. Past becomes present. Old friends, living and dead, people one's now. The dead die only as those who knew them forget or die themselves. To visit old friends is to bring into the

157

now all past nows—to wake and create a continued and expanded common now. It is all one's life and one must keep it all alive or one begins to die.

As a child I came to think of writers as people who lived differently—people who were not bound to the notions of others. The lives of writers, I came to think, were their major works, of which their writings were only a part. The more I know of writers the more it seems that few of their lives might be discovered in their works—only a few are able to write of their entire being. To read a man is not to know him. His writing reflects a limited vision—the mirror in which he himself watches the world and himself as the world watches him. Expect nothing of the writer beyond his good work—which is in fact all he expects you to expect—unlike the others, who can be expected to live with all their being at all times and in every situation, and who expect that you too will live as they.

My folks lived in Chicago. The first of my mother's family, Scotch-Irish, came to Illinois through Kentucky soon after Boone. My mother, Elsie Clark, was born in Princeton in 1913. My father's family, Austrian-Czech, found its way to Illinois in 1866. My father, James Koller, was born in Chicago in 1906. I was born in 1936 in Oak Park, at

*Parents, Elsie and James Koller, 1933*

the hospital closest to the apartment in which they lived. At the time I was born my mother had worked for wages hardly at all, except as a live-in caretaker for a rich cousin. My father was a union photoengraver for the *Chicago Daily News.*

My first recollection is sitting in a high chair in a kitchen similar to many in two- and three-room flats on Chicago's West Side. Much of my time was spent under the kitchen sink with the family dog. At a year and a half I was sent to live for two weeks with my mother's sister Laura in west central Illinois, on land the family had been near or on for over a century, farming. My sister Joan was born. When my folks came to get me, I called both my aunt and mother, Mother. Soon after I learned to walk I was sent, list in hand, to the corner store to buy single items the family needed. I always came back until once when a girl cousin, two or three years older, went with me. My folks discovered us several blocks from home, not yet knowing we were in totally unknown territory.

At three we moved to the suburbs immediately west of Chicago, just south of the CB & Q Railroad, which my father daily took to work. He wore a suit to work, carried his work clothes wrapped in newspaper. My sister and I would often meet him on the corner as he walked home in the evening from the train.

We spent a week in summer at a rented cabin in southern Michigan on the lake. My memory of going there was getting into the back seat of the car in the evening, falling asleep, waking in the dark when we got there. I remember the smell of the striped canvas awnings—the place was one room with a screened porch and the awnings rolled down to cover the screens when it was cool or raining. Once while I was peeling potatos on the porch with my father, he gave me my first knife. Another time he showed me a cabin once lived in by Carl Sandburg. "That's the kind of a house a poet lives in," he said. My first hammer came from the wreckage of the burned general store through which we rummaged. My father fit a new handle into the small hammer head. I can remember driving back home on Sunday afternoon through the smoke and sulphur of Gary, Indiana.

My mother's youngest brother, Robert, came to live with us just before the war. He worked as a mechanic, left on the doorjambs greasy fingerprints that my mother found infuriating. He enlisted in the army in early '41, the Coast Artillery, at the advice of the former WWI soldier who lived next door with his wife and pigeons. We visited often with my mother's other brother and sisters. Her oldest brother, Lyle, was a farmer, with four kids, who lost his farm after borrowing federal money to keep it going, and worked all through the war and after, trying to pay

*Young Jim on his fourth birthday,
Berwyn, Illinois, 1940*

James Koller, Sr.

back the money. He moved to California in the early fifties—drove all the way to Tucumcari, New Mexico, before he stopped, sent back a postcard. My aunt Laura and her husband, Ray, kept their farm, did general farming through the war, got into dairy farming in the early fifties. Their eldest son, Curtis, spent all of his time when not in school doing chores and fieldwork. Their eldest daughter, Elsa, kept house, cooked, and cared for the younger two children, Rita and Robert, while my aunt and her husband worked the fields, first with horses, later tractors. At one point it seemed they had a different dog each time we visited—the dogs kept getting killed by cars or trucks or machinery. Then for many years they had a brown chow who lived outside year round, looked like a fox when you saw him running through the fields at a distance. In winter when you approached him on the wooden porch, he would wag his tail and you could hear the ice in it thumping the boards. My mother's youngest brother was captured by the Japanese on Corregidor in '42. He survived the Bataan Death March and spent the remainder of the war in prison camps, came home unannounced in '45, and after a year in a VA hospital went to farming.

We also visited my father's mother, who seems old in my earliest recollection. She lived on the West

Side of Chicago, in the kitchen of a flat filled with her stored possessions. She seemed always to be sitting in the same chair. While my parents talked, my sister and I prowled the coal bins beneath the house. Then she came to live with us, just walked up one day with a shopping bag in each hand. I would sit and listen and she spent hours telling me of the evil folk who blew bad things at her, and how she survived. After my grandfather had died she'd remarried, moved to Missouri, to a remote farm. One of her four children died there. She left her husband, returned to Chicago. After she left us she went to live with her youngest son, Harry. My father's sister Em had moved to Iowa.

During the war we continued to visit in the country, my mother's people, but it took so long to get there that we didn't go as often. My father explained several times to me why he had to drive thirty-five miles per hour before it finally became clear. On more than one occasion we brought home chickens, which we kept in the garage until we killed them. I can remember my mother trying to make butter and cheese. We grew vegetables in the back yard, never joined in on the big community Victory gardens. I followed the war on maps in the newspapers my father brought home, listened to Roosevelt talk on the radio, was devastated when he died, thinking at that point that we would surely lose. My father brought home any photo that passed before him of prisoners in Asia, blown-up photos, which we searched for some sign of my uncle Robert.

My mother's father lived in Kankakee, where he lived alone in a basement apartment, and where he worked as a custodian at the state mental institution, a job he held after being a farmer, pool-room owner, and hotel keeper. He drank, had fires in house after house. My mother told of how Robert would lay out his clothes each night before he went to sleep in the order that they were to be put on. My grandmother left my grandfather when her youngest, Robert, was sixteen. She took up then with a man who died suddenly—traveled with him all through the country before he died. After him, she married and then divorced another drinker. She too lived with us for awhile, in her fifties, while working as a clerk in a local department store. She married once more after that. As I grew up, she was the only woman I knew who had been divorced. Once while she was married to her second husband and living on the Mississippi shore she became ill and we all spent a night thinking she would die at any time. On happier days we rode back and forth on the ferry boats across the river. She had two brothers and two sisters, all of whom had several children. I saw some of these people at family gatherings, but they were never close. Once we spent

*Grandfather Bertie Clark (at table), owner of Clark's Pool Hall, Peru, Illinois, 1908*

a week visiting them, chicken dinner every day at each new place. I saw for the first time the way I wanted to live when we visited my grandmother's youngest brother. He had a big family, they lived simply, the farm nestled into a hollow. Hunting provided much of the family meat. My grandmother's oldest sister, Ida, married Tom Travers soon after WWI and moved to California, where she raised their thirteen children. They came back each year in a truck that had been converted to a house on wheels, with an easy chair to drive from. The first time I saw Tom was just after the war. He was wearing laced boots that came to just below his knees, a pocketknife in a pocket in one of them. He wore a narrow brimmed western-style hat. I had never seen boots or hat like them outside the movies.

Hobos from the railroad passed by our house with some frequency, sometimes asking directions. I was always thrilled to talk with them. Walking home from the bakery, eating the center slices from a loaf of fresh rye bread, I saw several of them together, riding towards the enormous train yards that lay just east of us. I waved and they waved back and I worried they would get caught when they got into the yards.

When I got my bicycle my world grew bigger. I rode west to the Des Plaines, spent days along its banks, many riding in cement-mixing tubs converted to prams. There were many people who lived along

the river's banks—gypsies and bos mostly—in old cars converted to homes, cardboard shacks, vegetable gardens lost in the woods. With my bicycle I also found work, as a newsboy—first for three mornings a week and then every morning, and still later afternoons as well, after school. I kept up with world events reading bits from the papers as I wandered the early mornings. Usually I was the first on the streets since the night before, and telltale signs, usually clothing, told of goings on of the night before. Before I started work, I spent long periods each summer with my aunt Laura and her family on the farm. I took a bus or a train, was picked up by my uncle Ray in his '30s black Chevrolet—the floors covered with rags and feathers and mud, all the things of a farm. He always wore bib overalls, smoked a pipe, and never seemed to mind waiting. Once when the train was crowded I rode in the baggage car, felt closer to the exploits of the James gang, whom I read about under the covers at night by flashlight.

The first hunting I ever did was with my father and my cousin Curtis. My father owned a single-shot shotgun but seldom hunted—only this once in my recollection. We hunted squirrels, found none, but Curtis shot a raccoon. Soon afterwards my father gave his shotgun to me. I hunted often with Curtis—squirrels, rabbits, and pheasants. I tracked one rabbit, wounded in a rear foot, for hours through the snow until I finally discovered him behind a fence post and shot through the post to kill him. Another time Curtis and I tracked a pheasant, the one shot we had broke a wing, and we finally caught him alive where he hid in a clump of snow covered grass. There were no deer in that part of Illinois then—the farms were small and there was no cover. When the size of the farms increased, and fewer folks actually lived and spent time on the land, the deer moved down from Wisconsin. Hunting brought an interest in the guns themselves, and Curtis and I spent evenings in gun shops, talking with the gunsmiths and others interested in guns. We learned the fine art of silence in trading.

My father was an avid fan of prizefighting, told me of the great Dempsey, whom I read about and watched in old fight movies. Joe Louis was heavyweight champion then, and I listened to his fights on summer evenings on the back porch. When he lost I stopped listening. I boxed in high school, played church basketball (as my father had), played basketball in the streets, where usually when the shooting finished there were girls to stand and talk with until it was time to go home. I either rode my bicycle or walked the four or five miles to and from school. At times I walked home with a friend who like myself read a lot of history, who related in great detail all the battles he knew of, mostly WWII battles. He talked much of Rommel and the German generals who fought on the Russian front. My interest was in the American West and the War Between the States. I read biographies of Jeb Stuart, Stonewall Jackson, John Bell Hood, and Quantrill, thinking of the old photos of soldiers in gray in my grandfather's trunk. I never knew who these men were, who they fought with, my grandfather was dead and couldn't tell me, but I knew they'd been there. I studied photography in high school, wanted to learn to be an engraver, but was discouraged. No one in the immediate family had ever been to college, but they all thought it made sense to send me. I knew no one but my teachers who had ever been in college, had no positive point of view to balance the negative view of "intellectuals" that was common among my friends—and seemed completely consistent with the hopes I had for my own life. I wanted to learn something that would help me make the money I needed. Gunsmithing seemed a good possibility, one that would put me in school, satisfy my folks, provide me with income, while still being of interest to me. At some point in my senior year I talked myself into thinking that writing was how I would earn my keep. College could teach me the mechanics of that. I read and identified very strongly with Jack London's *Martin Eden.*

We traveled as a family, first in '48, to Wyoming and then down through Texas and Missouri, where my father had lived for three or four years before WWI. I saw the fields he had helped to clear, what was left of the buildings where they had lived and provided most of what they needed, putting things away for winter. I saw the small town, once a rail stop, where he had ridden horseback—a day's trip there and back—to buy what had to be bought. The place had been deserted for years. My father's stepfather, Joseph Kalcik, had lived out his life alone there after my grandmother returned with the children to Chicago. I traveled in '50 with my mother, her mother, and my sister to New Orleans and Florida. One of the men I worked with at the news agency had lived as a young man in New Orleans, and I wrote back to him that the place he'd mentioned was no longer there. When I returned home he was gone—came home one night, had taken only his pistol, and had disappeared, leaving behind his wife and two young kids. In Florida we visited the great swamps and the Keys. Driving out to Key West on the series of two-lane roads and bridges, we observed heavy artillery fire out to sea and tried to find some mention of it on the radio and were amazed to find nothing but Spanish spoken, which none of us understood. On our return we came north through Georgia and the Carolinas, through Boone's Cumberland Gap. I carefully noted the small farms, the poor who were everywhere, the chain gangs who worked the roads. We traveled to Washington, Oregon, and California in '52—my first view of country I knew I'd return to. On our way out we drove through Montana and Idaho, passed somewhere a several-tiered log bridge that I have looked for and never found again. We visited the public market in Seattle, the southern Oregon coast, San Francisco, and the Sierras. We turned east from Azusa, where we visited my mother's brother Lyle. We saw the Grand Canyon under a cloudy and snowy sky, saw the hogans and wagons that then lined old Route 66, drove down the seemingly endless street that was Albuquerque.

In '53 I drove west with Curtis and Dan Krakora. Dan and I spent much of our time when home drifting on the Des Plaines, hunting in the forest preserves west of Chicago, listening to the stories Dan's father, George, and his uncle Bill told of their lives. After camping in the Canadian Rockies in what seemed constant rain, we visited several ghost towns in Montana, drawn to the deserted cabins, where we pieced together what we could of former inhabitants. Once we ran through the rain to a cabin we thought deserted only to find that it was lived in, by someone with a gun, which we heard cocked as we neared the place. We didn't stay around to find out who was there. I returned to Canada in '54, to Bow and Peyto Lakes, to the Columbia Ice Fields, where I woke one morning to discover several inches of snow covering my tent. These were all summer trips and I worked summers as well, first at the news agency, then after breaking my hand falling from a moving jeep (into the path of an oncoming car—I rolled under a parked car to escape), worked as a copyboy and assistant pressman for the *Chicago Daily News.* One day as I sat on the curb eating my lunch near the News Building on West Madison, a man passed with his suit pant's fly open. I told the man his pants were open, from my seat on the curb, but he was in a suit and I was dirty and sitting on the same curb the Madison Avenue winos sat on and he didn't want to hear me. I followed him into a restaurant, to his table, and as he sat down, I told him again. He flushed, doubly embarrassed.

My photo teacher in high school, C.O. Druschel, was from Washington, had traveled east on the freights before WWI to go to college. I believe he and another teacher, Marjorie Diez, turned my thinking about college. Druschel lived in Naperville, had gone to North Central College there, where he knew of a man teaching English, Richard Eastman, who was well thought of for his ability to teach writing skills. I enrolled at North Central in the fall of '54. I made sure Richard Eastman taught my freshman English. He was good, taught me how language worked, what I could or couldn't do with it. As time went on, his analysis of what I did enabled me to formulate my own thinking. My major was English; what I studied mostly, literature. Hemingway, Zola, and early Tolstoy were my favorites. I studied philosophy too—Nietzsche, Camus and Sartre—and drama—especially Samuel Beckett.

In the summer of '56 I made my first trip by myself, drove west first to Seattle and Puyallup, where friends of my folks from Illinois owned an orchard, and then down the coast to southern Oregon, where a friend from college, Lyndon Viel, was working at the Oregon Caves National Monument as a bus driver. I found work in the kitchen for a month, then continued on down the coast to San Francisco, where I discovered City Lights Bookstore. The city was filled with energy and I felt it but couldn't connect. After a week I continued on down the coast to Long Beach, then inland into the Sierras, back to Monterey, and back to Cave Junction, up old Highway 99, where late at night in the Siskiyous I'm sure I saw a big old wolf waiting beside the road for a chance to cross the highway. I worked again, long enough to buy four

*Koller at Oregon Caves, 1956*

tires, and Lyndon and I drove back to Wisconsin, to Monroe, on two-lane roads, in forty-seven hours and fifty-three minutes. Traveling alone I read a lot—what I remember was Sandburg's *Complete Poems,* Dos Passos's *U.S.A.,* and Steinbeck's *Grapes of Wrath.*

Though Jean Rada and I were from neighboring towns, we went to different high schools and did not meet until we shared classes at North Central. We began dating in the fall of '56 and were married in the summer of '57, between our junior and senior years. We traveled to Quebec City for our honeymoon, then down to the Maine coast and back, moving to a converted chicken house in a town close to the college, where we resumed our studies, both of us in English and Drama. I read reviews of Kerouac's *On the Road* in the fall of '57 and ordered the book. The same reviews turned me to those people referred to as the San Francisco Poets, who were said to be in league with Kerouac. I ordered Ferlinghetti's *Coney Island of the Mind* when word of it reached me. I bought *Evergreen Review, No.2.* I tried to interest others in this work but had little luck. Jean and I traveled to San Francisco in the summer of '58, spent two weeks exploring the city from a cheap room on Ellis or Eddy Street before we returned to Illinois, where I expected to be drafted. I wasn't and we settled into the town the college was in, and Jean taught school for a year. I wrote what became *Brainard and Washington Street Poems,* read all of Pound, chasing down all the references I could, which led me into Chinese and French poetry. With the college close at hand I was able to direct a presentation of Beckett's *Endgame,* which Jean acted in. We spent the summer of '59 traveling around the country, doing museums and art shows (Jean painted) and bookstores in NYC and Boston (where I was introduced to Zen, by Alan Watts, on TV), camping in British Columbia (where one night we sat so quietly a bear didn't realize we were there until he was right next to us), and finally, walking and walking through San Francisco.

In the fall of '59 I enrolled at the University of Iowa, and Jean signed on with the Iowa City school system. I was there only a short time before I realized I was in the wrong place. On the first day of classes I met Marlene and Michael Fine. When I dropped out of the university in November, Jean and I helped Marlene and Michael open their bookstore, the Paper Place, the first all-paperback store between NYC and San Francisco. A friend in San Francisco, Carl Marcoux, who had gone to college with us, discovered Auerhahn Books, and sent us word of their new books as they appeared. My first reading was in a coffee house above the bookstore. In May, Jean and I left for San Francisco, arrived the day Francis Powers and his U-2 were shot down. I spent the summer working part-time at the Tides Bookstore in Sausalito, started full-time warehouse work with Paper Editions Corporation the day after our daughter, Deirdre, was born—August 21, 1960. I talked for months with the Apache kid who worked with me about blues and folk music. We lived on Hyde Street, 1317, third floor, walked up. We shared the place with Carl Marcoux, who introduced us to Bill and Laura Kwong, who lived a block away. Bill was just getting into Zen, and we talked a lot about Buddhism, Zen. A cable line ran in front of the apartment and we took the cable car or walked most everywhere we went. One day while I was walking home from work, on Fourth Street, near the train station, a black man, thinking me a wino, offered me fifty cents to help carry his laundry. I did it, and waited outside while he went in to get me my money.

While in Iowa I sent my writings to *Evergreen Review.* Irving Rosenthal responded, arranging a meeting with Don Allen in San Francisco, soon after I arrived. Don introduced me to Michael McClure, who lived above a garage, painted huge blue paintings, and was just beginning to write plays. We talked a lot of Blake. Don introduced me to Philip Whalen at McClure's reading of his *Dark Brown.* Philip had read some of the work I had given to Don, work from *Two Hands,* and told me I clearly had to write. I told him I

would get better. Don also introduced me to Richard Brautigan and Richard Duerden.

In March of '61 we went back to Illinois. Jean and Deirdre flew from San Francisco, and I drove, down to L.A., where I visited Jim Smith, another college friend, whose path has crossed mine again and again since we first met in '54. I drove from L.A. nonstop to Iowa City, to visit Michael and Marlene Fine, and a few hours after I arrived, ended up driving Michael on to Chicago, an all-night drive in fog, to get him to a train connection which he had to make for his induction into the U.S. Army. I worked for Paper Editions Corporation in Chicago, on West Jackson, from the spring into the fall, reading Henry Miller on the way to and from work, on the commuter trains between Chicago and Naperville, where we lived in a small house south of town. We spent a lot of time in these months with Pam and Fred Millward, whom we had known in college. We all wrote, had all studied with Richard Eastman. One night in April, Millwards came for dinner and were snowed in in a sudden and heavy storm. Snow plows totally buried their car where they left it beside the road to walk back after finding it impossible to return home. The snow was almost totally gone the next night. In summer, electrical storms made electricity jump from wall outlet to wall outlet. Hemingway killed himself that summer and I painted a huge black painting in the front yard. At the end of the summer we decided to go west again.

Smith had moved from L.A. to Seattle, and we headed for Seattle, thinking to go on to San Francisco if no work turned up. We stayed in Seattle nearly a year. Smith worked for Hartman's, a large bookstore near the University of Washington, a bookstore owned by the same man who owned Paper Editions. I found work as paperback buyer. Jean gave me an Alaskan malamute puppy for Christmas. The dog was a female and we bought her on an arrangement which provided that we were to breed her and give pick of the litter to her former owner. We ended up with several dogs. In March of '62 I started work for Warshal's Sporting Goods, inventorying their several outlets, carrying merchandise from the main store to the outlets. In the fall Jean went back to teaching, in Burlington, and we moved to Bow. I took care of my daughter, my dogs, and my garden. I wandered around in the mountains below Baker and Shuksan, and when there wasn't money to go that far, or the old Chevy wouldn't run well enough, I was on Chuckanut Mountain. I wrote a lot of letters, a novel (*Shannon, Who Was Lost Before*), and two books of poems (*The Dogs and Other Dark Woods* and *Some Cows,*

*Poems of Civilization and Domestic Life).* Don Allen sent out many of my poems to magazines and it was through his efforts that the first of my poems were published. In '63, after the Vancouver Conference, Philip Whalen wrote me and suggested I try some of my work with the *Northwest Review* in Eugene, Oregon. He had met Ed Van Aelstyn, who edited the magazine, in Vancouver. I wrote Ed, sent him work, and discovered his poetry editor was leaving. I suggested I could do the job and Ed put me on. The university suspended publication of the *Review* in '64 because of extreme reaction to an issue which contained work by Whalen, Antonin Artaud, and an interview with Fidel Castro. Van Aelstyn, Will Wroth, and I decided to begin a magazine, initially to publish those works we'd accepted for publication in the *Northwest Review.* *Coyote's Journal* began, branched almost immediately into book publication. Most of the work was done by mail, but we did meet together, made more than one fast trip together to the Bay Area. As I prepared to leave on one of these trips, I said good-bye to Jean, then looked for Deirdre. She was nowhere to be found. After looking for some time, I discovered her behind the seat in the car, stowed away. Christmas of '64, Jean and Deirdre and I drove down to Everett, took the train back to Illinois. We heard the Paul Butterfield Blues Band at Big John's in Chicago. In the spring of '65 we drove down to California to check out job possibilities for Jean, and she landed a job in San Rafael, at more than twice the wage she made in Washington. When her school year ended, we drove once more to Illinois, then back, to move. *Two Hands* was published as we made ready.

Jean stayed behind in Bellingham, did summer work at the university, and Deirdre and I drove down to San Francisco, the four-wheeled trailer hauling all of our belongings behind us. Coming over Siskiyou Pass the brakes overheated and we were without brakes on the two-lane road, cars swerving quickly in front of us in the face of oncoming traffic and there was no way with automatic transmission to slow down. We finally stopped in Yreka by dragging the trailer wheels against a long empty curb and waited until the brakes came back.

We found a house to rent in San Rafael, on D Street, near where Jean would teach and Deirdre begin school. There was a huge oak in the back yard, a bed of Naked Ladies against the back wall. I began *California Poems* at the kitchen table, listening to D Street traffic. Dick Baker, who had worked with me at Paper Editions, invited me to read at the opening reading of the Berkeley Poetry Conference. Bob Creeley introduced me. I attended very few of the lectures and readings, but I managed to meet Drum

Hadley, Charles Olson, and many others. I got to know Bill Brown and he suggested I help him clear up the field where his new house in Bolinas would be built. When we were finished he offered me a job, gardening and landscaping. My first recollection of Jack Boyce, who was living then with Joanne Kyger in San Francisco, was of him breaking up concrete with a maul and pick. Soon after meeting Jack, I had dinner one night with him and Joanne at their place on Pine Street. After too much alcohol and too many cigars I found myself in the bathroom being sick. I don't know how long I was in there, but Joanne eventually asked if I would like a pillow.

I first met Bill Deemer in Eugene, in '64, when he read with Ronald Johnson and myself. In '65 Bill lived in San Francisco, in a small room in a building where Max Finstein also lived. Bill and his sweetheart, Toby, and I went for dinner one night in Chinatown, met up with Philip Whalen, who came with us. We all ate with chopsticks from the same large bowl and we all hurried to keep up with Philip but we didn't stand a chance. Bill and Toby had an apartment on Fell Street, opposite the Panhandle, when they were married across the street in the park in March '66. I spent hours that day talking to Patsy Zoline, who had grown up in Chicago, who had graduated from the University of Chicago, and had been a graduate student in philosophy at Stanford. Zoline lived in a house on Du Boce Street with several others, including Karl Bruder, and it was there that I met Neal Cassady, who passed through while I was having a quiet dinner with Z.

Jack and Joanne were married in the summer of '66. We partied afterwards at the Doss house in San Francisco, a party that included champagne without end and dancing—at one point a circle dance ended with all falling to the floor. When the party ended Joanne waited on the curb while Jack carried out some cardboard cases of champagne and the case bottoms were wet and the bottles began to fall one after the other and several exploded before Jack finally realized what was happening. They went home to find their place on Pine Street filled with rice—their bed, every pot, every drawer—and Jack collected it all, filled a one hundred-pound bag, which they later ate. There were many parties, many at Brown's in Bolinas, where many of us often spent our Sundays, Bill talking as he worked in his garden. One Sunday, Jack introduced me to Kirby Doyle, who he had once worked with in Big Sur, packing tons of cement bag by bag up trails to a building site.

In the fall of '66, after her second summer in Bellingham, Jean moved with Deirdre to an apart-

*With Bill Brown in Bolinas, California, 1967*

ment in San Rafael and I to a house in Sebastopol. We lived apart for several months, then tried again and lived together in Sebastopol until we separated in mid-'67. Brown let me build a loft in his garage and I lived in it for two months before heading east, for a long trip through the summer of '67. I met Elizabeth Baker at a party at Muir Beach while she was visiting California. We wrote and arranged my coming to Detroit, where she lived. On my way I stayed briefly in Aspen with Patsy Zoline and had the luck of meeting Paul Blackburn and Robert Vas Dias and Bobby Byrd. Paul and I became friends immediately and talked at length of his translations from the Provençal, which he loaned to me in manuscript. Blackburn, of all my contemporaries, seemed to have learned the most from Pound. From Aspen I moved on to the riots in Detroit, where Elizabeth and I lay all night on the floor listening to the sounds of machine guns and rifle fire and screeching wheels and sirens. The television gave us instant coverage. The entire upper Midwest seemed under siege.

After a return to Illinois to help Curtis move his furnishings and farm animals (I remember trying to catch the ducks), Elizabeth, her son, Ben, who was three, and I traveled east. Jack and Joanne traveled in Europe for the six months following their wedding, then settled into a loft in NYC for another six months. Elizabeth and I arrived in New York in late summer. Jack and Joanne introduced us to many of their new friends, and then arranged for us to return in a few weeks, when we would all travel together back to California, which we did, all their things in the back of the pickup as far as Jack's mother's in

Michigan, Jack and Thomas Thomas (the one malamute I had kept) riding in the back with them. In Michigan we rented a trailer, so some might ride in the covered bed. We drove from Michigan to Wyoming, Yellowstone, and then to the Northwest. Jack shot movies of the trip. Somewhere in the Northwest, driving late at night looking for a place to park, Jack and I decided to head on home. The ladies slept through the night and in the morning found themselves far from where they expected to be. I again stayed at Brown's, worked with him. Elizabeth and Ben headed for Aspen, where they would settle.

I put Elizabeth on the bus in San Francisco the morning of September 21, 1967. I spent the afternoon with Patsy Zoline and Michael and Joanne McClure. That night, Cass Finley, whom Richard Brautigan had once brought to Brown's, and who was visiting now on her own, climbed the ladder to my loft. Cass grew up in New Jersey, outside of Philadelphia, started college in North Carolina, was married briefly, spent the next year in Philadelphia, and had flown to San Francisco in early '67, where she quickly met Brautigan, Peter Coyote, and the Diggers. After months in the city she traveled with others to New Mexico, where she had hoped to settle, and had returned to the city for what she had thought would be a short visit. She stayed on with me, and a few weeks later we drove to El Rito to pick up her belongings. When we returned we found a small house to rent on Sparkes Road in Sebastopol, the house where I wrote the screenplay for *If You Don't Like Me You Can Leave Me Alone,* and all but the last poem in the second section of *California Poems.*

We spent much of the time I wasn't working in San Francisco visiting Lenore Kandel and Billy Fritch, Peter Coyote and Sam, Peter and Judy Berg, and others of the Diggers—who then were at the peak of their activity. The Diggers functioned first as a community, then as social movers and shakers, focused much of the seemingly disparate energy running rampant on Haight Street. They staged many events, provided many people with a sense of community that has only been paralleled in my life by the poetic community, which Cass and I stayed a part of. I met Franco Beltrametti when I picked him up at Philip Whalen's suggestion at the pier where his ship came in from Japan, where Philip was and had met him. When Philip returned I met his ship, and moved his belongings from place to place. We visited often with Jack and Joanne, in Bodega (just around the corner from where I had once visited Brautigan), in the little blue house in San Francisco (where Lewis and Phoebe MacAdams, Tom and Angelica Clark, Lewis Warsh and Anne Waldman came when they came west, and where I got to know them, and where I introduced Jack to Patsy Zoline; a house which she and I had once almost rented), and later in Bolinas when they lived in the yurt on the land where Jack would build his house. When Gary Snyder returned from Japan with Masa, we met the boat, visited often before the Snyders moved to the Ridge. I first met Lew Welch at Philip Whalen's 123 Beaver Street apartment in '65, but never really knew him well before he too came to know the Diggers.

Drum Hadley hitchhiked up from Arizona in the summer of '68; I remember that the datura were in bloom where we walked under the apple trees. There were many late-night visitors, coming in from far and wide, off the road. I was reading Eliade's *Shamanism* and it found an easy place in most conversations.

When Brautigan learned that Cass was pregnant he wanted to know where she had conceived and was disappointed when he learned it had happened in bed. Our daughter, Jessie Aldebaran, was born in the Sparkes Road house, November 21, 1968. Sam, who was like a sister then to Cass, had come in a few days earlier from Colorado, to be there for the birth. Peter Coyote was in Olema, and I drove early that morning to get him, so that he might be there. Five weeks later, on the same winding back road, I was struck by a Volkswagen, out of control on the wet road, the woman driving thrown from her car and killed. While waiting for an insurance settlement, we traveled east by train, to Chicago and New Jersey, to show off the grandchild. We were gone a month, spent time in NYC with Lewis and Anne and Ted Berrigan and others. When we returned we bought a '62 Chevy Travelall, cut our belongings to what would fit and gave up our house, using Olema as our home base. We went first to Idaho and Montana, spent many weeks there, parking on the sides of logging roads, watching the melting snow seep into the ground. After a short return we went on to Tucson, and the Hadleys, stayed for weeks, in town and at Dart Ranch in the Chiricahuas where Drum first showed me the life of a cowboy.

The summer of '69 we were back in Olema with Peter Coyote. Deirdre spent a month with us, the four of us living out of the back of the truck. My folks came to visit, stayed at a motel in San Rafael. Before going to visit them, Cass and I walked into a local department store and the head cashier ordered all the others to close their drawers when she saw us— Bonnie and Clyde fresh in her mind.

In September '69 we headed north again, saw Deemers in Oregon, then headed east to Chicago, New Jersey, and then to Mountain Dale, New York,

arriving a few weeks after Woodstock. We spent several weeks exploring the fields and woods and made periodic trips to NYC. We were harassed by the police, who connected us to the others wandering the countryside. For Thanksgiving we drove to Savannah, Georgia, to visit a cousin Cass had grown up with, my first visit to the South in nineteen years. Somehow I had expected that it alone had not changed—would be as I remembered it. I was wrong. We spent December in Illinois, I skinning mink with Curtis, who raised them, living again out of the truck.

On Christmas day we headed south for Santa Fe, where Hadleys had just bought a house. We spent a few nights with them, then drove on to Olema, Bolinas, and San Francisco, to collect those belongings we'd left behind, and were back in Santa Fe by the end of January, where we rented part of a house on Camino Del Monte Sol. We lived there until fall. I rewrote *Shannon*, expanded *If You Don't Like Me You Can Leave Me Alone* into a novel, finished *California Poems*, wrote *Wind, Fragments for a Beginning*. I worked as well at carpentry and general construction with Tony Martinez, then at masonry with Felipe Gabaldon. Through Hadleys we came to know Keith and Eloise Wilson and Mona Sakiestewa, and through Mona many more, Jerome Rothenberg among them. Peter Coyote, Jack and Bill Brown, Lew Welch and Magda, and many others came to visit. Snyders and Nanao Sakaki came to Hadleys and I first met Nanao then, visited again with Allen Ginsberg, in that house on Monte Sol, which reminded him of one Ed Dorn had once lived in in Santa Fe. Deirdre was with us for a month that summer, and Jessie and I took her back to California, leaving Cass, who had found work, behind. The truck broke down several times going and coming, and though I drove straight through coming back, it took days. In the fall the landlord wanted the house for his daughter and we were forced to move. We stayed for awhile with Mona, then found a house on Garcia, around the corner from Hadleys. I had to clean and paint the whole house. In late December I helped Mona drive to Woodstock, New York, where her first husband-to-be lived. Except for an overnight with friends in Kansas City we drove straight through, arrived at dawn, the ground covered with deep snow, the temperature twenty-five below. I returned by train, train wrecks all through the Midwest, and I was routed far out of my way. When I returned, I found that it was over between Cass and me. I spent three weeks putting things in order before I left for San Francisco. The night before I left, there was a big poetry reading to benefit Black Mesa, and I came to know Peg Swift, who organized the reading, that night. I met Simon Ortiz at Hadleys' the next morning, where he had come to visit Gary Snyder who was staying there. I gave Simon a ride when I left, towards Albuquerque.

I was in California about six weeks. I went first to Olema, arrived at Coyote's as the last of the bikers straggled out after a party that had lasted for days. I learned that a caravan was forming and that Peter was going to move on, move out of Olema. I went on to Bolinas, and somehow Jack and I ended up going to Petaluma where we spent several days putting together a fence. Nights we hit the bars in towns nearby and talked a lot of other bars and Jack told of how he and Lew Welch got kicked out of every bar from Gazelle to Grants Pass when they had lived in the Siskiyou. Bill Brown was living with Wilma and others just north of Bolinas, truck farming, and I spent nights there, when Jack and I returned to Bolinas, sleeping in my truck, or at Jack's. Jack and Joanne were no longer together. Patsy Zoline was expecting Jack's baby, though she and Jack couldn't stand to live together—Lynn O'Hare and her children lived with Jack in the house he was building. My copy of *California Poems* arrived in the mail and I went up to Olema to show it to Peter, and found Peter and a small group finishing up their moving, and we all stood around drinking and I read the last poem in the

book to those there, and we all left together.

I went back to Santa Fe. I picked up a hitchhiker in San Bernadino, an ex-marine who had first seen duty in the Detroit riots, had shot a man as he climbed out of the bus in his hometown. We compared notes and decided that there was ample reason to believe that the riots had been incited. As we drove into Williams in the middle of the night we were stopped by a roadblock, twenty or so men with rifles standing behind parked police cars. They were looking for someone who had robbed a restaurant, and they thought I looked a lot like him, checked my arm for a telltale tatoo which wasn't there and we drove on. I left the ex-marine in Albuquerque, he was on his way home, and I drove north toward Santa Fe, and lost my fuel pump. Mona came to my rescue. I spent the next few days at Hadleys, looked up Peg Swift.

P eg Swift—Marguerite, after her mother—had lived in the Southwest for several years before I met her, mostly on the Navajo Reservation, mostly working as a journalist. She was born in NYC, spent her early years in Connecticut and summers for many years afterward in Maine. She had lived and traveled extensively in Europe and the Middle East, in Mexico and Central America. In April '71 she was house-sitting in Santa Fe, writing free-lance. After a two-week courtship we drove to Maine to visit her father who was dying. We were there most of May. Otis Swift had spent his early years in the newspaper world, as a writer, and then in the Depression years got into public relations. He had lived well a life of his own choosing. He died in June, we were gone, back to the Southwest on our way to California where I was to have done a reading which we found had been canceled. We traveled for several weeks with Deirdre and Jessie, back to Illinois, and then west again to take the girls home. We visited Peter Coyote, the caravan nearly ready. I worked in Petaluma, built a deck, and Peg went off each day to San Francisco, where she catalogued material for Julia Newman's Tenth Muse. In late September '71 I saw Jack for the last time. Patsy's baby had died at birth, Jack had gone to southern Mexico for several months. We talked of Lew Welch's disappearance—Jack had spent days helping in the search for his body, which was never found and which Jack hoped meant that he might still be alive. We watched Jack's movies.

Peg and I headed east to Illinois. We built a sixteen-by-sixteen-foot cabin in six weeks on my aunt Laura's land, a half mile from the road, on a wooded creek that ran through the property. We built the cabin of scrap wood, salvaged wood and a bucket of nails from a barn that had burned down. The farm

*"Thomas Thomas," Sante Fe, California, 1971*

James Koller

dump was close at hand and we found everything there we needed. The place cost, including the stove with a bad bottom, thirty-five dollars. We lived there through the winter, Jessie with us for six weeks. I began *Bureau Creek,* wrote "Message in My Poems." Peg left in March to help her mother return to Maine, I followed in May, after editing and annotating Peg's *Winter in the Illinois Woods.* After readings in Chicago I read my way east, where we stayed for several months in Wayne in a house loaned to us by Douglas MacDonald, whom I'd just met in Chicago, on the shores of Lake Androscoggin. Gary Lawless introduced himself and Ted Enslin and arranged several readings in Maine for Ted and myself. Peter and Judy Berg visited, and Peter Coyote was best man at our wedding in June '72, up from Pennsylvania where he'd come after his father died.

In August I went to NYC to work with Michael Fine, who had sold the Paper Place in Iowa years earlier and had returned to New York, and who now was beginning Bookthrift, a paperback remainder company. I stayed with Michael and Marlene weekdays, drove to Maine for the weekends. It was on one of those weekends in Maine that Lewis MacAdams called to tell me that Jack Boyce was dead. A few hours later Bill Brown and Patsy Zoline called. Jack died September 30, 1972, he was forty. He fell from a beam in his house, struck his head on a cast-iron stove. He was cremated, his ashes somewhere on Mount Tamalpais.

In October '72 Peg decided to move down to NYC too. The apartment we found was on Bank Street, right around the corner from the White Horse Tavern. We lived together in the city until Christmas, when Peg moved back to Maine. I stayed on in the city through February '73 back at Fines', Maine on weekends, until I went west in March trying to generate interest in Bookthrift. I was gone for two months. I drove through Wyoming, Colorado, New Mexico, Arizona, California as far north as Sacramento, and Nevada. Except in California, most of my time was spent in university towns. I hit a lot of bad weather, was snowed in briefly in Laramie and northern Colorado, hit bad ice near Flagstaff. I spent time with Wilsons, Hadleys, and Mona in the Southwest, with everyone I knew in California. Peter Coyote and I drove back together from San Francisco to Pennsylvania, where I left him, drove on to NYC, then to Maine.

Peg was pregnant. We decided to leave the East, move to Colorado. We packed everything into a trailer and drove to Morrison, stayed with old friends of Peg while we looked for a place to rent and work. We were there only a few days when I fell and broke

*With "Ülf" and daughters Jessie and Deirdre, Washington State, 1973*

both wrists—June 10, 1973. We bought a tent and camped with our friends for the next month, while my wrists began mending, then too restless to stay longer, I drove to New Mexico, picked up Jessie, and drove to California, where I picked up Deirdre. The three of us drove to Spokane, Peg flew up to meet us. We wandered, camping, over western Montana, Idaho, Washington, and Oregon for several weeks, then drove back to California, dropped Deirdre off, and drove back to New Mexico, where after taking Jessie home we camped another two weeks while we decided what to do next. My hands were still not fully operative—I couldn't do any heavy lifting. We decided to pick up our things in Colorado and return to Maine. We did.

Jedediah was born in Brunswick, Maine, November 23, 1973. The apartment we rented was in a building which had once been a hospital and now catered to mostly navy people. Many of the women who lived in the building were pregnant or had just had a child. Peter Coyote parked his trailer in the back yard that Christmas. I found work with a local book distributor who was opening a chain of stores, managing and establishing systems in each of the new stores. In April '74 we moved to Georgetown, south of Bath. I built a small shed for the sheep and goats we kept, a house for the chickens and ducks. We put in a large garden, three stone walls across it to terrace it. The house was not insulated and we used oil to keep it warm nights, and days burned wood, about five cords a year, which I bought in four-foot lengths. For the first few years we went almost nowhere, one quick winter trip to Illinois, Jedediah waving at all the big trucks. *O Didn't He Ramble* was finished here, and *Back River* written. Much of the writing from these years remains unpublished.

Bob and Susan Arnold discovered me working in one of the bookstores. They were down from Vermont to visit the coast, saw the new bookstore, and stopped in. Bob had known my work and when he learned I was there he introduced himself. We have written and visited with regularity since. Paul Kahn too came into my life in these years. Paul was managing editor of *Alcheringa* when my work appeared there, and once we began writing we never stopped.

In early '76 Peg visited the Southwest with Jedediah, and when she returned decided to have another child. Theadora was born December 27, 1976. I was invited to the Spring '77 Cambridge Poetry Festival, in Cambridge, England, and Franco Beltrametti, whom I've written since I met him in '67, set up readings in Amsterdam, Zurich, Biasca, Venice, and Munich. In Cambridge I spent much time with Bob Creeley, whom I hadn't seen since California in the late sixties, met Fielding Dawson, and Tim Longville, whom I had corresponded with for years. The Cambridge Festival lasted a week. I then flew to Amsterdam, found Franco at Harry Hoogstraten's. We read together in Amsterdam, then rented a small red Opel to continue the tour, and I drove, with Franco as navigator. We were on the road for nearly three weeks and between readings Franco made sure I saw those things an American Poet visiting Europe for the first time should see—we joked often of his "civilizing" me. Amsterdam and Venice were both cities I thought I could live in. In Munich as I walked toward the site of a reading in a park, I recognized in the distance Karl Bruder, whom I hadn't seen or heard about for eleven years. He had seen a flyer for the reading. Monika, whom he lived with and whom he had told of his life in San Francisco, had seen the flyer and had brought it home. We have been in touch since.

What most impressed me with Europe was that people had a different sense of necessity—people often lived without those things Americans thought of as necessary (the toilet was often used by more than a single family, there was often no central heating), and people spent their money for things we were likely to think of as luxuries.

Peter Coyote married while I was in Europe. I sent a poem written while flying to Europe, and the poem was read during the ceremony. Peter and Marilyn came east for their honeymoon and we canoed in the marshes off Back River.

In the spring of '78 Franco, Harry, and Giovanni Blumer came to the United States. We made a cross-country reading trip together that included readings in Maine, Boston, NYC, Buffalo, Cincinnati, St. Louis, Santa Fe, Las Cruces, and several places in California. We traveled in a rented station wagon, Peg and the kids riding with us. We visited many friends along the way, helped Drum Hadley build a corral, saw Peter Coyote, who had become Chairman of the California Arts Council, celebrated Bill Brown's sixtieth birthday. In the fall of '78 I flew again to Europe, to the first annual poetry event in Amsterdam, P78. Joanne Kyger, who had visited in the spring in Maine, Anne Waldman, Ted Berrigan, and many others I knew from America were there. Franco was there. Nanao was there. I met the Swedish translator and poet Reidar Eckner, the German poet Stefan Hyner. I was away about ten days. When I returned I took up with Leslie Burhoe and my marriage to Peg Swift ended.

Deirdre visited in Maine, Christmas of '78. Leslie threw a party and Deirdre went. When I picked her up, the driveway was icy and the front wheels spun; Leslie, who had seen her out, jumped onto the hood of the front-wheel drive car, giving us the traction we needed. The quickness and appropriateness of her response told much of who she was and I was impressed. She was born in Vermont, spent her early years near Ojai, California, and moved to New Jersey in the late sixties. She had summered in Maine, just down the road from where I lived, had moved up when she left home a few years earlier.

My third trip to Europe was to attend P79, but was longer and again included a wider area. I had moved in with Leslie, we were to have a child in December, and Leslie came with me, first to London, where we visited her mother's family, and where I read, then to Amsterdam, and after P79, where I saw many friends again, we took a train with Stefan Hyner to his place in Schwetzingen, then drove to Bern. After reading and visiting in Bern we took a train south through the Alps to Riva San Vitale, where we visited with Franco, before returning, via Amsterdam and London. We were gone a month. When we returned, I quit work, and we packed up and moved to Dover, Illinois, stayed with my cousin Curtis.

Bertie, our son, was born in Princeton, Illinois, December 28, 1979. Deirdre had moved to Illinois the summer before, was married the day after Bert was born. She and I worked together for five months in a roadside restaurant, before Leslie, Bert, and I headed west with Franco in May, to read in Boulder, Taos, Albuquerque, Washington, and California. We visited friends or camped along the way. Near Taos one morning we awoke to find we'd been covered with snow. Franco stayed in California, and on our way east Leslie and I spent a week house-sitting for Mona in Santa Fe. We met Arthur Sze, Mona's husband. When we left, Jed and Thea, who had been visiting in the West with their mother, drove with us to Illinois and Maine.

In September, Leslie and I headed west again, to Washington. I found work landscaping near Bellingham. We found a small house for rent on the edge of Ferndale, on the Nooksack flood plain. There was a grain elevator nearby, and we could hear the trains switching for hours, could hear the fast trains going through in the night for Vancouver or Seattle, sounds I hadn't heard since I was a boy west of Chicago. We stayed eleven months, Leslie working most of the time as a barmaid in a roadside bar, pregnant with our second child. Most of *Great Things Are Happening* and *One Day at a Time* were written in Ferndale. I edited with Peter Blue Cloud, Carroll Arnett, and Steve Nemirow a special Coyote issue of *Coyote's Journal,* which was published by Wingbow in Berkeley.

We returned to Maine in late August '81, found a cheap rent in the back of a house in Lisbon Falls. Ida Rose was born in Brunswick, October 14, 1981. We spent Christmas in New Jersey with Leslie's mother and brother and sisters, then went to visit my folks in Illinois, stopping along the way to see Jim Smith in Indianapolis. We saw Karl and Monika Bruder in Chicago, then on our way back stopped to see Bob and Susan Arnold at their place in southern Vermont—as we had stopped on our way to Washington and then again on our way back.

In January '82 we moved into a building in Georgetown that I had helped Darell Bidstrup build before leaving for Washington. Darell was a California boy who had come to Maine in the early seventies, and whom I met in '74. After knowing each other for years we discovered we had both known Wilma Hoefelfinger in California years before—Darell before she lived with Bill Brown, I after. I started landscaping and tree work in late March '81, in Boothbay Harbor. My second week of work I was caught in a snowstorm on the way home and the drive that normally took forty minutes took nearly four hours. I didn't make it up the final hill and walked

home the last half mile, looked like a snowman when I got there. In March '83 we visited New Jersey, saw Leslie's grandmother for the last time in Virginia, went on to Illinois, passing through West Virginia just hours before heavy storms closed those roads. In August '83 Stefan Hyner arrived on his way east from China, where he had been for two years, to help build, with Tom Chapin, a house we had designed. Tom Chapin is an artist—his structures are his art.

Over the years my mother despaired of my ever settling down and offered several times to give me money to buy or build a house—money she had spent her life saving. It would be my inheritance anyway, she said, why not take it—this way she could see how I spent it. Nineteen eighty-three seemed as good a time to accept as any, and we did, built a sixteen-foot-by-twenty-six-foot, two-floor frame structure, with a chimney in the middle, for the wood cookstove that heats the house and serves to cook on. My father wired the house for electricity. There is no water in the house, though there is a well. In October we all returned, Stefan with us, to Illinois, for my folks' fiftieth wedding anniversary. Stefan returned to Germany in December and we moved into the new house in January '84.

In the early spring of '84 we drove west, to Illinois, to Idaho, to see Darell and his place there, to California, where we visited my sister whose husband had died, and with Philip Whalen and Bill Brown. Brown had survived brain surgery that many had thought he wouldn't. Brown had a rat who visited each night, and one night we were there the rat tried to pull a loaf of bread through a hole a water pipe passed through. The rat was so loud that Bill finally left him food laced with Nyquil. We went on from California to the Southwest, stayed with Drum Hadley at his Guadalupe Ranch on the Mexican border for a week, then visited Mona and Arthur Sze in Santa Fe, before returning again to Maine. We saw Drum again in Cooperstown, New York, in September '84, when Leslie's father married again, to Peg Waller. Drum's grandmother had lived in Cooperstown, and he had come to visit with his parents at the homestead.

The winter of '84–85 we began extensive cleaning of the woods near our house, clearing out deadwood, burning brush, enlarging the area that had become our garden—a garden which because of the rocky ground and sparse soil had necessitated bringing in seven yards of soil. In the summer of '85 we visited several times with Bob Creeley and his family, who now summer in Maine. Leslie and I had seen Bob last in '80 in New Mexico. In December '85 Leslie and I married in the woods behind the house,

*Koller and children in Maine, 1983. From left to right: Thea, Jed, Bert, James, and Ida*

then traveled again to Illinois, picking up Stefan, who flew into Chicago and who returned with us to Maine. Darell returned for a visit and we were all snowed in over New Year, watched the Chicago Bears on TV. In March, after *Give the Dog a Bone,* poems from '85, came out, I flew to California, my first flight across the country, visited with Bill Brown, Joanne Kyger, and Peter Coyote. I saw Bill and Laura Kwong again after nearly twenty years, visited with Dick Baker for only the second time in nearly the same twenty years. I saw Magda Craig again. I gave a reading in Bolinas which was attended by a group that consisted almost entirely of folks I had known well since the sixties. In May I celebrated my fiftieth birthday. In the late summer I contacted Carroll Terrell at the University of Maine, arranged to once again publish *Coyote's Journal,* due for spring '87.

Leslie is back at work, waitressing, both Bert and Ida are in school. Theadora, ten now, Jedediah, thirteen, live with their mother in Flagstaff, Arizona. Jessie, just eighteen, is in Hawaii, where her mother now lives. Deirdre, divorced after seven years of marriage, lives with her daughter Tanya, who is five, in Illinois. It is an early winter, several light snows in November. The addition to the house we started this summer waits to be finished.

## BIBLIOGRAPHY

**Poetry:**

*Brainard and Washington Street Poems.* Eugene, Ore.: Toad Press, 1965.

*Two Hands: Poems 1959–1961.* Seattle: James B. Smith, 1965.

*The Dogs and Other Dark Woods.* San Francisco: Four Seasons Foundation, 1966.

*Some Cows: Poems of Civilization and Domestic Life.* San Francisco: Coyote Books, 1966.

*I Went to See My True Love.* Buffalo, N.Y.: Audit East/West, 1967.

*California Poems.* Los Angeles: Black Sparrow Press, 1971.

*Messages.* Canton, N.Y.: Institute of Further Studies, 1972.

*Dark Woman, Who Lay with the Sun.* San Francisco: Tenth Muse, 1972.

*Bureau Creek.* Brunswick, Me.: Blackberry, 1975.

*Poems for the Blue Sky.* Santa Barbara, Calif.: Black Sparrow Press, 1976.

*Messages/Botschaften.* Munich: S Press, 1977.

*Andiamo,* with Franco Beltrametti and Harry Hoogstraten. Fort Kent, Me.: Great Raven Press, 1978.

*O Didn't He Ramble* (bilingual edition, translated to German by Stefan Hyner). Schwetzingen, Germany and Brunswick, Me.: Bussard-Coyote Books, 1980.

*Back River.* Brunswick, Me.: Blackberry, 1981.

*One Day at a Time.* Markesan, Wis.: Pentagram, 1981.

*Great Things Are Happening* (bilingual edition). Schwetzingen, Germany: Bussard, 1984.

*Working Notes 1960–82.* Odisheim, Germany: Bussard/Falk, 1985.

*Give the Dog a Bone.* Brunswick, Me.: Blackberry, 1986.

*Openings.* Green River, Vt.: Longhouse, 1987.

### Fiction:

*If You Don't Like Me You Can Leave Me Alone.* Pensnett, England: Grosseteste Review, 1974; Brunswick, Me.: Blackberry, 1977.

*Shannon, Who Was Lost Before.* Pensnett, England: Grosseteste Review, 1974; North Fitzroy, Australia: Ear in Wheat Field, 1974.

### Editor of:

*Coyote's Journal* (anthology), with Peter Blue Cloud, Carroll Arnett, and Steve Nemirow. Berkeley, Calif.: Wingbow Press, 1982.

### Special issues devoted to Koller's work:

*Savage,* no.2 (1972).

*Falk,* no.25 (1986).

Koller has edited *Coyote's Journal* and edited and published Coyote Books since 1964.

# Michael Moorcock

*1939-*

I was born in Mitcham, a South London suburb, on 18 December 1939. My earliest memories are of air-raid shelters, dog-fights, searchlights, barrage balloons, collecting shrapnel and bits of planes on the Common—which we swapped as peacetime kids trade bubblegum cards—of ruined buildings, of endless landscapes where bombs had cleared eccentric spaces amongst shops and houses. We heard of little boys blown out of their clothes by the flying bombs, their bodies found in trees, of old women who survived direct attacks from a V-1 rocket, of girls who walked unharmed from factories set on fire by incendiary bombs.

Later the V-bombs were deliberately misdirected by Churchill into South London to save centres of government and industry. What was an almost unbearable strain on the adults never seemed very bad to us. We lived lives of constantly fulfilled adventure, climbing swaying staircases to the third storeys of houses, leaping from joist to joist because the floorboards were gone. I remember that one of my first toys not made for me by my father was a real Sten gun with its breach blocked.

By VE-Day the world I knew and thrilled to was ending. As we jumped over the bonfires on which effigies of Hitler and Goering burned, kids like us looked forward to peace as a new adventure, because we had grown into a world where only warfare was constant.

I think we were as disappointed by peacetime as we were by the first exotic pineapples, bananas, or tangerines which reappeared in the shops. Peacetime meant uninterrupted school (my first school had to our intense joy been hit by a V-2 on a weekend). We still had most of the inconveniences of wartime, such as long queues, limited travel, general austerity, but without the pleasures, that certain kind of freedom. Then, almost as soon as the war was over, my father left my mother. He went to live with a lady he had met in his drawing office (he was a draughtsman on "necessary war work"). My mother tells me he walked out on Christmas Day, 1945, as she was taking the turkey from the oven. I suspect the story's rather more complicated than that. Much of this period of childhood, however, remains a mystery, for there are many conflicting accounts and I wasn't told at the

*Baby Michael, at thirteen weeks*

*The Wykeham Studios, Ltd.*

time what was going on. Perhaps my persistently nagging fear of "betrayal," my most self-destructive trait, which usually reappears whenever I begin a major piece of work, has to do with those particular circumstances.

My mother, left with me and little money, sharing the rented house with her brother and his wife, went to the local timber yard, which employed women to yank nails from old wood so that it could be recycled. Before long, since she'd earlier been a bookkeeper in a shop, she was working in the yard's office, under the protection of the firm's owner, an Austrian Jew, a disciple of Rudolf Steiner's strange brand of Christian mysticism, who had escaped from the Nazis and, I later learned, had returned, risking his life and money helping others escape from Europe until the outbreak of the war. As an adult I met several people who owed their liberty and probably their lives to Ernst Jellinek. He was to become my guardian.

Ernst Jellinek counselled both myself and my mother, helped with my schooling, offering me a view of life both practical and moral which has never left me. My mother, volatile, pretty, neurotic, wildly generous, sometimes selfish, full of common sense

*Mother, June Moorcock, about 1950*

which her actions often denied, became, I suspect, first the object of his love and later his responsibility. He was a wonderful patriarch. He was also a married man, with children. I learned from his example and tried to follow it. Only years later did I realise the unconscious harm he had done my mother by responding so kindly to all her crises. I was a teenager, however, when I understood that in certain crucial ways I had become my mother's father substitute. An impulse towards patriarchy has haunted me most of my life, both creating and damaging friendships.

I remember my childhood as a happy one, with occasional desperate interludes, such as the period I spent at Michael Hall School in Sussex. It was an enlightened, liberal Steiner school, but I was horribly homesick, anxious about "secret" changes at home. I spent much of the time plotting escapes. I ran away several times from this benign institution, where I was instilled with further idealism and a morbid terror of vegetarianism, until they decided to expel me. I was the first pupil ever to be expelled. My mother was informed that I was not happy at Michael Hall and moreover I kept the other children up all night telling them stories (some of which I retailed as my own adventures wherein I had been raised by wolves in the Indian jungle; the school was too liberal to have Kipling in the library) or leading them on

midnight expeditions into the walls of the old Elizabethan building, which had a fair share of semi-secret passages, some opening on the kitchens where we ate outlawed white bread and "unhealthy" jam, the property of the staff.

I was sent to a small private "prep" school in Norbury, the next suburb on from Mitcham. My mother had moved from Mitcham to Shirley to Norbury during the time I was at Michael Hall. Norbury, also in South London, was a wonderful mixture of urban density and open spaces, of housing estates and woods, commons and parks. It was a short bus trip into the centre of London, yet summer holidays could be spent almost entirely in woods inhabited chiefly by myself and my friends. Sometimes I would visit my paternal grandparents (my maternal grandparents were dead, he of drink, she of diabetic complications); sometimes I would go to 10, Downing Street, where my uncle lived; and more rarely I would visit various aunts. My mother's family covered an astonishingly wide social range for the England of that period. We had diplomats, dog-breeders, telephone engineers, taxi-drivers, chemists. My mother's working-class to upper-middle class siblings gave me a far broader range of social experience than most children of my generation. This may not sound strange to Americans, but few English people have the opportunity to shift back and forth through the social spectrum as I did. One day I could be seeking my grandmother out at the conveyor belt where she sorted candy for the local sweet factory, the next I could be walking up the stairs of Downing Street admiring the portrait of Disraeli who was our legendary direct ancestor. An only child, I read a great deal and was fluent long before I went to school. As a result, school was dreadfully boring and the only subject I became enthusiastic about at the age of seven was Algebra, taught to young children on principle by Michael Hall. Later I added History and Geography to my limited range.

At the age of eight I began reading Richmal Crompton's "William" books and imagined myself their hero. My gang was called after William's, "The Outlaws." I had already read Dickens, G.B. Shaw, E.R. Burroughs, Clarence E. Mulford, P.G. Wodehouse, Bret Harte, George Eliot—almost anything which happened to be around our house or the houses of my aunts. The first long book I had read was called *Timothy Tatters* and was a tale of the Irish Land League in the nineteenth century. The book had been given to my father as a school prize. I still have it somewhere. Edwin Lester Arnold, H.G. Wells, Kipling, Arnold Bennett, Compton Mackenzie, E. Nesbit, William Faulkner, Rose Macaulay, Mervyn

*Ernst Jellinek, about 1960*

*Young Michael as hunter, with lion-friend,
Brian Alford, 1950*

Peake, J. Meade Faulkner, Marie Corelli, R.L. Stevenson, Mrs. Molesworth . . . My reading was so catholic it's impossible to respond to people who ask what my influences were, though Richmal Crompton was a considerable enthusiasm for years.

The first magazine I produced was also in imitation of "William" and was typed on a machine borrowed from my mother's office, using carbons to produce the copies. It was called *Outlaws Own*. It consisted mainly of material written by me. I was nine. The same typewriter was never returned. I used it to type all my novels until I was twenty-seven: an Imperial 50/60 "Utility" model, made during the war and completely indestructible. By the time I was eleven I had published a number of magazines and at fourteen was producing two "fanzines." One was called *Burroughsania*, for fantasy fans, and the other was *Book Collector's News*, mainly for people who collected prewar boys' magazines—*Magnet, Gem, Sexton Blake Library* and so on—which I sold at school and through small-ads. My first piece of publicity came through the *Croydon Advertiser*, which picked up on one of my shop-window advertisements and ran a story, with photograph, about my career to date.

I left school at fifteen, having distinguished myself only in English and Typewriting (the school was a Pitman's College, where young women, primarily, were prepared for life in offices; I had gone there because I failed the normal exams and by then knew I wanted to write). I went to work as an office boy for a medical publisher. This job, a few doors from Victor Gollancz's offices, lasted a day. I was shocked by the cynicism and foul language of my colleagues.

I got another job the following week. Jobs were easily available in those days in England and people from my background didn't consider issues like job fulfillment or prospects: I expected to earn my own living. My second job was as a messenger for a firm of shipping agents. I was disliked by some of the staff but adopted as a sort of mascot by others who saw my writing and magazine production as curious. I was encouraged to continue with it, although the job itself was ghastly. What was more, as I had found at school, my sense of amiable tolerance of the world and its illusions was regarded as dumb insolence by people whose egos depended on certain ritual responses and peculiar acknowledgements of their authority. I was fired after six months.

I got yet another job as an office boy at a firm of Management Consultants. The entire staff of this firm saw me as having all sorts of potential. I became the object of their aspirations and imagination. I scarcely

*With mother, looking at parrots along the
Thames, 1957*

did any work, so busy were they encouraging me to use my talents. The boss's hardest job for me was to ask me to go to the *Times* Library and exchange his books. It was mostly left to me what to pick. The kindness and encouragement of the staff of Harold Whitehead and Partners was one of the key supports in my teenage world where I expected to be drafted at eighteen and hoped to get a reasonable career-training in the air force. I had joined the Air Training Corps with the knowledge that it guaranteed one's entrance, often at a slightly higher rank, into the RAF. I had wanted to be a flyer or a reargunner, but was prepared to settle for a technical education, since nobody had yet suggested it was possible to earn a living from writing. My training was undistinguished. I had no aptitude with guns, light planes (even Link trainers), or drill. I stuck the whole thing out in misery until I could take no more. I had done enough training to qualify for the RAF. The crowning irony would be that by the time I was eighteen the "call-up" was abolished. I escaped being drafted by a matter of two or three days.

Encouraged by Whitehead's, I produced more and more magazines on their copying machines. As well as the two I started with, I did a music fanzine (*Jazz Fan*, later the *Rambler*), a bibliographical fanzine, and a whole variety of miscellaneous publications, including several science-fiction fanzines through which I was introduced to the world of sf "fandom." My Burroughs fanzine led directly to my being asked, at the age of sixteen, to write for a juvenile magazine called *Tarzan Adventures*. I began a series of articles,

some fantasy stories ("Sojan"), and various other "fillers," and had them all published. By the time I was seventeen I had been offered the job of editing the magazine. Alastair Graham, who had commissioned most of my stuff, was leaving. I hesitated, not sure I was qualified to do it. Again it was the encouragement of the staff at Harold Whitehead's which helped me decide. I became a fully fledged editor of commercial magazines (paid scarcely more than I had been receiving as an office boy!) and my career as an editor went from amateur to professional status. I was already a professional writer. I've been earning my living in the same way, with occasional breaks, ever since.

My other means of earning a living, never as successful, was as a singer/guitarist. As a teenager I'd become enthusiastic about American blues and folk music. An early hero was Woody Guthrie, with whom I corresponded until it became impossible for him to write. By the age of fifteen, playing banjo and guitar, I was appearing semi-professionally in a country-and-western trio called The Greenhorns. We wore grey stetsons, string ties, and short corduroy jackets. We couldn't stretch to the more expensive Western gear. We were never particularly popular, largely, I suspect, because of my insistence on playing and singing some of Guthrie's longer and more obscure songs.

This was the time when other British kids were producing a peculiar form of music which became known commercially as "Skiffle." In Liverpool The Quarrymen (later The Beatles) were doing the same thing as us. My friend Bill Harry, art editor and contributor to my fanzines, began his own magazine *Mersey Beat,* which eventually became *Disc and Music Echo.* He published a lot of John Lennon's early work. Much of the interchange on the music scene was between Liverpool and London in those days. Out of this came the first wave of seminal English rock bands, including The Beatles, The Rolling Stones, The Yardbirds, and others. It was a tremendous time to be involved in popular music. We all did what we did for the love of it. The idea of a career in rock and roll was not then regarded as much of a possibility. Part of rock's attraction for us was that there were no critics, no standards, no musical authorities, no historians, no music papers, as such, which would give anything more than a contemptuous mention to what we were doing.

I was attracted to science fantasy for much the same reasons. The stuff wasn't criticised (except in fanzines), you could produce it without some higher authority looking over your shoulder and judging you. Your judges, by and large, were your peers. Neither rock nor sf made you feel self-conscious. The

*Making music in the offices of* Tarzan Adventures, *1958*

possibilities were not proscribed. And, we began to discover, you could even sometimes get paid for doing it.

I dropped out of the rock-and-roll world as my writing began to get published. I'd grown temporarily tired of sleazy dressing rooms and cramped vans, of venues which ripped you off or told you, after a long drive, that a gig had been cancelled. In some ways I wish I'd stayed with it, into the Golden Age. It's a wonderful thing, being a rock-and-roll star. When I finally tasted what it was like, I was too old to enjoy the full euphoria.

I continued to play and sing with various groups during the late fifties and early sixties but appeared on stage very rarely. I did enough, however, for that particular world to become familiar, to make some good friends, to get the thrill of stage performing in my blood. I'm still doing music and still go on stage occasionally, but it's been several years since I performed with my own band, The Deep Fix, though we haven't stopped making the odd record, usually for obscure labels.

While I was editing and writing *Tarzan Adventures*

almost single-handed, I began to produce short stories for adults. These were varied (though not, I suspect, in quality) and since the short-story market was already shrinking I had little luck with them. People weren't interested in stories about teenage life in Soho. I began writing science-fiction stories because there was still a fair market in Britain and the U.S. My first sale was to *New Worlds,* a collaboration with my good friend Barrington Bayley, published in 1958 as "Peace on Earth." At about this time I was asked by Ted Carnell, editor of *New Worlds,* if I would consider writing a fantasy series for the companion magazine, *Science Fantasy.* Eventually, trying to produce something a bit different from the usual sort of sword-and-sorcery stories, I submitted the first Elric story, "The Stealer of Souls." I describe this in more detail in a couple of short essays included in *Elric at the End of Time.*

I had no idea how much of my future income would come to depend on Elric's success. Carnell liked the first one and asked for more. They became popular and he commissioned the other stories which were eventually published as *The Stealer of Souls* and *Stormbringer.* I owe a great deal to Ted Carnell, who was a wonderful man. He died suddenly in his fifties, the single most influential figure in British sf; he gave encouragement to the so-called "new wave" of British sf writers, including J.G. Ballard, Brian Aldiss, and Barrington Bayley, while publishing American writers considered at the time to be "too difficult" for the U.S. magazines. With his encouragement I soon began producing novellas and novelettes (my favourite form in those days) for all three of his magazines. The third magazine was the somewhat misnamed *SF Adventures* which published a great deal of the most introspective sf ever seen at that time!

Before I was twenty I was earning a good living from my work. I had left *Tarzan Adventures* and joined *Sexton Blake Library* (another contact gained through my fanzines), going from a tiny publishing outfit in a backstreet to the massive Amalgamated Press, which published more than half the commercial magazines produced in England and now, as IPC, publishes even more. Sexton Blake was "the longest running detective series in the world"; his adventures had started in 1889. I also worked on a number of children's annuals (hardback anthologies featuring the characters from the weekly comics) and strip papers, including *Lion, Tiger, Eagle, Thriller Picture Library, Cowboy Picture Library,* and many others. I found that I had a rare facility for writing comic strips and produced reams of scripts, including stories for Dogfight Dixon, RFC; Dick Daring of the Mounties; Captain Condor of the Space Patrol; Karl the Viking;

Robin Hood; Kit Carson; Buck Jones; Buffalo Bill; Strongbow the Mohawk; and Zip Nolan of the Highway Patrol; not to mention a score of others. I can't these days tell which I wrote and which others wrote except where my alliterative verse or rhyming couplets, done out of desperate boredom, were allowed to remain. I also wrote comic strip lives of Alexander the Great, Constantine the First, Genghis Khan, and other famous historical figures.

I claimed at this time to be working in the popular mythology business. It taught me how to write very economically, to plan scene, dialogue, and narrative so that they had the maximum effect. I also learned how people respond to their favourite myths, what they want from them. I think I utilised this experience in my ambitious fiction but the real problem I had was that I had developed a tremendous facility for writing quickly about almost anything. I'm envied for it and it seems ungenerous to complain that writing came easily, but this facility grew to be a burden. I've a talent for structure and can tell a good story, but the ease with which I wrote all those stories, comics, articles, the economy with which I was able to determine style, plot, character so as to give me minimum effort with maximum effect, was to hamper me later when my literary ambitions grew.

Meanwhile, between the ages of seventeen and twenty I was able to earn almost any amount of money by writing. I spent faster than I earned—most of it on the usual vices—and became a fairly dissolute teenager for a while. The bottom dropped out of this world when Amalgamated Press, about to be bought by IPC, preserved its cash assets by stopping payment on acceptance and changed to paying on publication (sometimes eighteen months or more in the future). As an active member of the National Union of Journalists, but because I was under twenty-one unable to hold any official position, I fought against this. What resulted was a series of encounters with management which led to two of my colleagues resigning and to my holding a beleaguered position where my bosses (who had conceived the ludicrous notion that I must be a communist agitator at very least) were too nervous of firing me (presumably because they feared that Red Hordes would swarm to my assistance) but attempted by various conventional strategies to make life hard for me. Eventually these strategies, together with my own fear of winding up as a company journalist, succeeded. After some fairly melodramatic months, I left.

A couple of weeks later I headed for Sweden, where my friend Lars Helander met me. I stayed chiefly in the Uppsala area, earning a living with my guitar in various bars and clubs. Later, having made friends with the geographer David Harvey, now Professor of Geography at Oxford, I travelled to the North where we explored the tundra and mountains of the European Arctic during a marvellous summer in which the sun never did completely set. My experience of Lapland did me enormous good. Returning to Uppsala, I pawned my guitar and sold books to get enough money to hitchhike to Paris where I understood money was waiting for me at George Whitman's "Mistral" Bookshop, today grandly retitled "Shakespeare & Co." The journey proved to be a hard one and I was in a very weakened condition by the time I reached Paris. George knew nothing of any money (it was for a short story), did not even recognise me, and I began to despair. Walking in the Tuileries at night I collapsed.

I awoke at the British Embassy. They took my passport, put me up in the bridal suite of the Hotel Madelaine, forgot to feed me, and in the morning presented me with a travel voucher for England. By the time I stepped off the train in London to be met by my mother and cousin, I was even more lightheaded. I had become too hungry to hold food down. The experience of being close to starvation and alienated in a number of countries seemed to have matured me, however, and given me a lot of material which I almost immediately began to use.

I had no job. I had been blacklisted as a writer at IPC. Of my old earning markets I had only the low-paying sf magazines left. I wrote more Elric stories, more fantasies, some science fiction. This last is a form I've never been much at ease in. Most of my work is not sf at all, though I'm often described as an sf writer. During this fairly difficult period, in which I lived chiefly at my mother's in South London, I met and proposed to a journalist working for the British Council, Hilary Bailey. I was twenty-one. I had few money-making projects. Even the Social Security office couldn't or wouldn't find me manual work.

Eventually, through the same person who had recommended me as his successor on *Tarzan Adventures*, Alastair Graham, I learned of an opening on the writing staff of the Liberal Party. The job would not come up for a month or two, but meanwhile I could work in the party's bookshop. For a while I was a sales assistant, part-time bookkeeper (a disaster), and general help to the various local political agents who required posters and publications for their constituencies. Later, when the job became available, I went upstairs and began writing broadsheets for the coming elections. I was also given the job of copy-editing the Liberal leader's latest book.

Jo Grimond was a pleasant, amiable, and worthy man, radiating soft good looks and decency, but logic wasn't his strong point and his political naïveté was astonishing, even to me. I began editing the book but eventually suggested it be rewritten. Nobody wanted to tell Jo. I argued, with others, that it could lose millions of votes. I came into conflict with the party's running committee and just after my wedding (September 1962) I was fired. We were living in two tiny rooms at the top of a hundred stairs in what had been a large linen closet of a house in Lancaster Gate. It was Christmas week. Hilary was pregnant. It was the worst winter since 1947. We looked desperately for a new flat while I wrote stories for Ted Carnell which, perhaps because I was trying my hand at science fiction again, were unsuccessful and consistently rejected.

By February 1963 we were in a friend's flat in Bayswater, where I spent most of my energy dealing with a roof which had collapsed under the weight of snow. That spring we found a flat in Colville Terrace, Notting Hill, a street mainly occupied by prostitutes, pimps, and West Indian steel bands which tended to rehearse at night. But we had two larger rooms, a cramped kitchen, and the toilet was only one flight down. There followed some of the most miserable months we'd experienced. By the time my daughter Sophie was born, in September 1963, I had sold my second book. The first, *The Stealer of Souls,* received an advance of £100 and was published in 1961. The second, *Stormbringer,* received £75 on condition I cut it down to a length suitable for an edition sold through circulating libraries, which were then just coming to the end of their existence. The full text was not published until the mid-seventies in the U.S.A.

I was now writing for IPC again but being paid under Hilary's name since I was still blacklisted. I worked for *Bible Story,* the best-paying glossy weekly, doing a series on cathedrals I'd never visited, interviews with various church personalities and organisations, articles on great Christian figures of history. I also worked for education magazines like *Look and Learn.* I continued to write some comics, though it was more difficult to find even the minimum of inspiration. I began, too, to fill Carnell's magazines with fantasy stories, with "imagist" stories usually termed "surreal" for want of a better word. Sometimes I virtually wrote whole issues of *Science Fantasy.* They paid badly, but they paid on the nail. My second daughter, Kate, was on the way in 1964, as I began to make some financial progress. I became anxious, however, when I realised I must soon support two children in our tiny flat. Then I heard the news that Ted Carnell, having lost a battle with his publishers,

had decided to fold the magazines. My chief source of revenue was about to disappear.

Ted bought the last Elric stories, a series of articles on fantasy, some marginally experimental work, but had to reject the sf serial I had written for *New Worlds, The Fireclown.* Hilary had her hands full with Sophie. I began to work at night so that at least one of us could sleep. I fed Sophie when she woke.

A few weeks later I was told by Ted Carnell that the magazines had been bought by a new publisher who had previously been best known for doing soft porn. The new publisher thought they might achieve a spearhead of respectability with the magazines and thus get W.H. Smiths, who then, as now, controlled the majority of periodical and book distribution in the United Kingdom, to take their other publications on. Ted had decided against continuing as editor and had recommended me as his successor. I was a little uncertain if I wanted to do the job, but Ted said I had the experience and the enthusiasm and he wanted me to take over. As it happened the publisher had a friend in Oxford, Kyril Bonfiglioli, to whom he had promised the job. In the end a compromise was reached. I would edit the magazine of my choice and "Bon" would edit the other. To everyone's surprise I chose the magazine I had been least associated with, *New Worlds.* I had plans to change its policies, to expand its range, and I wanted a title less specific than *Science Fantasy.*

I had already written some guest editorials in *New Worlds,* demanding more social and political engagement, better writing, better characterisation, more experimental prose, more urgent subject matter. Bayley, Ballard, and I met regularly once a week in a pub near Harrods, discussing the shortcomings of the form and what could be done with it. I determined to encourage newcomers and fresh techniques. I felt sf could become a genuine literary form whilst retaining its popular audience. My idealism was typical of the sixties, when popular music was growing more complex and interesting, when popular films grew increasingly ambitious, when it really did seem that "popular" and "quality" and "enlightened" could prove themselves compatible.

On this principle I began encouraging people to do experimental work and actively sought new talent. I believed many shared the frustrations felt by me and my friends. As it happened, I was wrong, certainly about the older writers. My early editorials spoke up a great deal for modernity, for unconventionality, but the contents remained fairly similar to Carnell issues. I attacked more of sf's icons and heroes, but couldn't find much to put in their place at first, except enthusiasm and idealism. It took at least a year before we began to publish something close to what we hoped to find. The details of this period are in my long introduction to *New Worlds: An Anthology* (1982).

I got about £20 a month from *New Worlds,* which was almost enough to cover our rent. Kate was born in September 1964. Things had begun to improve. By 1965 we were able to move to a much larger flat in Ladbroke Grove, where most issues of *New Worlds* were produced.

Earlier that year, still in Colville Terrace, I had attempted to break free of the sf form by writing a book called *The Final Programme.* I felt I was liberating myself and my prose, finding my original voice. I wrote the original draft at night, during the first ten days of January, with a nursing child in each arm during feeding times. I felt it was the best thing I'd ever done. It was rejected not only with disgust and concern for my state of mind, but with anger and hatred ("this evil book," said one editor). This made me reconsider my work and conclude that perhaps I was, after all, running before I could walk. I returned to more conventional forms for a couple of years, producing books like *Behold the Man, The Ice Schooner,* and *The Rituals of Infinity.* These were to prove radical enough for the sf fraternity. *Behold the Man* won a prize . . .

Later in 1965 I began to write fantasy novels to commission for U.S. publishers, primarily Lancer Books. I think I received $1,000 a book. It was a fortune. I could produce a full-length book in three days. Each manuscript was exactly 180 pages long. In what little spare time there was between issues of the magazine, I wrote these books to support my family and, by then, the magazine itself, since our budget did not meet our needs. The stream of writers, painters, poets, scientists, illustrators, and visiting editors seemed endless. They were heady, exhausting days which did not do much either for my family life or my emotional stability, but the excitement was intoxicating and we believed we were doing something worthwhile.

For two years or so, in a period others find nostalgic and which I remember as frequently nightmarish, we put out *New Worlds* and I wrote fantasy books. The series I produced then (Hawkmoon, Elric, Erekosé, in particular) have remained amongst my most popular and took the least effort to write. Because I put little value on them, I sold them cheaply on bad contracts. It would be a long time before I received a decent return on them.

Perhaps I overvalued *The Final Programme.* The novel had taken for granted, as I did, bisexuality and, if you like, homosexuality as perfectly ordinary expressions of human passion and love. It also present-

ed, in its protaganist Jerry Cornelius, an amoral antihero whose sophisticated knowledge of modern science led him to accept it all very casually. The book described a world, perhaps a model of our own, an "alternative" near future, in which the dreams of the sixties had turned to garbage, a world where sensation ruled and cynicism had completely taken over, where a wretched form of debased anarchism (I was then as now a proselytiser for Kropotkinism and its modern forms) prevailed. It was a moral tale about amoral people. It was a warning that the idealism of the sixties would produce no genuine change without considered and persistent engagement. It had strong female characters who dictated the action. It argued for a blending of "masculine" and "feminine" traits to produce a balanced human being.

*The Final Programme* was fairly crudely written, but I still find nothing much wrong with its underlying sentiments. It was eventually published in 1967 thanks to George Ernsberger, a brilliant editor at Avon Books in the U.S. George liked it so much he commissioned the other three books I had planned. I received an advance of several thousand dollars and for a while we were fairly solvent.

In 1967 I went to the U.S. to attend my first Milford Writers Conference. These events, held at the home of Kate Wilhelm and Damon Knight in Milford, Pennsylvania, played, together with Knight's anthology *Orbit,* a very important part in the inception of the American "new wave" of science fiction. By then *New Worlds* had already published some of the best young American writers, including Thomas M. Disch, John Sladek, Samuel R. Delany, and Gene Wolfe. I already knew Disch and Sladek and was glad of the chance to meet Delany again. I met Wolfe there for the first time. It was a pleasure to renew old acquaintanceships and make new ones but during the conference itself I found myself caught up in arguments I no longer found relevant. There was a clash between the "old guard" and the "young Turks" and I could see no point in preaching novelty to writers making a successful and contented living from traditional work. By now, it seemed to me, there was no need for converts: there were already plenty of writers keen to produce something different.

Eventually I escaped the conference to enjoy the wonderful wooded hills around the area and to go swimming. I have never officially attended another writer's conference since. I made some good friends, however, including Harlan Ellison and Norman Spinrad, both of whom were engaged in the forefront of the U.S. revolution in sf. I had by then become part-owner of *New Worlds.* The magazine had suffered circulation problems due to the bankruptcy of its distributors, and the old publisher and I had decided, after Brian Aldiss persuaded the Arts Council to give us a small grant, that we would continue the magazine. However, I was determined to go all out to produce what I had always wanted to produce— something which no longer compromised with traditional approaches, which was as experimental and risk-taking as possible. I had brought the first large-format issues with me to America to show what I wanted to do. By the time I returned to England my partner had washed his hands of the venture and gone to Scotland. I never saw him again. I was left with full responsibility for the magazine.

From that moment it was impossible to guarantee that the next month would see an issue. Yet somehow, with various kinds of help, chiefly with my own money, we continued to get the magazine out. Those issues are the ones I'm proudest of. I think we published some of the best work by writers now accepted as innovators and helped establish many of the best talents of their generation. We also acted as a catalyst, bringing writers from the more conventional literary world to a new audience and introducing the new sf writers to a more general public. This interaction was perhaps the most exciting thing.

When we published Norman Spinrad's *Bug Jack Barron* as a serial, together with Langdon Jones's story sequence *The Eye of the Lens,* we ran into attempted censorship from W.H. Smiths who demanded we drop such stories if they were to continue distributing us. There was an outcry in the Press. Parliament became briefly involved. Smiths pretended to take us back, but the distribution never really happened. The magazine was finished as a nationally distributed monthly. In the late seventies I produced some one-off issues and there's always a chance we'll do some more.

During the *New Worlds* phase of my life I also enjoyed my children growing up. I took them to the park and wrote in longhand while they played. My relationship with Hilary, however, went through a period of strain. I had an affair. She had an affair. We had a reconciliation. But our fundamental lifestyles, our specific needs, were beginning to alter and separate. Increasingly I needed to use our flat as a sanctuary from the excitement of producing the magazine. I had retired from much involvement and let the premises be moved to Portobello Road where a power struggle was taking place between various parties who felt they knew best what the magazine's direction should be. Hilary seemed unable or unwilling to help keep our flat free from the steady stream of visitors who continued to call, and disputes became frequent.

I was growing exhausted and desperate, finding it impossible to produce my books in the chaotic atmosphere I had helped create. By 1967 I had produced the second Cornelius novel, *A Cure for Cancer,* and had conceived the overall structure of the tetralogy, which was to be novel, very complex, and developed out of the needs of the subject matter. I needed more peace to produce such ambitious books. I also wanted to write some comedies. Comedy is a form I greatly enjoy but which I've never used as much as I'd like. I wanted to be free of other professional ties so as to get down to work, make a better life for the children, and provide an improved environment for us all. Perhaps a few years earlier Hilary would have shared this desire. Now she had no particular wish to go along with my needs. It didn't suit her, I suppose, that I was attempting to follow the principles of benign patriarchy learned from Dr. Jellinek. I asked her for positive suggestions. Either she had none or she didn't care to offer them. Possibly I didn't want to hear them.

My anxieties increased, together with fits of temper, wherein I tried to "drive away" the people who previously I had welcomed. Rows increased at home. The children witnessed them. I grew disturbed by my own behaviour and came to believe I was having some sort of breakdown. I recovered control of myself and went through a period in which I further attempted to understand the needs of my wife and children more thoroughly. By 1970 it seemed we had reached a closer understanding and were making progress in our relationship. We travelled to the U.S. together and had a great visit. For the first time we had been able to leave the kids behind. Hilary had a chance to assess her own ambitions and sort out what work she wanted to do. It looked as if the future was going to be better.

With an unexpected payment from a publisher who had forgotten to make it (and I'd forgotten it was owed) we decided to buy a house in Ingleton, Yorkshire. Houses in the Dales were cheap then and we had no other property, no means of buying anything in London. Ingleton, a few miles from the Lake District, lies in some of England's most dramatically beautiful countryside. I felt it would be worth living there at least for six months or so out of the year. Many of our friends enjoyed walking and climbing, as I did, and the house was in a perfect location for doing both. Hilary had found the place and bought it, but by then she decided she didn't want to spend so much time away from London, revealing that she only wanted to use the house as a "holiday home." I became resentful. There were further rows, attempted reconciliations. I went to the States in 1971 and telephoned her, as usual, to say I'd arrived safely. It was then that she told me she had decided to have another baby and was pregnant. This meant getting commissions for further fantasy series when I'd hoped not to write many more. Doing my best to see things from her viewpoint, I resolved to take the new baby and attendant problems in my stride. I sold the first "Corum" sequence to Berkley.

For the next couple of years, during which my son Max was born (February 1972), I continued to write a wide variety of books, including Cornelius novels, the first volume of "The Dancers at the End of Time" sequence, fantasies, and minor experimental work like *Breakfast in the Ruins.* I also continued my involvement with the so-called "underground" press, specifically with *Frendz* newspaper as well as *It,* and began to write for and perform with various rock bands, especially Hawkwind. Sometimes these performances were completely farcical, due to the amount of various intoxicants we'd swallowed. I vaguely remember one concert in which a band consisting of myself, Jon Trux, John May, and Paul Kossoff went on stage only to have Kossoff slide against the speaker stack and go peacefully to sleep while I somehow managed to fall several feet through a hole which had mysteriously opened under me. Perhaps as a rejection of my new responsibilities, perhaps because I was undergoing some sort of premature mid-life crisis, my lifestyle grew still further apart from Hilary's. I was back in my "old" element. I began another brief affair and for Hilary it was the last straw. We decided to separate. Ironically she moved up to Yorkshire for a year while I remained in London.

By the end of 1973 I had become involved with someone thirteen years younger, in a relationship which was to prove fairly disastrous for all concerned but which lasted for six years. Perhaps because I was curtailed by this relationship, with someone who was trying to live down a "wild" past and live a normal domestic life, I produced some of my very best work while Hilary, living in our old flat across the street so that we could both take responsibility for the children, also began to have success with her novels. This living arrangement was inspired by a mixture of idealism and self-interest. I think the idealism was misplaced, misconceived, and probably harmful. If there was a victim, it was the person whom I eventually married shortly before our break-up. My ego and self-confidence flattered, I suspect, by the attentions of an apparently compliant and younger woman. I wrote *The English Assassin* (the third Cornel-

*Moorcock, left, on the set of* The Final Programme *with "old card-playing friend" Jon Finch, who played the role of Jerry Cornelius, 1973*

ius book), the rest of the Dancers at the End of Time comedies, concluded all my various fantasy series with the books which brought them together into one "super-series" known as the "Eternal Champion" sequence, and enjoyed a measure of critical and financial success, especially towards the end of this phase with the publication of *The Condition of Muzak* and *Gloriana.*

Meanwhile I performed with my own rock-and-roll band, The Deep Fix, with Hawkwind, and made various appearances on TV and records. The abortive film of *The Final Programme,* with its messages translated into sexism and cheap sensationalism, appeared in 1973. I bought a massive Nash station wagon and became the terror of the highways. My record album *The New Worlds Fair* came out. I enjoyed the glories of being a minor rock star. I was a hippy prince. I had an entourage. We went to festivals together. We had Hell's Angels volunteer as body guards. We did drugs and sex and blew our minds. We kept on rocking. I was described as the Grove's own hip guru. Most of my old close friends found my company intolerable. I became pretty foolish for a while, absorbed in my own legend.

By 1975, however, I had given up the high life and returned to a rather reactive and overdone sobriety. I began to plan an ambitious novel sequence which would be my attempt to come to terms with the Holocaust. From being a glamorous bore I turned into a totally dull bore. My pious self-involvement increased but I must have become a little more tolerable to my friends, who began to reappear. Yet I

frequently waxed moralistic, in the manner of re-
formed persons. I gave myself monkish rather than
roguish airs. People said I seemed "more vulnerable"
(that's when one is at one's deepest level of self-
involvement!). I took myself, my duties and emotional responsibilities, and my work very seriously. I lost a
fair amount of humour. I became insanely responsible for the welfare of others. I was now described in
newspaper articles as saintly and wise. I almost
believed them. I believed them enough to begin
feeling I should live up to my publicity.

In 1976 I travelled to the U.S. aboard a Russian
liner. It was a marvellous trip, taking ten days in
rough seas, and I got to know several Russians in
more intimate circumstances than if, say, I had been a
tourist in Moscow. This experience gave me the angle
I needed for my Holocaust sequence, but now, having
won prizes and praise for my other ambitious work, I
worried that I would not be able to pull off the next
project. I began a period of intense research. I grew
obsessed with things Russian. I travelled on another
Russian liner, taking my daughters to New York, and
by now I'd grown almost Russian myself. Pictures of
that time sometimes frighten me. I wear a bearskin
"three-eared" cap. My eyes are hollow. I'm a character out of Gogol.

Through 1978 I planned my novel, which was to
be based on an old Polish man I had known around
Ladbroke Grove and whom I had already included in
my Cornelius books as "Colonel Pyat." I wanted my

*During his "Russian" period, 1978*

*The Moorcock children: Max, Sophie, and Kate, in
Ingleton, England. 1978*

acknowledgement of the Holocaust to bridge the
century, to trace its origins in the past, to draw
comparisons with the ancient world as well as the
modern, to show that almost the whole of our society
conspired in its inevitability and that few of us were
without some kind of involvement. The theme had to
do with yearnings for an imagined past, with the
appalling folly of attempting to recreate such a past,
both through personal relationships and political
action. It was to be an indictment of racism and
sexism, but to counter all this it also had to have its
comic aspects, its ironies. It also had to do with
imposition of imagination, of emotional demand, of
wish-fulfillment, over reality. I decided to write it in
the person of Pyat, a Jew-hating half-Jew, a Ukrainian
who had been terrified by the pogroms at the turn of
the century, a creature who is an exaggerated version
of all who deny responsibility for their own actions,
especially where those actions result in a massive and
terrible crime.

By 1979 I was writing the book. Its title has
several levels of meaning but was originally inspired
by the sardonic description of the Soviet Empire used
by people in the satellite nations of the Warsaw Pact.
They call the Empire "Byzantium." The novel is
*Byzantium Endures.* As Pyat took me over, my self-
obsession grew and grew. My relationships faded. I
had married for the second time in 1978, but by mid-
1979 my marriage was a travesty. I refused to accept
the evidence that my wife was seeing an old boyfriend, a man notoriously into sadism and other
forms of erotic sensationalism.

By July 1979, when the book was finished and I gradually came back to the ordinary world, I discovered that my marriage was in ruins. A series of nightmarish encounters followed, far worse than anything I might have imagined in fiction, in which my wife became increasingly involved in bizarre sexual adventures while at the same time calling on my emotional and financial support. I came to believe I was responsible for her state and hung on while I tried to convince her of the psychic damage she was doing to herself. I was further controlled by my own guilt, for there had never been anything like equality in our relationship. Eventually, having briefly returned to my first wife and realised, rather belatedly, that this was as confusing for the children as it was for us, I determined to remove myself from the whole scene so that I, at least, would no longer feel I was directly encouraging events. I went to visit Graham Hall, an old friend who was dying of cirrhosis and had settled in Los Angeles.

This action, taken in desperation and a wish to do something worthwhile for someone else, to end my own awful self-involvement, was ultimately to bring me a new and better life and a relationship with someone who at last felt like an equal both in her temperament and in her expectations of life. Much of this period is written about in a book called *Letters from Hollywood*. The book began as letters written to my friend J.G. Ballard, when I was living in North Hollywood with Linda, who was to become my greatest love, my most wonderful companion, illuminating and informing my life, teaching me more than anyone about human relationships and helping me to reach a much better understanding of myself.

In those early days, however, my behaviour became erratic as I was torn between past emotional connections and this fresh and better one. As I failed to live up to my own expectations of myself my self-esteem declined. It had already been seriously attacked by the events of the past months. I became dishonest. I knew I had become dishonest but, momentarily, I had lost any means of restoring myself. Soon I was lying to everyone, spending money I didn't have flying back and forth between ex-wives and my new love, attempting to find sanity and impose order while becoming increasingly fractured and uncertain of anyone's motives, including Linda's. Linda, unable to imagine the mess I was describing, continued to do her best to help me, eventually joining me in England during the early months of 1980. But the madness was by no means over. Both of us became infected. I had promised her that if I saw her "cracking" I would get her out of the situation. Eventually, when she decided to leave at one point, I

*With Linda Mullens at Tijuana Tilly's Bar & Grill & Dance Hall, Mexico, 1979*

encouraged her to go, telling her I'd rejoin her when I had sorted out what I could. The debts were increasing all the time.

I wasn't the only one spending nonexistent money. Indeed, I was spending less than anyone else. I'd left my ex-wives with bank accounts, credit cards, payments from publishers. I had given my second wife power-of-attorney since she argued she had no power, no familiarity with it. I thought this responsibility might help her get herself together. Instead she had continued with her adventures, buying more and more expensive clothes, ultimately at the rate of about £1,000 a week. Soon I was advised by everyone to file for bankruptcy. I was trying to write books to pay off debts which continued to increase. I briefly rejoined Linda until it became obvious I had not cleared up the mess and had to go back. We agreed that we would not get together again until I completed the books and wound up my affairs. She went to Mississippi to look after her grandfather. Linda was the most exceptional person I had ever loved. I loved her more thoroughly than anyone. Yet I must admit that after she left I began to lose almost any sense of the value of my own love. By mid-1980 I had written the books while my second wife alternatively tried to attack me with a butcher knife or took pills in unconvincing suicide attempts. I found myself giving her assurances I couldn't possibly keep in order to buy time. By giving these assurances, however, I was betraying my feelings for Linda. I grew weaker than I have ever been and my self-disgust continued to increase. I no longer knew other people's truth from lies (I knew my own lies). Lying myself, I trusted no-one. My betrayal was complete because I was now thoroughly betraying myself. I had learned a kind of cynicism completely at odds with my needs as a writer, my expectations of myself as a human being. Yet I continued to be motivated by my love for Linda, to whom I had already caused distress. I decided to rejoin her in America, accept a script-writing job in L.A., and try at least to help her restore her life. This was confused and stupid thinking, having much to do with my own lack of self-respect. By August, having remained in touch with my second wife, I left L.A. again. By September I was begging Linda to rejoin me, which she agreed to do, on certain conditions. I agreed to these conditions. I began separation proceedings with my second wife and moved up to Ingleton. Linda joined me in October 1980 and it seemed we were beginning life afresh, putting much of the terrible craziness of the past year behind us. Then in November Linda had to return to the U.S. to attend a dying relative. Our next-door neighbour committed suicide. In London I found myself again making unkeepable agreements with my second wife. I agreed to meet her secretly. The nightmare resumed. Linda returned and I now had a further deception on my conscience. By Christmas the strain had grown too great to tolerate and, convinced that Linda would decide to leave me, I told her what had happened. I was sure that I'd lost her and believed that I no longer deserved her love. Nonetheless, I determined to go to London and make a complete break. This I did, though not without further compromising myself. I still hardly had any of my former self-respect. I saw no reason for Linda wishing to carry on with me. Her own ego was badly wounded.

Within a month or two, however, after Linda had determined to give the relationship one last try, I was beginning to free myself finally from the past and restore my sense of myself as a reasonably moral and decent person. There were terrible rows and expressions of resentment, but I continued to give Linda my full commitment, which I've done ever since. It was the best decision I ever took. Life wasn't easy for us, especially in the early days, and I had to make several hard decisions, breaking almost completely with an old life which had many good associations and gave me a great deal of moral and emotional support in spite of its negative aspects, and losing touch with a number of people I had known for years. Yet I was doing no more than Linda had done by choosing to live with me in England.

A t the age of forty I felt I was starting all over, with a massive pile of debts, several impending

*Michael and Linda after their wedding in Fulham Town Hall, 1983*

lawsuits, nowhere permanent to live, since the house was owned by Hilary, hardly any outside support, and an almost tangible fear of doing serious work again, yet in a lot of ways I was more fulfilled than I had ever been, for I had Linda's companionship.

Together, Linda and I began to try to fight back, to build up enough money to move, to deal with a divorce becoming increasingly bizarre, to cope with a variety of legal cases, to make a decent life for ourselves. Linda's positive support was something I'd never known before. Her sense and her intelligence helped me with all aspects of my tangled life. My mother thinks she's Saint Joan, Florence Nightingale, and Wonder Woman rolled into one. This doesn't allow for her humanity, her vulnerability, and her remarkable sensitivity (or her anger, her frustration with the world's vices, her hot temper). She's lived in England with me for the past six years or more and we've been together for seven-and-a-half. Her generous American soul has sustained her through all kinds of difficulties, heartache, loneliness, and sometimes despair (especially living in London where people can be as ungenerous and as arrogant as any I know). Often she longs for California, her spiritual home, yet she is at last beginning to continue her own interrupted projects (she writes and illustrates) and make the best of things here in the cold. It will not be long, I hope, before we can spend at least six months in California every year.

During the difficult, fraught, and enormously happy years since 1980 I feel I've managed to get my life in better perspective. I'm still subject to self-destructive anxieties around work, but even these have subsided as our circumstances improve. Linda's particular sensibilities inform and amplify my own and I think I do the same for her. We now have a lovely flat in London which we feel is a blend of our tastes, a thatched cottage in the country, and we travel fairly frequently, almost to anywhere we want to go. Most of this is due to Linda's unstinting efforts on our behalf. I've written two or three fantasy novels since we've been together and enjoyed doing them. *The Warhound and the World's Pain* and *The City in the Autumn Stars* are fairly far removed from the earlier sword-and-sorcery adventures and I'm proud of other books, like *The Brothel in Rosenstrasse*, *The Laughter of Carthage* (the second Pyat novel), and *Letters from*

*Hollywood*, which have appeared during the years we've been together.

Currently I'm working on another book, the fulfillment of a long-term ambition to produce a kind of celebration of the virtues and charms of London and Londoners, *Mother London*. I'm writing this autobiography between completion of the first draft and doing the final draft. Next I'll be returning to *Jerusalem Commands*, Colonel Pyat's third volume, always a frightening prospect, since the horrible old bigot is inclined to take me over, and perhaps writing another fantasy or two. A recent offer to write a travel book, thanks to good reviews for *Letters from Hollywood*, means we might eventually get to Australasia and Malaysia. We've always enjoyed one another's companionship when travelling and somehow seem to get the most out of an experience together.

Certainly we shall continue to travel within the U.S. It's my ambition eventually to settle there, probably in Southern California. I have a particular liking for Mississippi writers and get a lot out of visiting Linda's parents in West Point or spending time in Jackson or Oxford, as well as Clarksdale, Mississippi, where so many great blues players come from. I'm also very fond of New Orleans. In 1986 I took my fifteen-year-old son, Max, on a Greyhound tour of the U.S. It was wonderful to see him get so much out of the trip, which did his morale enormous

*Onstage with rock band Hawkwind at the Oxford Apollo, 1984*

good. We completed about 8,000 miles in something under five weeks. It's now his firm intention to get back as soon as possible and continue his further education.

I still have a great deal of idealism invested in the United States. Compared to England, there is far more optimism, more willingness to support almost any kind of individual enterprise, to take people on their own assessment of themselves. England for me seems to be shedding her virtues as fast as she can, celebrating her vices, feeling proud of her most ludicrous traits; the society is as class-bound as it ever was and in some ways far more repressive than similar Oriental cultures. In Japan the rules rarely change. In England the rules change frequently and by these means those in power continue to maintain their authority.

As a committed supporter of the Women's Movement, I also find more hope in the U.S. than I do in England. A good many Americans I know are given to apologising for the crass aspects of U.S. society. As I'm fond of saying, there are many forms of good taste but bad taste is virtually universal. We have as much bad taste in England and as many awful politicians and hypocritical public figures. What we do not have is a Freedom of Information Act or an Equal Opportunities Act with muscle. We don't have a constitution and we don't have either greedy or idealistic lawyers willing to test new laws and amendments at every turn. There's a lot to be said for a country at least partially founded by a bunch of lawyers enthused by some of the better ideas of the Enlightenment! To me, America still has a great deal of real social progress left in her. I fear that England has only her fantasies.

I suppose it is out of this disgust for decadent imperialism (as opposed to America's dynamic imperialism) that I have written a fair number of my books. The Jerry Cornelius stories all returned to the theme of Empire-gone-sour. I've no brief for any form of imperialism, and the books also offer a warning against any form of paternalism, but England's hollow claims for herself are now embarrassing to me, so far have they drifted from any recognisable reality. These delusions, however, are also the stuff of comedy and my comedies are frequently about such things.

One can probably tire of satire, particularly as one gets older and realises it's virtually impossible to affect the smallest social change by it. Yet I feel greater affection for my funny books than for the melodramas, the sword-and-sorcery fantasies, which also attack imperialism. Two of these, comic thrillers, still give me pleasure. They are the stories of a sleazy secret agent called Jerry Cornell and his dreadful family, a more "ordinary" version of Jerry Corneli-

*With Dave Tate (center) and Jimmy Ballard, 1985*

us's, set in the real world of Notting Hill and Portobello Road. I've written far more ambitious books than *The Chinese Agent* and *The Russian Intelligence* and books which took somewhat longer to write than three and two days respectively, but they remain amongst my favourites.

I sometimes mourn the period when I used to claim that a book wasn't worth writing if it went longer than three days. Now books take months, sometimes years, and far more of my life is absorbed with writing them. This seems to me to be a failure on my part and I'm currently trying to find out what went wrong!

The job of a novelist has its own momentum, its own demands, its own horrible power over the practitioner. When I look back I wonder what I got myself into all those years ago when I realised I had a facility to put words down on paper and have people give me money in return. For ages the whole business seemed ludicrous. I couldn't believe my luck. Frequently, I still can't but it seems an unnatural way of earning a living. Of course, it's no longer easy. It's often a struggle. It spoils my health, it threatens my relationships, it absorbs time which could be spent in all kinds of more pleasurable ways. While I make light of this in conversation, Linda reminds me grimly just what sort of exhaustion my work can produce in her as well as me. It's left me utterly wiped out on

countless occasions. Once it was the direct cause of my contracting double pneumonia and nearly dying, had it not been for Linda's nursing. I suppose it must be an addiction. I'm pretty sure, though I deny it heartily, that I could now no longer give it up. I'm as possessed as any fool I used to mock.

I hate hard work. I am deeply suspicious of compulsive, even habitual behaviour. Yet there's a glimmering of truth which tells me I'm as thoroughly obsessed as another might be by a cruel lover. Nobody warned me of the dangers! Every real working day involves the taking of brutal psychic risks, of entering and reentering the war zones of human experience. Your self-respect comes to be based on how you conduct yourself in this arena, how you survive, and how much you achieve from taking these risks. You have no great desire to control the world; your fear is that you cannot control what you invent on the page. And you are really the only one who can appreciate your level of success, the degree of your courage. You yearn for outside acknowledgement, especially from your loved ones, but few can give it. Why should they? As far as most people are concerned you are crazy. No sane animal takes such risks willingly. Yet what you achieve for yourself, if you're lucky, is a saner understanding of the world. You can add a degree or two of genuine rationality to the little which already exists—a moment's illumina-

*The Moorcocks at an autograph session for* Forbidden Planet, *1986*

tion, perhaps, a couple of relatively fresh insights.

This is the irony of being a creative artist—why Tolstoy's books are so much saner than Tolstoy's life, how Conrad's wailings—"*Mes nerfs, mes nerfs*"—from behind a locked door can become translated into *Nostromo.* There are satisfactions. But are they worthwhile to your nearest and dearest? Have they any meaning to anyone but yourself? How much can you reasonably demand of those around you? These are the unsolved questions which remain after you have solved all the creative problems, and it could be that they are more important than anything to do with your work. Do your own children go unnoticed at times because you are contemplating the Holocaust, because you have elected to taste the ash of Auschwitz or the Cossack's lash? Why should they respect you or understand you or care to love you when nobody has conscripted you into these psychic battles; nobody has asked you to live so much of your life in misery; nobody has wanted you to be mentally absent for months while physically still present, sometimes wailing like a baby, sometimes weeping with exhaustion and self-pity, sometimes accusing those who offer you the most of betrayal and lack of respect.

You, of course, are the traitor, as far as they're concerned, and finally as far as you're concerned, even when you don't admit it. You are the greedy, whining, unrespectable, all-but unrecognisable monster of self-indulgence. When you fail—as often you must fail—in your voluntary tasks, your self-respect plunges, you are tempted to maintain ego and momentum—your courage—by all kinds of ludicrous strategies, most of which are demeaning or in direct contrast to your moral and artistic ambition, your ordinary human sympathies and desires. Yet, still ironically, you remain aware of the world and its injustices, for as a white middle-class male you know in your bones that you have learned to demand far more of those around you than any woman in the same situation. You have been allowed to become this monster partly as a result of your talent but largely as a result of an accident of birth which has placed you in a time and a situation astonishingly favourable to you. Why should you not feel guilty?

Why should you not try somehow to redress this balance, both in your daily life and in your work? Why—if you are a moral novelist—does everything else retain the tinge of hypocrisy, the smack of unreality, of lies? All you can do in the end, I suppose, is acknowledge your favoured status, keep some sort of humility and good grace when making assessments and judgements, when choosing your subject matter, as far as that choice is ever yours, and

*"Outside our favourite Indian restaurant, New Year's Eve, 1986"*

accept that much of what the world perceives as your virtue and your talent has a great deal to do with mere circumstance.

In the end you can hope to be judged and to judge yourself by the uses you make of your good fortune. Billions of individuals are in some way gagged or stifled, especially if they are women. That I'm allowed to sing at all is a miracle. That I'm applauded for it is a boon whose value can never be measured and, when rational, I am amazed and thankful to have been granted so much more than my fair share of the world's awards. And that's how one comes, in a way, full circle: I feel I have a duty to make the most of what I have. And that's doubtless why I go on, forever hoping to achieve a balance in my personal life which reflects at least a degree of the balance I achieve in my best work. Perhaps it should be the other way around? If it should, it's too late to change that, so I must do the best I can with what exists.

*Michael and Linda in Ouarzazate, Morocco, 1987*

I have no wish to live an alienated or isolated life. I don't believe it's good for me. So one of the things I tell myself is that I can give up writing any time I like. All I ask of a sympathetic world is that it not raise its eyebrows when I make that particular claim! It seems fair that we should all be allowed, at certain moments, some small form of self-delusion.

And all I ask of those I love and who, at least some of the time, love me, is a degree of forebearance, a smidgeon of pity. They could argue that I display more than enough pity for myself, at least when I'm working, and that I deserve no more. I couldn't easily argue with that. For the other thing you learn when examining the remorseless logic of this vocation is that in some profound sense you are almost always alone.

And if that doesn't make you laugh, nothing can.

---

*BIBLIOGRAPHY*

**Fiction:**

*Caribbean Crisis*, with James Cawthorn, under house pseudonym Desmond Reid. London: Fleetway, 1962.

*The Fireclown*. London: Compact Books, 1965; New York: Paperback Library, 1967; also published as *The Winds of Limbo*. New York: Paperback Library, 1969.

*The Sundered Worlds*. London: Compact Books, 1965; New York: Paperback Library, 1966; also published as

*The Blood Red Game*. London: Sphere Books, 1970.

*The Deep Fix*, under pseudonym James Colvin. London: Compact Books, 1966.

*The LSD Dossier* (ghostwritten for Roger Harris). London: Compact Books, 1966.

*Printer's Devil*, under pseudonym Bill Barclay. London: Compact Books, 1966; also published in a revised edition as *The Russian Intelligence*, under name Michael Moorcock. Manchester, England: Savoy Books, 1980.

*Somewhere in the Night*, under pseudonym Bill Barclay. London: Compact Books, 1966; also published as *The Chinese Agent*, under name Michael Moorcock. New York: Macmillan, 1970.

*The Twilight Man*. London: Compact Books, 1966; New York: Berkley Publishing, 1970; also published as *The Shores of Death*. London: Sphere, 1970.

*The Wrecks of Time* (bound with *Tramontane*, by Emil Petaja). New York: Ace Books, 1967; also published separately in a revised edition as *The Rituals of Infinity; or, The New Adventures of Doctor Faustus*. London: Sphere Books, 1970.

*The Black Corridor*, with Hilary Bailey. London: Mayflower, 1969; New York: Ace Books, 1969.

*The Ice Schooner*. London: Sphere Books, 1969; New York: Berkley Publishing, 1969.

*The Time Dweller*. London: Hart-Davis, 1969; New York: Berkley Publishing, 1971.

*The Distant Suns*, with James Cawthorn, under joint pseudonym Philip James. Bombay: Times of India Press, 1969; Llanfynydd, Wales: Unicorn Bookshop, 1975.

*Moorcock's Book of Martyrs*. London: Quartet Books, 1976; also published as *Dying for Tomorrow*. New York: DAW Books, 1978.

*The Time of the Hawklords*, with Michael Butterworth. Henley-on-Thames, England: A. Ellis, 1976.

*Sojan* (for children). Manchester, England: Savoy Books, 1977.

*The Real Life Mr. Newman*. London: A. J. Callow, 1979

*Gloriana; or, The Unfulfill'd Queen: Being a Romance*. London: Allison & Busby, 1978; New York: Avon, 1979.

*The Golden Barge: A Fable*. Manchester, England: Savoy Books, 1977; New York: DAW Books, 1980.

*My Experiences in the Third World War*. Manchester, England: Savoy Books, 1980.

"Elric" Series:

*The Stealer of Souls, and Other Stories*. London: Neville Spearman, 1961; New York: Lancer Books, 1967.

*Stormbringer*. London: Jenkins, 1965; New York: Lancer Books, 1967.

*The Singing Citadel: Four Tales of Heroic Fantasy*. St. Albans, England: Mayflower, 1970; New York: Berkley Publishing, 1970.

*Elric of Melniboné.* London: Hutchinson, 1972; also published as *The Dreaming City.* New York: Lancer Books, 1972.

*The Sleeping Sorceress.* London: New English Library, 1972; New York: Lancer Books, 1972.

*Elric: The Return to Melniboné,* with Philippe Druillet. Brighton, England: Unicorn Bookshop, 1973.

*The Jade Man's Eyes.* Brighton, England and Seattle: Unicorn Bookshop, 1973.

*The Sailor on the Seas of Fate.* London: Quartet Books, 1976; New York: DAW Books, 1976.

*The Bane of the Black Sword.* (contains some material from *The Stealer of Souls, and Other Stories* and *The Singing Citadel: Four Tales of Heroic Fantasy* ). New York: DAW Books, 1977; London: Panther, 1984.

*The Weird of the White Wolf* (contains some material from *The Stealer of Souls, and Other Stories* and *The Singing Citadel: Four Tales of Heroic Fantasy* ). New York: DAW Books, 1977; London: Panther, 1984.

*Elric at the End of Time.* London: New English Library, 1984; New York: DAW Books, 1985.

"Michael Kane" Series, under pseudonym Edward P. Bradbury:

*Warriors of Mars.* London: Compact Books, 1965; also published as *The City of the Beast,* under name Michael Moorcock. New York: Lancer Books, 1970.

*Blades of Mars.* London: Compact Books, 1965; New York: Lancer Books, 1966; also published as *Lord of the Spiders.* New York: Lancer Books, 1970.

*Barbarians of Mars.* London: Compact Books, 1965; also published as *Masters of the Pit.* New York: Lancer Books, 1970.

"The History of the Runestaff" Series:

*The Jewel in the Skull.* New York: Lancer Books, 1967; London: Mayflower, 1969.

*Sorcerer's Amulet.* New York: Lancer Books, 1968; also published as *The Mad God's Amulet.* St. Albans, England: Mayflower, 1969.

*Sword of Dawn.* New York: Lancer Books, 1968; St. Albans, England: Mayflower, 1969.

*The Secret of the Runestaff.* New York: Lancer Books, 1969; also published as *The Runestaff.* London: Mayflower, 1969.

"Jerry Cornelius" Series:

*The Final Programme.* New York: Avon, 1967; London: Allison & Busby, 1969.

*A Cure for Cancer.* London: Allison & Busby, 1971; New York: Holt, 1971.

*The English Assassin: A Romance of Entropy.* London: Allison & Busby, 1972; New York: Harper, 1972.

*The Adventures of Una Persson and Catherine Cornelius in the Twentieth Century: A Romance.* London: Quartet Books, 1976; also published in *The Cornelius Chronicles III.* New York: Avon, 1987.

*The Lives and Times of Jerry Cornelius.* London: Allison & Busby, 1976; also published in *The Cornelius Chronicles II.* New York: Avon, 1986.

*The Condition of Muzak.* London: Allison & Busby, 1977; Boston: Gregg, 1978.

*The Great Rock and Roll Swindle.* London: Virgin Books, 1980.

*The Entropy Tango: A Comic Romance.* London: New English Library, 1981; also published in *The Cornelius Chronicles II.* New York: Avon, 1986.

*The Opium General, and Other Stories.* London: Harrap, 1984; *The Alchemist's Question* also published in *The Cornelius Chronicles III.* New York: Avon, 1987.

"Karl Glogauer" Series:

*Behold the Man.* London: Allison & Busby, 1969; New York: Avon, 1970.

*Breakfast in the Ruins: A Novel of Inhumanity.* London: New English Library, 1972; New York: Random House, 1974.

"Books of Corum" Series:

*The Knight of the Swords.* London: Mayflower, 1971; New York: Berkley Publishing, 1971.

*The Queen of the Swords.* London: Mayflower, 1971; New York: Berkley Publishing 1971.

*The King of the Swords.* London: Mayflower, 1971; New York: Berkley Publishing, 1971.

*The Bull and the Spear.* London: Allison & Busby, 1973; New York: Berkley Publishing, 1973.

*The Oak and the Ram.* London: Allison & Busby, 1973; New York: Berkley Publishing, 1973.

*The Sword and the Stallion.* London: Allison & Busby, 1974; New York: Berkley Publishing, 1974.

"The Eternal Champion" Series:

*The Eternal Champion.* London: Mayflower, 1970; New York: Dell, 1970.

*Phoenix in Obsidian.* London: Mayflower, 1970; also published as *The Silver Warriors.* New York: Dell, 1973.

*The Swords of Heaven, The Flowers of Hell,* with Howard Chaykin. New York: Heavy Metal, 1978.

*The Dragon in the Sword.* New York: Ace, 1986; London: Grafton, 1987.

"Oswald Bastable" Series:

*The Warlord of the Air.* London: New English Library, 1971; New York: Ace Books, 1971.

*The Land Leviathan: A New Scientific Romance.* London: Quartet Books, 1974; Garden City, N.Y.: Doubleday, 1974.

*The Steel Tsar.* London: Mayflower, 1981; New York: DAW Books, 1982.

"The Dancers at the End of Time" Series:

*An Alien Heat.* London: MacGibbon & Kee, 1972; New York: Harper, 1972.

*The Hollow Lands.* New York: Harper, 1974; London: Hart-Davis/MacGibbon, 1975.

*The End of All Songs.* St. Albans, England: Hart-Davis/MacGibbon, 1976; New York: Harper, 1976.

*Legends from the End of Time.* New York: Harper, 1976; London: W. H. Allen, 1976.

*The Transformation of Miss Mavis Ming: A Romance of the End of Time.* London: W.H. Allen, 1977; also published as *A Messiah at the End of Time.* New York: DAW Books, 1978.

"Chronicles of Castle Brass" Series:

*Count Brass.* St. Albans, England: Mayflower, 1973.

*The Champion of Garathorm.* St. Albans, England: Mayflower, 1973.

*The Quest for Tanelorn.* St. Albans, England: Mayflower, 1975; New York: Dell, 1976.

"Von Bek Family" Series:

*The Warhound and the World's Pain.* New York: Timescape Books, 1981; London: New English Library, 1982.

*The Brothel in Rosenstrasse: An Extravagant Tale.* London: New English Library, 1982; New York: Carroll & Graf, 1987.

*The City in the Autumn Stars.* London: Grafton, 1986; New York: Ace Books, 1987.

"Colonel Pyat" Series:

*Byzantium Endures.* London: Secker & Warburg, 1981; New York: Random House, 1982.

*The Laughter of Carthage.* London: Secker & Warburg, 1984; New York: Random House, 1984.

**Nonfiction:**

*Epic Pooh.* London: British Fantasy Society, 1978.

*The Retreat from Liberty: The Erosion of Democracy in Today's Britain.* London: Zomba Books, 1983.

*Exploring Fantasy Worlds: Essays on Fantastic Literature,* with others; edited by Darrell Schweitzer. San Bernardino, Calif.: Borgo Press, 1985.

*Letters from Hollywood.* London: Harrap, 1986.

*Wizardry and Wild Romance: A Study of Heroic Fantasy.* London: Gollancz, 1987.

**Editor of:**

*The Best of "New Worlds."* London: Compact Books, 1965.

*Best SF Stories from "New Worlds."* St. Albans, England: Panther Books, 1967; New York: Berkley Publishing, 1968.

*The Traps of Time.* London: Rapp & Whiting, 1968.

*The Best SF Stories from "New Worlds" 2.* St. Albans, England: Panther Books, 1968; New York: Berkley Publishing, 1969.

*The Best SF Stories from "New Worlds" 3.* St. Albans, England: Panther Books, 1968; New York: Berkley Publishing, 1969.

*The Best SF Stories from "New Worlds" 4.* St. Albans, England: Panther Books, 1969; New York: Berkley Publishing, 1971.

*The Best SF Stories from "New Worlds" 5.* St. Albans, England: Panther Books, 1969; New York: Berkley Publishing, 1971.

*The Inner Landscape.* London: Allison & Busby, 1969.

*The Best SF Stories from "New Worlds" 6.* St. Albans, England: Panther Books, 1970; New York: Berkley Publishing, 1971.

*The Best SF Stories from "New Worlds" 7.* St. Albans, England: Panther Books, 1971.

*New Worlds Quarterly 1.* New York: Berkley Publishing, 1971; London: Sphere Books, 1971.

*New Worlds Quarterly 2.* New York: Berkley Publishing, 1971; London: Sphere Books, 1971.

*New Worlds Quarterly 3.* New York: Berkley Publishing, 1971; London: Sphere Books, 1971.

*The Nature of the Catastrophe,* edited with Langdon Jones. London: Hutchinson, 1971.

*New Worlds Quarterly 4.* New York: Berkley Publishing, 1972; London: Sphere Books, 1972.

*New Worlds Quarterly 5.* London: Sphere Books, 1973.

*New Worlds Quarterly 6.* London: Sphere Books, 1973; also published as *New Worlds Quarterly 5.* New York: Avon, 1973.

*The Best SF Stories from "New Worlds" 8.* St. Albans, England: Panther Books, 1974.

*Before Armageddon: An Anthology of Victorian and Edwardian Imaginative Fiction Published before 1914.* London: W.H. Allen, 1975.

*England Invaded: A Collection of Fantasy Fiction.* London: W.H. Allen, 1977.

*New Worlds: An Anthology.* London: Fontana, 1982.

# Carl Rakosi

*1903-*

*Carl Rakosi, 1974*

I was born in Berlin. My father had moved there from Budapest to go into a business manufacturing walking sticks, which every well-dressed man carried in those days. He had no money of his own to put in but he managed to find a silent partner who did and an active partner who knew machines and could run the plant. My father's position was to represent the firm and sell. He was immediately successful, not because of any extraordinary savoir faire, he explained, but because of the extraordinary rectitude of business practice. Everyone then, around the turn of the century, took integrity for granted and assumed that your product would be exactly as you represented it, no less, and that it would be delivered on time, and the merchant, in turn, paid you exactly what he said he would. Thus, all you had to do was to make a good product and the rest followed. It helped if it had some new,

attractive feature, however small, but it was not necessary. And since it didn't require salesmanship, it was a dignified occupation in which my father felt thoroughly at home. The rectitude suited his character to a T.

He was young then and on his way to a fortune, whereupon the partners, seeing how well the business was doing, bought him out. Thus, his own success led to his undoing. It was the one time in his life, he said, when he was almost a millionaire. He remembered these years affectionately and never tired describing them years later in Kenosha where he had a jewelry store. He would talk as he sat at his workbench fixing watches, a looped magnifying glass in one eye and the other eye squinting in sympathetic concentration, and I at his feet rapt in the glow of his recollections.

I can see it all: my father with his trim moustache and grey eyes and straight gentlemanly nose and fair complexion . . . looks, clothes, manner clean-cut . . . the voice big and resonant, unexpected in such a small man, and an air of utter integrity. An ideal Swede, as I imagined an ideal Swede might look. This man, Leopold Rakosi, setting out for the day, walks into a store with his sample case, introduces himself . . . educated Hungarians spoke an elegant German as a second language in those days . . . and hands the owner his card. The owner responds courteously, a sign that Leopold Rakosi is persona grata and can proceed, and Leopold Rakosi begins to show his samples, unhurried, dignified. Enough simply to show the merchandise. That is understood. The merchant could see for himself that the sticks were of the highest quality. The firm's reputation for rectitude stood behind every item. No need to say more.

Berlin with its wide, splendid boulevards shaded by trees, people out for a stroll in the evening (no motor cars yet), decked out in their best clothes, the men twirling their canes as they walked, the elegant carriages. Hadn't I heard of Unter den Linden? The Tiergarten? It was obvious that he admired that well-ordered, reliable society.

I have to remember that he was only thirty at this time and soaking up new experiences. He had one in particular which was in the nature of a revelation and forever changed his thinking. It happened somewhere near the Tiergarten, I think. A crowd had gathered around two speakers. He walked over to listen. One was a young man about his age. He was almost shouting, in order to be heard, about the terrible privations of the poor, working men included, the disabled, the homeless, the unemployed, the other Berlin portrayed years later by Kaethe Kollwitz, urging his listeners to band together . . . in union there was strength . . . and join him. Force the government to improve their condition!

My father was all ears and became more and more excited, dazzled by the power of the words, moved in every cell by the speaker's deep moral passion, which he felt at white heat, and his commitment to a cause from which he himself could not benefit, and the realization came to my father then that this was the noblest thing a man could do . . . he could not conceive of anything nobler . . . to have a great cause, to be a spokesman, an advocate, a champion of the oppressed and downtrodden. He never got over that. There was awe in his voice, almost reverence, and a hush, and his face became transformed when he mentioned the names of the speakers, and I, sitting at my favorite spot next to his right elbow by the workbench, basked in the glow of his idealism. And when he went on about the brotherhood of man and the necessity for justice, his favorite themes, a wave of emotion surged through me and lifted me up, and I was glad. Not wanting to disturb the alchemy of the moment, I did not tell him that I knew very well who the speakers were, they were well known in history, Karl Liebknecht and Rosa Luxemburg.

All his life my father was an idealist and a socialist at heart, and I'm afraid much of this has rubbed off on me.

He was born in Szilágymegye, a village in Transylvania, the most ancient part of Hungary, the son of Barbara Mayer and Abraham Rozenberg, neither of whom I ever saw. "Father Abraham," the peasants called him, out of affection as much as teasing . . . he was their Jew . . . and because of something different about his appearance, something biblical, his tall, patriarchal bearing and long beard and that he prayed in Hebrew, the sacred tongue. He dealt in grain and when I heard from my father that the peasants, who distrusted Jews, also had great respect for him, I knew that he must have been extraordinarily honorable in his dealings with them.

"Father Abraham" had two sons and two daughters, all of whom moved to Budapest at an early age, as there was no future for them in a village. The eldest, Jacob, went first. He had attended a Jesuit gymnasium, probably because there was no other secondary school in the village, and had done so well that his teachers urged him to continue his education at the

University of Budapest. But there was no money for this. Besides, it was very questionable whether, as a Jew, he could get into the University. So the Jesuits agreed to underwrite the costs and Jacob converted, apparently as part of the arrangement. My father was deeply disturbed by this because nothing offended his moral sense more than a Jew giving up his religion and identity to become a Christian, especially for practical reasons. He avoided talking about it because he was very fond of his brother and looked up to him.

Jacob graduated with honors from the University and went on to teach philosophy there for many years. What must have been for reasons of expediency he changed his name to *Rakosi,* a variant of *Rakoczy,* Hungary's great national hero. With that, he ended once and for all his connection to the world of Szilágymegye and "Father Abraham." In Budapest, however, it was not at all unusual for Jews to take on Magyar names, not necessarily because of expediency but because they had become Magyars in spirit and wanted Hungarian names to show it. It was he who, later, started the first movie studio in Hungary. The photograph he sent us of his wife, the country's most beautiful screen star, sent me into idolatry.

Towards my father he acted as a guardian. Knowing that my father would have to have some kind of a trade to make a living, Jacob arranged a watchmaker apprenticeship for him with a master craftsman in Budapest, a reputable Christian approaching retirement age. My father was only thirteen then. By agreement he was to work and learn under this master for the whole time, a period of seven years. In return he lived in the master's home, got room and board and pocket money, and agreed to behave decently, according to the life-style in the house. Living there, he came to feel like a member of the family, and the master felt the same towards him and looked out for his welfare.

My father found the regimen exacting and severe and too limited, but he wasn't complaining when he told me about it. When he was through, he had learned not only how to diagnose what was wrong with the most complicated timepieces and repair them but also how to make new parts from scratch, if necessary, on his lathe to replace the damaged ones. There was no such thing for him, therefore, as not being able to fix a watch, any watch. He was in control. By this time, you will guess, he had become a perfectionist, and that too, I'm afraid, has rubbed off on me. The severity became only a tiny memory towards the end, for when he too had become a master craftsman, he had also become a young man about town, enjoying the pleasures of Budapest, which sparkled in his telling like champagne. By this time he too had changed his name to Rakosi.

Now came a stretch as a hussar. *Stretch* is the

wrong word but I can't find the right one, one which would express pure romance, for in a small, homogeneous country with a long history like Hungary, being a hussar was, in my father's memory, pure romance: the brilliant crimson braided coats slung gallantly over one shoulder, the swords, the proud, dashing horses, everybody knowing—Wasn't it in all the books and daily papers?—that the hussars were the finest fighting cavalry in all Europe, nonpareil.

My father, always attracted to spirit, did his best to live up to this standard. He became a crack shot with a pistol, able to split a playing card down the middle along its edge at a hundred paces, and never took an anti-Semitic slur or look from any man without beating him down, and he had many stories to prove it. And I too have many stories to prove how I beat down slurs and deprecatory looks on the playground cast at me because I was small and looked slightly different, and bullies thought I would be an easy target. Bam! would go my fist at the first sign. It never occurred to me that I might lose. How could I? I was in the right. As I write this now, I realize that behind me was always the spirit of my father.

All this talk about him has made me run ahead of myself. Actually I have just been born. The address is *ein und sechzig Kommenandent Strasse,* which pronounced in German sounds like a no-nonsense Prussian order not to be countermanded. The day is November 6, 1903; parents, Flora Steiner and Leopold Rakosi. I am in a very long room, so long that I can not see its end. There is very little furniture. The ceiling is very high and vast. There are shadows. The further away they are, the longer and heavier. There is no one there. I lie in my crib. All I'm aware of is that I *am.* And the silence. The silence is loud. No one comes. The silence is all there is. The nothing is oppressive. Hours go by and it becomes harder and harder to bear. There is no end. There is only the silence. And nothing. But beyond what I can see is Something ominous looming.

This is not a dream; it's a memory, and I am bonded to it. It's a memory of no one being there and no one coming. A mother was not there. I'm sure.

I am bonded to the silence. Blessed silence in which poetry comes. Silence as my behavior, in which I say little and listen, always listen, in order to find out. That I do not mind. It has become my character. In it I find a strange, supernal ecstasy, related, it seems to me, to the magical inner quiet in a perfect poem, in the process of embodiment losing its supernal quality. Or to the absolute silence in the landscape behind the figures in some fifteenth-century Italian paintings, as if everything for some mysterious reason had stopped. Closer at hand the silence in Magritte's *A la Rencontre*

*du Plaisir.* Here there is both absolute silence and absolute emptiness, compelling the spectator, in the spirit of the painting, to ask:

Mother, why is the sky overcast?
Why is the building empty?
Why is the ball there?
Why is the ball so large?
Who are the two men?
Why can't we see who they are?
Where are they destined?
Why aren't they talking to each other?

I would be surprised if Magritte could tell you why he painted this picture this way. The reason is buried in his early experiences, as my own style, whatever it is, is buried in mine. The larger point I deduce from this is that any style, any aesthetic taste, originates in life experiences which long antedate any experience one has with the arts and which have nothing to do with them.

The same applies to those hushed moments in a Beethoven symphony when he arrives at something mysterious at the center of things, the great forces all around held in suspension. This overwhelming quiet is explained and dismissed as inspiration. It would be more accurate to perceive it as a greatly enlarged artistic re-creation of an early experience, large and great in proportion to the imagination and inspiration.

I am also bonded, however, to the aloneness of that distant room, aloneness on a scale beyond physical bounds, the unbearable shadows in the distance, the bodiless, terrifying Something looming out there. That's always with me. It was there in the short story I started to write years ago. I started with where I was in the story, in an empty house, and as I went on to describe what was in the house, I felt myself being pulled further and further into its extremities until I was sure that just beyond the last, looming shadow I was going to encounter it. At that point I had to stop. I was too scared.

It's there in my meditation on Christopher Smart:

Yet I have been
                                  in the same presence
alone at night
                         in the forest,
spellbound in the un/
                                      conscious
where there is no
                                   perception
of purpose
                      in the universe.

It was there in a secluded farmhouse in Pennsylvania which a friend had loaned me to work in over the weekend. The drive from New York was sunny and uneventful. When I reached it, however, I noted that the nearest farmhouse was beyond sight. I was alone, and when the night came on, darker and darker, the daemonic spirit of the whole house, which my mind tells me could not be there, came down on me, and I fled in terror.

It is there to this day in my own apartment in San Francisco when I'm alone there at night and become aware of the unending silence facing me, and the aloneness creeps closer and closer to the moment when it will leap into a far greater aloneness, that utter aloneness in the universe, derived, I feel, from my aloneness and helplessness as a baby in that enormous room long ago. It does not help me to know this, however. The supernatural continues to have me in this thrall. It is not fear of anything physical, for I do not have this fear when anyone is with me, even a dog. This thrall affects what I like in poetry. Although I am a rationalist through and through, I am held in a similar thrall by the approach to the mystical in poetry, which seems to be in poetry's nature to express (to be *in* the mystical is to be in the occult and that is quite a different world). Another case example of what we mean when we say, literary taste is a personal matter, as against its being the product of one's literary influences.

In any case, I think now that it was my mother's inability to function as a mother which led to my parents' divorce, a thing unheard of in those days. I suspect she suffered from what was called melancholia then, and now deep depression, and that it was simply more than she could bear to mother my brother, Lester, and me, and finally even to be with us. It could not be ruled out even that my father and her parents thought that in her condition it was dangerous for the children to be with her and kept her out. How else can I explain never seeing her, even in Baja, Hungary, where we lived next with her parents, Rosalia and Samuel Steiner, until I was six, and never remember her ever touching me all that time?

I have considered other possibilities and have had to rule them out. The Steiners were a fine, upright couple, greatly admired by my father. The likelihood, therefore, of her being unfaithful in a small provincial town like Baja, where the Jews lived in their own neighborhood, was practically nil. Besides, she was extraordinarily beautiful, both my father and stepmother agreed, with rich black hair falling to her waist and very full, expressive dark eyes; the kind of beauty that my daughter Barbara too has, who at the age of nineteen won two beauty titles, Miss Minneapolis and Miss ROTC. Knowing my father, I'm sure only something as impossible to cope with as her melancholia and in-

capacity to function as a mother would have made him break with her.

Furthermore when her name came up in conversation, which was not often, there was never the slightest suggestion that they had been incompatible. On the contrary, he would stop a moment as if this was a special case and he had to find the right words for it, and his voice, and my stepmother's too, would become gentler than I heard at other times, and they would both look sad and sympathetic, as if what they would have said if they had not held back was, "Poor woman, because of a condition she couldn't help, she lost her two boys forever."

My father did not volunteer information on the subject, perhaps out of delicacy, not wishing to say anything against her, because he had nothing against her, and I never asked. It never occurred to me. She wasn't *in* my life, after all, and I felt no need to know. Besides, I would have been reluctant to make waves by asking something that might have been embarrassing all around and have led to other questions even more embarrassing, and who knows how destabilizing. In my later years when I was far enough away from these early events to be free of possibly suppressed feelings about them, I perceived what was basic and unchangeable in the situation, that we were of common stock and that I did have questions to ask about her whose answers might have restored some lost knowledge about myself. By that time, however, it was too late. There was no one left alive to ask.

The next thing I'm aware of after Berlin is that I'm in Baja, Hungary (if I were literary I would add, "a dusty, sleepy town on the Danube," but I don't know for a fact that it was that). It is 279 Fo Utca. There is a fence in front of our house and a cobbled street. The street is usually quiet. Occasionally a troop of hussars rides by, their coming announced from a distance by the sharp clatter of the hooves on the cobblestones, and the kids rush outside to watch, all eyes, mouths agape. And once in a great while the street explodes. It's a rock fight between older, invading Christian boys and defending Jewish boys on the block. I watch but it's much too fierce for me. I'm only a little kid then and it's as if the mighty forces of nature had broken loose and were rushing at me, and I run into the house. But my brother, who is five years older, is out there among the defenders and holds his ground, small as he is.

Back of the house is a large yard, and that's where the main action and the wonders are. I know them only in the summers when the heat induces a throbbing in the air, tiny heatwaves almost tactile. And a single high, perpetual note, a tone rather, too airy and pure to emit from an instrument, seems about to emerge . . . a sister note to singing, a fundamental tone under it . . . a zinging? . . . yet imaginary like the fundamental bass in music.

It is summer, man's element, and nothing can keep me indoors. There's a large barn in the back that has a touch of mystery about it but I never go inside to investigate. The mulberry tree is more important. There all along its branches are planted caterpillars chewing the tree's leaves. At first nothing seems to be happening but if I watch patiently, I can see a thread of silk extruding by millimeters as slow as summer from its rear. I can't believe silk is coming out right in front of my eyes!

And chicken and geese wander around the yard. One goose is tied up and from time to time our maid goes over, forces its jaws open and shoves in a handful of corn kernels. Then she holds the jaws shut and with her other hand squeezes its throat and pulls downwards until the corn is too far down to be regurgitated. A peasant girl.

Then a moment I can't forget. She has climbed up on the swing and with her legs apart and skirts up, she swings back and forth relentlessly, and Lester stands facing her, looking up her legs, transfixed. Something electric is going on but I don't know what.

Throughout all this, I have a sense that my mother is somewhere around, somewhere in the back. It is persistent as the summer and hangs in the atmosphere, a vague rumor, slightly mesmeric. But I never see her.

Once a year at different times Grandfather Steiner's two sons visited us from Munich. They were now middle-aged but as young men they had caused my grandparents great heartache and worry with their carousing and sponging and squandering and shady deals, never willing to work. In desperation my grandfather, who had been successful in business, loaned them his reserve funds in order to put them into a business and set them on their feet once and for all. But they squandered that like everything else and were dishonest. This ruined him. He had no capital left with which to recuperate and in his last years had to start all over in a small store, repairing umbrellas.

This is when I knew him. What I did not know, of course, as a young child, was why he was always so somber and preoccupied. When Grandmother took me downtown through the darting, confusing traffic to visit him in the store, I was cautioned not to bother him but to just watch. There he sat at his workbench, like my father at his, bent over, repairing an umbrella.

As I was saying, when the Munich sons visited, they came with a large retinue of wives and children and presents for everyone . . . for Lester and me a large, extravagant box from that exciting foreign world of chocolates with various liqueurs inside. You can imagine the excitement and commotion: my grandparents standing at the door, smiling and looking pleased, the welcoming, the embraces, but they were just going through the motions. There was an unspoken distance between us in which we could not move towards each other, for the sons after moving to Munich had converted to Christianity and married German wives, and the children were Christian and had always been that.

"Carl (Karoly in Hungarian), meet your cousins," someone said.

We looked at each other. We were expected to feel something.

Grandfather had a third son, Karoly, after whom I was named. He was the good son, a sweet, likeable man. He was youngest of the three and remained in Baja. Grandfather, however, was unlucky in him too. Karoly lost his life in a building collapse before I was born.

There's not much more to recount. In Hungary the state regarded the Jews as a separate community and provided funds to them for education. Thus, there were Jewish public schools administered by the local Jewish community body. It was in one of these that Grandmother enrolled me when I was five. All I remember of it was the confusion of that first day, the older boys on the playground doing breakneck acrobatics on the trapezes, yelling and shouting back and forth, and finally tearing off in my direction to get back to class on time, so close that for a moment I had the sensation that they were going to run me down and trample me.

I remember too what I should not remember, it is so trivial. It is summer again. A Serbian workingman has just sat down on a bench to have his noon lunch and I smell something overpowering. He takes out a pocket-knife and holding a slab of smoked bacon in one hand, he slices it with the other the way one would slice a peach, and the way he slices his country bread too, and eats with gusto, a thousand years of peasant life . . . the peasant and his pig . . . behind him. Apparently the body has a memory not plugged in to the screening intellect because that aroma, which could not possibly be important, is still in my nostrils.

And finally there is my departure. I can not improve on what I have already written about that.

I have never been able to remember, even in analysis, what I felt as a boy of six when I parted from my grandmother. She had been my mother, but more gentle and kind than a mother. Her presence has always been with me. The eyes are sad and reflective, the face

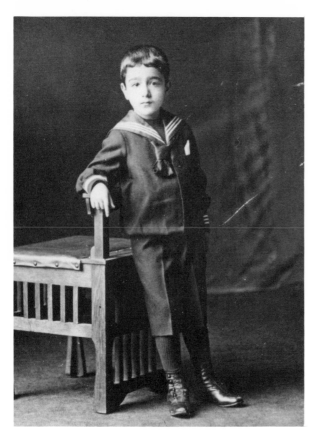

*At age seven, in Budapest, Hungary*

tired, beginning to show wrinkles, but the mouth smiles and an incomparable sweetness that is her character exudes from her, holding back nothing, and envelops me. She leans towards me, attentive, smiling, and I respond in like, as I had learned to do from her, also smiling, and inside me all is light.

Now my father had remarried and this woman had come to take my brother and me back with her to America, where I had never been. I do not know now whether I suspected that I would never see my grandmother again but I did know it was an important parting, yet all I remember of that last day is the hustle and bustle and a great silence and my extraordinary calm and robustness of spirit.

I found the explanation for this many years later in a passage of a book. The author was describing how the political prisoners in a Siberian detention camp during the Stalin terror managed to preserve their sanity. "The main thing," she wrote, "was in a certain self-control: it was important not to think about

the future. Expect nothing and be ready for anything. The only other thing was to scream, but no one would have heard."

With that formula I managed my transition to America quite well. But my poor grandmother, what was there for her to hold on to?

I can imagine the final moment. The bags are packed. We are all dressed, ready to leave. The time has come. All I am thinking of is the going and the necessity to act as if this were like any other day. She has suppressed her tears so as to make the parting bearable to me. I walk up to her and like my granddaughter Julie, also six at the time I wrote this, let myself be hugged and kissed with that self-possession and vigilance which protect children. And I leave without recognizing her grief or even acknowledging that this is a separation.

Forgive me.

I had a chance in 1980 to visit Baja when I was in Budapest to give a lecture to the PEN club on American poetry of the 1930s but chickened out. What happened was that when I told my host that I would like to see Baja again, where I had lived as a child, but would need an interpreter to go with me because I had lost most of my Hungarian, he looked blank, as if he couldn't comprehend why anyone would want to go there. Typical for a Budapestian, I learned later, but I didn't know it then. His look fazed me. What was wrong with Baja? What had happened? In any case, an interpreter who would be interested and have the time couldn't be found at the moment, so I let the matter drop. I told myself that I had done the right thing, that the Communists had probably changed all the street names and I wouldn't have been able to find my old house anyhow; that in seventy years the town would have changed so much that I wouldn't have been able to recognize it; and that the houses, like the great old public buildings in Budapest, would probably look terribly neglected and shabby. I was afraid what little I remembered of Baja would be demolished. But I don't know.

In that connection I have a story to tell. Before going to Budapest I gave a reading at Cambridge and visited with my friend Jeremy Prynne, most rigorous and intellectual of British poets. When he heard I was going to Budapest he gave me the name of a young man he knew there that he thought I would find interesting, Dr. Mihaly Szegedy-Makas. When I got into the city I called Dr. Szegedy-Makas and told him about my lecture at PEN, and he said he would meet me there; he would be carrying a copy of *Amulet* under his arm so that I would be able to recognize him.

After the lecture, when he learned I was from Baja, he told me this. Years ago he had spent a year at Cambridge studying American poetry with Prynne. Prynne, who had been introduced to my work by Andrew Crozier, a former student of his, and had come to have a high regard for it, introduced his Hungarian student to *Amulet,* an early book of mine. Dr. Szegedy-Makas subsequently returned to teach poetry at the University of Budapest and one year had a student who was similarly interested in American poetry, and he introduced him to my work. After graduation the student went to Baja to teach . . . my work, hopefully, among others. And thus I lie, cushioned, on the bed of fantasy that I have become re-connected to my past in actuality because things of my making, of my self, therefore, objective doppelgangers, have returned to Baja.

I was now in the hands of the woman from America whose mission was to take me safely to my father, whom I didn't remember ever seeing, and she looked as if she had every intention and the competence to do so. All I had to do was listen to what she told me to do. At six, with nothing between me and what was now going to happen, there was nothing else I could do, and I did it.

Our first stop was Budapest, where Lester and I were outfitted with new clothes. Then Vienna where, for a treat, we sat in an outdoor cafe and had pastry and coffee under an equal layer of whipped cream, which I was urged to drink because it was so special to the city. Our next stop was our point of embarkation. Was it Bremen? Hamburg? Rotterdam? I don't remember. It was a city so congested and bustling that I was glad to board ship.

We went second-class. I remember Lester leading me down a forbidden flight of stairs to see what it was like in third-class. It was more crowded there and the talk was thicker and louder and more of it, but otherwise not different that I could see. We tried also to see what it was like in first-class, what the rich people looked like and what they were doing, but the steps were barred to that deck.

The only other thing I remember is throwing up night after night at the dinner table on the clean white tablecloth, and my father's wife . . . I didn't think of her yet as a stepmother . . . rushing me outside. It must have been a trial for her but she didn't reproach me. She just handled it efficiently. It was her responsibility, she had taken it on, and she went about it with what I was to learn later was her characteristic common sense.

Then an enormous excitement seized the ship.

Everyone was out on deck, babbling away, and looking out into the distance. I had trouble seeing anything but I finally did. It was the Statue of Liberty. After much tooting from small vessels all around and men scurrying and shouting, the ship docked and the next thing I knew we were on Ellis Island.

There, into what looked like an enormous, barren barracks, the immigrants poured and stood around, waiting nervously in their best clothes to check out their papers and to go through the required medical examination, and it hit them head-on for the first time that no one knew exactly what state of health they had to be in order to pass. The room became all waiting and tension, and in the suspense they all burst out talking at the same time, relating dread stories about people they knew who had failed to pass and and had been sent back.

Our guardian was worried too. She was worried about Lester. He was small and skinny and a hunchback. A medical examiner might well think he was a poor risk. Her face looked tight and anxious. We waited. We heard it could take weeks. Finally our names were called. Our guardian explained to the examiner that Lester and I spoke no English, and he asked her a few questions, examined Lester carefully, then me, less carefully, and waved us on. At the immigration desk the officer looked down on me and smiled kindly, and we passed through.

Was my father outside to meet us? I don't remember. Our destination was Chicago, where he had a position as master craftsman with Moore and Evans, a large wholesale jewelry firm, where he was assigned to work on returned, complicated timepieces difficult to repair.

How did I learn English? I haven't the faintest idea. It occurred as if one day I didn't know a word of it and the next day I was speaking it like everybody else. Only one small incident marred the process. A kid on the playground made fun of my accent. In a flash I was on him and chased him into the schoolhouse. I don't think he expected that.

The plan was not to remain in Chicago but to open up a jewelry store in some town nearby, where competition was less fierce. Moore and Evans was willing to supply the stock on credit, and my father had saved up enough for store rent for the first few months. During that time, he figured, he would be able to bring in enough from repairing watches to support the family. With that in mind, he opened up a store in Gary, Indiana, which was booming then.

Gary's school system was better than you'd expect in such a rough steel town. That was because it happened to have a bold, innovative superintendent at the time who assigned children to grade levels not on the basis of age but mental ability. Thus, one day I was sent to a room I had never seen before and given a test; I had not the foggiest notion why. The next day I was called out of class to the principal's office and told I was going to be moved ahead a grade. I couldn't understand it. Then a month later, the same thing, another grade ahead. I had no difficulty doing the work in the upper grades, but now everybody in the class was two years older than I, and that did make a difference in my life because henceforth everybody in class would always be two years older and bigger and I would always be two years younger and smaller, even at the university.

I think my father would have done all right in Gary . . . in fact, if he had stayed long enough and bought a few lots, which were selling for under a hundred dollars then, he would have made a fortune . . . but he thought he could do better in Kenosha, Wisconsin, and we moved there. That was his last move.

I grew up in Kenosha and have been affected by its particular Middle-West character . . . industrial, some sixty miles from Chicago, on the southwest shore of Lake Michigan, which we could see from our front window, population 50,000, heavily German and Polish, and the way of speaking that goes with that.

Our house was a house of daily scrimping and worry because of the nature of my father's business. As I said, he had started in Gary with only a credit line from Moore and Evans. He earned enough from his watch repairing to provide us with food and part of the other necessities; he could depend on that, but he never knew whether he would sell enough jewelry to provide for the rest and pay his bill at Moore and Evans on time. As long as I knew him, when that time approached, my father and stepmother would stop everything else and absent themselves for days, trying to figure out how they could pay that bill, where the money was going to come from. It was all worry. They usually made it, but just barely.

Sometimes they would have to ask for an extension, and those were the most anxious moments because their credit was at stake. If they lost that, they were finished. In good times, what was left over after paying Moore and Evans was put into enlarging the stock to attract more customers, and in the best times, into putting up a new building with a more attractive store and with living quarters for us upstairs, a saving in the long run. All very nice, but now on top of the constant debt to Moore and Evans there was a monthly mortgage payment to make. Thus, no matter what happened, there was never anything left over for the family. And it was in the nature of the situation that there couldn't be. A jewelry store in a working-class neighborhood could never bring in enough from

sales to be able to accumulate the capital for moving to an expensive downtown location where there would be a chance for greater profits.

There was the additional worry that years of concentrated use of his eyes on minuscule watch parts was bringing on symptoms of glaucoma in my father and we didn't know when he would lose his sight and have to stop work entirely.

This is what had my parents locked in and dominated their lives, subsuming their softer, convivial qualities. It locked me in, too. It locked me into a life-long concern about making a living and affected my personal habits and the way I deal with practical matters. For example, not so long ago, Ed Dorn was telling me that he was thinking of moving to San Francisco with his family, and I asked him the thing that would be foremost in my mind, what job was he going to?

"Oh, no job," he replied.

"How can you move," I asked, "if you don't have something?"

"Oh," he said, "I can always find something."

I have never been free in that way.

Outside the store, the streets and empty lots and beaches were teeming with boys, and perhaps in somewhat the same way that I had learned English, one day I was just a little kid playing by myself around the house and the next day I was one of them, playing baseball and basketball and soccer and ice hockey, and swimming and roller-skating and ice-skating, flying along in long musical lines, and riding a bike without hands, all my natural medium—my song of summer, turned crystal in winter. I was utterly content and absorbed.

After school, I found odd jobs. I washed dishes in an ice-cream parlor, I did menial chores in a barbershop, things like that. Summers, I worked with the men, assembling chairs and bedsprings at the Simmons Bed factory and reading house meters for the electric power company. I was in fact an all-American boy.

Although my father and stepmother were intelligent and had a high regard for learning, she was too practical and literal to be interested in more than a newspaper, and his eyes at the end of a day were too tired to be able to read. Thus, there were no books in our home. That didn't bother me because I didn't know I was missing anything, until one day I discovered the public library on the other side of town.

The library, courtesy of Andrew Carnegie, was a charming building in the style of a graceful Grecian temple. It was set in an equally charming and well-kept park. You approached this distant sanctuary from a long and winding path that looked lonely and a bit melancholy because no human figure was to be seen on it. When I started out across it, I too felt a bit lonely and melancholy, and the venture felt as if it would take a bit of daring. As you entered the portico, a high, massive bronze door carved in the Renaissance manner confronted me, and the pillars, which from a distance looked so graceful, now loomed over me, as massive in their Grecian way as the door, and cowed me with their majesty and austere, imperial spirit.

Now to pull open that heavy door and enter. All inside was cool and quiet, illuminated by a golden glow from vaulted lights. Before me was an open space that looked like an atrium. It was so cool and quiet that I would not have been surprised to hear water murmuring as in a glade. At the far end two ladies were sitting at a desk and when they saw a small boy approaching, they looked a bit surprised and smiled encouragingly. There was only one other person in the library, a lone man in the periodical room, absorbed in reading.

"Could I look at the books in the stacks?" I asked in a subdued voice to go with the subdued air, expecting to be told, with the well-bred manners of such a place, that I was not old enough.

"Oh yes!"

They looked pleased and continued smiling. I gathered from that that it was safe to be bolder.

"Could I take some home with me to read?" I asked, again expecting to be rebuffed.

"Yes. Yes."

They looked even more pleased and as one of them led me to the adult books, they were positively beaming. But I couldn't quite believe it. There was a mistake somewhere. When it came right down to it, they weren't *really* going to let a little kid like me take adult books out of the library. Furthermore, how could precious books like that be free? So when I brought back five books from the stacks to check out that first day, I stood mute and avoided looking at anyone, hoping in this way to appear as if I was unaware of the error and that it would go unnoticed. But the lady checked the books out without any hesitation, smiling all the while, and I hurried out with them before she could change her mind.

Now, however, I had the problem of how to get them home unobserved, for if I ran into Jewish boys of my acquaintance, who altogether unlike Jewish boys of their age in New York, read only schoolbooks when they read, they'd razz me and I'd never hear the end of it, and I had no way of protecting myself because the razzing hid under the guise of masculine humor. So I'd slink through downtown very fast on my way home, hoping they wouldn't be in their father's store to see me.

There was another reason I didn't want to be seen: in all the time I was in Kenosha I don't remember ever seeing a grown man carrying books on the street, and I knew they weren't reading. So I couldn't help feeling embarrassed, suspecting that they might think me peculiar, and I avoided looking at them when I was carrying my embarrassing cargo so as not to draw attention to myself.

Once I was across the bridge on the immigrant North Side I was safe. During the day there was no one in the long block of saloons on the way to our house, and if a lone figure did happen to be in one and looking out at the street at that exact moment, books were so far outside anything he was interested in that I passed by, invisible. The few who knew me as Rakosi's boy already knew I was different, and beyond that they weren't interested. As for my folks, they didn't object to my secreting myself in my room with my books as long as I did my chores.

The library now became my secret home and my secret vice. When my parents asked me where I had been, I referred vaguely to it or to some other place, always in a casual way as if it were of no importance, not wanting them to suspect that my life had changed or that I was different from before. With my friends the matter never came up, so my secret life was never found out.

The stacks where I made my home were illuminated like the atrium by a soft glow and were quiet, too, and deserted. There was a small table and chair under a window for sitting and reading as long as you pleased, without intrusion or question, and all around a great collection of the classics in literature and philosophy in almost mint condition, most wonderful of all a complete set of of the old Scribner's edition of Dickens with the original illustrations; ditto Thackeray; and the great Russians . . . Maxim Gorki's unforgettable *My Life* comes to mind; and Huneker who introduced me to the wonders of music and the cross-cultural currents in the arts. To make a long story short, I read everything, everything. And I found there the mental universe which suited me, and I discovered its scope and depth and excitement, but I had no one to share this with or the wild nature of my excitement.

I had no inkling of anything in me beyond this until I was sixteen and wrote a piece in high school in senior English on George Meredith. To my wonderment the teacher wrote back a long enthusiastic response as to an intellectual equal, with comment after comment indicating that she respected my literary mind. That is how I learned that I had one and that I could express it.

I was now beginning to be fixed in my future course. I had been a B+ student until then, except in English, which had been A, so it made no sense to my parents to end my education there. They thought they could manage to support me at a university if they were very careful and if I lived frugally and worked during the summers. They would send me as much as they could.

It was decided that I would go to the University of Chicago because there was a Jewish family not far from the University with whom I could room and board cheaply, an elderly couple that our boarder, Samuel Kleinman, had lived with for many years when he worked in Chicago and spoke of very highly and affectionately. I had already been attracted by the University's somewhat Byzantine aura, so I was jubilant, and my parents, who had been concerned about leaving a sixteen-year-old on his own in such a big, impersonal city, felt reassured that I would be under the eyes of a responsible couple.

My first sight of the University was exciting. There before me was old England, a quadrangle of Gothic buildings more severe and cloister-like than Oxford or Cambridge, possibly because the interiors seemed to be always in shadow, and passing unhurriedly in and out, older students, at one with the atmosphere, in very serious dialogue so monkly quiet as to sound like murmuring.

By the term's end, however, my spirit felt as if it was being dragged against its will into a cloister and began to retreat. More and more it was a relief getting back to the city. The students broke up after classes and dispersed like buckshot so quickly that there was no opportunity to make friends. As a consequence I felt lonely and crimped, and was too young to get much out of Chicago on my own. By the end of the second term my spirit was in full revolt and I decided to transfer to the University of Wisconsin.

Before I did, however, I wrote poetry for the first time in an English class, along with George Schuyler, my only friend then, a black student who wrote Kiplingesque verse and later became a well-known columnist in the black press. Again, like the invisible way I had learned English, one day I was a reader of literature and the next day, there was the knowledge, as if it had always been there, that I wanted to be a writer and that I could best express myself in poetry, not prose. It happened in this class.

In Madison, in order to save money, I moved in with some older Jewish acquaintances from Kenosha who were preparing for the law and medicine and who already had rooms. We had our meals on the other side of town with a youngish Jewish widow with a slew of small children. She was a cheerful, stocky little woman with ruddy cheeks. As soon as we sat down to her table and saw spread out before us all the dishes heaped high, steaming hot from the kitchen, and rich spicy

smells all around, like at home, we unwound and started jabbering away, joking and bantering and laughing, and she stood by our chairs with a big smile, as if entranced, and took in every word, laughing hard along with us and making herself a part of us without intruding. How she enjoyed seeing us eat heartily! And when the food ran out, how happily she ran into the kitchen for more. The place had the jovial spirit of Dickens when she was there, and the warm, giving spirit of a genial mother who knew how to keep hands off. How much she gave us! And how uncertain her own future was.

Despite this connection, I had no question in my mind by this time that I was a poet, that that was the authentic *I* and that my life would be determined by that. Thus, when I was being a poet, I felt as unconnected to being a Jew as if I were on another planet which admitted no extraneous body. This had me in such a powerful fix that it shut out the reality of my father's support and I acted as if it would go on forever, taking only courses that fitted this planetary purpose, with no view to a vocation.

It was in this state that I met my new friends. By the time I got to Madison, Leon Serabian Herald was already established there on a Zona Gale fellowship for talented young writers. We formed an immediate bond. It was he who told me about Margery Latimer, saying that I'd like her. She was the other Zona Gale fellow on campus. Leon was an Armenian whose parents had been killed in the Turkish massacres. He had been brought up by an uncle in Cairo and had come to the states on his own at the age of what he thought was twenty. He couldn't be sure because the Turks had destroyed the vital statistics in his village. When I met him, he had learned to speak a faultless English.

He was a gentle friend with a sunny, open disposition. He had an endearing simplicity. All he wanted was to be a poet. The only other thing he needed was a woman, and to her he wrote paeans of lovely, exotic metaphors. Neither Margery nor Leon at that time had intellectual interests outside literature, so they didn't bother to go much to classes except to William Ellery Leonard's writing course. Leonard was Madison's Man of Letters, as well known then as a poet as Carl Sandburg.

Margery came from Portage, a small town near Madison, and as God-awful a place to her as Gopher Prairie. She was descended from the great Bishop Hugh Latimer and from Anne Bradstreet and John Cotton. What struck one immediately about her was her radiant presence: a great shock of golden hair falling free to her shoulders, gold with more life to it than auburn and more serenity than red; a radiant smile, full, warm, committed, trusting, guileless; a mellow, vibrant voice, the most earthy part of her, coming as if from the deep; a hearty laugh with a musical lift at the end; unusually large, observant eyes, always curious . . . a presence that would have made Blake sing.

Embellishments seemed false to her and demeaning. As a consequence, she wore no makeup or lipstick or high heels and only the most plain dresses, and her walk was very straight and direct, unself-conscious. Not that she was not womanly, but it was not in her nature to act any differently with men than with women. When we were together, Eros was in Blake country, and woman as Blake envisions her, but earthy and hale, was Margery herself.

From the start I was drawn into a deep relationship in which, to borrow Blake's imagery, our souls contemplated each other happily, sporting and embracing. She accepted everything I felt and imagined and aspired to and delighted in its uniqueness and gave it a radiant affirmation. Yet her conversation was not exceptional, but there was an overpowering depth and perspicacity in her intuitions which called for the same in me. I remember being with her one afternoon not long after we met. As I talked, I noticed that I was feeling extraordinarily free, as if for the first time I was in the presence of a *wholly* congenial soul.

This went to my head. As I talked on and the afternoon light became dimmer, time seemed to slow up. Deeper and deeper I probed for this other-soul until all restraint was gone and time stopped, for I found myself before the awful prospect of boundless potentialities on a universal scale. It seemed as if my understanding, deeply buried until then, could grasp *anything* in the world. I had to draw back: the scale was monstrous. But our spirits had been in a deep union and a quasi-supernatural force had been present.

Even in our pedestrian contacts her great confidence in my work shone on me like the sun. In fact, she was responsible for my first success. She had gone on before me to New York to look for a publisher for herself and had learned that Jane Heap had taken over as editor of the *Little Review,* in which Joyce's *Ulysses* was running serially at the time along with new work by Yeats, Pound, and Eliot, and that she was looking for new talent. Margery told me about it but I couldn't believe that could mean me. I was only twenty-one. Except for a few poems in the *Nation,* nobody had heard of me. But Margery persisted: I ought to try. Finally one thing she said clicked: "Jane Heap," she said, "likes to meet young, unknown writers and just talk with them. Really!" That convinced me.

But how do you do this sort of thing? I didn't know anyone who knew her. Do you call in advance? I didn't have enough confidence for that. Margery kept reassuring me with an impish smile that all you had to do was walk in on her, that other young poets had done it, and that I was exactly the kind of person Jane Heap had in mind. She left me no choice. But what did I have to say that would be interesting to such an editor?

Apprehensive, I climbed the circular staircase one afternoon to the *Little Review* office, which was then in the Village. It was dark in the hallway. At one end on the first landing was a small white name-card, *THE LITTLE REVIEW,* and a push button under it. I rang the bell, there was silence for a moment, then the door opened and a pudgy figure appeared in a red velvet smoking jacket, smoking a small cigar, the face very round, the hair bobbed to look mannish. For a moment there was an astonishing resemblance to Oscar Wilde. It was Jane Heap.

This startling appearance, for some reason, at once put me at ease. I simply gave her my name and she invited me in. It was not an office at all but an apartment she shared with Margaret Anderson. She was pleasant, served tea, and we talked—she as to a fellow writer. I found myself stimulated and was not lacking for words. I remember our conversation as lively and straightforward. At the end, she said, "I suppose you brought something with you," and I said, "Yes," and pulled out a batch of poems from my coat pocket. She read them closely, thought for a few moments and then said, "We'll take these."

That was it. I was in. I had made it into that illustrious company! I got up and left right after that while I could still hold in my exultation. I wanted to get out of there fast before she changed her opinion of me, and rushed to tell Margery about it. She listened with a happy smile, relishing everything, my anxious climb up the stairs, the dark hallway, the surprisingly small, neat name-card on the wall, the sudden apparition of Oscar Wilde in the doorway, Jane Heap's simple courtesy, the quick way our conversation took off . . . the whole thing. "Oh Carlos," she said at the end, she called me Carlos when she felt affectionate, her voice dropping to that low, pulsating resonance so characteristic of her, as if no greater pleasure were possible to anyone. She had known this was going to happen.

Margery Latimer, Leon Herald, and I were a threesome at first. Kenneth Fearing joined us a bit later. Kenneth and I must have been together a lot in Madison. Charles J. Duffy, writing in the *Wisconsin Alumnus* in 1967, refers to us as "the Fearing-Rakosi circle," and recalled him with "his great shock of uncut, unkempt hair, which was the talk of the campus." As I write, I can hear his low, gravelly voice, like Humphrey Bogart's, and see again his thin, loose-jointed frame, the tiny, short-sighted eyes behind very thick glasses, and the familiar quizzical, amused look on his face, the limp, black hair falling low over his forehead, almost covering one eye. He seldom left his room. In one corner his dirty laundry lay piled up on the floor, chest-high. In the other, he reclined far back in his chair, almost on the small of his back, with his knees up. He was already a heavy drinker and did his writing at night with a bottle of whisky at his side and an unlit cigarette dangling from the corner of his mouth, and slept all morning, skipping classes the next day, a bold thing to do in those days. He had admirers even then who hung around him, basking in his bohemian boldness and waiting for his next bon mot, which dropped in a flawless idiom sounding like Thomas Carlyle. When asked in the *Wisconsin Yearbook* for a summary of his achievement, he wrote, "Indian Reservation."

Madison in those days was a very clean, respectable small town of one-family homes with well-kept lawns. The University had some ten thousand students, mostly from Wisconsin farms and small towns, blond young Babbitts, their hair cropped close. Time was suspended for these boys and girls from the country while they looked each other over and saw that they were comely, and flirted and horsed around. And the big events were football and the Big Ten pennant ahead, and standing guard was a smugness hard to imagine these days, although Nancy Reagan comes pretty close to it.

Entered I, poor little Jewish boy, stewing in an inner life, sensitive, mystical, full of Tolstoy and Nietzsche, feeling as if I had been branded by a stigma. Duffy in the *Wisconsin Alumnus* recalled me as "a little fellow with an intense manner and tragic eyes" and my verse as "soulful." I myself had this to say in 1923 for the contributor's column of *Palms,* a little magazine published in Mexico,

> I am sure sex chose me for destruction; that my trop-semitic savoir will defeat itself in the way a poetic technique, too conscious of its facture, defeats itself. Since 1920 I have tried to fend off oblivion and the domination of trifles and quasi-poets by a life of exact ritual. Nothing can convince me that my passive attention will not sometimes surprise depth and novelty; nothing but a feeling of non-existence, a humour of calculation. Yet can these defining words frame anything but the words, *Carl Rakosi?*

And an early poem, "Orphean Lost," recalls my deepest inner tone then:

> The oak boughs of the cottagers
> descend, my lover,
> with the bestial evening.
> The shadows of their swelled trunks
> crush the frugal herb.
> The heights lag
> and perish in a blue vacuum.
>
> And I, my lover,
> skirt the cottages,
> the eternal hearths and gloom
> to animate the ideal
> with internal passion.

The bestial evening of alienation and insecurity, of mysterious depths and longing. With that, I graduated in 1924 and re-entered the world of work.

A grim prospect faced me. I had not prepared for either a profession or a trade and the moment of truth had come, as my father knew it would but could not persuade me. It gripped me in the gut. What was I going to do? Who would want me? The labor market was tight, and my folks had done as much as they could and as much as I had a right to expect. I was on my own. On my own! For the rest of my life? A great dread and a revulsion as from nausea swarmed up in

*Rakosi in Madison, Wisconsin, 1927*

me. This passed, subsumed in the ordinary busyness of figuring out what to do, inquiring of people, doing things.

Into this hopper dropped a rumor that social work was looking for people to train, men in particular. The American Association of Social Workers was interviewing applicants in Chicago. Social work? The term was new to me. As I didn't know anything about it, I didn't know whether I had anything to offer but it was the only opening and I was willing to try anything and went for the interview, without being able to prepare in any way for it. As it turned out, I didn't need any preparation.

The nature of social work immediately became apparent: I was treated with great respect as if I were a precious commodity. The interviewer asked me a few simple questions to sound out my feelings about people, conveying in his tone that this was not an intellectual activity in which I was expected to come up with the right answer. In that sense, there was no right answer. So nobody was going to criticize me. It was just that I had something important to say and he was eager to hear it. All I had to do was be myself and look inside and tell what I thought and felt. There was plenty of time. It was very quiet as I looked inside and spoke. Would I be willing to go through the two years it would take to finish my training? he asked. Would I be willing to go to Cleveland, where there was an opening with the Associated Charities? Sure. (I would have gone anywhere; it was a way to see the country.) I was hired on the spot. Thus, I did not have to return to Kenosha to live off my parents in shame, like a child, which for a while I was afraid might happen.

The Associated Charities needed a trainee right away, so I moved at once to Cleveland. This was 1924, before a professional postgraduate curriculum and faculty for social work had been developed in universities. One was just starting at Western Reserve in conjunction with the Associated Charities. Members of the agency's supervisory staff taught courses in theory part of the time and supervised and helped the trainees with their cases the rest of the time. The trainee was paid a modest salary. I found the courses rather dull but immediately became deeply involved with my clients, more deeply and disinterestedly than I had ever been involved with anyone before. And I discovered in myself a great urge to listen deeply to their distress, to understand it, my *whole* attention in it, and be helpful. In this I discovered a great excitement and a gay self-fulfillment unknown to me before.

However, I was still a writer and my heart was set on living in New York, there was no other place for a writer to be, that was the epicenter, where things would happen. With my brief Cleveland experience as a cre-

dential I was able to get a job in New York with the Jewish Board of Guardians, a psychiatric social service for disturbed and delinquent boys, and left the Associated Charities after a few months, to the disappointment of the executive, who was the only man on the staff and had been looking forward to having another man to be with and talk to occasionally.

New York was all I expected and I learned a great deal of Freudian theory in my new agency, which had the best clinical reputation in the country at the time, but I had to give it up. It was too much of a good thing, too absorbing, too demanding, too rigorous. It was making it hard for me to write. I decided I would try something less demanding. I would study psychology and go into personnel work. And that's what I did. I went back to Madison and got an M.A. in educational psychology. I was unsure about this, however, and thought that if that didn't work out, I'd fall back on university teaching, and with that in mind, I changed my name legally to Callman Rawley. For one thing, Rakosi was forever being mispronounced and misspelled, but the main reason was that I didn't think anyone with a foreign name would be hired, the atmosphere was such in English departments in those days. I kept Rakosi as my pen name, however, and no one who knew me as one, knew me as the other. This suited my purpose, as I didn't want professional colleagues to know that I was a writer. It was not just that I wanted to keep that private: I thought it would color and con-

*Carl and Leah Rakosi with daughter, Barbara, and son, George, in Minneapolis, Minnesota, 1946*

taminate their perception of my understanding and practice of the profession. I saw no point in their knowing in any case. In later years, after I had retired and was using Rakosi again in daily contacts, I forgot sometimes by which name I had introduced myself to a person and had to keep my mouth shut until I got a clue from the conversation as to which it was.

With my new degree I got a job with the Milwaukee Electric Railway and Light Company in their personnel department, testing motormen. Physical equipment was used, simulating the equipment on a streetcar, and a projector flashed street scenes on a screen, cars and people darting in and out unexpectedly. I checked the motorman's responses . . . his speed, accuracy, endurance, and the like, and made out a psychological profile from that. And on that the poor fellow's employment or future in the company depended.

This was not a function that interested me for long . . . neither did the city of Milwaukee . . . and I left after a year and picked up a job as psychologist in the personnel department of Bloomingdale's department store in New York. Here I was entirely on my own. Nobody paid the slightest attention to me. The store had never had a psychologist before and the store su-

*In Oaxaca, Mexico, 1974*

perintendent who had hired me assumed if I was a psychologist, I knew what a psychologist should be doing in a department store. He didn't know. He was a merchandiser. So I had to figure it out, and I was beginning to—starting with a plan to make a job analysis of every position in the store—when a poor Christmas season stopped it all, and the superintendent was fired right after Christmas, and I and a host of others along with him. That ended my career in industrial psychology.

Under the circumstances, I naturally fell back on what I knew, social work, this time in Boston with the Massachusetts Society for the Prevention of Cruelty to Children, a very old-fashioned name for a very fine children's protective agency which was a working adjunct of the juvenile court, of which I was an agent. As such, I had police powers to force entry into a home where there was evidence of child neglect or abuse. I never had to use this power but I did threaten to use it once in a particularly egregious case and felt ashamed at what I had done because when the children's mother, a washed-out, copped-out young woman, finally opened the door to admit me when I threatened to call the police if she didn't, I found the father, a small, wiry Portuguese workingman cowering in a closet like a rat. I was agitated by the indignity I had forced on him but the children were in great peril and I had to remove them into the custody of the court, the mother standing by, weeping and drunk, the father glowering and threatening. There was nothing else I

*Leah Rakosi, 1948*

could have done. The situation was too far gone to be helped.

A calm, benign spirit presided over this court, the white-haired, elegant Judge Cabot, of the Boston Cabots. Everything about his person was aristocratic but when he was talking to a child, you didn't see that, you saw only how considerate and sensitive and sagely proportioned he was and glowing with kindness.

Again I felt the need to protect my time and resources for writing by work that was less compelling, less absorbing. I thought the other route, university teaching, would be easier and less demanding, so I left Boston and got myself a job as an instructor in English at the University of Texas, teaching freshman composition to engineering students, a cruel assignment, and taking graduate courses in the department towards a Ph.D.

But this didn't work out either. The work was easier, all right, and there was time for my writing, but now it was the young prigs in the department I couldn't stand. They acted as if they had brought Oxford to Austin, and unlike young professors these days, were so affected and British high-toned that I felt nauseated and was faced with having to spend the rest of my life with clones. I could see too that what I would be doing as a professor would be so specialized and of so little value except in English departments that I would be like Tom in the old English joke:

"What are you doing, Jack?"
"Oh, nothing."
"And what are you doing, Tom?"
"I'm busy helping him."

So I called it quits after a couple of years and entered law school, but I didn't go far there either, not because I didn't find it interesting . . . on the contrary, I was captivated by the insistent practical base of jurisprudence and found the logical and philosophical reasoning supporting it as clear and well-proportioned as the Parthenon . . . but because for me to stand up and speak in public was nerve-wracking then, an ordeal, and I realized too late that that's what a lawyer did. The sons of instant Southern oratory in the huge class in which I was called on to stand up and analyze a case and found myself tongue-tied, were waiting, rarin' to go to do just that the moment I sat down.

No contest. I wasn't going to throw myself into that pit of crocodiles. So again I had to change course. This time I decided to go for broke. Why not become a psychiatrist? Wasn't the study of human nature and therapy what I was most interested in? Psychiatry would give me the best opportunity to keep my working hours down, plus a good income and prestige. So I took the required chemistry, biology, and physics in

Austin and entered the medical school in Galveston. I was immediately engulfed in the maddest race in my life for facts, physical facts that were perfectly within my power to memorize but only if I slaved away at it every day, Sundays included, until one or two in the morning. I did it, along with the other students, and probably would have found the second year a little easier, but my money ran out and I had no one to borrow from. The dean was sympathetic and wanted me to continue but the medical school had no financial loans for needy students at that time, so at the end of the year I had to give up. I had only one tiny pleasure to remember the experience by: I had gotten the highest grade in the anatomy class, a 98. How tenacious the memory can be when it has to.

After teaching for two years in a high school in Houston and working in a settlement house with Mexicans, I rode back north to Chicago on freight cars, partly for the experience, partly to save money. It was during my worst feeling of debacle in Houston that I received an invitation from Louis Zukofsky to rush him my best poems for a special issue of *Poetry* which he was editing under the sponsorship of Ezra Pound. Here began my association with him and with two of the others in that issue and, later, in *An "Objectivists" Anthology*, George Oppen and Charles Reznikoff. Zukofsky called us Objectivists. We are still known by that name.

It is now 1932. The Great Depression has set in and I'm back in social work in Chicago, working for the Cook County Bureau of Public Welfare. People are desperate. For example, one day I'm out making home visits and when I return to the office, I find that an agitated client waiting for word of his eligibility for financial assistance has stabbed a case worker to death in the waiting room. At the Depression's most desperate point, a million men a day, it was estimated, were on the move, going from city to city by freight cars, looking for work. My poem "New Orleans Transient Bureau" is drawn from my experience as case-work director in the New Orleans Transient Bureau in 1933, one of the transient bureaus set up by the federal government in large cities to try to deal with the problem.

In 1935 I left the South for good and spent the next five years in New York, working for the Brooklyn Jewish Family Welfare Society, which had a staff of brilliant practitioners and theoreticians then, among them Dr. M. Robert Gomberg. He and I were the first in our field and in psychiatry to conceptualize and practice family therapy, as against individual therapy. During this time, too, I pursued my graduate studies in social work seriously and received a Master of Social Work degree in 1940 from the University of Pennsylvania.

*Robert Duncan, Charles Reznikoff, George Oppen, and Carl Rakosi at the National Poetry Festival, 1973*

Living through the Great Depression I had become convinced by 1935 that capitalism was incapable of providing jobs and justice to people and that the system had to be changed, that there was no other way. Normally, this would have remained in my mind as just an idea, but I was seeing a lot of Leon Herald, my old friend, then. He was a starry-eyed Communist from way back, and prodded and cajoled me until I ventured in, hesitantly. I found the best minds in my agency already in. After a couple of years, however, I stopped going to meetings, and that ended it. Nobody noticed because all I had ever done was listen, and march occasionally on picket lines with people I didn't know, and cheer and feel uplifted at mass rallies.

In 1938 I met Leah Jaffe. I liked her immediately. We were married in 1939. A few years ago, in a letter, Cid Corman had remarked that he couldn't visualize Leah or me without each other, and I, to confirm that there was a solid base to that, wrote back that ours must be one of the great marriages of all time. When I told Leah what I had written, she looked at me in disbelief. I was startled. Didn't she believe the same thing? I examined her face. It looked serious. But something told me she was going to lower the boom on me. With a straight face, after a moment of suspense, she said, "If you feel that way, why don't you bring me more presents?" We burst out laughing. She has a great spirit of fun. You can see why, in the words of

young Mozart to his father, I hope she lives "till there is nothing more to be said in music."

By 1939 writing was coming harder and slower to me as more of me became involved in social work and in reading and writing professional articles . . . I wrote some sixty . . . and my evenings were swallowed up by the things that a man who is not a writer normally spends his time on in a big city: the theater, concerts, professional meetings, friends, girlfriends. It was impossible to pile on top of this daily regimen a night of writing. When I tried it, I turned into such a live wire that I could neither sleep afterward nor do my work right the next day. In addition, my Marxist thinking had made me lose respect for poetry itself. So there was nothing to hold me back from ending the problem by stopping to write. I did that. I also stopped reading poetry. I couldn't run the risk of being tempted.

When it came to me what I had done, that there would be no more writing in my life, I was stricken by what Kierkegaard, for a different reason, had called a "sickness unto death." Living became a dreadful existential state, something grey and purposeless between living and dying, and so physical that for a while I was sure I was going to die. This lasted about two years and then stopped, and I went on with my life as a social worker and therapist. This was 1940. The next year my first book, *Selected Poems,* was published.

In 1940 we moved to St. Louis, where my daugh-

*Leah and Carl Rakosi, George and Mary Oppen in San Francisco, California, 1975*

ter, Barbara, was born. Here until 1943 I worked as case-work director of the Jewish Social Service Bureau. Then on to Cleveland as case-work director of Bellefaire, a residential treatment center for disturbed children. My son, George, was born here. And finally on to Minneapolis where for twenty-three years I was executive director of the Jewish Family and Children's Service.

Towards the end of this period, in December 1965, I received an unexpected letter. As it changed the course of my life a second time, I quote it in full. It came from a young English poet studying under Charles Olson at the University of Buffalo.

Please excuse me if I make any intrusion upon your privacy but I would like to write to you about the poems you published under the name Carl Rakosi. I have your address from the Hennepin County Welfare Department, to which I wrote at the suggestion of Charles Reznikoff in New York.

I have been interested in your poems since I saw your name mentioned by Kenneth Rexroth some three years ago, but until I came here last autumn was only able to turn up "A Journey Away" printed in *Hound and Horn*. I have now been able to find about eighty poems of yours, published between 1924 and 1934, and what immediately strikes me is the discrepancy between that body of work and your *Selected Poems*. And the way, say, long poems like "The Beasts" and "A Journey Away" are chopped up into smaller units in that volume.

I wonder, too, why you have stopped publishing since 1941 and whether you have been writing since then or not.

Again, please excuse me if this letter is an impertinence, but I like and admire your poems very much and feel impelled to write to you now, my interest is so engaged with them.

Yours sincerely, Andrew Crozier.

I almost wept when I received this. It made me start writing again. I have been at it ever since.

Space now compels me to end. Looking back, it seems to me that three things in my life have made a man of me . . . humane, that is . . . the example of my father, social work, and Leah. Not poetry. I had to struggle to make a man of it. I see too that what I have related are mostly my difficulties and shortcomings, not my achievements and pleasures. My sense as a writer must have guided my hand in this.

## BIBLIOGRAPHY

### Poetry:

*Two Poems.* New York: Modern Editions Press, 1933.

*Selected Poems.* Norfolk, Conn.: New Directions, 1941.

*Amulet.* New York: New Directions, 1967.

*Ere-Voice.* New York: New Directions, 1971.

*Ex Cranium, Night* (includes prose selections). Los Angeles: Black Sparrow Press, 1975.

*My Experiences in Parnassus* (includes prose selections). Los Angeles: Black Sparrow Press, 1977.

*The Rakosis at home in Minneapolis, Minnesota, 1978*

*Droles de Journal.* West Branch, Iowa: Toothpaste Press, 1981.

*History.* London: Oasis Books, 1981.

*Spiritus I.* Durham, England: Pig Press, 1983.

*Collected Poems.* Orono, Me.: National Poetry Foundation, 1986.

**Prose:**

*Collected Prose.* Orono, Me.: National Poetry Foundation, 1983.

# Aram Saroyan

*1943–*

*Young Aram Saroyan (center) with neighborhood pals
in Pacific Palisades, California, about 1954*

ture or a game or practice most any time. I remember losing my timing for hitting pop flies for fielding practice after I seemingly had mastered this skill. It was around this time too—I was now almost twelve—that my mother moved my sister and me to New York City.

New York was as different from Pacific Palisades as anything I could imagine. On one of our first evenings in the city, Al and Dolly Hirschfeld (the caricaturist and his actress wife) drove my mother and Lucy and me through Times Square and I was dazzled by the variety and magnitude of the neon lights. It seemed like some great man-made wonder, the Great White Way, as indeed it is.

But the change from suburbia to Manhattan was anything but smooth. In effect, my childhood turned into the equivalent of the old-fashioned "double feature," with the individual movies having even less in common than they usually did. That I was a preteen added to the malaise. At the same time, there were bonuses.

At Robert F. Wagner Junior High School, I fell

T he first thing I ever wrote that wasn't at someone else's bidding, but rather because the sound and sense had come to me and I thought it might be worth preserving, was this:

> The whistle of the wind
> and the crinkle of the trees
> made everything sound
> like the birds and the bees.

I was ten years old and had my own room in the ranch house in Pacific Palisades, California, that had been a part of the second divorce settlement between my mother and my father. I lived with my mother and my sister, Lucy. My father had a house on stilts on Malibu Beach and we saw him frequently, but not enough to satisfy my craving for a father's companionship, support, and instruction.

I was in the Little League, where I played outfield and, at least once, pitched. In addition to this supervised play, our neighborhood was full of other boys around my age and it was easy to find adven-

*School portrait: "the new New Yorker," 1955*

*"Snow Study." Photograph by Aram Saroyan, about 1957*

in with a group of fast-talking, witty, and good-natured classmates: Jimmy Peck, Jimmy Fingeroth, Jay Feinberg, and Matthew Zukerman. For a year or so, I became a clown. I also encountered a teacher, Herb Greenhut, who introduced me to photography, which became my first overriding interest. At the East Eighty-sixth Street RKO and Loew's movie theaters, I saw, among other movies, *The Benny Goodman Story* (my friend Jimmy Peck was an avid collector of Benny Goodman records), and *Rebel without a Cause*. Greatest of all, my mother managed to get me into a sixth-row center seat at the Winter Garden Theatre for a performance of *Damn Yankees*, starring Gwen Verdon and Ray Walston.

My mother's friend Gloria Vanderbilt and her then husband, Sidney Lumet, had an annual Christmas Day party and it was at one of these—in the Lumets' Gracie Square penthouse—that I met Richard Avedon, who, when I eventually asked him if there was anything I could do to help out at his Manhattan photography studio, hired me as an apprentice. I worked after school, and my immediate boss was Avedon's young assistant, only recently emigrated from Japan, Hiro Wakabayashi, later the renowned photographer Hiro.

This taciturn young man, already possessed of a portfolio of unmistakable distinction, became a friend and mentor. In the darkroom, waiting for film to develop in the dim glow of the red light bulb, we discussed everything from photography to my school pals. I realize now how much I must have monopolized the conversation. Yet Hiro may have allowed this only because to him I represented a sort of instant composite of American manners and mores, which he could study, as it were, at firsthand. I remember one stormy winter weekend we agreed to meet at my mother's apartment on East Ninety-third Street near the corner of Madison Avenue and from there go to photograph the snow in Central Park.

But the snow proved unexpectedly heavy, and Hiro, a hundred blocks south in his Village apartment, told me over the phone it looked like he wouldn't be able to make it uptown that day. I was disappointed, but from our apartment window the snow looked like it had brought the city to a virtual standstill. I spent the day inside, trying, I imagine, to avoid coming to terms with my heavy homework assignments from Trinity, where I had started high school. Then in the late afternoon, the buzzer rang and it turned out to be Hiro. What a friend! And what a liberation from the dire straits of Latin, Science, Algebra, et al.

It all caught up with me in June. I flunked the ninth grade, and the following fall was sent to make up the year at Trinity Pawling boarding school in Pawling, New York. I was fifteen years old and poorly prepared to be on my own among a school full of boys and masters. Boarding school proved to be the familiar nightmare, a long, deeply unnerving encounter with my own character as mirrored by my classmates. After losing a fistfight because I was afraid to use my fists, I was driven to a kind of sickly introspection.

Even so, I earned good grades in my make-up year at Pawling, and the following year I was back at Trinity in Manhattan. In the interim, photography had fallen away as my primary interest, to be eventually replaced by poetry. I also did a successful turn in a school production of *You Can't Take It with You*, and this had me wondering, momentarily, whether acting might be my path. During the summer of 1959, my mother had married Walter Matthau, then a successful Broadway actor, and Walter was a steadying presence through my adolescence without ever encroaching on my father's place.

The summer I was sixteen, in my first attempt at "going all the way," I got befuddled and, instead of trying again the next day (we were trying during the afternoon when my girlfriend's mother was at work), I took it as a sign and retired. I went back to my room in my mother and stepfather's new apartment on West End Avenue with the idea of discovering who I was. Once again, I'd known a loss of generic timing, as it were: first for hitting pop flies, then for throwing a punch, now for making love. In adolescence, the answer seemed to lie in a conscious retreat during which one could shore up the self.

It was at this time that poetry became a factor. Poetry, after all, was said to contain the deepest truth about man and I may have thought, pragmatically, why not look there? As it happened, I could scarcely have looked at a moment of more extraordinary ferment: the late fifties and early sixties. Reading *Howl*, and equally, Allen Ginsberg's early poems collected in *Empty Mirror*, was a major event in my life. It was as if an interior membrane suddenly broke inside me and I discovered my own deeper reality. The line between poetry and life itself effectively disappeared: this writing was simply the deepest expression I knew of the common humanity each of us shared, even in alienation. The following excerpt from an early poem by Allen Ginsberg might have been written, I felt, in my very room:

> I suddenly realized that my head
> is severed from my body;
> I realized it a few nights ago
> by myself,
> lying sleepless on the couch.

In the poetry of Robert Creeley, which I found in an early small-press edition one evening in the Eighth Street Bookstore, I encountered such a spare and, at first glance, relentlessly "unpoetic" vision that I bought the book that night on the instinct that work so wanting in the externals I associated with poetry must contain a secret. I kept the book *A Form of Women* (Jargon Press) in my room for the rest of my high-school years. And indeed, the poet's terse, "New England" style gradually yielded up a world—of men and women, marriage and children.

I'm speaking of finding, in essence, a window on the world that had eluded my father, as much as he had emphasized to me its importance. The fact that Creeley wasn't, at least stylistically, a "romantic," but more careful, and at times even contorted in carving out his statement, only further validated him for me. For my father himself, a freewheeling improvisatory prose stylist and playwright—one of the first influences on Kerouac, as it happens—had somehow failed in his own life to make the connection with wife and family that he himself held most

*Carol and Walter Matthau, 1961*

*Aram Saroyan*

*Robert Creeley, Placitas, New Mexico, 1964.*

important.

I'm speaking, then, of looking from my father to another writer, of a distinctly different style, as a model. Implicit here is an equation of style and substance, an underlying assumption that life and literature are in a continuum and that one's way in one is related and perhaps critical to one's way in the other. Today, it seems to me that this fundamental assumption was one my father himself had made in his work, as indeed Kerouac had ("Write as you would live," he says somewhere), as much as had Robert Creeley. But I took Creeley for my model because he seemed more self-conscious, more analytical, about it. Above all, his work was different enough from my father's, and its family reference pronounced enough, to promise me a passage into the life I wanted for myself, as my father had wanted it.

During my last years of high school I sometimes went walking through the streets of the pre-gentrified Upper West Side, and these walks had a way of filling me up. The little children, the sidewalk chalk drawings, the hopscotch games, the ra-

dios blaring, the men and women out on their stoops, and the afternoon sunlight touching it all—if I could take the feeling of it home, I thought, I could write a poem. Over a period of months, working with this experience, I arrived at my first high-school poem, which was printed in Trinity's literary magazine, *Analysis*, which I edited:

*Small Poem*

a woman
somebody drew with chalk

sat laughing
on the sidewalk

with strange teeth
showing in her mouth

with her dress on loose
and amazing hair

someone somebody
drew on the sidewalk

sat laughing
as small as your hand

This poem pleased my father, among others, and is still among the poems of mine most likely to elicit a favorable comment. Yet today the chief interest of the poem for me is the fact that I was almost immediately suspicious of it. Steeped in the personal candor of the new American poetry, and the Beat Generation in particular, this poem's "romantic" slant seemed a sort of too-perfect cul-de-sac. I might be able to match its pleasing effect once or twice again, but where could I go from there? Hence, although it's in my collection of early work, it wasn't until several years later that I felt I made my genuine beginning as a poet.

It was the summer I was nineteen, the summer of 1963. I had dropped out of the University of Chicago and for the moment was living again in my mother and stepfather's apartment on West End Avenue. It was some time after Martin Luther King's Freedom March on Washington, which I'd participated in with a couple of New York friends, riding one of the chartered buses down and back the same day. The apartment was for the moment empty, my mother and Walter out of town. On an impulse one afternoon, I went to my stepfather's desk in the corner of the living room and, writing in hand, composed three or four poems in succession. The first of these set the tone for the others:

I have spent a year mostly alone.
Walking a lot.
With a poetic attachment

to street drawings.
Staring at concrete.
My shoes.
And going over my life.
Situations.
Walking
and sitting in my room.
Or movies.
Or reading.
Working. Practicing the
new patience.
The year has been good.
With long thoughts.
Care to myself.

This poem and the others that followed were written out of what seemed in me, just then, an unusually calm and contained center of self. As I went along, each word arriving, as it were, just in time for me to write it, I needed neither to hurry up or slow down, but only to keep to my own natural pace. Hence, writing the poem was in itself a satisfying, validating experience. At the same time, an interior critic warned me not to melodramatize my life. I wasn't, after all, Allen Ginsberg—only Allen Ginsberg was.

Less than a year later this poem and five others appeared in *Poetry* magazine, along with my review of Robert Creeley's novel *The Island,* and this constituted my debut as a writer. Coincidentally, it was during the spring of 1964, when the issue of *Poetry* containing my poems and the review appeared, that I first began to encounter the poets of the New York School, and most importantly among them, Ted Berrigan.

I had up to this time been chiefly influenced by Creeley and other Black Mountain poets. The New York School poetry of Kenneth Koch and Frank O'Hara I tended to distrust for its romanticism. Ted Berrigan, however, changed all that, and his presence in New York was an important factor in enlarging my idea of what to write, and how to write.

Today, in the eighties, the work Berrigan did and the influence he exerted during the sixties, and, in fact, to the end of his life (at forty-eight in 1983) has still not been properly recognized. We are in a period of conservatism, in poetry as well as in politics, that harks back to the days of the New Criticism during the Eisenhower era. On a practical level, what this seems to mean is that poetry has receded significantly in public consciousness. I had my arguments with Ted and others of my peers in the New York School, but it seems a shame and a waste that their work is less known and honored than the

*Ted Berrigan, 1983.*

more remote, but not more accomplished or genuine work of so many others. In over two decades as a writer, I've learned that the truly gifted in any generation aren't very many in number. Ted Berrigan, I would venture, was among the two or three most gifted poets of his generation, and the anthologies have yet to bear that out.

How did my work change in Ted's sphere of influence? I started playing, experimenting, being more willing to fall on my face for the sake of learning something; I began, I think, to be less tortured and to have a better time. Simultaneously, as the sixties went into gear, I started to use marijuana as a part of the process of composition and continued to work with it, off and on, for about two years. Everything got much closer up. Suddenly a single word had a resonance, not only inside a line or stanza, but all by itself:

lighght

This one-word poem, written one night in my new apartment on West Eighty-fifth Street during the fall of 1965, and subsequently the subject of two decades of government debate and censure from the Oval Office to the halls of Congress, was and is, to me, simply an expression of the stop-time sensibility of the sixties. The light expanded—an extra, silent diphthong came into it, as it were—while we all for the moment forgot what time it was. Andy Warhol attested to this by putting Elizabeth Taylor's identical portrait in eight places in the same work. Donald Judd attested to it with his identical metal boxes, all in a row against a wall. In writing, however, it was an affront, at least after Robert Duncan chose the poem for a National Endowment for the Arts Poetry Award (for 1967) of $750.

By the time of the first wave of controversy regarding this poem, I had met my future wife, Gailyn McClanahan, in Cambridge, Massachusetts, and had for all intents and purposes stopped writing poetry altogether. In one sense this was only the logical extension of the minimalist work I'd been doing. On

*Aram and Gailyn, St. Mark's Place,*
*New York City, 1970*

Jayne Nodland

another level, it involved a recognition that my previous work represented a period of being alone and that whatever followed now would be changed by the fact of my no longer being alone. My father's work seemed to have foundered when he attempted marriage and a family, and no doubt that knowledge, too, played its part in my putting my writing aside. In the end, it was more important to me that my life work out than that my writing continue. In a certain sense, as my father's son, this was a critical issue.

Gailyn and I became a couple, and then, a year and a half later, got married. Two years after that, our first child, Strawberry Cara, was born on October 20, 1970, in Stoneham, Massachusetts. (We were living in Marblehead, but the hospital was in Stoneham.) Having a family, of course, changes one's life irrevocably and, for the first time, the issue of employment for me loomed precipitously.

The following year, back in Cambridge again, I worked as a Poet in the Schools in the National Endowment for the Arts program. A year after that, by a circuitous route that involved a trip to London and a commission from BBC Radio to do a program on the burgeoning California poets' colony, we arrived in Bolinas, in Marin County, California, where we settled for the next twelve years. It was here that our two other children were born: Cream on November 26, 1973, and Armenak on October 12, 1976, both of them at home. It was here, too, within weeks of our arrival, that I began to write again, five years after I'd stopped.

I remember a poetry reading I gave in Bolinas on one of our first evenings there. It was at the town's Community Center and the audience wasn't a large one, no more than two dozen people. But among that number it seemed that half or more were friends and fellow poets whom I'd known for years, among them Tom Clark, Lewis MacAdams, Lewis Warsh, Larry Fagin, and Bill Berkson. As I read my old poems I felt at the center of an almost palpable emanation of affection and approval. I was now twenty-eight years old, married and the father of a little daughter, and that night there were people in the room with whom, it seemed, I had found a place.

What seems to have happened to me the night of the reading is that the atmosphere of approval was so strong and heartening that, speaking in Freudian terms, my ego and superego effectively merged. It was as a result of this, I believe, that I began to write again—this time more fully and directly out of my own life. Another way of looking at

*Daughter Cara, 1971*

At the same time, in a figure like Kerouac one seems to see both tendencies—speaking broadly, both the extrovert and the introvert—at once: a burgeoning Hemingway figure periodically retreating to Emily Dickinson's attic. In my father's career, too, both tendencies are apparent, this time divided between the exuberant first half of his career and the more brooding, contemplative second half.

Curiously, this split in and of itself is a theme I find repeated over and over again in the work of contemporary American artists from Edward Albee to Martin Scorsese. For example, in Albee's breakthrough work, the two-character one-act play *The Zoo Story*, the wild, anarchic Jerry forces the conservative, orderly, and sedate Peter to stab him with his own knife. One reading of this play might be that Jerry, the artist *maudit* figure, makes a conscious choice to submit himself to the discipline cultivated by his less creative, but more settled and self-protective interlocutor, Peter; that Albee is saying, in essence, that the artist must have both his wild and domesticated sides, his masculine and feminine

it might be that it was now that my apprenticeship ended. Over the course of three days in the late summer of that year, 1972, I wrote a poem called "Lines for My Autobiography" that later appeared as a full-page poem in *Rolling Stone*. A few months later, I began *The Street: An Autobiographical Novel*, my first prose book.

I subsequently worked as a journalist for *Rolling Stone* and wrote reviews for the *New York Times Book Review*, the *Nation*, and the *Village Voice*, among other publications. During the years we were in Bolinas, I also published *Genesis Angels: The Saga of Lew Welch and the Beat Generation; Last Rites: The Death of William Saroyan;* and *William Saroyan.*

In all of these books, an essential theme is the position of the writer in American society, a position I'd been exploring myself now for some time, in addition to observing it at firsthand in my father's career as well as the careers of other writers, both elders and peers. It is, I think, an extremely perilous position, and it seems to engender two broad strategies of response. The first might be exemplified by, say, Ernest Hemingway or Norman Mailer, and the second, perhaps by Emily Dickinson or Eugene O'Neill.

*With Gailyn and Cara, during the writing of* Lines for My Autobiography, *Bolinas, California, 1972*

sides, if you will, in some kind of balance and harmony in order to be a whole figure. In a way, the most telling commentary on the symbolic enactment of this theme in *The Zoo Story* is the fact that it was followed only a year or so later by Albee's three-act masterwork, *Who's Afraid of Virginia Woolf?*

An artist like the filmmaker Martin Scorsese, on the other hand, seems to restate the theme of *The Zoo Story* again and again without ever quite making up his mind or heart about it. In *Mean Streets* the anarchic, wild brother played by Robert De Niro gets himself and his more cautious, practical-minded brother, played by Harvey Keitel, both killed. In *Raging Bull*, De Niro as Jake La Motta, having aged and put on sixty pounds, is seen delivering jokes at the microphone in his nightclub. Here is a figure who seems tamed more by time than by any conscious choice of his own.

Yet in a way the question has to do with time. After all, the young artist may need to allow his intuitive, overreaching side free reign in order to begin at all. But as he goes on, unless his other, survival-oriented, disciplined side begins to assert itself, he is likely to have a hard time developing and maturing. When I wrote the long poem "Lines for My Autobiography" and a few months later, my first novel, *The Street*, it was as if I was catching the last wave of my youth and, as it were, riding it out in these works.

*Genesis Angels: The Saga of Lew Welch and the Beat Generation* followed in the fall of 1977, three-and-a-half years after *The Street*, and after numerous other attempts at writing a second book. In the interim, I had, I think, gradually come to terms with myself as no longer a young man. Indeed, in the figure of Lew Welch, I found someone who helped to shepherd me through this passage. Welch's humanity and candor about himself, as I encountered it in his writing and correspondence, as well as in tape-recorded conversations and interviews, reassured me about myself at this crossroads and taught me, I would say, something about how to let go, about how to melt a little. My book is an homage to the style of Beat writing as well as the story of the Beat Generation, a fact that seemed to puzzle or elude certain critics. The first draft of the book, however, was a dry, academic rehearsal of the ideas that seemed important in the story. But only after I'd done this, and put it aside, was it possible to move into the real writing and a rather different story than the one I'd sketched out in the first draft. I remember the beautiful afternoon I started the book in Bolinas. I walked from our garden into the house with the color of the sky in my mind. Just this blue, I thought, as I sat down to write, and the first pages followed from there.

The hardest part of the book proved to be the last chapter, about the early deaths of Kerouac and Neal Cassady and the presumed suicide of Lew Welch (who disappeared with his gun into the foothills of the Sierra Nevada in 1971). The book is primarily a celebration of art and friendship among the Beats and I found it hard to give the proper weight to this dark side of the story. In the last chapter, I had, as it were, come up against another threshold in myself. At my wife's prompting and with her support, I wrote it three times before we were satisfied.

*Last Rites*, written as a journal over a period of three weeks as my father was dying during the spring of 1981, proved to be a *book* about the dark side that had troubled me at the end of *Genesis Angels*. By the time I wrote it, I had in fact decided to work henceforth as a screenwriter, but the book literally burst from my hand before I had time to consider the career choice.

*Steamboat. Courtesy of David Kherdian.*

*Signed photograph of Lew Welch, Marin City, California, 1968*

Now a word, if I may, about our American critics. Character assassination, as I discovered in the reviews of *Genesis Angels*, is not unknown to them. Interestingly enough, I'm speaking less of the critics and reviewers of the American provinces, whose response is often more measured and thoughtful, than of those in the New York media axis, where positively awful, *personal* things may be said about a writer and no one will look sideways at the reviewer.

We might take the case of Jack Kerouac, for example, since *Genesis Angels* is in the nature of a stylistic tribute to Kerouac and in the reviews of my book I seemed to sniff out some residual resentment at its progenitor. Here was an ex-football star, the American hero in looks and deeds, as it were, who dared to have a sort of long, tender nervous breakdown in prose. He broke through his own American dream, so to speak, and told us of its dark underside: his doubts, his foibles and failures, his—to use a phrase of Robert Duncan's—"darker dearnesses."

The response of the critics to this writer who took such bold risks proved to be devastating. In fact, sometimes our professional corps of writer-critics seems to comprise a kind of palace guard around the hallowed ground of the American Dream. If an artist comes along who says he's been inside it and actually it's a little different than he'd expected, his father was disappointed, his mother got fat, his sister married an s.o.b., and he himself is feeling a little down and/or a little playful within the sanctions of his art, the elite print corps are likely to jump on him with phrases that reflect not on his work, but rather on the artist personally. Words like "immaturity" will be thrown around—words like "bathetic." A favorite word is likely to be "infantilism."

All this seems to me not so very different from the attacks of the literary henchmen of the Soviet Union in their denunciations of Boris Pasternak, Osip Mandelstam, and Anna Akhmatova. The terms are a little different—as are, crucially, the consequences of such attacks—but "decadence" seems a more or less fair trade for "infantilism." It also seems quite probable that the Stalinist henchmen half-believed their own critiques, as it's apparent many of America's writer-critics believe in the terms of their attacks. But we know that in Russia everyone was caught up, or trampled down, in the myth of building socialism.

A more complicated question is what the operative American myth is. In my books about my father, I grappled with a figure whose public and private sides reflected a profound ambivalence. Here

was a man whose deepest wound—his father's death and his own subsequent confinement in an orphanage from the age of three to the age of eight—had somehow alchemized in him an amazing strength of character. In the thirties, in the midst of the Great Depression, the young man who had been an orphan wrote stories of such sweetness and high spirits that they helped to keep hope alive in an ailing nation, and catapulted the writer to the literary equivalent of a movie star.

My father had, in effect, known the psychological equivalent of the Great Depression at the time of his father's death and his confinement to the orphanage. How he survived that crisis became, in a sense, his lifelong message. To simplify but I hope not to falsify, he did it by *deciding* to survive, by discovering his own capacity to be strong, to keep on, to brace up, and get on with life.

In its personal way, this may be the American answer at large. To get here in the first place, there was most likely in all our families someone who had to put pain and sorrow behind him or her and move

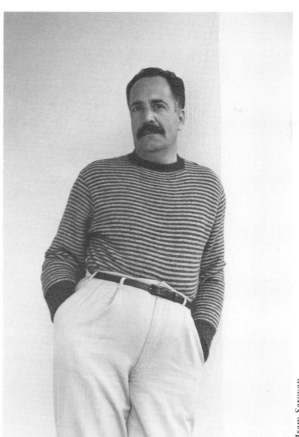

*William Saroyan, 1958.*

on, for life's sake. As a result, for some of us, a part of our unconscious inheritance may be a transmitted habit of neglecting a reckoning with the darker dimensions of our experience. No doubt, at the beginning, there was good reason for it. But this course has its own dangers and deprivations. In avoiding a coming to terms with pain that may seem too great to bear, it may be impossible not to dismiss at the same time one's vulnerability and openness to experience at large, not to dismiss, in effect, both pain *and* pleasure, since each seems to come through the same door.

My father was a man of great complexity, a man of genius, I think, who knew these dilemmas intuitively and tried to deal with them as best he could as long as he lived. Some of his finest moments in life are in the pages of his writing, where the struggle assumed proportions that perhaps made it more manageable. At the same time, he suffered profoundly for the very alchemy by which he transformed an early wound into a skein of steel, so to speak; and it was this transformation, too, I think, that lay at the bottom of the pain he inflicted on those who were closest to him.

For while it may be expedient, or even absolutely necessary, to turn pain into a capacity to endure, there is something irreducible in pain itself that begs for, and, in the end, seems to insist on recognition. Isn't it, in fact, an inextricable part of the substance of our humanity—pain and pleasure in us being a part of the same "mortal taste," as Allen Ginsberg put it?

Recently, when Nancy Reagan, with President Reagan at her side, addressed the nation on television on the subject of drug abuse, and made a special, heartfelt plea to young people in particular, one felt moved and heartened by her concern. Yet at the same time, it seemed curious that while she told young people that life was a wonderful experience, she didn't say that it could be a very painful experience, too. After all, a significant part of the attraction of drugs is their proven effectiveness in obliterating pain, and, in a certain light, the drug problem might be viewed as yet another facet of our national penchant for the denial or avoidance of pain.

The paradox of my father's life was that in denying his own pain, he seemed helpless not to perpetuate it in others' lives. And this circular, centrifugal process, which sometimes appears so characteristic of us as Americans, seems to have its parallel in America's identity as an international power. How is it possible, one asks oneself, that most of the beef for McDonald's Big Macs could be raised in

Central America and at the same time the percentage of beef in the diet of Central American peasants could be lower now than before the huge rise in beef production? How could we support the murderous regimes we have supported in the Philippines and in Haiti, and currently support in Guatemala and El Salvador? Why does our president call the Nicaraguan *contras* Freedom Fighters? How could President Reagan make a speech at the grave site of Nazis as well as their victims?

These questions can stun the mind in their unanswerable multitude. And yet it seems to me that the same denial of pain at a personal level may lie at the heart of any answer. A study of my father's life suggested, in the end, that there was no easy moral judgment to be extracted: that he did what he had to do, some of it wonderful, some of it sad and painful indeed. What I think I learned, finally, was that it was useful and perhaps even healing to study and think about his life, to reflect on it; that while his own life may have made it impossible for he himself to do this, a part of his legacy to me was a life far

*Aram Saroyan*

*Gailyn with newborn Armenak, Bolinas, California, 1976*

*Cara, Armenak, and Cream Saroyan, 1979*

less painful than his own: one from which I could turn around and try to take some measure of our history as a family.

After the two books about my father, I wrote *Trio: The Intimate Friendship of Carol Matthau, Oona Chaplin, and Gloria Vanderbilt*, and this was like coming through the dark back out into the light. The first and, in a very real sense, the *only* question with regard to the writing of that book was the question of the writer's approach: social history, celebrity biography, or nonfiction novel being only three of the more obvious choices. My special position with regard to the three ladies—being the son of Carol Matthau and having known the other two all my life —made the choice, if anything, even more critical. For, of course, implicitly it involved the delicate issue of the spirit of the project. Would I exploit an admittedly privileged access to the three for my own benefit? If I did, how would I ever face Oona and Gloria again, not to mention my mother?

The contract with the publisher was signed. I began talking with my subjects, and taking notes, but I hadn't yet written anything. Then one morning in the fall of 1982, while in Manhattan on busi-

ness that had to do with the book, I went to the Whitney Museum to see the retrospec  exhibit of the paintings of Milton Avery. It was here, coincidentally enough at the museum founded by Gloria's aunt, Gertrude Whitney, that the solution first began to dawn on me.

I was walking the rooms of a whole floor of the museum, all of them hung with paintings by an artist who had lived through the era of Abstract Expressionism and gone on resolutely painting the recognizable: landscapes, interiors, still lifes, and the human. Of the last group, often the subject was a woman, and even more frequently two or more women together, talking.

Milton Avery, I would venture, is as superb a colorist as we have had in the history of American painting, and seeing his paintings had a profound effect on me, joyful and moving at the same time. My God, I thought, *that* was how to paint women. The way he handled their presences implied so much: a sense of the light they brought into a room, a suggestion of their grace in movement, their wit, and even—almost—a whiff of fragrance. If the two books about my father have a gritty, documentary, and, speaking of their essence in retrospect, a somehow black-and-white quality—now, in the presence of the Avery paintings, it struck me that I had an opportunity to write a book with a full palette of color.

In effect, Milton Avery's paintings provided me the first glimmer of the idea of approaching Carol, Oona, and Gloria as a novelist, rather than as a journalist, in any of the various incarnations of that term, including social historian, biographer, or even memoirist. Surrounded by the portraits he had painted of women I had never known and never would know, I realized some common denominator in them with the women I was to write about. They too possessed these subtle essences of color. Of course, in the end, a writer's medium is words and not paint, but that was technical. The important thing was to try to render these women as I had actually known them and also as I might imaginatively expand that knowing. Taking stories they told me and writing them with a different member of the

*Gailyn and Aram Saroyan, 1986*

*Gailyn with Cara on her fifteenth birthday, Ridgefield, Connecticut, 1985*

trio as the protagonist of each, gave me the opportunity, like Dustin Hoffman's in the role of "Tootsie," to play a woman, in fact to play three quite different women.

During the summer of 1984, at about midway in my work on *Trio*, we moved from Bolinas to Ridgefield, Connecticut, where we now live. I was able to work more closely with my editor on the book; Gailyn, a painter in the East Coast "painterly realist" tradition of Fairfield Porter and Jane Freilicher, could be closer to the New York galleries and museum exhibits; and our children, who had spent their whole lives in a small town, would have a standard for comparison and a broader horizon. We eventually sold our house in Bolinas and bought one in Ridgefield in a neighborhood not unlike the one I had known as a boy in Pacific Palisades.

After *Trio* I wanted to get away from family history for good, and my first impulse was to explore the novel purely as fiction. Our first year in the new house, I wrote a novel about contemporary family life cum mid-life identity crisis, and worked on a play about Pasternak and Mandelstam, an idea I've been researching for years.

Now in the fall afternoons after school, out on our front lawn beside a hundred-year-old sugar maple whose leaves have turned a bright yellow, I sometimes hit pop flies to my son, Armenak, ten years old and an avid baseball fan and player. More than thirty years later, I discovered that as a boy part of my problem with hitting pop flies had to do with my swinging too much *up* at the ball, with not swinging at it evenly enough.

It would be nice here, in conclusion, to be able to summarize, as if from some stable eminence, sure of my terms. But at forty-three, I find my only real stability in my family. After more than twenty years as a writer, I'm more than ever aware of the risks and outright absurdities of my position. I'm not a member of a strong union, and the business side of the profession is a nightmare for the writer of my generic type who doesn't have another trade, like teaching, by which to carry himself and his dependents.

Then too, I've watched the tide of literary politics turn on my generation, in essence the generation of the sixties, and, as I've said, some of my most gifted peers are currently excluded from the anthologies. In any case, perhaps as a consequence of my background, I have a virtually inborn distrust of the essential instincts of our cultural climate; I'm not convinced that our established cultural arbiters are more than public trustees of an implicit and largely unconscious status quo. At the same time, I consider myself as corruptible as the next person, if not more so. A writer's greatest liability, it seems to me, is his or her distance from the work-a-day scheme of society. Therefore, to yield to the temptation to throw off solitude for the sake of money, company, and other benefits, might prove to be, in certain circumstances, nothing less than a saving grace.

Or perhaps I'm speaking here from the perspective of one whose commitment to writing has always been secondary to a commitment to survival beyond the terms of a literary career per se. Indeed, as a second generation writer, this perspective may have been an inextricable part of my legacy from my father.

---

## SELECTED BIBLIOGRAPHY

**Poetry:**

*Aram Saroyan.* New York: Random House, 1968.

*Pages.* New York: Random House, 1969.

*Words & Photographs.* Chicago: Follett/Big Table, 1970.

*Cloth: An Electric Novel.* Chicago: Follett/Big Table, 1971.

*The Rest.* Philadelphia: Telegraph Books, 1971.

*Poems.* Philadelphia: Telegraph Books, 1972.

*O My Generation, and Other Poems.* Bolinas, Calif.: Blackberry Books, 1976.

**Nonfiction:**

*The Street: An Autobiographical Novel.* Lenox, Mass.: Bookstore Press, 1974.

*Genesis Angels: The Saga of Lew Welch and the Beat Generation.* New York: Morrow, 1979.

*Last Rites: The Death of William Saroyan.* New York: Morrow, 1982.

*William Saroyan.* San Diego: Harcourt, 1983.

*Trio: Carol Matthau, Oona Chaplin, Gloria Vanderbilt: Portrait of an Intimate Friendship.* New York: Linden Press/Simon & Schuster, 1985; London: Sidgwick & Jackson, 1986.

# Susan Richards Shreve

*1939-*

*Susan Richards Shreve, 1981*

M y parents were married on New Year's Day in 1937 in the parlor of my grandmother's house. No one, so I have been told, approved.

First off, my father was from the wrong side of the tracks. In small midwestern towns there are, even today, two sides. He was a man of unpredictable genes. No midwestern farmer. And for years, my mother had been engaged to marry a splendid young athlete whose pictures in basketball shorts doing jump shots and lay-ups are in my attic. She agreed to leave the basketball player several weeks before the wedding, but my father, committed as he was to emergencies, found Donna, a tall, voluptuous blond, late-thirties Harlow,

in mid-December. On Christmas Day, a week before the wedding, he maintained in earnest that he was undecided about marriage.

I think he made it up. My father saw my mother when she was twelve years old, sitting on the veranda of her house with the quiet and contented air of the well-born on the bottom side of the century, just after the First War. He decided about marriage then. He crossed the tracks on Valentine's Day to bring her chocolates which he gave to her father because my mother wouldn't come to the door.

"He was too small," my mother said, "and skinny as a pole. Anyway," she insisted, "my friends would have laughed. He was younger than I was and didn't play sports. Instead," she said, "he wrote stories."

I expect my father found Donna just in time to protect himself with understudies in the wing, to seal my mother's commitment to this persistent dark horse.

Besides, as I have said, he liked emergencies. A simple wedding in the company of outraged relations was not enough.

"I suppose," my mother said on Christmas Day after the news about Donna, "that if you come on New Year's Eve, I'll know the wedding is on."

"I'll try my very best to let you know before then," my father said.

Twenty-one years later, my parents were announcing my engagement to a man not unlike the basketball player who lost out in his list of accomplishments—a young man of his time whose talents, unlike my father's, were perfectly suited to the moment. My parents had planned a large party with friends and relations from out of town, but the day before the party, the man I was to marry broke his leg playing football and could not attend the celebration. Immediately, my father sent out telegrams to everyone invited. "ENGAGEMENT OFF," he said. He was a writer, known for absolute clarity.

For weeks I received small notes on blue Crane's stationery, on sheets with violet borders from well-meaning aunts. How sorry they were to hear about the trouble, advising me to get busy and put the man out of my mind, to look for someone else more loyal.

"Jeez," I said to my father. "What did you tell Aunt Lindsey and Grandmother and Mrs. Henry?"

*Sally Stone Halvorson*

*Father, Robert Kenneth Richards, 1935*

*Mother, Helen Elizabeth Green, about 1933*

"That the party was off," my father said. "That's all."

"You said the engagement was off," my mother said with surprising sharpness. She had, after all, dedicated that year to the careful arrangement of her daughter's future and did not want slip-ups. "You forgot the word 'party,'" she said.

"By accident," my father said sheepishly.

It may have been because the man I married was tall and blond, unreasonably successful for a boy. Or that he reminded my father of the ex-basketball player or his own impossible dreams for himself. Or that I was his daughter.

All of these reasons and more that I don't know yet or don't understand. What I do know is that we inherit from the lives of our parents a complex of patterns which can give a sense of order to our lives. When I write, I am looking for these patterns.

My mother didn't know my father well before she married him although they had grown up in the same Ohio town. He was a crime reporter for the *Post* in Cincinnati and she was teaching school in Urbana, waiting for the basketball player to get a job and marry her. Her own father said she had to wait. He also said she must teach school. Not go to New York to be an artist or a model or a dancer, in that order, as she wished to be. In New York, she would be, he promised her darkly, open to false advances, low-life companions. She must have a serious profession teaching school.

When I got my first job teaching school, my mother told me fiercely that I was throwing my life away. And with all my opportunities. I could be an actress or television writer. I could produce plays. Something worthwhile. I mention this so you will understand why a careful and old-fashioned woman, as I describe my mother, could be carried off by a crime reporter, a Welshman from the wrong side of the tracks.

On their way to Cincinnati, driving at night, after the wedding ceremony and the disappointed relations, my father spotted a brown paper bag in the middle of the highway and stopped.

There was, he claimed in dead earnest, a baby in the paper bag.

"A baby?" my mother asked incredulously. "How do you know?"

"*Look*, for heaven's sake," he said to her, as though her sense of sight had failed her in an instant. "Can't you tell?"

She looked. There were lights on the highway and headlights on their car so she could see the paper bag perfectly. It appeared to be a brown paper bag which gave no evidence of concealing a baby. But it did move, she noticed, as my father rushed to rescue it from the middle of the road.

Filled with a sudden and unfamiliar excitement, she began to believe that he was right and would return with a small baby which he'd dump from the paper bag onto her lap. She straightened her skirt in anticipation.

"Well?" she asked as he opened the door by the driver's seat. "What is it?"

My father got in, tossed the paper bag in the backseat and turned on the engine.

"Nothing," he said and drove off into the night with his new bride, headed for Cincinnati.

"Why," my mother dared to ask sometime later, "did you think there was a baby in the paper bag?"

"There could have been a baby," my father said simply.

Anything, of course, is possible and so my reasonable mother agreed that "yes," there could have been a baby.

"Besides," my father said later. "I couldn't imagine that it was simply an empty paper bag."

Our house was full of stories. Every night when my father came home from work, I wanted to be there, not to miss my role in whatever high drama might be played out in our kitchen. It was not so much that he told us stories, although he did that too, but he made our lives into stories. I grew up believing that there could be a baby in an empty paper bag.

My parents moved from Toledo, Ohio, to Washington, D.C., in 1943. I was three years old. We came because my father, who had wanted to go to Europe as a correspondent, was made head of radio censorship for the wartime office which cleared the news before it reached the American people. He moved my mother and me into the only place we could find, which in the winter of 1943 was occasionally heated and always full of soldiers, passing through Washington on their way to Europe. I had rheumatic fever shortly after we arrived, followed by pneumonia. I'd already had polio before we left Ohio. I mention this not for itself but to say that my early life was attended by a certain amount of drama of which I was the center. It wasn't a bad time and I wasn't bored. There were plenty of soldiers and my mother was good company. I listened to soap opera on the console radio and played out melodrama of my own design with paper dolls on my bed. I expected, as children do, that my life was ordinary. I expected as well that it was easy to die. A child must be armed for it, ready for combat. I remember one angry winter, fed up with staying in bed, that I undressed my doll, Ann Shirley, named for the healthy, dimpled child idol of the time, and asked my mother to put the naked doll out in the snow so she

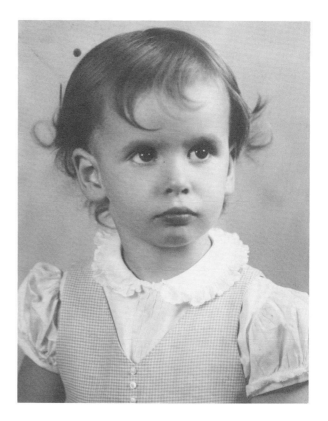

*Susan, age three*

would die. My wonderful mother did just that: walked around the house to my window so I could see her and put Ann Shirley in the snow where, I had determined, she would catch pneumonia and die.

For several years after I got well, I went through a ritual with my mother before I went to sleep. "Promise me that I won't be poisoned," I asked. "That I won't be kidnapped in the middle of the night or bitten by the poisonous snake under by bed. Promise me that I won't die."

My mother was an honest and literal woman and would not make promises she couldn't keep. But after staying up nights with me, she compromised and promised me faithfully that I would make it through the night.

I see dark shadows everywhere, even now. Roach poison mysteriously in the orange juice, kidnappers lurking in the basement thinking our house belongs to the wealthy senator from Colorado, viruses transmitted by pigeons which flood Washington every fall. Living, I instinctively believe, requires energy, a readiness to fight.

I have been careful with my children. They are not growing up with my father's stories from his crime-reporter days or my precarious childhood. They do not need to believe, as I seem to, that we live in a state of emergency. But, of course, however careful we are as parents, these legacies outdo us.

Recently, when I was in New York, I spoke long-distance with my eldest son who told me about the fine day he had had in school, about lacrosse, and a new girl friend with long, yellow hair—a conversation punctuated by black reminders of the dangers of New York. Was my door locked? Did I go out at night alone? Did I remember the woman from Washington struck by a taxi as she waited for the bus? Did I ever travel by subway?

When I was a child, I made up events as if I were in the midst of them, turned them into stories in my mind, casting myself in the heroic role. Once, at Garfinckel's, waiting for my mother to try on suits, I spotted a child hiding under the dress racks. I imagined the kidnapper of the Lindbergh baby in the dressing rooms, waiting for the child's mother to move out of sight so that he could whisk the little girl away. In the nick of time, I warned the mother and pulled the child, chewing Juicy Fruit, from under the dress rack.

"That didn't happen," my mother told me in distress as we drove home from Garfinckel's.

"Yes, it did," I said. "I was there. You were in the dressing room."

"You made it up," my mother went on.

"I think it happened," I said. "Anyway I did find the little girl in the nick of time."

"She tells lies," my mother told my father at dinnertime, her sadness absolute.

"She exaggerates," my father said.

"Whatever," my mother said, exasperated. "She doesn't tell the truth."

My mother used to telephone about a book of mine she was reading.

"Look at page 96," she'd say. "Aunt Lucy doesn't drink too much. She's going to be furious."

"The woman on page 96 isn't Aunt Lucy," I'd say. "I made her up."

"She has lavender hair," she'd insist. "What other woman do you know with lavender hair?"

I was rigorous about honesty when I was growing up. I never cheated in school or stole Lifesavers from G.C. Murphy's or lied regarding my whereabouts when I skipped classes or blamed another child in the class for my own, not infrequent misbehavior. I knew hypocrisy in myself and others as though it were painted turquoise. But even when I was small, invention seemed to me as true as the facts of things, truer because it showed the facts for what they were.

My father was a reporter not only by profession but by temperament as well. He knew there were enemies camouflaged under ground cover; that the only protection a man has is to expect these enemies behind the bushes, expect the worst of them. So armed, it becomes possible to live well and generously and dignify the human spirit.

I recall one of the last visits I had with him before he died, at which I insisted with false gaiety that he would be home soon. He looked at me directly and with no pleasure, discouraged that I had missed the point. We were not brought up with fairy tales.

When I think of him now, seventeen years since I've seen him, I remember a remarkable sense of humor that lit our lives, which is the dividend of knowing there are enemies in the home camp without losing the energy to thrive among them.

I went away to college in the late fifties and took it seriously. I took myself seriously and the professors and the history of English literature seriously, as though it were fundamental to our well-being.

"I want to be a serious writer," I told my father in the middle of my junior year.

"It sounds very dull," my father said.

"I don't want to be a journalist," I continued, "or any other kind of hack writer."

"I should think not," my father said amused. "It would be too frivolous a way to spend your time."

Later, the following summer, I was sitting at the breakfast table beside him. He had the newspaper open and was reading the center section, but the paper was folded so that I could see the front page on which it was announced that Ernest Hemingway had died the day before of a self-inflicted gunshot.

I burst into tears. With great concern, my father put the paper down and asked me what was the matter.

"Hemingway shot himself," I wept.

He looked at me for a long time with a disapproval I hadn't known since grade school.

"I did not know," he said quietly, "that you and Mr. Hemingway were such good friends."

"If you're going to be a serious writer," he told me later, "you'll have to be serious about what is true and what is not."

I went to a Quaker school in Washington, D.C., and in my last years there, post McCarthy and the 1954 Supreme Court decision on integration, amid the liberal whisperings of the next era, the senior class would spend hours in small, earnest groups discussing issues.

"My uncle came over last night," one boy said in the senior shack, "and we discussed the crisis in the Middle East."

"We have ongoing debates every night after dinner," another girl said, "about the conflict between science and religion. It can be incredibly tense."

Another claimed to spend hours talking with his father about civil rights and the nature of God and the influence of Puritan morality on the twentieth-century state of mind.

I was at a loss. Dinner was not a serious occasion at our house. It was important to have good food and tell good stories. It was important to laugh a lot and accept with grace the stories told by others at your expense. There were often unimpressive guests. A painter who left a life-sized nude and a life-sized Lincoln in our attic; he changed his name from time to time if he found a new one in the obituaries. An exquisite woman, a former actress, with her great dane; she drank herself to death after my father died. A black man given to the occasional shooting of his relations; for him my father created jobs at our house whenever he was fired from a proper job my father had found him downtown. These were regulars, but there were others in and out who stayed for dinner and sometimes didn't leave for days. My father had a deep affection for decent people down on their luck—not the usual hand-licking variety who wander woefully from one free meal to the next, but odd people and good ones who simply did not get on well in the world as it's arranged.

It was not, however, a group for intellectual discussions in the parlor after supper.

"Other people in our class have real conversations at dinner," I told my father one night. "They learn something."

"What would you like to learn about?" my father asked.

"For example, today at lunch we were talking about civil rights and whether there were intrinsic differences between blacks and whites."

The painter was there that night and the actress with the great dane, the woman called Rosemary. My brother sat at the table carefully collecting his supper in a linen napkin, and Jimmy was there on parole, having recently made the front page of the *Post* after major difficulties with his wife.

I knew the story my father told that night because it was true and I had been there when it happened. It went something like this:

At the end of the war, my parents bought a farm in Vienna, Virginia, then rural and Southern. The farm included three tenant farmers with piles of children, crops, and animals tended by the black families who had lived there for generations, under owner protection, barely paid—a not uncommon post-slavery arrangement. My father was a Northerner, a Midwesterner from that vast central expanse between the oceans, peopled by ordinary Protestant farmers of moderate disposition who grew up in small towns knowing a handful of Jews, some Catholics, and one or two black families; a score of Polish jokes. They believed in democracy the way fundamental Christians believe in Genesis. He left home at seventeen, but you don't leave everything behind.

My father set about treating those tenant farmers decently, to show the other white Southerners in nearby farms what democracy was all about. He paid the farmers equal wages, had them to supper, to sit at the table with us; and even I knew they weren't comfortable taking meals in our dining room. He went down to their places and played poker, had their children up to play with me. Nobody in the village said much, but one woman warned my mother at the market that trouble was afoot, she'd heard from Mrs. Able at Bailey's Crossroads.

"The neighbors are hoping for trouble," my father said.

On the Fourth of July, my father butchered a pig who'd grown so fat he had to be cut out of his pen. From the back porch of the house I watched him shoot the pig and cried for the sweet pig and for my father who had to shoot him.

When my father came back to the house, he told my mother it had taken all the ammunition that he had to kill that pig.

That night after supper we heard shots, the same as the ones I'd heard when the pig was shot. Shortly afterwards, the women and children from the houses on the farm streamed into our kitchen, full of bruises, spilling blood on the floor.

"They're going to kill us," they said. "They've beaten us. They're crazy with drink." And my little friend, Janie, wrapped her arms around my mother's white skirt, striping it like candy cane.

My father bolted the door, turned out the lights, and sat on a chair with the empty pig-shooting rifle across his knee. The men came soon.

"Let them go," they shouted at my father.

"Not on your life," my father shouted back.

"We'll kill you if you don't."

"I'll shoot the first one who walks through this door," my father said.

They must have known he had an empty gun. They had been with him when he shot the pig. In fact the gun belonged to one of them.

My mother called the police. They said they wouldn't come.

"We don't ever get involved," they said.

"Not even when there are guns?"

"Let the women and children go," the officer said.

"They'll be killed," my mother said.

"They won't be killed, but you ought to know it's not your business anyway," he said.

"Let them go," my mother said to my father when she put down the phone.

"Those men are drunk," my father said. "They could kill someone."

"It's not our business," my mother said, and she unbolted and opened the back door, motioned to the women, who then filed out of the dark kitchen into the silver light of evening and their men.

No one was killed. Contrite, my father sat in the chair at his bedroom window all night watching the farmers' houses, which were quiet until dawn.

"Some civil rights discussion," I said later to my brother, but he was not sympathetic.

When I grew up in Washington, D.C., it was a small, sleepy, Southern town, populated largely by people whose allegiances were elsewhere. There was an "old Washington" whose children attended Episcopalian schools and dancing classes, went to law school and practiced in respectable firms. But their lineage was political as well—defeated or retired senators who couldn't leave the town and stayed after their terms were up. The rest of us came to Washington because our fathers were elected or got someone else elected or were good, as well as noted, at what they did.

I wanted to be famous. It was not a pipe dream. It seemed that everyone I knew was famous or had once been famous.

It was a segregated city in the years I was in school. White families, even Northerners like ours, had "live-ins" at little cost. Lula lived with us for years, and her children often lived with us as well. She was a college-educated black woman who couldn't get a federal job in postwar Washington and we got on terrifically: I spent weekends with her as the only white child at a black movie theatre or birthday party or chicken supper at the Baptist church.

I went to a school noted for its liberal education, its respect for individual rights, its tolerance of alien points of view. Nixon's children went there; the children of one of the most reactionary senators from the South went there. But the school turned down the children of Ralph Bunche because they were black. As a young girl, I was aware of paradox and so were most of those with whom I grew up. I didn't have unquestioned faith in anything except my family. Nothing was absolute.

We were not a religious family, although I always thought my mother believed in God and Heaven, probably not Hell. She never would admit there was not a Santa Claus.

"I've never seen him," she'd say, "but I believe in the spirit of Christmas." It drove me crazy. I wanted the facts. No Santa Claus. Period. No God.

There was a splendid man in the waiting room of the hospital the first time my father was brought in critically ill. While we sat there together in that futile state of waiting that goes on in hospitals, he gave my mother his Bible and told her to read every night certain passages he'd marked for her about the promise of eternal life.

My mother took the Bible, marked at the passages, and kept it on her bedside table during the last year my father lived. I knew she read those passages. I'd catch her reading them quietly to herself as I passed her bedroom at night. I was touched by her conviction that it would make some difference; but I was annoyed as well—jealous that she had something I lacked—and probably frightened because it seemed an innocent faith and made her vulnerable.

I never mentioned the old man to her or the persistent Bible reading until my father died, and as we walked out of the hospital into a bright April afternoon, I asked her.

"Did you think you'd save him by reading those passages from the Bible every night?"

She looked at me with astonishment. "Of course I didn't think that I could save him," she said. "I read those passages to save myself."

She seemed to me invincible that afternoon as she had seemed when I was a small child.

My father wanted to be a fiction writer.

"He was a fine nonfiction writer," my mother has told me, "but not much good at fiction." And that may be true. It is also true that he was a fatherless boy who came of age at the end of the Depression and he would have been crazy to be a fiction writer. He wanted to make money and eat well and ride in taxicabs. And he did all that while I was growing up.

On television, during the sixties, I recall seeing an immigrant Jewish father distressed about his son. "Everything I work for, he throws out," the father said. "The new house, the carpet, the television set, meat on the table. He lives in a ghetto without a bed to sleep on, eating vegetables—the way I grew up—like it is some kind of wonder to be poor."

It was possible for me to be a fiction writer in a way that was not possible for my father in 1931.

I didn't write fiction while my father was alive. Perhaps it is true that I was only free to write after he

*With brother, Jeffrey, 1945*

died. It is also true that in the manner of families, my parents set me up in this business: I have inherited my father's shop, passed from father to child, with the responsibility for maintaining its essential character in changing times.

I was born in Toledo, Ohio, on the second of May, 1939, the first child of Betty and Bob Richards who named me variously at birth: Janet, Letitia Janet (the Janets for an unrelated Aunt), and Sharon. The Sharon lasted longest, until my mother read that "Sharon and Her Girls" were dancing topless at a club in Toledo and changed my name to Susan Lynn, to be called Susan if my eyes turned brown (as they did) or Lynn if they remained blue. My mother was a methodical woman who kept her options open.

I have been told many stories about my childhood and, in each case, the protagonist of the stories is a lot of trouble. I never used to run away from home without taking along my baby brother, Jeffrey, born when I was five, and thinking with some justification that, although my parents might be relieved at my absence,

they would certainly miss Jeff.

There is one story in particular which I find mysterious and somehow related to the childhood of a fiction writer. My father worked nights in Toledo managing a radio station; my mother and I were at home alone and I was still in a crib. One night I woke up quite late—although I have been told I never slept at all—and called my mother, who turned on the hall light and came into my dark room. I was standing in my crib. I believe I remember this moment exactly, or it may only be that the story was so often retold. According to my mother, I looked just beyond her into the hall as she walked towards me, gripped the crib rail, and said in a voice she described as theatrical, "Who's that man behind you, Mommy?"

My mother panicked, grabbed me from my crib, turned around. There was no man. She searched the apartment. The door was locked as it had been and the apartment was empty except for us.

My father thought I showed early signs of developing a sinister nature. My mother, who always believed I was innocent, was inclined to agree.

Years later, my third child, Caleb, awoke in the middle of the night and couldn't breathe.

He had, he told me in a tiny voice, swallowed his father's ring—a large school ring—clearly caught in his three-year-old esophagus. We rushed to the hospital. He was taken to X-ray and we were told they would perform emergency surgery as soon as they determined the exact location of the ring. We were not permitted to go with him.

Shortly after, a doctor returned with the X-ray which he held up against the light.

"No ring," he said coldly. "No evidence whatsoever of a ring."

"What about his breathing?" I asked.

"He had a bad dream," the doctor said. "There is no other explanation."

"Bad enough to make him unable to breathe?" I asked.

"That depends on the size of his dreams," the doctor said.

In the car going home, Caleb sat quite contentedly on my lap. "Are you breathing easily now?" I asked him.

"Just fine," he said happily.

"Well, what do you think happened?" I asked.

He looked at me as if I'd lost my sense. "You know what happened," he said to me. "I swallowed Daddy's ring."

I believe I actually saw a man in the hallway behind my mother all those years ago and was warning her of danger.

In the afternoons, before I was old enough to go to school, my mother and I used to play paper dolls on my bed. We had families of paper dolls spread all over the quilt into a small town; their flimsy lives we sustained month after month with Scotch tape. My mother liked the paper clothes carefully cut, the tabs bent over the shoulders, around the sides and legs of her dolls; her families were elegantly dressed and changed for every occasion. I did not bother cutting out the clothes. I was interested in the invented characters of these dolls, the drama of their relationships; each day would be another episode like a soap opera or a continuous dream. We'd sit together side by side, my mother cutting out clothes while I imagined serious episodes with miraculous solutions. There were no unhappy endings. These reassuring afternoons occurred in the years of my life called formative, and I look back to them now as significant to my writing as well as my life.

I wanted to have a bedful of real children—a team, in fact—on whom I could count in battles, there with me for the whole dance as a stay against loneliness.

"Did you have so many of us so that we can take care of you when you get old?" my eldest son once asked, adding that it hadn't been necessary to have so many. He would have been glad, gladder in fact, to take care of me alone.

I collected the stories of orphans and homeless children from the "*New York Times* Neediest Cases" published during the Christmas season. I wanted to save as many of these children as possible. I named my unborn children years before their arrival. I believe this instinct for children was more than maternal or sentimental, a serious passion born of early years trapped in a bed and sustained by the compensatory life of paper dolls—and a mother willing to play them with me.

Some time ago, I found a five-year diary I had kept for a month in 1949 when I was nine years old. Every entry in that month of January, the only month recorded, begins, "We are all well and happy." Day after day, the coldest month of the year: "We are all well and happy."

It is no wonder, I thought reading that diary, understanding the quiet desperation of the child who wrote it, that I couldn't make it through recording the first month of the first year. I must have known that the wonderful promises we had been given by the world we entered as children could not be kept.

I have a picture of myself at about six, walking down F Street in Washington, holding my father's hand, although my father is not in this picture, only his hand. I have on a coat with a velvet collar, incorrectly buttoned, cockeyed in the front; the collar of my dress is sticking out of the collar of my coat and I have an expression of great seriousness. I look like a child in borrowed clothes—too thin, with black circles under my eyes. It is exactly the wrong kind of picture for the time. And my mother must have kept it for the same reason I am glad to have it now, because it joins more predictable pictures of a child in organdy pinafores with carefully done curls and ribbons, occasionally taken with my baby brother, in gestures of affection invented for the occasion. Although I indeed loved him, I showed it then, not in the adoring glances captured by the still-life photograph, but rather by experimenting with my lost tooth in his small mouth.

It is as though we were recording pictures for cookbooks, painting the cherries and strawberries and apples bright red, the goose and cheese sauces golden as the sun, so the poor cook following the recipe line by line cannot hope to match the promise of the photograph.

I grew up expecting to fulfill advertisements of happy families, fine-looking mothers, impeccably dressed, preparing supper for fathers who rushed in the front door, good-humored and on time, to children who had been coloring or cutting out paper dolls in blissful fraternity all afternoon. In the movies, people only kissed and lay hand in hand in rowboats under a full moon. When I was thirteen, I thought I understood that passion had to do with holding hands, and I wanted to lie forever in a rowboat with a Persian patrol-boy named Sergai, pretending he was blond. I kept pictures of heroes in a box under my bed and expected to be a hero myself in time. A modern-day Joan of Arc is what I had in mind, in case the occasion arose again for military heroes, although I was not interested in a martyred death. Or any death for that matter.

When I was twelve and in a hospital in Georgia, I received an emergency call from my grandmother very late at night. She was looking for my mother and aunt who had left Georgia that day, driving North: did I know where they were spending the night? "No," I said. "What is the emergency?"

"Oh, no emergency, really," my grandmother said. "I am expecting them tomorrow and wanted to know would they arrive in time for dinner."

"No emergency," I said. "Then why did you call in the middle of the night?"

Of course it *was* an emergency, and later I found out by accident that my uncle had died. My grandmother insisted that they didn't want to worry me while I was in the hospital. I don't know when they planned to tell me—Christmas, perhaps, when I asked why Uncle Henry hadn't sent his usual box of nuts and butter cakes. "Oh dear," my grandmother would have said. "I forgot to mention it to you."

"Don't tell the children," was the serious warning of the time as though the children of my generation were made of a brittle substance which could, if tested, disintegrate. The first time I was in the presence of a dying person, I left the room when the dying was imminent. I don't know what I expected to happen to me when his heart stopped in that hospital room, but death had been kept such a terrible secret that I expected something from which I might not recover.

I wasn't going to recover from making love either. Something wonderful was supposed to happen between the frame of the beautiful boy and girl in the rowboat and the frame of the full moon. Something sweet and gentle from which I had no wish to recover.

I knew Sally Thackery once as a girl and then not again until she was a woman, a mother, thick with a third baby. She was a slender and lovely girl, an athlete, and I can see today my memory of her untroubled eyes during summers we spent together. There was a look about her, not arrogant, not wise enough for that, but a look which expected to win—probably then a swimming race, a tennis match—because winning was a part of the bargain.

When I saw her again, we were in a different town and she was Sally Something Else. I didn't recognize her and made a friendship without memory of a past friendship because she had grown fat and absent-minded. I was married at the time, without children, and remember one afternoon sitting in a room with her, watching her diaper her baby softly but without joy, putting the baby back in a playpen, tossing some plastic toys in with the child, and collapsing on a couch.

"Did you . . . ," she asked me in a moment of rare intimacy, "before you were married?"

I don't have a predictable answer to that question and I don't recall which one I gave at the time, but I do remember a sudden recognition of the slender innocent girl expecting victory, lost in that ungainly body out of sorts with itself slouched across from me.

"I thought it would be miraculous," she said, her eyes alive with recollected magic.

In my senior year in college, I took seminars in literature and writing; and I read with every other woman in my house, *Bride's* magazine every month. If asked, I wanted a career. I had written two novels and taken them to the Paul Reynolds agency in New York; these were the early days of Françoise Sagan, and I imagined that I too at twenty would be published. Paul Reynolds suggested that Miss Sagan had lived a

great deal more at twenty than I had, and perhaps I ought to consider working in a five-and-ten to get a look at what life is all about. I wasn't much in favor of the five-and-ten and decided to be a television producer instead of a novelist and produce the plays I had written for television. But my dreams, between acts of Shakespeare or Shelley's sonnets, were of me, radiant, in full flower, wearing one of the dresses from that month's *Bride's*. By the time I had graduated from college, I had set the hour of my wedding, named six children born at two-year intervals from that hour, and planned my life and my husband's exactly, including the houses we would live in until we were forty. Beyond that, it was difficult to imagine the future of a beautiful boy and girl side by side in a rowboat. I did not give any thought to my career as a television producer except to assume that it would be waiting for me when the six named babies were older.

I married Porter Shreve on May 26, 1962, at the Washington Cathedral. For years, in grammar school and Alice Deal Junior High School, I had collected photographs of high-school football players from the sports page, and my only serious ambition in those years was to be a cheerleader. Amongst my books, my favorite title is *Dreaming of Heroes,* for it names the condition of my childhood. Porter Shreve was a football hero—he was the best football player in Washington and had been offered a contract to play professional baseball at fifteen. We met on a blind date when we were sixteen years old, which I describe in a short story called "Double Exposure," written specifically about his mother:

> Her son, who was the only reason I had for searching her out between the silver urns at St. Alban's School, was tall and blond and an All-American Football player in 1956 when that combination of virtues was unsurpassed. I could not believe my good fortune.
>
> Some days, I'd sit in the bay window in our living room staring out at winter and honestly think that I was beautiful and witty, with an intelligence so understated as to be imperceptible. That I was a woman of my time and had a future.
>
> The first night that I went out with Elsa Gordon's son I wore a red taffeta dress that made my hips the size of row houses. He didn't kiss me but when I got inside the house and shut the door, I whirled around from room to room, the taffeta cracking and cracking like brown paper. Halfway between the floor and ceiling, I danced to a wild tune without music in my head.

The Philadelphia Inquirer

*Porter Shreve, playing tailback for the University of Pennsylvania against Brown University, 1960*

Once, I went into my daughter Elizabeth's dark bedroom when she was a baby and found her crying and wet. I lifted her up to change her and she grabbed my hair, pressed her face into my shoulder. "I don't want to take my dreams off," she said. Nor did I.

I lost weight in the year before I was married. Once the date was set and all arrangements in order, I reassumed the figure of a young girl, hoping, I suppose, in the body of a child to ignore the challenge of advertisements for happy families in the magazines of the time, to dismiss my responsibility for reproducing them in my new life.

After our wedding, we went on a trip, a gift from my parents because they hadn't had a trip, and by the fourth day, I was counting the time until we could board the plane for home. In this long trip with just the two of us—and though we were very young, surely I loved him—my misgivings were of a different kind. The days stretched out before me like open plains with a huge sky, too much landscape to fill with the imaginings of a child who grew up to a world no longer at war, overprovided, protected from danger by fairy tales without dwarves and goblins, where the princes

were never toads but princes to begin with.

The other morning in a fit of anger at my children, brought on less by anger at them than at myself for allowing their innocence in a foolish effort to perpetuate a myth of happiness, I threw open the *Washington Post,* confident that it would provide me with dark reminders from every corner of the world. "See," I said. "Look at these people in Afghanistan." They did. "And Cambodia. They haven't eaten for a very long time." I turned to the obituaries.

"Please Mummy," my youngest child said to me. "I don't want to hear such bad news about life before breakfast."

When I was growing up, our stories had happy endings.

There was a hill in the back of the junior high school where the boys from the home for juvenile delinquents gathered during free periods to smoke cigarettes and, according to rumor, to flash their switchblade knives. No one went up there. They had no trouble from the police or the teachers at Alice Deal, simply a bad reputation which I thought was unjust, believing in the concept of goodness that was popular at the time. And certainly I knew that boys with hair greased into the high tail of a black duck, with leather jackets, and the unmistakable beginning of beards, could be redeemed from bad reputations. I realize now that I loved danger but at the time, in keeping with its spirit, I thought I loved mankind and set about getting to know this group of wronged boys, to save them from trouble by offering them friendship with a nice girl. It didn't occur to me that they weren't interested in being saved.

"They're really wonderful boys, basically," I'd tell my mother. I expect I was having rowboat dreams again which were more compelling than social-worker fantasies.

Just about that time, on the hill behind the junior high school, a member of the group was killed in broad daylight by one of his friends with a switchblade knife.

I saw a switchblade knife for the first time last year. Closed, it was about five inches long, black with deep grooves running lengthwise and a small silver button. "Push the button," the friend who had shown me the knife said. "Away from you." I did. I no longer have trouble imagining the death of that young boy on the hill when I was fourteen. Now I look back on those dangerous boys in their black jackets like the black sheaths of the switchblades concealing a weapon which can kill easily without a struggle. But I was brought up with *West Side Story,* believing that danger was romantic, not dangerous, in love with James Dean and Marlon Brando. I expected miracles.

I was expected to marry and have children, to have a profession which used my education, to leave home and make an independent life—constructed like rainbows, a confetti reproduction of recommended dreams—to fill my days as though they were a glass jar whose contents in their splendid order were easily visible to any passerby.

The summer after we married, we went to a boys' camp near Lake George in the Adirondacks where I had a job as a secretary from which I was fired for incompetence and Porter had a job as head counselor from which he was fired for permitting the boys' camp and the girls' camp to have a sleep-out together.

In the fall, we went to England to live in a village outside Liverpool where the Beatles were establishing a minor reputation at the time. I gained weight on tea and biscuits, and drank sherry to keep warm. We slept in a single bed, the only bed we had, and wore clothes to sleep in because it was too cold to change. In the short days of winter, I went to work before the sun and came home after it had gone down, living a night life by candlelight. We drank lagers after work by a small coal fire until we were rosy with the heat and warm drink. Our small lives were hushed by the gentle reminders in the village where we lived, by the fine faces of the people along the quay where our house was, by the house itself which had stood centuries—a small thatched house, simply built. One would not suspect long life in so small a place built on a sea wall. Even the sea had disappeared.

In pictures I have of myself at that time, I look thirty-five, like English women look for years, and plump, padded like a squirrel in winter, with bright cheeks which in America had always been the color of brown pears.

In the spring we stripped off layers of clothing and spent weeks in pensions in Italy and Spain, knowing, we told ourselves, believing, that we were different than the other creatures of a modern ark, poured out of *Bride's,* two by two, in June, to Wall Street or Scott Paper or law school. Leaning over the bridges of the Arno, lying in the gardens of the Tuileries, in a small room in a bed half my height, looking through the leaded window which framed the Canterbury Cathedral, we believed, awash in the permanence of old civilizations, spinning with our young love, that we could make a perfect life.

We lived and worked in Europe until our money ran out, traded in our return ticket for a last trip to France, and went home steerage. My husband was seasick for six days and spent the voyage next to the smokestack in the only space of deck allowed steerage, and I ate meals with an Italian-American from Sicily who wore undershirts to dinner and ordered every se-

lection on the menu: three soups, two main courses, three desserts—mentioning, between bites, his money's worth. And I knew in such company that I was going home.

Everyone my age has stories of where he was and what he was doing the afternoon that President Kennedy was shot. I worked in Philadelphia, an hour away from the boarding school where Porter taught and where we lived at the end of a corridor of boys. Our bed was against the same wall as the beds of the boys in the next room; and once, they taped an argument we had and played it in the dining room. The tape did not clearly reproduce what I was saying, only the fact that I was crying, which pleased the boys. My father who visited us at the boarding school told my mother he was glad to see us safely there, in a small apartment, which was part of the bargain, and meals on a regular basis, as if we would not have made it in the world alone.

On the afternoon that Kennedy was shot, I left work early and drove home on a narrow country road with a student who commuted with me. We listened to the radio and she asked me questions about what would happen now the President was dead and why was my leg shaking on the accelerator.

I turned off the radio. By the time we reached the young girl's house, I was holding my leg as though it were the wind-up leg of a mechanical toy drummer who wouldn't stop marching. At home, Porter was in bed following surgery for a football injury his senior year in college which had ended his athletic career. He is a man of reserve and dignity who does not complain or register disappointment, but certainly we believed as children do that the world was in our hands.

The history books I read in school recorded assassinations as though they were part of an early outlaw civilization, not our own, recorded a violent history in America like didactic fiction invented for instruction. Wars were fought in other countries.

On the way home, I drove into a ditch, accelerating by accident, as though my leg were designed to fail me on a curve.

For months, I didn't look at the newspapers, cautious of bad news. I stopped reading serious fiction because it told the truth about our lives. I read instead cheap magazines with sentimental stories, romantic gothics, and skimmed the pictures of happy families still used for advertisements—holdovers from an earlier time.

I wanted to have a baby.

After all, I told my husband, we had been married three years and that first-named baby should have already come with a second in the making. I wanted to recapture those pictures of families for my own life as a protection against bad news.

When I wasn't pregnant by the third month, I went to a fertility doctor.

"How long have you been waiting?" he asked.

"Three years," I lied, and he agreed I had been extremely patient and deserved his attention.

The fertility doctor was located five miles from the school, which meant that if he were to help me, I had to get up at 5:30, go to his office for examination to determine whether in fact it was the time for conception, rush back to my husband in the room next to the boys who were at that moment getting up to the gong of bells for breakfast, and hasten, after that romantic interlude, to be out of the apartment and at work by eight.

It should come as no surprise that I didn't get pregnant in those years.

After my first son was born, the pediatrician made an initial house call to check us out. I dressed my baby in a fine-knit suit, blue booties, and brushed his yellow hair with a soft-bristled brush.

The pediatrician took off the suit and booties.

"Do you have an undershirt?" he asked. "Keep him in one." He looked at the baby's head. "Cradle cap," he said. "And that," he added, "is a diaper rash. Keep his legs warm." As he left, he folded the fine-knit suit and handed it to me.

"This is for photographs," he said; "it's not useful for a growing boy who'll ruin the front if he spits up and catch cold with his legs bare." He patted my shoulder as he left. "It's a baby, Susan," he said. "Not a doll."

In 1970, we moved into an old house in a changing neighborhood in Philadelphia with two small children, my younger brother, and a few of his friends. They were war resisters on their way to Canada who stopped by to visit for a week and stayed a year. They were children of the late sixties, silent revolutionaries, committed to communal living, vegetables, and natural love; we were fine decoys on which to practice their ideas without the responsibility for failure. They took over the garage, got a wood stove, built lofts, became house painters and church janitors. We ate together (an excess of vegetables and homemade bread), spent weekends sleeping out, hiking through the woods. We even took a trip to Key West in a truck. They had long hair and beards, one set of clothes, and lived on the road in a Volkswagen bus. They went to war rallies in Washington, at City Hall, talked about the revolution and their unhappy childhoods. I remember being intrigued by their sense of lawlessness and exasperated all the time.

Once I threw a pot of vegetable soup straight off the stove at one member of the group who was reading philosophy in the kitchen while I cooked supper. He stood up quietly, picked some of the vegetables off his sweatshirt, returning them carefully to the pot one by one, and said to me sadly, "You will die early of a heart attack."

"Good," I replied. "Maybe tonight."

They believed in fundamental good and the purity of children, suggesting that we should raise our children naturally, let them come to their own decisions by intuition, like animals. For example, they were against bedtime.

"Children go to bed when they get tired," they insisted.

"Fine," I said. "You stay up with them."

The following morning, my son was still up when I got up.

"You've ruined their natural instincts," they said to me, bad-tempered after no sleep.

One evening while we were sitting at the table, a group of boys raided the Volkswagen bus parked in front of the house and one of our members rushed out to protect, so I thought, his possessions.

"So," I said when he came back, "what did you do?" It was evident there hadn't been a struggle.

*Son "Po," 1985*

"Nothing," he said.

"Nothing?" I asked.

"If they wanted something that much?" he shrugged.

"You let them have it?"

"That's right," he said and looked at me without hope. "You miss the point."

The next morning we had planned our usual weekend hike through the Wissahickon woods and it was raining. I asked the protector of street criminals if he would call the weather to see if it was going to rain all day.

"Rain all day," he said putting down the phone, lying on the couch and covering his legs with an afghan. "Rain and turning colder. More rain tomorrow."

I lost my temper.

"Listen man," he said to me, closing his eyes. "It rains everywhere. Think of it. You could be in Portland."

"You act as though the weather is Rick's fault," my brother said in a rare moment, bridging the two camps between his friends and his family.

"It is," I said.

They left that afternoon, headed to Canada again, a year late, although the signs were good that the war in Vietnam would be over soon. They packed sleeping bags, a towel or two, some dried food, and washed their only outfits, sitting naked in the kitchen waiting for them to dry. Then they left on foot down Gowen Avenue, heading north.

I hadn't missed the point altogether. I had learned to bake bread and cook from scratch, to live simply and on very little. I realized after they'd been gone a month, that I wasn't thinking crazily about the future any longer, as though the only truth about our lives is what we will become.

In the first five years we were married, we lived in ten houses, in England, then at the Hill School in Pottstown, Pennsylvania, in Philadelphia, and then in Washington. Our first son, Porter Gaylord Shreve III, called Po, was born on the 13th of September, 1966, at five in the afternoon, forced to arrive before he was ready so the obstetrician in attendance could vote for Spiro Agnew for governor of Maryland before the polls closed. Even as a little boy, Po had, to quote Robert Frost, a "lover's quarrel with the world," his own strong sense of the way things ought to be. He is the original character in my life and funny besides. We lived in a gingerbread house in Chevy Chase the first year of Po's life, and then moved to Dyke, Virginia, a village described in sociology books as a hollow in the Blue Ridge Mountains, where Porter had been made

*Daughter, Elizabeth, 1982*

Assistant Headmaster of the Blue Ridge School, a former mountain mission-school. We lived in a farmhouse just below the Skyline Drive, and for three years we lived a strange rural life, forming the deep friendships possible in places without diversions, living out of doors. We each got a Master's degree at the University of Virginia where I studied with Peter Taylor and began to write in earnest. My father died two days after Easter in 1969, and our daughter Elizabeth Steward was born February 19, 1970, on a cold, icy night just after midnight. I almost didn't make it to the university hospital.

We moved that year to Philadelphia to a huge house with an acre of land in a changing neighborhood—and the hippies moved in. I taught English in high school and we had a second son, Caleb Richards, born just before Christmas on the 20th of December, 1971. My mother moved into a small house attached to ours, and shortly thereafter Porter's mother moved into our house. The summer after Caleb was born, we had our first real holiday since we had gone to Europe in the summers. With my mother and uncle and our own family, we went for a month to St. Thomas, where I wrote the first one hundred pages of a novel. By the time the book came out in 1974, Porter, my brother, and I had started an alternative high school with some

Cynthia Brumbach

*Caleb and Kate Shreve, 1979*

other teachers. Porter's mother—a Scottish woman of great drive and ambition for her children, widowed early, whom I alternately admired and competed against for her son—died without any alleviating drugs for a rampant cancer.

On the 8th of November, 1973, our fourth child, Katharine Taylor, was born, three months to the day before we were expecting her. Her life was precarious for what seemed to be centuries, and she is now, like children of such experiences, fierce and competitive. The first day of nursery school, some years later, I picked her up to find that she had a poor little boy, somewhat larger than she was, flattened against the wall.

"Help," she said, although certainly it was Anton who needed help.

I helped by removing her body lock and carried her stiff form to the car.

"What happened?" I asked her when I put her in her car seat.

"A terrible thing," she said to me. "You would have spanked him if you'd been there; but the teacher is always too busy to pay attention to trouble like kissing."

"Kissing?" I asked.

"Kissing," she said. "That's what he tried to do to me. I could have been killed of course."

"Of course," I agreed.

The summer of 1974, we sold our house, left our jobs, and moved to Houston, Texas, where Porter started a new life as a family therapist. We moved with our four children, two dogs, and a young woman named Mary who had been a student of mine, into a tiny two-bedroom house above a bayou, with rats in the air-conditioning units. Houston was a boomtown in those years like memories of what America used to be, as foreign to an Easterner as India or Japan. At dinner, you could be seated with a stockbroker who had just declared bankruptcy, a plumber, a man recently out of prison for smuggling, a painter. I lived in Houston for less than a year and we made more friends than we had made in ten years in Philadelphia. Everything was in bright colors.

After that year, we decided to come home. To a casual observer of our lives, it must look as though we moved home to repeat our own childhoods in the lives of our children, and certainly that was part of the reason though we would at the time have denied it. We moved to a house around the corner from the house where I grew up—sent our eldest son to St. Alban's, where Porter had gone, and the next three to Sidwell Friends, where I had gone. My brother married and moved to an apartment three blocks away from the apartment where he had been born. My mother married William Schaub and lived nearby. Our house was full of friends, of cats and kittens, children and dogs, writers, many others who came to visit Washington, and tenants, because the house was large and we rented to students. It seemed always to be Halloween or Christmas or Valentine's Day. I took a job teaching at George Mason University and wrote books. Certainly there was something about the smell of moss on the old brick sidewalks, the sultry heat of Washington, the soft sounds of a city built on a swamp, which flooded my mind with memories of childhood.

I love stories. When I was a little girl walking down the street from school, I engaged in imaginary conversations. I ran a theatre in our living room for years for which I was the director, playwright, and major actress. I published, to my parents' distress, a newspaper full of moral stories which I sold for twenty-five cents to neighbors, selling door-to-door so they couldn't refuse. I like writing novels best because there's space in a novel and they can be written in bed without assistance or equipment. Some time ago I found a picture I had drawn of myself when I was in the second grade. "This is me as a fairy," I had written under the picture.

*The family, about 1974: in back, from left to right—Susan's mother, Helen, Susan, Elizabeth, Porter holding Kate, and friend Mary Tonkinson; in front—dog Traffic, Caleb, and Po*

"Only I was much better still." Which is how I feel about writing as well as fairies.

In the years in Washington, we have lived on the edge of respectability, and these years have passed with such swiftness I am out of breath. My novels have been described as photograph albums of black-and-white pictures spilled randomly on the living-room floor so the years have no sequence except as time frames caught in memory.

In 1981, my mother died.

When I was about six years old, I was taken to one of those medical meetings by my pediatrician, a wonderful odd woman, Dr. Margaret Nicholson, to see Sister Kenny, the Australian woman who was the leading authority at the time for victims of polio. My mother and aunt were in the audience and I was wheeled in front of the groups of physicians and examined by Sister Kenny whom I remember as being the size and shape of a hotel.

"This child won't be able to walk by the time she's twelve," Sister Kenny said, shaking her enormous head. "No one has used my methods on her."

Recently I told this story and was asked wasn't I devastated by what Sister Kenny had said. I shook my head.

"I knew she was wrong," I said.

"How did you know?" the friend asked.

"My mother told me I could walk," I said. "And I believed her."

I went to Disneyland one summer on the day in August that the crowds broke record attendance. I hadn't wanted to go but I was visiting Los Angeles for the first time with seven children. There was no possible excuse.

We hadn't been there very long, just on the train that runs through the place and the Haunted House, when my youngest daughter asked with genuine concern, "Are we going to die, Mummy?"

"Of course, Kate," my older son said, not wishing to miss an opportunity to deliver dark news. "Everybody does."

"I mean today," Kate said.

And I realized that I was expecting trouble: one of the boats that travel through tunnels to go off the

*Cynthia Brumbach*

*At mother's wedding to William Schaub, 1979. Susan is far right; brother, Jeff, far left; Kate, Caleb, and Po in the foreground; and husband Porter, in the back, center.*

track, a roller-coaster car to jam halfway and catapult children into the sky, the cable to break on the cable car as it passed between fantasylands over the record-breaking crowd, heart attacks and runaway horses, a stampede to get in line for "It's a Small, Small World."

"Of course not, Kate," I said, but I wasn't sure and these children in my charge would have had a better time with another mother whose childhood diary hadn't recorded in such desperation, "We are all well and happy," for here I was caught inside the gates of a make-believe city promising short-term happiness.

I wrote a book a few years ago about a family; the book is called *Miracle Play*—the "play" has to do with our invented lives and the "miracle," with life. In it, the protagonist takes on the responsibility of keeper of her family's stories, understanding finally that one cannot rewrite the end or revise the sequence of time or alter the characters—only be careful and pay attention. The book ends after a large family party like many of the ones I attended when I was growing up or ones that I've given since:

That night, after the festivities and the cleaning up, the Howells children lay around the living room half sleeping in exhaustion, talking very little. But there was in the room a wonderful spirit of accord that must come to soldiers in the trenches after a long volley has been survived—a company knowledge that the treasure of living comes in moments and is prized because the moment does not last.

## BIBLIOGRAPHY

**Fiction:**

*A Fortunate Madness.* Boston: Houghton, 1974.

*A Woman Like That.* New York: Atheneum, 1977; London: Hamish Hamilton, 1978.

*Children of Power.* New York: Macmillan, 1979.

*Miracle Play.* New York: Morrow, 1981.

*Dreaming of Heroes.* New York: Morrow, 1984.

*Queen of Hearts.* New York: Simon & Schuster, 1987.

**Juvenile fiction:**

*The Nightmares of Geranium Street.* New York: Knopf, 1977.

*Loveletters.* New York: Knopf, 1978.

*Caleb, Elizabeth, Kate, and Po*

*Family Secrets: Five Very Important Stories.* New York: Knopf, 1979.

*The Masquerade.* New York: Knopf, 1980.

*The Bad Dreams of a Good Girl.* New York: Knopf, 1982.

*The Revolution of Mary Leary.* New York: Knopf, 1982.

*The Flunking of Joshua T. Bates.* New York: Knopf, 1984.

*How I Saved the World on Purpose.* New York: Holt, 1985.

*Lucy Forever and Miss Rosetree, Shrinks, Inc.* New York: Holt, 1986.

# Jon Silkin

*1930–*

## THE FIRST TWENTY-FOUR YEARS

*Jon Silkin, 1984*

Five major pogroms took place in Russia during the last twenty years of the nineteenth century and the first years of the twentieth, impelling my grandparents, on both sides of the family, from Baltic Russia (Lithuania) to Britain. My maternal grandfather, Harris—"Matilda dear, have the goodness to pass the mustard"—was on his way to America, but the ship got short of water and docked at Swansea. That is how my grandfather entered Wales, and how it was that my mother's family were brought up, first in Llanelly and then (from 1928) in

Swansea. "It might as well be here," he said, shrugging his shoulders, as he left the boat. It has been a continuing source of wonder to me that some of the warmest most familial parts of my psyche have been turned out on the lathe of geographical accident rather than grown from a genetic inheritance handed down from generations of English persons rooted in an Island landscape. None of that. My memories of the *Nurse* are created out of chance—the South Wales of my mother, and the East London of my father. My maternal grandfather drank whisky, not in quantities—at least, I don't think in quantities—but discernibly drank it—Haigh's, I think—and that smell and demanding strength, male and strong, is certainly a part of a drink I not only like but one I feel links me to a world that is friendly.

My father's family were more intellectual, and less friendly (in fact my father does not drink). I have always thought that the nature of Welsh people in their love of what is local has also warmed the Jews; it has shed some warmth on the Jews notwithstanding the anti-Semitism my mother claims she experienced, both from the prejudice of teachers in her school, and her fellow students. (The word "Jewess" can be used bitingly.) My father, however, had no such dispensation. No-one is so parochial as a Londoner, who, at the same time, adheres to an unshakeable belief that London is the radiating centre of Britain, and therefore—at that time—of the earth. Ignorance, reinforced by prejudice, whether in the mind of an educated or barely literate person, is a chilling environment for nurturing the children of immigrants. Although since I have never experienced the ghettos of London's East End, which was my father's environment, I cannot say what positive nurture was available.

My mother's father made some money during the First World War when his decorating and wallpaper business inadvertly profited from the wartime shortages. But a family of eight took care of much of that, and what remained was depleted by indulgence towards some of the sons (there were six sons, and two daughters, my mother being the younger daughter and the youngest but one in the family).

My father was one of eight children—five girls and three boys, and his father cleaned the toilets of the Synagogue, gave Hebrew lessons, and sold fruit off a barrow. My father writes:

My mother died in 1924 just before my twenty-first birthday. . . . I remember my sister Bessie dimly. She was sitting in a baby chair at table and reached out for a crust which we all thought was clever. Later there was a mourning candle in a glass tumbler. I asked where was Bessie and was told she had gone. I asked no further questions. This tumbler was on the mantelpiece of the basement bedroom occupied by my father and mother and Goldie [his sister] and me. As you can guess we were miserably poor.

My mother was a great reader both in English and German. A great admirer of Charlotte Brontë, particularly *Jane Eyre*. She also admired Queen Victoria and read about her and was always interested in what (from my history) I could tell about her. She gave me all the information I asked for including dates to help me make up our complicated family tree. My father was not interested in his family connection. He was also a reader, but mainly of love stories. I won't add more. All this may not be material.

The eldest son, Lewis, who had been born not in England but Lithuania, became a lawyer, and it was through his efforts and gradual affluence that the whole family professionalized itself—the men, I mean (the women did not professionalize themselves beyond their getting married). My uncle Lewis had been a clerk in the London Docks (Millwall) and, after that, a clerk with the haulage firm Carter Paterson. A lawyer spotted his intelligence and took him into his firm. He subsequently took on a political career and became a Labour member of Parliament for the Peckham constituency in London.

My mother's sister got married. The eldest of her siblings, a brother named Moss, died shortly after the end of the First War from some disease contracted, in part, from four years in the trenches of the western front. Two other brothers were also in the Army but "refrained from dying" in the War through their being garrisoned in Egypt. Subsequently, these brothers went to University College at Aberystwyth—to train as chemists. They enjoyed this experience and it has sewn in my mind a melancholy affection for Wales because the country seems permanently tinctured with my uncles' lives. Did

they handle women when they were at University; were they industrious; did they experience Welsh anti-Semitism; did they go for long walks in Cardigan? Did they professionalize themselves as a protection from the Welsh, or did they like them and mix with the townspeople? Did they drink beer? These, and a host of questions will remain unanswered, for they are dead, and my family do not readily give up their secrets, even supposing that such knowledge concerning the boys was to be had. What I do know is that a faint but recognizable pain attaches to my thought of Wales in a way it does not to London. It may be to do with my sense of a minority culture dominated by the larger English one. It may not be an entirely Welsh version of Wales, but the Jewish tincture is not imbued with anything English, on that side of the family. A more or less easy and not especially profound warmth distinguishes that brood, most of whom are now dead. The strongest, and most penetrating of them was my grandmother, who seems to me to have been someone apart from the rest of the family. "And some there be which have no memorial; who perished, as though they had never been; and are become as though they had never been born; and their children after them." Is that particular melancholy to do with immigrant families? I fancy it is, for when they die, they are like orphans in that no trace of their progenitors survives the transhipment from one country to another.

On the other hand, if my mother's family provided an image of warmth (and squabbling excitement) my father's side provided not merely intellectual presence, but energy. Some of this may, I suspect, have come from the Jewish East End as well as from themselves. "Get on, and prosper; the mind is alive." I have inherited a snobbishness from my father's side—a respect for intelligence—perhaps more respect than is right (for me it is also a weapon); and making money on the other hand has always seemed to me, not worthless, but unintelligent. It is one or the other, it seems. Thus the Anglo-Jewish community, despite its having produced many excellent writers, is not especially marked for its intellectuality, and its own Press is not remarkable either (it may once have been). I judge, from my experience, that most encouragement to Jewish writers has been given not by Jewish Organs and Institutions, but by English ones, even if the English have inherited a curious mixture of suspicion towards Jews as well as a tradition of hospitality and generosity.

My sharpest memory of my father's energy is connected with his professionalization. The living symbol of this was represented in the electric suburban trains which took Father from a railway junction named Herne Hill to the terminus in the City, Holborn Viaduct. My father was for years a junior partner in his brother's firm, situated, after I was born, in Giltspur Street in a building opposite Saint Bartholomew's Hospital, and close to the Central Criminal Courts—the Old Bailey. By train, to one of the most professionalized nerve centres of London. It never occurred to me in my middle-class, early childhood to ask if life might be different and less secure. And the energy of those electric trains, the turning over of the strong engines when we were stationary, but waiting to move, or the dashing past of the trains from the Continent as they swished on through our junction towards their terminal on the smart edges of London, Victoria, was a confirmation of the energy I felt growing inside me. "I have an engine inside me that will never run down," I unoriginally declared as I started running down the street to the station. My father, on the other hand, gave free advice to working people who had got hurt in industrial accidents, and all the time that Britain abused its work force, underpaid them, and never properly compensated or protected them with respect to industrial accident, my father, like other socialist professionals, gave free advice, I think it was every Thursday night. I wrote about this in a recent poem:

### For a Man's Head

Leaving his eating-house refreshed, my father
carries the flimsy cash, most likely in
his inside pocket, buttoned to admit
his fingers. It is for a man's head
crayoned by fumes, a page of shapes
over the foundry wall.
And will the head come with me, and will it
concentrate a nation's charity?

(From *The Ship's Pasture*. Copyright
© 1986 by Jon Silkin. Reprinted
by permission of Routledge &
Kegan Paul)

The mind grows, and becomes aware, in its tottering progress towards adulthood, that the entire world saving oneself is outside one; which realization is, Freud says, the true (perhaps only) mark of adult perception. That, maybe, is what women are in fact protesting—the failure of men to become adult in their relations with women and thus treat them as autonomous beings. But in the Jewish family of the diaspora, the woman enjoys, as in many peasant and working-class communities, a more powerful position than she does in English middle-

*Parents, Dora and Joseph Silkin*

class families. The matriarchal power exists; I have felt it.

Memories of pity. Aristotle is right to couple pity with terror. Shortly before the War my father's father became ill. He lived, or so I felt, in loneliness, and more than any other member of my two families—with the possible exception of my maternal grandmother—he seemed the most Jewish, the most starkly European Semite of the whole double tribe. Indeed, had I been able to marry off my lonely father's father, whom the younger generation seemed slightly ashamed of, to my mother's mother, I should have made of them a perfect Jewish couple. But chance only gave me this dictatorial insight: not life itself. When he was ill, Father and I went to see him in—either a hospital or a home. There he insisted on giving me a large bag of hexagonal threepenny bits. My heart contracted with pity and terror, not only because of his condition, although that as well—ill and alone—but because I could not think what to do for him, or with my feelings, which seemed stronger than myself. My father demurred, but I wanted that bag, and I believe I was permitted to clutch it and take it with us when we left. In fact my father's father did not die until 1948, when he was eighty-three plus.

At this period—between six and seven—I became susceptible to bullying, and although my mother taught me aggression I remained timid within, and from within. Recently, I received a letter from a Romanian Jewish woman I had met in Bucharest, in 1986, and to whom I had sent my *Se-*

*At a National Poetry Society meeting, 1979: Silkin, center, talking with his mother; father on right; Pamela Clunies-Ross on left*

*lected Poems.* On the cover of which is my photograph. She wrote—"you—with two parallel furrows between the bushy eyebrows, and looking half-defiantly half timidly at the world."

A year earlier (I was five and a half), I witnessed with horror a young boy being publicly beaten in our school, the Dulwich Hamlet School, with a cane gaily coloured like a barber's pole. I remember the boy howling, and again, my pity and terror, this time the terror being uppermost. After being taken from that school, I endured for a year the rigours of home education from my mother, whom I tried sorely, but whom I wished—consciously at least—I could appease. My biggest trial was forming the figure 8 which in half its character is like the letter S. When I had formed the letter S I could not somehow bring myself to ascend the invisible unapparent back part of the S which would make it into the figure, and back slid my pen to the point from which it had started. Besides which, S's were S's and figures were figures. How could you mix the two? To rise with the pen upwards was to invite vertigo and the pain accompanying heights. I could not. In vain my pen traced the figure S back to its starting point, again and again, until my mother, stung by my incapacity (or was it stubborness), her inability to convince me that the figure eight was kosher and permissible, and her failure in the face of an inept

child, lost her temper. Her anger only spurred her to a greater scalding anger, the experience of which was like my being plunged, as I once was by my nanny, into an absurdly hot bath. Even so, back went my pen on a track it had already created for itself. One adventure was enough, and I could not bring myself to provide the courage for its sequel— the completed 8, or the transformation of its S. A sort of stutter of literacy I might describe it as now. Then, it was torment.

Two more memories predate the Second World War. When I was nearly seven, my mother, whose parents were conscientious but not fanatical Orthodox Jews, felt I should receive as much Hebrew education as she could obtain for me, which was not much. I attended classes in religious education. I remember the grey, dull Synagogue, and a hall attached to it, to which I went for a dance years later. I remember nothing of that education, and I seem moreover to remember my father, the humanist sceptic, openly making fun of these attempts. I vacillated. On the one hand I respected my father, and in any case when invited to rebel against my matriarchal mother, I did so. But part of me felt, independently of my mother, that, since my grandmother valued it, here was something I must also value. For two years I was also taught Hebrew, at home, by a pretty redheaded young woman named

Miss Silverstone, who looked at this monster child with the melting and pitying eyes of love. I confess I liked the eyes more than the Hebrew, but, in any case, I made some progress in my aleph bet. What I also remember is my father, after the departure of Miss Silverstone, perhaps to covertly annul the religious and Hebrew element of my education, telling me that he did not believe in God. On the one hand, this could readily be construed as courageous honesty. But here was a proposition I had never considered and I felt that he, and I, would be punished; he for believing in his nonbelief, I for the knowledge I had wispily acquired. Suddenly I felt relieved of all structure and security and I believe I started to weep. My mother was furious with him, as furious as he had been some years before with her when she, having put on makeup, had refused to remove it. I was puzzled. If my pretty mother looked well in it, what was wrong?

My parents were members of a branch of the League of Nations, and my father organized meetings on Foreign Affairs from 1937 to 1939. Meetings were held in the local church but members often came back to the house for discussion and review afterwards, and I seem to remember that some of my father's but not my mother's family attended these discussions. It was not only because my mother's family—most of them—lived outside London that they never attended. Or rarely so. But perhaps I misremember. My uncle Jack, who drank himself to death on brandy, and whom I loved, kept a chemist shop by Paddington Station (like the Irish who live close to the London Terminal that will let them slip back home—thereby keeping a tangible link with their roots). Jack never attended these meetings, but they were attended, as I say, by the Silkin family, and this, once again, marked off the one family from the other—the father's side being the avowedly interested, the intellectual, the political, and, probably, the committed one. Certainly they rallied to the cause of political amity, and were genuinely moved and excited by what they hoped they were working for—peace between nations. Mussolini had gassed the Abyssinians in 1935, and none had prevented him. The signs of a European war were gathering. But for me these Isaiah-like meetings, perhaps tinged for my League of Nations family members with a tincture of their nebulous Jewishness, were a delight, irradiating an inexplicable, unexplained warmth which united fire and intellectuality when, in my life, as I have tried to suggest, they rarely were united.

Refugees. As the War England dreaded and tried to forestall, or ignore, slowly assembled its apparatus, Jews fortunate enough to escape Nazi Germany and Austria, or any other part of Europe they were farseeing enough to leave, began to reach England. My father specialized not only in Workman's Compensation now, but in Naturalization, a process by which he hoped to convince the British Home Office that these strange, passportless Jews, and other representatives of European disintegration, would make good, useful British citizens in what must now have been regarded as the inevitable War.

It came. The refugees that passed through our house, or were housed in it, ceased arriving. When War was announced we were holidaying in Torquay, and I had been playing table-tennis with my father. The image that rests in my mind is not so much that of my father telling mother and me about the declaration of war, in that intense, cold, reproving voice he reserved for serious things, although I recall that too; what I best picture is a small waterfront and, as my father is speaking, coiled and dead on the small bracket-shaped quay, a huge serpentine black eel. Inextricable with its vulnerablity its menace, a product of its large, powerful, sticky body. These two attributes, of menace and vulnerability, remained braided in my mind, reinforcing, contradicting, and echoing each other. How could such a huge, heavy creature be so vulnerable?

Two years later, in a different age it seemed, the German submarine UA 81 sank the British aircraft carrier *Ark Royal* (November 1941). This, when things were going badly for the Allies, was demoralizing. I seem to remember that several British warships pursued, and sank, a German craft, to even the score and attempt to restore morale. When the news of that was delivered, I remember how all the children in this small room—it was during afternoon break—became delirious with joy—and cheered—and danced. I just stood. (See the poem "We Were Evacuated," in *Autobiographical Stanzas*.) My big knees, which I associated with my being Jewish, became larger and even clumsier. And leaden. Was it from a need to be different that I stood immobilized; or was it that somewhere in me the pitiful image of that eel, so noxious, and so dead, supplied my feelings in such a way that I stood joyless amid the whirling merry-go-round of other children? I was afraid they might notice my immobility, and misinterpret, or rather, partly understand it, and I be accused of being pro-German. Which I was not. Just sad for the lives, and unable to explain my feelings, or account for them in a rational way. There lay the German ship sunk. I was not even able to grin. I willed myself to believe that this was a good thing, and felt entirely counterfeit. However, I have jumped two sets of experiences.

Like a million other children I was evacuated—from London—when war was declared, and the familiar, home-associated electric train became, when we changed at Paddock Wood in Kent, a rumbling, retired large tank-engine drawn train made up of antique carriages that might have and probably had done service during the First World War. Corridorless carriages, pulled by an engine that had probably, like an overfed colonel, gone into retirement. Breathless, slow, and remorseless, the traction finally got us to—a number of huts that had done service as an Army camp, and there we were billeted, until this school evacuated itself yet again, to North Wales (1940). But by this time I had been given the chance to say Yes, I wanted to leave that school; and since it coincided with my parents' wishes, I did so. However, at this point we were in rural Kent. It was, I think, the coldest winter of the War and each day we had to walk, in short trousers, from camp to schoolhouse—I think about a mile and a quarter each way—and the backs of our legs got badly chapped. One took it as normal. Grumbling seemed unpatriotic, and unmanly. I cannot dissociate the huts we were then in from those I experienced ten years later during my National Service Infantry Training at Dering Lines, Brecon.

In this first camp, bullying started immediately. N——, though hardly bigger than I, terrified me. Once, he stirred in me, during a wrestling bout, the entirely new feelings of masochism. But the climax of this series of episodes was of a double character, and different from the fighting, though that was the means he used to achieve power. I cannot dissociate him from the Nazis, although at that point in the War, I had no idea what they were, or what the true character of those we were fighting was. And British propaganda I almost immediately discounted. What I do remember, shortly before the War, is listening to my father's account of Fascism, and its organizational capacities. I realized that I was supposed to respond to what he was telling me, and I said, but that is good, isn't it. What he had told me sounded impressive, and I said as much. No, that was not right, and I was rounded upon for saying so. I suppose I earned my rebuke; but found it hard to reconcile the capacity to organize—if we were doing it (good) with their capacity to do so (bad). But perhaps from this I learned to distrust bureaucracy, and so my father's rebuke stood me in good stead.

He was a keen stamp-collector and got me interested. Amongst my most treasured though perhaps unworthy items—had I known it—was a set of Italian colonial stamps—large, colourful, pictorial.

That no political implications had made themselves understood speaks for my societal naivety, yet they were in fact the instrument of an experience that was to educate me in precisely that area in which I was deficient. I was about to become a Jew and a wiser human being. N—— had an older, larger brother who collected stamps and I was persuaded by him, under the guise of a much-needed friendship and the promise of intercession between his younger brother and myself, to exchange my Italian stamps for others of his I did not at all want. The older N—— was less ferocious and more phlegmatic than his younger brother, but I suspect he got his way by guile, and I learned, by the template of this experience, the value or usefulness of inwardness and design. An hour later in rushed the whole hutment of boys shouting "Jew, Jew, you've Jewed him." Had I? The word was new to me but the implication of what they were yelling, without cessation, was clear. Here was another valuable lesson to be learned, though perhaps I postponed digesting it for years, and instead, insisted on sticking to the letter of understanding rather than, because of my fear, understand and square up to its full meaning. Jew meant swindler. How was that? Either it was true or it wasn't true. Was it true? It never occurred to me to go beneath the ascription to ask if a deeper hatred than that expressed for a mere swindler was being acted out. My vocabulary, and my understanding, were being extended, not by a proud father impatient for my education, nor by a mother frantic for me to take on the metropolitan values of an urbanized (and apparently anglicized) Jewry she had married into, but, quite simply, by the intractable experience of life, in the form of an equally intractable prejudice.

Flung onto the bed were my Italian stamps, one of which had a huge corner (newly?) torn off. Had I, or the older brother N——, failed to notice this during the exchange? Had I Jewed him? I wondered, in terrified stupefaction. Had I? At a loss, I faced the yelling boys—Jew, Jew. I cannot remember what happened to the stamps, but I think I gave the older N—— back his and received my humiliated ones. Shortly after that, initiating a long-lived disguise, I discovered that I might make myself "less Jewish," less despised, if I became less scholarly, less a swot. Nothing of course infuriated, and threatened, my Jewish parents more, who had seen scholarship or, at any rate, education as the means to obtaining not merely a bogus respectability, but some protection in the Gentile world. I went just the opposite way about to get the same results. Where they relied, perhaps on what at that time was the more Jewish mode, of the letter, I relied on the body, muscles, resistance, and affected to despise scholastic achievement. Always wrong from the start, it took years to reorientate myself to achievement in education, when that, in middle-class fashion, became the way to achieve survival if not the capacity to get on. In the midst of this, another Jew arrived in the hut, one whom N—— inevitably, and to his downfall, drew into a fight. Miller, though rattled, showed a physical knuckle-hard courage that N——, once beaten, never again challenged, and Miller remained unmolested. So did I, and the hut settled into a peevish half-relieved resentment when all who had secretly stood behind N—— realized that he no longer fulfilled the role of gang-leader, champion, or representative. Then indeed I felt almost sorry for him and experienced a half-formed dismay and contempt for those whose aggression and prejudice he had fulfilled without their having to do anything but line up behind him. I also learned that a Jew could resist and succeed. I began to think that I, too, must learn to fight could I find the courage, or simply, the audacity. As my friend the intelligent Kevin Fitzpatrick said, years later, there comes a moment when it is inappropriate to be afraid, and give way to fear.

The school I next attended, in Swansea, was called Parc Wern, and to my delight I stayed with my aunt Selina, her husband Goodie, and their only child, Rona, two-and-a-half-years older than I. I had been in love with Rona for as long as I could remember, but had not the means or the capacity to love her: though that, too, I would have done if I could. Swansea got bombed because of the nearby Skewen oil refineries and the steel works at Port Talbot, and the school evacuated. Just in time, for it soon suffered a direct hit.

What the summer seaside is to many, Swansea was for me; and when we evacuated to Dol-au-Cothi —the house in the plains of the river Cothi—something curious occurred because, I suppose, of the location being Wales and my relatives a part of it. Pumpsaint, the tiny village to which Dol-au-Cothi is marginally attached, is some sixty miles from Swansea (which was now my lodestar); though as the train would go, from Lampeter through Carmarthen and Llanelly, rather more. At any rate, this seventeenth-century house belonging to the Johnes family, lit by its own home-manufactured acetylene gas, was never in my mind far from the sea. We were, it seemed, both in the midst of this silent country, so silent it almost choked you, and at the same time on the fringes of the sea. London was of another world (even at nine I was aware that Wales was a different

*Dol-au-Cothi, Wales*

country, much larger it seemed then than it is in reality). This summertime "arcadia" composed not of grass and tree but sand and tide was in some way joined not only with my cousin Rona but also with the cheerful radiance of my aunt Selina who missed, I think, the intellectual opportunities London would have otherwise provided for her. And I think that probably some good-natured rivalry existed between Selina and her younger sister, Doris, my mother. In fact, my parents were receding in immediate importance, and no doubt this contributed to my sense of both holiday and adventure.

One way to describe Dol-au-Cothi is to provide a photograph, especially since, through a series of grotesque misfortunes, the house no longer exists. One master of the house, I believe in the eighteenth century, balked his servant's marriage and got stabbed for his doing so. Thereafter the house was said to be under a curse that would eventually see to its destruction by fire. (See the poem "We Were Evacuated.") After Parc Wern was temporarily closed, Dol-au-Cothi was taken over by the Ministry of Munitions for the storing of huge shells. Stupid, surely? For the floors buckled under their weight, and shells and floors had to be removed. Thereafter, much of the house stood like a husk, until it suffered a fire, and the curse and its fate became one. Many of the poems in *Autobiographical Stanzas* renew my experiences in this house.

Pumpsaint is a tiny village composed of the Dol-au-Cothi Arms Hotel, where the poet Edward Thomas stayed, and wrote his prose, a blacksmith's (as it then was), a post-office and general store, and a green-painted corrugated iron hut which, I think,

may have served as a chapel. It was of no consequence to the students however (the chapel I mean)
for I cannot remember us ever in the year that I attended the school enduring any religious instruction. And for that matter, until my last three
months there, no educational attention either. Miss
Hall, our headmistress, was a large lady who taught
the girls ballet. Each morning she would assemble
the children and declare invigoratingly: "Tomorrow
children we start work." We never did, and eventually Miss Hall left under what was probably a quite
unfair opprobrium. Getting staff during the War
must have been next to impossible, and it was only
in the last three months of my year at Parc Wern
that the literacy we had lost was coaxed back by a
new teacher, a Miss Harding, a gentle woman with a
slight back deformity—beyond doubt the gentlest
woman I have ever known, and who, by implication,
taught us not only how we might recover our literacy but how we might be cared for.

But we had also acquired another education—at
least the boys had, for we roamed the countryside incessantly. Underneath each boy's bed reposed
a chamberpot full, not of piss, but gold: in reality
"fool's gold" or iron pyrites. But it gleamed with a
dull brassy eye, and in places you could see where
the fanged saw had left its herringbone tear marks.
Pumpsaint means "five saints" and there exists a
stone in the village whose indentation attests to the
fact that five saints had reposed there for a night—
while sheltering from a storm. A little further down
the road, going south, you turn off to the left and
then on the right is a track embedded with quartz
stones. You entered a space enclosed by small hills
and were in the site of two gold mines.

The first is a gold mine worked by the Romans,
tunnels—adits—shoved straight into these hills,
from which they extracted the gold embedded in
quartz in hexagonal deposits. According to an article I have, recording the sixty-third field day of the
Carmarthenshire Antiquarian Society, held on July
1, 1937, "it was said, that many inhabitants of the
parish considered themselves descendants of a Roman colony, and prided themselves on their Roman
descent, and Roman names were prevalent, there
being at that time a 'Paulinus,' a day labourer." To
pride oneself (unless I have misunderstood) on
being a labourer instructed by one's conqueror
seems not to me a distinction worth having, but it
thrilled me then to think that these long gloomy galleries were worked by "the Romans." It never occurred to me that the Welsh were probably the ones
who did the graft. In the floor of this site a shaft

had been sunk and, in recent times, good Welsh
gold had been extracted, which provided metal for
the Queen Mother's ring. Although, in our time,
the flooded mine was closed. We ransacked the
spoil-heaps, crushed the quartz and panned the
"fool's gold," and then embarked on the more difficult task of rendering it down. We never did, but
had we done so we planned to sell this gold and with
the proceeds escape from the school. We broke test
tube after test tube trying to render the foolish gold
into a consolidated lump. Why we wanted to escape,
I cannot tell. It was not just the fantasy of adventure, though that was part of it. We longed to escape—from happiness. Because truly, I maintain
that the year in Dol-au-Cothi was the best year of
my childhood—as I grew older, and the older children left, and I gained some respect both from my
teachers and peers. It was during this time that I
emancipated myself, or so I felt, from my parents
and, as I now think back, from the siren-like entice-
ments of Swansea which, however, always held me
in the inferior supplicant position that, I felt dimly,
was not what I wanted. That seemed to be the
wrong price to pay for my desires. The relationship
I had with those adults at the school, extremely caring adults I must add, could not be one of equals but
it was one in which I was taken, all in all, for what I
was. I felt as if I had earned my relationships because of my person, not from the privilege of any
kinship.

Another memory. When the homemade gas did
not supply enough pressure to keep the lamps lit,
they would extinguish, and we would be left in darkness, and would have to "rush" about the house
turning off the taps in order not to choke from the
shreds of gas that nevertheless continued to squeeze
through the pipes. What a strange, advanced, modern house it must once have been. The pride of Carmarthenshire, surely.

Then, food-shortages being what they were,
there began a craze of shaking up milk in a medicine bottle until we had "churned" it to a white but-
tery substance. It was edible, but the activity bored
us. There was a pony that the school had somehow
acquired, and our gym mistress, with whom I had
fallen in love, a Miss Hawthorn I think, supervised
our rides on this patient creature. She enticed me
onto its back and gravely led us both by the bridle
back and forth in front of the house. Then I supervised the building of a Morrison shelter; the hole in
the earth that we all dug must surely be an indentation somewhere on that site.

Through ignorance I almost destroyed myself.
One of the students had discovered a cache of solid

methylated spirit tablets which she, and those to whom she offered them, mistakenly thought were peppermints. They didn't taste like peppermints and didn't smell like them as they slowly, and lethally, dissolved in the mouth. They took some dissolving, too, but the four or five of us managed it in the end. And in the end, as night approached and we grew tired, the teachers, when they discovered what we had done, frantically worked to prevent us from falling asleep, for that is what the dose does to you—puts you to sleep, for ever. And at the same time we had to be made to vomit the contents of our foolish stomachs. I was the last to be made to do so. I clung resolutely to my approaching sleep, and I could see that the teachers were frantic, though could not work out why. We survived, only to catch jaundice from, it was said, the stagnant duck-pond, at the back of the house, outside its marvellous cobbled and protected courtyard, within which we did so many of our childish transactions—the back-lane of our lives. This round stagnant water clung to by a dense scum of green, almost lawn-like, but treacherous to the tread, provided, it was said, the means of us contracting the illness. We went bright orange. I fished (elsewhere), I am glad to say, with complete unsuccess; and I have never felt again the lust to catch a life by exerting my skill upon another creature. Vengeance I have felt; but that, I think, is different.

One winter's day in 1941 my mother turned up in a taxi. It seemed unexpected, but it must have been planned, for we left Dol-au-Cothi and drove the wintry seven miles to the market town of Lampeter.

My next school, in this town, was what is incorrectly termed by present-day terminology a Public School. Wycliffe College was Methodist in complexion, and it was here, in the Junior School housed within a bright red-brick building called *The Bryn*, that I learned all the Christian hymns I know. They had pleasant tunes, but the language of many of them puzzled me. Some were, for instance, militant. I had no trouble in reconciling these bloodthirsty sentiments concerning victory, with the War, since that, in any case, was how we were expected to feel. But was this love? Such, I was being told, was the creed of the Christians. Had I known that, at that moment, Christian Europe was active in torturing, burning, starving, and experimenting on, the Jews, I might have been more puzzled. But I did not know. On the other hand—to return to these hymns— some of the words gurgled with love that, I had to admit, promised a delight I could not properly fathom but which I knew was—delightful. Yet I

dimly sensed that this love, whose scent I had undoubtedly picked up, was not what these hymn-writers intended. This puzzled me even more because I expected no inconsistency from adults. I expected what they said to be what they meant. I knew about lying, of course, but that was straightforward. You merely said the opposite of what you intended and hoped for the best. What I could not digest was the adult inability to say what you meant, or the failure to assemble words into the meanings one intended. There seemed no-one with whom to discuss these problems, even supposing I could have voiced them. What I do remember is being troubled by these inconsistencies. Perhaps it was this as much as anything that drove me to assert my independence, in one respect at least.

I went to the Headmaster, who was soon, I remember, to be married—a Mr. Bird—and told him I did not want to worship as a Christian any longer. I cannot imagine how, as a ten-year-old, I put it to him, but at any rate, to my surprise, he agreed, accepting my scruples immediately. Thus on Sunday mornings when the other children went to whichever denomination they glumly accepted as their lot, I was left to discover what inner resources I had, which were few. In the wooden hut which served as a classroom—wooden huts seem to have been the functional architecture of my childhood and youth —I might have been slaughtered in a wooden hut had I been born on the Continent rather than in Britain—there, I asked myself, "Now what?" The answer came in what was probably my first experience of inspiration. The obvious thing was that when they were reading their New Testament, I would read our Old one. I think I can honestly say that although I read the Jewish Bible obsessively I understood nothing. But thirteen years later I wrote a poem on the death of my child Adam. It seems that by a process of osmosis I had acquired, and so, used, the form of Hebrew parallelism. It was a form I had no idea I was using until, several years later, a friend pointed out the fact to me. Donald Keene took me to task for the totality of my poems in Michael Schmidt's *Poetry Nation Review*—among other things for having no form. But this (and other poems of mine) have a form, Mr. Keene and Mr. Schmidt notwithstanding. However we are well-established enemies, Mr. Schmidt and I; after all, from *Stand Magazine* and *Northern House* I feed him a number of his best poets whose work he subsequently turns into books.

Prayers were also important to me. My mother had fed me the Twenty-third Psalm and this was what I said, silently, before slipping into bed. Even if it was a tedium to do this, I always came away conscious of the beauty of the feelings expressed in the Psalm. The purest language was after all spoken by the Psalms. So that when I knelt by my bed, conscious of my enemy, the Polish boy Modelski, I said the Twenty-third unison of praise in English. But I could not suppress the egotistical notion that my lot had lent sense and music to English.

These pearly animosities disrupt my narrative, and narrative was of importance because, after the nightly dose of radio malt and codliver oil, in lieu of much else that was nourishing in the country's diet, we went to bed. There I became the dormitory's storyteller. "And then, and then" they would exclaim when sleep, rather than boredom, was pulling down my invention. Where did these stories come from, and what was the spring—mental spring—that issued forth verbal energy? Who was I? The homesickness I felt was humiliating; but perhaps it can be explained not so much by a love for one's parents, though I do not doubt that in my strange way I did love them, but by my constantly having to start life over, and establish myself in a context that was neither constant nor continuous. This applied both to my schools and to my holidays, during which I would be, now in one home and, in the next holiday, in another. But for whatever reason, I was, at a slighty earlier stage, the briny milksop of the school, whose grief nothing at that point could assuage. But it passed, as it always does, and nothing worse befell me that I could then detect than the wrath of my parents for becoming immersed in the achievements of sport—I loved running—rather than scholarship. Thus I failed to win a scholarship to the Senior School (housed in what was then St. David's Theological College); which meant that my parents must continue paying in full for the expensive education I did not appreciate. Taking it in the whole Wycliffe was not a bad school, although I have never been sure of the value of any school. Schools undoubtedly fill a needed role as a caretaker, but I do not know if they fulfil their claim to educate. Children are creatures filled with curiosity. Maybe some of the learning processes are dull and must be doomed to bore the learners, but that cannot account for all the disillusion and dejection which many students apparently feel, in Britain, and whose curiosity the educational system rarely restores. I do not blame our teachers, but I wonder about our system.

In the Junior School I had been obsessed, for a period, with sin; and I ran to one of our teachers, a clever man, and a conscientious objector, I believe, a Mr. Waterman, and asked him if treading on ants

was a sin. I think this inquiry must have summated a long list of such anxious questions, and for this I earned the public minor disgrace of a black-mark for being, it was announced in assembly, self-centred. Darkly it was hinted that I, rather than the school at large, would know what this mark was for, and indeed I did know. Although it did not seem entirely fair. To whom must I apply, if not to myself with such questions? And if I could not answer them, then to whom but a master who seemed sympathetic? I was probably a trying child, but no nonsense masculinity was also the day by day rule. Still, preferable to Mr. Waterman was a Mr. Lloyd. Mr. Lloyd's unfailing routine joke was: "A fine day for the race," to which one had to ask, "Which race?" —to which the answer came, "The human race." At a time when the human race was busy inflicting the most unthinkable and calculated grossnesses upon its kind, I beg to question if the day was a fine one. Perhaps for the patient Mr. Lloyd it was since here he was, not having to kill, or be killed (Mr. Lloyd had lost a leg in the First War), but simply to share an affectionate and manly Welsh nature with these fairly reasonable young boys. He taught us *Julius Caesar*, and we enjoyed his devotion to the narrative. Indeed, his tuition established in my mind a bridge, or is it a link, between the specialized literary work and the life outside the life of literature—to which the most accomplished literature must refer. He made literature and life seem a natural part of each other, and I believe that this has been of permanent value to me, indeed to all the boys he taught.

One incident darkens my image of Wycliffe. No better but no worse, I think, than any Public School in that dark period, its official attitude to homosexuality would seem to have been stringent, and wanting in sympathetic understanding. A boy had been found in bed with, I think, a younger boy. The older boy was caned on a platform before the whole school—and then cast out. It constituted not merely punishment for this young man, but a threat to the rest of us. I can remember the fear and horror generated by this incident served up as it was in the manner of a public execution; and also, its resemblance to that earlier corporal punishment in the Dulwich Hamlet School. The boy howled, not only with pain, but fear, and the shame of his being exposed to the whole school. What made it worse was that, this time, my pity for the boy was muted by *my* fear and horror as the punishment took place. Would what was happening to him ever happen to me? What made the incident reprehensible was that the punishment, corporal and spiritual, was delivered by the Headmaster, whose name I shall omit, but who was a practising vegetarian, and the head of a *House* that I believe catered for the sons of similarly minded humanitarians. What kind of humanity, I asked myself, was it that inflicted such severe punishment on a young man, with such contempt for the person? It seemed, and it still seems, as if the master was protecting his property—the name of the school—as conscientiously as any capitalist; and with as little humanity. Indeed, pupils suffered in both directions, because were you caught going out with a girl in the town, you were expelled. Masturbation was discouraged. What then remained? And one must remember that with respect to the older boys, we are considering young men who were about to have their heads blown off by way of participation in the War.

One episode I remember with relish involves the Methodist minister the School employed. He was an opponent of pacifism. One Sunday, a Mr. Clapham, a pacifist, I believe, a cello player, and a teacher employed in the Junior School, spoke of the immorality of killing. That was not how he put it, and indeed, considering the War and its nature, and that he had to thread his way between simple expediency, destruction (which was what Britain was threatened with), and vengeance, it is a wonder that what he had to say emerged with any intelligibility at all. It also says much for the School that Mr. Clapham, a gentle man, was allowed to voice any of his convictions. But he was allowed, and that must attest to the nonconformist strength of the school's beliefs. At any rate, Mr. Clapham spoke up against killing. The next Sunday, our minister, from the pulpit of the Senior School, declaimed wrathfully against those who advocated pacifist doctrines and, I suspect, although I cannot be sure, spoke of how the practice of his opponent's beliefs would, if carried through, make a travesty of the sacrifice made by those who had already lost their lives in defence of their country "against the enemy." The enemy was, I think, a word he used but, significantly perhaps, I cannot remember his ever using the term "fascism," or any such word that touched upon the politics of the contemporary world. That would be asking too much of spirituality, which apparently operated on a vaguer, grander time-scale. Good and evil were the sole concessions to the world's profane terminology.

Our minister, during a period of prayer, would slip from one pulpit in the school chapel to the other so that when we uncovered our eyes and rose from our kneeling he would be stood, miraculously transported, and ready to deal the next blow in the Christian cause. I disliked, and feared, his Christian

militancy, as well as its associations with an English middle- (and upper-) class ascendancy from which I was partly alienated, and which (I hope) I would have rejected had any minor place in it been offered me. Fortunately there was no danger of this isolated and on the whole unbefriended young adolescent being accepted into the minor establishment of the school, and my instincts warned me, rightly I think, against taking any further part in the socio-Christian institutions of the school. I was a Jew, and that was the end of it. Whatever authentic morality and ethics there remained to gather from Christ's teaching—and no amount of lukewarm appraisal from my mother could put me off seeing the value of it— could be got from reading the Bible.

However, the incident I am about to relate happened as a result of the minister's being a few minutes late for the afternoon period of religious knowledge, when two boys, to dispel their disappointment at not receiving his instruction, started to fight with chairs, lifting them up and clashing them against each other in a manner that looked dangerous. It was certainly noisy, and then the Minister arrived. He was not a big man but his slightly hooked Phoenician nose, in his bony querulous face, conveyed that he was in no mood for gentle persuasion. "Put down those chairs," he said, quite loudly. "Any two fools can make a child; it takes a craftsman to make a chair." The chairs we used in the classrooms did not bear out the point about a "craftsman," but the sexual comments got home, since, as he must have known, we were most of us into masturbation, and an appreciation of girls. I had been given a small magazine-cutting of a beautiful young girl, nude, sitting with her feet curled under her, and smiling sadly, and beautifully, as if she had no idea she was naked, or, that if she knew, then it was all that could be expected of her considering the nature of the world. I masturbated madly with this image, and used my narrative powers to construct a story in which I told her I was in love with her, which I felt I was, and would she sleep with me. I knew that that last part would be hard to ask of her, but I hoped I would manage it. It never occurred to me that she might want to make love with—not me perhaps—but someone.

In the meanwhile childhood and its world drew off, rapidly, and for ever, and as the War and its horror came apart, my parents gave me the choice of either staying at Wycliffe as a boarder (it was about to return to its native village of Stonehouse near Stroud in Gloucestershire) or return to London, and enter Dulwich College as a day-pupil. Before I come to that portion of my life I should mention one other incident of my childhood. And in case the word horror seems too easily used, I ought to record that I was ten. I was in London for the holidays, and I discovered a paperback which induced, or confirmed, my worst fears about what it meant to be a Jew. The book offered an account by a concentration camp inmate of his experiences in —I forget which camp. He had escaped but, unable to rid himself of the imprint of the experience, had killed himself. The book I was reading was by a dead man. That in itself was sufficient to impress a child of ten. I remember his describing how the inmates (or the group in his hut) were made to stand to attention for hours on the square, without relief, with the urine dribbling down their legs. If they moved they were clubbed, and I cannot remember if in fact they weren't clubbed if it was perceived they were dribbling piss. There was no question of mercy being a constituent of this life. This was another world but not, I felt, one with which I was completely unfamiliar. That conjunction of brutality and humiliation affected me. My mother was at work in the Ministry of Fuel and Power, and I was therefore able to read the book with care. I cannot remember in detail what else the inmates endured, but that, I believe, was the mere tip of the ice. The hulk of experience drifted beneath the conscious surface.

The only anti-Semitic experience in Wycliffe came from a pupil in the Junior School, the boy named Modelski, son of a Polish General. The son dispensed poppycake as a mark of his favour—not to me I remember—and then he called me a dirty Jew. Par for the course, I would say in retrospect. We had a small scrap which, in fact, I won. I remember my subsequently being offered, and accepting, his poppycake; and it was delicious. Shades of my fellow-Jew, Miller. But that incident was exceptional. Wycliffe had its share of middle-class louts of which I may well have been one, but never, I am sure, any touched with anti-Semitism. I wonder if this was to do with the students having been recruited not so much from metropolitan England, but either from provincial Gloucestershire, or Wales. For the most part, not withstanding the attitudes of baiting cruelty towards students suspected of being homosexual, for which they had no better example from their elders and betters, I remember my fellow-students as composing an easygoing, tolerant and, on the whole, decent community. Is that time, or is it true?

My next academic experience was in Dulwich College. I joined it in 1945, after the War, when I was fourteen. It was, in the main, composed of London day-students, mostly middle-class and jacked-up with not aristocratic disdain but with a southern-English hauteur and self-importance. It is a school for which I feel no affection or resentment—although I liked a number of the students and, at last, formed two friendships which, however, I never felt deserving of. Gilkes, the Headmaster, was attempting to imbue the school not with his socialist principles, God forbid, but with a few modest egalitarian ideas, such as the cautious leaching into the pupil community of working-class boys who, by scholarship (not money) were to enter the College. This concession had brought in a few boys, but the students as a whole treated them badly. One boy, a short stubby person with a cockney accent, had been admitted, and subsequently promoted to a dubious and insidious alliance with the School authorities by his being made a Prefect. All the resentment against this form of deputized and divisive authority was visited upon this adolescent whose authority was flouted, and his person, his nature, in fact everything about him, mocked for his indefensible working-class character. (I was to experience the same prejudices in reverse when I came to work as a labourer seven years later.) Here indeed was complexity, for although I loathed the Prefect system, and could not like those who took the system upon themselves, yet equally I loathed the cruelty and prejudice of my middle-class students. I lacked the courage to remonstrate on his behalf, and could not have explained my position, rationally, even if I had tried.

The school had at least one double-standard. Tolerance, that easy virtue the English claim for themselves, was proclaimed for the school; so that you were free to join, or not join, either of the Corps and participate in their military activities. It was not compulsory, it was said; but on Field Days, you were punished with a day's detention if you were not a member. The majority of the students joined—this one must remember, within the context of a recently ended war where, one might think, few would welcome voluntary military duties.

I suppose I was a bad scholar, although—with some coaching in maths—I matriculated with modest success. I must frequently have swung the lead with regard to my willingness to work hard. I also bluffed. I spoke of my love of poetry to one or two teachers, and my hard-currency knowledge was called, and found wanting. I did not perform diligent intellectual work at that time. I never knew what it was to be rigorous, and all my true energies went into athletics—rugby—and then, suddenly, into one and then another relationship with a girl. All the girls seemed marvellous, and, as I think of them again, I still feel that they were—kind, generous with their sexuality, and probably more questioning intellectually than I was.

Eventually my truancy registered. Gilkes called me into his study and said: "You don't seem to have much use for Dulwich, Silkin, and frankly I don't think Dulwich has much use for you." Then he beat me. I should have refused, and I still occasionally relive my failure to resist his corporal punishment. "Leave at the end of term," he told me, and I did. I can see the egotism sheltering behind my timidity, but I am unable to redeem either; my failure to say "no" to Gilkes still dogs me.

One more incident belongs to this two-year period. I wanted by now to be a composer (I had not yet got to poetry) and at fourteen I had started to have lessons in the clarinet. I tried; but I did not give the tedious hours in practice that the instrument required. Nor did I apply myself to the theoretical mastery needed if one is to compose, and, in truth, I knew I was inadequate to the demands. Or rather, the testing of my ability never occurred because I never reached the stage where such a test could be applied. I wanted to express myself, and I badly needed admiration, and approval, for my would-be productions. Would it do if I were a critic of others' music? It would not. I composed a Mozartian melody which I tried to transcribe, but I did not succeed. I read about sonata form which I believe I understood, but harmony was beyond me, for the simple reason that I had not taught myself to read music. I was not manually effective with the clarinet, and at the end of the year, though I had tried, the results, I had to admit, were unimpressive. I did want to continue, but my parents felt that too much effort was being spent on lying about in somewhat degenerate fashion listening to music, and too little effort put into active study. They were probably right in the latter. They withdrew their financial support for the lessons and, instead, insisted on my putting all my efforts into passing my matriculation exams, in particular Latin. Latin was vital (I failed it) because one needed Latin in order to enter the Law, which was what they wanted me to do; enter the Law, and become a partner in my father's practice. My sense of inadequacy with respect to music (and much else) reinforced my sense of grievance at being so deprived of music lessons; and then, in despair, I asked myself an authentic question: what can I do now that's useful and creative. The answer came directly, as it had come once before: I can write poetry.

My first, at fifteen, was an attempt to turn the *Book of Exodus* into verse, but it is already rendered in powerful, efficient prose, and my attempts were unsuccessful. I rushed up to my bedroom and opening my grandfather's small bureau, which acted as my desk (it always felt amateurish), I set to work. Of course, lacking confidence, I attempted to do the least personally demanding thing. I had assumed, moreover, that I had the right to tamper with a Jewish book. Perhaps, had I been living in a Jewish society, I might have been less presumptuous. My next was a more modest attempt on the seasons. But I was all the time haunted by my failure to achieve anything in music, and suspected myself of turning to poetry in lieu of any achievements in a superior medium. "Articulate energy" I had not even considered yet, although by now I was, outside of school, reading—under the scourge of teachers' appraisal —Milton, Eliot, and Joyce's prose. A few years later, I was enjoying the poetry of Lawrence and Spender. But whatever the negative self-appraisal, I was getting some depth into my poetry. Years later I came upon two assertions, or confessions, in Isaac Rosenberg's letters. Writing to his patron Edward Marsh from an Army camp in England, late 1915, he declared: "I believe in myself more as a poet than a painter. I think I get more depth into my writing." And to Gordon Bottomley (who was to become one of Rosenberg's editors after the War) he wrote, in July 1916: "I am always afraid of being empty." Rosenberg expressed in those letters the negative feelings I had both about my poetry and myself. I had, of course, put into my music only a fraction of the labour Rosenberg had put into his art.

After my expulsion from Dulwich College, I worked for three months as a filing clerk in an Insurance Office in the City. "Let the fire of insurance take hold of you," said my section-manager. It did not. I left, and worked as a journalist in a small South London news agency. I was seventeen, and my National Service call-up was one year away. I was by this time quite desperate to prove myself as a writer, and like most apprentices, proof of achievement meant publication. To the question "what do you do?" I said I wrote . . . poetry. To my reply came the next question: "Have you published anything?" It was most of the time kindly framed, but it hurt, and its effect, of humiliation, got in the way of my seeing what little I had done. I tried to delude myself into imagining that if I wrote journalism, and published it, that would be an achievement. Several things were wrong with this. In the first place, I didn't believe it. In the second, although I knew that poetry was what I most wanted to achieve, I secretly downgraded even the most proficient journalism, thereby doing myself the double disservice —of attempting to substitute journalism and the publishing of it for the publishing of my poetry, and then, of depreciating another medium because I had not succeeded in the one in which I wanted success. To keep abreast of my multiple self-deceptions required not only much energy but also a painful violation of honesty, in order not to collapse into defeat. My parents were surely right. The proper course was to become a partner in my father's firm of solicitors. That meant returning to my Latin, and, more importantly, following my father's advice to "give up this bee in your bonnet about writing poetry; there have never been any Jewish poets." My persistence with my writing caused all kinds of —lesions—painful disturbances, and on one occasion there was a physical struggle with my father. After that, relations settled into coldness and hostility. My failure of courage, when I was fifteen, to take the furnished room I had found for myself in Victoria, made me feel further humiliated; but the worst passage of arms, which is what it felt like, was between my self and my mother. My growing sexual activity displeased both of them.

I was not a good journalist. I had neither the cool head needed to assemble facts quickly, accurately, and shrewdly; nor the will to press people into yielding information when they were in the midst of troubles. I was appalled at what made news, and what this agency was called upon to do by way of supplying items to the national London papers. Its busiest hour came when the agency, which was opposite a hospital in East Dulwich, witnessed, outside its front door, a gruesome crash between a London double-decker and a car. No need to find the news: there it lay. Yet when I and other employees knew that I had not much longer to work there, one of the journalists said: "You have always earned your money here." It provided much comfort to remember those carefully-said words.

I had asked for a quick call-up, at eighteen, and got it. I did my basic infantry training with the *Welch Regiment* in a camp called Dering Lines, Brecon, not far from the Brecon Beacons. I hated the servile way in which it became a matter of pride for us recruits to bullshit, shine, or blanco our equipment to perfection, but it was awkward to defect from this communal diligence and compliance because then one "let down the platoon." Why one should feel loyalty to an institution that bullied you if you didn't comply was something I could not work out. Compulsion and loyalty, I felt, were incompatible. I was back in the situation where group and in-dividual were at odds, and this bind in which I repeatedly found myself consisted of demands being made on me which I was either to comply with out of fear, or resist out of self-respect.

The bullying was not intolerable: you had to tolerate it. What made it bearable, for all of us if the truth is told, was the presence of a sergeant who, without being soft or lenient, made our existence seem a normal, credible one. He comforted us by what he was; not by trying, but by being. His was the truly untypical presence in the Army, the opposite of what Private Rosenberg described in the First World War as the way in which duties were served on one—with "brutal militaristic bullying meanness." I remember yet another incident of anti-Semitism, and the fact that I can remember and not have to distinguish it from any others says much for the absence at that time of such racism. There was a fair-haired tall cockney man with a nice-looking narrow long-drawn face. He had a whine in his voice, and as soon as he could he started to make references to "Welsh Jews"—by which he meant to compound his inflictions. I started to tremble with rage and fear and as soon as I found the opportunity, which was in the urinal, I said, while pissing, my voice, I am sure, shaking, that I was sorry to say it, and I expected to lose the fight, but that if he persisted in making these remarks, and throwing them in my direction, I would have, out of sheer self-respect, to fight him. To my relief, and amazement, the threat, which was no bluff, moderated his aggression. He tried it once more, glancing towards me with his head lifted up, like a cat, as if scenting me, the light from the ceiling of our wooden hut gleaming upon his uplifted glasses. But I continued bulling my boots, and the incident died away. I learned afterwards that he had failed to qualify for subsequent training in the Education Corps, and had wept. One more incident in this three-months period stays in my mind. One of the recruits in our hut was an Egyptian, and he had been trying to convey to all of us the quality of the colours of the sea, and sands, and sky in his country. The colour is mathematical, I said suddenly. That's exactly right, he declared with enthusiasm, and I felt proud to have matched this sudden insight with a landscape he was clearly missing; and a potential hostility melted. So writing, or words, or a way with words, had its uses, I reflected; as if this could substitute for my doing no writing. The business of survival in the Army made so great a demand that, for the time being, there seemed no energy remaining for what mattered more. For writing, too, implied, though on a less immediate level, survival.

Yet another incident from this period. My grandfather was now living with his daughter Selina, in Swansea, and he loathed my making the occasional visit. Perhaps his daughter did too, although she laughingly excused her father's dislike of my presence. I began to question myself as to what offence I had committed, on this or any other visit, the more so since it did not occur to me that although I might take intense pleasure in visiting my Swansea relatives, it might not be reciprocated. I also began, for the first time, to wonder if my Rubenstein maternal family were as warm as that ready demonstration of warmth was the supposed warrant of. This was all the more embarrassing, and confusing, because on this occasion I had brought with me a young Jewish friend who, although dubious of the timing of our visit—would we be able to get back on time to camp—had been persuaded, ill-advisedly in fact, that we had time and to spare. I was in the meanwhile trying to be hospitable, with my aunt's kindness.

We did not have time enough. When we reached Merthyr Tydfil, "the next bus had gone." All of a sudden my friend started to run, and the slim, diffident young man showed an energy, and stamina, I could not keep up with. I began to panic, and shouted for him to wait, but fear, though of another kind, had also taken possession of him. The night was bitterly clear, as if any guilt that one hid could no longer be concealed; and the moon lit the countenance of the earth and the spaces of the sky with a flashing coldness, everything in this landscape rendered immobile by this blazing clarity, except for two young men running and clattering in the night. The lake we now approached, him in the lead, looked as if gashed into the earth, and the zig-zag pines, so distant, so sharp, dark, viridian, looked like toys, one moment, then a condensed version of reality, the next; and so the scene alternated between horror, fear, reality, and play, in a manner that made me feel fearful and unstable. His head worn by its khaki badge bobbed up and down as his strides lengthened and he took off past the lake in its dark low-lying vale, low, and sinking even more as he ran and I followed. I have only a confused memory of whether we got a lift or simply arrived back to camp, eventually, sweating and frozen, and in a state of panic; whether we were late and excused, or on time, but badly shaken. Either way, I recollect no punishment, but a sense of failure on account of my being afraid, and a coldness on my part for feeling deserted by him. Fear had separated us. I believe that, in fact, we did get a lift, and that I, being behind him and therefore the first to en-

counter the lorry, had contrived to get us back to camp. And so my efforts (I said to myself) finally prevailed upon a situation deteriorating through my enthusiasm to reach Swansea, and my ineptitude at working out the logistics of the return journey. We never made the trip together again, and our friendship gently came apart. He had the mild head of a worn-down greyhound, aristocratic in his diffidence, which no amount of warmth and busyness on my part could change. (See the poem "The Armed," in *Autobiographical Stanzas*.)

On an earlier occasion, I had made a similar miscalculation (also see poem named above). The sky was as black, and emptied of light, as on the second occasion it had had the ferocity of day. Suddenly, as I turned the corner out of town, there were no lights. The orange sodium lamps simply blacked, and I went down on my hands and knees, crawling on the road to avoid spilling over the steep bank into a ravine I knew was somewhere below me. This is ridiculous, I reflected. As abruptly, I stood up and, with a panic like the one immediately preceding it, and heedless of the drop to my left, hurtled back to town. On this occasion I managed to hire a taxi; the man was good enough to consent to take me back, and to my shame I was slow to discharge my debt, which I was forced to clock up since I had on me insufficient money to pay for the hire. On we went into the night, the beams breaking up the darkness, past, almost immediately, the point on the road where my determination had so easily failed me, and so, into camp, safe and no wiser.

I began to despise myself, once more, and distrust the pithy character I had thought I possessed. On the contrary, panic and fear. I determined to change that.

I had occasion to test this resolution six months or so later. I was garrisoned in Bodmin, on the first lap of my training to become a Sergeant Instructor in the Education Corps, and I had failed to pass out. "Return to Unit?" I was faced with stiff questioning as to what I would do if confronted with such and such a situation. Suddenly I found myself barking back my answers, believing them, all civility, middle-class politeness, and deference gone. My wet-lipped overweight Captain said, when we came out of the interview, I didn't think you had it in you, and I didn't think you'd be given a second chance; but you have been given it. He didn't say he hoped I would pass, but when I eventually did, I did not forget the capacity I had found for standing up in the face of what looked like failure. I made myself unpopular, yet again, in my hut, which was filled with similar borderline cases, like myself, of soldiers who stood a fair chance of being returned to unit. I used, on what were now summer-weekends, to leave camp and wander round Cornwall. I had never seen such seascapes before, and the sun and colours astounded me. My senses were waking up. On my return, I discovered that the hut had on this occasion held sentence on my absence and had decided to pull me down a peg or two. My uniform had been done up into the form of a guy, stuffed with my bedclothes. The whole thing was ingenious and I started to pull it to pieces as quietly as I could, for everyone seemed asleep. Of a sudden a hut-mate was starting to box me, and I to wrestle with him (the man had confided in me that when he came out of the Army he was going to become a priest). Yet again, my simple wrestling helped me to survive, so much so that he appealed for help to another, sturdy recruit who announced he had judo and I had better stop this, which I did. The rest of my time in Bodmin was spent on camp, and I was glad to leave my peers behind, with the possibility that some would not pass the course. Vengeance is mine, saith the Lord. My worst fears about "the group" had been realized. I more than ever wished to be by myself and merely of myself.

After three attempts to get a posting abroad, I was in the end stationed in Hawthorn Camp, on the edge of the Wiltshire village of Corsham. There I taught illiterate soldiers from the Pioneer Corps, and those noncommissioned officers, veterans of the War, who had now to pass exams in order to substantiate the rank they had gained in the War. It seemed grossly unfair that men who had proved themselves should now be put through this humiliation and ordeal. Had they not earned their rank through their wartime conduct? It would appear not, said the Army. My sense of this injustice was no doubt compounded by my embarrassment at taking on these seasoned men, but whatever they may have said of me afterwards, and whatever resentments they may have felt at what seemed an injustice, after the first round of difficulties, I never had further problems. I was a sergeant instructor, and messed with these noncommissioned officers. They never made my life feel anything but compatible with theirs. And when I returned once, when my Army life was done with, complete with beard, suntan, and short-sleeved pullover, one of the sergeant-majors whom I respected, a dour Devon man, simply said to one of the orderlies, "Get the sergeant a cup of tea." Thus was my inadequate service given its tacit acceptance.

In fact the one truly hostile incident occurred when a huge aggressive Sergeant-major, whom I

was not instructing, confronted me about violence the Israelis had committed on the Arab village (in Israel) of Deir Yassin. They had murdered the villagers because of some confusion over the curfew. It remains *of course* a blot on the life of Israel; but the Sergeant-major also insisted on connecting it with the blowing up of the King David Hotel in Jerusalem, and the hanging of the British sergeant—with these words: "That's your lot that did it." Then a Sergeant-major, who had taken an avuncular liking to me, retorted quietly: "He didn't, so lay off him." Such kindnesses I have to report.

As for the privates to whom I tried to teach reading and writing, I remember, after three months, one of them saying in a gentle voice, "It's very interesting, Serge, but what's the difference between a large 'A' and a small one?"

By this time I must have gained some desperate measure of confidence because I started to write again, in sufficient amounts for me to put together, with the one poem I had kept from my sixteenth year, thirteen poems all from this Army period. I collected them under the title of *The Portrait and Other Poems* (1950) and I believe eight hundred (or was it four hundred?) were printed by a pay-for-it-yourself publisher called Arthur H. Stockwell, of Ilfracombe. Although I had contracted for it while I was in the Army, it did not appear until I was out. Twenty-three copies were sold at a price of nine pence (old money). It had sixteen pages.

There was always the chance that the statutory eighteen months National Service would be extended to two years. Such was my case, and by the time I had finished my full-time conscripted service, the Korean War had started, and I was committed to Z reserve with the possibility of my having to kill Koreans, on behalf of our American allies. I could think of no reason for hating Koreans, and even less for killing them whatever the commitment to Z reserve, and the more I thought about it the less I could square it with my moral and political beliefs. True, I had already served in the Army. True, it might be that my belated pacifist principles, and my newfound political ones, might each be a function of cowardice. But this possibility notwithstanding, nothing could justify war. One might find it expedient; that is all. And this was not a war I could even square with expediency. The Army had taught me one thing. That I knew nothing whatever about working-class existence. Apart from my long-lived adolescent relationship with a girl from Peckham, I had no idea how working-people managed to survive, what their expectations were, how they lived, and what was the quality of their lives. My relationship with Doris had not given me the understanding at the right time in my development. But it seemed to me now that I had to learn these things; without such understanding how could I consider myself a writer, and begin to grow into a complete human being? It began to seem as if being a man, and I was very anxious to become one, entailed making moral choices. This may sound self-righteous, but the choices were real enough. I wanted the experience of working with working-people, and of having the conditions they had. Whatever middle-class sophistry may make of the phrase "working-people," I knew the kind of life to which I was orientating myself, and it seemed there was no choice but to become a labourer—in the event, an unskilled one. Becoming a marketable item however was not easy. The first job I managed to get, after a miserable period on the London streets, was as a grave-filler and gardener in Fortune Green Cemetery, West Hampstead.

The alternative seemed to be to fight in the Far Eastern War. I told the Army I was not prepared to serve in the Korean War. (I had in my mind conceded that I would have had to fight in the Second World War.) I also told the Army that I was not prepared to do further Z reserve, and that they must try me if they felt I was in default of duty—which they certainly did feel. They accused me of running away, to which I replied that although it must seem like that, the problem was that I was "moving about" London, living in different furnished rooms. I felt ashamed to admit that I kept being chucked out of these places. In one of them, I had a fight with the landlord (an ex-colonial policeman) who, for some trivial offence I had committed, insisted that prior to my quitting his premises at the end of the week he must expropriate my record player. It belonged, in fact, to my friend Philip Inman, and in the ensuing struggle as to who would have possession of this valuable piece of property, we ended up on the floor with me uppermost. At this moment his wife burst in and, seizing my small but useful metal kettle, hit me over the head. The next thing I remember is my being on the ground, on my back, bleeding copiously, feeling faint, with the pair of them bending over me with alarm. I took the afternoon off from the cemetery, and the doctor put some stitches in my scalp. He did not believe that I had fallen onto the pavement, and was solicitous; but I had given my word to my landlords, and foolishly kept it. Nevertheless, I wrote a poem to celebrate the whole event, and inked it onto the otherwise drab cream wall. I remember nothing of it

except these two lines which expressed the experience succinctly:

You hit me over the head with a tin
You let the blood out and you let the germs in.

I was not angry, only miserable.

I can understand why the Army thought I was on the run, but I tried to correct this impression by giving them the address of every new furnished-room I occupied. They must have had a fat file of comic documentation. Indeed the episode's absurdity grew. The Army sent a charming officer to my parents, or so Mother told me, to plead with them on the one hand, and threaten me with jail on the other. They also threatened me directly, with jail. I replied, having got advice from Civil Liberties, that they must try me first. Things now possessed the gravure quality of nightmare, and I found I could think of little else. Even the room I lived in reflected this bare, limited, divided life—a room cut in two by a partition—half a room for sleeping in, and the other half for my meals. Then the waters broke, and they released me. I received a letter from the forebearing Army, its typed terse message on pale-green bank paper. It read: "Subject TA discharge: send back your uniform."

It was just at this time that I started to sleep with Cynthia and thus form my first adult relationship. Outwardly, I rejoiced. But for years after, I had this, my second, recurring dream. The earlier one had been of my escaping from a concentration camp, but of always being captured and returned. This Army dream consisted of my being called up, and of my being unable to find all my equipment necessary for imminent parade. Sometimes it was my belt that was missing; sometimes my gaiters. Sometimes my beret was gone, and at other times I barely had more than my tunic. I mention these details to suggest the powerful effect dereliction and its consequences had upon me; and years later, when I read of Sassoon, an Army officer in the First War, defecting from service out of moral scruples, I could only put the book down, close to tears, in admiration at the man's courage. How slight, in comparison, was my action.

The work in the cemetery was hard but invigorating. I had a physical breakdown in the first or second week of employment because, through lack of money immediately prior to taking the job, and because of their rule of holding the first week's pay by, I had not eaten properly and still, the hard work notwithstanding, was not managing to do so. I landed up in hospital pissing blood. Here, in Hampstead—the date is September 1951—my friend

Philip Inman bought me a present of Auden's *Collected Shorter Poems*, and these I eagerly devoured. By the time I resumed work, I was fit. I got thrown out of this job after nine months for being found sitting on a tombstone reading Shaw's *Saint Joan*, and laughing. I think it was my laughter that our conventional foreman found insupportable. And I left. A cemetery is a place of tears.

It was, in fact, a living example of class distinction. The upper part of the cemetery was reserved for the middle-class, whose graves were six feet deep and held one person privately. The paupers' graves, in the physically lower part of the burial ground, were about twenty feet in depth and, like inverted sky-scrapers, housed as many bodies in them as you could comfortably stack. After you had buried the first, and dropped enough London clay to cover the coffin, you waited for the next. And on, until you filled each grave with, I think, some five dead. The London clay baked hard in the summer so that when you dropped it in lumps onto the flimsy wood coffins they burst open and you saw the corpse wrapped in white sheets of rough cloth. But you covered it over. In the winter, however, the clay was soft and oozed, so that the bones of the bourgeoisie, which had by this time decayed and become bluish green and semi-fluid, worked their way down to mingle with the ooze of the paupers. So that you got democracy, but in a somewhat belated fashion. "Don't handle the stuff," one of the older diggers said to me when I expressed surprise at the half-sweet smell. "Why, what is it?" I asked.

I seemed to get on with the Irish who, I think, must have felt some kind of solidarity with a member of another minority. It was always unspoken, but it existed—at a time when the notice boards of newsagents held cards advertising rooms to let with the proviso, "No dogs, Jews, Irish, or children." The community of those discriminated against was a pleasure to belong to, even if it made finding furnished rooms more difficult. A fine, comic poem by Wole Soyinka called "Telephone Conversation" touches on this very hazard. At any rate, I liked the Irish. I was affecting a rough manly exterior at this time, and they found this both amusing and, so it appeared, acceptable. There were several incidents which ended in friction (none of them with Irish people), and one of them, which must have been provoked by my cockiness, resulted in a wrestling bout and humiliation. Another incident was caused by a man called Spike, who could neither read nor write, and who caused some discreet hilarity one break-time, in our hut, by his holding a newspaper before him, studiously, but upside-down. A minor

but unhappy episode, but though I was not one of those who gestured and winked, it was me that was guilty, because I spoke with a middle-class accent which I would not modify. Finally he provoked me into a fight. I had been terrified by this oncoming prospect and had been taking boxing-lessons in a club. I was not keen on boxing and would willingly have stepped aside from the situation, which now divided the workers in the place—those for and those against—those who said I would win, and no doubt those who said Spike would. "He's soft," one of my kinder supporters said quietly. "Don't you worry." I did worry, but there was no stepping aside. The lessons in boxing discontinued after I had my nose badly messed, but the conflict with Spike took place nonetheless. In the event, that too turned into a wrestling bout, but this, to my astonishment, I won. I had expected a much stronger man. Perhaps aggression renders one weaker in the event. Whatever the cause, the fight that I subsequently lost was to a friend of Spike's. One tumble makes another.

Later, I tried to write Babel-like stories about these incidents, for I had been reading Isaac Babel's *Red Cavalry*, which I greatly admired. I wanted to emulate the brevity and concision of these stories. But could not.

By the time Cynthia and I had got together, my job with the cemetery was over, but not my experience with cemeteries or death. However, our life filled with excitement and incident. Also, with terror and creativity.

I had been working for the National Cash Register Company. This American firm appeared to be anti-union, perhaps out of unthinking habit more than deliberate animosity, and when I tried to form a small union of janitors so as to fight a command for overtime without overtime rates, they were so enraged that they gave me the sack. What enraged *me* about the episode was the bullying bogus politeness of the foreman: "And if, gentlemen (he said to the five janitors), you don't want to do the overtime, perhaps you might like to find a job elsewhere." At any rate, my resistance brought me the sack. But not before they had paid me two days' holiday pay, which amounted to five pounds. Only a pound less than a week's wages. Was it fear or play-safe that prompted this payment; or fairness? I believe the former. But for whatever reason there I had, for the first time since the Army, five pounds in my hand, for which I had no immediate use other than for my plan, which was to start a literary magazine. For besides the fact that hardly anyone would publish me, I also felt that there was an apathy in England, both in social relations and towards new writing. I therefore called the magazine *Stand,* because it was meant as a *Stand* against this double malaise. And indeed, *Stand,* which I started in London in February 1952, when Cynthia and I were living in Strathray Gardens in Swiss Cottage, has continued with the double focus it originally deployed. Before I left NCR I purchased, with the help of the friendly head of the stationery department, some pale green duplicating paper. With this and the use of a friend's duplicating machine I produced the first issue, which contained poems by Philip Inman, Thomas Blackburn, Maurice Hurst (Capitanchick), Jon Wynne-Tyson, and Iris Orton. Cynthia provided the spur of intellectual discrimination. I was used to my father's questioning mind, but hers was questioning and literary, and it constituted a parallel driving energy. When we were living in Swiss Cottage, our first child, Adam, was born.

Shortly afterwards, we moved to Blackheath where we had managed to find what was so difficult to obtain—an *unfurnished* flat. This was my first security since coming out of the Army; and the result of no longer feeling as if I were on the run, and of having a beautiful companion who possessed an active intelligence, was that, for the first time, I stopped moving through the world. It was as if, for the first time, a stillness had descended on me, and instead of my moving and the world being a backcloth to my movement, my life became still—like a screen—and the world flowed across it. My paranoia, which before had been both incipient and pressing, now came out into the open, a fully fledged neurosis—as if now I could afford the energy, the leisure, and the strength for it. I could therefore begin to grapple with it, and I believe that it was in some way intimately connected with my poetry which, also for the first time perhaps, I began to write in earnest. Of these poems, the first to be written was "The Cunning of an Age," which I sent to the *New Statesman;* and although it was rejected I had an encouraging note from the literary editor, Janet Adam-Smith. It certainly set the theme, or one of them, for those poems that formed my first book, *The Peaceable Kingdom,* so-called after the work of the American primitive artist Edward Hicks. Chatto and Windus published my book in 1954, and five more after that. C. Day Lewis was then reader at Chatto.

"The Cunning of an Age" is a fluid, narrative poem but in addition to poems like this, I was writing colder two-line stanza poems of which "Carved" and "A Death to Us" are instances. I started to publish and broadcast poems, but all the time my employment never varied: I was an unskilled worker. Sometimes I hodded bricks, sometimes I measured parts for telephones in a machine shop, or I worked in a badly ventilated mill in *British Ropes,* where I helped to cause an accident. But I was an unskilled person.

It now became clear that Adam was not making progress like other children, and soon, though no doctor would tell us what was wrong, it became evident that in "normal terms" Adam was not normal, not equipped to function with all his senses intact and fully continuous. This seemed the remorseless counterpoint to my poems. Or I should say that my poems provided that positive distillation of pain and exultation counter to Adam. Adam who could not grow like other children, and who seemed the badge of our failure.

At this time I formed a friendship with one who has since consistently helped, encouraged, and actively criticized my work, the fiction writer and poet Emanuel Litvinoff. I first met him in 1952 at the Ben Uri Art Gallery with Louis Golding, and Litvinoff was then working as a journalist for the *Jewish Observer and Middle East Review,* edited by Jon

*Emanuel Litvinoff*

*Silkin, Iowa City, 1968*

Kimche. It was Litvinoff who remarked of my poem "The Coldness," written in 1959, that the other half remained to be added (it had first ended with the thirty-second line). That was the kind of criticism Litvinoff provided me with and he was invariably correct (the other person who helped, and published, me at this time was the poet Dannie Abse). Litvinoff helped me focus my consciousness, and then, focus my attention on my Jewishness—an act that in turn helped me to focus my attention on what I was as a human being. In turn, that helped me to focus on the nature of my intellectual capacities.

Litvinoff belonged to quite another part of my life. He hardly impinged, I hardly dared have him impinge, on my working-class life. For although Litvinoff came from a working-class family, and was brought up in the poverty of the Jewish East End, by the time I met him he had been married for some years to this beautiful and elegant woman who ran a model-agency; and he was settled with children and a home in Golders Green. He had published two books of poems and was now writing plays and fiction. The milieu of his life made me feel that my

working life was at once more real (or do I mean actual) and substantial than my life as it connected with his—more basic, that is. Yet at the same time, I wanted to have the comfort and sense of well-being his life radiated, as well as that feeling, intellectual substance, which my own life was just beginning to develop. And still, where my life seemed real, if desperate, the coin of his life, had *I* succeeded in replicating it, would have seemed counterfeit.

Two other friendships of an entirely different quality were formed at this time: with Alan Brownjohn and Bernard Bergonzi. Alan lived in Catford and Bernard in New Cross, and they came regularly to our flat in Blackheath. I envied their steadiness and calmness, but they managed to share that, and my respect for them increased.

And all the time, Adam made at best only intermittent progress, so that as my small pile of poems grew, so did his uncommunicating life, with its life that my mother forbade. I was angry with her, and yet I could see what she and others were saying, and I could also see that Adam's condition frightened her. I could not, alas, afford her any sympathy be-

*Merle Brown, 1968*

cause I was myself far too desperate. Her fear made me frightened, yet made me love Adam the more. Slowly my life was braiding into an almost intolerable tussle, except that it had to be tolerated. In Rosenberg's incomplete play *The Amulet*, which he composed in the trenches, the Nubian says to Lilith:

> None can exceed their limit, lady:
> You either bear or break.

Precisely. And as the life of Adam grew in its apparent deficiencies, and my poems accumulated, and my relationship with Cynthia became more ruffled, so my other friendships with Litvinoff and Day Lewis, always friendships in which they gave infinitely more than they received, grew, until my life seemed to reach a choking point with both the rich and positive, and the failing things. Full to satiety.

And then came the event that seemed to tear up but not cancel life. Adam was being looked after in hospital and he and Cynthia were summoned to County Hall, the authoritative building of the London County Council, so that doctors could test him. If, as a result of these tests he was deemed educable, he would remain in the hospital where, so it seemed to Cynthia and me, he was making a little intermittent progress. But still, progress. But if these tests were negative, and he was considered ineducable, then he would be put into a mental institution. With all this balanced in her mind, Cynthia had to wait with Adam in County Hall, in a draughty corridor, for four hours, until eventually doctors contrived to see Adam and test him.

Adam was transferred to a mental hospital. We received this hospital telegram which said that he was critically ill and that we had better visit him. (We had no telephone.) When we arrived, the hospital, which was in large grounds, was filled with mad people, as if the world had crammed into a huge field, and were walking about in it. (See the poem "Air That Pricks Earth." in *Selected Poems*.) One of the mad, a woman of about forty, came up to me and gently taking my hand, raised it to her lips and kissed it. Then she as gravely and as gently released me, and we were free to go to Adam in his ward. He lay in a large, adult bed. This small child slowly turned towards us and with these huge tears slowly gathered in his eyes, he shed them, and in such a way that, as they fell out of his eyes, he died. It was over very slowly, but almost done before we had realized it. There seemed nothing to do and nothing to say. I could not weep, and nor did Cynthia do anything but kiss him. The last line of the poem composed itself as he shed his huge tears:

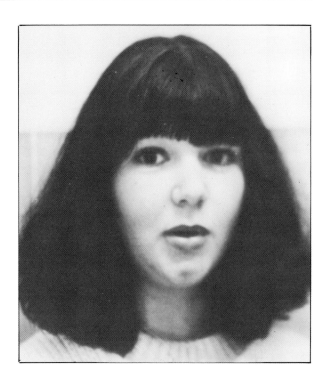

*Daughter Rachel, age twenty-three*

> And out of his eyes two great tears rolled,
> like stones, and he died.

I knew it was a line of a poem as soon as it had, in an involuntary way, formed in my mind; and I knew that as soon as we got home, I would write the poem to vindicate Adam against all those who had said he should have died at birth, oh, much sooner than he did; or that perhaps he should not have been born. And I had to write the poem because the two tears, that he had shed, seemed to weep, not for himself, but for us, and therefore that weeping was an act of generosity, a supremely conscious, intelligent, and generous act. And it vindicated Adam's being, always supposing, that is, that his life needed such vindication. Thus Adam, and our second child, David, are the only two human creatures in *The Peaceable Kingdom*, a collection otherwise devoted to animals, because it was animals, I felt, who were innocent in this sense: that unlike human beings they killed only to eat, and not out of pleasure, not out of what the Germans, who have a word for it, call *Schadenfreude* —a love of inflicting or witnessing pain. It was this book which the American critic and teacher Merle Brown was to read, and like; and because of his liking it, Merle was to invite me to his University for a six-week stay, in 1965. My first visit to America, with Catherine Lamb. But that is another and different story.

*Jon and Lorna Silkin, Jerusalem, 1980*

Strangely enough, my life has gradually become more and more involved with Americans. In the fifties I developed a friendship with the American poet and art critic Gene Baro. Merle is dead and so is Gene. I am now married to the American fiction writer Lorna Tracy. By 1986 we will have been together seventeen years. But this sketch of my life, and my development as a man who writes, ends at the point when I had entered my twenty-fourth year, and *The Peaceable Kingdom* had been published only a few months previously.

*BIBLIOGRAPHY*

**Poetry:**

*The Portrait and Other Poems.* Ilfracombe, England: Stockwell, 1950.

*The Peaceable Kingdom.* London: Chatto & Windus, 1954; Boston: Yorick Books, 1969; Boston: Heron Press, 1975.

*The Two Freedoms.* London: Chatto & Windus, 1958; New York: Macmillan, 1958.

*The Re-ordering of the Stones.* London: Chatto & Windus, 1961.

*Flower Poems.* Leeds, England: University of Leeds, School of English, 1964.

*Nature with Man.* London: Chatto & Windus, 1965.

*Penguin Modern Poets 7,* with Richard Murphy and Nathaniel Tarn. Harmondsworth, England: Penguin, 1966.

*Poems New and Selected.* London: Chatto & Windus, 1966; Middletown, Conn.: Wesleyan University Press, 1966.

*Three Poems.* Cambridge, Mass.: Pym-Randall, 1969.

*Vernon Watkins and Jon Silkin: Poems.* London: Longmans, Green, 1969.

*Vernon Scannell and Jon Silkin: Pergamon Poets VIII.* Oxford, England: Pergamon, 1970.

*Amana Grass.* London: Chatto & Windus, 1971; Middletown, Conn.: Wesleyan University Press, 1971.

*Killhope Wheel.* Ashington, England: Mid Northumberland Arts Group, 1971.

*Air That Pricks Earth.* Rushden, England: Sceptre Press, 1973.

*The Principle of Water.* Cheadle, England: Carcanet Press, 1974.

*A "Jarapiri" Poem.* Knotting, England: Sceptre Press, 1975.

*The Little Time-Keeper.* Ashington, England: Mid Northumberland Arts Group, 1976; New York: Norton, 1977; Sydney, Australia: Wild & Woolley, 1976.

*Two Images of Continuing Trouble.* Richmond, England: Keepsake Press, 1976.

*Jerusalem.* Knotting, England: Sceptre Press, 1977.

*Into Praising.* Sunderland, England: Ceolfrith Press, 1978.

*The Lapidary Poems.* Knotting, England: Sceptre Press, 1979.

*The Psalms with Their Spoils.* London and Boston: Routledge & Kegan Paul, 1980.

*Selected Poems.* London and Boston: Routledge & Kegan Paul, 1980.

*Autobiographical Stanzas: "Someone's Narrative."* Durham, England: Taxvs Press, 1983.

*Footsteps on a Downcast Path.* Bath, England: Mammon Press, 1984.

*The Ship's Pasture.* London and New York: Routledge & Kegan Paul, 1986.

## Nonfiction:

*Out of Battle: The Poetry of the Great War.* London and New York: Oxford University Press, 1972; London and

New York: Routledge & Kegan Paul, 1987.

## Editor of:

*New Poems 1960,* with Anthony Cronin and Terence Tiller. London: Hutchinson, 1960.

*Living Voices: An Anthology of Contemporary Verse.* London: Vista, 1960.

*Poetry of the Committed Individual: A "Stand" Anthology of Poetry.* London: Gollancz, 1973.

*New Poetry 5,* with Peter Redgrove. London: Hutchinson, 1979.

*The Penguin Book of First World War Poetry.* London: Allen Lane, 1979. Revised edition. Harmondsworth, England and New York: Penguin, 1981.

*Stand One: Winners of the "Stand" Magazine Short Stories Competition,* with Michael Blackburn and Lorna Tracy. London: Gollancz, 1984.

*The Penguin Book of First World War Prose.* Harmondsworth, England: Penguin, 1988.

## Translator of:

*Against Parting,* by Nathan Zach. Newcastle upon Tyne, England: Northern House, 1968.

# Andrew Sinclair

*1935-*

*Andrew Sinclair, 1977*

I always wanted to scribble from the first time that I covered my bedroom wall with scrawls from my mother's lipstick, and was spanked for it. The war made it likely that I would write, the divide between the dream and daily life, the desire and the conditions, the need to describe the differences and reconcile them.

War children, we were not the same. The adults remembered peace, they thought the war abnormal. To us, wartime was forever, in Oxford. We listened to a fairy story, often told, but always good to hear. Instead of "Once upon a time . . ." the story would begin,

"Before the war when . . ." I was four years old when it began and I had no memory of peacetime. In those magic days, there were all the toys money could buy; but in the war, our tin soldiers were taken away to make Spitfires. Before the war, there was all the food we could eat, even chocolate and trifle; but in the war, there was the weekly cake queue at Oliver and Gurden's, where we could buy two shillings' worth of dry Madeira cake off ration, if we hung about the baskets and waists of housewives for a whole afternoon. It was no accident that the first very short story of mine published in the school magazine when I was six told the story of a small boy starving to death, nursed in his final illness by his mother in rags. I still remember the last sentence. "'Give me an orange, an orange,' said the boy, but there was none, and the cottage on the moor fell into silence again."

There was also the blackout. Before the war, the night streets were as light as day and the skies blazed with fireworks to remember Guy Fawkes on the Fifth of November even more brightly than the searchlights laying grids on the dark after the sirens sounded. But in the war, we felt our way along the pavements by touching the garden walls under the dead street-lamps, and we traced the numbers of strange houses in braille with our fingers. The blackout was for ever, in Oxford.

Rationing was our existence. Coupons set the limits to what we wore and ate. Our desires were cut into coloured squares by the scissors of grocers. Children cannot live in last year nor imagine next year; the present is, is and always will be until they grow up and remember forever what their youth was. So we were war children and our world was too dark and too cold, always makeshift and short of things, a world of the fourth-hand, the worn, the patched, and the drab. Our fathers were away fighting and our mothers tried to protect us from the war, but it squeezed them and us, reaching into every home in khaki gloves to pinch and scrape.

We had fled to Oxford when war was declared because there was a rumour that a secret agreement had been reached with Hitler. Although Hitler was no gentleman, we did have the riposte of the Royal Air Force to make him keep his word. The pact was said to be that, if we did not bomb Heidelberg, he would not bomb Oxford and Cambridge. The perfidious British naturally surrounded the university cities with aerodromes and filled the Oxford suburb of Cowley with war factories. But Hitler kept his promise; the nearest bombs fell at Boar's Hill and only killed some earthworms. So the war for me did not mean blitz and ruins, but shortages for ten years until rationing ended.

My mother, my elder brother, and I lived in an old brick semidetached house in Polstead Road, a mile north of the city centre, and a few doors down from where Lawrence of Arabia had spent his youth. He had a hut at the bottom of his family's narrow garden, where he used to dream of a desert empire from his tiny shed. Our garden, a few yards wide and a cricket pitch long, had a hen run behind the stumps. We had eggs for the duration, and the fact that we named each hen individually Whitey or Brownie did not stop us from enjoying them when they finally reached the pot. Eggs, pickled in great pitchers; hundreds of Kilner jars of bottled plums and apples and jams; occasional salt-dried meat *biltong* from South Africa and Spam from America, these were our luxuries, and Marmite on fried bread. The war made us all pioneers. My mother made and preserved food from scraps and ends, and she darned clothes until jerseys and socks were joined patches. We built whole battle fleets and tank armies out of pins and wood. What we could not make ourselves, we had to do without. So we learned how to fix things and imagine them into what they were not. Deprivation is a great improviser.

Memories of war. The androgynes in the ARP in dark blue fat-rumped trousers checking our blinds to see no streak of light showed. The mysterious airmen in lighter blue, flown from nowhere, about to go on their missions. The Yanks stopping me to give me gum, tasting of rubber and peppermint.

"Are you sure you can spare it, sir?" I asked as I was taught to ask, and they laughed from great heights at such odd politeness from a kid with chilblains on his bare knees. The Spitfire grounded in St. Giles, where we could sit in the cockpit and pull the joystick, if we had sixpence to help buy another Spitfire off the conveyor-belt. The doctor who stitched up my cut thumb without anaesthetic because it had all gone to the soldiers. "Don't cry, boy, there's a war on," and I bit my lip as the needle and thread went through the flesh, and I did not cry because I was eight and the soldiers did not cry, did they? Then the lodgers who were billeted on us, and they cried louder than children. They were the wives and parents of the wounded dying in the head hospital in St. Margaret's Road, where my mother visited, and where I used to sneak past four times a day on the way to school in case the nurses rolled out Frankensteins on wheelchairs with only a ball of bandages above their dressing gowns and slits to represent mouth and eyes. They almost always died in there, but the one survivor in ten would be rolled out as a mummy to scare a small boy witless.

Everyone worked and had no time. And when I first became old enough to understand the war, we had begun to win. In fact, we won so often that a sense of fair play made me wish for a few German victories. My games were filled with tanks and guns, dogfights and flak, convoys and submarines on the battle-map which my mother called her carpet. But there was a private world out of wartime behind the drawn blinds, when the coal fire scorched the grate and blackberry jelly covered the toast and my mother read us Dickens, *Oliver Twist* and *A Tale of Two Cities*. He and Walter Scott, whose total work I read between the age of ten and eleven, were my interior escape routes under the barbed wire, the first a tunnel to slum and blood and thunder, the second a refuge of chivalry and fair ladies and gentlemen with maces.

Yet I had my little concentration camp for eight months of the year, an educational institution called the Dragon School, which taught me admirably, French at six, Latin at eight, Greek at ten, and precious little science. For obvious reasons, German was not then an option on the curriculum. The school fitted me to take a scholarship to Eton, where I decided to go because I lost an argument about the best of schools in the playground. I had a photographic memory until I was twelve, reading a poem at night, and remembering it perfectly in the morning. But puberty put holes in my head, and on the final speech-day, I burst into tears at last, completely forgetting how to continue with "O wild West Wind, thou breath of Autumn's being. . . ." Since then, I have been just as good at forgetting as remembering, and both are essential.

My best escape of all was down Polstead Road, across Walton Street, and up a little track called Aristotle Lane. There I ran away every holiday to fish for silver roach with scarlet fins in the onyx canal under the humped brick bridge. From time to time, a red and yellow and black barge was pulled past by a clopping Shire horse, on to London, on to London, down to the Thames, and as far as Rio, where did the canal end, how did I know? And further up Aristotle Lane was the higher hump of the railway bridge with its sides of corrugated iron, where I could stand in the middle while the steam trains shuddered the boards beneath my feet and sent up smoke on either side to make a cathedral of cloud above me. And beyond was Port Meadow, where the horses and the cows grazed on the common land, rolling away and away to the bright river, with the swans so strong they would break a leg with their beaks or fly away gracefully to the ends of the earth.

So I escaped the war at Oxford. And the war was over when I reached College at Eton. My parents were divorced now and gone to Africa, where my mother had married again. Many holidays were spent with steprelations, who did not want to bother with me. So my room at Eton College became my home, with its folding bed and elementary desk. The scholars were set apart from the rest of the private school; in my case, because my family were not rich, my education was free. The school had originally been endowed by King Henry VI for seventy poor scholars, and so we were, the strongest and meanest of us pitted every year in the Wall Game against the best of the Oppidans, the eleven hundred Etonians whose rich parents paid fees for their sons' exclusive education. If the Battle of Waterloo was won on the playing fields of Eton, Passchendaele and the Somme were fought to a draw in the Wall Game. Brutish, immobile, nasty, long, and without result, the Wall Game was a mudbath and a class war each St. Andrew's Day between the cleverest youths in the country and the most privileged ones. I ended as the leader of the game, the Keeper of the Wall, although the memory I keep of it is when I felt a still body beneath my boots, shouted the traditional "Air," the scrimmage broke up, and we hauled out a boy just alive who left his death-mask imprinted face down in the mud.

It was a classical education. By seventeen, we were writing Greek hexameters and Latin lyrics. Homer was our Chaucer, and science was a joke, a faint smell of rotten eggs in a test tube. So many contemporary writers had been Collegers at Eton that my dreams of becoming one had a track record. Cyril Connolly had written a famous essay, *Enemies of Promise,* to try to prove that an education at Eton was the crippling of literary inspiration, but he was only trying to excuse his own failed promise. George Orwell, then called Eric Blair, was a Colleger. The Sitwells were from Eton, Henry Green, Anthony Powell. When Somerset Maugham with his old lizard's face came down to talk to our Literary Society, he declared that one in five of England's leading novelists came from Eton, as high a proportion as sat in the average Conservative cabinet: Harold Macmillan was an old Colleger too. Maugham discouraged us from becoming writers before the age of forty, recommending us only to copy out Swift and Defoe and his own works before then, but we reckoned that he feared our competition.

My last year at Eton, I had won a history scholarship to Trinity College, Cambridge, although I had to do two years National Service in the army before going up to the university. I was writing bad poems, although one was printed in a defunct magazine called *Truth,* and trying short stories. Fortunately, I edited the school magazines. I was also in "Pop," a self-electing group of school prefects in gaudy waistcoats, who disciplined the rest of the school and were envied as only the very exclusive are by the exclusive and excluded. Yet I was penniless and homeless in the holidays, my father on colonial service in East Africa, my mother with my lawyer stepfather in West Africa. I had twenty pounds to cover the four weeks of an Easter holiday. I ventured into the boardinghouses of Bayswater, had my first affair with a South African student pianist who played the Park Lane bars to earn a living, thought I had plunged into low life and real life, and astonished my contemporaries in "Pop" with my adventures during the luxurious weekends I spent in their families' country houses. I was living at extremes of new experience, and I was hungry, with little to eat from the gasrings of Bayswater and less in the country houses, because I did not dare take much from the butler's passing silver tray and could not select from the armoury of knives and forks that flanked the crested plates. Only at the last meeting of the Literary Society did I read out an account of myself down and out in London and Bayswater, which provoked the headmaster out of slumber. "Oh dear," he told a friend of mine when I had left, "I see Orwell strikes again."

My stepfather died, and my mother came back to England, distraught and needing me. I had to listen all that summer and realize that I had become the only man in my mother's life: my elder brother was wasting out his National Service behind barbed wire by the Suez Canal. My stepfather had been a Major in the Coldstream Guards; his wish was that I should try to join the Brigade of Footguards and his old Regiment. By a combination of toughness, risk, and luck, I managed to survive the Brigade of Guards' training camp at Caterham and do well at the Officers Training School at the old ducal home of Eaton Hall. I was accepted as an Ensign in the Third Battalion of the Coldstream Guards, then posted on Public Duties in London, which meant living in Wellington Barracks by Buckingham Palace, and guarding it, St. James's Palace, the Tower of London, and the Bank of England in a succession of quaint ceremonies and military rituals that made us both the security and the chorus line of the London scene and season.

The debutante dances and the Royal Garden Parties, the Trooping of the Colour and the Ceremony of the Keys, the manners of London Society and the Officer's Mess, these arcane observances were the material for my first novel, *The Breaking of Bumbo,* written in five concentrated weeks in a summer vacation at Cambridge at the age of twenty-two. I had been shocked as if I were still a child in the war. The state imposed its conflict and authority upon me. As a Cambridge undergraduate, I was an Army Reserve Officer, and I was called up during my second year at Cambridge for the Suez crisis. I refused to go and set off to fight for the Hungarians against the Russians instead. I had been reading political philosophy as well as history at Cambridge, and the intervention at Suez struck me as imperialism and murder, while the Hungarian revolt against Russian control seemed in the just cause of liberty and human rights. I never even reached Budapest owing to the intervention of my mother. I returned, my heroism between my legs, to Trinity. The Brigade of Guards in its wisdom decided not to court-martial me for desertion, and I was left to write a black comedy about a young Brigade of Guards officer who fails to lead a mutiny at the time of Suez, and is blessed and received into the British Establishment.

The short novel was an immense critical and commercial success. It was published at the right time and on a left subject. With John Osborne's play *Look Back in Anger* and Kingsley Amis's *Lucky Jim* and John Braine's *Room at the Top,* my little novel was held to be the work of the *soi-disant* "Angry Young Men." It was the only one of these works written from within the Establishment. I used to explain the difference between myself and the other Angry Young Men—all older, incidentally, and in their thirties—by saying that they were kicking their way in, while I was kicking my way out. They did, indeed, all move towards the right wing while I moved towards the left.

Cambridge was my time of trial, of change, of awakening. In an essay for an unpublished collection written by young Oxbridge contemporaries to be edited by the blind Indian writer Ved Mehta, I analysed at the time what I thought the university had done for me.

Two and a half years at Cambridge had taught me that conviction was another name for prejudice, that the closed book of the probable truth was only visible to the open mind, and that Socrates was always right by never saying that he was. I had learned a little of the amused, suspicious, responsible, sceptical tolerance of English humanism. My chief commitment seemed not to be committed, especially to any unseen fiction. Creeds were only for those weak enough to need them; they should not be imposed on others. Even my subject, history, was meaningless except for the meaning that I wanted to give it. I had been taught reasoned doubt and reasoned belief. For a difficult person like myself, who could only envy those cradle-believers, the pure in heart, both doubt and be-

lief needed to be approached warily. I began to learn this approach at Cambridge.

In another summer-long vacation, I wrote my second novel, *My Friend Judas.* It was about an orgiastic May Week at Cambridge after the Tripos Examination and my first frustrated love affair. It was written in an overwrought prose, a mixture of J.D. Salinger, Dylan Thomas, current slang and the King James Bible. It was also successful, and I found myself, with William Golding, as Faber and Faber's leading novelist. My contemporaries were breaking through into the theatre and the media as rapidly as I was. In a piece I wrote at the time about why the war children burst through so easily in the late fifties, I used the word "satire" as the reason that we succeeded.

*Sinclair at twenty-four*

Our glory was to knock, knock, knock. And as we knocked, from *The Breaking of Bumbo* to *Beyond the Fringe,* the walls came tumbling down. For the whole edifice of class and Empire and the great white gentleman was rotten and was garrisoned by men, who had lost heart and were tired. There was no resistance to the war gang. As we knocked

Britain and its institutions, we found we were knocking at a creaky door that swung open at the first bare knuckle. And our knocking proved to be more for our own opportunity than for our elders' doom.

So came the nineteen-sixties. And the war gang swept into the media. My Cambridge contemporaries were media professionals almost before they left university—Jonathan Miller, Michael Frayn, Trevor Nunn, many others. The war children were inventive and adaptable and took to the new communications techniques like sparrows to a dust-bath. They were used to risk and improvisation, skilled in the daily survival that war imposes on the young. They were contemptuous of the mistakes of the past that had given them such a harsh childhood and adolescence; but that same harshness had schooled their takeover and had whetted their greed. So the war gang hooted and sneered and carved out its own positions of power. As they attacked the Establishment, they replaced it.

In my first two novels, I had exhausted the material of my life. Tony Richardson wanted to put on a musical version of *The Breaking of Bumbo* at the Royal Court Theatre, starring the emerging actors Peter O'Toole or Albert Finney. But I had taken a Double First in History at Cambridge, and graduate work in America lured me across the Atlantic. I was given a Harkness Fellowship to do research on my subject, Prohibition. I chose to study under the best of the social historians, Oscar Handlin at Harvard and Richard Hofstadter at Columbia. The two years I spent in the United States, travelling by car from coast to coast, made me see it as a continent of vast diversity, and Great Britain as two small islands with large pretensions and a larger literature.

I married a French girl, Marianne, who had nothing in common with me. Her different values and American values made me question all my own assumptions. Going abroad does not always make the heart grow fonder of the home country. It can make the fatherland seem dull and strange.

I returned to live with Marianne in a small apartment under the roofs of Soho Square and to become a Founding Fellow of the new scientific foundation at Cambridge, Churchill College. Soho was still its bohemian, raffish self, and we loved it, while most of the Nobel Prize winners in science passed through Churchill College. My social history of *Prohibition* was pub-

lished and received well and gained me a doctorate. Another career as an American historian opened up. Although I left Churchill College after two years to spend another year travelling on a fellowship in the United States in order to write a prophetic book on *The Emancipation of the American Woman,* I returned to lecture on American history and political philosophy at University College, London. My twenties were years of a growing reputation as a social historian, but three more short novels showed that I had run out of material. My married and donnish life was without the fire and brio of my military and student days. Only a move to a house on the river in London's bombed dockland provided a terrible isolation, where I might do good work.

Until I wrote my first long novel, *Gog,* I thought that experience was something that happened casually to me. The material for my fiction would come from my normal life. But gradually, as I felt more in command of my style in the novel, and as I grew more to recognize my obsessions, I realized that I did not have to wait around for experience to occur. I could go out and find the experience I wished for the themes that I needed for my novel. *Gog* took three years in gestation and another two to write. It demanded a great deal of research into the byways of mythology and the details of popular revolt in Britain; it also demanded a huge grubbing into the facts of being alive in 1945, something which I had largely forgotten. But it made me do another thing, which I began in terror and ended in gratitude. It made me tramp some four hundred miles without any money along the old right-of-ways in England and Scotland.

This experience of tramping, which gave me all the details I needed about season and sight and hunger and cold and just moving, was not a *real* experience of being a tramp, as George Orwell's was, when he described his years of poverty in *Down and Out in Paris and London.* I was tramping towards a perfectly good house in the London docks and a perfectly secure income from academics and writing. I was only playing at being the tramp, with my shorn hair and assumed accent. Yet the sensations which I experienced were all true enough. An empty belly is no forgery, sleeping on a moor, soaked to the skin, is no lie. Lying out in a gale all night on the site of an old Roman camp by Hadrian's Wall gave me a better picture of the feelings of a Roman sentry on guard duty nineteen hundred years ago than I could reach in my imaginings or researches in London.

Approaching somewhere with the same physical sensations as one's hero makes all the difference in the description of a place. York Minster does not look the same to a fat man after a good night as it looks to a hungry man after a week out. People do not behave the same towards a dirty stubbled hiker as they do towards a car driver with a crease in his trousers. These are all simple observations, but vital ones. Until I had condemned myself out of my own mouth to a host of friends, and until shame drove me out to tramp as I had boasted that I would, I was one of the complacent authors who claimed that memory or plagiarism or inspiration could provide a far better description of a thing than the thing itself. It would be convenient if this were true, and far more comfortable. But it is not true.

Good novelists may make bad newspaper reporters, and good reporters may make bad novelists. Yet the novelist has to stir his stumps and become something of the reporter. There are two lines of W.H. Auden's which long ago influenced me before I had written my first novel. Auden wrote that the novelist

> . . . in his own weak person, if he can
> Must suffer dully all the wrongs of Man.

The gifted may, perhaps, suffer all these wrongs by a process of telepathy, a sympathetic transference of themselves into the condition of other men. All novelists have to do this in some small degree; it is the necessary trick of their trade. Joyce Cary could not have been further in character from Gulley Jimson or Mister Johnson; but his characters breathe as if the author had puffed the air of their paper mouths. Yet without his detailed knowledge of Africa and of the life of the failed artist, would Cary have convinced us about the truth of his two major creations in character?

It is fine if a writer can suffer at a distance for others; but it is better and more sure if he suffers close. It is fine if the ordinary course of life brings the experience and material which are necessary for writing novels; but it is more sure if the writer goes out to experience and gather material on the theme that he has chosen. The deluge of suburban and university and business and young-married novels that flood the book stores with what Benjamin Franklin once called "happy mediocrity" would be channelled into more original pools if writers looked out for the detail needed to describe their dreams rather than submerged themselves under the detail of their rutted lives.

It is difficult to plan a novel on an original and curious theme, and then to find the time and money and energy to pursue that theme to the limits of mind and body. But it is that very difficulty which forces the writer into more originality, it is the *chosen* experience that becomes the different experience and distinguishes one particular novel from all others. The will to write should dominate everything, even a way of normal life; it did mine only when I wrote *Gog*. During the two

years of its walking and writing, hardness was all, and a vision as blinkered as the Blackwall Tunnel.

I ended the book to find myself losing my wife to one of my friends, a long slow sharing that seemed to have no turning. I used to say that every woman needed two men to give her enough time and conversation, while every author needed half a woman to give himself enough time to write alone. My statement was only a defence, which did not even convince me. For company, I had an Abyssinian cat called Mishkin, which used to sit on my lap while I typed until it decided to join in with its paws, making my manuscript rather surreal, or it would sleep in my bed with its head on my pillow, waking me in the small hours by walking across my face as it left on its nightly errands and me to my solitude.

I was offered three professorships in American history in England, the United States, and the Antipodes; but they all meant running a Department and gave me no time for my double life as a historian and a novelist. I had no reason to choose security, half a wife, and no child, so I decided to become a free lance and break my spears wherever there was a fight. I was chosen by the executors of the Estate of Dylan Thomas to adapt for the stage his unfinished novel, *Adventures in the Skin*

*"Acting in a film I wrote,* Before Winter Comes, *1968"*

*Trade.* It was put on in the tiny Hampstead Theatre starring an unknown actor called David Hemmings. Then the hazard of celebrity changed all our lives. Michelangelo Antonioni saw Hemmings's charismatic performance as the young Dylan and made him the star of *Blow-Up.* Tennessee Williams saw the play and pronounced it the best in London. I was offered a serious original screenplay to write for a fortune, and I took the offer. Incredibly, the film went straight into production for Columbia Pictures. It was called *Before Winter Comes* and starred David Niven, Topol, John Hurt, and Anna Karina. I became a script doctor for Columbia and CBS Films and spent a couple of years travelling between Hollywood, New York, London, and Paris. I was overpaid, overrated, overseas, and under the weather, doing what writers tended to do for the money and knew they should not do.

Then another political crisis changed my life, the failed revolutions of 1968, that year when the young and the workers were in revolt and most of the capital cities of the world thundered with protest and blazed with petrol bombs as they had in 1848, one hundred and twenty years before. I was in the Beverly Hills Hotel removing the warts from some script when I received a telephone call from Havana, where the cigars come from. It was from my wife: we had been reconciled for a time the previous year. I had to go to Havana to rescue her. She was pregnant and had run away to Cuba to present the child to Fidel Castro and the Revolution. If born a boy, it was to be called Che. If a girl, Tania the Guerrillera. She had lost her nerve, and the Cubans had taken away her passport. Could I get her out?

I have never looked for drama nor danger. They were wished upon me, as they were wished upon Graham Greene's hero in *Our Man in Havana.* My telephone calls to Cuba from Hollywood were so heavily monitored that my wife might have been Mata Hari. "Baby" to the eavesdroppers seemed the code for "bomb." I was followed round Hollywood by a football squad of American Agents, while half the passenger list of the aeroplane to Cuba were British or French security men. In the event, baby meant baby, and I had to bring him out of there in the womb, or he would be born a Cuban citizen, perhaps for his good, certainly for our ill.

My fortnight in Cuba was a black comedy beyond credulity. My heavily pregnant wife had made friends with Eldridge Cleaver and the Black Panthers, who usually arrived in Cuba after hijacking a plane because they had broken jail and could not afford the fare. As they were considering the invasion of Mississippi in a reverse Bay of Pigs adventure, four against America,

they were embarrassing Fidel, who did not fancy the odds or the retaliation. They had barricaded themselves in their Havana apartment with all their weapons. Paranoia ran high. They thought the Cuban army would come to take them out. My wife and I seemed to be their only visitors. They seized upon my past in the Coldstream Guards and at Cambridge and Harvard. I gave them lessons in stripping automatic weapons, in fire positions, in African history, and in political philosophy. A strategy then presented itself to me. If we all became unpopular enough, Fidel would not attack us, he would deport us. And so it proved to be. My pregnant wife, breaking all airline regulations, was flown out with me, while Cleaver and his criminal comrades were expelled a week later. I have never felt so happy to be an undesirable alien in all my life.

This display of Cuban roulette, however, did not mend my marriage. My wife could give up the Revolution, but not my friend. She simply could not choose, and I could not stand sharing any more. My son was born in Paris, but I sold my dockland home in a week and bought one of the largest mansions in London on a short lease, a Nash terrace house in Regent's Park, vast and six stories high with a mews at the end of the garden. "There's one thing about Andrew," my friend William Golding always says, "he needs space to write."

For the next fifteen years, I lived in these spaces piled upon spaces, and I tried to write, publish, and make films. I had started a company to print the illustrated texts of classic screenplays such as *Grand Illusion* and *The Blue Angel, Greed* and *The Third Man.* I used to joke that I doctored bad screenplays in order to publish good ones. My Hollywood career ended suddenly after my Havana caper. The studios in the late sixties were no different than those in the early fifties: they wanted nothing to do with those who meddled with revolutionary countries. I used all my screenwriting money, however, to buy the rights to classic films and to publish them. The list grew to a hundred titles: more than a million copies were sold across the world: a whole generation of filmmakers learnt to appreciate the well-made screenplay. Unfortunately for me as a writer, the publishing firm gobbled up too much of my time and my income. It is the folly of writers to believe that, because they are good at words, they are good at business. I was not. The publishing firm always made a loss because of its good intentions and bad management. As its reputation grew, its fortunes fell. Its survival is a tribute to the survival of the virtuous and the unfittest.

*Gog* was the novel of my life, and I always meant it to be part of a trilogy. It had been the story of the struggle of the people against power, of Gog against his half brother Magog, both nicknamed from the twin giants of Ancient Britain who used to guard the city of London, mythologically built by King Ludd. *Magog* was to be a novel about the corruption of power, about a man who joined the Establishment, about the decline of England in the two decades after the end of the Second World War. Magog was even to live in my own huge house in Regent's Park, although I was not he. Yet half of me was Magog, a man who knew about power and the waste of it. Half was Gog, the anarchic fighter for liberty and self-expression. It seemed to me a struggle for some people throughout history that could not be resolved, even in the book intended to complete the trilogy, *King Ludd.*

The seventies for me were the years of Magog, and in the course of those years, I wrote *Magog*. Novels of disillusion and social decline are rarely as good as those of creation and prophecy. I felt the divine spark dying in me. I began to make films of my own. I directed a version of *The Breaking of Bumbo*, updated to the "swinging" and radical London of 1968. Then I bought the rights to Dylan Thomas's radio play *Under Milk Wood* and made a film of it: as talking pictures go, there was more talking in it with the pictures than any other film ever made. The Italian subtitles looked like a withered

*Directing the film* Under Milk Wood, *1972*

forest when the film opened the Venice Festival in 1972. René Clair shook me by the hand and said he wished he had made it. I replied that I wished he had made it too. I had directed the three biggest British stars of the time in the world—Richard Burton, Elizabeth Taylor, and Peter O'Toole, and two of them had given magnificent performances. There was a magic in the film and a trick, the use of a panning camera which slid between shots so that the film appeared as continuous as the words of the First and Second Voices, rolling like one wave from the living to the dead, from dream to reality, as if all were in one sea of imagination.

The making of *Under Milk Wood* was the unmaking of me. Having made one good film that did not coin money, I thought I could make more. I was wrong. I was offered worse subjects and had to take more financial risks in trying to shoot new films. On one catastrophic occasion, I found myself in Athens with the two weightiest actors of them all, Orson Welles and Oliver Reed. I was trying to shoot a modern Faustian legend. The English stock market crashed, the producer ran away, and I was left with two megaliths who took my credit card out of my pocket, sat me between them in the best restaurant in town, consumed every dish in the place and twenty-two bottles of wine during the next fourteen hours, while they were discussing who would murder me first. Films were no longer my *forte,* but my ruin. I persisted in trying to make them for too long.

I married again, a younger English woman, fresh from the counties, apparently the sort of debutante that I had pilloried in *The Breaking of Bumbo*. I knew her to be intelligent, quick, a funny and fabulous liar, and what the Mitford sisters called "a bolter." She stuck with me for ten years, filling up the emptiness in the Nash terrace, and she gave me another splendid son, who grew to love his French half brother. The disaster that my friends had predicted for my second marriage was a slow one, the story of a woman trying to escape from my shadow and live as a writer in her own right. She left in the end, and I was alone in my vast spaces again.

We had also bought a Venetian ruined villa in Corfu, and I had to earn too much money to keep up a style of life that I did not deserve, unless the film money flowed. As that money ususally flowed in the wrong direction, I found myself dependent on writing biographies for a good living. I had written a political biography of Warren Gamaliel Harding. Now I wrote on Jack London and John Ford, the film director, and J.P. Morgan. I also was permitted to enter the Royal Archives at Windsor Castle to write the biography of Victoria, the eldest daughter of Queen Victoria, later the Empress of Germany for ninety-nine days.

The writing of biography is more than a discovery of another person. It is a matter of self-discovery. If the subject of the biography is not too alien or repugnant, the writer goes through a painful process of immersion in another's life, a baptism by research. There is the following process of separation and definition, painful and discriminatory. He or she, the subject, is not I, the author. I do know myself better. I am not he or she. Even if I do understand another so well, I must not pardon, but explain and judge. As Randall Jarrell wrote:

> Forgive, forgive, forgive no one,
> Understand and blame.

That is the role of the biographer.

For me, both literary and historical biography are a plunge, an identification, and a divorce. I try to choose subjects with whom I have sympathy and whose society I have considered. The process begins by an inquiry, whether there are papers and what are the terms of access to them. Biographers may not always have the troubles detailed in *The Aspern Papers,* but they do have the problems of family or state censorship. If and when I am given access on reasonable terms to papers and witnesses, then I plunge. First, I try to fill my own library shelves with everything written about my quarry and his background. Then I go to my favourite libraries, the London Library or the Widener at Harvard, where topics are still listed by subject and are put in the stacks by subject, and I am given entry to the stacks. There I read books by the yard and have the relevant pages copied. Then a rough filing system, then the preparation for the quest—an inquiry by place and time and survivor.

There have been admirable works of imaginative biography, in which the search for the truth by the biographer is almost as significant as the subject of the biography. The voyage in the Odyssey fascinates me more than the historical accuracy of Ulysses, King of Ithaca: Boswell is more intriguing than Dr. Johnson. *The Road to Xanadu, The Quest for Corvo,* and the recent *The Man Who Was B. Traven* illuminate the inquirer, who comes like Childe Harold to the dark tower, or knocks like the traveller on the moonlit door, asking, "Is there anybody there?" It is essentially a journey to all the places and people who can answer the right questions. And it is an imaginative journey, on which the biographer can stand and stare, look and hear with the same eyes and ears as the person he seeks to describe.

The journeys I took while writing on Jack London and John Ford were a discovery of America as well as of my subject and myself. So was the journey I had to take in order to write a short novel, *The Facts in the Case*

*of E.A. Poe,* for it contained a short biography of Poe. It pretended to be written by a modern man who identified himself totally with Poe. His therapy was to visit all the places where Poe had been and to write a biography of Poe so as to separate himself from his *alter ego.* The act of visiting all the areas of Poe's life gave me personally as well as my hero/biographer an exact opportunity to compare ancient and modern sensibility as well as historical awareness. A black comedy, the novel itself mocked at psychiatric techniques as used in biography, but contained a valid method of writing both historical and literary biography by description of place and comparison of time.

Autobiography, even the short one that I am attempting, is notorious as a method of whitewash and blindfold. The memories of Bismarck, for instance, rival those of Gypsy Rose Lee in hiding more than they reveal. The proper study of mankind may be man, but not myself. Even the writer of a secret diary such as Pepys hoped for its posthumous discovery, or else he would have destroyed it before his death: he too wrote not only for himself, but for the eyes of others and possible publication. If there were no biographers, the writers of diaries and autobiographies would have to invent them. Or who would ask the right questions and set their records straight?

I do not distinguish overmuch between the writing of political or literary or artistic biographies. These all depend on the materials available, the approach to those materials, the ordering of them, and the nature of the biographer and his time. A biography is, after all, never finished. It exists only to be rewritten. From lack of other documentation and competition, the lives recorded by Plutarch and Tacitus will always remain seminal and basic to Roman studies. But their judgements have been questioned by playwrights and historians, from William Shakespeare to Michael Grant. No biographer can escape from the sensibilities and values of his age. We are caught in the same process of time from which we seek to rescue our subjects. As we explain others to our contemporaries within their terms of reference, so we date ourselves in front of our sons and daughters. For when they become adults, they will demand biographies written in the terms they understand.

The last climacteric in my life was a separation from my second wife and two years of solitude rebuilding the Nash terrace in order to sell it. I lived in the gutted ruin in the one habitable room, feeling like the hero of Robert Louis Stevenson's *Kidnapped.* I would walk up a stair to find it ended in nothing. I was desperate and unable to write, in debt and without inspiration. Then at the only cocktail party I had at-

*Yachting with wife Sonia, 1985*

tended in a year, I had what I call a recognition. I looked at a woman of extraordinary beauty and intelligence and sympathy and grace, and she looked at me. She had been widowed ten years before and courted by hundreds of desirable men for a decade. But our recognition was total and absolute. We had both given up the idea of love, or commitment, or sharing, or living closely together. But in a year, we were married and happy beyond the dreams of romance or destiny. We were, as they say, made for one another and had been looking for each other all our lives. We met too late, but perhaps hurt enough to appreciate our good fortune.

I moved to a house in Chelsea, long and low, beautiful and spacious. I gave up any involvement in the cinema, and I am lessening my involvement in publishing. I wrote *The Red and the Blue* about Cambridge University between the twenties and the fifties, the time of inconsiderable traitors and scientific discoveries. I agreed to write a last biography on the last of the great creative film producers, Sam Spiegel, a friend of my wife. But I was clearing the decks to write *King Ludd,* for the time had come historically to tell about the Luddites, who first wrecked the new textile machines, through the story of the printers like Francis Place who defended liberty, on to the sad end of the print unions through new technology, locked out by barriers of barbed wire while journalists set their own copy for the *Times* at Wapping. Contemporary events have given *King Ludd* its shape.

I am happy now, and inspired. The good years of a novelist are in his fifties, when he has still something

of the fire of youth and more of the experience of age. I hope that I have revealed a little of myself and my writing in this piece, but I feel rather like the scientists trying to observe Heisenberg's Uncertainty Principle. As they describe it, so it has gone. The discovery of myself may be like Emily Dickinson's warning about trying to find out too much in a writer or in his works.

> Finding is the first Act
> The second, loss,
> Third, Expedition for
> The "Golden Fleece"
>
> Fourth, no Discovery—
> Fifth, no Crew—
> Finally, no Golden Fleece—
> Jason—sham—too.

## BIBLIOGRAPHY

### Fiction:

*The Breaking of Bumbo.* London: Faber, 1959; New York: Simon & Schuster, 1959.

*My Friend Judas.* London: Faber, 1959; New York: Simon & Schuster, 1961.

*The Project.* London: Faber, 1960; New York: Simon & Schuster, 1960.

*The Hallelujah Bum.* London: Faber, 1963; also published as *The Paradise Bum.* New York: Atheneum, 1963.

*The Raker.* London: J. Cape, 1964; New York; Atheneum, 1964.

*Gog.* London: Weidenfeld & Nicolson, 1967; New York: Macmillan, 1967.

*Magog.* London: Weidenfeld & Nicolson; New York: Harper, 1972.

*Inkydoo, the Wild Boy* (for children). London: Abelard-Schuman, 1976; also published as *Carina and the Wild Boy.* London: Beaver, 1977.

*The Surrey Cat.* London: Joseph, 1976.

*A Patriot for Hire.* London: Joseph, 1978.

*Sea of the Dead.* London: Joseph, 1978.

*The Facts in the Case of E.A. Poe.* London: Weidenfeld & Nicolson, 1979; New York: Holt, 1980.

*Beau Bumbo.* London: Weidenfeld & Nicolson, 1985.

*Farthest Distant: The Last Novel of Them All.* London: Lorrimer, 1986.

### Nonfiction:

*Prohibition: The Era of Excess.* London: Faber, 1962; Boston: Little, Brown, 1962; also published as *Era of Excess: A Social History of the Prohibition Movement.* New York: Harper, 1964.

*The Available Man: The Life behind the Masks of Warren Gamaliel Harding.* New York: Macmillan, 1965.

*The Better Half: The Emancipation of the American Woman.* New York: Harper, 1965; London: J. Cape, 1966.

*A Concise History of the United States.* London: Thames & Hudson, 1967; New York: Viking, 1967.

*The Last of the Best: The Aristocracy of Europe in the Twentieth Century.* London: Weidenfeld & Nicolson, 1969; New York: Macmillan, 1969.

*Guevara.* London: Fontana, Collins, 1970; also published as *Che Guevara.* New York: Viking, 1970.

*Dylan Thomas: Poet of His People.* London: Joseph, 1975; also published as *Dylan Thomas: No Man More Magical.* New York: Holt, 1975.

*Jack: A Biography of Jack London.* New York: Harper, 1977; London: Weidenfeld & Nicolson, 1978.

*The Savage: A History of Misunderstanding.* London: Weidenfeld & Nicolson, 1978.

*John Ford: A Biography.* London: Allen & Unwin, 1979; New York: Dial, 1979.

*Corsair: The Life of J. Pierpont Morgan.* London: Weidenfeld & Nicolson, 1981; Boston: Little, Brown, 1981.

*The Other Victoria: The Princess Royal and the Great Game of Europe.* London: Weidenfeld & Nicolson, 1981.

*Royal Web: The Story of Princess Victoria and Frederick of Prussia,* with Ladislas Farago. New York: McGraw, 1982.

*Sir Walter Raleigh and the Age of Discovery.* Harmondsworth, England and New York: Penguin, 1984.

### Plays:

*My Friend Judas,* adapted from the novel by the author, produced in London, 1959.

*Adventures in the Skin Trade,* adapted from the novel by Dylan Thomas, produced in London, 1965. London: Dent, 1967; New York: New Directions, 1968.

*The Blue Angel,* adapted from the screenplay by Josef von Sternberg, produced in Liverpool, 1983.

### Screenplays:

*Before Winter Comes,* adapted from "The Interpreter," a story by Frederick L. Keefe. Columbia, 1969

*The Breaking of Bumbo,* adapted from the novel by the author. Associated British Pictures, 1970.

*Under Milk Wood,* adapted from the play by Dylan Thomas. Timon Films, 1971. London: Lorrimer, 1972; New York: Simon & Schuster, 1972.

*Malachi's Cove.* Timon Films, 1973.

### Television scripts:

*The Chocolate Tree,* 1963.

*Old Soldiers,* 1964.

*The Voyage of the Beagle.* CBS Films, 1970.

*Martin Eden,* adapted from the novel by Jack London. RAI, 1981.

### Translator of:

*Selections from the Greek Anthology.* London: Weidenfeld & Nicolson, 1967; New York: Macmillan, 1968.

*Bolivian Diary: Ernesto "Che" Guevara,* translated with Carlos P. Hansen, introduction by Fidel Castro. London: Lorrimer, 1968.

*La Grande Illusion,* by Jean Renoir, translated with Marianne Alexandre. London: Lorrimer, 1968.

### Editor of:

*The Call of the Wild, White Fang, and Other Stories,* by Jack London, with an introduction by James Dickey. Harmondsworth, England and New York: Penguin, 1981.

# Robin Skelton

*1925-*

*Robin Skelton, twelve months old, with his
grandfather, William Robins*

*In the garden at Filey, 1928*

I was born in the early morning of October 12, 1925, in the red brick schoolhouse of the village of Easington on the east coast of Yorkshire, or so I am told. When I emerged my right thigh was found to be broken; it was put in a splint for some time, and when the splint was removed I ignored the wishes of my mother and the doctor and, instead of lying still, I kicked and kicked and kicked without cease. I have been kicking ever since.

My father was the village schoolmaster, and my mother taught the infants' class, in which, at the age of four, having already found out how to read, I was placed out of the way at the back of the class while my companions struggled with their letters. I finished my book on the first day and advanced to the front only to be told sharply to return to my seat. "But, Mother, it's

Robin!" I expostulated tearfully, for she had clearly forgotten me. That was my first experience of the difference between private and public behaviour, and the first of my many failures to appreciate the importance of conformity.

My childhood was solitary but not unhappy. For a long time I was not permitted to play with the village children, but only with the vicar's son and the son of a regular summer visitor from Hull. My parents were Victorian in attitude and almost in age, my father having been born in another Yorkshire village schoolhouse in 1879 and my mother in a Cumberland lighthouse nine years later. They met during an amateur performance of *The Mikado*. I have been devoted to Gilbert and Sullivan all my life, and sometimes I wonder if in some mysterious way my facility with verse was not influ-

*Robin, left, with the Vicar's son, about 1934*

enjoyed the brightly coloured weekly comics, especially *Tiger Tim's Weekly;* one special Guy Fawkes issue had so much colour on its cover I almost fainted with ecstasy. This kind of reading was tolerated by my parents, but they preferred tougher stuff. I was given Arthur Mee's *Children's Encyclopedia* in which I greatly admired the Greek statues and imitated them in plasticine. I also read, with delight, *The Wind in the Willows, Treasure Island,* Ballantyne's *Coral Island* and *Gorilla Hunters,* and most of Dickens.

There was no cinema in our village; only during the Second World War were there occasional showings of films in the Village Institute which had been turned into a forces club, ruled over by my iron-handed mother. I saw my first movie on one of our regular family summer visits to stay with my father's mother at Filey. My father thought that at nine I was old enough to be subjected to this novelty, and took me to see *Man of Aran,* which enchanted me. (Is that where my love of Synge began?) He had intended to take me to see *Treasure Island,* but had got the week wrong. I saw it the next week and was exhilarated by Wallace Beery's Long John Silver and terrified by Blind Pew and his death.

I had by now written my first poem on record; it

enced as much by my father's tuneless singing of "Tit Willow" when I was small, as by my mother's reading aloud of the verses of A.A. Milne.

I spent a typical country childhood, wandering the seashore and the fields, collecting birds' eggs and, later, moths and butterflies, but the greater part of my leisure was spent in my room playing with toy soldiers of the brightly coloured metal provided by Messrs. Brittain and reading everything I could lay my hands on. My taste was eclectic. I staggered through bits of Chaucer before I was ten, and was hugely puzzled by references to pubic hair in *The Miller's Tale,* as I did not know such growths existed and dared not enquire. I read Scott, and Baroness Orczy and Tennyson, and Wordsworth, and the *Boys' Own Paper* (oh the excitement of W.E. Johns' "Biggles" stories—maybe that was why I joined the Air Force) and I read all the "William" books of Richmal Crompton. I was also excited by the "bloods," weekly periodicals filled with adventure stories. I still remember half their names: *Hotspur, Champion, Adventure.* As a smaller child I also

*The Schoolboy, 1943*

was called "The Storm," and is lettered as "by Robin Skelton 8 yrs 2 mns." When, just before my eleventh birthday, I was sent off to Pocklington Grammar School as a boarder I had quite a collection of verses which swelled as the years went on. Early subjects included a ballad about digging for gold and fighting Indians "in Canada so bold" where my Uncle Will Robins had emigrated in 1907. Other verses reveal my devotion to Rider Haggard, John Masefield, Scott, and *The Last Days of Pompeii.*

My boarding-school days were mostly miserable. I was no good at gymnastics, only discovering later that my broken thigh had caused one leg to be shorter than the other so that I was developing spinal curvature that made physical precision difficult. ("Hold up your Head! Don't hang it to one side like that! Stand up straight!") I also developed my talent for other forms of incompetence. As a Boy Scout I made sausages that exploded; as a cricketer I neither struck nor caught any ball; as a member of the school Officers' Training Corps, and, later the Air Training Corps, I could not dismember and reassemble a Browning gun without finding pieces left over. I also developed a healthy distrust of all forms of authority, a small talent for drawing vicious caricatures of my oppressors, a sharp tongue to deal with those who bullied me, and a certain ingenuity in evading duties I disliked.

By this time I had made many literary discoveries, most of them by myself, though my English teacher, Tom Pay, did encourage me a good deal, and made me read *Erewhon.* My other major discoveries during those seven dreadful years included Carlyle's *Sartor Resartus,* Jane Austen's novels, the *Essays of Elia,* Kinglake's *Eothen,* Rupert Brooke, and, inevitably, Shakespeare. I won a prize for writing verse and for elocution and also learned, on stage and off, how to play a part, which explains how I managed to get myself selected to go to Cambridge University as one of a small number of Air Cadets regarded as officer material, even though my academic standing was only high in Maths and English, and my knowledge of Latin, Physics, and Chemistry was abysmal.

I enjoyed Cambridge. It had misfits too. I shared a "stair" with Anthony Caro, then a student of engineering, and encouraged him in his early sculpture and listened to his woes. He and his friends also encouraged me in my verse making.

I studied Economics, Civics, and Politics, which was a standard diet for those whose school performance did not entitle them to specialize. In fact, I studied very little. I read a lot, joined the Mummer's Dramatic Society, had poems published in *Christ's College Magazine,* and haunted the second-hand bookshops. I emerged with an undeserved second class. My Air Force studies

were less successful. I achieved a seven percent solution to the problems of Aircraft Recognition, never fully understood the positions of the stars, and continued to have trouble with the Browning gun. My squadron Leader, a Scot whose favourite reading, it was rumoured, was the prophet Isaiah, told me at the end of the course, "Skelton, you'rrre temperrramentally unfitted for the RRRRRRoyal Airrrrrr Forrrrrce!" I agreed with him, but I had already been accepted as a volunteer and there was nothing we could do about it.

I joined the Air Force proper (or improper) in June 1944 and it was discovered by way of an aptitude test that I possessed marked mechanical ability. I therefore went into training as a Flight Engineer, and was managing to fiddle my way through (in spite of a total failure to understand the internal combustion engine) when the Authorities (no wonder I still distrust them) informed us all that there was little need for more Flight Engineers and we must find other trades. I chose to be a Code and Cypher Clerk, which meant (if I contrived to slide through successfully) an immediate promotion to Sergeant and an overseas posting. In spite of only adequate touch-typing on the electrical coding machines, I got through and after brief, hilarious, and occasionally drunken periods at embarkation centres in Blackpool and Morecambe (off-season, alas, but there were still girls), I was sent off to India.

In New Delhi I was set to work on the electrical coding machines, and it was soon discovered that not even our side could decode my messages, and so I was posted to a Care and Maintenance Unit near Quetta in what is now Pakistan, where I suppose I assisted in the care and maintenance of a small airfield and wrote more poetry. I had bumped into Sergeant Terence Ian Fytton Armstrong, more generally known as the poet and bibliophile, John Gawsworth, in my barrack block in New Delhi, and in between drinks and listening to him rant colourfully about the government, I had helped him put together a collection of his poems to be published by Susil Gupta, who at that time was known for disseminating such dreadfully risqué works as *Mlle de Maupin.* I picked one of John's more erotic poems to open the book and christened it "The Susil Gupta Special." He read my verse and told me that I had talent and when I had written a thousand more poems I might get somewhere. I reckon he was right to within a hundred. Thus encouraged, I wrote and wrote and wrote—stories and essays as well as verses, all of them terrible.

Of RAF station Samungli the space at my disposal only enables me to say that when I read *Catch-22* I did so with a shock of recognition, but thought it all a little understated. The German War was now over. I

*In the RAF, early 1945*

had celebrated V-E Day in a Delhi cinema where, having just emerged from hospital after a bout of heat exhaustion, and having consumed two festive brandies, I vomited unhappily over the seat in front of me. V-J Day was more fun. I was up in Waziristan at Ziarat and the local British Authority invited a group of us round to play tennis. I had only played badminton before—in the school yard at home with shuttlecocks found on the beach (we were all avid beachcombers in that village), and I tried to use the tennis racket in a similar fashion. I sent half-a-dozen balls out of the court and into impenetrable forest before they intimated that perhaps someone else might play now.

At Samungli I recalled *The Mikado*, for, as the station's population dwindled due to demobilization, I became a kind of Pooh-Bah, being at the same time Station Cypher Officer, Station Signals Officer, Officer in Charge of the Motor Pool, Station Librarian, Station Education Officer, and for two dizzying weeks Officer in Charge of Flying Control. That the one plane I ushered to land did not crash I can only ascribe to the good sense of the pilot who ignored the gesturing figure on the roof of the control tower attempting to flash Morse code with an unplugged Aldis lamp. Had he even seen the signal it wouldn't have helped. I had

forgotten the Morse code and was simply flashing at random and as fast as I could to suggest expertise.

There was little to do at Samungli. We all drank a great deal, and I personally wrote and read continually. There were some excursions such as the occasion when three of us stole the fire truck and went into Quetta to a brothel someone had heard about. It was shut. And then there was the time our C.O. decided we should drive to Afghanistan over the trackless mountain country behind us, so we got into trucks and managed maybe two miles before one truck got stuck and we ran out of drink.

I was hospitalized for a couple of times while in Samungli, once for a mysterious undiagnosed ailment which I am now sure was food poisoning, and once for severe depression. I was lucky enough to go home for mid-tour leave, however, and would have enjoyed the voyage had not my cunning failed me so completely that I found myself working nights in the ship's bakery, the second hottest part of the ship. Off Massawa the ship's ventilation system failed. It is as close as I ever hope to get to Hell.

I spent some time in Ceylon on a course to teach me to be a teacher, which like almost all such courses was absurd. Either one can teach or one can't. Happily, I found that I could. I enjoyed Kandy, and especially the Temple of the Tooth, though my skimpy reading of Buddhism had not prepared me for one graphic fresco of the damned in Hell. I still have somewhere an inscribed bo-leaf from that temple. Drink was cheap in Ceylon, and I had spent all my money before the time came for my ten days' rail journey back to Baluchistan, so I was obliged to live on railway tea and bananas. I could not look a banana in the face for some years after that.

In 1947 I was posted back to New Delhi where the Codes and Cyphers section was wise enough not to tax me with any coding or decoding. I sat in the office pretending to keep the log books straight and wrote scripts for All India Radio, for I had made friends with the head of the Western Music Section of Station Delhi and I moonlighted as a radio broadcaster. Radio was live in those days, and very confused. One evening when a production of my potted version of *The Beaux' Stratagem* was due to be aired in ten minutes time, it was discovered that almost all the cast could not turn up because of the flu. I played five parts that night, in an assortment of accents. The morning paper reviewed the production without enthusiasm.

I returned to England in 1947 and, Cambridge having told me they would have no room for me for twelve months, I applied to enter Leeds University. On registration day Bonamy Dobrée, then Professor of the

Department of English Language and Literature, said I didn't have the necessary entrance qualifications, and why did I want to study literature. I told him because I was trying to write it, and with a grin he let me through.

The four years at Leeds were full of discoveries, though not always in the lecture rooms, even though my instructors included the dazzling talents of G. Wilson Knight (who was vatic), Kenneth Muir (who was precise), Bonamy Dobrée (who was exciting), and dear Wilfred Rowland Childe, whose poetry was by then unfashionable, and whose lectures were largely inaudible, but who was a wonder. Outside the classroom during those years I edited the University magazine, the *Gryphon,* edited the first annual collection of University poetry outside Oxbridge, published it myself, and sold it (after I'd paid the printer) for beer money. I produced *The Second Shepherd's Play,* was Drama Critic for the *Union News,* and took over the publishing firm The Lotus Press, from which I and my co-conspirators issued what may have been the first series of new poetry in paperback in Britain (Erica Marx's Hand and Flower Press being either just before me or just after me).

The Lotus Press produced the first collection of drawings and poems in translation by Max Jacob to appear in Britain, James Kirkup's long poem *The Creation,* and a volume by Wilfred Rowland Childe, the first he had published for a number of years. I am surprised that I did not publish my own work as most young writer-publishers do these days. It never occurred to me to do so.

I also fell in love a number of times, and became left-wing in politics, as who did not in those days.

Another part of my education was at the hands of Geoffrey Keynes with whom I had corresponded from India as I had to get permission to broadcast a piece by Rupert Brooke, and he was the active member of Brooke's trustees. I visited him in Hampstead and for the next fifteen years I stayed with him regularly either in London or the country, at first alone, and then with my wife and children. Staying with Geoffrey was itself an education. The house was filled with paintings and fine prints, and crammed with books from all centuries. I examined incunables. I read Marvell and Donne in their original editions. I was introduced to the wonders of William Blake and Samuel Palmer, and Geoffrey took me to first nights in London, especially to the ballet. I think that my own house, a big one, also crammed with books and pictures, owes much to him. He gave me a model. He also taught me to work on several books at once. He himself always had eight or ten books in various stages of production, and since then I have followed his example. He taught me how to edit a

*Master of Arts, 1951*

text and I helped him with his labours on the letters of Rupert Brooke. I met fascinating people, including Siegfried Sassoon, who slaughtered me at croquet, and who scared me silly in London by dashing across streets in full traffic as if he were still leading a charge in the trenches. I learned the art and mystery of book collecting and we spent many days "book-crawling" antiquarian bookshops, in one of which I began my collection of Yeats and Synge. Geoffrey also taught me bricklaying and there is a depressed portion of the paving outside the front of Lammas, his country house, with which I have been credited.

In 1951 I was hired by Manchester University's English Department in the teeth of sixty-nine other applicants. H.B. Charlton was responsible. He wanted a poet on strength, I think. I passed the interview largely on gall, and a bland agreement with Professor G.L. Brooks that I was totally ignorant of Anglo-Saxon. The Professor of English Language had fought against my getting a first class at Leeds, on the grounds of my inability to translate *Beowulf,* and there had been a real dust-up, I discovered later. Nevertheless I did get a first and did my M.A. with Wilfred Childe on the work of Francis Quarles, discovering a hitherto unascribed poem by Quarles in the process. It was a very dull thesis.

The Manchester Years were not wholly without pleasure. I enjoyed teaching, but my poetry was ignored by most of my colleagues (one of them always left the staff lounge whenever it was mentioned) and I was never invited to meet visiting poets (who sometimes asked after me), or to give readings. H.B. Charlton tried to turn me into a real academic by getting me to edit some Ruskin letters in the Rylands Library, which I did, after a fight with the Chief Librarian about how to print the footnotes. I also produced my first book of verse which was a Choice of the Poetry Book Society, and my first book about poetry, *The Poetic Pattern*, thanks to the help and support of Herbert Read.

I did a lot of extra evening teaching in those days, both for the Extra-Mural Department and the Workers' Education Association, for my salary was tiny, and I enjoyed working with non-captive audiences that turned up because they actually wanted to learn. I taught one class in Stockport for five years, and they were wonderful people, though travelling back and forth through fog, taking two buses each way, was no joke. Manchester evening classes, however, brought friendships, and particularly one with Tony Connor, who came to my first class thinking I was someone else. He was painting as well as writing at that time. Later I put together his first book of poems and got Oxford University Press to publish it. I also edited the first book by that wonderful and still unrecognized poet, John Knight. I began to paint and make collages. Tony Connor, Michael Seward Snow, and I founded the Peterloo Group of artists and writers which met monthly in the upper room of a pub. There were no membership fees, and we three were the only full members, but the world and his wife were welcome to join us. Each evening began with a talk or reading by an artist, writer, or composer, and then there was a discussion, and finally an hour of talk and drink, the cost of the room being covered by passing round the hat. We put on exhibitions in the city, organized the first display of open-air sculpture it had ever seen, contrived to bring in lecturers and speakers, and, eventually were instrumental in founding the Manchester Institute of Contemporary Arts, of which I wrote the constitution (the British Arts Council asked me what lawyer I had used!) and was the first Secretary and Programme Director. In this capacity I became friends with a number of most entertaining people, including John Betjeman (who was wonderfully funny and generous) and Norman Nicholson, who was and remains a marvellous man and poet.

On occasional forays into London, while working on *The Poetic Pattern*, I talked to a lot of poets about how they wrote their work, and thus began a long and still warm friendship with Kathleen Raine. I also had entertaining and slightly baffling encounters with William Empson, David Gascoyne, T.S. Eliot, and G.S.

*With Margaret, 1953*

Fraser (who had recently been in America and startled me by smoking in between courses at dinner).

By this time I was married to my first wife Margaret, and living in a flat in Manchester which was tumbling about us (one afternoon the main window fell in). I was also writing reviews and doing various broadcast talks, including a series on how to write poetry, which formed the basis of my book in the "Teach Yourself" series. I even wrote a play that originated in the experience of J.D. Jump, my most supportive and warmhearted colleague, in Carthage during the war. The Arts Council of Great Britain agreed to subsidize its performance by any theatre that wished to put it on; no theatre did. Kitchen Sink Drama had come in, and I was out of step.

My poetry was out of step, too. Philip Larkin's *The Less Deceived* emerged at the same time as did my own first book and the so-called "New Movement" was in full flow as I continued perversely to write in less ironic modes. When Anthony Hartley, the originator of the term "New Movement," became literary editor of the *Manchester Guardian* I lost my job of reviewing poetry for the paper, though not before I had given rave reviews to Theodore Roethke's first British collection and the first books of Ted Hughes and Thomas Kinsella. I was transformed into a Drama Critic and had the luck to see the first British production of *West Side Story* as well as Orson Welles' *Othello* and Gielgud's Japanese-style *Lear*. I was also sent out to far places and on one occasion placed Sam Wanamaker's production of *The Rose Tattoo* in Liverpool in the wrong theatre and an apology had to be printed. Not all plays were rewarding. I recall, with bitterness, an amateur production of *The Duke in Darkness* which lasted four and a half hours.

My marriage to Margaret came to an end in 1957 and I had the extraordinary good sense and fortune to marry again later that year. Sylvia had been married to an artist and lived in Cornwall, which Margaret and I had loved to visit. I spent a good deal of time there in the West Penwith area, where I met W.S. Graham, and started my collection of his books, notebooks, and manuscripts. I also met many artists, including Barbara Hepworth and Ben Nicholson, who later contributed to the *Malahat Review*. Cornwall also provided me with the subject of the first of a series of ballads that landed me into difficulties with Oxford University Press, who thought two of them were too bawdy to be published by their respectable house. I therefore published the *Two Ballads of the Muse* myself from Will Carter's Rampant Lions Press in a limited edition. Thanks to Tom Driberg who commented on OUP's Grundyism in a Sunday paper, the book sold out rapidly. I have enjoyed creating finely printed limited editions of poetry ever since.

In 1959 I also became interested in another art and wrote the words for two motets and a cantata by the Manchester composer David Freedman, and attended the first performance of one of them, *The Wheel of Stars,* with some astonishment at my own temerity. I also, around this time, wrote a number of songs for the guitar with Frances Webber, a Cornish friend; these, however, have never been publicly performed.

It was in the late fifties that I became deeply involved in the Irish Renaissance. My new father-in-law wanted me to go to Dublin with him for personal research into the virtues of Guinness. I could not afford it, but having bought some first and early editions of Synge, I realized that his work was almost all out of print. Cheerfully I told OUP that a "World's Classics" edition was needed, that I was the man to do it, and that I needed fifty pounds advance to go to Dublin and talk to the Synge Executors about unpublished papers. I went. I found masses of unpublished verse and other material, made friends with Thomas Kinsella, John Montague, and that publisher of genius, Liam Miller, and, on returning to London, met Ann Saddlemyer,

*Contemplating, 1959*

*Michael Seward Snow*

from what was then Victoria College on Vancouver Island, who was doing a Ph.D. on Synge. I talked OUP into doing a *Collected Works of J.M. Synge* in four volumes, having first been obliged to explain to Stanley Unwin how important the project was, and betray such fanatic idealism that he would turn the project down for publication by his house, which had been the main publisher of Synge till then. He did turn me down. As General Editor of the series I gave the play volumes to Saddlemyer to edit, and Alan Price got the prose, while I did the poems, and Saddlemyer arranged for me to teach a summer school at Victoria, where I fell in love with Vancouver Island. It seemed like a paradise. It still does.

The Irish connection certainly treated me well, and I did my best to be of use. For a number of years I was a sort of poetry talent scout for Oxford University Press, and was instrumental in getting them to publish Thomas Kinsella, as well as Charles Tomlinson and Tony Connor. I also helped in getting OUP to distribute Dolmen Press Books, and had great fun organizing the book part of an exhibition devoted to W.B. Yeats in the Whitworth Galleries, Manchester, later taking it all over to Dublin. Inevitably, I wrote two books about

Synge's work, edited his translations, did a brief biography of him, and published a variant text of *Riders to the Sea.* All my life I have found I can only learn something by writing about it.

Indeed, a number of my books emerged simply because I wanted to understand something. I became cross with existing translations of Corbière, so I did some of my own. I was profoundly irritated by the current humorless translations of the poems of the Greek Anthology, so I produced a collection of two hundred in my own versions. I wanted to read the work of John Knight, David Gascoyne, and Philip O'Connor in other than rare volumes and typescript, so I edited them and got the books published. My much later collection of translations of George Faludy arose from the same impulse, as did my various anthologies. I have always felt that if you really want something done you had better do it yourself.

I was still on Vancouver Island that summer of 1962 when I was suddenly invited to the University of Massachusetts for some months in connection with the celebration of their Centenary. I was, and I remain, puzzled why I was chosen. But Amherst was a turning point for me. There, for the first time, I read my poems to a huge audience, and even those sitting in the aisles did not go away! It gave me courage. Maybe I could take risks with my work. I date my "mature" poetry from that day, and I enjoyed my New England stay enormously. I had practically no duties (they didn't know what to do with me, I think), so I produced a mimeographed fortnightly magazine of poetry by Amherst writers, students, and others, called *Poetry Circular,* and talked such splendid poets as Robert Francis and Rolfe Humphries into giving me material. I also plotted, with David R. Clark, an Irish Renaissance issue of the *Massachusetts Review,* which eventually emerged. I was offered a job in New England, the first four-college appointment they'd contemplated. I would be hired equally by the University of Massachusetts, Amherst, Smith, and Mount Holyoke. I foresaw that it would be a peripatetic job and I don't know how to drive a car (mechanical ability indeed!) and also that my small shreds of glamour would soon be tattered. Besides, Victoria also offered me a job, and I could not resist the lure of the sea, the lakes, the mountains, the forests, and the fact that I would take up my appointment on July 1, 1963, the very day Victoria College became a University. Moreover my son Nicholas, born in late 1957, was suffering from annual bronchitis, as was I, and I feared for him as for my daughter, Alison, born two years after Nicholas. The doctor told us that Manchester smog was taking ten years off all our lives. It was clearly time to head out for cleaner and preferably sea air, so out we went. Sylvia and the children went

*With son, Nicholas, 1958*

ahead of me, for I had more marking to do than usual, as Manchester had not given my classes to anyone else during my absence, although I had been on unpaid leave, and obliged me to do them all when I returned. I flew out and Sylvia took ship and train, and I caught up with her on the very day she arrived, enormously excited, for after the years of conservative thinking at Manchester I looked forward to working at a place where there were things to be done for the first time. I insisted that I be given a course on the writing of poetry (at Manchester there was none) and it was agreed, and so at last I found my home.

In 1964 I had news from England that my father was dying. I could not get any relief from my lectures at the University, so I tape-recorded two weeks' worth of lectures in two days and Sylvia played the tapes to my classes. My father was still alive when I got to Hull, where my parents had retired in 1946. I spent much time by his bed. He looked at my recently published Penguin anthology, *Poetry of the Thirties,* and asked me, "Was it worth all the work?" He had a way of making quietly challenging comments. At the age of eleven or so I dashed into him one day and announced, "I've written a poem!" He looked at me over his glasses and said, "I hope to goodness you're not going to turn into a poet." Many years later, after I had published three books of verse, I reminded him of this and told him that this had decided me. "Yes," he said, "and you *tried.*" I left him there in bed, the bed in which I had been born, and he said, "Cheerio." He went into a coma two days later and had to be transferred to hospital where he died. My mother came out to live with us, and we had to buy a bigger house to provide room for her.

The sixties in Victoria were exciting. The University was in its beginnings and new ideas were welcomed. Saddlemyer and I and others decided that we must celebrate the centenary of the birth of W.B. Yeats and took over the Art Gallery of Greater Victoria for an exhibition of books, drawings, paintings, and memorabilia, utilizing our private collections. Several plays by Yeats were also produced and there were, of course, lectures both on campus and on CBC radio. The book *The World of W.B. Yeats* emerged from this festival and I contrived to get it published simultaneously in Canada, Ireland, England, and the U.S.A. where a paperback version still exists. The library at UVIC was still small, but, thanks to the book-finding genius of Roger Bishop, the then head of the English Department, it contained many books of considerable value and rarity. There was no rare book room, however, so they were in the stacks, and many had been disfigured by rubber stamps. I therefore made it my habit to go round the stacks with a cart every week or so and collect eighteenth-century books, signed editions, and books of rarity and deliver them to the Chief Librarian with the comment that these were too valuable to be left in the stacks. His office became chockablock with books. When *The World of W.B. Yeats* exhibition ended, I loaned my huge collection of Irish material, which included many great rarities, to the University and a special room had to be found to house them. Not too long after that a "Special Collections" division was created, and I helped it to acquire the complete Dolmen Press archive to that date, and, later, other collections.

I was also busy on the committee for buying art for the University, and was writing a weekly column on art for the then *Victoria Daily Times*. I got this job because the editor thought I had been an art critic for the *Manchester Guardian*. I did not disillusion him. I was fired after a couple of years for writing a very rude review of an edition of the journals of Emily Carr at the same time that a Carr exhibition was taking place with much fanfare. It may not be a coincidence that the book was edited by a person with lots of strings to pull. I got my own back by so organizing my final column that the first letters of all the sentences when read consecutively spelled out "Truth is a Bad Investment, Friend."

In 1966 I was elected a Fellow of the Royal Society of Literature, and that same year John Peter, the novelist, and I decided that Canada needed an international literary quarterly, not only to introduce new foreign writing to our country but also to publicise the work of Canadians in those countries which our magazine would reach, and in due course the *Malahat Review* did indeed reach over two dozen countries. The University paid the whole of the costs during the first years, and our contributions included previously unpublished work by D.H. Lawrence, Lady Gregory, and W.B. Yeats, translated poems, plays, and stories by Rafael Alberti, Ugo Betti, Jorge Luis Borges, Zbigniew Herbert, and August Strindberg, reproductions of worksheets from John Betjeman, James Dickey, Thomas Kinsella, and Robert Graves, and fiction and poetry in English from Lawrence Durrell, Paul Theroux, Margaret Atwood, Kathleen Raine, and John Wain, among many others known and unknown. The art pages contained work by Henry Moore, John Piper, Paul Delvaux, Barbara Hepworth, David Jones, Joan Miró, Edward Weston, and Graham Sutherland, to name but a few.

In 1975 the University's new President, Howard Petch, queried whether or not the *Malahat Review* should be continued. I told him it was prestigious. He asked if I had letters in my files to prove it. I told him that I had not, but could get some. I got letters of enthusiastic support from all over the world, and from writers and artists whose names were sufficiently well known to impress even the most ignorant member of the committee created to deal with the matter. Henry Moore, Samuel Beckett, Robert Graves, George Woodcock, Graham Sutherland, and Lord Clark were among the 149 writers, artists, and academics who wrote enthusiastic letters in support of the *Malahat*. The *Review* continued. Later the President felt there should be an enquiry as to the magazine's efficiency compared with other literary quarterlies of a similar size. I was obliged to do the investigation myself as nobody else knew how to conduct it. I played fair, and the *Malahat Review* turned out to have fewer staff (myself and a part-time secretary) than any other, to have sales around the middle of the scale, and contributors' payments around the middle as well. After that I only suffered a series of budget cuts which prevented me from travelling in search of foreign material, and obliged me, at last, to get regular assistance from the Cultural Fund of British Columbia and the Canada Council which I had previously only asked for help in producing expensive double-size special issues, such as those on Herbert Read, Raphael Alberti, Margaret Atwood, Robert Graves, and Western Canadian Writing. I was also deprived of my Editorial Committee which consisted of senior academics who supported the *Review* in times of stress and helped me over general policy matters involving finance.

In 1969-70 I took my first and only year of leave

from teaching, and wandered Europe with my wife, leaving my children in London with their maternal grandparents. We took in the PEN Congress at Menton (I had been a member of PEN for some time), Corsica, France, Ireland, Italy, and Switzerland (where we visited Ben Nicholson and were given an etching), and, of course, much of England. I wrote many poems, and two books about Synge, got bronchitis in Paris when my wife was away in London, and, finding my halting schoolboy French inadequate for coping with the situation, I developed a new understanding of Kafka's nightmares.

In 1970 my father-in-law suffered a heart attack and had to retire from his position as an organizer for the National Union of Journalists, and so he and my mother-in-law emigrated and travelled with us back to B.C. on the *Oriana*, which took fire while still in Southampton Water, so that we lived in a floating hotel for two delightful weeks before the voyage actually began. The fire itself was quite alarming. Brigid, aged three and normally uncomplaining, voiced the sentiments of all the passengers when, swaddled in a life jacket, she wailed, "I thought this was going to be a fun trip." It was a fun trip, in fact. We called in at Bermuda and Florida and Acapulco and San Francisco, and I wrote a detective novel, with Sylvia's help, for each lunch time I would show her the morning's work, ask her what was going to happen next, and then, the following morning, make sure that it didn't. I was able in San Francisco to smirk at George Cuomo, who takes years over each splendid novel, and say casually, "I wrote a novel on the ship." The novel itself, however, remains unpublished.

Back home again, I decided that it was time to carry out a long-standing plan to divorce the Creative Writing Division from the English Department and create a Department of Creative Writing. It took three years of diplomacy and deviousness, but in 1973 I became the founding Chairman of the new Department, with only two colleagues, Derk Wynand and Lawrence Russell. Over the next three years I hauled in a good many visiting teachers including John Montague, Peter Russell, Jeni Couzyn, Ken Mitchell, and Madelyn de Frees, and hired W.D. Valgardson. I was still editing the *Malahat Review* and by myself, for John Peter had left it in 1971, and I was teaching more than a full load. I also founded an annual series of small anthologies of student writing, and edited most of the early ones. And in 1971 the art collection that Sylvia and I had gathered together was exhibited in the Art Gallery of Greater Victoria, the only time that institution had ever given up its space to a single private collection. I continued making collages and exhibited them in one-

*"The Poem Waiting," a collage by Skelton, 1975*

man shows from time to time, and also made a number of soapstone carvings, which sold rather better than my collages. They started because one of our collection of Inuit carvings fell and was chipped. I decided I could smooth it back into shape with a file and sandpaper, and, on doing so, found pleasure in working with the stone. For some considerable time after that one half of our basement was white with talc and the sound of the saw and drill were heard in the land. I was elected that year to the Board of Directors of the Art Gallery and served it for several years. In 1975 I also served on the executive of the Canadian Periodical Publishers' Association.

In 1972 I made my first (and possibly last) foray into the movie business. William David Thomas and I were commissioned by the Drug Abuse branch of the Provincial Government to write, direct, and produce a movie for educational purposes. It was the end of the financial year and they had money left in the kitty. We had ten days to prepare it. We sat down together and constructed our script, and then, time running out, we cast it by dragging in a number of our friends and portions of our families. William's eldest daughter was the star and my three children also played significant roles. We shot it for the most part in an as yet unused floor of the Eric Martin Institute for Psychiatric Care, and were occasionally visited by disturbed and de-

*Working with soapstone, 1972*

ranged people from lower floors. Their confusion was, however, as nothing to ours. Halfway through shooting, all our camera equipment was stolen and we ceased work for two days. I also may be the only movie director who ever attempted location shots during an eclipse of the sun. (Nobody told me it was to happen.) The movie got finished, however, and we were pleased with it, as it dealt largely with diagnosis, cure, and rehabilitation, and did not merely tell a horror story; moreover we had the sense to use a real psychiatrist to talk to the parents of the disturbed girl at the centre of the film, and two real parents to argue over their child's predicament, and we allowed them to improvise. The movie itself, however, fell victim to a change of government; the Drug Abuse program was abandoned and I have never seen the final edited version. It is lost somewhere in the government archives. I do not, however, regret the experience, and I wonder now whether it has anything to do with my son's choice of television as a career.

I took up stamp collecting again, too, in the early seventies. My Uncle Bill Sykes had given me his stamp collection before he died, and it was in chaotic condition. Sorting it out and adding to it my schoolboy collection, which my mother had not sold when I was

away in India (though she had got rid of my huge collection of toy soldiers and three half-sovereigns given me by my grandfather), was a kind of therapy, being a relatively mindless occupation and totally unconnected with the stresses and strains of my University work; it was my escape at a time when I desperately needed one.

Another escape took the form of two months in the Cariboo area of B.C. where my Uncle Will Robins had settled and where my cousin Nellie and her family still lived. I had visited them before, but this time I was determined somehow to express my allegiance to a country I had heard so much of as a child, having been regaled with stories of my Cousin Rose (now dead) who was a famous bareback rider at the Williams' Lake Stampede. My book *They Call It the Cariboo* began its slow progress towards publication that summer.

In 1976 I fell from grace. I knew that I had been heading for a fall. I had instituted so many new courses, and invited so many visitors, without the usual rituals of committee meetings, that I was certain to come to grief. But I knew that the only way to get the Department to be a real success was to work quickly before the boom times were over or the University became wholly entangled in red tape. In 1976 I received harsh criticism from one of my colleagues, and no support from the others, so, following my principle that a Chairman must not continue when he has lost the support of his department, I resigned and took a month or so off to have a very minor breakdown. That year I was made a Fellow of the English Centre of International PEN and elected a Knight of Mark Twain, filling the vacancy left by the death of C. Day Lewis.

The seventies had begun with a real upheaval. My ticky-tacky box of a house had become too small for us and our three children, and even though my mother had left for England on the birth of Brigid— our third, unplanned, and marvellous child—in 1966, the acoustics made it hard to work, for a word spoken in any room could be heard in most of the others and teenage record players made quiet thought impossible. The University had asked me several times to sell them my Irish collection and I had always told them that I would do so only when I needed the money. And then one morning Sylvia found a house, a huge and elegant mansion, with room for all of us, walls for our art collection, and space for whatever we wanted. I had to make up my mind in half an hour, or the house would be put on the open market. I walked round it. It was a place I could write in. I said, "We'll take it," and did not even ask the price. I had to find $20,000 cash for the down-payment in ten days and there was nothing in the bank. I sold my Irish collection with the delight-

*Marcia Willis*

*With Sylvia, 1985*

ful feeling that Yeats, Synge, Lady Gregory, and their friends had bought my house for me. I also sold some of my personal archives and thus started the hideously large Skelton Collection at the University, to which I now add new material every two or three years, by donation. That way I both get an income tax rebate and, thanks to the Curator of Special Collections, can actually find material which would otherwise be lost to me in the welter of papers and books which is my study.

It was in 1972 that my mother returned to Canada, no longer able to look after herself or continue looking after her brother-in-law for whom she had been acting as housekeeper. She lived with us until progressive Alzheimers disease caused her not to know who we were or where she was, and also inflicted paranoiac delusions. In 1980 she went into a home, where she died in 1982 at the age of ninety-three. It had been a difficult time, especially for my wife, for round-the-clock nursing was required. We could no longer hold our weekly "Thursdays" for friends to drop round for wine and cheese in the evenings. We had kept these going for seven years. Some Thursdays provided only two or three people; some found us with fifty or more. Our highest score was 108. We never knew whether we were facing a conversazione, a party, or a dance. Our friends were, and are, a fine mixture of academics, writers, artists, and people who fit into no category save that of friendship. I was at that time organizing the Poetry Reading Series at the University, and I held

these on Thursdays also, so that visiting writers always found a good party to go to after they had given their performances, and we had the room to give them a place to stay, which reduced expenses and increased our pleasure.

In the early seventies, too, a group of these friends, all artists, decided to form the Limners Society of Artists of which Sylvia was and remains Honorary Secretary. I was initially Vice-President. The founders were Maxwell Bates, Herbert Siebner, Elza Mayhew, Nita Forest, Robert de Castro, Richard Ciccimarra, and Myfanwy Pavelic. The Limners have been giving exhibitions in Victoria and elsewhere in Canada ever since, and our infrequent meetings are invariably occasions of great hilarity. Maxwell Bates, Richard Ciccimarra, and Robert de Castro are now dead, but others have joined the group and it continues to enliven my days. I wrote a number of articles on these and other artists in the *Malahat Review* and also contrived a full-length monograph on Siebner, with whom I collaborated in creating two collections of poems with accompanying hand-coloured pictures. The second of these was published by the Pharos Press which Sylvia and I founded in 1972 to produce fine limited editions of works that excited us. So far it has included Robert Graves' *Marmosites Miscellany* (first published pseudonymously), a collection of *Kiskatinaw Songs* by Susan Musgrave and Sean Virgo, and a collection of translated poems by George Faludy.

These books were printed by the firm of Morriss Printing in Victoria with whom I have worked ever since *The World of W.B. Yeats* was published, and who are the printers of the *Malahat Review*. In 1976 the one-man publishing house Sono Nis Press failed and Richard Morriss took it over in lieu of monies owing. He then asked me to be Editor-in-Chief of the firm, and I agreed with enthusiasm. I decided that the press, while continuing the poetry list which had been its main concern, should also concentrate upon books of Northwestern interest, histories of our coast, memoirs, and journals; this series continues to be successful. I also introduced some art books to the list and some literary criticism, and am happy to say that the firm is now one of the most respected small houses in the country, thanks particularly to the high quality of the books' design and printing.

It was in 1977 that I decided that it might be my last chance for some time to travel to Europe with my wife, for my mother's health was deteriorating. Moreover, the University Library had asked me to sell it another big parcel of my manuscripts and this would make it possible to finance the trip. The day before the cheque was due to be issued the University President cancelled the sale on the grounds that no University bought archives from its employees. I was furious. I did not, in any case, believe him. So I brought the matter to the attention of the Writers' Union of Canada, found myself heading a committee on authors' archives, and discovered that only one university in the country had placed such a ban, and that this was being reconsidered. I wrote a pamphlet for the Union on how authors should turn their archives into cash, and I then, perversely, donated my own material to the University. This pamphlet led to another committee and another pamphlet on Authors' Wills, and I was elected to the Union Executive and became Chairman of the Union for 1982-83. I asked my University for some relief from teaching and a small travelling grant to help me get to Toronto for meetings. I was refused. I therefore commuted from Victoria to Toronto throughout the year, the Union paying for some airfares, and others being covered by Canada Council-supported readings in the Toronto area. It was important, I felt, that I should not give this position up. I was the first Chairman to be appointed who lived outside Ontario, and I was fearful that the Union would become centrist if "provincials" were unable to take high office within it.

In 1975 William David Thomas and I collaborated again on two Robert Graves projects. We edited a special issue of the *Malahat Review* in celebration of the poet's eightieth birthday and arranged for every copy to contain a signed serigraph portrait of Graves by William Featherston—the first time an original print had been included in a magazine in Canada. The BBC also commissioned us to visit Graves in Mallorca and build a programme from the interviews. This was not wholly a success. I did the interviews round the vast table of the poet's friend Martin Tallents over afternoon teas for several days. Robert's memory was becoming shaky. He would tell half a story and then appeal to Martin to complete it, which Martin (well off-mike) would do. Moreover Robert contrived to cough into his neck mike, to pour tea on it, even once, I believe, to butter it. The five hours of tape we got were fascinating but were unusable, so, back in B.C. and in the CBC studios we constructed a programme from existing tapes of Graves made over the years and I did a linking script and a description of his splendid eightieth birthday party. The BBC gave the programme an award for excellence.

In 1978 I visited Europe again, with William. Sylvia had to remain home, for my mother was unwell and we could not afford two tickets. (Sylvia got her own trip, with an eighteen-year-old Brigid in 1985, while I stayed home.) We spent time in France, Spain, and Italy as well as England and Wales, and in Rome became friends with Marino Villalta about whom I wrote an essay in the *Malahat Review*. I also spent a

couple of weeks in Cambridge, which had given me so much, and which I still enjoy. It was there, however, that I was taken aback by a statement that still troubles me. A lady who had been present at a dinner gathering the previous night, came upon me in King's Parade, and said in a loud shrill voice, "But I didn't realize last night! You're FAMOUS!" I didn't know how to handle that. I still don't. I muttered, "Maybe well-known," and passed on as soon as I could. Like many artists I distrust admiration slightly more than I desire it.

A chunk of bread I had cast upon the waters in 1956 came back to me in 1983, when my play *The Paper Cage* found first a publisher, and then a theatre. The remarkably imaginative and talented group of players in William Head Prison put the play on for the general public and got deservedly excellent reviews. I was much moved, for the play itself deals frequently with the feelings and thoughts of Regulus as a prisoner in Carthage and the whole play is about kinds of imprisonment. The cons were enthusiastic about it, so I must have done something right.

During the seventies I gave more poetry readings than before and also spent two weeks each summer for three years in Wells, B.C., teaching the writing of poetry and fiction and living in a log cabin. I enjoyed, and still enjoy, these workshops away from the big cities, for the students are of all ages and are keen on their work. Indeed, I found myself working a twelve-hour day one way or another, though I must admit I held my afternoon individual discussion and criticism sessions in the Jack o' Clubs pub. From these classes, and of course from University classes, I have seen many writers of real quality emerge, and am gratified to list a number of now well-established writers among my sometime students. The next best thing to writing a book, I have always felt, is getting a book out of someone else. Perhaps that is why I enjoyed editing the *Malahat Review* and working for the Sono Nis Press so much.

In 1983, the University authorities decided that the *Malahat Review* should not be run so autocratically, and also that its budget should be severely cut, perhaps even cancelled entirely. Rather than fight yet another battle, which I realized I was certain to lose, and knowing that my successor (Constance Rooke, whom I had already acquired as an Associate Editor) would succeed where I could not, I resigned. I could have simply caused the *Review* to die, but no editor should allow his proprietorial feelings or his ego to kill a literary quarterly in these days. Besides, I could no longer get the international material I wanted, as I no longer had a travel allowance, and the magazine was to be deprived

*Poet with Hat, 1980*

of even a part-time secretary. At the same time I resigned from the Sono Nis Press. In seven years I had done what I wanted to do, and I felt new perspectives were needed. Then, in order to make a clean sweep of things, I handed over the task of organizing the University Poetry Readings to a colleague, and, my stint as Chairman of the Writers' Union being over, I decided to settle down to concentrating upon writing and teaching.

It was at this time, however, that another obsession took over a portion of my life. I had met the great George Faludy in 1982, and, having seen how his usually rhymed and metrical poems had been presented as flat free verse by his translators, I decided, as an experiment, to see if I could do better. He agreed to give me literal line-by-line translations in English from the original Hungarian, and began with a series of sonnets. I got them into sonnet form all right and they were published by the Pharos Press in 1983. This led to my working for a couple of years on translating Faludy. Some of the challenges were very exciting. I had to imitate Mayakovsky and Villon, write in sapphics and the Rubaiyat stanza, construct sixteen-syllable lines, and even, once, adopt the vocabulary and diction of the eighteenth century. Faludy's *Selected Poems 1933-1980*, which also included some translations by others whom I had dragged into the project as well as a few

revised versions of the best earlier translations, appeared in 1985, and I shared the first F.R. Scott Award for Poetry in Translation with Roger Greenwald who had produced a wonderful version of the poems of Rolf Jacobsen.

I could not make my own poems while entering so thoroughly into Faludy's work, but I found a new zest in writing short stories, one of which won another prize. I also completed a novel set in the Stone Age, and a collection of aphorisms. I was not, however, to remain too securely tied to my typewriter (my mechanical ability does not extend to word processors), as the Ministry of External Affairs sent me off to tour Ireland with Susan Musgrave. We did nineteen readings in twenty-one days, with Susan's husband driving the car, and her small daughter—whom Irish barmaids considered "a little doat"—enlivening and complicating the proceedings. We had great fun on the whole, but it was exhausting. Our organizers had not realized that a one-hour drive on Canadian roads may take four in Ireland, as the roads are narrow, the villages frequent, and slow-moving herds of cattle ubiquitous. Both of us were surprised when our audiences expressed astonishment that we were entertaining and cracked occasional jokes. Irish poetry readings appear to be usually sombre affairs. There were a number of misadventures, of course, but as we both knew and loved the country and its eccentricities we were not especially fazed.

After Ireland (which enabled me to make a side trip to London and visit my son who was working there) I was delighted, a year later, to be sent off to Sweden, where I visited writers' groups, talked to writers' organizations, and gave readings in Stockholm, Lund, Uppsala, and Göteborg. The Swedes were enormously hospitable and I enjoyed myself in spite of a perpetual jet-lag, for it took me twenty-six hours to get there from Victoria. I also did a brief tour of colleges in the Puget Sound area of Washington, where, again, the hospitality was splendid and the audiences responsive. Tours of this kind I find invigorating, if not particularly remunerative. It is good to try one's voice and one's words out on members of other cultures, and also to feel part of the world community of writers for a little while.

The eighties brought some sadness. My father- and mother-in-law moved into our house, where we had prepared rooms and a separate kitchen for them, as they no longer felt able to cope with the house and garden we had been providing for them since 1970. My father-in-law died in the house, after many months of pain, in October 1984. It was a great loss; he was not only a friend but also our household's beer and wine maker. He challenged me to put him in a short story, which I did. "The Importance of Being Percy" is a joke at his expense, but an affectionate one, and he relished it.

It was in the early eighties too, that, at a massive Toronto banquet called "The Night of a Hundred Authors," I met Barbara Turner, a writer whose sister I had once taught, and we became friends. Our friendship led to her deciding to construct a book about me, and *Skelton at Sixty* finally emerged, filled with serious essays on my work, less serious and sometimes scurrilous anecdotes, and drawings, poems, and paintings by sixty of my friends not only in Canada but also in England, Ireland, and the U.S.A. At first it felt like an obituary. Perhaps I was finished. But then I remembered Geoffrey Keynes telling a gathering at Barts for his seventieth birthday that they would be certain to regret it in ten or twenty years, for he came of a long-lived family and eightieth and ninetieth birthdays were to be expected. He died when he was ninety-three, and was making books right to the end. I hope I may last as long.

*Robin Skelton, 1985*

*Marcia Willis*

## BIBLIOGRAPHY

**Poetry:**

*Patmos and Other Poems.* London: Routledge & Kegan Paul, 1955.

*Third Day Lucky.* London and New York: Oxford University Press, 1958.

*Begging the Dialect: Poems and Ballads.* London and New York: Oxford University Press, 1960.

*Two Ballads of the Muse.* Cambridge, England: Rampant Lions Press, 1960.

*The Dark Window.* London and New York: Oxford University Press, 1962.

*A Valedictory Poem.* Privately printed, 1963.

*An Irish Gathering.* Dublin, Ireland: Dolmen Press, 1964.

*A Ballad of Billy Barker.* Privately printed, 1965.

*Inscriptions.* Privately printed, 1967.

*Because of This and Other Poems.* Manchester, England: Manchester Institute of Contemporary Arts, 1968.

*The Hold of Our Hands: Eight Letters to Sylvia.* Privately printed, 1968.

*Selected Poems, 1947-1967.* Toronto: McClelland & Stewart, 1968.

*Answers.* London: Enitharmon Press, 1969.

*An Irish Album.* Dublin, Ireland: Dolmen Press, 1969.

*A Different Mountain.* Santa Cruz, Calif.: Kayak, 1971.

*The Hunting Dark.* Toronto: McClelland & Stewart, 1971; London: Deutsch, 1971.

*A Private Speech: Messages 1962-1970.* Surrey, B.C.: Sono Nis Press, 1971.

*Remembering Synge: A Poem in Homage for the Centenary of His Birth, 16 April 1971.* Dublin, Ireland: Dolmen Press, 1971.

*A Christmas Poem.* Privately printed, 1972.

*Hypothesis.* Toronto: Dreadnaught Press, 1972.

*Musebook.* Victoria, B.C.: Pharos Press, 1972.

*Three for Herself.* Rushden, England: Sceptre Press, 1972.

*Country Songs.* Rushden, England: Sceptre Press, 1973.

*The Hermit Shell.* Privately printed, 1974.

*Timelight.* Toronto: McClelland & Stewart, 1974; London: Heinemann, 1974.

*Fifty Syllables for a Fiftieth Birthday.* Privately printed, 1975.

*Georges Zuk: The Underwear of the Unicorn.* Lanzville, B.C.: Oolichan Books, 1975.

*Callsigns.* Victoria, B.C.: Sono Nis Press, 1976.

*Because of Love.* Toronto: McClelland & Stewart, 1977.

*Three Poems.* Knotting, England: Sceptre Press, 1977.

*Landmarks.* Victoria, B.C.: Sono Nis Press, 1979.

*Collected Shorter Poems, 1947-1977.* Victoria, B.C.: Sono Nis Press, 1981.

*Limits.* Erin, Ontario: Porcupine's Quill, 1981.

*De Nihilo.* Toronto: Aloysius Press, 1982.

*Zuk.* Erin, Ontario: Porcupine's Quill, 1982.

*Wordsong.* Victoria, B.C.: Sono Nis Press, 1983.

*Collected Longer Poems, 1947-1977.* Victoria, B.C.: Sono Nis Press, 1985.

*Distances.* Erin, Ontario: Porcupine's Quill, 1985.

*Openings.* Victoria, B.C.: Sono Nis Press, 1988.

**Fiction:**

*The Man Who Sang in His Sleep.* Erin, Ontario: Porcupine's Quill, 1985.

*The Parrot Who Did.* Victoria, B.C.: Sono Nis Press, 1987.

*Telling the Tale.* Erin, Ontario: Porcupine's Quill, 1987.

**Plays:**

*The Paper Cage.* Lanzville, B.C.: Oolichan Press, 1983.

**Nonfiction:**

*John Ruskin: The Final Years.* Manchester, England: Manchester University Press and John Rylands Library, 1955.

*The Poetic Pattern.* London: Routledge & Kegan Paul, 1956; Berkeley and Los Angeles: University of California Press, 1956.

*Painters Talking: Michael Snow and Tony Connor Interviewed.* Manchester, England: Peterloo Group, 1957.

*Cavalier Poets.* London: Longmans, Green, 1960.

*Teach Yourself Poetry.* London: English Universities Press, 1963; New York: Dover, 1965.

*J.M. Synge and His World.* London: Thames & Hudson, 1971; New York: Viking, 1971.

*Paintings, Graphics, and Sculpture from the Collection of Robin and Sylvia Skelton.* Privately printed, 1971.

*The Practice of Poetry.* London: Heinemann, 1971; New York: Barnes & Noble, 1971.

*The Writings of J.M. Synge.* London: Thames & Hudson, 1971; Indianapolis: Bobbs-Merrill, 1971.

*J.M. Synge.* Lewisburg, Pa.: Bucknell University Press, 1972.

*The Limners.* Victoria, B.C.: Pharos Press, 1972, 1975, 1978, 1986.

*The Poet's Calling.* London: Heinemann, 1975; New York: Barnes & Noble, 1975.

*Poetic Truth.* London: Heinemann, 1978; New York: Barnes & Noble, 1978.

*Explorations within a Landscape: New Porcelain by Robin Hopper.* Victoria, B.C.: Robin Hopper, 1978.

*Spellcraft: A Manual of Verbal Magic.* Toronto: McClelland & Stewart, 1978; London: Routledge & Kegan Paul, 1978.

*Herbert Siebner: A Monograph.* Victoria, B.C.: Sono Nis Press, 1979.

*They Call It the Cariboo.* Victoria, B.C.: Sono Nis Press, 1980.

*House of Dreams: Collages.* Erin, Ontario: Porcupine's Quill, 1983.

*Talismanic Magic.* New York: Samuel Weiser, 1985.

**Editor of:**

*Leeds University Poetry 1949.* Leeds, England: Lotus Press, 1950.

*Translations,* by J.M. Synge. Dublin, Ireland: Dolmen Press, 1961.

*The Collected Poems of J.M. Synge.* London: Oxford University Press, 1962.

*Four Plays and "The Aran Islands,"* by J.M. Synge. London and New York: Oxford University Press, 1962.

*Selected Poems,* by Edward Thomas. London: Hutchinson, 1962.

*Six Irish Poets: Austin Clarke, Richard Kell, Thomas Kinsella, John Montague, Richard Murphy, Richard Weber.* London and New York: Oxford University Press, 1962.

*Viewpoint: An Anthology of Poetry.* London: Hutchinson, 1962.

*Five Poets of the Pacific Northwest: Kenneth O. Hanson, Richard Hugo, Carolyn Kizer, William Stafford, and David Wagoner.* Seattle: University of Washington Press, 1964.

*Poets of the Thirties.* Harmondsworth, England: Penguin, 1964.

*Collected Poems,* by David Gascoyne. London and New York: Oxford University Press-Deutsch, 1965.

*Irish Renaissance: A Gathering of Essays, Letters, and Memoirs from the "Massachusetts Review,"* with David R. Clark. Dublin, Ireland and Brattleboro, Vt.: Dolmen Press, 1965; London: Oxford University Press, 1965.

*Selected Poems of Byron.* London: Heinemann, 1965; New York: Barnes & Noble, 1966.

*The World of W.B. Yeats: Essays in Perspective,* with Ann Saddlemyer. London: Oxford University Press, 1965; Dublin, Ireland: Dolmen Press, 1965; Victoria, B.C.: The Adelphi Bookshop, 1965; Seattle: University of Washington Press, 1967.

*Poetry of the Forties.* Harmondsworth, England: Penguin, 1968.

*Introductions from an Island: A Selection of Student Writing.* Victoria, B.C.: University of Victoria, 1969, 1971, 1973, 1974, 1977.

*Riders to the Sea,* by J.M. Synge. Dublin, Ireland: Dolmen Press, 1969.

*Collected Verse Translations,* by David Gascoyne, edited with Alan Clodd. London and New York: Oxford University Press, 1970.

*Herbert Read: A Memorial Symposium.* London: Methuen, 1970.

*The Collected Plays of Jack B. Yeats.* London: Secker & Warburg, 1971; Indianapolis: Bobbs-Merrill, 1971.

*Some Sonnets from "Laura in Death" after the Italian of Francesco Petrarch,* by J.M. Synge (bilingual edition). Dublin, Ireland: Dolmen Press, 1971.

*Six Poets of British Columbia.* Victoria: Sono Nis Press, 1980. Boston: David Godine, 1973.

*From Syria: The Worksheets, Proofs, and Text,* by Ezra Pound. Port Townsend, Wash.: Copper Canyon Press, 1981.

**Translator and Editor of:**

*Two Hundred Poems from "The Greek Anthology."* Toronto: McClelland & Stewart, 1971; London: Methuen, 1971; Seattle: University of Washington Press, 1972.

*George Faludy: Twelve Sonnets.* Victoria, B.C.: Pharos Press, 1983.

*Selected Poems of George Faludy, 1933-80,* translated with others. Athens: University of Georgia Press, 1985.

*George Faludy: Corpses, Brats, and Cricket Music* (bilingual edition). Vancouver, B.C.: William Hoffer, 1986.

# Kate Wilhelm

*1928-*

## A TAPESTRY

*Kate with the 1968 Nebula Award for her short story "The Planners"*

I was born into a sea of confusion, out of the amniotic sea into a sea of argument and dissension. My father wanted to name me after a cousin, Katie Downs, and my mother was unprepared with a counter name, or perhaps she was simply tired. In any event, he won. Katie Gertrude Meredith went on the birth certificate, June 8, 1928. They could have called me Katie, or Kate, or Gertie, or Trudie, or some other variation, but they called me Catherine from the start. I was sixteen before I knew my name.

I worked at the telephone company while in high school as a long-distance operator, during the last year of World War II. One day the personnel manager sent for me. My first thought was that I was being fired because I never could remember the little set phrases we were supposed to deliver: *Sorry, that line is busy. Shall I try again in ten minutes?* or *The circuits are busy now, please*

*try again later.* The one that bothered me most was the response: *Operator.* Now that should hold no mystery for anyone, but I never could seem to remember exactly what it meant. It identified who was speaking, no more than that. I would try to put through a call to Texas, for example, and this voice would come on the line and say, "Operator." I would say, "Yes." And the other operator would repeat her one word and I would too. Presently she would say angrily something like, "This is the operator. Who are you?" The mystery would be cleared up. The supervisor more often than not would tap me on the shoulder for a little chat. So it was that when the personnel manager sent for me, I was prepared for the worst.

I was told by her secretary to go on in, and I did so, cautiously. It was in the fall; Christmas was coming up. I did not want to lose the job, and I knew there was little reason for them to keep me. She looked up from paperwork on her desk.

"What's your name?" she demanded.

That was the only response I definitely knew I knew. "Catherine Meredith."

"No it isn't."

"Then what is?" I was astonished and disbelieving.

She told me my name officially was Kate and that it had to be changed on my income-tax records, my employment records for Social Security, and so on. She did not threaten to fire me. When I asked my mother to explain all this, she also said they had named me Kate after the distant relative. And so the matter ended, I thought.

I did not adopt the name publicly, not yet. It became my escape hatch. When things got to be too much over the next ten or twelve years, as they frequently did, I became Kate in secret. No one could touch me as Kate, because that person did not yet exist. I could hide in a name.

Fifteen years later I learned how inefficient the security check had been. They got it wrong, after all. I had moved to Pennsylvania where I applied for a driver's license, using the name Kate. By then I was no longer hiding. I had become a writer, and that was my official name. The bureaucrat in Harrisburg did not approve. My application was returned with a scrawled note saying they could not accept diminutives, and I

had to use my full name, Catherine, or however I
spelled it. He had drawn a black line through Kate.
I wrote back that I had used my full name. He replied
that I would have to furnish a certified birth certificate.
I wrote to Toledo, Ohio, for that. Eventually it arrived
and I learned my real name. During all this time, five
months or more, I had been driving illegally, carrying
copies of all the correspondence in my purse, to justify
my criminal behavior if I should be stopped by the
police.

I was number four of six children, four boys, two
girls. The first born was, almost by definition, the
most precocious; that was Edwin. Two years younger
than he there was Eula, the prettiest, with curly blonde
hair and a petite build, fragile looking. Two-and-a-half
years later came Kenneth, the cleverest and most en-
terprising. I came into the family nearly three years
after him, and there followed, again separated by
about two-and-a-half years, Russell, an erratically brilliant child, and last, five years later, David, the steadi-
est of all. For whatever reason, the grouping was usually referred to as the three older children, then
Catherine, and the two youngest children. Russell was
born on Kenneth's birthday; Kenny promptly sold
him for a dollar to a neighbor. He was quite bitter
about the birthday joke present.

*The author's parents, Jesse and Ann Meredith
(right), 1918*

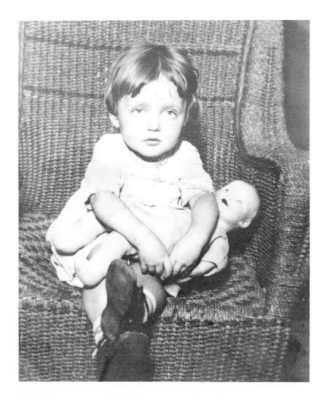

*Catherine Meredith, age two*

I have thought a lot about the spacing of the children in our family. With five years separating all the
boys and five years between my sister and me, what
happened was that we never formed the tight friendships based on gender that might have been expected.
Five years is hard to bridge until adulthood. Ed and
Eula were friends to a degree; Kenny and I were
deadly enemies until we were both grown. I was always
much closer to the two younger boys. This has something to do with being a middle child—too young to be
allowed the privileges of the older children, too old to
be allowed the peccadilloes of the younger ones. It had
more to do, I think, with the fact that for the first five
years of my life no one could understand a thing I said.

By the time Russell was born, suspicions had
grown that there was something wrong with my
speech. I talked a lot, they tell me, but in tongues. Now
and then my mother could decipher my words, or my
father could, but no one else. It must have been an
embarrassment to the older children; I know there was
a certain amount of teasing from Kenny, and scorn
from Eula. Very early I stopped trying to communi-
cate, thinking, I suppose, there was little point to it. To
a certain extent I became an invisible child, and this
continued for most of my life before I left home. When
I got very good grades in school, no one noticed. When
I stayed home from school for no particular reason, no
one noticed. As a teenager I was never severely questioned about the hours I kept, the many activities I was
engaged in. I don't think anyone noticed.

I don't remember the process; no one taught me,
but I cannot remember a time when I could not read.
Every week my mother went to the library with a shopping bag and brought home the world. She read to us
all until we were too old to sit still for it. I have vivid

memories of the illustrations, of her finger moving along the words for me to follow. I loved the Palmer Brownies the most. All those hundreds and hundreds of busy Brownies swarming over bridges, building snowmen, riding horses. There was a blue overstuffed chair in our living room that I hid behind to read the library books for myself in between her readings.

The other pastime I loved was cutting out pictures of furniture from magazines and newspapers. I kept my collection in a cardboard box. It was very complicated, finding pieces in scale, organizing the colored pieces, the black-and-white illustrations, which had to be colored with crayons. When the older children were in school, I got out my furniture and arranged rooms all over the living-room floor. I furnished mansions, castles, and lived in them all.

One incident filled me with terror during those early speechless years. My mother always took one of us with her to the library. This day it was my turn to go. We had moved to Cleveland by then, and the library of choice was the big main one downtown that we reached by streetcar. I remember it as an imposing gray building with wide steps up to the entrance. My mother took me to the children's room and left me there with orders to wait for her. I sat on the floor and read for a long time, I thought, and then went looking for her. I could not find her anywhere, and eventually I decided she must have forgotten about me and was even then on her way home. I left the library with the intention of walking home also. And I left it by a different door. When I reached the street, it was like awakening in a foreign land, with buildings I never had seen before, traffic patterns I could not recognize, no familiar landmark anywhere. I had planned to follow the streetcar tracks all the way to my street, West Seventy-second. I might even have made it if I had exited the only way I knew. But I was lost and I wandered for a bit and began to cry and was picked up by a policeman who took me to a station house where they let me sit on a motorcycle and on a horse. They gave me ice cream and tried to calm me down enough to tell them my name and address. I told them both many times and gave up when they failed to understand. By then I was not frightened any more, and was even enjoying the attention and especially the horse. I did manage to make them understand a name, Rafferty, a city alderman who lived next door to us, and through that name they located first him and then my parents, and presently my father arrived to collect me.

In kindergarten I was placed in speech therapy and the teacher listened to me for a few minutes and knew exactly what was wrong. She made me slow down and pronounce each syllable. My tongue had been put on fast forward at birth, and it was relatively

*With brother Russell, 1937*

simple to change it to normal speed. She was the first one who realized that I was really reading, not just memorizing the words I had heard, or looking at pictures. Part of her method was to read from children's books and have me repeat words, phrases, and then sentences. One day I continued to read past the point where she had stopped, and she let me go on for a page or two, then closed the book, said I was all right, and sent me back to class. She put her arm around me as she walked me to the door, then gave my shoulder a little squeeze, and I loved her fiercely. Later, I would walk past her door slowly, dawdling, hoping to catch a glimpse of her, but I never did. I don't even know her name, but she was the most important person in my life at that time. She saw me, heard me, understood me, made me feel special; she opened the world to me.

My memories of the first few years in school consist of the various constructions I made with building blocks. While the other children were struggling with Dick and Jane I built castles and in my mind's eye furnished them with the wonderful pieces of furniture I had collected. I built highways to my mansions, houses with many wings, apartment buildings, towering skyscrapers, and furnished them all. I also drew mazes by the hour. Done with my work, required to sit at my desk, my books all read, I drew ever more complicated mazes, filled pages with them. Later, when we had to start reading aloud in class, I planned in advance exactly how long I would read, where I would make a mistake. Sometimes I read only a paragraph, then again pages, and once or twice until the teacher told me to stop. It was a silly system. Making a mistake ended your turn and consequently the ones who needed help most got very little. As soon as our reading books were handed out, I read mine from cover to cover, and at home I read my brothers' pulp magazines—*The Shadow, Doc Savage,* mystery magazines, flying stories; whatever they read, so did I. I read my father's books—Ellery Queen, Erle Stanley Gardner, Zane Grey. I read the newspapers and magazines that came into the house—*Blue Book, National Geographic, Saturday Evening Post, Ladies Home Companion.* And I read fairy tales, all of them, over and over.

Our house had a wide porch with a swing and several chairs. It opened to a staircase on the right, the doorway to the living room on the left. A hall led to the dining room, and the kitchen. My parents' bedroom and the one bathroom was also on the first floor. Upstairs were three bedrooms, one shared by Ed and Kenny, one for Eula and me, and one for Russell. David was still in a crib in my parents' room. There was a connecting closet between the boys' room and the one my sister and I had. It was a long, narrow closet with a sloping roof and no lights. Only if both doors were left open was there enough light to see anything. I would go upstairs and into my room, close the door, then sneak through the closet to the boys' room and sneak out a book or magazine. I never prowled through their other belongings, or snooped generally, although they suspected that someone was doing that. At one time Ed accused me of going into their room and I stoutly maintained that I had not touched their bedroom door. As long as I could distinguish the bedroom door from the closet door, I felt safe. They never caught me. I felt then that they didn't have anything else of interest anyway, but my sister did.

Eula had secrets all her life. She was five years my senior, and I must have been a terrible burden for her. Sometimes my mother made her let me go to the store with her and her friends, or to the library. Eula hated it. She made me walk well behind her and her best friends so I couldn't overhear their conversations. She pretended she didn't know me. She had secrets in the closet we shared, too. I was forbidden to touch anything on her side. Of course, I did, and never found anything as interesting as I'd expected, although there were mysterious objects. I tore a sanitary pad apart trying to figure out what it was and what it was for. She called me a snoop and hit me. She drew a picture on the ceiling over our bed and said it was me. It was a moon-faced pumpkin. She drew a line down the center of the bed and warned me not to cross it, not even in my sleep, and to turn my face the other way so I

*The Merediths, 1939: Kate, Russell, and David in front; Father, Mother, Edwin, and Eula behind. Missing is brother Kenneth*

wouldn't breathe on her. She had curly blonde hair; mine was straight and brown. She was fragile and delicate looking; I was a sturdy tomboy. She was always clean; I was always dirty. She was artistic, and could draw very well, and liked pretty pictures, and studied piano. Those virtues eluded me. By the time I was seven or eight, she was already always washing her hair and curling it, and I thought it was plain dumb, that everything she did was dumb. I never played with dolls. I must have had them although I don't recall any of my own. Eula had several beautiful dolls, porcelain with blue eyes, blonde curly hair, of course. I do remember deliberately throwing one of them down the stairs and watching it break into pieces. I remember the satisfaction it gave me.

I never was afraid of the dark; my favorite hiding places for the games of Hide-and-Seek we played indoors were in the closet that linked the two bedrooms, behind out-of-season clothes, or boxes, and in a cold-storage room in the basement, on an upper shelf in the dark. But I had other terrors. Eula and Ed took me on a Ferris wheel when I was very young, and I panicked when it reached the top. The seat was swaying, and Ed made it swing more wildly by leaning forward, then back. I became hysterical, screaming out of control, and they had to bring me down. I refused to ride anything at the amusement park for many years, and tried again only when I was a teenager among teenagers, and I hated it. The merry-go-round is my speed. Another time Ed decided to teach me to swim and took me to a sandbar in Lake Erie. It was not far from shore, and I doubt the water was very deep. Ed told me I had to swim back, and I started, but when I wanted to stop, I could not reach bottom, and I panicked again. Somehow I got ashore, dog paddling, terrified, but I still want to know where the bottom is when I swim. I don't like murky water, or unknown water.

Our street had single-family houses with big yards. There was not much traffic. It was a good place to spend childhood. We were bounded by Franklin Boulevard, on one end, and Euclid Avenue, on the other. Past Franklin there was the lake shore, the beach where we spent most of our time in the summer. Euclid had the streetcars, trips to the library, to the Twenty-fifth Street Market, a farmers' market my mother visited weekly. I loved to go with her. The vegetables smelled good, and were plentiful. It was exciting in a disorderly way, with stalls, produce spread out on the ground, shops, long tables of juices and fruits, wagons and truck beds with pumpkins and squashes. There was the poultry store, a fish market, butcher shops. It was smelly and dirty and noisy, just the right sort of place for a child to visit now and then.

On the block was an ethnic mix of Lithuanians, Swedes, Irish, Germans, Italians. The religious mix was wide also: Catholics, Jews, Baptists, Lutherans, and heaven alone knows what else. One time Kenny announced that he was going to become a Catholic priest, not out of religious conviction, but because the Catholic children had more school holidays than we did. We all played together. In the summer twilight we played Kick the Can, or Red Rover, or Red Light, Green Light, or, my favorite, Hide-and-Seek. In the winter we built snow forts and, at least once, a real igloo. The best times were in the summer when many of us would gather in our backyard and the Swedish boys would tell stories.

A stone cutter had occupied our house at one time, and when he moved on, he left many blocks of cut granite, slabs of a smooth rock, slaty and shiny, and miscellaneous odds and ends. These were all in the back corner of our yard, and it was the best place on the block. The rock pile was a theater, a ship, a castle, a rocket ship, an airplane, whatever was needed for any fantasy. Those were magic times when the sky was clear, turning cerulean blue that deepened to darkness so slowly that when the first star appeared, it too was like magic. One moment the sky was sunlit, the next it had a star, then another, another. As if on cue the lightning bugs began to flash on and off. The rocks radiated the heat of the sun and somehow felt softer than rock, yielding. And the older boys told folktales, or adventure stories. I was beneath their notice, naturally; they were Ed's age or slightly older. I didn't dare move, to draw attention to myself, for fear Ed would make me go inside. I was entranced over and over by

their stories, the setting, the mystery of words working such magic.

The rock pile was a very special spot; I read there, or played with my own friends there, played with Russ on them, baby-sat David out there, and it was on them that I experienced one of the worst terrors of my childhood. I had started to read newspapers very early, and that has continued all my life. At that time the *Cleveland Plain Dealer* was full of stories about the war in China, the invasion of China by Japan. Of course, I read as a child with the understanding of a child. Yet the stories filled me with a vague dread and fear that I could not express; neither could I resist reading them every day. There was an airshow in Cleveland at this time. My grandparents came from Kentucky to attend it; my mother and father took them, and perhaps Ed also. It was never even considered that the younger children attend. But everyone in Cleveland saw the airplanes. It was unavoidable. I was on the rocks when I heard the noise of aircraft, and I was seized with absolute terror. I stood up and watched half-a-dozen airplanes cross the sky and I felt I knew something that the newspapers had not told me. I was terrified and could not tell anyone why, because I didn't know myself, but the terror was real.

There was a very large German woman who came to help my mother in the house sometimes. She was intimidating, brusque, forceful, and had little patience with a bunch of spoiled brats, as she called us. She baked bushel-basket cookies, called that because she made enough to fill a basket. They were heavenly. She made vinegar pie, and we would not touch it. She made chicken and dumplings and I would not touch that. I would not eat anything doughy: noodles, dumplings, biscuits, spaghetti, macaroni, and so on. I would not touch anything with visible fat on it. I had little use for mashed potatoes, and positively loathed gravy. We always had an extra two or three people at our table—Mrs. Moyer who helped out, a relative or two, a boarder now and then, my father's friends. Every dinner—we called it supper—was a major production. Sometimes there would be two fried chickens, and a roast, or a couple of roast ducks. We all wanted the drumsticks, and there were never enough to go around. One time Mrs. Moyer gave me the duck neck and insisted it was a leg. I started to eat it and pulled out a very long thing that looked to me like a worm. I ran shrieking from the table and would not touch duck or chicken again for many years. I grew well, was healthy and sturdy, and did not suffer from my pickiness. My mother was a good cook. The food was plain and plentiful, with many vegetables, fruits, simple meats, never any sauces, seldom any salads, homemade breads of all sorts. I loved cornbread then and still do.

Coming home from school in cold weather to a house scented with freshly baked yeast bread was one of the great pleasures of childhood. My mother would make us hot cocoa, and that, with hot bread dripping butter, spicy apple butter on top, was delightful.

We were not a very religious family. My mother was a Baptist; the church was at the end of our block, and she took us to Sunday School and church services regularly. My father never went. I considered the Sunday School stories just that, more stories. They were no more, no less true than the other stories I had read. I much preferred the Saturday matinees at the movies.

It was at a Saturday matinee that I came down with acute appendicitis. I left the movie house and went home. I have no memory of telling anyone I was ill; it is quite possible I didn't. When I arrived home, the house was empty and I was in agony. We never locked doors then; I went in to my parents' room and fell across their bed, doubled up in pain. I woke up in a strange bed, with fires burning all around me and a devil and witches in black mumbling. I knew I was in hell. Actually my mother's closest friend, knowing I was not yet baptized, arranged to have extreme-unction rites for my salvation. The next time I woke up it was to see a tent all over my bed, an oxygen tent I knew later, but then I was completely mystified and terrified. I was in hell, burning up, and perishing of thirst. I climbed out of bed and started down an endless corridor looking for water. After that my mother was at my bedside almost constantly. One of the few times she was not there at mealtime, a nun brought in a tray and arranged my bed, and then sat on a chair by me to wait for me to eat. I would touch nothing on the tray, all blobs of pasty-looking stuff that I would not have touched in the best of health. The one thing on the tray that I wanted was ice cream, and she would not let me have it unless I ate the other food first. We both watched the ice cream melt and turn to slush, then to a puddle; she stood up and took the tray out. I hated her. I think she hated me, too. She was one of the witches who had wanted to burn me in hell, or she was just like them. I must have taught David my fear and hatred; when he was about four some nuns got on a train we were on and he screamed that they were witches.

Later, convalescing at home, I was allowed to sleep for weeks in my parents' room because I could not yet go up and down stairs. My mother read to me a lot, and my father played with me, and I read, and colored pictures, and it was very nice. I could eat whatever I wanted without any fuss being made about it. The only bad thing, in the beginning, was that every day my mother appeared with a tall glass of foaming liquid that I was supposed to drink, and after one look at it, I knew I couldn't. I told her not to watch, to go away and come back, and I would drink it. As soon as she was out of the room, I poured it down the side of the bed. That went on for a week, at least. She worried that I had reverted to bed-wetting, and coaxed me to the bathroom frequently. As soon as she stopped bringing that glass of foaming something, the "bed-wetting" ended, and my recovery proceeded without incident. It probably was just as well that I didn't drink it. I have since found out that I react very badly and unpredictably to medications; who knows what that would have done to me?

My next encounter with religious mercy came about during the summer I turned twelve. We had moved to Louisville, and I was sent off to visit some of my mother's relatives in the country around Mammoth Cave. Aunt Maud was a kindly, gossipy woman who never stopped talking, and never forgot a thing in her life. She could describe events, down to the color of hair ribbons, from year one. My cousin was a simpleminded boy of eighteen or so who would not keep his hands off me. This was the first time I had suffered from attention of that sort and I didn't know what to do about it. Intuitively I knew I shouldn't tell Aunt Maud. I tried to avoid him, dodged out the back when he came in the front, refused to go with him to do any of his chores, and just tried to keep out of reach. Aunt Maud said I was being selfish.

The week I was there a tent revival was underway. I attended with my aunt one time. It was very hot in the tent, and very crowded. The preacher was red-faced and fat, and he shouted and yelled and waved his arms about in a way I never had seen before. That was not how the preacher had acted in Cleveland. After the interminable sermon the preacher began to exhort the congregation to come forward to be saved. All around me people got up and moved forward. Aunt Maud went to be saved. I did not move. The preacher yelled louder; he was working himself up to a real state by then, his face redder and redder, sweat dripping from his jowls. He was going on about the wicked woman from the city, damned to eternal hellfire, and it dawned on me finally that I was that woman. He stared at me, came closer and yelled in my face, and I sat there and stared back. I never moved. My aunt was crying, begging me to be saved; he was waving his arms and yelling; most everyone else in the tent had stood up and gone to the front. I never moved. He ranted about defiance in the face of the Lord's love and mercy. He raved about the evils of the city, the fall into sin of those who lived there, the wickedness of the woman from the city. He yelled that the devil had hardened my heart, that the devil's grip on my heart must be broken and only God could break those bonds. And so on. I sat and stared back into his face and did not budge as he got louder and louder, and what he saw in my face was hatred, pure and simple. He was the second person I came to hate during those early years. I hated him for humiliating me like that, for calling me names, making accusations that were false, for calling me corrupt, the temptress, the tool of the devil. He knew what he saw in my face that day. Before the ordeal ended, the only expression I could read on his face was hatred also. He finally saved the faithful who had come forward, another hymn was sung, and we were allowed to leave. My aunt bawled me out for being stubborn and embarrassing her in front of her friends, and I said I was going home. The next day I left.

The two experiences, having a nun refuse to give ice cream to a sick child for the sake of a principle, and the evangelist bullying a defenseless girl, bracketed my feelings about organized religion. Within the year I declared myself an atheist and have seen nothing to this day to make me reconsider.

That week in the country introduced me to several new aspects of life. My cousin with the busy hands assumed I was wiser than I was. Another cousin, a teenage girl, told jokes that I did not understand and knew I should not repeat at home. They were very obscene. She too made the assumption that I knew more than I did. Actually I knew nothing about sex, or sexual innuendoes. In our family, sex was never discussed or referred to. My oldest brother examined me early on, and later I examined my youngest brother, driven by the same curiosity, baffled by the mystery I sensed all around me. One day when I was about eight I went home from my best friend's house and asked my mother if it was true that Beatrice's mother had taken something to kill the baby in her stomach. My mother slapped me. I don't think she ever hit me except for that one time. Years later when I was about thirteen my mother kept chickens in the backyard. I was at the door looking out and I said, "Those chickens are fighting again." My mother said, "Catherine, don't you know what they're doing?" Instantly: "Yes!" But I hadn't known. No one had told me anything. No one did then. At eleven I had become moody, wept a lot, fought with Kenny constantly, and generally suffered as only a prepubescent child can suffer. My mother sent my sister to tell me about menstruation. I ran from her and locked myself in the bathroom, certain she had come upstairs to scold me for something or other. It seemed at that time in my life I could do nothing that didn't merit a scolding. She stood on the outside of the door and asked me if I was bleeding. I wasn't, and did not understand what she was getting at. She said I might start bleeding and when I did I should tell her. That was my education about the menses. More puzzled than ever, I tried to piece it together without any information. I decided my mother bled from the breasts. I had seen her in bed, with her breasts flattened out, and made the assumption that that was what happened. I did not have breasts yet and I could not understand why Eula was telling me anything like this. I did not ask a question, and she never referred to it again.

We had moved from Cleveland to Louisville; we moved again to Kansas City, Missouri, and then back to Louisville where we stayed. Those were bad years for all of us; I had no real friends any more, no one I could talk to about sex. When we did talk later in high school, it was ignorance multiplied by the number of the girls in the conversation. We were all ignorant, and kept ignorant. The subject was taboo, period. Some girls I knew studied biology for a term or longer, hoping to find a clue. They didn't. We studied flowers and bees, no higher organisms. Our schools were segregated; blacks kept from whites, girls kept from boys. If a teacher in my high school had brought up the matter of sex, no doubt she would have been fired. Two girls in my graduating class got pregnant. One quit voluntarily, and it was said, "She had the decency to drop out before it showed." The other was expelled. One of them had been in a sorority; she was booted out of that too.

Back to Cleveland and the period when all the lines of my life were being introduced to the tapestry, some of more importance than others, some long since lost to me, others traceable from the beginning until now. I was catching the world in snapshots, in isolated glimpses of people and places. I was learning things that had no names, no words; many of them are still in my head. Pictures of Lake Erie: somber gray and flat, heavy looking; alive and dancing, flinging up wisps of white frills here, there, everywhere; long gloomy rollers that rose and crashed like thunder; brilliant blue, blue-green, almost white; wavelets whispering on the sandy shore; ooze and mud between my toes; towering clouds that looked as if the water had reached up to the sky and it was all the same black. The buckeye trees on our street: the way they arched and met over the street here and there; the first blooms in the spring that made me ache with a nameless response; the dense shade, and the way they tossed and blew in the summer storms. Gathering the buckeyes in the fall to make necklaces, to store in boxes, to use as ammunition in a street war. I know how they felt, as smooth as satin, and I remember the rich brown gloss. Burrowing into mountains of leaves, and, later, staring into the bon-fires. Dancing in the leaves, scattering them to the wind. The sounds: the guttural deep accent of Mr. Gorman who sprayed me with a hose when I skated on his sidewalk. The melodic sing-song of the Swedish boys when they told stories. The nearly unintelligible cries of the Lithuanian woman when Kenny fought with her sons. And the magic of radio.

*Easy Aces, Burns and Allen, One Man's Family, Jack Armstrong, the All-American Boy, Amos and Andy* . . . Two shows were forbidden to me because I was too young— *Lights Out* and *The Inner Sanctum.* I listened to them too, sitting on the stairs in the dark. Those two were my favorites, naturally. I sat on the stairs and watched my parents put together a table and chair set for me when I was seven, my Christmas present that year.

But there was an unease in our family by the mid-thirties. My father was a millwright; he worked through the worst of the Depression and we were un-touched by it, except for the stream of people who flowed through our house on their way to look for work, or between jobs, or because they had nowhere else to go. My mother did not approve of my father's friends. She called them all bootleggers, bums, or de-generates. I know some of them must have been boot-leggers. I remember the quart jars of alcohol—gin, moonshine, whatever it was that appeared on our din-ing-room table when my father and his friends played poker there. The rotating poker game was as much a part of our routine as trips to the market, or to the amusement park in the summer. Our house, then somewhere else for the next few weeks, back to our house. We scrambled to get up first the next morning to find the coins dropped under the table. Gradually, however, a change was setting in. My father's health was failing, and he was drinking more than he ever had before. Which came first I don't know. He had been in the army during World War I, had suffered from influenza, pleurisy, and pneumonia, and he had not been treated. Twenty years later the aftereffects caught up with him. He lost his job in Cleveland first, and we moved to Louisville where he found another job right away. A year later he was transferred to Kan-sas City and we moved again, but he was ill and losing weight, and within months, he collapsed and was hos-pitalized with empyema, an inflammation of the lung lining. He never really recovered; he suffered through surgery several times, and was an invalid the rest of his life, until his death in 1952.

Ed did not move to Kansas with us. He remained in Louisville to finish high school. Eula went with us, but she would not stay, and went back to Louisville also, to live with an aunt and go to school. That left Kenny who was thirteen; me, eleven; Russ, eight; and

David who was three. Our father was in the hospital and we were all very frightened. Every Sunday my mother went to the hospital and I made dinner. All I knew how to cook was meatloaf, stuffed baked pota-toes, and chocolate pudding. That was the menu. Kenny and I fought more than ever, and, in fact, had our last rolling-on-the-floor-trying-to-hurt-each-other fight that winter. I think we were both frightened by the intensity of our battle that time, and without de-claring a real truce, we simply stopped that kind of behavior although our hostility did not abate. I realize now that he was even more unhappy than I was, that his position in the hierarchy was worse than mine. Ed was the favored child; he was intelligent, and he had a streak of cruelty that was more subtle than physical abuse. He was cruel to Kenny who could not retaliate in kind. Ed was almost five years his senior, and he had an innocent look that our parents trusted. He was ma-nipulative in a way that always resulted in Kenny's being punished when they had trouble. In turn, Kenny took out his frustrations on the younger children. Russ was too small to fight him; the spread of five years that kept Kenny from getting back at Ed, was the same spread of years that prevented Russ from retaliating. In size Kenny and I were not mismatched too much. We did the physical blow-by-blow fighting. Kenny was forthright and understandable. I never was afraid of him, but I was always a little afraid of Ed.

One time when I was about five our parents went out for the evening, leaving Ed in charge. We hated those times because he turned into a tyrant as soon as they left. That night when it was my turn to take a bath, I took a box of soap powder with me and dumped in what I thought was enough to make a bub-ble bath. It did bubble, and bubble, and bubble. The suds filled the tub and overflowed to the floor. I locked the door and tried to get the suds back in the tub, tried to stop more from forming, all to no avail. Half the bathroom was filled with soapsuds by then. Presently one of the others banged on the door and yelled for me to get out of there. I said I wasn't done. Someone else pounded on the door. They were all yelling at me by then. I thought someone might try to come in through the window and I locked the window and pulled down the shade so no one would see all the soapsuds, and I refused to open the door. The banging and pounding went on and on. Eventually Eula and Kenny went to bed, but Ed was still out there, waiting for me, and I was afraid of him. I didn't open the door until our parents came home. I knew my father wouldn't let Ed hurt me. He picked me up and took me to bed. There was some talk, of course, the next day or two. My mother and my father both said something like, "You know your brother wouldn't hurt you." But I didn't know that at all. And Kenny didn't know it either. A couple of years later Ed got a new bike for his birthday, and I got new roller skates. I was a good skater by then, and loved skating more than anything. Ed offered to tow me down the sidewalk, and it was great fun as he went faster and faster, but then he turned off the sidewalk onto gravel and I fell and was scratched and cut up on my arms and legs and one cheek. Somehow he put the blame on me.

I wasn't sorry he didn't go to Kansas City with us, but after Eula left to return to Louisville, I was very resentful. I thought it unfair for her not to help somehow. It was a very bad winter and spring. We never had been poor before, but now we had our own private depression. We were growing children in need of clothes, shoes, school supplies, and there wasn't any money for them. In spite of the hardships, which were immediate and real, I fell in love with Kansas City. I loved the hills and the trees and the heavy snow and even the wind. I loved the people, the children in my school, my teachers. I would have stayed there forever, I think. Somehow my mother held things together for us to finish the school year, but then she had to take us back to Louisville. My father had been moved to a veterans' hospital near Chicago where he was to undergo more surgery. My mother had to take us someplace where there were relatives, where someone would stay with us when she went to Illinois to be with our father. I wept bitterly for days when I realized we were going back to Kentucky.

*With brothers Kenneth, David, and Russell, 1983*

Childhood crashed in many ways that year. Our family was totally disrupted, totally different. Ed graduated from high school and got a job with the telephone company. They sent him out into the state as a lineman, and he was never really home again. Eula had dropped out of school and was working, and dating, and she was not home much at all. Kenny had a part-time job after school, and was gone most of the time. In some ways Kenny and I began to grow together that year that I turned twelve and he became fifteen. We might have snapped and snarled at each other still, but we did not fight. Before, in Cleveland, I had teased him in various ways, and he had teased me; that stopped. I remember that I could whistle as a child and he couldn't. I waited until he was entering the house and I started to whistle, pretending to be deeply engrossed in my book, my paper furniture, my crayons, whatever. He knew. He would yell to our mother, "Make her stop that!" and our mother would look bewildered. "She's not doing anything." But he knew, and so did I.

Also, I grew much closer to my two younger brothers. My mother got a job that year and I was in charge of the house and the two smaller children until she came home every day. And I kept them inside most of the time. I became a story teller. I learned how to cook. I learned how to bake cakes and pies and make bread. I have clear memories of mixing cakes while David sat in the middle of the table and Russ prowled about the kitchen getting into things. I told them the stories of books I had read, of movies I had seen, and when those ran out, I began to make up stories. I reinvented the serial, every day leaving our hero in an impossible situation, to be continued the following day. I held my audience. And the cakes weren't bad, either. We became a three-children family that year and the

*Kate with her mother, Ann Meredith, 1981*

three of us got along rather well.

That was the year the world opened its door for me in the form of an adult library card. Until the age of twelve, children were not even permitted in the adult section of the library, and suddenly it was all mine. I couldn't go to the main library often because it was downtown and I never had money for the streetcar, but I read everything in the branch library. For several years I think I was intoxicated with words. I judged nothing and read everything with equally rapt attention. Mysteries, travel books, westerns, classics, best-sellers. I loved them all.

The worst thing that happened that year was having our grandfather come to live with us. I don't know what discussion took place first; we were not consulted, naturally. Just suddenly he was moving in. Grandpa Meredith, our father's father, to keep those children from running wild. Whatever reason there was in the beginning, that was the reason he muttered repeatedly. He was trying to keep those kids from running wild. We all hated him. This was the third hatred I felt, and stronger than the first two by far.

He wore long underwear summer and winter, a three-piece suit, white shirt and tie day in and day out. He bathed once a week. He had worked for the Louisville and Nashville Railroad until his retirement, and he was proud of a gold watch that he boasted kept railroad time. He got up early and went to bed early and wanted everyone else to do the same, and complained constantly that we kept him awake at night. He wanted someone to get up and make his breakfast before seven, and he wanted a real lunch at eleven, and supper at five. If I was cooking, he would stamp into the kitchen, pull out that gold watch, check it against the kitchen clock and mutter supper was getting late.

I think we would have forgiven all that; other guests had been peculiar, and we were all peculiar in our own ways, and tolerant up to a point. He crossed that point. Every afternoon he went for a walk with his dog. Her name was Patsy, an obese, short-haired, short-legged dog with a belly that nearly scraped the floor. He always stopped by a store and bought a little bag of candy on the way home; then he sat on the porch in the summer, in the living room that winter, and he fed the candy to the dog. One time David asked for a piece of candy and he said, no, it was for Patsy because she was good. If he found me reading the newspaper, he simply picked it up and walked away with it, to the porch or the living room where he dozed with it on his lap. Eula and I both tried to keep all the way out of his way. He would sidle up to one or the other of us every chance he got and drop his arm on our shoulder, let his hand fall as if by accident on our breast, and then feel us, squeeze a little. When he came

in one door I tried to leave by another unless I was occupied and couldn't, and then I openly kept the table between us. He had a cane that he used to sweep things off the table if they were in his way, or clear a chair if he wanted it. He used it to push Russ around, not hitting him, just pushing with the cane. In a way, that was even worse than if he had hit him. At least that would have given us something to complain about to our mother. As it was, none of us complained, or said why we hated him, but it showed. I refused to make his lunch, one of the first small signs of rebellion. That was a bad time of day; usually Russ and David were out playing, or busy somewhere or other, and Grandpa seemed to assume a girl alone in a room was his for the fondling. I would not tell why I wouldn't make his lunch, I just said I wouldn't. My aunt, his daughter, told him to come to her house for lunch every day and the matter ended there. But Russ took more drastic measures against him.

Russ had always been a difficult child, tempestuous and unpredictable. He had a short temper and was uncontrollable when enraged. He was also very bright. He did experiments with kitchen ingredients, had a chemistry set, made balsa wood airplanes and painted them with extraordinary care, made a radio set, played with batteries and wires, and so on. He read popular-science magazines regularly. One day Grandpa swept something of his off the kitchen table with his cane, an airplane probably. Normally Russ's reaction would have been a tantrum, a throwing fit, or something else instant and dramatic. Instead, he started a campaign of retaliation.

He would hide the old man's glasses, just put them in a place where they didn't belong, but a place accessible to everyone where Grandpa might have put them and forgot. He tied knots in his shoe laces, again nothing too outrageous, just an annoyance. Grandpa smoked a corncob pipe and used wooden kitchen matches to light it, then flung the match down in the general direction of the woodbox by a wood-burning stove. He also emptied his pipe bowl in the same general direction, never actually getting the ashes in the box, and then growled at Russ, or me, or no one in particular, "Clean up that mess."

He always bought three boxes of matches at a time, and kept them in his bedroom. One day Russ took one of the boxes from the bedroom out to the garage. He opened it and carefully removed the band of cardboard that held the matches in place, and then dumped them all out. One by one he soaked them in a salt solution and laid them out to dry again. When they were completely dry he repacked them, replaced the band, and took that box inside, brought out another. He repeated this with all three boxes. Nothing showed afterward to indicate any tampering. I watched a good bit of the process; it took two days to complete. Then we waited for Grandpa to empty the current box of matches.

He tossed the empty box in the direction of the woodbox and got up, stamped to his bedroom and returned with a new box of matches. He pulled off the cardboard wrapper and took out a match and tried to light it. The phosphorus head crumbled and fell apart. He threw the match after the empty box and took out another one. The same thing happened. Another one. None of us looked at him. Russ was in the living room, I was, David was. I don't know if anyone else was there but the three of us knew Russ had done it. My mother was home, I think, possibly in the kitchen. Match after match after match. The floor was littered with them; the front of his vest was covered with powder. He got up and left for another box. The same thing. Then the third box. He tried every single match in all three boxes. None of us looked up at him or at each other.

I don't know if he suspected Russ, but soon after that he raised his cane as if to hit Russ when my mother was home. Always before, he had been very circumspect when she was there, but that was enough. She knew he was the cause of the high level of tension in the house even if we hadn't told on him specifically. She told him he had to leave, and was firm in the face of his protests. He returned to his daughter's house where he spent the rest of his life. He was a vigorous man in his mid-sixties when he lived with us, and for the next fifteen years until his death I made certain I was never alone in a room with him. When he came to visit, I went to my room, or left the house altogether. So did my brothers.

The next year Pearl Harbor finished splintering the family. Ed joined the Navy; Kenny joined as soon as he was seventeen. Eula joined the WAVES, then got out and married. Ed married as soon as he was out of the Navy and moved to Chicago where he lived for the next twenty-five years. When Kenny came home we became good and close friends. I married soon after high school, and the next year he married also; he and his new wife lived with me and my husband for almost a year without ever a cross word passing between Kenny and me.

All through high school, teachers encouraged me to write. I was the editor of the school paper, and sometimes wrote the entire issue. One teacher in particular was very good for me. Miss Walsh had a standing assignment: we had to turn in a three-by-five index card daily with original writing on it. I described shoes on the bus, the way rain fell, how it was to be awake when the world was asleep, little poems, character

*With son Douglas Wilhelm, 1978*

sketches, vignettes . . . Very good training. She knew I read everything, but still I had to read the class assignments, and ended up disliking everything we studied. Dickens, Shakespeare, Kipling. The list is long. It took me many years to go back to some of them with appreciation; some I still don't like. What a pity. The class in which we studied Shakespeare had about twenty-five girls and an octogenarian teacher who dozed as long as voices droned. We would start reading at the front of the room, read a page, then the next girl would take over. Certain murder for Shakespeare.

What I liked best in school was science and math, not English or literature. When I told the dean I wanted to be a chemist, she discouraged me. She said I would end up teaching chemistry, and I knew very well I did not want to be a teacher. I believed her although I did not believe any of the teachers who told me to work at becoming a writer. I don't know why I couldn't accept that, unless it was because I was so worshipful of writers and the books they produced. Godlike figures, all of them, and most of them quite dead.

My attendance at school was abysmal. I made straight A's and went four days a week. I worked from the age of fourteen on, after-school jobs, weekends. By

*Son Jonathan Knight, 1985*

then I had rediscovered roller skating, this time figure skating in a rink, and I had to work to support that. I joined a skating club; we put on shows for charity, and I loved it. Probably I skated twenty hours a week or more for four or five years. I was not good enough at skating to ever consider doing anything with that. I was in the chorus and that was enough for me. I modeled at a department store at that time, the last two years of high school, and briefly I thought of going into fashion design, or trying to model for a living. But I hated it too much. It paid more money than anything else I could find on a part-time basis, but it was thoroughly demoralizing and dehumanizing.

I drifted through school, made good grades, won competitions, and it was all too easy to believe in. I won a merit scholarship and went to the university to register and never went back. That wasn't what I wanted. No writing classes, no journalism, no literature, the only language available for the entering freshmen was Russian, the only P.E., square dancing, and both were required. I got a job at an insurance company instead. The underwriter suffered a disabling heart attack a few months after I started working there, and they trained me as an underwriter in a crash

course. I learned that insurance salesmen will insure corpses if no one oversees what they are doing. Then I got married and the second phase of my life crashed to a halt.

By the time I was thirteen, fourteen at the very most, all the motifs of my life were in place, the tapestry design laid out, the colors decided upon. Ever since, I have been filling in, adding very little that is really new. My childhood fears are the concerns of my characters; the snapshots my mind recorded keep surfacing, seen through the eyes of fictional people. My loves and hopes were being shaped fifty years ago; they endure, and my characters share them today. I have a lot more data now, but no more emotions than I did then. I have come to recognize that the only heroic figure in our family drama was my mother. My father was a casualty with no reserves left to him to fight with. The children were helpless in the winds that blew. My mother refused to be defeated, refused to yield; her dignity remains intact. Born into a family of twelve, daughter of a strict Scots farmer/homesteader, she grew up in the wilderness of Kentucky, married young and bore six children of her own, and only then was thrust into the world to make her own way. And she did. Untrained, unschooled, a country girl, she survived and thrived and grew, and is still growing, although she was ninety in October of 1986. She is my heroic figure, the model for the women I write about, strong women all, determined women, unconquerable women.

When I began to write at the age of twenty-eight, it was like going home, as if all my life I had been lost and speechless, and was only then finding my way back home, finding I could talk. Possibly I was intimidated by the teachers who urged me to be a writer because I was afraid they expected great works from me, and I did not for a minute believe I could do great things. What they didn't know and couldn't tell me was that it was like going home, and in your home you don't have to be great or do great things. It's enough to be there.

## BIBLIOGRAPHY

### Fiction:

*More Bitter Than Death.* New York: Simon & Schuster, 1962; London: R. Hale. 1965.

*The Mile-Long Spaceship* (short stories). New York: Berkley Publishing, 1963; also published as *Andover and the Android.* London: Dobson, 1966.

*Damon Knight and Kate Wilhelm with their Hugo Awards, 1984*

*Kate with son and coauthor, Richard Wilhelm, 1986.*

*The Clone,* with Theodore L. Thomas. New York: Berkley Publishing, 1965; London: R. Hale, 1968.

*The Nevermore Affair.* Garden City, N.Y.: Doubleday, 1966.

*The Killer Thing.* Garden City, N.Y.: Doubleday, 1967; also published as *The Killing Thing.* London: Jenkins, 1967.

*The Downstairs Room and Other Speculative Fiction* (short stories). Garden City, N.Y.: Doubleday, 1968.

*Let the Fire Fall.* Garden City, N.Y.: Doubleday, 1969; London: Jenkins, 1969.

*The Year of the Cloud,* with Theodore L. Thomas. Garden City, N.Y.: Doubleday, 1970.

*Abyss: Two Novellas.* Garden City, N.Y.: Doubleday, 1971.

*Margaret and I.* Boston: Little, Brown, 1974.

*City of Cain.* Boston: Little, Brown, 1974; London: Gollancz, 1975.

*The Infinity Box: A Collection of Speculative Fiction* (short stories). New York: Harper, 1975; London: Hutchinson, 1979.

*Where Late the Sweet Birds Sang.* New York: Harper, 1976; London: Hutchinson, 1977.

*The Clewiston Test.* New York: Farrar, Straus, 1976; London: Hutchinson, 1978.

*Fault Lines.* New York: Harper, 1977; London: Hutchinson, 1978.

*Somerset Dreams and Other Fictions* (short stories). New York: Harper, 1978; London: Hutchinson, 1979.

*Juniper Time.* New York: Harper, 1979; London: Hutchinson, 1980.

*Better than One,* with Damon Knight. Boston: Noreascon II, 1980.

*Listen, Listen* (short stories). Boston: Houghton, 1981.

*A Sense of Shadow.* Boston: Houghton, 1981.

*Oh, Susannah!* Boston: Houghton, 1982.

*Welcome, Chaos.* Boston: Houghton, 1983; London: Gollancz, 1986.

*Huysman's Pets.* New York: Bluejay Books, 1986.


**Nonfiction:**

*The Hills Are Dancing,* with Richard B. Wilhelm. Minneapolis: Corroborree Press, 1986.


**Editor of:**

*Nebula Award Stories 9.* New York: Harper, 1974; London: Gollancz, 1974.

*Clarion SF.* New York: Berkley Publishing, 1977.

# Colin Wilson

*1931–*

## AN AUTOBIOGRAPHICAL SKETCH

*Colin Wilson, 1984*

Isaiah Berlin divided writers into hedgehogs and foxes: "The fox knows many things; the hedgehog knows only one." Shakespeare is a fox; Tolstoy and Dostoevsky are hedgehogs. By this definition, I am undoubtedly a hedgehog. All my work has been about the same subject: those strange moments of delight in which we feel "All is well." Ever since I was a child, I have experienced the same profound sense of the *authenticity* of these moments. They do not seem to be some temporary flash of euphoria; on the contrary, they are always accompanied by a sense of calm objectivity. It is like seeing the solution to some problem, and recognising that this *is* the correct solution, and that there can be no possible doubt about it. But if I solve some mechanical or arithmetical problem, I can be certain that the solution will still be valid next week and next year. In the case of these flashes of total certainty, the "answer" seems to vanish within an hour or so.

In retrospect, I can see that my whole life has been an attempt to analyse and solve this problem, and that, like any scientist who devotes his life to the same investigation, I have accumulated a great deal of interesting information about it, and reached a few conclusions that seem to me objectively valid. In these pages I shall try to present these conclusions in the context of personal experience.

I was born in Leicester (pronounced *Les*-ter), England, in 1931. My background was working class, but I do not feel that this is of any particular importance. Some writers, like D.H. Lawrence and Jack London, have been deeply influenced by their working-class background. In my case, it was simply a nuisance that I wanted to escape and then ignore. Bernard Shaw once said that the workers are dull, narrow, and bigoted, and that was why he wanted to

311

see them abolished; I have always felt much the same. If I try to define what I disliked so much about that Leicester background, I suppose I would say that it was an *assumption of ordinariness*—the feeling that life is rather dull and rather predictable, and that "that is all there is." Abraham Maslow once said to his class: "Which of you intends to do something extraordinary in life?" and they all looked at him blankly. Maslow said: "If not you, *who* then?" And they began to understand. I have a feeling that if he had asked the question in Leicester, they would have continued to stare at him blankly.

My father was a worker in the boot-and-shoe trade, who earned about three pounds ($5) a week throughout the 1930s. His own father had been killed in the First World War and, as the eldest male in the family, he was forced to take over the role of protector to four sisters and a brother. It made him into a rather dominant character who liked his own way. My mother told me that she was attracted by him because he seemed more grown-up than the other men she knew. When she was nineteen, she went on a holiday to an aunt in Doncaster with her elder sister, my aunt Connie, and with Connie's boyfriend Frank and my father. She and Connie slept in a double bed. On the first night, Connie got out of bed and announced that she intended to go and join Frank, who was sharing a double bed with my father. So my father was obliged to get into bed with my mother, who was a virgin at the time. A few weeks later, I was on the way. They married at Christmas, and I was born 26th June 1931.

Theirs was not basically a happy marriage, although it could have been worse. My father was a hard worker, but I think he resented being forced to get married. He was happiest sitting in the local pub with a pint of beer in front of him and a game of dominoes, or taking long cycle rides into the countryside looking for mushrooms. My mother, like most young working-class girls, was a romantic whose expectations of the opposite sex had been formed by reading *True Romance* magazines and seeing sentimental films like *Wuthering Heights* and *Smiling Through*. Her first great disappointment in marriage was on the first Friday evening, waiting for my father to come home with his pay packet; he came home drunk and fell asleep on the bed—with its new eiderdown—in his boots. Only nine months after I was born, she was pregnant again with my brother Barry. I think they both found marriage a kind of treadmill. My father was fond of his children, I suppose, but by the time we were six or seven, he was bored, and seemed to regard us as nuisances. At the beginning of the war—in 1939—

he went into the army, and for a few months we missed him, and looked forward to weekends when he came home on leave. After six months or so, he was discharged from the army—they discovered he had duodenal ulcers—and we were delighted. But he had only been home a day or so when we remembered how much we disliked him and slipped back into the old routine of trying to avoid him. Later, when my first book came out and I was suddenly "famous," he began to call me "son," and was obviously proud of me; but by then it was too late.

I learned to read fairly late—at about seven or eight—but as soon as I made the amazing discovery that I could read most of the words on a page, I began reading everything I could lay my hands on—comics, my mother's *True Romance* and *True Detective* magazines, the *Just William* books, Leslie Charteris's "Saint" and P.G. Wodehouse. During the summer evenings, I sometimes went to bed as early as seven o'clock, and went on reading until the light failed. I spent most of my time in a dream world. When an aunt took me on holiday to Doncaster—the house where my mother had met her downfall—I ignored the open fields and the farm next door, and spent my days in the front room reading *Weird Tales* and other pulp magazines that I had discovered in a cupboard. My uncle was furious and gave me a long talking-to. He didn't seem to understand that I didn't particularly like the physical world, and found most of the grown-ups I knew unutterably boring. I was never invited back there again.

When I was ten years old, my grandfather gave me a tattered and coverless science-fiction magazine. The opening story, I remember, was about a scientist who learns how to synthesise some crude form of life, a little blob of cellular matter. A piece of it gets washed down the laboratory sink, and begins to feed on the algae in the sewers; then it gets washed down to the sea and eats the fish. It grows bigger and bigger until it can engulf ocean liners, and threatens to go on expanding until it can crawl up on land and depopulate cities. I forget how its creator finally destroys it, but I can still remember that almost painful feeling of excitement I experienced as I read through the rest of the magazine, the recognition that I had entered a new dimension of imaginative experience.

At about the same time, an uncle presented me with half-a-dozen copies of a magazine called *Armchair Science*, and I can remember the same feeling of excitement as I read an article about the possibility of atomic energy—and a warning that smashing atoms could cause a chain reaction that might destroy the whole world. It suddenly seemed to me that the world was full of all kinds of knowledge that had so far been kept from me. I had felt the same at about the age of seven when our schoolmistress had told us that the earth had once been populated by dinosaurs and flying reptiles—it seemed incredible that no one had ever before offered me such an important piece of information.

Now, suddenly, I began to read in earnest—no longer for entertainment, but to try to learn all I could about the extraordinary universe that surrounded me. When I stared at pictures of the Milky Way or the Andromeda nebula, I experienced the same "magical" sensation that I would later experience on listening to Bruckner or Mozart's *Magic Flute*. It was a sense of *leaving behind* my personal identity, of becoming simply a perceiving mind. It also seemed clear to me that this is the basic aim of all human beings: this is why people went to football matches or sang the National Anthem or joined in "Auld Lang Syne" on New Year's Eve. But football matches or patriotism were relatively inefficient ways of escaping the sense of personality. Science was obviously the real solution. To read about the depths of space or the interior of the atom or the mysteries of the earth's magnetic field was to catch a dazzling glimpse of what the human mind was intended for: *to grasp objective reality*.

My mother bought me a chemistry set for my eleventh birthday. I converted an empty bedroom into a laboratory, and spent every Saturday afternoon making liquids change colour and producing disgusting smells. Chemicals were difficult to obtain during the war; I cycled all over Leicester until I was familiar with every chemist's shop. If I succeeded in buying half an ounce of potassium bichromate, or a few grams of cobalt chloride or sodium iodide, I felt like a prospector who has struck gold. I borrowed huge volumes on inorganic chemistry from the library, and read them from end to end. Science had given me a sense of purpose, and life was suddenly endlessly fascinating.

I soon noticed that there were other circumstances in which I could experience this ecstatic feeling of "impersonality." On most Saturday afternoons we went to the children's matinée at one or other of the local cinemas. Again and again, I can remember coming out of the warm darkness into the blinding glare of a summer afternoon, and experiencing a sudden feeling of enormous contentment with my own life. My mind had been "elsewhere" for two or three hours, and now there was a sensation like coming back from a holiday and discovering how delightful it is to be home again. I felt the

same when I learned to ride a bicycle, and pedalled out into the countryside—sometimes as far as Warwick, with its old castle, or Stratford-upon-Avon, or Matlock Bath, where there are underground caves. As I set out early in the morning, when the air smelt fresh and there were still patches of mist on the surface of the river, it was as if my imagination was being charged with a peculiar energy of excitement, not unlike the sexual tingling I was beginning to observe in my loins at this time. And just as, when this sexual energy made its presence felt, I could use it to fuel all kinds of erotic fantasies, so this vital energy that was aroused by the smells of the countryside seemed to invite visions of fame and achievement and travel to distant places. When I was a child, the daydreams had been heroic: rescuing pretty girls from Red Indians, capturing Hitler single-handed, and so on. Now I daydreamed of being the first man to make an atom bomb, or build the first spaceship capable of landing on Mars.

At the age of thirteen I had a girlfriend for a few months—I had met her while doing a newspaper round—and used to travel on the same bus to school with her, and sit with my arm awkwardly around her in the cinema. But just before my fourteenth birthday she "chucked" me for my best friend. That August, feeling miserable and at a loose end, I began to write my first book. It started simply as an attempt to write a brief summary of all I knew about physics and chemistry—I originally thought that it should be possible to condense pages of exposition into a few dozen formulae. Then I grew more ambitious, and decided to include astronomy and geology. I knew nothing about the latter, but borrowed elementary textbooks from the local library. In a six-volume work called *Practical Knowledge for All*—acquired at a church bazaar—I read articles about psychology and philosophy, and decided that they also ought to be included. I had originally believed that it could all be compressed into one pocket-size notebook; by Christmas it had swollen to six.

There was, of course, nothing original in all this; but it taught me how to work for my own pleasure. It also taught me how to think. At first I found philosophy completely baffling; it seemed to me quite irrelevant whether there were Platonic forms or ideas below the surface of reality, or whether change is real or illusory. But when I read Joad's account of the ideas of Bishop Berkeley, I suddenly became intrigued. Berkeley was obviously right to say that colours are the creation of the senses. In that case, it was hard to see how we can avoid the conclusion that our senses also create shape and size and density, and that this apparently solid world exists only in our minds. And if objects are a creation of my mind, how about other people? Then, for the first time, I experienced a sinking sensation, a sudden fear that this was not just an intellectual game, but a reality. It was a frightening experience for a thirteen-year-old who had always taken it for granted that the universe rests on solid foundations.

It was also at about this time that I began to read Einstein. The science-fiction magazines that I read so avidly often mentioned him as the greatest of modern scientists, and when I read somewhere the comment that only half-a-dozen men in the world understood relativity, I saw it as a challenge. I found Einstein's own popular book on relativity incomprehensible—he forgot to explain what he meant by a coordinate system—but I soon came upon simpler accounts written in language I could understand, like Bertrand Russell's *ABC of Relativity*. But, like Bishop Berkeley, Einstein seemed to be removing the solid foundations of my universe. It seemed to me obvious that it is a meaningful statement to say that some event occurs simultaneously on earth and on Arcturus. Einstein and Russell assured me that this was old-fashioned Newtonian thinking and that I had to get used to the idea that two events might be simultaneous in one coordinate system but not in another. A man on a train has a right to assert that the platform is travelling at sixty miles an hour.

Ideas like these began to produce a sense of intellectual vertigo. There is an essay by G.K. Chesterton called "The Mad Official" that begins:

> Going mad is the slowest and dullest business in the world. I have nearly done it more than once in my boyhood, and so have nearly all my friends, born under the general doom of mortals, but especially of moderns; I mean the doom that makes a man come almost to the end of thinking before he comes to the first chance of living.

At the age of thirteen, I had come very nearly to "the end of thinking" and had not even started to live. Berkeley and Einstein and Freud and Adler seemed to have undermined my universe. It would have been delightful to go back to the old, comfortable universe of childhood, but it had obviously gone forever. Instead, there was this alarming feeling of living in a universe without certainties.

In childhood, I had often had the sudden feeling that the world is basically delightful and wonderful—that the sense of magic that we experience

at Christmas or on a clear summer morning is somehow more real and truer than the "ordinary" world we see on a wet Monday morning. Now, suddenly, I began to suspect that this was just a comforting delusion. This reached a frightening intensity one day in the clay-modelling class at school, when we were discussing the question of the size of the universe. We agreed that the visible universe of stars has to come to an end somewhere. But how long does space go on for? If you were in a spaceship as fast as light, and you reached the end of the galaxies, would you simply go on forever and ever into total emptiness? As we talked about this, I suddenly experienced a sensation of cold fear in the pit of my stomach. It was obviously impossible that the universe could go on forever and ever; it was equally impossible that it could suddenly stop. Reason, which had always seemed so reliable, now seemed to contradict itself. I felt emotionally drained and totally alone. It was no good turning to my parents or grandparents, as I had when I was a child, no good appealing to teachers or vicars. No one knew the answer. There was something oddly shocking and unpleasant about this thought, like a sudden violent blow. In *The Outsider* I was to quote the experience of the French philosopher Jouffroy when he also destroyed all his own intellectual and emotional certainties:

> I shall never forget that night in December in which the veil that concealed from me my own incredulity was torn. . . . Vainly I clung to these last beliefs as a shipwrecked sailor clings to fragments of his vessel; vainly, frightened at the unknown void into which I was about to float. I turned with them towards my childhood, my family, my country, all that was dear and sacred to me: the inflexible current of my thought was too strong: parents, family, memory, beliefs; it forced me to let go of everything . . . . The days which followed this discovery were the saddest of my life.

I also felt that I was carrying around an intolerable burden of knowledge, a burden that seemed far too heavy for someone of my age. It seemed clear to me that all these people walking through the streets, going about their business, were impelled by delusions. Parents, schoolteachers, city councillors, members of Parliament, saints, philosophers—even scientists—were motivated by "feelings" that would not bear examination.

What worried me, of course, was not uncertainty about the universe, but the fear that *reason it-*

*self* might be unreliable. And that would rob me of everything I had gained in the past few years. All human beings crave certainty and security—it is our most basic need. My discovery of science had been like a religious conversion; it had given me what seemed an unshakeable foundation of belief. There is a feeling of tremendous comfort in knowledge for its own sake—even apparently useless knowledge, such as that days of the week are named after Norse gods, that Wednesday is Woden's day and Thursday is Thor's day and Friday is Freya's day. If, as a child, I thought: "Today is Thor's day, and Thor was the son of Odin, god of the dead," the reflection produced an odd feeling of satisfaction, as if I had pushed reality to arm's length, and thereby gained a certain mastery over it. *That* was the basic function of reason—to push everyday reality to arm's length, to gain power over its "ordinariness." If reason was unreliable, then I was again the victim of the futile world of everyday reality. And for all my knowledge of Einstein and Freud and Plato, I was really no better off than the boy across the road who was always getting into trouble with the police for stealing and vandalism. When I first read *Faust*, I understood precisely what he meant when he said that all his study of philosophy, medicine, law, and theology has only forced him to recognise that we can know nothing.

This was an appalling period; I felt as though my mind was churning away in a void. The powerful erotic desires of adolescence were also a torment, accentuating the feeling of being out of touch with reality. I had discovered the plays of Bernard Shaw, and they were a tremendous stimulant; but what was the good of being stimulated if there was nothing to do with your energy? I longed for experience and felt as though I was locked in an airless room. Life seemed totally futile—not just mine, but all life. I began to read T.S. Eliot's poetry—because the English master had told me he was "difficult"—and it seemed to me that he had grasped the ultimate truth about human existence:

> Remember us—if at all—not as lost
> Violent souls, but only
> As the hollow men
> The stuffed men.

One day during the long August holiday I had been reading Janko Lavrin's book on Russian literature, depressed by his descriptions of the work of Chekhov and Andreyev and Artzybasheff, and I went into the kitchen to make a cup of tea. Standing up after sitting down for so long caused a blackout, and I stood swaying, holding on to the stove, as my

consciousness seemed to dissolve away. It made me feel that even our apparent control over our own minds is an illusion, and deepened the feeling of futility. I had fallen into the state that William James calls "anhedonia," a permanent state of interior greyness.

I left school at sixteen, vaguely intending to become a scientist and work for Imperial Chemical Industries. But I gained only a pass instead of a credit in the maths exam—not a sufficiently high mark to matriculate. There was no question of returning to school for another year—my father was determined that I should start contributing for the household expenses. So I took a job in a small local factory, where a couple-of-dozen women wound wool from hanks on to bobbins—my job was to weigh the wool when it came in, weigh it when it went out, and keep the women supplied with hanks and bobbins. It was a nine-hour day, with an hour for lunch—when I cycled home. I loathed it. Life had suddenly turned into a treadmill. But there was one compensation. In the evenings I retired to my bedroom and read poetry—Spenser, Milton, Cowper, Byron, Shelley, Wordsworth, Poe, Tennyson. Since I always felt depressed to begin with, I would always begin with the gloomiest poetry I could find —Eliot's *Waste Land*, James Thompson's *City of Dreadful Night*, and Poe, Beddoes, and Dowson. Then when I had been soothed into a mood of savage but resigned disgust, I would read Shelley and Keats—*Adonais, Ode to a Nightingale, Endymion*. By this time I was feeling thoroughly cheerful, and would read *Paradise Lost* and *The Prelude* and *Don Juan*. By the time I went downstairs to make myself a cup of cocoa, I was usually in a mood of buoyant optimism. Moreover, there was an odd sensation of floating—a sense of freedom. In one of his poems Aldous Huxley used the phrase "the high liana-ways of thought," and my mind felt as though it had turned into a monkey that could swing freely from tree to tree in any direction.

After I had been in the factory for a month or so, my old school offered me a job as a laboratory assistant. I took the maths exam again and this time gained the credit I needed. But it was a mistake to try to return to science. The months of poetry had made me determined to become a writer, and I was halfway through my first play—heavily influenced by Shaw's *Man and Superman*. I know my old headmaster must have been disappointed. I had been one of the best science students the school had ever had, and now, apparently, I had totally lost interest in the subject. The physics master, an exceedingly petty-minded individual, made life thoroughly unpleasant. And I found myself sinking again into the depression of my last years at school. The factory had been hard, but at least the physical exercise had exhausted me. Now I felt I was back in the airless room.

One day I decided to commit suicide, and wrote about it in my diary before I went off to night class. It seemed to me that I was trapped in a vicious circle. I would induce a mood of optimism by reading poetry, but it seldom lasted beyond midday the next day; then I had to start from the bottom again. It felt as if God, or some hidden fate, was deliberately taking pleasure in forcing me to keep moving, like a donkey with a carrot dangling from a stick tied to its collar. Suddenly I experienced a sense of rage and disgust, a determination not to put up with it a moment longer. On the way to night school—it was a class in analytical chemistry—I told myself what I would do. I would go straight to the reagent shelves, take down the bottle of potassium cyanide, and drink it straight down. When I walked into the classroom—late as usual—I ignored the crowd gathered around the master's desk and went and took down the cyanide. As I pulled out its stopper, I could suddenly *see* myself raising it to my lips, and feel the agonising pain in the pit of my stomach. It was as if I had turned into two people. One of them was a self-pitying little idiot called Colin Wilson who was sick of life, and another was a stranger—the real me. I didn't really care if Wilson committed suicide —he seemed such a fool that it didn't matter. The only trouble was that he would kill *me* too. And that was serious. I experienced an overwhelming sense of relief and joy as I replaced the bottle on the shelf, the recognition that all life is good and that there are no real problems. The feeling lasted several days before it gradually faded away.

When the exam results came through at the end of the year it was obvious that I had not been working. The headmaster offered me another chance, but I knew it was pointless; I gave in my resignation. Then I found myself a job as a civil servant in the local tax office. Again, it was a bad choice—a return to boredom and frustration. I continued to write, and to send off stories to magazines, and to experience days of anger and despair when they came back through the letterbox. But life was beginning to open out a little. I joined a local drama group, and became friendly with a young married woman who was a member of it; she also worked in the office. Inevitably, I became emotionally fixated on her—it would be inaccurate to say that I fell in love, for I always maintained a clear-eyed realism

about my emotional and physical needs—and daydreamed about becoming her lover. Returning from a day trip to Stratford-upon-Avon on the bus, she fell asleep with her head on my shoulder, and it seemed one of the most delightful experiences of my life. But although she admired my intellect, she obviously found me too immature and awkward even for mild sexual experiment. And when I passed the exam to become an established civil servant, I was transferred to a tax office in Rugby; after that, I saw little of her.

I found Rugby as boring and frustrating as Leicester. I spent my evenings cycling round the country lanes and reading Shelley and Rupert Brooke—Brooke's father had been a housemaster at the famous Rugby school—and trying to write a novel whose style was tiresomely Dickensian. My landlady disliked me and I returned the sentiment. Finally, she threw me out, and I found a room in a local hostel. It is a pity I had not discovered it earlier—there was a marvellous sensation of freedom in being allowed to come and go as I liked, and to eat my meals in the canteen whenever I felt inclined. I had suddenly become interested in the visual arts, deciding to learn about them as I had decided to learn about geology and psychology at thirteen. I read Maugham's *Moon and Sixpence*, and daydreamed about escaping to Tahiti.

Then came my eighteenth birthday, and I was summoned to register for my National Service. I decided to enter the Royal Air Force, hoping to learn to fly. Quite suddenly, life became real. It was exhilarating to get out of bed at 6:30 in the morning and march up and down a parade ground. I hated the NCOs and the restrictions, as I had always hated authority; but at least I was never bored. Not, at least, until we had completed our initial training, and I was assigned to a part-time antiaircraft unit near Nottingham as a junior clerk. Then, once again, I sank into the old condition of disgust and resentment.

It all ended quite suddenly. One day, when I came into the office, the adjutant, a Flight Lieutenant named English, waved a letter under my nose and asked if I was not ashamed of my messy typing. Suddenly, I was sick of being hectored and nagged; I looked him in the eye and said no. He looked startled, and told me to go and wait in his office. I was prepared to be confined to camp for a month; but to my surprise, he looked concerned and sympathetic when he finally came into the office. I suspect he was as anxious to see the last of me as I was of him. At all events, he told me that he understood my dislike of office work, and said that if the Medical Officer would certify that I was emotionally unstable, he would do his best to get me transferred to a medical unit—I was hoping to become a medical orderly in a hospital, since a brief stay in an RAF hospital convinced me that this offered the maximum freedom. On my way to see the MO, I had an inspiration. I told him that I was homosexual, and that I was finding it a dreadful strain to have to undress at night among all those splendid male bodies. In fact, one of my closest friends in Leicester had been homosexual, although I had never experienced the slightest inclination in that direction.

My plot backfired. The Medical Officer was as sympathetic as I had hoped, and promised to try and get me transferred. But later that day, I was summoned to the office of the RAF police. They wanted to know the names of other homosexuals on the camp, and whether I had been importuned by any of them. Everyone knew the "queers" in the camp, but I had no intention of admitting it and causing problems. They spent hours questioning me, and told me that they would keep on questioning me until I decided to cooperate. When I got back to the office, and told the adjutant what had happened, he was appalled; he had reported me to the RAF police, and now felt responsible. He told me to go home on leave, and to stay there until he sent for me. A few weeks later I had to see a senior medical office at Wendover, a sympathetic Wing Commander with a bald head, who told me that the best thing would be to discharge me from the RAF. I was naturally delighted, although I tried to conceal it. Later, I learned from a Flight Sergeant who had known him well that he was a homosexual . . .

When I was finally discharged from the RAF, I was determined that I would never again work at a job that I found boring; I would rather become a tramp. Throughout that summer of 1950, I took casual work as a farmhand and a ditchdigger. I had learned that hard physical labour left me no time for boredom. I had also undergone a curious kind of conversion. A reference in T.S. Eliot led me to buy the *Bhagavad Gita*. I began to practise meditation and mind-control, and to spend hours sitting cross-legged repeating:

> Brahman is the ritual
> Brahman is the offering
> Brahman is he who offers
> To the fire that is Brahman.
> When a man sees Brahman
> In every action
> He shall find Brahman.

I had recognised, in effect, that the miseries of my teens were due to negative emotions and to desires, and that the answer was to cultivate detachment. Once again, I had found a method for getting reality "at arm's length." And I found, to my astonishment, that once I had become accustomed to spending an hour or so every day in a state of concentration, I began to experience a feeling of vitality and strength. In my early teens, I had often been taken unawares by "sinking feelings," like an aeroplane that hits an air pocket. Now I began to experience equally unexpected "lifting" feelings. I might be standing at a bus stop, or merely staring at a cracked windowsill, when the world would suddenly become more real—as if a black-and-white television picture had suddenly turned into Technicolour. I realised then that the secret of happiness lies in mind-control.

That summer I also had my first love affair. I was working on a fairground, selling tickets for a gambling machine called a spinner, when a pretty girl who looked about thirteen began to talk to me. I walked her home later—she lived in a slum street not far from the fairground—and kissed her goodnight. The next day I took her out for a day in the country, and was shocked when she told me that, although only fifteen, she was no longer a virgin. About two days later, this was also true of me. Now, quite suddenly, I felt that I had finally emerged from the "airless room." Life was self-evidently delightful. I walked around with the *Bhagavad Gita* in one pocket and the poems of Walt Whitman in the other, and felt that I only had to concentrate hard to achieve direct contact with objective reality. My only minor problem was that Sylvia was determined to marry me, and I had no intention of marrying anyone. Ever since I was nine or ten years old, I had been convinced that I was a genius and was destined for great things. Throughout the miseries of my teens, that certainty had never left me. Now I felt that I only had to maintain my optimism and vision of purpose, and nothing could stand in my way. Sylvia's desire to get engaged made me feel vaguely uneasy; there was a gentle persistence about her that rang alarm bells.

I finally escaped by fleeing. Ever since my schooldays I had maintained contact with a pen friend who lived in Strasbourg; now, with only a few shillings in my pocket, I set out to go and see him. I arrived in Paris without any money, and heard about an eccentric millionaire who ran an "academy" on the Left Bank; his name was Raymond Duncan, and he was the brother of the famous dancer Isadora. Raymond dressed in a Greek toga and preached a philosophy he called "Actionalism"— the conviction that man can only contact reality through action, not through mere thinking. Since I had already arrived at the same conclusion myself, we found ourselves in warm agreement, and he offered to let me stay in the Akadaemia Duncan and to teach me printing and hand-loom weaving. A few weeks in the Akadaemia Duncan convinced me that I had no real desire to learn printing or weaving— my real ambition was still to write books. When my friend in Strasbourg sent me some money, I said a grateful good-bye to Raymond, and once again set out to hitchhike eastward. I arrived in Strasbourg in October, spent a few weeks with my friend, and discovered that we no longer had anything in common. He had become a communist; I was half-inclined to become a Catholic so I could enter a monastery. Before Christmas, I was back in Leicester.

I had not particularly enjoyed wandering around France without any money; but at least it made me grateful to be back home again. I found a job in a local steelworks as a clerk, and was soon as bored as ever. To combat the boredom, I began to flirt with the resident nurse, an attractive, rather "ladylike" girl who was ten years my senior. She had her own flat—supplied by the firm—and I found it pleasant to call on her in the evenings and eat the chocolate rolls wrapped in silver paper that she brought from the works canteen, and drink endless cups of tea or coffee. I soon overcame her natural prudery, and she allowed me to stay overnight. But even this could not compensate for the boredom of the office job. I resigned and again became a common labourer. I was trying to write my first book, a novel called (at that time) *Ritual of the Dead*, based on the Jack the Ripper murders; I also wrote a series of essays on subjects that interested me—Hemingway, Eliot, the Diary of Vaslav Nijinsky. That Easter, Betty told me she thought she was pregnant. A week or so later, a doctor confirmed it. We talked halfheartedly about getting an abortion. But when my parents heard about it, they took an unexpectedly moral stance, and demanded to meet Betty. After that first meeting, my mother seemed shocked. "But she's a *lady*." And they ordered us to get married. The day after our wedding night, I set out for London to look for a home for the two of us.

The marriage lasted only eighteen months. It was not that we quarrelled or found one another incompatible; only that it was practically impossible for a penniless married couple with a baby to find a home. Advertisements for double rooms often ended: "No children or pets." In eighteen months of married life we had four different homes. Finally,

in January 1953, we separated "temporarily" while I looked around for another flat; meanwhile, Betty returned to Leicester to live with my parents. One day, I saw an advertisement for a flat in east London, and Betty came down from Leicester to look at it. We liked the plump, good-natured Irishwoman who wanted to lease it, even though she wanted several hundred pounds "key money," and we agreed to sign the lease. But by the time she was back in Leicester, Betty had changed her mind, and sent me a telegram to cancel the deal. That was, in effect, the end of our marriage.

I had taken a job as a porter in a hospital in Fulham, west London, and I soon disliked it as heartily as I had disliked every other job since I had left school. That autumn, I left for Paris again. I spent only a few weeks there, making a small income as a salesman for an American-backed magazine called the *Paris Review*. I had hoped to stay in Paris and finish my novel; but by November, it was clear that I would probably starve before I found some way of making a regular income. Reluctantly, I returned once again to Leicester.

I went to the Labour Exchange, and found a job as a carpet salesman in a big store; it sounded rather less dreary than an office. On my first morning there, I joined two or three other new recruits in a room at the top of the building, where we were supposed to learn to use a cash register. Our teacher was a tall, slim girl with a dazzling smile and a pleasant, sweet voice. She was not particularly pretty, having a rather Romanesque nose, but she seemed to radiate serenity and good nature. She had a ring on her finger—I could not tell whether it was a wedding or engagement ring, and felt greatly relieved when her supervisor addressed her as "Miss Stewart." At lunch-time that day, we sat in the canteen with her, and when I saw her smile, I experienced a sudden sinking feeling—the realisation that it would be easy to plunge into a state of hopeless romantic thralldom to her. Then I told myself that that would be stupid—that she was already engaged, and would probably not be interested in me anyway. So I took the emotion by the scruff of the neck and firmly thrust it from me.

But a few days later I began to suspect that such self-denial was perhaps not going to be necessary after all. One of the other new recruits was a young ex-army officer named Martin Halliday; he was the son of a bookbinder, and had a flat of his own in the centre of town. It was Martin's ambition to seduce a pretty girl called Pat, who worked on the perfume counter and was a close friend of my dazzling Joy Stewart. Martin had the cunning idea of asking Pat if she would like to spend Saturday night and Sunday at his flat, bringing Joy as a chaperone; I was asked to make up the foursome. So I found myself unexpectedly thrown into her company for thirty-six hours. By the end of that time, I was fairly certain that she found me interesting—although she was so cool and reserved that it was hard to be sure. But at least we were now sufficiently well-acquainted for me to be able to ask her out.

I can still remember the moment when I decided she was the kind of girl I had always been hoping to find. We were crossing Victoria Park one evening and I asked her what books she had in her room; she mentioned *Ulysses*, the plays of Yeats, and *Du Coté de Chez Swann* (in French). That settled it; she was obviously intelligent enough to understand the books I wanted to write. I began using all my powers of persuasion to induce her to come to London with me.

The only problem was her engagement. She was a graduate of Trinity College, Dublin, and intended to marry a fellow student and emigrate to Canada. In fact, she went to see him off from Liverpool in January; but when she came back, I could sense that she was no longer so certain about her marriage. I renewed my arguments, and finally persuaded her that she would find her last few months in England more enjoyable in London than in Leicester. I went to London in February; she finally gave way and joined me there. A few weeks later she wrote to break off her engagement.

I preferred London to Leicester, but it still presented the same problem of how to make a living. I tried working in the office of a wine company, then in the office of a spare-parts garage; but it was so obvious that I detested the drudgery that both sacked me within weeks. The same thing happened when I tried working in a plastics factory. I began to feel as if I was being persecuted by fate. In that spring of 1953, I decided to try to save rent by buying a tent and sleeping outdoors. The first night, I erected the tent on a golf course in north London, but it was too obviously conspicuous. Then a friend suggested the obvious solution: a waterproof sleeping bag. It was, in fact, a kind of rubber envelope that went over the ordinary sleeping bag. When it rained, I could pull a kind of hood up over my head, and sleep warm and dry. The only problem was that the inside of the waterproof bag became damp with perspiration; I had to turn it inside out every morning and allow half an hour for it to dry.

By this time, I was sleeping on Hampstead Heath, in the centre of London. I usually woke up at about eight o'clock, and packed my belongings on the back of my bicycle. Then I cycled down Haverstock Hill to a busman's café, where I could get a huge mug of tea and a slice of bread and dripping for a few pence. I arrived at the British Museum for opening-time around ten o'clock—I had started using the Reading Room in the last year of my marriage, no doubt inspired by romantic tales of Marx, Shaw, and Samuel Butler writing masterpieces there. I left my haversack and sleeping bag in the cloakroom, then spent the day working at my novel, now entitled *Ritual in the Dark*. I was still obsessed by the idea of Joyce's mythological method, and by Eliot's remark that Joyce's use of the *Odyssey* had been an attempt at "controlling, of ordering, of giving a shape and a significance to the immense panorama of futility and anarchy which is contemporary history." I had decided to use the Egyptian *Book of the Dead* as the basic structural framework of my novel. In its original version, it had been a grim story about a man who kills a prostitute, but is then unable to decide whether it was all some kind of delusion. But, like Dr. Johnson, I found that "cheerfulness kept breaking in," and that in later versions, my hero became less of an obsessive. By the time I began rewriting it—for perhaps the tenth time—in 1953, the novel was a study in three "outsiders" (a word I had borrowed from Bernard Shaw). One was an "intellectual outsider," like Nietzsche, one an "emotional outsider," like Van Gogh, one a "physical outsider," like the ballet dancer Nijinsky. I wanted to show the different ways in which all three responded to mental stress. The "physical outsider" expresses his frustration through sadistic violence, like Jack the Ripper, or the Düsseldorf murderer Peter Kürten.

The superintendent of the Reading Room was the novelist and short-story writer Angus Wilson. One day, I asked a librarian to try to help me track down Eliot's essay "Ulysses, Order and Myth"; he had no success, and it was Angus Wilson who finally located it for me. He asked me what I was writing, and when I told him it was a novel, he offered to read it. Christmas was only a few weeks away, and I rushed to complete the first part, so Angus could read it over the holiday. I handed it to him just before he left.

By this time, bad weather had driven me back indoors again. I had found a room in New Cross, and a labouring job in a local laundry. That Christmas, alone in my room—Joy had gone to see her parents—I began to sketch out the idea for another book, to be called *The Outsider in Literature*. It sprang out of an increasing dissatisfaction with my novel, which was too overloaded with intellectual references. The sensible thing, I decided, was to write a separate book about the ideas, and to try to turn *Ritual* into something more like a traditional novel. In an hour or so, I had outlined *The Outsider* in the back of my diary—chapters on Sartre, Camus, Hemingway, Hermann Hesse (whose work was then almost completely unknown in the English-speaking countries), Dostoevsky, Tolstoy, William Blake, Ramakrishna, Gurdjieff, and so on.

As soon as the British Museum opened again, I cycled there with the outline in my saddlebag. On my way there, I recalled a reference to a novel by Henri Barbusse, about a man who finds a hole in the wall of his hotel room, and spends his days peering through at the people who come and go in the next room. Here was obviously a perfect symbol for "the Outsider." When I got to the Museum, I ordered the novel—Barbusse's *Enfer*—and read it straight through in about four hours. Then I copied out a sentence from it at the top of a sheet of paper: "In the air, on top of a tram, a girl is sitting . . ." By the time I cycled home that afternoon, I had written the first half-dozen pages of *The Outsider.*

The job in the laundry was exhausting—it involved lifting baths-full of wet laundry from a continuously moving belt—and when my journal was stolen out of my pocket one day, I gave in my notice. The next day I saw an advertisement asking for staff for a new coffee house that was opening in the Haymarket. I went and applied, and was engaged as a washer-up. I worked every evening, from half past five until midnight, so I could spend my days in the Reading Room. And for perhaps the first time in my life, I found myself enjoying a job I was being paid to do. Most of the other employees were drama students and out-of-work actors, so the atmosphere was pleasant. I was soon promoted to working behind the counter, serving coffee, and found that even more enjoyable. In retrospect, I find myself half-suspecting that some destiny was trying to drive me to write *The Outsider,* and allowing me no peace until I did it. And now the book was at last safely under way, I could be allowed to relax.

Angus Wilson, meanwhile, had read the opening section of *Ritual,* and was encouraging; he told me to go ahead and finish it, and then he would show it to his publisher. But I decided to finish *The Outsider in Literature* first. One day, in a second-hand bookshop, I came upon an anthology of religious mysticism called *A Year of Grace;* it was edited by the publisher Victor Gollancz. I decided to type out the first chapter of *The Outsider,* and to send it to Gollancz, together with an outline of the rest of the book. To my delight and astonishment, he wrote back an encouraging letter, saying he liked it, and would be glad to read it when it was finished. I began to get an odd feeling that life was about to change for the better—the kind of feeling animals probably get when they smell the first breath of spring.

Then, suddenly, my mother was rushed into hospital with peritonitis. It sounded as if she might not recover. I went to Gollancz's office, left the half-completed typescript with an unwilling secretary—who told me Mr. Gollancz never read unfinished books—and rushed up to Leicester. I stayed there until my mother was off the danger list. When I returned to London, I found a letter from Gollancz waiting for me; he said that he would definitely like to publish *The Outsider,* and offered me an advance of seventy-five pounds.

A few days later, he invited me to lunch. He was a large man with a bald head, bushy eyebrows, and a booming voice. The first question he asked me was how I had succeeded in reading so much; I told him that I'd had nothing else to do since I was about thirteen. After lunch, I met Joy and took her to a cinema in the Haymarket. They were showing a film called *Daddy Long Legs* with Fred Astaire, and as we walked into the cinema, he was dancing to a tune called "Something's Gotta Give." I had not heard that kind of blaring brass since the last time I saw a Harry James film in childhood; suddenly, I experienced an overwhelming sense of sheer delight, a curious certainty that *The Outsider* was going to be a success.

That August, Joy and I sent our bicycles on ahead, and hitchhiked down to Cornwall. We took the coastal route via Lyme Regis. As we were climbing the steep hill out of Lyme Regis, looking at a tremendous cliff that was full of gulls' nests, I again experienced the feeling of overwhelming happiness. At the same time, I felt that this was more than mere happiness: that in some way it involved an insight into the nature of reality. Ever since my early teens, I had had a feeling of being on a treadmill; life had seemed to be an endless series of depressions and disappointments. But the real problem had been suprapersonal: that suspicion that life is fundamentally meaningless and futile. By the time I was eighteen, I felt a deep certainty that this is not so: that somehow, "meaning" is an objective reality, completely independent of our minds. But I was in the absurd position of feeling that I had intellectual reasons for optimism, while my everyday life remained boring and frustrating. When I found Joy, I had the feeling that fate had offered me something "on account." But my everyday life remained intensely frustrating. And now, staring at the cliff to the west of Lyme Regis, I had a feeling that I was not merely looking at beautiful scenery, but contemplating a proof that meaning is an objective reality. And I continued to feel this as we meandered around Devon and Cornwall, sleeping in a tent, wandering into fish-and-chip shops for a meal, drinking cider in old pubs with smoke-blackened beams, swimming in the sea. In my childhood I had daydreamed about fame and it had seemed very distant; now I had an odd feeling that it was about to become a reality.

In May 1956, a month before my twenty-fifth birthday, *The Outsider* finally appeared. Joy was by now living with me in a room in Notting Hill Gate, in a bohemian household where Dylan Thomas had once lived. We got up early on that Sunday morning, for we knew that the book would be reviewed in one of the two "highbrow" newspapers, the *Sunday Times* and the *Observer*, for an advertisement in the newspaper on the previous evening had mentioned that Cyril Connolly would be discussing the subject: "Are men of genius Outsiders?" We went down to the newsstand on the corner and bought the *Sunday Times* and *Observer*. Both contained highly favourable lead-reviews. And when we got back home, someone pointed out that we had overlooked a review in the previous evening's newspaper. It was headlined: "He's a major writer, and he's only twenty-four!" A few moments later, the telephone rang—it was our neighbours' phone, but they had agreed to let us give the number to my publisher. It was my editor, ringing me up to congratulate me, and asking me if he could give the number to the press. Our neighbours agreed—and probably spent the rest of the day regretting it. The telephone went on ringing until evening. The next day I was on television and radio, and being interviewed by the London correspondent of *Time* magazine, then photographed in my sleeping bag on Hampstead Heath by *Life*. A film star named Jean Seberg, who was in London making a film about Joan of Arc, asked me if I could go and have dinner with her, but I was so busy that I had to refuse. (I have often regretted it—we never succeeded in getting together.) The fame I had always dreamed about had arrived, and the irony was that I was unable to appreciate it. So much publicity seemed to knock the breath out of me.

In fact, after a few days I realised that, far from enjoying it, I detested the sensation of being "in the public eye." It seemed a total contradiction of everything I stood for. I had spent years reading Nietzsche and Rilke and Dostoevsky, and looking at the paintings of Van Gogh and Cézanne, and seriously thinking about entering a monastery. Now, suddenly, I was being taken to dinner by publishers and pursued by gossip columnists and invited to cocktail parties. It seemed a betrayal of the things I had written about in *The Outsider*. Fundamentally, I felt about London society as Kierkegaard had felt about Danish society a century earlier; it seemed to me boring and brainless. My "success" itself was an absurd paradox; I was being rewarded for telling society how much I detested it. But the journalists who interviewed me seemed to have no understanding of that. For them, I was some kind of intellectual freak, like a calculating prodigy or idiot savant. And I became aware of another strange thing: that the interview, when it appeared, seemed to have no relation to what I had actually said. It was not that I was wilfully misquoted; only that the writer seemed to have given prominence to all the things I thought unimportant, so the end result was a mangled travesty—like a drawing of someone where every feature is recognisably accurate, but where all have been magnified or reduced in different degrees, so the end result is like a fairground distorting-mirror.

Another young writer named John Osborne had "arrived" at exactly the same time; his play *Look Back in Anger* had been presented at the Royal Court in the week before *The Outsider* appeared, and the Sunday newspapers hailed it as the most exciting play of its generation. (I went to see it and hated it—it seemed to me self-pitying verbiage.) For a few weeks the newspapers seemed unable to decide whether to describe myself and Osborne as Outsiders or Angry Young Men, but finally settled on the latter as being more self-explanatory. We were supposed to be the voice of the younger generation, and since we arrived in midsummer—the "silly season" when there is a lack of hard news—we found ourselves in the gossip columns every other day. Journalists would ring me up to ask: "What do you think of the seams in ladies' stockings?" On one occasion I went to the local cinema to see *The Cruel Sea*, and the next day, an item appeared in the *Daily Express* gossip column saying that I had been seen standing in a queue outside the cinema. It was all incredibly silly and irrelevant.

Within a week or two, I became aware of a change in the atmosphere, an unmistakable sense of hostility. The day after *The Outsider* appeared, the *Sunday Times* asked me if I would like to become a regular reviewer. Although my first review appeared promptly, they took several months to print my second one, and thereafter sent me no more books for review. But their gossip columnist mentioned that there was a rumour that most sales of *The Outsider* were "furniture sales"—that is, people bought it to leave around on their coffee tables to show they were intellectual, but seldom actually read it. It gradually became clear to me that the *succès fou* of the book had infuriated the serious critics who had been responsible for launching it. It was reported to me that Cyril Connolly had been assuring his friends that he had not actually read *The Outsider*, but had simply glanced at it and decided it deserved a good review. Angus Wilson asked me to dinner to warn me that if the publicity continued, people would cease to take me seriously; he urged me to keep out of the newspapers. I told him I would be delighted, but had no idea of how to do it. When someone wrote to ask me about my publicity methods, I replied that I had no more idea of how to obtain publicity than a football had of how to score goals.

Gollancz himself was partly responsible for the increasing hostility; his advertisements continued to quote the good reviews (Edith Sitwell: "I think Colin Wilson will be a truly great writer") and to announce that the book was going into yet another new impression. (The *Sunday Times* gossip columnist reported that there was widespread cynicism in the trade about the size of a Gollancz impression.) In fact, *The Outsider* sold about forty thousand copies in the course of those first few months, and was translated into about a dozen languages in its first year. In America it immediately went to the head of the nonfiction best-seller list. The impresario Sol Hurok cabled me asking if I would do a lecture tour of America, but I refused; I was sick of "fame." I was beginning to suffer from what I called "people poisoning." The increasing bitchiness made it worse. At Christmas, leading writers are asked to give their opinions of the best books of the year. No one mentioned *The Outsider* with the exception of Arthur Koestler, who went out of his way to comment: "Bubble of the year: *The Outsider*, in which a young man discovers that men of genius suffer from *Weltschmerz*."

Early the following year there was further bad publicity. One evening when Joy and I were giving dinner to a bizarre old chap named Gerald Hamilton—the original of Mr. Norris in Isherwood's *Last of Mr. Norris*—Joy's parents suddenly burst into the room. Joy's father was flourishing a horsewhip and shouted, "The game is up, Wilson." Joy's parents had always objected to me, and her father had once told me that I would "end in the gutter." Now Joy's

younger sister had told them that she had read my diaries, and that I was a homosexual and had several mistresses. In fact, the diaries—which I had left around on a visit to Joy's home—contained notes for *Ritual in the Dark*. I finally got to a telephone and rang the police, who pointed out to Joy's parents that she was over twenty-one and could do what she liked. But a few minutes after they had left, the doorbell rang: it was the *Daily Mirror*, complete with a photographer. Gerald Hamilton had made for the nearest telephone and rung every newspaper in Fleet Street. We gave them an interview, but no sooner had they left than the doorbell rang again; we looked out of the window and saw a crowd of reporters and photographers. So we sneaked quietly out of the back door, and caught a train down to Devon. This proved to be a mistake; the story of "runaway lovers" caught the imagination of Fleet Street, and we were pursued over England and Ireland. When I finally returned to London, Victor Gollancz sent for me and said: "For God's sake get out of London or you'll never write another book." We took his advice and moved down to Cornwall—the tenant in the next room told us we could rent his cottage near Mevagissey for thirty shillings (about two dollars) a week. That was almost thirty years ago, and we have been here ever since.

The "horsewhipping" publicity proved to be as disastrous as Gollancz had predicted. A year after the publication of *The Outsider*, there was probably not a critic in England or America who still regarded me as a serious writer. It had become fashionable to describe *The Outsider* as a collection of quotations. My reaction to all of this was to make my next book a study in religious mystics and "world rejectors." In a sense, Kierkegaard is its central figure, with his revolt against his own society. "Let others complain that our age is wicked; my complaint is that it is wretched, for it lacks passion." Yet I was not, like Rousseau, arguing against civilisation itself; this would have struck me as stupid. The basic problem is that most "Outsiders" seem born to be "in opposition," and that this position is intolerably lonely. That is why so many of the Outsiders of the nineteenth century ended tragically; most of them felt that the tragedy was inevitable, a kind of martyrdom. In *The Outsider*, I argued that the martyrdom is unnecessary. If Van Gogh and Nietzsche had held out for another ten years, they would have triumphed. The Outsider simply has to learn to *stand alone*, and to avoid falling into the trap of despair and self-pity. The real danger is what Shaw called "discouragement."

In my second book, which I wanted to call *The*

*Rebel* (and which Gollancz persuaded me to call *Religion and the Rebel*), I proceeded to extend this argument. I wanted to show that in ages of religious faith, the "Outsiders" had been able to find a place inside the church, where their dislike of society and craving for spiritual intensity were perfectly acceptable. Since the rise of science had destroyed the basis of orthodox religion, the Outsider was simply an uncomfortable misfit, regarded by the "Insiders" as a hopeless failure. I remained convinced that this was a mistake. If he could generate the strength to stand alone, the Outsider could still exert an important influence on society. I cited Shaw, Wittgenstein, and Whitehead as modern examples: men who had dared to express their deepest values and had never compromised.

When *Religion and the Rebel* appeared in the autumn of 1957, Gollancz's worst fears were realised; it was universally hatcheted. A *Daily Express* journalist, Nancy Spain, expressed the general view when she wrote: "We are sick of the boy Colin, sick of hearing about his domestic problems and his finances and his love affairs . . ." Philip Toynbee, one of the critics who had launched *The Outsider*, dismissed the book as a "rubbish bin." *Time* magazine announced my downfall with an article headed "Scrambled Egghead" which began "Colin Wilson's game of intellectual hooky is well and truly up. . . ."

In retrospect I can see that the attacks were not entirely unjustified. I made one major mistake: instead of concentrating on my main theme—religion and mysticism—I tried to begin with a summary of *The Outsider*, then went on to discuss Spengler and Arnold Toynbee before I settled down to my major theme: "religious Outsiders." The result is undoubtedly a badly constructed book. But this was not primarily why it was attacked. The real reason was that everyone was heartily sick of the Angry Young Men, and wanted to see the last of us. (Osborne's musical *The World of Paul Slickey* was booed off the stage and he was actually chased down Shaftesbury Avenue by an angry crowd.) The popular journalists who had been impressed by the praises bestowed on me by their intellectual betters were delighted to hear that it had all been a mistake and that they could safely dismiss my work as pretentious rubbish.

But if it was upsetting to be regarded as some kind of intellectual fraud, it was also a relief to be off the pedestal and standing on solid ground again. I had been working alone, without much encouragement, for the past twelve years, so it was not as daunting as it might have been. A few weeks after

publication of *Religion and the Rebel*, I went to lecture in Oslo. When a journalist met us at the airport, I had to conceal a feeling of suspicious hostility; but it changed to astonishment when he began to question me about my ideas, and how my existentialism differed from that of Sartre and Camus. It took some time for it to sink in that Norwegian journalists had no intention of asking me about my love life or my income, and that the insensitivity and sheer nastiness of British journalism was not universal. By the time I left Oslo, I had ceased to feel defensive, and begun to recover the inner certainty I had experienced as I wrote *The Outsider*. And as I began to achieve some kind of objectivity about the past eighteen months, I began to understand the irony of the situation. Before *The Outsider* came out, I had reread Nietzsche's first book, *The Birth of Tragedy*, which had been received with contemptuous hostility; and it had struck me that I could probably expect the same reception. Instead, to my astonishment, I was hailed as a major writer. Within weeks, it had all turned sour, and I had realised that my success was, in fact, a cunningly disguised form of failure. I could now understand what had led T.E. Lawrence to refuse a knighthood and driven him to try to take refuge in the anonymity of the tank corps.

But at least I had made the discovery fairly early, and could now understand what lay ahead of me. Now the success of *The Outsider* had evaporated, I saw it as my task to try to demonstrate the truth of its central argument: that it *is* possible for an "Outsider" to work alone. I could see that "success" is, in a basic sense, a contradiction of what he stands for. (It would be possible to write a book about modern Outsiders who have been destroyed by success: Utrillo, T.E. Lawrence, Jackson Pollock, Dylan Thomas, Tennessee Williams. . . . .) What, then, is he supposed to do?—refuse all offers of publication or exhibitions of his paintings or performances of his music? Obviously not. His problem is simply to continue to work at his main task; and in a certain sense, "society" is the enemy. If he accepts the kind of success it wants to bestow, he will lose that peculiar inner-pressure that drives him. He has to learn to *choose* isolation. When Kierkegaard said "Truth is subjectivity," he was not denying that truth is also supreme objectivity; merely insisting that it involves what I have called "access to inner worlds." And where "access to inner worlds" is concerned, success is more dangerous than failure because it is more insidiously distracting.

So although it was a traumatic experience to be dismissed as a has-been at the age of twenty-six, I was detached enough to realise that it had all been for the best. I was back in the position where I could get on with my real work. And there was at least one respect in which some degree of success was better than failure: it offered me a lifeline of income. At least I was in a position to make a living doing something I wanted to do. I was living in a pleasant country cottage, with a stream running past the door, and the sea a few hundred yards away down a green valley; it was the kind of life I used to dream about in my teens. Joy was an ideal person to live with: serene, good-natured, and undemanding. It was true that we seemed to be permanently broke, but there was just about enough money to run a car and buy a few bottles of wine. I never ceased to be grateful that I no longer had to work in factories and offices—occasionally I dreamt I was back at the factory bench and woke up sweating. And although my books continued to be attacked or ignored, publishers seemed quite happy to go on commissioning them and giving me advances.

Luck also favoured us when we decided it was time to move out of the cottage. Our landlord was a poet who worked for a London publisher, and longed to return to Cornwall. In 1958 we heard rumours that he had decided not to renew our lease. I wrote to ask him about it but—being a poet—he was too lazy to reply. I was trying to finish *Ritual in the Dark*, so it was Joy who went house-hunting. She saw a house advertised for sale about two miles from our cottage, and wandered up the long drive. A glance at the place convinced her it was too big; then she saw someone looking at her out of the window and decided to go and make enquiries. They asked her in and gave her tea. When she came home, she told me that the place was too big and too expensive—it cost almost £5,000. But I liked the idea of a large place—the cottage was already jammed from floor to ceiling with books and records. I wrote to Gollancz to ask him if he could give me some sort of general advance on future books; to my delight, he told me that I already had several thousand pounds due on *Religion and the Rebel*; in spite of bad reviews, it had sold fairly well. So we were able to buy a house just before the property-boom trebled the prices. It stood on two acres of land on which there was building permission for more houses, so in due course it became invaluable as collateral at the bank. And after all that, it turned out that the poet had no intention of returning to Cornwall; the cottage stood empty for long after we left it. . .

*Ritual in the Dark* finally appeared in 1960, and sold unexpectedly well. But reviews were lukewarm;

the critics had no intention of reconsidering me as a novelist. A film director, Brian Forbes, wanted to option the book, and for a few weeks I thought that our problems were at an end. But the deal fell through, so our finances remained as unstable as ever. It was a disappointment; I realised that if *Ritual* had been made into a successful film, most of my subsequent novels would probably have been filmed, and life would have been a great deal more comfortable. As it was, we staggered on from crisis to crisis. During the next six years I went on to complete my "Outsider cycle"—with *The Age of Defeat, The Strength to Dream, Origins of the Sexual Impulse*, and *Beyond the Outsider*—but the critics remained indifferent. Fortunately, these books also appeared in America, and went into various foreign translations, so we were able to live precariously off advances. It was a discouraging sensation: I once compared it to dropping a stone down a well and hearing no splash. Yet I found deep satisfaction in the work itself, and knew that this was the real answer—to be so absorbed in the ideas that it made no difference whether they were understood or not.

Even my own anomalous situation made me aware of the real nature of my obsession. My work made little headway, and the sheer stupidity of the critical attacks sometimes made me rage. Yet I was now happily married to Joy, lived in a pleasant home, and was able to take walks on the cliffs or swim in the sea when I was tired of writing. It would have been stupid to indulge in self-pity or indignation. I had to make the effort to "perspectivise," to grasp my situation objectively and count my blessings. *This* had always been my basic obsession: what one writer called man's "fundamental alienation from the source of power, meaning, and purpose." Again and again we experience the moments of what G.K. Chesterton called "absurd good news," the insight that made Proust write: "I had ceased to feel mediocre, accidental, mortal." And each time we experience it, we realise that the power to induce such states lies within *the mind itself*, and it is absurd to sit waiting passively for it to happen.

Another important clue was provided by an American professor of psychology, Abraham Maslow, who discovered my work through *The Age of Defeat* (called in America *The Stature of Man* because the publisher wanted an "upbeat" title). Maslow told me that, as a psychologist, he had got sick of studying sick people, because sick people talked about nothing but their sickness. He decided instead to study the healthiest people he could locate. And as soon as he began to study healthy people, he discovered something that no one had ever discovered before: that all healthy people have, with a fair degree of frequency, what Maslow called "peak experiences"—experiences of sudden overwhelming happiness. He made another important discovery. When he began to talk to his students about peak experiences, they began to recall peak experiences they'd had in the past, but half forgotten. (For example, a young man who was working his way through college as a jazz drummer recalled how, late one night, he began to drum perfectly, and went into the peak experience; a marine who had spent a long time on a Pacific island had a peak experience when he was posted back to base and saw a nurse—because, he said, it suddenly struck him like a revelation *that women are quite different from men*.) But he made an even more important discovery. When his students began thinking and talking about peak experiences every day, *they began having peak experiences all the time.* In other words, the reason we seldom have peak experiences is that our basic attitudes are negative; we don't *expect* them. If we could actually grasp this, we would immediately become capable of inducing "peaks" at will.

In this connection, I was also fascinated by Graham Greene's story about "the revolver in the corner cupboard." In his teens, during a period of grey depression, he found his brother's revolver, and took it out on to Birkhamstead Common to play Russian roulette. He inserted one bullet, spun the chambers, pointed it at his head, and pulled the trigger. When there was just a click, he looked down the barrel and saw that the bullet had now come into position, so he just missed death by one pull of the trigger. He wrote: "It was as if a light had been turned on . . . and I saw that life is full of infinite possibilities." But if a light is turned on, you only see what was already there *before* it was turned on. The peak experience always brings this insight: that life is infinitely rich, and that only the sheer *feebleness* of our perceptions prevents us from grasping it —our lazy assumption that there is nothing to see. It was the surge of *effort* induced by the closeness of death that made Greene aware that life is worth a hundred times as much effort as we normally assume. To some supervital being from another planet, depression and boredom would seem ultimate absurdities, like a millionaire committing suicide because he has lost a penny down a drain.

This sudden surge of a more powerful type of consciousness enables us to tear aside those curtains that normally separate us from reality, and in such moments we seem to grasp the reality of other times and places as if they were as real as the present. This is what happened to Proust as he tasted the cake

dipped in tea, and suddenly became aware of the reality of his childhood in Combray. In *A Study of History*, Arnold Toynbee described a similar experience as he was sitting in the ruined citadel of Mistra, overlooking the plain of Sparta. The thought suddenly came to him that two centuries earlier, barbarians had poured over *that* wall he was now looking at, and that ever since then, this place had been a ruin. Quite suddenly, it was real, as if he could actually see the barbarians; time had ceased to exist. I labelled this ability "Faculty X," the ability to grasp reality *with the mind.*

But if we already possess this faculty, then what prevents us from making use of it at will? The answer is: automatism, or what I came to call "the robot." The robot is a kind of valet who lives in the unconscious mind, and who helps us to master all kinds of complicated tasks. When I learn to type, or ski, or learn a foreign language, I have to do it painfully and consciously; then my "robot" takes over, and does it far more quickly and efficiently than "I" could do it. The trouble is that he not only does the things I want him to do, like typing and driving the car, but also the things I don't want him to do. When I go for a country walk for the first time I thoroughly enjoy it; when I go on the same walk for the fiftieth time I no longer enjoy it so much because I am "used to it," which is only another way of saying that the robot has taken it over. Sometimes, when I go for a walk on the cliff, I can *see* that the scenery is beautiful, yet I feel nothing whatever. This is because I am tired, and when I am tired, the robot "switches on" automatically, like a thermostat. The robot can sit on my shoulders like the old man of the sea in the Sinbad story, throttling me and destroying all appreciation of life. When Graham Greene pointed the revolver at his head, the old man gave a shriek of alarm and leapt off—which is why Greene suddenly realised that life is full of infinite possibilities. Faculty X is simply another name for consciousness unimpeded by the robot.

There was another aspect of it that fascinated me. In his autobiographical book, *Legends*, Strindberg describes how he was feeling homesick in Paris, and longing to be back in his wife's home in Germany. The feeling was so powerful that for a moment he actually felt that he was in her sitting room, and could see his mother-in-law at the piano. Then the intensity faded and he was back in his room in Paris. But a short time after, he received a letter from his mother-in-law asking: "Are you all right? The other day as I was sitting at the piano I thought I saw you standing in front of me." Was it possible that Faculty X is not simply an unusually active state of imagination, but that it also releases some curious "paranormal" power?

It was at about this time that an American publisher asked me if I would be interested in writing a book about "the occult." It was not a subject that had interested me deeply, although I had read many books about it in a lighthearted and sceptical spirit. But as soon as I began to study it closely, I became increasingly absorbed. It was clear to me that my investigation of the mysteries of consciousness led straight into the heart of the paranormal. The book grew to three times the size I had originally intended. And when it finally appeared, in the autumn of 1971, it was successful beyond my expectations. Philip Toynbee and Cyril Connolly, the two critics who had launched *The Outsider* then recanted later, gave it glowing reviews. During the week of its publication there were newspaper interviews and appearances on radio and television; it was all a little like the publication of *The Outsider*, but on a more dignified level. And since it cost four times as much as *The Outsider*, I made a great deal more money. And it was at about this time that I began to realise that I had a wide audience of regular readers, even when my books received no reviews. They were not the type who wrote letters—regarding themselves as Outsiders—but they bought my books and borrowed them from libraries, and even advertised for second-hand copies in magazines. I even learned from an advertisement in the *New Statesman* that there was a Colin Wilson Society in London, and that a group of them held weekly meetings to study *The Outsider*.

The more I studied the paranormal, the more I became convinced that Faculty X is the key to man's future evolution. There is strong evidence that civilised man has lost a "sixth sense" that is still possessed by animals and primitive people. I was particularly fascinated by the case of the Dutch housepainter Peter van der Hurk, who fell off a ladder and fractured his skull; when he woke up in hospital he found that he had become telepathic, and "knew" things about people as soon as he spoke to them. His problem was that this sixth sense prevented him from being able to concentrate on the practical problems of everyday life. In effect, his mind was like a radio set picking up half-a-dozen stations at the same time; it was not until someone suggested that he use his peculiar powers on the stage that he was again able to make a living.

*This* is why man has deliberately got rid of his "paranormal" powers. They are incompatible with the kind of sharp, clear consciousness that he needs to achieve success in a civilised society. Yet although these powers have been placed in cold storage, they have not been lost. We could reactivate them if we needed them. But most of us have no desire to reactivate them. What we are aiming at is a different kind of power. An animal possesses a kind of "wide-angle consciousness," a sense of direct contact with nature; but this is not the kind we want. The kind of "wide-angle" awareness that came to Toynbee in the citadel of Mistra was basically an intellectual vision; it depended on an immense wide knowledge of history. Faculty X turned this intellectual awareness into *living knowledge*. No animal could achieve a similar vision because no animal possesses Toynbee's intellectual knowledge. Man has abandoned the animal's "wide-angle vision" in favour of a kind of "microscopic" awareness, which enables him to deal with the minutiae of everyday existence. But the ultimate aim is a *different kind* of wide-angle vision, in which intellectual knowledge is transformed into a direct sense of reality.

Our greatest problem is a certain inborn negativity. Mephistopheles tells Faust: "I am the spirit that negates." And in human beings, this "Mephistophelean" tendency takes the form of an assumption that "robotic" experience is more real than the moments of intensity and "peak experiences." Flaubert comments that when Charles Bovary is first married to Emma, their love life is delightful; but after a while, he begins to treat lovemaking as a kind of after-dinner dessert. Moreover, Charles would feel that this is only to be expected. Now he has made love to Emma a hundred times or so, he "knows" her in much the same way he might get to know a favourite book; and now he knows the book, it can never again produce the same impact as on first reading. In the same way, Dylan Thomas compares the female sexual organ to a "foul mousehole" from which the male withdraws "pouting" when the "limp time" arrives. Yet this "Mephistophelean" vision is insidiously false. All that has happened is that the "robot" has taken over and is draining the experience of its reality. Every peak experience, every flash of "absurd good news," makes us clearly aware of this. Then we can see that if only we could find some way of *galvanising* the mind into a state of alertness, we could live at an altogether higher level of intensity. Dr. Johnson said that the knowledge that he is to be hanged in the morning concentrates a man's mind wonderfully. Sartre said that he had never felt so free as when he was in the Resistance during the war and might be arrested and shot at any moment. But "crisis" is not the only way of forcing the robot to relinquish his stranglehold. Maslow's students achieved it merely by talking and thinking about peak experiences and recognising that peak experiences can be induced by an *attitude of mind*—the non-Mephistophelean attitude.

In *The Outsider* I asked repeatedly: "Why does life fail?" I was thinking of Auden's lines:

> Put the car away; when life fails
> What's the good of going to Wales?

as well as of Shaw's remark in *Back to Methuselah*: "Even at the moment of death their life does not fail them." Then why *does* life fail us so often? The basic answer is that we are labouring under two disadvantages: the "robot," and the "Mephistophelean point of view," which tells us that it is inevitable for our experience to deteriorate so that life becomes increasingly dull. Both these problems can be remedied. The robot is, after all, only a kind of thermostat which switches on when we feel tired or low, and *we can set the thermostat ourselves* by changing our attitude. And the Mephistophelean point of view is an unexamined assumption that we tend to take for granted. Therein lies its danger. The moment we begin to study and actively question this assumption, it begins to lose its power over us, as it lost its power over Maslow's students as soon as they began to assume that peak experiences are perfectly normal.

The more I thought about this, the more it struck me that the phrase "access to inner worlds" should be taken quite literally. While we think of "inner worlds" merely as a "manner of speaking," we are missing the point. When Proust's Marcel tasted the cake dipped in herb tea, that strange feeling of ecstacy was not due simply to a vivid memory of childhood. It was due to a sudden revelation of the vast extent of the world inside us. He could be compared to Aladdin, pulling up a large stone slab and descending a flight of steps into an underground kingdom. This kingdom exists quite literally. The neurologist Wilder Penfield discovered this when, during a brain operation, he touched the patient's temporal cortex with an electric probe, and the patient suddenly relived a memory of childhood in photographic detail. But even this recognition is only a step in the right direction. Rudolf Steiner insisted throughout his life that the "spiritual realm" lies inside us, and is a universe in its own right—that, for example, when we die, we enter this inner universe just as Aladdin entered the magician's cave. Proust's excitement was due to a glimpse of this truth, and he spent the rest of his life searching for the stone slab. It is our intuitive recognition

of this truth that produces the feeling of "absurd good news" in the peak experience. It is a recognition that we are not slaves of the material universe, "creatures of circumstance," but inhabitants of a realm that was also "the source of power, meaning and purpose."

It was not until the late seventies that I came across an important clue to the mystery, in the realm of split-brain physiology. It came through a reading of Ornstein's *Psychology of Consciousness* and Julian Jaynes's *Origin of Consciousness in the Breakdown of the Bicameral Mind*. I had known about the differing functions of the two hemispheres of the brain for a long time—that the left deals with language and logic, while the right deals with intuition and pattern-recognition—but what I had not realised is we quite literally have *two people* living in the two hemispheres, and that the person you call "you" lives in the left. The person a few centimeters away is virtually a stranger. This—as everyone now knows—becomes apparent after a "split-brain" operation to cure epilepsy. One split-brain patient tried to hit his wife with one hand while the other held it back; another tried to unzip his fly with one hand while the other tried to zip it up. When a woman was shown an indecent picture, with the right half of the brain, she blushed; asked why she was blushing, she replied truthfully: "I don't know."

As a writer I had always been aware of these two selves. When I was learning to write, I would often do an evening's work which I thought was magnificent; but when I read it again the next morning, it made me wince. It was as if, in turning the intuitions into words, I had somehow crushed them flat, so they looked like so many squashed flies. I began to suspect that it is impossible to grasp intuitions and turn them into words—they simply evaporate in the process. Yet I persisted, and finally, I began to realise that it *can* be done. Sometimes I'd read what I'd written the night before, and *it was still there*. And then there were times when I felt so alert that I could grasp the intuition while it was still on the wing, and turn it into words, and the words were so obviously apposite that I'd experience a glow of self-congratulation, and turn the next one into words even more precisely. And suddenly, the two "me's" —the intuitive and the verbal halves—were like two first-class tennis players, or two lumberjacks at either end of a doubled-handed saw.

What is obvious is that the left brain—the "everyday me"—tends to move much quicker than the "other self." He is naturally impatient. And that means he is always losing touch with his intuitions.

The continual pressure of modern society makes things worse. When I am at my best, I somehow relax deep inside myself and then the "verbal me" becomes dimly aware of the existence of that "other self," and suddenly relaxes into a mood of blissful collaboration. *This* is what produces the peak experience—the recognition of the existence of that "other me," and the insight into the tremendous powers it can call upon. If modern man wants to escape the trap imposed by his self-division, he will have to learn to recognise the existence of that "other self" as an objective reality, and learn the trick of entering into instantaneous cooperation with it. When he loses touch, he begins to feel "mediocre, accidental, mortal," and is easily defeated. The moment he regains contact, he feels a surge of power and confidence. And since this "other self" is *really there*—it is not a "manner of speaking"—it is absurd that we should waste so much of our lives in a state of nervous exhaustion. Auden writes:

> In headache and in worry
> Slowly life leaks away.

But this is only because we have forgotten that we have a powerful helper who lives in the Aladdin's cave.

I have always felt that the very essence of the human problem was grasped by that fine music critic, J.W.N. Sullivan, in his classic autobiography *But for the Grace of God.* He writes about the First World War:

> The only assimilable "lesson" taught by the war was the extreme desirability of the ordinary commonplace civilised life. Even as seen from the relative security of a war hospital that life seemed desirable almost beyond imagining. Looking out on those dark, alien Serbian hills, after a day spent amongst the sights and odours of suppurating flesh (for all our wounded, on the long journey from the front, developed gangrene), I have had visions of Paradise. I have pictured the lighted Strand, one of the golden streets of Heaven, and longed for its ambrosia, two poached eggs on toast, in those dazzling halls of light called Lyons' restaurants. It was inconceivable to me that I could ever have been discontented with life in such celestial surroundings. The thought of a London bus on a rainy evening, its windows steamy with the breath of its crowded passengers, splashing its way through the dark space around Trafalgar Square, filled me with a yearning that perhaps an exiled cherub would experience for his chariot of fire. I felt that I had learned my lesson. If ever I were permitted to live again my ordinary life I would never, I reflected, permit the blasphemy of thinking it dull. It seemed incredible to me that I should ever have been blind to the bliss of working in a London office, and of living in two amazingly beautiful rooms in idyllic Richmond. And on top of these there were my serene, wise books, and my dramatic, untamed pianola! I have never quite lost that vision. I am a little impatient of those people who find the whole of our "material" civilisation merely sordid and ugly. A London bus is not quite the miracle I thought it in Serbia, but it is, nevertheless, a most delightful, friendly and interesting object. And I can still sometimes experience a mood of pure exultation at my incredible good fortune in being alive, and privileged to sit on a high stool at a delicatessen counter in the Strand, consuming a Bismarck herring and (as I believe) genuine German lager beer. Perhaps I would enjoy riches. I might like to possess a Rolls-Royce, a country house, a flat in town, and a villa in the south of France. But I can still feel, at times, that the transition from an overcrowded Serbian hospital even to a life of one room, a bed and a chair, and a penny newspaper every morning, is so vast that the millionaire's extra advantages are hardly perceptible on that scale.

Sullivan adds: "It is a pity that one cannot preserve this attitude. One becomes so debilitated that even a bus-ride down the Strand is taken for granted. . ." And in that word "debilitated," Sullivan has gone to the heart of the problem. Man has taken about three million years to struggle to his present position on the evolutionary ladder; he has survived ice ages and fought mammoths and sabre-toothed tigers. Yet he has achieved this amazing, wonderful civilisation far too quickly—almost overnight. He takes it for granted, and needs the misery of war or violent catastrophe to remind him of how lucky he is. He responds magnificently to challenge, but the moment a challenge has been conquered, his robot murmurs: "Nothing to worry about now—relax," and he promptly *over*-relaxes into a state of "debilitation" and boredom.

Yet he also possesses one tremendous advantage

when compared to the animals—the force known as imagination. It is a pity that the word has come to acquire all the wrong connotations—connotations of fantasy and "escapism." In fact, imagination is merely the power *to conjure up realities that are not actually present*. It is, in other words, what Pierre Janet called "the reality function"—the power to grasp reality *with the mind*.

Insects and animals have no power to take an interest in anything that is not directly connected with their welfare. Most insects live so briefly that their lives are entirely controlled by a set of instinctive responses; they are little more than machines guided by a computer-programme. Man is the first animal who takes an interest in all kinds of things that are quite unconnected with his physical existence. The Greeks thought about philosophical questions *purely for the fun of it*. When an artist says that a scene is beautiful, he does not mean that it is good to eat, or for any other practical purpose; he is appreciating it purely for its own sake. And when minstrels learned the art of holding an audience around a camp fire with tales of ancient battles or tragedies, they were teaching their audience to *fly away* from the physical world on a kind of magic carpet. The Greek drama gave these imaginary realms a new reality, for the audience could see the deaths of heroes before their eyes. But the greatest advance of all was the invention of a self-made businessman, a printer named Samuel Richardson who, in 1740, began to tell a story about a wicked squire and his attempted seduction of a maidservant. *Pamela*—the first real novel—taught thousands of readers to fly away on magic carpets, and from then on, man learned to take mental journeys as casually as he now takes a train or an aeroplane. *This* is his salvation and the key to the next step in human evolution: this curious power we call imagination, which is actually merely an undeveloped form of Faculty X.

I have been obsessed by these problems for as long as I can remember; they are the subject of every book I have written (and the number now approaches sixty). My life has been a continual search for the entrance to the Aladdin's cave. And in the past few years—I am now fifty-five—I have begun to feel that I am often very close to uncovering the Great Secret. I have been concerned with the same insights all my life, but sometimes, in a mood of mental clarity or excitement, two or three insights suddenly coalesce together like raindrops, and I am aware that I am a step closer to the Great Secret. At other times, I feel disgusted that it has taken me so long to learn so little. Yet I never doubt that a day will come when young children will absorb within weeks or months what has taken me a whole lifetime to discover, and that my own life's work will have played its part in bringing men to this level of control over their own destiny.

---

## BIBLIOGRAPHY

### Nonfiction:

*The Outsider*. London: Gollancz, 1956; Boston; Houghton, 1956.

*Religion and the Rebel*. London: Gollancz, 1957; Boston: Houghton, 1957.

*The Age of Defeat*. London: Gollancz, 1959; also published as *The Stature of Man*. Boston: Houghton, 1959.

*Encyclopaedia of Murder*, with Patricia Pitman. London: Arthur Barker, 1961; New York: Putnam, 1962.

*The Strength to Dream: Literature and the Imagination*. London: Gollancz, 1962; Boston: Houghton, 1962.

*Origins of the Sexual Impulse*. London: Arthur Barker, 1963; New York: Putnam, 1963.

*Brandy of the Damned: Discoveries of a Musical Eclectic*. London: John Baker, 1964; also published as *Chords and Discords: Purely Personal Opinions on Music*. New York: Crown, 1966; revised edition published as *Colin Wilson on Music*. London: Pan Books, 1967.

*Rasputin and the Fall of the Romanovs*. London: Arthur Barker, 1964; New York: Farrar, Straus, 1964.

*Beyond the Outsider: The Philosophy of the Future*. London: Arthur Barker, 1965; Boston: Houghton, 1965.

*Eagle and Earwig* (essays). London: John Baker, 1965.

*Introduction to the New Existentialism*. London: Hutchinson, 1966; Boston: Houghton, 1967; also published as *The New Existentialism*. London: Wildwood House, 1980.

*Sex and the Intelligent Teenager*. London: Arrow, 1966; Boston: Houghton, 1967.

*Bernard Shaw: A Reassessment*. London: Hutchinson, 1969; New York: Atheneum, 1969.

*A Casebook of Murder*. London: Frewin, 1969; New York: Cowles, 1970.

*Poetry and Mysticism*. San Francisco: City Lights, 1969; London: Hutchinson, 1970.

*Voyage to a Beginning: A Preliminary Autobiography*. London: Woolf, 1969; also published as *Voyage to a Beginning: An Intellectual Autobiography*. New York: Crown, 1969.

*The Strange Genius of David Lindsay*, with E.H. Visiak and J.B. Pick. London: John Baker, 1970; also published as *The Haunted Man*. San Bernardino, Calif.: Borgo, 1979.

*The Occult*. London: Hodder & Stoughton, 1971; New York: Random House, 1971.

*New Pathways in Psychology: Maslow and the Post-Freudian Revolution.* London: Gollancz, 1972; New York: Taplinger, 1972.

*L'Amour: The Ways of Love.* New York: Crown, 1972.

*Order of Assassins: The Psychology of Murder.* London: Hart-Davis, 1972.

*Strange Powers.* London: Latimer New Dimensions, 1973; New York: Random House, 1975.

*Tree by Tolkien.* London: Covent Garden Press, 1973; Santa Barbara, Calif.: Capra, 1974.

*A Book of Booze.* London: Gollancz, 1974.

*Hesse—Reich—Borges: Three Essays.* Philadelphia: Leaves of Grass, 1974; also published separately as *Hermann Hesse, Wilhelm Reich,* and *Jorge Luis Borges.* London: Village Press, 1974.

*Ken Russell: A Director in Search of a Hero.* London: Intergroup Publishing, 1974.

*The Craft of the Novel.* London: Gollancz, 1975.

*Mysterious Powers.* London: Aldus, 1975; Suffern, N.Y.: Danbury, 1975; also published as *They Had Strange Powers.* Garden City, N.Y.: Doubleday, 1975; revised edition published as *Mysteries of the Mind,* with Stuart Holroyd. London: Aldus, 1978.

*The Unexplained,* edited by Robert Durand and Roberta Dyer. Lake Oswego, Ore.: Lost Pleiade, 1975.

*Enigmas and Mysteries.* London: Aldus, 1976; Garden City, N.Y.: Doubleday, 1976.

*The Geller Phenomenon.* London: Aldus, 1976; Suffern, N.Y.: Danbury, 1976.

*Mysteries: An Investigation into the Occult, the Paranormal, and the Supernatural.* London: Hodder & Stoughton, 1978; New York: Putnam, 1978.

*Science Fiction as Existentialism.* Hayes, England: Bran's Head, 1978.

*The Search for the Real Arthur* (published with *King Arthur Country in Cornwall* by Brenda Duxbury and Michael Williams). Bodmin, England: Bossiney, 1979.

*Frankenstein's Castle: The Right Brain, Door to Wisdom.* Seven-oaks, England: Ashgrove Press, 1980; Topsfield, Mass.: Merrimack Book Service, 1982.

*Starseekers.* London: Hodder & Stoughton, 1980; Garden City, N.Y.; Doubleday, 1981.

*The War against Sleep: The Philosophy of Gurdjieff.* Wellingborough, England: Aquarian Press, 1980; York Beach, Me.: Weiser, 1980; revised edition published as *G.I. Gurdjieff: The War against Sleep.* Wellingborough, England: Aquarian Press, 1986; North Hollywood, Calif.: Newcastle, 1986.

*Anti-Sartre, with an Essay on Camus.* San Bernardino, Calif.: Borgo, 1981.

*Poltergeist!: A Study in Destructive Haunting.* London: New English Library, 1981; New York: Putnam, 1982.

*The Quest for Wilhelm Reich.* London: Granada, 1981; Garden City, N.Y.: Doubleday, 1981.

*Witches.* London: Granada, 1981; New York: A & W Publications, 1982.

*Access to Inner Worlds: The Story of Brad Absetz.* London: Rider, 1983.

*Encyclopaedia of Modern Murder: 1962–1982,* with Donald Seaman. London: Arthur Barker, 1983; New York: Putnam, 1985.

*A Criminal History of Mankind.* London: Granada, 1984; New York: Putnam, 1984.

*Lord of the Underworld: Jung and the Twentieth Century.* Wellingborough, England: Aquarian Press, 1984.

*Psychic Detectives: Story of Psychometry and Paranormal Crime Detection.* London: Pan Books, 1984; San Francisco: Mercury House, 1986.

*Rudolf Steiner: The Man and His Vision.* Wellingborough, England: Aquarian Press, 1984.

*Afterlife.* London: Harrap, 1985.

*The Bicameral Critic: Collected Shorter Writings,* edited by Howard F. Dossor. Bath, England: Ashgrove Press, 1985.

*The Craft of the World.* Topsfield, Mass.: Merrimack Book Service, 1985.

*The Essential Colin Wilson.* London: Harrap, 1985; Berkeley, Calif.: Celestial Arts, 1986.

*Existentially Speaking: Essays on Philosophy and Literature.* San Bernardino, Calif.: Borgo, 1985.

*The Goblin Universe,* with Ted Holiday. St. Paul, Minn.: Llewellyn, 1985.

*The Laurel and Hardy Theory of Consciousness.* Mill Valley, Calif.: Robert Briggs, 1986.

*Scandal! An Encyclopaedia,* with Donald Seaman. London: Weidenfeld & Nicolson, 1986; New York: Stein & Day, 1986.

**Fiction:**

*Ritual in the Dark.* London: Gollancz, 1960; Boston: Houghton, 1960.

*Adrift in Soho.* London: Gollancz, 1961; Boston: Houghton, 1961.

*Man without a Shadow: The Diary of an Existentialist.* London: Arthur Barker, 1963; also published as *The Sex Diary of Gerard Sorme.* New York: Dial, 1963.

*The World of Violence.* London: Gollancz, 1963; also published as *The Violent World of Hugh Greene.* Boston: Houghton, 1963.

*Necessary Doubt.* London: Arthur Barker, 1964; New York: Simon & Schuster, 1964.

*The Glass Cage: An Unconventional Detective Story.* London: Arthur Barker, 1964; New York: Random House, 1967.

*The Mind Parasites.* London: Arthur Barker, 1967; Sauk City, Wis.: Arkham, 1967.

*The Philosopher's Stone.* London: Arthur Barker, 1969; New York: Crown, 1971.

*The God of the Labyrinth.* London: Hart-Davis, 1970; also published as *The Hedonists.* New York: New American Library, 1971.

*The Killer.* London: New English Library, 1970; also published as *Lingard.* New York: Crown, 1970.

*The Black Room.* London: Weidenfeld & Nicolson, 1971; New York: Pyramid Books, 1975.

*The Return of the Lloiger.* London: Village Press, 1974.

*The Schoolgirl Murder Case.* London: Hart-Davis/MacGibbon, 1974; New York: Crown, 1974.

*The Space Vampires.* London: Hart-Davis/MacGibbon, 1976; New York: Random House, 1976; also published as *Lifeforce.* New York: Warner Books, 1985.

*The Janus Murder Case.* London and New York: Granada, 1984.

*The Personality Surgeon.* London: New English Library, 1986; San Francisco: Mercury House, 1986.

*Spider World: The Tower.* Aldershot, England: Grafton Books, 1987; also published in three volumes as *Spider World: The Desert, Spider World: The Tower,* and *Spider World: The Fortress.* New York: Berkley Books, 1987.

*Spider World: The Delta.* Aldershot, England: Grafton Books, forthcoming; New York: Berkley Books, forthcoming.

## Plays:

*The Metal Flower,* produced in Southend-on-Sea, England, 1958.

*Viennese Interlude,* produced in London and Scarborough, England, 1960.

*Strindberg.* London: Calder & Boyars, 1970; New York: Random House, 1971; produced as *Pictures in a Bath of Acid,* Leeds, England, 1971; also produced as *Strindberg: A Fool's Decision,* London, 1975.

*Mysteries,* produced in Cardiff, Wales, 1979.

## Editor of:

*Crimes and Punishment* (twenty volumes). London: Phoebus Publishing, 1973.

*Fiery Angel,* by Valeri Briussov. London: Neville Spearman, 1976.

*The Supernatural,* edited with Christopher Evans (twenty volumes). London: Aldus Books, 1976; Garden City, N.Y.: Doubleday, 1976.

*Colin Wilson's Men of Mystery.* London: W.H. Allen, 1977; also published as *Dark Dimensions: A Celebration of the Occult.* New York: Everest House, 1978.

*The Book of Time,* with John Grant. Newton-Abbot, England, and North Pomfret, Vt.: David & Charles, 1980.

*The Directory of Possibilities,* with John Grant. Exeter, England: Webb & Bower, 1981; New York: Rutledge Press, 1981.

*The Great Book of Mystery,* with Christopher Evans (selections from *The Supernatural*). London: Robinson, 1986.

*Marx Refuted,* with Ronald Duncan. Bath, England: Ashgrove Press, 1986.

## Sound Recordings:

*The New Analytic Philosophy.* Big Sur Recordings, 1967.

*Human Evolution and a New Psychology.* Big Sur Recordings, 1968.

# Keith Wilson

*1927-*

More than I should, probably, I have puzzled over the various patterns my life has taken. To this day, its contradictions make only partial sense to me—I grew up mainly in New Mexico of Irish, Scot, and Welsh heritage, graduated from the United States Naval Academy at Annapolis with an engineering degree, served three years in and out of the Korean War, did a tour on a destroyer in the Caribbean, resigned from that life, went to graduate school in English, became a technical writer for Sandia Corporation, decided to become a writer/teacher, have done so. I write only when I am compelled to, teach only when required. I am obsessed with modern technology, yet would prefer to live a life reminiscent of the nineteenth century and have a fascination with weapons and other artifacts of that era. I try to teach in exactly the same way as I write: compulsively, using my inner, subconscious forces, with no real external plan at all. I am really writing in the air, when I teach. Yet I crave order, rarely attain to much of it.

I've always been what I term a "compulsive" writer—I write out of an inner pressure, a fascination with the process of naming—of seeing the object and then translating it into my own brain's energies, using the code of language. Ever since I can remember, I have had these drives, even before I was "literate" (and I learned to read and write, primitively, at around three)—even before that I remember words as chants in my head. Some word I would hear would come back and back to me as almost pure sound, almost detached from meaning. One word that came later to me in this way was "chemistry." I remember running to school and singing to myself "chemistry, chemistry, chemisTRy!" Later, when I found out what it meant, I decided to become a chemist (and very nearly did!) simply because I loved the sound of the word so much, liked the way it felt on my lips.

But what may have made me a writer, almost in self-defense, was partly the family I was born into.

Both my mother and my grandmother read to me a lot. My grandmother used to tell me that she would read me a nursery rhyme if I would listen to her read a poem by Bobbie Burns, her favorite poet. She would read them out of an old leather-bound volume that had belonged to her husband. I quickly,

*Keith, age seven, with sister, Marjorie Ann*

according to her, liked the poems more than the stories and she then began to insist that I hear a story before I could hear another poem. She read with her finger tracing the word she slowly spoke. Thanks to her, I was reading everything I could understand in our library when I was about four. By eight I knew I loved the act of writing, doing the work, and showed my mother a poem I had written. It was a pretty terrible parody of a Kipling poem and I remember my mother being embarrassed by it. She was silent for a little while and then handed it back saying, "That's very nice, Keith." I didn't show her any more for a long, long time, not because I didn't want to but because I too felt embarrassment. I do to this day,

*Author's mother, Marjorie Valentine Edwards Wilson*

lived, because the Clovis Baptist Hospital was the only hospital in that part of New Mexico. And my mother badly needed doctors because she was forty-two years old, and nearly died having me. My father responded to the nurse who told him that I was a boy by saying, "I don't care if it's a goddamned chicken! How's my wife?" thus beginning our long yet distant relationship with each other.

My mother, Marjorie Valentine Edwards, was directly descended from a long line of New England landed gentry that stretched back to around 1632 in the Massachusetts Bay Company. Before that, the family (Edwards or MacEdwards) had its roots in Scotland and—from its name—Wales. From this background my mother carried the burden of New England mysticism and, though she was Anglican, New England puritanism. She was a member of the Daughters of the American Revolution and the only reason she was not a member of the Colonial Dames, as my grandmother was, was that she did not have the

*Young Keith with father, Earl Charles Wilson*

when I show my writing to others.

At about this same time, another incident occurred that shaped my writing life for years to come, silly as it was. I was busily reading an anthology of poems that had come down to me from my grandfather and, as I would find something that appealed to me, I would take the book to Mother and ask about the author. Once I remember asking about Kipling, where he lived, what he did, etc. Mother replied, "Oh, he's dead." A few more inquiries about other authors were met with the same reply. At that point I knew deep within myself that I was some sort of writer and since it seemed that most of the writers of the world were dead—maybe all of them—and if anybody found out that I was a writer, maybe they'd come and make me dead too. As I said, silly, a boy's logic, but it shut me up for many years. I was in my middle twenties before I admitted, even to close friends, that I wanted to be a writer, much less was one.

But my family. I was born in the small city of Clovis, New Mexico, on December 26, 1927. My mother and father had driven there several days before from Fort Sumner, New Mexico, where they

*Uncle Keith Wyman Edwards*

the rails reached Fort Sumner, Territory of New Mexico, in about 1905, he felt that he had found the place he was looking for, resigned his position, and hung up his sign "Attorney at Law." With only a few exceptions—to serve in World War I, to act as advisor to his friend and former law partner Senator Carl Hatch, and to become commanding officer of the Houston Recruiting District in World War II, he spent the rest of his life there, becoming Democratic Party chairman for De Baca County and the local *Patron.* To me, he was an extremely good and gentle man. He really acted as my father, instead of just an uncle, and I loved him very much. When he died, just as I was leaving for my second tour in Korea, I'm sure he still believed that that tiny village beside the Pecos River would one day become a great city. Perhaps it will.

The three ghosts of my family for me were James Keith Edwards (dead), my maternal great-grandfather; Herbert Mead Valentine (alive until I was thirteen), my grandmother's brother; and Rear Admiral Allen Victor Reed (dead), my maternal great-great uncle, who raised my mother after my grandfather killed himself. James Keith Edwards was the only writer my mother's family had. A second son, he had

money for the fees. She dreamed of joining that organization all her life. It was a great disappointment to her, I'm sorry to say, that I had no interest whatsoever in joining anything like that.

My father, Earl Charles Wilson, on the other hand, was a cowpuncher and much younger than she when they finally met in New Mexico. His ancestors had been landed farmers (probably named McLiam) in county Cork, Ireland, and had only immigrated in the 1840s. My mother was the product of a finishing school; my father had only an eighth-grade education, and that from a one-room New Mexican schoolhouse.

An important influence in my early life was my uncle Keith Wyman Edwards who had been a page at the United States Senate, working there until he graduated from Georgetown Law School. He was also a reserve army officer who had always wanted to go to West Point. Instead, he took a job as an attorney with the Panama Canal project, staying there about a year. He then signed on as an end-of-the-line lawyer for the Atchison, Topeka, and Santa Fe Railroad. When

*Great-grandfather James Keith Edwards*

*Great-uncle Herbert Mead Valentine*

It did not help that he had been late to her wedding and, according to her, had—drunk and reeling in the saddle—ridden his English hunter into the hall of their old home and right up to the altar, where his horse's excited breath blew two of the wedding candles out. According to Grandmother, for reasons I never understood, his actions brought terrible bad luck upon the marriage, causing the Edwards family also to lose its money and its land and, in the end, forcing my grandfather to kill himself. It wasn't until many years later that I found her wedding certificate, while going through a box of old pictures and documents. She and my grandfather were married in Washington, in the Admiral's home on the old Dupont Circle. I think it would be even beyond my uncle Bert's sense of malicious humor to have ridden his horse clear from Massachusetts, through the streets of Washington (while drunk), just to curse his sister's wedding. But, in our family, what might have happened often got confused with what actually

*With grandmother Anne A. Valentine Edwards*

gone to Canada straight from the University of Edinburgh and become a journalist, winning the prize of the Canadian Parliament when he was in his early forties. That prize, a huge silver samovar with a silver serving plate extolling his literary virtues, sat on the sideboard in our living room all of my childhood. I was always reminded that it was only because he was a second son that he became a writer, and a journalist at that. Later, he became a senior press correspondent at the White House, and died in Washington, D.C.

Great-Uncle Herbert Mead Valentine, Uncle Bert for short, was a different sort of a character entirely. He, the last of the landed Valentines, had—rather happily I always thought—squandered all the land and three fortunes: his own and those of his two wives. His sister, my grandmother Ann Valentine Edwards-Winton, hated him and sometimes referred to him as a throwback to the Scottish border lords of their mutual ancestry. That was when she was being polite. His eternal sin was that he had lost the ancestral estates through his drinking and wenching.

happened. I am sure that Grandmother believed that story, and Uncle Bert never contradicted her. In any case, to my grandmother, everything was all Uncle Bert's fault. He, on the other hand, reveled in his sins, real or imagined by my grandmother, and remained unrepentant to the absolute end. I, of course, adored him.

### Woodcarver

Nobody's uncle but mine, he cut
whistles from slippery mountain
birch, carried them home in his
pocket, for me

        —a drunk, he lived
by his wits, an old robber, he stole
books, told lies for bootleg whiskey.

sitting very straight, frosty, winter-
eyed he stayed in his room, sipped, a
gentleman drunk at noon, calling for
me, shouting my name: and when I
came, he just looked at me, four,
but not ashamed before his eyes.

When he died he filled the longest
casket old John Allen had, plain white.
They stuck a naked pink bulb above the
open lid, for color. They said he
only slept

        Eyes shut, he didn't look
asleep, his pale face, thin fine hair
slicked down, he looked ready to rise.
Pink light streaming along his beak of
a nose, he looked ready to get up staring,
blue-eyed, the crisp woodchip smell of him
darkening all the roses.

Another member of my mother's family was also a favorite of mine—Alexander Edwards, my beloved uncle Sandy. Uncle Sandy was another charming disgrace to my mother's family. My maternal grandfather's brother, he had graduated from Virginia Military Institute at a time when only VMI and West Point could grant regular Army commissions. On graduation day, though, Uncle Sandy didn't show up for the commissioning exercises. When the family finally tracked him down, he was an enlisted man in a cavalry regiment serving in the far West. Later, he led a cavalry patrol chasing Pancho Villa in the area around Las Cruces, New Mexico, and further south into Mexico. He won battlefield commissions in both the Spanish-American War and World War I, turned

*Granduncle Alexander Edwards*

them both down, and lived most of his life as a Master Sergeant (though he was broken to Private twice for his drinking).

He came to see us, as I remember, about once a year after he retired, and always his arms were loaded with presents for me, his only grandnephew. He never married and retired to the Old Soldier's Home in Washington, gracefully refusing my aunt Pick's invitation to come and live with us. He was probably the only member of either side of the family who was unreservedly loved by all. I think I get some of my stubborness from him, and he, like my father, was a fine storyteller.

And what could I do, after all, but write down all this sweet yet tragic foolishness?

It was the Rear Admiral though that had the worst and most lasting impact on me. He was a graduate from the first class of the United States Naval Academy, was a classmate of Admiral Dewey, and had won the Academic Sword as top man in his Class. When I was born and my mother saw I was male, she rose through her pain and said, "He'll go to West Point or Annapolis." That goal became her obsession more and more as her marriage to my father slipped toward the disaster it finally became. The only choice that ever seemed open to me as a child or young man was the Army or the Navy.

*Great-granduncle, Rear Admiral Allen V. Reed, U.S. Navy ( photographed when he was still a captain)*

Probably because I had never seen the sea, I chose Annapolis. She had wanted that, because she worshipped the Rear Admiral. She often told a strange story about him. When I was only a few months old, and he nearly ninety, he had taken the train from his home in Washington, D.C., clear out to Fort Sumner. He wired ahead and the whole family met him at the train and drove him out to our house. He went into my room, pulled my covers back, and punched and examined me for some time. Then he snorted and demanded to be driven back to the train station where he sat, attended by the whole family, until the next East-bound train showed up.

I was never told what he thought of me; I don't think my mother knew either. The incident has puzzled me most of my life. He died shortly after he returned to Washington, but his ghost has walked with me a long time.

I don't mention much about my father's family through here, because they had little to do with my growing up. My father was often away hunting or working and my mother and grandmother disapproved of my father's background. Farmers of any sort were peasants to them. My paternal grandfather was Charles Foster Wilson, my grandmother, Emma Frye Wilson; both died before I was born. My

grandfather was a well-remembered figure in Fort Sumner driving his wagon, his Bible under his arm. His reputation was that of a good and kind man. I've always regretted that I didn't get to know him. He and my father were estranged though, because of my father's drinking and carrying on, so it is probable that I wouldn't have seen much more of him than I did of my uncle Vance, my father's brother, or Aunt Bessie, his sister. About the only half-way kind thing Grandmother ever said about the Wilsons was, one day when she was reading to me, "Well, your father's family is not much but at least there's not one drop of English blood in your veins—you're all Celt." I am truly sorry that I wasn't permitted to know them better then. My uncle and aunts, my cousins, were and are fine, hard-working people. Irish, but not drinkers.

Drinking was a major problem in my father's life. Sober, he was a hard, intelligent man who could be quite ruthless, and very much a loner. He went from a cowhand to a job carrying a chain, learned surveying around the campfire with the Chief of Party, moved up to rodman, and then to surveyor. He was a natural born leader, engineer, and his men seemed to love him. Drunk, he was a crazed loser. And each time he would be right at the point of real success, off he would go on a two-or-three-week binge. Sometimes he'd be found in a motel, in a coma, other times he'd just get lost—once for a month—down below the border in Mexico. Towards the end of his life he was District Maintenance Engineer for the New Mexico Highway Department until he got fired in a statewide scandal of which he was probably more the victim than the villain, at least that time. Because of our very different natures, he and I had almost no real relationship until the closing years of his life when we at last talked at his small farm in the Pecos Valley. Now I suppose he too is one of the ghosts that walks with me. Certainly I know that whatever storytelling abilities I have came mostly from him.

*Growing Up*

A big Jack, cutting outward toward blue,
little puffs of my bullets hurrying him.
Sage crushed underfoot, crisp & clean—

My father, a big Irishman, redfaced & watching,
he who could hit anything within range,
who carried a 150-lb. buck three miles
out of the high mountains when he was 57

—a man who counted misses as weaknesses,
  he whipped up his own rifle, stopped the Jack
  folding him in midair, glanced at me, stood
  silent

My father who never knew I shot pips from cards
candleflames out (his own eye) who would've
been shamed by a son who couldn't kill. Riding
beside him.

His life must not have been easy. He was shut
out rather totally by my grandmother and her crazed
dreams of past splendors and glories—neither he nor
I, for that matter, could either cope with or understand what was going on there. My poor grandmother
was, among other things, addicted to phenobarbital,
and especially when the drug was in short supply
became confused. (This is my father's story, told to
me much later when I was grown. He said she had
been given the drug when she was a young woman, as
was common for young women of good families when
they had nervous problems. I don't know how true it
is, but I do remember the purple bottle that always
stood by her bed, remember her taking spoonfuls of
it. And one terrible night I awoke to hear screaming
coming from her bedroom, heard my father dress and
disappear into the night. He returned with that
purple bottle full and the screaming stopped.)

Sometimes she would tell me at the dinner table
of how careful I must be when I grew up and
inherited the estates. She'd glare at Uncle Bert sitting
beside her and say how the men of our family were
always drinkers and that that was the downfall of us
all. Then I would have to solemnly swear that I would
never touch a drop. As I grew older, I began to
perceive that there were no estates, no money,
nothing to inherit, but when I was four and five I
remember being much burdened and worried by
these nebulous responsibilities that I seemingly had
to face.

Those evening dinners linger in my mind.

Grandmother was always late, we all standing
behind our chairs, men, women, and child, waiting.
The dark room was only partly lighted by two coal-oil
lamps. The heavy silver samovar, the place settings,
and the tureen ran yellow with rivers of lamplight. I
stood there in my sailor suit usually, short pants, hair
stuck down with Wave Set watching my father's set
face as he adjusted his unaccustomed tie.

One night I remember particularly, the wind
howled outside, roaring off the Llano Estacado and
the windows banged and rattled with its blows against
the frame, clapboard house. She entered, tall, pale,
very straight, emeralds and sapphires around her
neck.

Looking back, it seems a scene out of a bad
romantic novel. We sat down surrounded by solid
silver service, candlelight with my grandmother wear-

ing enough jewels to, at that time, buy a considerable
chunk of the village we were living in—and what we
were eating was macaroni and stewed tomatoes.
There wasn't money for anything else, for we were
poor and the only money we had came from my
father's part-time construction job and his bounty-
hunting for predators. It was the height of the
Depression: ranchers couldn't sell their beef, farmers
had no markets for their crops, and there just weren't
very many jobs. Yet my grandmother's jewels would
have kept us in comfort for several years. Naturally no
one suggested her selling them.

Those nights were rituals, seances calling back
older days my grandmother's mind clung to in her
growing madness. It was a long time before I
understood that, though.

Always the talk turned to her family's history—
the long traditions of lawyers and military men. An
Edwards had been with Washington at Valley Forge;
Valentines had fought in every war this country had
since the French and Indian War. She spoke of her
uncle, the Admiral, and looked significantly across
the table at me.

As a consequence—and to me I mean that almost
literally—my grandmother's look held a command—I
was raised to go to Annapolis. Every detail of my daily
life was carefully oriented to that goal: my teachers
were chosen for me from the better ones available,
especially from those who taught mathematics; Mother and I sang "Anchors Aweigh" and "Don't Give Up
the Ship" endlessly about the piano that she played
so well; and by the time I was ten, I was aware of the
basic requirements for entrance into the Academy.
My teeth were fixed regularly, though no one else's
were, including my sister's. Nor was any provision
made for her to go to college, only me. Through the
years, this continuing injustice separated me more
and more from my sister, my cousin Mary Patricia and
my aunt. Though I was not truly aware of it during
those years, I am most conscious of it now.

Marjorie Ann, my sister, was born when I was
seven. She and my cousin Mary Patricia Edwards, who
was slightly older than she, were only "girls" to the
male-oriented (but female-dominated) family we
grew up in. I was, to my increasing discomfort, more
and more the subject of the family's dynastic plots. I,
according to my grandmother, was to regain the
power and prestige of her family, become an Admiral
in the United States Navy, accept the Scottish title
(another of her completely believed myths), and
nothing else much mattered, especially not women,
young or old, saving herself of course. It was, of
course, impossible for me to even become a midshipman, much less a commissioned officer or an admiral

and hold a foreign title, even if one had existed, which it didn't. But I didn't know all of that then.

Plans were made for me then to attend college before trying to get in Annapolis, to make the process easier and less likely to fail. All of this was paid for by my uncle Keith. I was terribly excited about their dream for me. For one thing, it made me different, special to the teachers who treated me with exaggerated respect and probably helped me get the very high grades that I did get. All this also helped separate me from whatever friends I might have had. I was a "brain" to the other kids in the small villages of New Mexico and since we moved a lot, I was the "new kid" to boot. This naturally led to many fistfights and challenges.

Unfortunately (looking back) I turned out to be very good with my fists and fought with what I can only describe as a cold fury. Usually I won, which only separated me more from the boys I would really have liked to have been friends with. I had noticed, of course, that boys who were whipped in a fight were usually welcomed back into the group eventually, often right away. I wasn't. I gained respect, maybe fear, from them, but they stayed away from me. Then, usually, my dad would get another job someplace else and the whole process would begin again. I couldn't seem to learn. A fight would shape up, the challenge given, and I would think to myself, "This time I'll let him win." Then he'd hit me and my reflexes and my anger would take over.

As the years passed, I stayed more and more to myself, scribbling down what I felt on scraps of paper. I spent a lot of time reading and walking in the desert. Usually I pretended to be hunting, an acceptable pastime for an adolescent boy in that society, but actually I would be dreaming about writing, reciting out loud to the lizards, I guess, whatever I had done or was worried about. And merely carrying my rifle.

When I was thirteen, World War II broke out and when I was sixteen, we moved away from New Mexico to Portland, Oregon, so that my father could work at Oregon Shipyard as a rigger. We lived in Vanport, the shipyard's housing development, which was something of a shock for all of us. No matter how little money we had had before, we had always lived in clean, spacious houses with good neighbors. Now we were in what amounted to army barracks, with muddy streets (for it rained all the time), surrounded by men and women from all over the nation, most of whom were hired simply because the real working force was off fighting World War II. It was a tough place, and I learned a lot, fast, about how to walk through those streets. So did my sister.

We moved there in the early summer and when fall came, I was enrolled at Jefferson High School, which at that time was the school for upper-middle-class students in Portland. It also had the reputation of being one of the best and most progressive high schools on the West Coast. When we got off the bus the first day, we were met by a delegation of football players, frat boys and girls, and told that we'd better keep our noses clean and stay out of the clubs and the activities that were theirs alone. I took this as a challenge, outraged because they associated me automatically with the rest of that bunch. It actually did me good. I found out about prejudice first hand, had to face the fact that I *was* one of "that bunch" and would have to make it on my own merits for a change. My first class left me staggered. I didn't even know what the teacher was talking about. As I remember, it was a math class taught by a Miss Katherine Piggot. She was a very old German lady with a sharp, clear

*Keith Wilson at University of New Mexico, about 1946*

*As midshipman at the U.S. Naval Academy,
Annapolis, about 1946*

voice and by the end of the class, I was terrified. I simply knew I'd never pass it. I, with my straight "A" average, couldn't understand even what she wanted us to do! I went to her after school and found her to be warm, helpful. She grilled me for the better part of an hour and said I had no real background, that was the problem, and arranged for me to sit in on her first-year geometry and algebra classes. I worked harder than I ever worked, came to adore her, and still remember her as one of the finest teachers I ever had.

The problem was that I had memorized problems and solutions: that was the way mathematics was taught in the smaller schools of New Mexico that I attended. To this day I hate memorization and refuse to memorize anything, especially my own poems. I discovered back then that the process was deadly to my mind at least. By the end of the term I was in the Honor Society and doing fine.

I graduated from Jefferson High School in May of 1945. I had hoped to get to go to Reed College, where I intended to study chemistry for my preparatory semesters toward Academy admission, but I had no money. My father was neither interested nor able

to send me there. Uncle Keith came through again, though he attached a condition that I must go to the University of New Mexico at Albuquerque.

At that time I was seventeen, terribly naive, and immediately fell in love with campus life. I enjoyed everything about the place. World War II was still on and, since I had a deferment from the draft thanks to my Annapolis appointment, I was one of the few able-bodied civilian males on campus. The Naval ROTC men were very restricted in their free hours, so we lucky few had a pretty full run of girls. I had no idea in the world what to do about that situation. I was terribly shy, had little money, and lots of other excuses, so I mainly ran around with my buddies, smoked my new pipe, and tried to look like a young writer. That too was something of a failure.

I entered the United States Naval Academy as a member of the Class of 1950 in the summer of 1946. The Academy was, for me, four years of desperation. I had come to hate engineering courses during my preparatory semesters at the University of New Mexico, though I still loved the idea of building things. And I once again found myself an alien, this time to my complete surprise. Raised the way I had been, I had expected to be welcomed into the company of my true peers: well-born young warriors from the Eastern Establishment. One of my room-mates, and a dear friend, was a Du Pont; old names studded our class roster. To them I was a hick, some sort of barbarian who spoke a strange sort of English, and no one had heard of my "old" family. It was then that I discovered how many Spanish words (I had thought them English, if I thought about it at all) were in my daily vocabulary. I also used some Indian words. My language, my thinking, my ways were the subject of endless jokes. I was truly shocked and felt betrayed by my family—why, I didn't belong here at all. They had lied to me.

Yet Annapolis did a great deal for me—I met young men who knew about literature, music, the world beyond New Mexico's border, and ideas I had never thought of. I was again subjected to high standards. Since the Academy did not accept credits from any other university or college, every midshipman entered directly into the Plebe (freshman) class. In my class there were several men who had already graduated, some with honors, from such places as Yale, Harvard, MIT, and Princeton. The professors based their passing grades on the performances of the best students in the Class. I nearly flunked out the first year. But I learned, and I stayed—partly out of pride (for by that time I knew I didn't want that life) and partly out of a guilty desire not to hurt my mother and my uncle so deeply. During those days, also, it was necessary to have your parents' permissions to resign. The only other way out was to flunk out. That I couldn't seem to do. And I knew, for I begged her in my third year, my mother would never sign those papers and she wouldn't let Daddy do it either.

I spent my time writing, mainly short stories, and reading, reading. In my second year I went into a bookstore just outside the Main Gate and met a lovely old lady whose father had been ambassador to the Court at St. Petersburg. There she had met a Russian nobleman and had married him. The two of them had fled Russia during the Revolution and after his death she had opened the bookstore. We became friends almost immediately and she took over my real education. She first introduced me to Tolstoy, loaning me his *War and Peace.* Tolstoy spoke, or so I saw it, straight to the heart of my dilemma: I had been raised to be a naval officer, a warrior, yet my own nature recoiled from the thought of it. I wanted to become a writer. At the same time, I was drawn to the excitement of a naval officer's life, the sea, the challenge.

I have read that book many times since, and am sure I will read it again many times. It changed the whole pattern of my life, slowly but inexorably.

From Annapolis on, I felt that my world was dominated by the themes and questions of *War and Peace.* True, I was no wealthy, titled Pierre or Andrei but it seemed to me that I faced the same problems. But I discovered, and not for the first time, that things read and believed in books rarely adapted themselves directly to immediate experience.

I was granted a thirty-day leave after graduation in June of 1950, returning home on the bus with my mother and was enjoying the freedom. At that time the family was living in Tucumcari, New Mexico, a very small town on the old Route 66. And I was restless. I just didn't know what I had gotten myself into. I had not been accepted for flight training at Pensacola, something I dearly wanted, and instead had been ordered to carrier duty, Pacific—I had wanted Atlantic, but that was the way the Navy was I thought. In any case, one night in June I was sitting in a small bar on the main street of Tucumcari drinking a Tequila Sunrise when the radio in the bar broke into its music program with a news bulletin: the Korean War had broken out, units of the Seventh Fleet were in action and the USS *Valley Forge* (CV-45) was involved in that action. I had orders to that ship in my inside jacket pocket. All my thoughts of a peacetime duty in the Navy vanished and to me, to those of us headed out there, it looked like World War II starting up again. I particularly remember my

*Wilson at the time of the Korean War, 1951*

mixed feelings of apprehension and excitement.

I left for the West Coast almost immediately, was given priority travel orders, and joined my ship in Buckner Bay, Okinawa (another jog to the memory of World War II). The ship was already at combat status and we got underway the next morning for a series of strikes off the Korean coast. I have written about much of this in *Graves Registry,* so I will only summarize here. From that day on, I spent three years off and on in the combat zone. The *Valley Forge* came home once, I had leave coming, and the Second Communist Offensive broke out. Forty-eight hours later we were underway back to the combat zone. When we returned to the States many months later, my orders for Naval flight training had come through and I was ordered to report, after thirty days leave, to Pensacola Naval Air Station.

It was at that time that Jean Marsh King and I were married in Washington, D.C. Jean and I had met and dated during my senior year at Annapolis; she had attended June Week with my mother and seen me graduate; and, by the time that I left for Korea, we were sure that we wanted to be married.

We were married at the National Cathedral of the Episcopal Church in Washington, with a full naval wedding, crossed swords and officer attendants. The bachelor party was held at the Army and Navy Club and the wedding reception at the Blackstone Hotel, owned by my new father-in-law, Roland King. He and his wife were immensely kind and loving to me and

Roland was probably the only real father I ever had.

Jean and I had a wonderful time—the life of a young officer and his bride in the fifties could appear like something out of a Hollywood movie of the same period, and perhaps that's what our marriage was. Dancing at the Officer's Club till midnight, then walking along the beach afterwards, the whole swirl of young pilots and their wives and girlfriends, uniforms and salutes—it was heady wine for two as young as we.

Jean was always more mature than I. She saw things much more clearly. She truly loved the Navy and the life of a naval officer's wife. To me, it was a trap I was in—something I had to get out of if I were to become a writer. She had had security all of her life; I had only rarely known it, and hadn't cared much for it when it had come along. I was a desperate gambler; she preferred a reasonable bet. Leaving the Navy and the promise of that career for who could know what was foolish but what I felt I had to do.

I have never been an easy person to live with. I seem to have a little boy who lives forever within me. I can feel him stirring now. On the other hand, as my father once said of me, I was born old, worried, concerned. Add to that a fairly placid nature which conceals a violent temper that can be unleashed in a flash if I am pushed too far and, yes, I can be unpredictable and certainly not easy to live with. Then there was my driving compulsion to write, regardless of the cost to me or others.

Though I had done quite a lot of flying at Annapolis in the old biplane N3Ns and had loved it, I found training flights at Pensacola boring. I also found out what a daydreamer I was. After several near misses in midair with other student pilots and after having nearly killed my instructor and myself by getting into a progressive spin, we all decided I would be safer at sea.

From Pensacola, I got orders to the LST 1123, based at San Diego, had a leave, and reported for duty. Several months later we got orders to join the Seventh Fleet as part of the Amphibious Support Group. For the most part, we supplied guerrilla groups north of the Bomb Line. There was a great deal of fighting going on and we were in a state of continuous emergency most of the time, but we saw little action directly. It seemed that we were forever coming into a beach or a port immediately after action—bodies were strewn about or floating on the now calm sea, but there was no living soul about. I guess it was during this period that I began to think of us as being similar to the Graves Registration people who came in after the battle to register and count up the human wreckage. Or we sailed by, sometimes in the middle of someone else's firefight, but with the participants far too busy trying to destroy each other to notice our Long Slow Target limping along, trying to pretend we weren't there. We had some old-fashioned 20-mm and 40-mm guns, but nothing really to fight with or even defend ourselves with. Normally we carried heavy loads of rockets, fuel, ammunition for the units we serviced. It was a joke among us that a North Korean with a pistol could have blown us out of the water.

*Und bebende Trommeln*

the captain:

Army of the United States. About 40,
small, lean. Colt .32 Auto
snug under his armpit, the kind eyes
of somebody's uncle.

His men: tall for Koreans, all
carried M-1's (because there, big men
have big rifles, it is the custom)

& what happened to his eyes
the changes when he spoke of their raids
of villages flaming, women & children
machinegunned as they ran
screaming from their huts:

> his own sense of the stillness
> (which he told of) as the Gray
> Marine engines caught & they
> drew away, leaving the bodies
> in their white clothes
> sprawled here & there, big
> & small, blood seeping into
> white, junks slipping
> smoothly away

My experiences there haunted my mind for a long time—to a certain extent, they still do. After awhile the incidents were like still photographs held in my mind. At the oddest times a picture would flash, bringing with it all the emotions I had felt back there in the Zone. Or I would dream them and wake up shaking and sweating. I was not innocent. I had chosen that life, was a regular officer, and accepted my responsibility for what I had seen, what I had done. My repulsion and sorrow was always mixed, even at the times when the experiences occurred, with excitement, a kind of singing in the blood. I saw that excitement everywhere among the men and the officers I knew. One part of a man was naturally afraid, unsure, the other parts were exhilarated, exalted by being in battle, the legendary testing of ancient heroes (though there wasn't much heroic going on around us most of the time). I watched reserve officers and petty officers come aboard, secretly so glad to escape from the boredom and grimness of life as a shoe salesman or a bank clerk— to get away, frankly, from the wife and the kids, to drink and tell sea stories, maybe get laid, have a good time basking in the reflected glory of the war.

(Korea, 1952)

*guerrilla camp*

We arrived at Sok To
before dawn, caught the last
of the tide & slipped the LST's bow
high on the beach.

> he was waiting, bent
> slightly over, hiding
> his hand. he didn't
> wave.

Later, after a good breakfast
aboard, an Army captain took
us on a tour of the guerrilla
camp:

> & he followed, tagged
> along like somebody's
> dog. a tall Korean,
> patient.

We were shown the kitchens & the
tent barracks, the specially built
junks with their concealed engines

> & he watched, never
> leaving us with his
> eyes

Through the hospital, saw four
sheetcovered bodies from the
raid the night before, didn't
ask whose men they were, spoke
kindly to the wounded & gave
them cigarettes

> until he strode up,
> stuck his shattered hand
> in my face, anger & hatred
> flaming in his eyes & shouted
> & shouted & shouted & shouted

> waving that hand, the
> bones crumpled by
> a rifle slug & pushed
> almost through the skin,

> hardened into a glistening
> knot

He was one of ours, a retired fighter,
about my age, my height. They told me
he wanted to know how a man
could farm
with a hand like that.

with a hand like that.

In Japan on R & R, or later back in our home port of San Diego, a naval officer could walk into a bar with his dress whites and ribbons on and nearly every woman in the place would turn around and look, to the annoyance of her escort. War was horrible, destructive, but I discovered that it was exciting, terribly exciting, to the human animal. And I believed we would continue to have war as long as that excitement existed. I could see no way of changing that, but if we as a race on the planet could understand once and for all that we were predators, blood-hungry, stirred by the images and rhythms of war—if we could look at it honestly and try, perhaps like the Aztec and the Maya, to compensate more for those violent needs in our lives, wouldn't that work? There is, of course, no answer in me. But to try to answer that I wrote the eight Books of *Graves Registry,* using quotations from the beautifully terrible *Lay of the Love and Death of Coronet Christopher Rilke* by Rainer Maria Rilke as epigraphs for my work. Writing *Graves Registry* has occupied most of my adult life. I am haunted by it as I am haunted by the experiences and thoughts that were born in the Korean War.

*the ex-officer, navy*

the man, in whose eyes gunfire
is a memory, a restless dream
of stuttering mouths, bright flame

a man, who no matter how long the days
faces still the combat, the long night's terror—

beyond the shoreline, gray muzzles train,
the destroyer's bow breaks cleanly, all mounts
at ready, general quarters: racing feet
grunting, rasping horn. tight stomach.
knotted muscles in the shoulders, neck.

on white bare feet, with flaring eyes he greets
the morning, peace—advancing age, the dead
    faces once
again firm, smiling, ready for battle fade
grey smoke against a city's sun.

Yet I cannot say that I wrote *Graves Registry* consciously attempting to solve that question of war. I don't think I have often written poetry or fiction with a conscious purpose. I just started writing and afterwards found that the poems I had written fitted neatly in the growing collection of graves registry poems. I believed sincerely, for example, that I was finished with it all when I published the first volume with Grove Press. Then I was absolutely certain that I had done with it when Sumac Press published *Mid-Watch* (the second collection of books), until an editor friend pointed out that the last poem was not an ending but a gate swung open to admit more. Now four books later (at this writing unpublished), I do think—and hope—that all of it is over, and most of it is out of me.

While I was on that third trip to the battle zone, we were ordered out on the second invasion of Kŏje-Do. The situation looked very grim indeed and, rationally, I couldn't see much prospect for us returning from it. I wrote my first will and composed a letter to send to my wife, Jean, who was with her family in Washington while I was away. I never mailed it, for in the last mail call came a letter from her saying that she wanted out of the marriage and would not be waiting for me when I returned home.

A day or two later I received a wire from my father telling me that my mother had been diagnosed as having terminal cancer, that there was no chance for her, but that I didn't have to hurry home immediately. The next day we set sail for the invasion, which turned out to be a "mock" invasion. We came under heavy coastal battery fire but took no casualties.

The LST 1123 returned to the States in the spring of 1953 and Jean met me at the dock. She wanted to try again, at least for a few months. New orders had arrived for me to report to a destroyer mine-sweeper, the USS *Ellison* (DMS-43), whose home port was Charleston, South Carolina. At last my desire to join the Atlantic Fleet had come through. Jean accompanied me back and—through a grim circumstance—we drove through Indian Springs, Nevada, on the exact day that my Annapolis roommate and best man at our wedding, Captain William B. Taylor, USAF, was killed in his jet at that same place. A telegram was waiting for me in Washington when I arrived.

The reconciliation did not work and we broke apart. I resigned my commission and got the divorce through a lawyer back in New Mexico.

When I came back from the Korean War, I never intended to return to New Mexico except to be with my mother as much as possible. After that, I planned to leave and come back only to visit my sister. As soon as my resignation as a regular naval officer had been accepted, I bought a little blue-and-white Henry J and drove from the East Coast to New Mexico. I grew more excited with every mile, finally only catnapping beside the road and driving away as soon as I was partly rested. By the time I arrived I thought of New Mexico as home, for the rest of my life.

My family was then living in Las Vegas, New Mexico, on the other side of the Sangre de Christos Mountains from Santa Fe—and far from the ghosts that had haunted me in Fort Sumner and on the Llano Estacado. I began more and more to feel the force of New Mexico, Nueva España, and the older land of the Peoples—the several tribes that had lived there for thousands of years. They seemed to me to have no voices or, perhaps, it was I who had no voice, but could hear theirs. In any case, I began to dream of writing for and about them all—especially to try and blend my own two tongues, Spanish and English, into poetry.

I began trying, at least on the surface of things, then, to create a new formal structure in poems that would fit my rather strange, fantastic land—as well as find some way to work our local Spanglish (Spanish + English) into verse. Formal matters such as these were to occupy my head for more than fifteen years. New Mexico was at that time, and to an extent remains, almost another country to most other Americans. When I am in the East reading I am sure to have to repeat at least once where I am from, because the questioner may then ask: "What part of Mexico do you live in?" We also sometimes have trouble cashing checks or ordering magazines because banks and publishing houses don't accept "foreign" checks and have a higher rate for out-of-country subscriptions. Part of their confusion is based upon something quite real. For a long time New Mexico did seem like another tiny country. We remain one of the two states who are, by law, bilingual. If there were any fairness, we would be required to accept at least six languages, for then we could accept the tongues of our fellow New Mexicans, the Indian nations.

New Mexico also remains a strange land of mountains and deserts, with a very ancient history and a deep sense of religion and mysticism. I wanted to try and handle that, somehow, in poetry. I also wanted to write honestly about it, rather than romantically, as so many other poets—mostly late visitors to the state—had done. I had only one model during this period—now my friend the novelist Frank Waters. A truly great writer, Frank treats every thing with honesty and respect. And that was what I set out to try to emulate.

That fall of 1954, I enrolled as a graduate student in English at the University of New Mexico and drove home each weekend to be with mother and my sister.

Mother was dying of cancer very slowly, but with very little pain. All of my life she and I had loved each other deeply, but we had never really known each other. Now I was grown. I had disappointed her greatly, it is true, by resigning my commission. Up to that point, I suppose I had been her little boy, someone she dreamed of accomplishing something that would make me happy and make her proud of me for doing it. She was very much a romantic, never permitting herself to dwell on bad things (and she had many in her life). She could always look around, perhaps not see, the poverty we lived in in spite of my father's good salary, his heavy and sodden drinking, his women friends, his seemingly congenital lying. Now she was face to face with something she couldn't look around or say, like Scarlett O'Hara, "I'll worry about that tomorrow." She was meeting her death. The doctors had given her only a few months, but she fooled them all and lived more than two years.

Oncoming death transformed, revealed her. I couldn't get over how well we could talk. We spent hours together, discussing everything in the past. Always before, I had felt that she simply didn't hear what I said, if it revealed a side of me that she didn't wish her dreamed child to have. (Now that I am a parent, I certainly understand the temptation toward that.) She listened, she understood, even about the writing. I guess she knew it was something I couldn't help, a sort of terminal disease like hers.

She died early one morning in April, two years after the doctors' prediction. My sister held one of her hands, I the other.

### The Arrival of My Mother

She got off, according to her diary,
dressed in a lovely beaded gown, fresh
from Washington with sixteen trunks of ballgowns,
chemises, blouses (4 Middie), shoes and assorted
lingerie. She was at that time about 25, old
for an unmarried woman. Her stiff mother was at
her side, she also wildly overdressed for
New Mexico sun and wind.

What must she have thought, seeing my uncle
    standing,
hat in hand in the dust of that lonely train
    house,

cracked yellow paint, faded letters of welcome
for passengers that rarely come?

The buckboard was waiting and they rode out
    into
the darkness of coming evening toward the tent
    and that half
built frame homestead house, wind dying as the
    sun
sank, birdcries stilled.

I see her now outshooting my father and me,
    laughing
at our pride and embarrassment. My sister, as
    good a
shot, waiting her turn. Or that picture of her
on horseback, in Eastern riding clothes beside the
    Pecos.
A picnic when I was small and how my father
    lifted me up
to her and she carefully walked the horse around
rock and sand.

I suppose she finally arrived in New Mexico
in the April of one year when my sister and I sat
    beside
a rented bed, each holding one of her hands and
    watched
her eyes grow childlike, unmasked as a *kachina*
entering the final *kiva* of this Dance. The graceful
the slim laughing woman of my childhood. The
    old mother
heavy with years slipped away and the woods of
New England dimmed as these dry hills ripened
    and caught
her last breath, drums, drums should have
    sounded
for the arrival of my mother.

After Mother's death, I finished my master's degree in 1954, the same year my sister completed her B.A. at Highlands University in Las Vegas, New Mexico. An old friend, Jack Griffin, gave us a triple party (he graduated too) at his house on the Santa Ana Indian Reservation. Shortly afterward, I accepted a position as instructor of English at the University of Nevada for one year. While there, I met and briefly married Verda Boyd Ostensoe. We had one child, our daughter, Roxanne, who is now happily married to Michael Anspach. They have three lovely children—Jeremy, Jennifer, and April.

It was at the University of New Mexico that I met the most important person in my adult life—Heloise Brigham. Through the twenty-nine years we

*Heloise Brigham Wilson*

have been together, she has become my best friend, my most trustworthy literary critic, *la alma de mi casa* ("the soul of my house"), and the mother of our four children. Then she was the lovely and rather wild daughter of a pair of writers, Besmilr and Roy Brigham who had traveled like gypsies through most of North America, Mexico, and Central America for the past ten years. I was twenty-eight and she, eighteen, when we met. And I think I was pretty well along the trail towards becoming a social drunk. She changed all that, taking hold of my life very firmly, as if she were the older one, not putting up with a bit of my damaged-war-hero nonsense (which it was). I was feeling terribly sorry for myself in those days.

### To My Wife

There are beauties and beauties.
Yours are simple, rough
irregular

The boned lines of your face
stand, in certain light, severe
almost harsh

You worry about seeming old

while I've watched your hands

sewing, seen the strong arcs
they make

              needle passing through
materials drawing firm together
thread lost in weave:

a wholeness, coming together
lost in itself from attention.
We are what we piece together

beauty after beauty the hand
your hand turns in the light, the tuck
is made

There are these beauties & then
there is you, lined fingers following
the silver needle, sewing light
into place

Heloise and I were married February 15, 1958, in the last year of my formal studies for the doctorate at the home of our friends Jack Griffin and Kenny Wells in Coralles, New Mexico. Thanks to Jack we were able to rent a spacious house on the Santa Ana Indian Reservation and spent the first months of our marriage there, among the ghosts and beauties that seem to live along that section of the Rio Grande.

### Santa Ana House

where we leased from Indians,
Heloise (part Choctaw), I,
born of this Indian State

—its flagstoned walls
rose to gleaming *vigas*
the huge main room bristled
in firelight

              & outside
shadows, low hills, the moon
struck out a history, a *campo
santo* of ghosts, old battles

              (In the 1600's two fights
between the Spaniards & Isletas
happened here & even older burial
grounds ring those hills)

              —where the two of us,
newly married, walked among
dead eyes, the sharper points
of the night, hatreds from
the past

              & saw the moon
silver the hills, toward Placitas
it glistened on the river

                    old Masks moving
round the house, as we slept,
Kachinas slipped forward, terrible
rattles

                    in the night the moon
blazed cold with silver; the rock
named "Serpent's Head" lay a mile
away; recent prayer sticks there,
eagle feathers fluttering

                    —this solid house
where we held each other, sure in
the love we brought, a respect for
those gods, we caught ourselves in
similar rituals, dualities of
earth spinning beneath our bed
a vision of brightness, old dreams
to guard us, darkly, darkly through
the reaches of an ancient night.

We were involved in a serious car wreck the following summer, just after we had discovered that she was pregnant with our first child, Kathleen. As a consequence of the wreck, I was nearly paralysed. I went in a few seconds from a young man in pretty good physical shape to a cripple—two vertebrae were cracked, I had a serious hematoma over one of my kidneys, and some of the major back muscles were torn loose from the bones they were supposed to be attached to. And we were broke. All we had was my last GI Bill check. I had to be helped to drink a cup of coffee and it looked like I would be an invalid the rest of my life.

Amazingly enough, we both look back on that time as one of the happiest in our marriage. We were then living in the Old Town section of Albuquerque, surrounded by the old adobe village and the church of San Filipe de Neri which had later grown into the city of Albuquerque. I had begun a study of Yoga in the university, but had concentrated on Hatha Yoga (the Yoga of the body). It suddenly came to me that Raja Yoga might help me now, since I certainly could not do exercises. Heloise would read to me and I would try with all my being to do the healing exercises of the mind. I still don't quite believe it myself, but I walked—not well, but could make it down the street—within two weeks.

During this time and the time that followed, I read a great deal. The only meaningful study of prosody and poetics that I had encountered was in a class on Chaucer, offered by my advisor for my master's degree, Dr. William Albrecht. He taught me a great deal, and was a godsend in many other ways. For one thing he, too, had a degree in engineering

and had gone on to become a brilliant teacher and a writer, so maybe I could give it a try.

Obviously, I needed to know more though—isolated as I was, I really didn't know where to turn. Universities then more than now, I think, tended to lag behind current developments, especially in English. I was lucky to find someone who knew Chaucer so well, and also men like George Arms and the late Thomas Matthew Pearce who continue to help me by their examples, but I needed to find out what was happening in current poetry. At that point in time, I bought the just printed *New American Poetry*, edited by Donald A. Allen from Grove Press. It was a magic book to me. I discovered with real joy men and women who were, wonder of wonders, writing very much like the way that I was trying to write and solving problems I could not yet solve in prosody.

Most of all, I devoured the essay "Projective Verse" by Charles Olson in that volume. My whole writing life changed and picked up an insistent, driving pulse to it. Materials started surging through my typewriter and onto the page. Really, much began then.

Since I was still a little uneasy on my feet, I thought it better to apply for a job where I could sit down some of the time. Sandia Corporation in Albuquerque had a position open for a technical writer and one of the qualifications was a technical background and the ability to write. It seemed heaven-sent. We were expecting our child to be born in November and we had no money—the salary there was excellent. I applied for the position as Staff Member, Technical Writing, and was hired. For the first, and perhaps the last, time my engineering degree fed us. And I got to work with men and women who were professional writers. I learned about honest writing there. We didn't usually shade anything—we tried to write it as it was. I discovered to my joy that I was capable of sitting eight hours at a typewriter day after day and I loved the kind of exploration of language that a growing technology demanded. There simply weren't words in the hoary old Anglo-Saxon-based English that a transistorized world needed. We no longer wore horned helmets and carried spears, but our language did.

Lorna Kathleen Wilson was born November 20, 1958, in Albuquerque. Neither Heloise nor I had spent much time around babies and I, to the best of my memory, had never held one in my arms before. It remains a miracle to me that Kathy survived our well-meaning ignorance. Or at least mine, for Heloise quickly learned and her very fine maternal instincts took over. We both absolutely adored Kathy and viewed her as a true miracle that had come into our lives. We both now had a centered purpose in our lives.

### The Gift

—for my daughter Kathleen

This is a song
about the gift of patience
of opening

the need to walk alone
ever deeper, into

This is a poem
against light

a recommendation
to darkness

bring a candle
the room is warm

This is a song

Eleven months later, on October 23, 1959, Kristin Mavournin Wilson was born to us, and Heloise and I entered baby-raising in a big way! The two of them constantly amazed and defeated us. One would progress, the other regress, and indeed we had our hands full, but I would not exchange one memory of that time with anything I can think of. They were simply gloriously happy years.

While I was at Sandia Corporation, three of us—Lloyd Alpaugh, Bob Rhodes, and I—started a small magazine called, partly from the way we were all feeling, *Targets.* Again a door opened. After the first two issues, submissions flooded in. On a business trip, I took some copies to City Lights Bookstore in San Francisco and touched bases there, meeting Lawrence Ferlinghetti for the first time. We gave readings, not of our own poems, but of poets in the issues at various coffee houses in Albuquerque to publicize the magazine. It was a heady time for all of us, but I and the others began to see that we were not really interested in continuing the editing. The duties of editing were getting very much in the way of the little time we had free for our own writing, but we didn't want to let the contributors down. Along came Lee Garner, who also worked at Sandia. He wanted to take over the magazine and we gave it to him. He carried the magazine on for several years afterwards, doing a much better job than I certainly would have done.

After Korea though, and because of my growing commitment to peace, I couldn't handle the bomb-making. It seemed that I had escaped right back into the prison I had come from. So I resigned after our bills were paid and our two babies were born, to take a job at less than half the pay as an instructor of English, teaching for the University of Arizona, Tucson.

I had no idea in the world what I was getting into; I just wanted out of the nightmares that my job was causing me every night. When we arrived with our two babies, our pit bulldog Tyger, our female Poppie with her new litter of pups, we were tired but happy creatures. The money was barely enough to live on and we could have gotten almost as much on relief, but we all loved it. We rented a university-owned house about a block from campus and settled in. I rediscovered how much I loved teaching and I found out that there was a newly established poetry center on campus. A wonderful woman, Ruth Walgren Stephan, the former editor of *Tiger's Eye,* had given money to establish the Poetry Center and to make the small house where she had once lived a place where poets could come and stay. I was invited to join the board and spent three very rewarding years there as the host board member for the various visiting poets. I first met Robert Duncan, Kenneth Rexroth, Robert Creeley, Richard Wilbur and many, many others when acting as their guide during the days they spent at Arizona. Three of my now dearest and lifelong friends were there as students: Drummond Hadley, now probably the best cowboy poet I've ever encountered and the closest thing I've ever had to a brother in all senses of the word; David Slagle, a truly fine farmer and poet; and Robert Byrd, a poet, editor, and writer who at that time was running a wonderful little magazine called *Through a Window.* My officemate for awhile was Barney Childs, a student of Ivor Winters, a most knowledgeable prosodist, and a fine modern composer. It was a great period. I got to hear readings by some of the better poets in America, had access to a growing library of poetry books that were rare indeed in the Southwest.

During part of the time we were at Arizona, Roy and Besmilr Brigham also lived there. Besmilr, a fine fiction writer and poet, was a continual source of ideas and concepts about the art of writing fiction and poetry. Her book *Heaved from the Earth* was published by Knopf shortly after she left Tucson and remains a book that has influenced me greatly.

It was also at Arizona that Heloise and I began to receive visits from fellow artists. Our first visitor was Cid Corman. Ed Dorn had written me and asked me to help him get a reading. But the people at the new Poetry Center had never heard of him and were unwilling to invite him. Heloise and I decided to give a reading for him in our living room, the first of many, many readings through the years. Cid stayed with us and I probably learned more about poetry from him in two days than I ever had before. He kindly added my name to the subscription list for *Origin,* an extremely important poetry magazine of this era. Since one could not buy the magazine—it was a free gift from Cid—I took it as a real honor and as a sign that Cid considered me worthy of being a reader of it, a compliment I badly needed at that time, with all the rejections flooding in.

From then on until today, there have been many visitors in our house, many readings and parties for men and women who have become some of our closest friends, surrogate uncles and aunts for our children. People often speak of artists as neurotics, and—in the sense that they are driven people, people who choose a life of constant concern and work in their arts—I suppose they are. But we have found in them our brothers and sisters: warm, exciting people—generous beyond all expectation. They have deeply enriched our lives.

Heloise opens our house like a flower to them. She truly loves people and no matter how busy she was with our children or how worried she was about money, all guests became, instantly, members of the family. Though this may embarrass her when she reads it, she has truly been the center of our lives. I with my reserved shyness and doubts could simply never have pulled it off alone. Whatever else poetry and writing has brought us, and it has brought us much, the shared life of art and artists will always be for me the major reward we have received.

Through Robert Creeley, one of those early visitors, I heard of the "floating" magazine *Wild Dog* then in Salt Lake City. I sent them eight poems and, much to my shock, they took them all and, according to Drew Wagnon, one of the editors, they were going to put them in the issue then going to press. My first real publication. A lot followed from that—the first card I got was from Theodore Enslin saying that he liked them. There began a correspondence and a friendship that lasts until today. Soon other editors wrote, wanting poems and I began serious publishing.

While we lived in Tucson, our son, Kevin O'Keith Wilson, was born on August 30, 1962, and our third daughter, Kerrin Noel Wilson, was born December 24, 1964.

*A Poem for My Newest Daughter*

Among the Navajos

*Keith and Heloise, San Francisco, 1984*

the baby's first laugh
is a signal

for celebration: a rising
of laughter
—of holiness close to the gods
    who also walk, laughing.

This day you laughed & I sang
to you, whose eyes fill song;
being much aware of those
Old Ways, I get taught anew
by my child laughing, bright
blonde hair, greenflecked eyes,
head tossed back, laughing.

                    —for Kerrin

All in all, I spent five years at Arizona, failed to get tenure primarily because I did not finish my Ph.D.

In the summer of 1965 we packed our belongings into a U-Haul truck and set off back to New Mexico where I had been offered a position as assistant professor in technical writing at New Mexico State University, Las Cruces, New Mexico.

I have been here in Las Cruces for twenty-one years, and they have been, mostly, good years indeed. The year after I arrived an old friend from the Arizona days named Carlos Reyes published my first small book, *Sketches for a New Mexico Hill Town,* from where he was back in Orono, Maine. It seemed to take an immediate currency—I heard from many people about it; it received a surprising number of good reviews; and two of the poems were anthologized in Scott, Foresman's *Some Haystacks Don't Even Have Any Needle,* and later other anthologies picked up the poems too. Around that same time, Ron Schrieber selected me to be one of the 31 New American Poets in the anthology by the same name that Hill and Wang was publishing. Some poems were taken by *Poetry* (Chicago) from my new *Graves Registry* series and I sent the manuscript for the whole series to Grove Press through the slush pile. Through some sort of magic the manuscript made it through to an editor and the book was accepted.

I mention all this primarily because these events radically changed my life. First, I abandoned my pursuit of the Ph.D. in American Literature that I had been working on at the University of New Mexico. Then I began the teaching of creative writing. As I mentioned, I was hired as a teacher of technical writing. After some of the publications had come out, a few graduate students got together and came to see me about teaching creative writing. I basically said that the department already had a teacher of creative writing and that I didn't know anything about teaching something like that anyway, since I had never had a course in it myself. They said they wanted to study with me and would I mind if they talked to the Department Head? I said no, he said yes, and that started a whole new world for me. By this time I was giving a number of readings around the country and everywhere I went, I studied the writing programs there, lugging back little techniques and approaches that seemed useful to me. Then I modified them hopelessly and tried them out.

The result was that I grew more and more known at NMSU as a teacher of creative writing (a term I have always disliked), won the university's only award for research as a writer—the first time that the award had been made outside the sciences. The same year, I won the D.H. Lawrence Creative Writing Fellowship and we spent a wonderful summer at the Lawrence Ranch near Taos, New Mexico, where I wrote my novel *Martingale* and began the series of poems that led to the collection *While Dancing Feet Shatter the Earth.*

I was still bothered in my teaching of writing because I had had no creative writing classes at all. Of course there were few such classes—so common now—when I was at the university or Annapolis or later only one undergraduate course in graduate school. If there had been one I could have taken, I probably wouldn't have had the guts to be in it. They scared me then, and now. I was, am, too private, too alone in my writing to share or expose myself, my poems, prematurely. I didn't even call what I did in the early days "poems"; I called them "things," and I once sent a few off under a flamboyant pen name and was relieved when they came back rejected. In truth, I had rejected them myself when I used the pen name.

My training had taken place, but within myself and by myself (a practice I recommend always in the workshops). I tried to learn discrimination, the essential act of the artist. What to put in seems less the question than what to leave out. With all that beauty out there, how am I to pare it down, enclose only this one thing in words and hand it to someone? Looking at my much-loved desert always gives me nervous twinges. How could a man begin to write about all that? So I pick a snake or he picks me and the voice speaks, something happens on paper and in the tones of my mind's tongue—resulting in poems like "Yellow-Green" or "Sidewinder," or more generally, "The Voices of My Desert." But each is like the dust particles on a pottery shard, so small in relation to the desert that held them that they could blow into your eyes without making you blink.

*The Voices of My Desert*

Beginning this new trail, with the resonance
of shifting earth about me, I hear calls
distancing the crow voices of my childhood,

the wolf cry of my middle age. The sun
is an ancient symbol above me and God knows
what the mountains, spirit blue on the horizon

mean. Silence stands within me as without
desert stirs to its own subtle communication.
There is time, always, to wonder, doubt.

New Mexico is a myth, an ancient whirlpool
of time where moments stand still just before
being sucked down to other planes, other hours.

We hold time back through rituals, dances
that stir the seconds like flecks of sand
beneath our feet, eternities of the possible.

I write down the words I hear, but I know

it is the Dead who speak them. Our ears
are tuned to the past, hear, hear the days

less clearly than the flute-songed nights
with their last owls whitefaced as moons
swooping low for the poisoned, dying mice.

The ghosts of wolves ring our hills.
Those birdcries? Comanche songs drifting
up from wartrails. The click of steel

in the night? Prospectors or old soldiers
sharpening the edge of darkness to a keen
wind that blows all the stories away.

I became more and more involved in the act of
oral poetry and story-telling. New Mexico in the
thirties and forties, was a place where story-telling
was still common and natural to all of the cultures.
There were few radios or movies and men and
women generally relaxed and entertained each other
with stories. Since I was comfortable with Spanish, I
also got to hear tales in Spanish. But I wanted my
stories and poems written down too. Originally using
some of Charles Olson's techniques, I tried to
construct poems and short stories that were notated
for the voice of a reader. In my first little book,
*Sketches for a New Mexico Hill Town,* I had intended to
echo the folk stories in Spanish and English that I had
been told as a child by some old man or some old
woman.

I listened a lot to the old men like my father's
friend Virginio—he told me *cuentos* and joked with
me, took the time to teach me how to become a man.
There were many other old ones. Old men and
women take on special reverence for me. I listen to
what they have to say, even now when I am rapidly
becoming one myself.

Above all, I sought awareness. If I taught anything through the twenty-eight years I taught, I hope
that I taught how to become aware, to defeat the
blindness and deafness that society with its "manners" and "discipline" imposes upon us. I tried to
listen (with ears damaged in the war), see (with
myopic eyes), taste (even though I smoked heavily),
feel (I did that well), and trained myself as a runner
trains, practiced as a cabinetmaker would practice.

I have a kind of tape-recorder memory for what
is said to me or around me. I have a literal, though
spotty, memory of things that were said to me as far
back as three years old. I use that constantly. To a
certain extent, thus, my poems are plagiarized from
the lips of the living and dead people I have known.

Through this period, I continued to publish and,
though we had not intended to stay at New Mexico

State, I found myself more and more drawn into my
old world of New Mexican concerns and now, of
course, teaching. I was continually warned by well-
meaning writer friends that teaching and writing
could get in the way of each other, and I certainly saw
many examples where it had. I don't think it did, in
my case. I thought a lot about the problem and came
to believe that the real difficulty was in trying to
separate oneself from either the teaching or the
writing, so that one would drain energy from the
other. I decided that I would treat both writing and
teaching the same way: as activities that I was
committed and driven to. Further, I would teach as I
wrote, compulsively and as honestly as I could.
Lesson plans, superficial organization, following the
rules of teaching were out for me—whatever literature I taught, I approached as a writer, not as a critic,
and I clearly identified my stance to my students. It
seemed to work for me, and a rather large number of
former students seem to think it worked for them.

*Classes*

they should be held in the open.
free. you should talk, then I:
we will have communion, here under
the bright green leaves of a Spring
all will remember this as our awakening.
class, I'm talking to you.
it's important we touch each other,
no matter how foolish the gesture
(this connection, couldn't matter less—
who but a fool cares about commas?)

                I am here,
you, there. ah, but you sleep.
& I drowse. at least we share
that room, let that be recorded:
together, we dream these hours
and, perhaps, each other.
class, I hear your names
like strokes against ancient cymbals,
ghosts, voices answering to a role.
class, we are dying, do you know
that? mustn't we speak now? or
for God's sake let's end this farce,
let tree roots claim us, spreading
its branches to the sky, let us live
that way, if we can manage no other.

The act of writing took priority always. Papers
didn't get graded if I were in one of my writing
outflows. To this day I seem to write in a kind of
frenzy of activity on the typewriter (in the old days)

and now on my word processor—I would explain this to my students and, surprisingly, I never had a single protest; they seemed to understand almost instinctively.

Much of what I discovered about how I should teach and write, I found during the years of 1965–68, when we lived in the small town of San Miguel, fifteen miles south of Las Cruces. It was wonderful, we loved it, and I had for the first time hours to write and think in my second-floor study that overlooked the Mesilla Valley. And I began to worry about why I taught and wrote the way I did. I think I have always been introspective about my writing and my life, at least as an afterthought. First I act, and then I wonder why I did it just that way. Since writing was my first priority and teaching followed from the manner in which I attacked that activity, I concerned myself mostly with that.

Then, some of the reasons I write as I do also stem from my own nature as a basically intuitive person who does things very, very fast. And, like most writers, I think, I tend to be a split-person, one a participant, the other an observer; both ruled by intrusions from the dream world, the unconscious. My poems begin with a feeling, a nervous, almost apprehensive awareness of something about to happen—then maybe I will actually hear a tune in my head, see an image, or see clearly the first line or the title—after that it is all drummed out by the driving pounding of the typewriter keys. I am rarely aware of what I have actually written until I have finished it. This continues to amaze me. Often, after I have written the night before, I will awaken and remember only the act of writing and not anything specific that I wrote. If anything about it should come to mind, the memory will be foggy, unclear, and I will resist thinking about it. Sometimes I wait weeks before returning to the page to see what is written upon it.

When I write poetry, I always hear a voice in my head speaking the lines just before I write them. I have heard voices all my life, have used them for advice, guidance. My best poems seem to emerge from that speaking voice, as if I were taking dictation. When that voice begins to speak, I drop everything and head for my study or a piece of paper.

And once something is written, I never get involved with extensive revisions on the page. I think I revise constantly in my mind, though, before the act of writing seizes me. I would love to revise my poems, but I don't—I damage them. My friend Drum Hadley revises his poems many, many times and each time he does, I can see clear improvement. Once he talked me into revising a poem I had just written called "My Daughters, The Seas." I made such a horrible mess

out of it that to this day I cannot face that mangled heap of words and rhythms or look at the original from which I started. Drum revises beautifully on paper. I cannot. If the poem is not nearly perfect when it comes, I put it in what I call my gunny sack (actually one of several boxes) and leave it, often for good.

It was also there that I decided to gamble. Up until that time, I was in the habit of jotting down whatever came to me on tiny scraps of paper—matchbooks, torn-off sheets from note pads, whatever—and stuffing them into my pockets. One of Heloise's jobs in those days was to rescue them before the trousers hit the laundry. I rarely took them out myself. Naturally, one day she missed and brought me a soggy ball of paper. I was devastated, until I suddenly realized that I had NEVER used those hundreds of notes for anything—the poems that I had written had always come fresh out of my mind. True, I had a couple of drawers stuffed with notes, but they were as dead as the leaves of autumn.

So, the next time such an impulse hit me, I said, "No, I'll gamble, I'll wait to see if this notion comes back in a fullness of development that I cannot resist." The gamble of course was that it might not come back.

I suppose that during this time I learned to live with and accept myself as I am, at least a little.

In 1972 I was selected as a consultant to the Coordinating Council for Literary Magazines (CCLM) and spent two years getting to know more about the writing world in the U.S. and left, for a time, my self-imposed exile.

I n 1974, I won both the Senior Fulbright-Hays Fellowship to Romania and the National Endowment for the Arts Fellowship. As a consequence, we spent eighteen months traveling in Europe and living at Cluj-Napoca, Romania, where I was visiting professor of American literature at Babes-Bolyai University (formerly King Carol University). People often ask me why I picked such an out-of-the-way place. First, I had been fascinated as a very young child by any mention of Romania—Queen Marie was mentioned in my hearing several times and each time I would become excited and try to learn as much as I could from the speaker who usually knew nothing more than the news clip he or she was quoting. I used to have dreams about what I can only term "another me" who had lived there. These dreams haunted me for years, along with many other similar ones. Recently someone asked if I were interested in reincarnation. I replied, "No, I'm terrified of it." Yet the yoga doctrine of Karma or reincarnation remains, to me, as one of the dominant themes of my work. Inescapable, in a way.

### Seadream

Romania is too much a part of me,
of nightgulls that sweep
the Black Sea and cry about
the breakwaters of Constanta.

Queen Marie was right.
No one can resist the love
these hill bring to darkly
touch your face and seek
the centered marrows of your bones.

Light has a peculiar quality here.
Fingers brush your face as you sleep.
There are pipes in the hills, and bears,
Great bears that walk the seas in moonlight.

That year of 1974–75 significantly changed our lives. I have always thought of myself as a Celt and a New Mexican who lived in the United States. Whatever shadowy karmic past I had was deeply buried in my involvement with my family, my work, and the land and peoples of New Mexico. Now I was forced into an awareness much closer to the bone than even all that.

### Romanian Thoughts

*When I turn to you transfigured*
*Why do you grow so silent?*
Mihai Eminescu (1850–1889)

Am I so different from Eminescu?
A solitary man, landlocked in Romania
caught to dreams of universality. A brain
dissolving in the disease of existence, trying
to write, overwhelmed before I begin?

I too have walked along his shores,
as sleeper have known the shock of waking love
the quick surrender of defeat when the child
is born to her and damns me for not going
where I could not go, where I never dreamed.

The shores fill with shells and beating
waves. The moon a perfect circle on a thin line.
I walk away because I cannot understand
dare not feel more than my flesh and the sea.

—Constanta, Romania

We all discovered so much there. The children

were enrolled in Romanian schools and quickly learned, as children do, to rattle off pretty good Romanian; Heloise learned to shop and to cope with the terrible food shortages that haunt that land; I found teaching in that world a bit different from anything I had experienced before. And I discovered something about the history of my ancestors, the Celts on the Danube Delta.

### The Celt in Me

In a museum here I saw a Celtic swordblade,
rusted, bent in combat. No handle.
These men who built what are now shadowed
   ruins,

my ancestors: from deathmasks, carvings
I see similar features. Gaiety, defiance,
lost causes, futile wars. Indians of Europe.

Always the High Goddess, Moon Lady of White
streaming with light with eyes that touch
as the breeze moves through the Holy Tree.

From ancient barrows, dim men with old robes
walk gravely through the Danube mists
their arms outstretched for me.

Dej, Romania

We were, of course, up to our eyebrows in secret agents. Our phone was bugged as was our apartment. We were followed on the streets and visited at our home by known agents, just checking up.

### Secret Agent

Those who follow
step-by-step
through the Autumn night

find echoes across
this old bridge, moon
lit arc of the Somesh River.

He wears a trenchcoat
like mine, a small beard
and, by God, a beret—too

many movies—his eyes
are Orson Welles he thinks
and they cannot avoid

that clear Hollywood suggestion
the quick leer that lets me know
he, he alone, is my shadow

his footsteps predictably
out of step with mine the silent
concrete slapping to his shoeleather.

My wife, streetlights catching her
unawares, smiles but I pass him by
silent, do not nod, for it would break

his whole illusion (not mine)
to let him know I lived with shadow
had always walked this way.

In spite of all this, and also because of this, we met and made good friends. I was welcomed as a poet and friend by the great Romanian poet Aurel Rau and others. I wrote a book of *Graves Registry* and most of *Stone Roses* while there, and we took fascinating trips to Constanta beside the Black Sea, to Radauts to see the monasteries of Moldavia, and naturally to Bucharest, the capital. I also got the rare opportunity to be guided through the royal summer palace of Sinaia, a place Queen Marie had loved.

We returned in late summer, 1975, to find that I had been made poet-in-residence and the next year, promoted to full professor. I continued to teach, write, and publish. Our children grew up, married, and left home. Kathleen is married to Walter Fox; both are finishing Ph.D.'s at Indiana University—she in Balkan History and he in Nuclear Physics. Kristin and her husband, Ryne Palombit, are in the Sumatran rain forest studying gibbons. She is an accomplished cellist and he is finishing his Ph.D. in Animal Behavior at the University of California at Davis. Kevin is a painting contractor in Albuquerque and his son, Jeremiah, is three years old. Kerrin has returned home to finish her degree in Social Welfare at NMSU.

### In Sere & Twisted Trees

—El Rito, New Mexico

Walking the small trails of the stonecropped hills,
my son and I read with the grains of our skins
the old language, its tongues of night and day,
toned winds and the watching trees and skies.

How it all grows easy and secure when one
   realizes
everything is alive in the summer's sun, listening
watching. I speak to my brothers. I tell them we
   are
coming, meaning no harm. Wait. My son, 10,
is a fisherman, and he hopes to catch trout.
I tell them this, promise he will eat what he
   catches.

I will see to this.

                A prayer for the trout.
A prayer for my son, whom I love more than
   ever
watching his graceful figure dance to the rod
and fly he made. I needn't have bothered the
   trout.
He was wiser than my son. We walk back, Kevin,
still excited, apparently not caring about the lack
of fish, full of the adventure of the day.

He no longer holds my hand now, and I
   understand.
His embraces are quick, embarrassed, his eyes
shifting warily away towards the hills. It won't
be long, as this canyon's time is measured,
before he leaves me. Pray for me, Trout.
Pray for me, Mountain Stream.

Now, as I write this, on November 18, 1986, I am in my last semester at New Mexico State University. Looking back over the years, I am aware that a large share of my accomplishments have derived from my teaching, that writing-in-the air of the twenty-eight-year-long classroom. I have also spent a long time trying to deal with the central verbal and emotional confusions that stem from my early life at Fort Sumner, there by the Llano, listening to its winds. Some stories nurtured my manhood, as they were supposed to. Others challenged my central existence, became divisive, and left me searching. I remain, perhaps consequently, an emotional historian who has tried very hard to write aware, honest, accurate poems that describe those histories as I saw and felt them. Like most other men and women I have failed to accomplish those goals. If I am permitted the years, I intend to go on with such failures, all the time dreaming of at least partial success.

I don't know how valuable fame or being well-known in one's field is. I do know that a life in art, amongst artists, has written its own warm histories inside me and my family. I can't think of a better way to live one's life. If God so permits, I will continue to live that life, to write and publish and teach, but at other places—and in other times.

### Revista

Now in these years when looking back
becomes blurred, uncertain, the days
too much like the nights, faces,
always reminding of another, thus
dismissed in their own certainties
because of a chance resemblance

*Wilson family portrait. Front row, left to right: Keith, Kerrin, and Heloise; back row: Kevin, Kathleen, and Kristin*

to someone long dead, or lost.

—buoys on a still sea. Gullcries
haunt my head and still I long
for that seafall that will announce
my coming home, my sailing in

—this windy mesa, no sea at all,
yet the waving grass, even the stubble
catches at my heart with the old
longing. How far is the home the heart
needs, how long the night's dawn
that awaits the passing of light.
Behind me, the moon rises.

## BIBLIOGRAPHY

### Poetry:

*Sketches for a New Mexico Hill Town.* Orono, Me.: Prensa da Lagar-Wine Press, 1966.

*The Old Car, and Other Blackpoems.* Sacramento, Calif.: Grande Ronde Press, 1967.

*II Sequences.* Portland, Ore.: Wine Press, 1967.

*Graves Registry, and Other Poems.* New York: Grove, 1969.

*Homestead.* San Francisco: Kayak Press, 1969.

*The Old Man and Others: Some Faces for America.* Las Cruces, N.M.: New Mexico State University Press, 1971.

*Rocks.* Oshkosh, Wis.: Road Runner Press, 1971.

*The Shadow of our Bones.* Portland, Ore.: Trask House Books, 1971.

*MidWatch: Graves Registry Part IV and V.* Fremont, Mich.: Sumac Press, 1972.

*Psalms for Various Voices.* Las Cruces, N.M.: Tolar Creek Press, 1972.

*Song of Thantog.* New York: Athanor, 1972.

*Thantog: Songs of a Jaguar Priest.* Dennis, Mass.: Salt-Works Press, 1977.

*Desert Cenote.* Fort Kent, Me.: Great Raven Press, 1978.

*While Dancing Feet Shatter the Earth.* Logan, Utah: Utah State University Press, 1978.

*The Shaman Deer.* Dennis, Mass.: Salt-Works Press, 1979.

*The Streets of San Miguel.* Tucson, Ariz.: Maguey Press, 1979.

*Retablos.* Los Cerillos, N.M.: San Marcos Press, 1981.

*Stone Roses: Poems from Transylvania.* Logan, Utah: Utah

State University Press, 1983.

*Lovesongs and Mandalas.* Los Cerillos, N.M.: San Marcos Press, 1984.

*Meeting in Jal,* with Theodore Enslin. Hobbs, N.M.: Southwestern American Literature Association, 1985.

# David Wright

## *1920-*

*Composed at thirty, my funeral oration: Here lies*
*David John Murray Wright, 6'2", myopic blue eyes;*
*Hair grey (very distinguished looking, so I am told);*
*Shabbily dressed as a rule; susceptible to cold;*
*Acquainted with what are known as the normal vices;*
*Perpetually short of cash; useless in a crisis;*
*Preferring cats, hated dogs; drank (when he could)*
    *too much;*
*Was deaf as a tombstone; and extremely hard to touch.*
*Academic achievements: B.A., Oxon (2nd class)*
*Poetic: the publication of one volume of verse*
*Which in his thirtieth year attained him no fame at all*
*Except among intractable poets, and a small*
*Lunatic fringe congregating in Soho pubs.*
*He could roll himself cigarettes from discarded stubs,*
*Assume the first position of Yoga; sail, row, swim;*
*And though deaf, in church appear to be joining a hymn.*
*Often arrested for being without a permit,*
*Starved on his talents as much as he dined on his wit,*
*Born in a dominion to which he hoped not to go back*
*Since predisposed to imagine white possibly black:*
*His life, like his times, was appalling; his conduct odd;*
*He hoped to write one good line; died believing in God.*

*Phillipa Reid and David Wright, 1951*

Thus did I see myself, with as much honesty as you might expect, at the age of thirty. At sixty-five I would have to paint a different portrait. That poem was written in 1950, my annus mirabilis. I remember waking up in Great Ormond Street one May morning to the euphoria of realizing that a long adolescence was over, that I was master of a disability that had hobbled me since 1927. Then, out of the blue, came the news that I had been given one of the last of the Atlantic Awards in Literature donated by the Rockefeller Foundation to help young writers. It was worth three hundred pounds. Half of it I spent on a long sojourn in Italy—Brescia, Sirmione, Verona, Padua, Venice; thence to Florence, Perugia, Assisi, and Rome. The result was a profound cultural shock that stopped me from writing verse for more than a year. The other half of it was spent drinking and talking with poets and painters in Soho. The result was marriage. One Sunday in the spring of 1951, at the beginning of the Festival of Britain, I met Phillipa Reid in the Lamb, my local pub in Lamb's Conduit Street. She was very beautiful, and like me a colonial; the daughter of a New Zealand sheep farmer. Her age was twenty-three and she was a student under Michael St. Denis at the Old Vic Drama School. The moment I set eyes on her I knew that this was for ever. And so it was till she died thirty-four years and six months later.

Poetry has been my vocation since I lost my hearing at the age of seven through a bout of scarlet fever and became, as George Barker once put it, deaf as the womb. It was an accident that shaped my life but which failed, I think, to distort it—a matter discussed at length in an autobiographical book called *Deafness* that I wrote nearly twenty years ago. The subject now rather bores me, so I will not revert to it except where necessary.

The other main shaping influences on my life were the usual ones—ancestry and environment. Each was characterised by a certain polarity. My mother, born in Dumfriesshire, was pure Scots, while my father, born in Kimberley, was authentically South African, being descended on both sides from the 1820 Settlers—English emigrants sent out to create a kind of buffer state between the Boers and their cattle-raiding neighbours, the Xhosas. And while I was born in South Africa and remained there, save for two visits to England, till I was fourteen—these being the impressionable years—thereafter, and for all of my formative years, Britain was my home. Yet, as will be seen, it was due to my Scottish mother that I never lost touch with South Africa.

One of my father's Settler forbears is said to have come from Newcastle-upon-Tyne, and to have been a musician. Certainly my father and his two sisters were given an unusual upbringing for South African colonials when they were sent to Dresden, before the Kaiser's war, to obtain a musical education. Music is in my blood, I think; for it is my belief, or delusion, that after I became deaf I took to the reading, and then to the writing, of poetry as a substitute for the music I could no longer hear but still remember. Even now it is the sound of a poem that first communicates, rather than its "meaning." For me the best definition of poetry is Dryden's: "articulate music."

Of my father's people I know little, owing to his parents' Victorian reticence in front of children. My father's grandmother married twice; her second husband was a man called Nordern who, when diamonds were discovered at Kimberley in 1870, trekked there from Grahamstown, four hundred miles away, in an ox-waggon with his stepson, my father's father, then a boy of fourteen, walking behind; while his wife followed in a buggy. Ten years ago, when I was in Grahamstown as a guest of the poet Guy Butler, I discovered that the Norderns were locally famous. In the cathedral is a tablet commemorating a Lieutenant Nordern killed in one of the Kaffir Wars: I was told it is probably the only memorial to a Jew to be found in a Christian church.

Another Settler forbear was a Captain Manley from Yorkshire, who has left his name on a railway station, Manley Flats, not far from Grahamstown. He is said to have altered the climate by introducing Australian blue gum and wattle (now a pest!) into the area with the object of inducing an increased rainfall. My grandfather David Ormson Wright, the boy who followed the ox-waggon, married Captain Manley's daughter. He made the first of his fortunes in diamonds at Kimberley, sold out to the Cockney millionaire Barney Barnato, and moved to Johannesburg where he became a stockbroker. When the Boer War broke out in 1899 he escaped with his family to Kimberley,

*Grandfather David Ormson Wright (seated far left), Grandmother Wright (standing far right) in Kimberley, South Africa, about 1898*

which the Boers soon invested; my father, then a boy of eight or nine, had many stories to tell me about this surprisingly humane and lackadaisical siege. After the relief of Kimberley my grandfather took the family back to Johannesburg. He celebrated the end of the Boer War by making the grand tour of Europe—to find himself penniless when he came home: a business partner had absconded with the firm's capital. But money was not hard to make in Johannesburg in those days. He was soon master of another fortune. I remember him in the days of his grandeur, immaculate in top hat and morning coat: they called him "the best-dressed man in South Africa." Even when broke he always managed to look as if he had just stepped out of a bandbox.

When the Kaiser's war began in 1914 my father joined the Transvaal Horse Artillery to serve in the short-lived Boer Rebellion, and then under General Botha in German South West Africa (now Namibia) which surrendered after a brief campaign—the first Allied victory in that war. Thereupon my father sailed for England to join up again, this time with the Royal Artillery. He fought at Passchendaele, was mentioned in despatches (what for, I never knew; my father wouldn't talk about his experiences on the Western Front), and was finally invalided out of the army minus a foot, which misfortune he did not owe to any malice of the enemy but to having coincided with a goods-train at a level-crossing in France while riding a motor-bicycle with faulty brakes.

To which accident I may be said to owe my existence. Certainly it helped to shape my own attitude when in turn I became a cripple: for my father refused to knuckle under, but swam, walked, played golf and cricket to the end of his days. His crushed foot brought him to Guy's Hospital in London to have it amputated. Hence my emergence on the scene: he fell in love with the ward sister, married her, and took her back with him to Johannesburg, where I was born on February 23, 1920.

My mother, Jean Murray, was descended from a line of tenant-farmers whose ancestors had fled from the Highlands after the battle of Culloden in 1745 and settled in Ayrshire. Cousins of her grandfather, Archibald Murray, were neighbours of the Burns family at Alloway; one of them, when a boy, is said to have "held the plough" for the poet. Archibald Murray, a stonemason, married one Margaret Bone, cook to the Earl of Cassilis at Culzean Castle. His son John Murray, my mother's father, was born in the last year of the reign of George IV. Beginning as a stonemason, he launched out as a builder, and made his fortune with his first major contract, the building of Loch Inch Castle, seat of the Earl of Stair: one of those Brobdingnagian exercises in Scottish baronial gothic which have to be seen to be believed. He then leased the Corsehill Quarries near Annan in Dumfriesshire, which produced a red sandstone much in demand for building, and until President McKinley clapped a tariff on it made a great deal of money exporting it to America in

a sailing-vessel, the *Margaret Murray,* which he built and owned; the stone was carried as ballast and sold off at the ports where she touched. It is my grandfather's Corsehill stone that forms the base of the Statue of Liberty outside New York harbour.

He died in 1903, when my mother was twenty-two. Determined to escape from the stifling little provincial burgh of Annan, she took up one of the few careers open to women in those days, and trained as a nursing sister at Guy's Hospital. Here she met the painter Henry Lamb, who for a time was one of her patients. He introduced her to the fringes of that bohemian world her son was afterwards to inhabit; took her to tea in his studio, where his great portrait of Lytton Strachey still hung unfinished; it was with him that she attended what must have been one of the first of Edith Sitwell's poetry readings.

But when she married my father she was taken far from this kind of life. My father's friends were mostly business associates—he had joined my grandfather's stockbroking firm—and except for music, he had no interest in the arts. Johannesburg was then a raw city of office-blocks, bungalows, red corrugated-iron roofs, trams, and dust; still congested by long, magnificent ox-waggon trains, each drawn by eight span or more of extravagantly horned oxen, which were even then a major form of transport in South Africa. Its only beauty was a necklace of white mine-dumps, floating like gulls on the wide ocean of the high veld. These I could see from the house where my childhood began:

*Margaret Murray; Grandmother Janet Kerr Murray; Ronalyn Murray; Grandfather John Murray; Mother, Jean Murray*

*Father, Gordon Alfred Wright, and Mother, Jean Murray Wright, Johannesburg, 1925*

*Grandmother Murray, Mother, David, Margaret
Murray, about 1925*

*Father, Mother, and Grandfather, Johannesburg, 1932*

an iron-roofed bungalow half-way-up the eastern end of the Witwatersrand koppies, with a magnificient view, which will remain with me till the day I die, over the vast plain of the high veld to the Magaliesberg hills forty miles away, behind which stands foreign Pretoria, the Afrikaner capital. The blue line of distant Magaliesberg, notched by Moselekatse's Nek—where, only ninety years before I first set eyes on it, the warrior king of the Matabele, who laid waste the Transvaal and eliminated nearly every living soul between the Vaal and the Limpopo, had built his royal kraal—haunted and still haunts my imagination.

Up to the age of seven my childhood was intensely happy. Then one day in 1927 I went down with scarlet fever, at that time a dangerous disease: there were no antibiotics. In the end my life was saved at the expense of my hearing. I underwent an operation for the removal of the mastoid bones and have ever since been totally deaf. But I was lucky in becoming deaf when I did, if deafness had to be my destiny: for unlike the deaf-born I had learned speech naturally by ear and already had a good vocabulary that was easily extended by reading. As my father was then very well-off, he could afford to send me to England with my mother to run the gauntlet of Harley Street in a des-

perate and quite hopeless effort to find some means of restoring my hearing. The real bonus of this trip was my mother's discovery of Miss Neville, a talented teacher of the deaf by the oral method, who took my education in hand with spectacular success. My mother engaged her assistant, Miss Ruth Holland, to be my governess, and it was with her we returned to South Africa.

The year was 1929, the year of the Wall Street Crash: my father's and grandfather's stockbroking firm went down in ruin—a ruin abetted by their confidential clerk, who embezzled scrip, leaving my father and grandfather bankrupt. The grand house my father had built on the site of our former bungalow was sold with every stick of furniture, and we moved to a tiny cottage on the outskirts of Orange Grove; Miss Holland, my excellent governess, had to be dispensed with; and my father spent his days tramping round Johannesburg looking for a job while my mother put her nursing experience to use by earning a little money as a midwife. We did not exactly starve but lived on very short commons for a year or two, till my father obtained an executive post with the Legal and General Insurance Company which was then beginning to operate in South Africa. This led to my being sent to P.T.S., a well-known preparatory school where, if I did not learn much, I had the great advantage of finding my feet among ordinary boys, my hearing contemporaries. The short period I spent at P.T.S. turned out to be invaluable in counterbalancing the five unhappy years I was to endure at the famous Spring Hill School for the Deaf at Northampton, England.

That deaf school was another world. The deaf-born, who have to be taught slowly and painfully the use of words and how to speak, are liable to have very limited vocabularies and little general knowledge of the kind one takes for granted, e.g., that hens lay eggs. This is because their information is not picked up casually, as in the case of hearing children, but acquired with trouble and effort. So difficult is the education of the deaf-born, that it was not till the sixteenth century that any attempt was made to teach them to speak. As for their higher education, the Northampton school to which I was sent was a pioneer in that respect. The first deaf-born person ever to graduate at a university had been educated there—and for that matter, was still alive (Abraham Farrar, 1861-1944); so recent is the beginning of secondary education for the deaf. That school represented my only chance of getting into a university.

The headmaster was a brilliant teacher, a short, rotund Welshman with a handsome face, who wore a gold monocle and was often mistaken for Sir Austen

*At P.T.S., Johannesburg, 1930 (The school can be seen on the top of the hill at extreme right.)*

Chamberlain. At that time no deaf school anywhere in the world could rival the academic successes of his pupils. Yet the school was a small one: never more than twenty-four boys at the most, their ages ranging from seven to twenty-five. It was housed in a stucco-fronted late Victorian dwelling on what were once the outskirts of Northampton; further up the main road stood the lunatic asylum, where in summer we played cricket against the local grammar school, and where the poet John Clare spent the last twenty years of his life. There James Joyce's daughter Lucia was later to live and die.

Without that school I should not have entered Oxford University; for which I shall always be grateful. The experience of living with others as deaf as myself was also salutary, for it inhibited any tendency to self-pity or trading on the infirmity—the others were deaf too. But it is so much easier for the deaf to converse with one another than with the hearing that the danger is that they tend to become a community isolated from the larger world, to cut themselves off from ordinary people and ordinary life. It is a matter of communication—for though the school was strictly oral, with any form of sign-language or even the use of the deaf-and-dumb alphabet strictly prohibited (in fact I never did learn any of the finger-alphabets), when we talked among ourselves we would be incomprehensible to an outsider. Very few words were spoken, or mouthed, and those bare substantives; gesture, mime, and grimace did the work of verbs and adjectives; on top of which, we had many signs and gestures private to ourselves, a kind of dumb-show slang or argot invented by, and peculiar to, the school. While there, among my deaf coevals, I became one of them: a different persona from the "normal" one that I wore when at home or among hearing folk.

Unfortunately the headmaster made it impossible for his pupils to mix with ordinary hearing people for nine months of the year. We were forbidden to leave the school precincts except for prefect-escorted two-hour walks on Sunday afternoons, and for an hour-or-so's shopping in the town on Saturday mornings. To speak to the cook or the two maidservants was to risk a caning. I do not exaggerate: the headmaster was insane on the subject of sex, perhaps as a result of Victorian upbringing. Now and then, as happens in all schools, two boys would be found in bed together: whereupon they would be taken to the study, soundly thrashed, shown lurid illustrations of persons in the last stages of venereal disease, and told that that was what would happen to them. One lad of eighteen, who lived in Belfast, arrived at school a day late for the beginning of term—he was taken to the study the moment he arrived and flogged there and then. (I saw the weals on his back next morning.) The boy had stayed overnight

*Northampton School for the Deaf, 1935: David standing behind the headmaster
(front row, center)*

with his brother in London: the headmaster would not accept this explanation, insisting that the delinquent had passed the night with a girl—no such luck, as my friend said. Eventually the headmaster did go mad, and was confined for a year or two in the Retreat at York, whereupon the school closed down. This was during the war, long after I had left. He returned to his family; but whether he was ever entirely compos mentis again I do not know. One of my fellow-pupils went to visit him and stayed for lunch. Nothing odd took place, he said, until lunch was over, when everyone left the room except the headmaster and himself. Whereupon the headmaster turned to him and said, "Do you still play with yourself?", unbuttoned his flies, and peed into a bowl of roses on the table.

All this to explain, in brief space, why after five years at that school I found it extraordinarily difficult to rejoin normal society. When I went up to Oxford in October 1939 it was—to quote from my autobiographical book, *Deafness*—

> like emigrating from Tristan da Cunha. I was totally ignorant of the manners and mores of the males of my own generation. As for the other sex, I found myself incapable of the most perfunctory social relationships with any unattached member of it under the age of thirty-five. Introduced to one, I would shake hands, say nothing whatsoever, slowly

and remarkably assume a sunset tinge, and stand there thinking furiously, until such time as the girl's nerve broke and she fled, leaving me undisputed master of the field.

It took time and experience to disembarass myself of the inhibitions produced by that extraordinary Northampton establishment. Looking back it seems to me that mine was a protracted adolescence, that not till I was thirty did I really grow up. It was at Oxford I began that process.

I went up to Oxford in the first October of the Second World War. Half the colleges, including mine, had been wholly or partially requisitioned by various governmental bodies evacuated from London. Oriel College, to which I belonged, lost one of its quads to the Prison Commission; later it was to lose another to the Intelligence Corps. As a result, I and other freshmen of my year were boarded out in Hertford College, where I was assigned rooms in its New Quad, built only ten years previously, but all the same authentically medieval in plumbing and what are called conveniences. None of the rooms had any of the former; as for the latter, these were represented by a corrugated-iron shed in a back alley.

My first term was spent in painfully finding my feet; my second, in acquiring friends. Here I was wonderfully fortunate. Though no games-player I decided

*Punting on the Cherwell at Oxford, 1941*

I had better go in for something, and chose rowing, partly because it seemed the romantically appropriate thing to do at Oxford, and partly to please my father, who had rowed for a Thames boat club in his youth. Thus I came to know the public-school rowing men, whom I found myself admiring immensely—the 1939-40 crop at least. Nearly all were waiting to join the air force, and nearly all were killed in the Battle of Britain or shortly after. They were, I suppose, "bloods," while I was an oddball. But to me they behaved with the greatest kindness and would even ask me to their rooms for drinks and parties, a thing that meant much to me at that time. Theirs was the Hillary generation[1]—some may have been his friends. They owned a magnanimity of spirit which I never again encountered. They lived with zest, as if they felt in some way set apart, which in fact they were.

Most of my friends, however, were offbeats like myself. For some reason many of them were biochemists—Gerhard Schmidt, now a distinguished researcher in that field, was one. He had come to England as a schoolboy, a refugee from Nazi Berlin, knowing no word of the language. Because of this he may have understood my communications problem better than most. English he mastered by a simple and Teutonic expedient: he learnt a dictionary by heart. "The first week, everything I said began with A." Through him I later had the experience of sitting out one of the first air

raids on London in a cellar full of Germans—his mother ran a lodging house for refugees—which gave piquancy to the self-congratulatory eulogies of British phlegm under fire that I read in the papers next morning. Another odd man out I came to know well was an engineer, a Rhodes scholar from Malta, the son of a sea-cook (literally: his father had been one in the Royal Navy). He was at Hertford, and like myself rather a fish out of water. We got into the way of talking far into the night over pot after pot of tea—the same tea leaves wetted again and again for the sake of economy and rationing—sessions wherein he would speak of the poetry of Leopardi and expound what he meant to do when he returned to Malta: raze the slums of Valletta, reorganize its Labour Party, and generally get things moving in the right, or properly speaking, left, direction. I didn't believe a word of it; but the last time I saw Dom Mintoff all this had come to pass and he was the then prime minister of Malta.

In my last year at Oxford I moved into digs at 52 High Street. This proved my introduction to the university literary set, which I had more or less avoided, because poetry was my sacred or at any rate secret preoccupation. For the room under mine was taken by Sidney Keyes, who was then, in succession to Keith Douglas, the reigning Grand Cham of Oxford poets. He had edited an anthology called *Eight Oxford Poets* in which appeared the verse of Keith Douglas, Drummond Allison, Michael Meyer, and Keyes himself. No. 52 High Street naturally became their headquarters.

---

[1] Richard Hillary, fighter pilot and author of *The Last Enemy*.

An inauspicious address as it turned out: nearly all the Oxford poets who took digs there in the forties were allotted early and violent deaths. It might have been an omen when, in the first month that Keyes and I lived there, the third lodger, a Magdalen undergraduate, threw himself into the Cherwell and drowned. Barely a year after he left Oxford Keyes himself was killed at the tail end of the Tunisian campaign, while his friend Drummond Allison, who inherited my room, died a few months later in the Italian landings. Some time after Allison's death his room was taken over by William Bell, a poet whose potentiality may have been greater than that of either. Bell died at twenty-four, killed while climbing the Matterhorn. This last fatality was too much for our landlady, Mrs. Taylor, who thereafter refused to take on any more undergraduate poets.

Keyes's poetry—he was only nineteen—was extraordinarily assured and polished; it hypnotized his contemporaries. As the first young poet of any note to be killed in the Second World War, Keyes became its Rupert Brooke: his posthumous poems were awarded a Hawthornden Prize, and he was compared with Donne and Rimbaud; yet today he is practically forgotten. Nonetheless he had the luck to have enjoyed, as it were, his posthumous reputation while still alive; for at Oxford his name was legendary. It was through him that I was introduced to the poems of Dylan Thomas and Vernon Watkins. Though I had read a great deal of poetry at school—where, in the long light summer nights, when I found it difficult to sleep, I would amuse myself by reciting aloud from memory (knowing my companions could not hear me) what seemed to me marvellous harmonies from Milton's *Lycidas,* Dryden's *Ode to St. Cecilia,* Donne's *Holy Sonnets* and *Hymn to God in My Sickness,* as well as bits of Tennyson, Browning, Kipling, and so forth—I came across no modern poetry bar that of Yeats and Thomas Hardy. Contemporary verse was not so publicised, or so easily available, then. Thus it was at Oxford I first discovered—and immersed myself in—Eliot, Hopkins, Pound, and Joyce. As always it was the verbal music that hooked me. To begin with I did not "understand" much of Eliot or Dylan Thomas, but they communicated through my enjoyment of their euphony.

My own first poems had been written at the age of eight, in an attic flat off Paddington, at the time when I was being dragged up and down Harley Street. At school I wrote a lot of Byronic and Tennysonian verse, but at Oxford and for long after I wrote verse that was hopelessly neo-romantic, melodious, word-obsessed and arcane: much of it I now find indistinguishable from that produced by a contemporary, essentially ersatz, school of poets that called themselves, or rather

got themselves called by their promoters Henry Treece and G.S. Fraser, the New Apocalypse; though when at Oxford I never heard of it, and when I did, took exception. Yet I was open and reacting to the same influences, which for that generation were firstly the shadow of the Great War in which our fathers fought, and our conviction, ever since the emergence of Hitler, of the imminence of the next; secondly, the publication of the poems of Gerard Manley Hopkins, of Yeats's last collection, of Joyce's *Ulysses* and *Finnegans Wake,* and—more marginally—of Christopher Smart's *Jubilate Agno,* Lautreamont's *Lay of Malodoror,* and the Nonesuch edition of Blake.

It was about the time I met Keyes, though not because of it, that I decided poetry was to be my vocation. I never had any idea, throughout boyhood, what I was going to do for a career. Deafness, as good an excuse as any, ruled out most jobs. Inability to answer the telephone crossed out the idea of office or business employment. I had no aptitude for and less interest in most of the trades and professions in which deafness would be least a liability: farming, architecture, engineering, printing, and so on; though at a pinch I could always find work as a dishwasher. But my targets had always been limited ones—first to matriculate, next to get into a university, then to get a degree. Having decided, rightly or wrongly, that the writing of verse was to be the main preoccupation of my life, made the question of a "career" of less importance. Somehow or other, I supposed, I would make or get enough money to live on. Looking back I am appalled at this optimism and its justification. In life, if you want a thing badly enough you are liable in the end to be given it by the ironic gods. So be careful what you want.

But it was not through Keyes and his circle that I began to find my way to the people under whose aegis I finally grew up. Through Cyril Frankel, who founded the university ballet club, I became close friends with two members of the Ballet Rambert, the choreographer Walter Gore and its ballerina Sally Gilmour, who had created the title role of Andrée Howard's *Lady into Fox;* and with Honor Frost, who designed some of their ballets, and who many years later became a pioneer of underwater archaeology. It was to her that I owed three introductions that afterwards proved decisive.

The first was to the poet David Gascoyne, tall as a pylon, intensely nervous, beautiful as a derelict angel escaped from the illuminated margin of an Anglo-Saxon psalter. From him I learned that poets do not have careers. The second was to Tambimuttu, then operating from a ratty old basement cellar in Chelsea, where he lived on visions and unsold copies of *Poetry London*—one of the two "little magazines" devoted entirely to verse that kept going throughout the war. His

*David Wright with Julian Orde at the York Minster, a
"French pub" in Soho, 1957*

function was that of catalytic agent; the influence of his magazine, good or bad, was nothing. Tambi's service lay in his role as a kind of peripatetic rendezvous, a one-man Institute of Contemporary Arts through whom, at a time of scattering and regimentation, poets, painters, and musicians met one another. In the pubs of Soho, sleazy and rumbustious, he dispensed Dutch hospitality and kept the lines of communication open. The third and last introduction was to the York Minster in Soho, where I was to be found, on and off, for the next forty years, and in whose radius I was to make the most important friendships of my life.

In June 1942 I gained a second-class honours degree in English. I didn't deserve a first; but could reflect that I was only the fifth or sixth pupil from a deaf school to graduate at a university. My mother was then staying in the village of Broadway at the foot of the Cotswolds, where she had been marooned since the outbreak of war prevented her from returning to South Africa. I went to London, ostensibly to look for a job, and stayed with Walter Gore and Sally Gilmour in their tiny flat in Montpelier Street. We were very broke and at one time lived entirely on kippers for a fortnight, a box of them having been sent from Scotland by a friend working on a documentary for the Crown Film Unit. Then in November I landed a job, through no effort of my own.

It was the headmaster of my deaf school who managed the affair. He was a friend of W.W. Hadley, editor of the *Sunday Times,* though nearly eighty years

old; its proprietor, Lord Kemsley, had asked him to stay on for the duration. Mr. Hadley, a kindly man, agreed to take me on, and even stood me lunch at the Reform Club to celebrate—though owing to the war and rationing, the lunch consisted of sausages and mash. He had really no idea what to do with a deaf man; it is my belief he invented a job for me. This was to make an index of the *Sunday Times* week by week. As a job, it was a doddle; all I needed was a card index, a typewriter, and paper; all of which were supplied me, plus an office to myself, in the converted boot-factory in Grays Inn Road where the *Sunday Times* was edited and printed. For this I was paid seven pounds a week, an ample wage.

Simultaneously I acquired a mistress and a flat—having obtained the one, I needed the other. The flat was in Great Ormond Street opposite the Children's Hospital, and was an affair of two rooms and a kitchen-bathroom. The ground floor was occupied by an electrical appliance shop, its windows boarded up, having been blown out by a bomb. Here too was the lavatory, shared by all the tenants of the house. The rent was miniscule. I was to live in this flat, on and off, for nearly thirty years.

The lady who relieved me of my virginity and much else that I needed to be disembarrassed of was twenty years older than myself. Like Balzac's *femme de trente ans* she taught me much. Through her, or rather her friend Peggy-Jean Epstein, I first met Dylan Thomas, "nattily dressed, not unlike an unsuccessful commercial traveller" or so I described him in a contemporary letter home. This encounter was in the Swiss pub in Old Compton Street, and one of the few times I saw Dylan really drunk. But by 1943 "Soho" was abandoning the Swiss (a Black American soldier had been stabbed there) and moving north of Oxford Street to the Rathbone Place public-houses, the Wheatsheaf and Black Horse. These pubs became a meeting-place for writers, painters, musicians, and all sorts and conditions of people from every quarter of the globe. "Soho" was the lineal successor of pre-war Montparnasse, many of whose survivors, e.g., Nina Hamnett, mistress of Modigliani, had transferred there. One could run into literally anybody—the "rightful king" of Poland, clad in gown and crown; a Cambridge Senior Wrangler; the librarian of the House of Lords; not to mention burglars, prostitutes, and the fighting forces of half of Europe. In those days "Soho" constituted the kind of "convivial" university that Ivan Illich was later to advocate. Among the drinkers there you could find an expert in almost any art or science. My most valuable friendships were made in Soho—John Heath-Stubbs, whom I had met, rather than known, at Oxford; W.S. Graham, Roy Campbell, and George Barker, to name four poets who in their very different ways helped the person I became to break through the chrysalis.

W.S. Graham, word-possessed and language-obsessed, with a head like Beethoven's, taught me craftsmanship. We met in 1943 at the Wheatsheaf, along with the two Roberts—the painters Robert Colquhoun and Robert MacBryde—Julian Orde, and the nervous, generous, inarticulate, spectacled David Archer, "quivering like an aspirin tree," a *New Statesman* tucked under his withered arm. They had just emigrated from Glasgow after the collapse of one of Archer's bookshops—which always succumbed because while Archer would stock, he would refuse to sell, books he disapproved of; those he admired he generally gave away. Though Archer read no poetry, he published it, relying on an intuitive perception of talent. Thus he brought out the first collections of four notable poets: Dylan Thomas, David Gascoyne, George Barker, and W.S. Graham.

Roy Campbell, still wearing his King's African Rifles slouch hat, I met through Tambimuttu at the Wheatsheaf; but, believing all the propaganda about his being a Fascist, I was wary to begin with, and did not get to know this gentle, magnanimous, self-doubting man—for such Campbell was behind all that bluster—till much later. Again it was through Tambimuttu that I first met George Barker—the Byron *de nos jours*—and his then companion Elizabeth Smart. At that time I was more or less ensorcelled by Barker's poetry, of which for all its indisputable eccentricities I still consider to be among the finest of our time. In those days it overwhelmed me much as Swinburne's early verse overwhelmed the young of his generation.

When I met George again one evening, to my astonishment he accepted an invitation to tea at my flat—and even more astonishingly, he kept the appointment. In his turn he asked me to visit his parents' home in South Kensington, to look at the paintings of his brother Kit. This I did one winter afternoon in 1946. He was not there—having gone off to live in Ireland—but nonetheless I was welcomed by his three sisters and brought into the great Chinese drawing room where I instantly recognized that marvellous woman, his mother, "sitting as huge as Asia, seismic with laughter, / Gin and chicken helpless in her Irish hand." The room seemed crammed with her children and grandchildren. There I met the painter brother, Kit; we became friends; in time I felt myself part of that hospitable family, even approved of (comparatively speaking) by old Colonel Barker, who was as English as his wife was Irish—hence tension—and had no time for artistic layabouts like his two sons.

Perhaps that was because I had a job: which I proceeded to lose. Wartime paper restrictions had re-

duced the *Sunday Times* to five or six pages; consequently, an issue could be indexed in a matter of hours. This left me with three or four days with nothing to do. I got into the way of letting the weekly issues pile up, then demolishing the backlog with a few days' frantic work. No one came near me, no one ever asked to see the index. The weeks, months, and years wore on; till one day in 1947 I woke up to the fact that I was three years behind in my indexing. Thereupon I decided to resign, and went to see the editor. On my appearing at the door of his office Mr. Hadley looked up. "Are you still here?" he said. "I thought you went back to South Africa two years ago."

So ended the first and last job I ever had. Now I was free, but in the usual condition of the free, i.e., broke. My generous father came to the rescue with a monthly stipend of ten pounds (this was in fact his wound pension), which enabled me to survive. About this time Kit Barker went to live and paint in Cornwall, where cottages could be rented for as little as twenty-five pence a week. There his brother George, who had separated from Elizabeth Smart, decided to join him near Zennor with his new girlfriend, Cashenden Cass. When in the summer of 1948 John Fairfax, one of his innumerable nephews, said he was going to

*Cove Cottage, Gunnard's Head, Cornwall, 1949*

*Kit and Ilse Barker's wedding, 1950, London: Maurice Carpenter, Monica Humble, Cashenden Cass, David Wright, Eileen Jackson, Kit Barker, Ilse Barker, Mrs. Marion Barker, George Barker, John Fairfax, Colonel George Granville Barker, Wendy Humble*

hitchhike to Cornwall to pay his uncles a visit, I went with him. We meant to spend no more than a week in Cornwall but stayed a year.

Zennor in 1948 was a derelict mining hamlet. Kit had a cottage up in the moors two miles away, reached by no road; on the hill above him lived the painter Bryan Wynter, whom I had met long before with W.S. Graham; in St. Ives, and hamlets round about, were young painters like David Haughton, Peter Lanyon, and Willie Barns-Graham, besides grand folk like Barbara Hepworth, Bernard Leach, and Ben Nicholson. George and Cass found a cottage in Zennor: John Fairfax and I rented, for a while, Higher Tregerthen, where Katherine Mansfield had lived next door to the D.H. Lawrences; but soon left this depressing house for a magical cottage perched on the cliffs by Gurnard's Head, so remote that not even a track could reach it. It was here, conversing with George Barker and visiting poets—among them John Heath-Stubbs and Michael Hamburger—that I continued the education begun in Soho, and first began to write poems in my own voice—the "Seven South African Poems" were begun at Cove Cottage. It was this experience that later gave John Fairfax the idea for the Arvon Foundation, which now has two remote country houses where those who wish to write or paint muck in with established artists for a week or two at a time and so gain understanding of their art from informal conversation as well as precept and practice. And it was here at Cove Cottage that I received a bundle of copies of my first collection

of poems that Tambimuttu had accepted for publication five years before. As usual he had begun by losing the typescript; unluckily he found it again, and here, when I had forgotten all about them, were my jejune neo-apocalyptic verses staring me in the face. I nearly threw the lot over the cliff into the Atlantic.

In the spring of 1949 I returned to London. John Lehmann had just published a pioneering anthology of Victorian verse, *The Forsaken Garden,* that John Heath-Stubbs and I had edited. With my share of the advance—£35—I made my first trip to the continent. It lasted three weeks: the first I spent in Paris, the remainder in Provence. All was a wonder: the cornucopias of food and drink (in England austerity still ruled); the people; the light; Tarascon, Arles, Aigues-Mortes, Nîmes, and Avignon, where I accidentally put up in a brothel. I vowed henceforth to let no year pass without visiting Europe: and kept that vow.

As I have related, 1950 was my *annus mirabilis,* when at long length I found myself, and found my wife. We were married in October 1951, with George Barker as my best man, at the registry offices in Russell Square next door to Faber and Faber.

Almost immediately I was hauled off to South Africa to pay a long promised and long deferred visit to my parents in Johannesburg. In December I sailed from Tilbury, desperately sad to leave England and my new bride. The voyage lasted three weeks; the food and the passengers were rebarbative; I spent my days

*Wedding photograph, October 6, 1951: Julian Orde Abercrombie, Donald Harwood, Robert Pocock, Ralph Abercrombie, Cashenden Cass, George Barker, David Wright, Phillipa Reid, unidentified woman, Honor Frost, Sheila Pocock, John Fairfax, David Archer*

© *Topical Photos, London*

making a prose translation of *Beowulf,* which I hoped I might sell to Penguin and make a little money.

After so many years in England, the South African set-up—apartheid had just begun—I found horrifying. In February 1952 I returned home, and in the following year made three crucial friendships—again in Soho—with the Irish painter Patrick Swift, his friend Anthony Cronin, and finally with their totem, the poet Patrick Kavanagh, a being as rugged, forthright, and down-to-earth as Samuel Johnson. In England Kavanagh was then more or less unknown; but he has now been recognized, rightly if posthumously, as the greatest Irish poet since Yeats. Cronin, besides being a poet, possessed one of the finest critical intelligences I have come across. As for Patrick Swift, whose prodigious and multifarious talents made him the most remarkable person I ever knew, he was to develop into a painter in the class of his friends Lucien Freud and Francis Bacon, while eluding their celebrity. It was not dislike of fame but of famousness that held him back from showing his paintings after his first and highly acclaimed exhibition in Dublin in 1950.

My first real book of poems, or first collection of real poems, *Moral Stories,* was published in 1954 by Derek Verschoyle. A second collection, *Monologue of a Deaf*

*Man,* came out in 1958. Meanwhile I had become acquainted—yet again in Soho—with a young businessman, Tristram Hull, who had begun a pamphlet-sized "little review" called *Nimbus.* He asked me to help find him contributors. At first my connection with *Nimbus* was as tenuous as the magazine itself, but grew with its circulation and format till I found myself appointed coeditor in 1956. Which appointment lasted a twelvemonth. The first number under my aegis printed fourteen pages of poetry by Stevie Smith, picked from a batch of fifty or more which she had sent when I wrote asking for a poem. No editor, she explained, would touch her stuff. The next number performed a similar service for Patrick Kavanagh, nineteen of whose poems we printed from a thick typescript volume of his unpublished verse, which had been picked up from a scatter of papers on the floor of the poet's Dublin flat by Patrick Swift's brother James, who had them typed and bound and sent to me. The poems that we printed in *Nimbus* led to the publication of Stevie Smith's *Not Waving but Drowning* and Kavanagh's *Come Dance with Kitty Stobling* and to their belated recognition by the English Reviewage. But my half-share of the editorial seat at *Nimbus* was insecure. Christopher Logue took my place, and thereafter *Nimbus* concentrated on the products of politically committed afflatus.

It is not to be thought that I spent all my days in London and Soho. My wife Phillipa had joined the Century Theatre, a unique mobile theatre that toured the northern industrial towns. Most weekends I would spend with her wherever the Century happened to be situated, and sometimes help with its dismantling, transportation, and re-erection elsewhere. In this way I got to know England better than most Londoners, who seldom venture further north than Watford or Potters Bar.

It was while we were living on fish and chips in one of the dressing rooms of the derelict Theatre Royal at Castleford in 1959 that I received a letter from Patrick Swift inviting me to come in with him to edit a new quarterly magazine. The backing was to come via Mrs. St. John Hutchinson. Mary Hutchinson was then in her eighties, a cousin of Lytton Strachey, and an intimate of George Moore, Sam Beckett, Matisse, and Giacometti. In the event she got Michael Berry, now Lord Hartwell, the proprietor of the *Daily Telegraph,* to back the magazine. He was the ideal patron and never interfered, which is more than could be said for Mrs. Hutchinson. We called the magazine *X*—"the unknown quantity" and were out to provide a platform for individual vision rather than second-hand avant-gardisme or accepted attitudes. To begin with, *X* became an outlet for then-neglected poets like Stevie Smith, Patrick Kavanagh, and Hugh MacDiarmid, as well as later "discoveries" who could not have been

*Wright at Leeds University, 1966*

published elsewhere at that time, so counter to current trends was their verse: C.H. Sisson, Brian Higgins, and Cliff Ashby. Higgins's first book was disallowed the Poetry Book Society Choice because the Arts Council considered it libellous (but the selectors made his last, and posthumous, collection a Choice in 1965, and this time it was permitted to stand). On the art side, under the guidance of Patrick Swift, *X* launched a series of torpedoes at the official art of the day (those were the boom years of abstract), and drew attention to the work of then unknown figurative painters like Frank Auerbach and Michael Andrews, and to the as yet uncanonized David Bomberg, Lucien Freud, and Francis Bacon.

*X* survived for two years and seven numbers, although to begin with Michael Berry had only committed himself to backing the first four numbers. In any case I felt the job we had set out to do was done—and the work was later carried on by magazines like *Agenda, Ishmael,* and *Poetry Nation.* Then in 1962 Patrick Swift departed for Algarve in Portugal to devote himself to painting. The Century Theatre, after ten years of travelling, came to a halt at Keswick in the Lake District. In the summer months of every year Phillipa, as leading lady, lived in the theatre caravans at Kes-

*At Hearne Farme, 1951: George Barker, John Fairfax, Phillipa Reid, David Wright, John Heath-Stubbs, Cashenden Cass*

*Cumberland, 1967: "Near Goldscope mines at head of Newlands Valley. You can see all the way down it to Skiddaw and Saddleback in the distance. Braithwaite is behind the shoulder of the hill to the left—about four miles from the spot where I am sitting."*

*David Wright and Patrick Swift working in Sesimbre, Portugal, 1969*

*Wright with Lionel Abrahams, Johannesburg, 1979*

*the North.* At the same time family ties brought me back to South Africa. In 1957 my father died, as so many do, shortly after his retirement. In his will he left me nothing, having nothing to leave but a pension for my mother: he had already provided for me more than generously by affording the best possible education at that expensive deaf school and at Oxford, to say nothing of the small monthly allowance that enabled me to survive until the royalties from my translation of *Beowulf* began to furnish an income. But in 1969 my mother entered her ninetieth year. Imagining that every visit would be the last, I made repeated trips to South Africa during the seventies to see her. Most of the time I spent in Johannesburg, where my mother lived. Here, against all expectation, I found that a philistine and illiberal environment had excited a stimulating and vigorous artistic reaction. With no governmental or academic financial aid—far from it!—"little reviews" and small publishing houses were proliferating. It was the decade that saw the Soweto massacre and the emergence of Black poets like Oswald Mtshali, Wally Serote, and Sipho Sepamla, the last of whom

wick, where I joined her. Then in 1965 we bought at Braithwaite, a nearby village, a cottage with windows looking out at Skiddaw and Helvellyn.

We meant it to be a holiday home: but at once became permanent residents. Already the diaspora from London had begun. The painters and the poets had departed to take up creative chairs in Africa and America, or to teach at polytechnics. Never again would Soho be the rendezvous of the arts.

For twelve years, from 1965 to 1977, my wife and I lived in Cumberland. With Patrick Swift I collaborated to produce three travel-books covering the whole of still-untouristified Portugal, a venture undertaken out of curiosity and for the fun of it. During this period I published four books of poetry, and in 1976 my collected poems, *To the Gods the Shades.* Apart from editing *The Penguin Book of English Romantic Verse* (an anthology which I am told helped to secure John Clare his rightful seat among the major Romantics), De Quincey's *Recollections of the Lakes and the Lake Poets,* Edward Trelawny's *Records of Shelley, Byron, and the Author* and *The Penguin Book of Everyday Verse*—an anthology of social and documentary poetry from the middle ages to the Great War—I published *Deafness,* an autobiographical account of my own experience of the disability, including a brief but comprehensive history of a little-known subject, the education of the deaf.

The experience of living in Cumberland, in the last of its mining villages still to have a working mine, produced a collection of poems that I called *A View of*

*Phillipa Reid, 1951*

*David Wright, Phillipa Reid, Ivor Bowen, near Bassenthwaite Lake in Cumberland, 1982*

became my friend. In Johannesburg I got to know young poets and writers like Lionel Abrahams, poet and courageous publisher of the Black writers mentioned above; Peter Wilhelm, Cherry Clayton, Stephen Gray, Patrick Cullinan, Ahmed Essop, Nadine Gordimer, the architect Michael Sutton, and Barney Simon, who created the now famous Market Theatre and threw it open to mixed audiences in defiance of apartheid laws. I also visited Rhodes University under the wing of the poet Guy Butler, who showed me the haunts of our Settler forbears. Many poems, including the sequence "A South African Album" and "Letter to Isabella Fey," resulted from these visits.

At the end of 1977 we left the Lake District, driven out by tourism and the new motorway. Cumberland is heaven from October to Easter, hell thereafter. We did not go far—not more than thirty miles—having discovered an old Westmorland farmhouse overlooking the river Eden. Here I began a verse translation of Chaucer's *Canterbury Tales,* which was published in 1985 by Oxford University Press. But before this consummation, three deaths: in 1983, that of my mother at the age of 102, and of Patrick Swift, at 55; two years later, at 58, my wife, Phillipa, generous and

innocent, a brilliant actress, a woman of many talents. To her I owe what I am, to her I owe more than I can say. But—"I shall find time." Meanwhile

> *a, te meae si partem anima rapit*
> *maturior vis, quid moror altera,*
> *nec carus aeque nec superstes integer?*

## BIBLIOGRAPHY

**Poetry:**

*Poems.* London: Editions Poetry, 1947.

*Moral Stories.* London: Verschoyle, 1954.

*Monologue of a Deaf Man.* London: Deutsch, 1958.

*Adam at Evening.* London: Hodder & Stoughton, 1965.

*Nerve Ends.* London: Hodder & Stoughton, 1969.

*A South African Album,* edited by C.H. Sisson. Cape Town, South Africa: Philip, 1976.

*To the Gods the Shades: New and Collected Poems.* Manchester, England: Carcanet New Press, 1976.

*A View of the North.* Manchester, England: Carcanet New Press, 1976.

*Metrical Observations.* Manchester, England: Carcanet New Press, 1980.

*Selected Poems.* Johannesburg, South Africa: Donker, 1980.

**Nonfiction:**

*Roy Campbell* (literary criticism). London: Longmans, Green, 1961.

*Algarve,* with Patrick Swift (travel). London: Barrie & Rockliff, 1965.

*Minho and North Portugal: A Portrait and a Guide,* with P. Swift. London: Barrie & Rockliff, 1968.

*Deafness: A Personal Account* (autobiography). London: Allen Lane, 1969; also published as *Deafness.* New York: Stein & Day, 1969.

*Lisbon: A Portrait and a Guide,* with P. Swift. London: Barrie & Jenkins, 1971; New York: Scribner, 1971.

**Translator of:**

*Beowulf.* Harmondsworth, England: Penguin, 1957.

*The Canterbury Tales,* by Geoffrey Chaucer (prose translation). London: Barrie & Rockliff, 1964; New York: Random House, 1965.

*The Canterbury Tales,* by Geoffrey Chaucer (verse translation). Oxford: Oxford University Press, 1985.

**Editor of:**

*The Forsaken Garden: An Anthology of Poetry, 1824-1909,* with John Heath-Stubbs. London: Lehmann, 1950.

*The Faber Book of Twentieth-Century Verse: An Anthology of Verse in Britain, 1900-1950,* with J. Heath-Stubbs. London: Faber, 1953.

*South African Stories.* London: Faber, 1960.

*The Mid-Century: English Poetry, 1940-60.* Harmondsworth, England: Penguin, 1964.

*Seven Victorian Poets.* London: Heinemann, 1966; New York: Barnes & Noble, 1966.

*The Penguin Book of English Romantic Verse.* Harmondsworth, England and Baltimore: Penguin, 1968.

*Recollections of the Lakes and the Lake Poets,* by Thomas De Quincey. Harmondsworth, England: Penguin, 1970.

*Records of Shelley, Byron, and the Author,* by Edward Trelawny. Harmondsworth, England: Penguin, 1973.

*The Penguin Book of Everyday Verse: Social and Documentary Poetry, 1250-1916.* London: Allen Lane, 1976.

*Selected Poems,* by Thomas Hardy. Harmondsworth, England and New York: Penguin, 1978.

*Under the Greenwood Tree,* by Thomas Hardy. Harmondsworth, England: Penguin, 1978.

*Selected Poems and Prose,* by Edward Thomas. Harmondsworth, England: Penguin, 1981.

# Cumulative Index

# CUMULATIVE INDEX

For every reference that appears *in more than one essay*,
the name of the essayist is given before the volume and page number(s).

**INDEX**

INDEX

INDEX